CONTROVERSIES
IN AMERICAN
VOTING BEHAVIOR

CONTROVERSIES IN AMERICAN VOTING BEHAVIOR

Edited by **Richard G. Niemi** and **Herbert F. Weisberg**

UNIVERSITY OF ROCHESTER   CALIFORNIA INSTITUTE OF TECHNOLOGY

W. H. FREEMAN AND COMPANY, San Francisco

Campaign buttons are from the collection of Jeffrey B. Shellan, California Institute of Technology. Photographs by Floyd Clark.

Library of Congress Cataloging in Publication Data

Main entry under title:

Controversies in American voting behavior.

Bibliography: p.
Includes index.
1. Elections—United States—Addresses, essays, lectures. 2. Voting—United States—Addresses, essays, lectures. 3. Party affiliation—United States—Addresses, essays, lectures. I. Niemi, Richard G. II. Weisberg, Herbert F.
JK1967.C675   324'.2   76-13564
ISBN 0-7167-0536-2
ISBN 0-7167-0535-4 pbk.

Printed in the United States of America

9 8 7 6 5 4 3 2 1

To Angus Campbell, Philip E. Converse, Warren E. Miller, and Donald E. Stokes, without whose work this would have been impossible.

Contents

ELECTORAL CHANGE

Preface

When *The American Voter*—or later *The American Voter* plus minor elaborations—said it all, a reader on voting was unnecessary. But today a diverse group of authors is contributing to a resurgence of voting behavior studies. New technical developments, new data sources, new theoretical models, and changes in the real voting world all have combined to provide renewed interest and growth in the area of voting behavior. As a result, not only is there a need for a reader, but this is the ideal time for one.

Selecting articles for this reader has been a welcome task because it forced us to read widely and to make sense out of a wide array of new studies. We hope that the organization and integration we have provided will be useful to a wide audience—students, professional political scientists, and others who simply want a guide to current work on American voting behavior. In addition to the work reprinted here, the interested reader will want to delve into material which we have cited but have not been able to include, for we could not reprint all of the top quality research of recent years.

Our introductions are intended to be more than minor scribblings with a sentence about each selection. Rather, we have tried to provide the background necessary for a full appreciation of current work, and to do it in such a way as to highlight what controversies exist, to call attention to the underlying scholarly disputes, and to indicate what has been learned in spite of the remaining controversy. Our hope is that our essays are themselves of considerable use—especially to those who are unfamiliar with the previous literature or who want an up-to-date picture of the new directions in voting behavior research.

Some of the work represented here is technically complex. But we believe that political science students are becoming increasingly expert at understanding such techniques and that professors are becoming more skillful at explaining them. Our introductions should also be of some use in this regard by summarizing major points which might go unnoticed as readers concentrate on understanding the methods used.

Finally, we would like to express our appreciation to those who have made this volume possible: to Richard Lamb and the entire production staff at W. H. Freeman and Company, to Paul Abramson, Herb Asher, Lance Bennett, Sam Hodder, and Jacob Hurwitz for their helpful comments on the manuscript, to Michael Yosha and Nancy Niemi for assistance in preparation of the manuscript, to Catherine Street for inspiration, and to the Niemi women for their hospitality when we meet to work together in Rochester. But, above all, this reader owes a unique debt to two sets of scholars—those who dared provide the original brilliant insights in a field and those who have not been willing to accept the conventional wisdom in the field. If the later work challenges the original insights, it also underscores their importance. And lastly we acknowledge the contribution of those who make election analysis so much fun: the inscrutable American voters.

R. G. N.
H. F. W.

January 1976

List of Contributors,
with Current Affiliations

Paul R. Abramson, *Michigan State University*
Kristi Andersen, *Ohio State University*
Paul Allen Beck, *University of Pittsburgh*
Richard A. Brody, *Stanford University*
Thad A. Brown, *University of California, Los Angeles*
Walter Dean Burnham, *Massachusetts Institute of Technology*
Philip E. Converse, *University of Michigan*
Anthony Downs, *Real Estate Research Corporation, Chicago*
Barbara Hinckley, *University of Wisconsin, Madison*
C. Richard Hofstetter, *San Diego State University*
M. Kent Jennings, *University of Michigan*
John H. Kessel, *Ohio State University*
Arthur H. Miller, *University of Michigan*
Warren E. Miller, *University of Michigan*
Norman H. Nie, *University of Chicago*
Richard G. Niemi, *University of Rochester*
Benjamin I. Page, *University of Chicago*
Gerald M. Pomper, *Rutgers University*
Alden S. Raine, *Rutgers University*
Jerrold G. Rusk, *University of Arizona*
Richard M. Scammon, *Election Research Center, Washington, D.C.*
Mark A. Schulman, *University of Maryland, Eastern Shore*
James A. Stimson, *State University of New York at Buffalo*
Donald E. Stokes, *Princeton University*
Edward R. Tufte, *Princeton University*
Sidney Verba, *Harvard University*
Ben J. Wattenberg, *Washington, D.C.*
Herbert F. Weisberg, *California Institute of Technology*
Arthur C. Wolfe, *University of Michigan*

CONTROVERSIES
IN AMERICAN
VOTING BEHAVIOR

INTRODUCTION

1. The Study of Voting and Elections

Why Study Elections?

We could try to justify studying elections simply by referring to classical democratic theory. That theory tells us that we should be interested in elections because of their role in a democracy. Elections select the government. They also provide a brake on the government, which realizes that it must behave responsibly because the electorate will pass judgment on its actions when it seeks re-election. The electoral process thus simultaneously puts the government in office and limits its actions when in office. Elections also provide a "linkage mechanism" by which public attitudes can affect government policy. It is important in a democracy that government actions correspond to public desires, and elections are one of the means of linking the two.

Democratic theory tells us that elections also perform a number of "latent" functions for the political system. They legitimize the government's authority. The fact that the government was elected makes citizens accept it and rally behind it even when they disagree with specific governmental actions. Elections serve to contain political conflict. As long as the electoral arena is open, the need to resort to force is diminished. In this respect, there is a stark contrast between countries with an electoral tradition and those with a tradition of military coups. Elections also help restrain social conflict.

Social groups inevitably have conflicting needs, but they have usually been willing to engage in open elections rather than in open warfare.

We could also try to justify elections by referring to their "symbolic" role. Elections constitute an important ritual of democracy. Just as performing a religious ritual makes a person feel more a part of the religious group, so voting makes the person feel more a part of the society. Thus voting helps integrate the political system while at the same time reaffirming and displaying its basic principles. By providing a means of participation, voting gives people a stake in the political system. Citizens are made to feel they have contributed to the government and have affected governmental actions, regardless of how large or small that actual contribution or effect is. Elections thus help maintain democracy, and voting makes the citizens feel they have performed their civic duty.

We *could* justify election studies in these terms, but for many people today that would not be good enough. After years of racial strife, Vietnam, and Watergate, so many people are turned off of politics nowadays that voting hardly seems important. In the eyes of many people, the government will do what it wants to anyway, regardless of the election. The candidates do not differ very much, and when they do, the election is only a matter of selecting the lesser of two evils; regardless of campaign promises, after the election the winner becomes just another politician. As for the effects on citizens, many people do not vote anyway, and election fraud and unrepresentative institutions like national conventions misrepresent the votes that are cast.

In light of such criticisms, can we really justify studying elections? We think we can—for a number of reasons besides the classical arguments given above. The most important reason may be to see whether or not the critics are right. Are elections useless? Are they useful for elite groups that run them and not for others? Do candidates really represent the public's viewpoints? As long as there is controversy about these matters, they deserve study. And we think that there is sufficient evidence of the impact of elections on recent governmental behavior that even confirmed cynics would have to admit that the matter was at least debatable. For example, President Johnson's decision not to seek a second term seems clearly related to the existence of elections even though he was not actually defeated at the polls. Johnson decided against seeking another term when it became apparent that he would have a difficult time winning re-election and had no chance of uniting his own party. The 1968 election did not force an immediate end to the Vietnam War, but President Nixon clearly realized that American troops had to be virtually out of Vietnam and "peace" had to be near if he was to win re-election in 1972. The electoral process thus seems to provide a powerful restraint, even if it is not totally effective.

In similar fashion, cynics might cite Nixon vs. Humphrey in 1968 as an example of "Tweedledee and Tweedledum." And yet it would be hard to deny that the 1964-1972 elections offered serious alternatives to the public. Although many people rejected both Goldwater's and McGovern's ideas, that simply proves the point that a real alternative was available. And in 1968 Wallace offered a genuine alternative, though even more voters seemingly rejected that option. Moreover, it was elections—primary elections such as in New Hampshire—that helped lead to President Johnson's decision in 1968.

We could go on at length, but our purpose is not to present a full-scale discussion of the role of elections. Rather, we are simply suggesting that, for all but the most dedicated cynics, elections *are* or *may be* an important determinant of what happens in our political system. To determine whether elections really do have an impact on governmental behavior is justification enough for studying them.

But there are other reasons for studying elections, which we shall mention only briefly. If we take seriously the political scientist's goal of generalizing about human political behavior, then we can focus on elections as one of the most pervasive and widespread kinds of behavior. It is far from the only kind of behavior which we could investigate, but the frequency of elections and their real or possible importance make them a good candidate for study (no pun intended). We shall see examples throughout this book of some rather surprising discoveries that have already been made about political attitudes and voting behavior.

If we are convinced that voting is good and/or here to stay, then we have an additional reason for studying voting. There are many possible ways of improving elections, but to do so intelligently requires considerable knowledge about voters and their knowledge, interests, and behavior. The answer to a "simple" question, such as whether or not to establish a national presidential primary, may depend heavily on what we know about voting behavior in primary and other types of elections.

One further justification for studying elections is a pragmatic one. In recent years candidates have increasingly turned to specialists of various kinds to run their campaigns. Even local campaigns now depend on some specialized knowledge about voter behavior. Anyone interested in influencing public opinion or in helping candidates get elected would be well advised to know something about electoral behavior.

All of these reasons together suggest the importance of studying voting and elections. But there are many ways of studying voting, and the way chosen by political scientists is not always the easiest. Hence, the next section indicates why political scientists study elections in the particular way they do.

How to Study Voting

Why Study Public Attitudes on Voting?

If elections are to be studied, why aren't the election summaries by authors such as Theodore H. White sufficient? White's series on *The Making of the President, 1960, 1964, 1968,* and *1972,* provides interesting and discerning summaries of the specific events of each election. The dry election statistics come to life in vivid personal conflicts. Why aren't these enough?

One difficulty is that the White approach is more subjective than it sometimes seems. There are no clear criteria for choosing between alternative interpretations. In 1968, three British journalists collaborated on a book on the American presidential campaign, and their view of *The American Melodrama* diverges considerably from White's. In 1972, *Rolling Stone* magazine reporter Hunter S. Thompson provided his own view of the election in *Fear and Loathing on the Campaign Trial, 1972,* a turned-on portrait which bears little resemblance to White's account. Which interpretation to accept is left largely to the whim of each reader.

A second problem is that most such accounts emphasize elite behavior. White offers much insight into the behavior of candidates and their staffs and a glimpse of the attitudes and reasoning on which that behavior is based. This often involves evaluations of public opinion, but there is usually no direct assessment of that opinion—only White's interpretations. But elections depend on the public, and if we are to understand election results, we must understand the electorate. Its knowledge, attitudes, information sources, candidate evaluations, and much more must be investigated.

At one level the elections reflect strategic battles between candidates. White excels in describing those strategies and the personalities involved. But at another level the elections involve public reactions to events, issues, and candidates. And the only way to gauge those reactions is to ask the public. If we want to understand why the public voted as it did, we must ask a cross-section of citizens why they voted as they did. And this leads inevitably to survey research—public opinion polling.

Why Not Use a Journalistic Approach?

Journalists frequently write about public opinion, so why not study it simply by following newspaper accounts of election campaigns? Actually, for many purposes we regard this as the most sensible approach. If what you want is current, day-to-day accounts of a particular campaign, or if you want to know who is the current front-runner in the presidential race, then you should consult the newspapers.

There are questions and problems, however, that journalists don't consider. Two examples illustrate this nicely. One concerns journalists' periodic discovery that many Americans reject statements which are regarded as fundamental to our political system.[1] A reporter, for example, will stand on a street corner and ask several dozen people whether they would allow an atheist to address a meeting of public school children. Invariably, a large

---

[1] True to form, as this book was going to press, a reporter in Rochester, New York, used July 4 as the occasion to ask people to sign a petition that happened to be the Declaration of Independence without the title. Few people signed it, and the reporter heard comments such as, "You can't be too careful about what you sign these days." Rochester *Democrat & Chronicle*, 6 July 1975, p. B1.

number of people would prevent the atheist from speaking. The reporter will dutifully express shock at this because, after all, wasn't this country founded on the principle of freedom of speech? This makes good newspaper copy and is, no doubt, the kind of writing that the reporter should be doing if he or she wants to keep a job. However, any number of questions go unanswered in this sort of report.

You might well ask, for example, whether most people feel the way the reporter's informants did. A simple question—but before you can answer it, you have to examine a variety of things, such as how one designs a survey, whether respondents' answers to survey questions are reliable, and so on. Newspaper reporters don't write about these topics, and rightly so, because they would lose their jobs if they did. Few people, including well-educated people, want to sit down and relax with the newspaper and encounter a lengthy discussion of the principles of survey research. Yet it is obvious that the reporter's story may really be creating a false impression of American public opinion. And we'll never know unless we consider such "technical details" as we mentioned.

Moreover, there are lots of other questions that we might be interested in. For example, are some types of people much more in favor of free speech than others? This might not just be idle curiosity. If educational level is highly correlated with support of free speech—that is, if support of free speech goes up as the level of education goes up—this has all sorts of pro-grammatic implications for the future of education. It also has implications for historical interpretations, which are another thing that might interest us. If low educational level goes along with lack of support for free speech, consider what the reporter would have found fifty years ago when levels were much lower than they are now.

We could go on and on, but let us ask only one more question—an interpretative one. Suppose we accept the reporter's results at face value. Does this mean that Americans are indeed undemocratic? If not, how can we make such a judgment in the face of the reporter's evidence? Clearly, such interpretations would have to rest on other information, such as other polls that seem to explore other aspects of democratic ideals.

All of this is not to say that the reporter's findings should be ignored. Clearly, what the reporter found was of interest. But the point is that there are many questions which have not been answered and which educated people should be and are concerned with. We should read newspapers, but we shouldn't stop there.

Let's turn to the other example, this one concerning day-to-day accounts of an election campaign. In 1972, a number of prominent columnists pro-duced reports which said, in effect, that it didn't make much difference what the candidates did, because research showed that voters didn't know any-thing about politics anyway. This was doubly interesting—first, because the columnists were drawing directly on previous studies done by political sci-entists. Some reporters even quoted directly from *The American Voter*, a book which we shall have much to say about later on. But the other reason for our interest was the fact that by 1972 political scientists were becoming convinced of just the opposite of what the reporters were saying—in other words, that voters were considerably attuned to what was happening in the campaign.

Now, surely, columnists would rather be right than wrong, and few would knowingly print facts, or interpretations of facts, that they believed to be dead wrong. Yet there is a difference in that political scientists much more than journalists are seeking generalizations that withstand relatively extensive, objective attempts to disprove them (and in this limited sense can be tentatively accepted as "true"). Plausible conclusions—people are antidemocratic or people do not know anything about politics—cannot be accepted without testing. Rather, tentative explanations such as these must be tested in a variety of ways, by a variety of methods, and in a variety of settings. Only if they are continually supported (i.e., not disproved), do we begin to believe that explanations might be valid.

Obviously, it is not an easy matter to develop, test, and retest all of the competing explanations that can be made of a given event. And this is where the journalist and the political scientist usually part company. Journalists are primarily interested in today's news. They typically cannot afford to wait until 1978 for an analysis of voters in the 1976 election. Public reactions to the Korean War would hardly make headlines today. And even "timeless" topics such as civil liberties have ebbs and flows in public interest. Moreover, the journalist must typically appeal to a wide audience. Complicated analyses, even of current topics, would leave many readers just plain bewildered. This emphasis on today's news and on general audiences means that journalists must be more content with subjective interpretations and tentative explanations than political scientists. Careful analyses of public opinion require months, if not years, of work. The results are often highly complicated and hardly the kind of material that will sell newspapers.

None of this is meant to disparage the work of journalists. For day-to-day coverage of political events and for "investigative reporting," journalists' work is clearly superior to what political scientists might have to say. But when it comes to analysis, interpretation, and explanation of political matters, the political scientist's more precise, more systematic, and (ideally at least) more objective studies are also needed. This is what we attempt to provide here.

Why Not Use Gallup- and Harris-Type Polls?

You will notice that the articles on this book are based on special surveys rather than on Gallup and Harris polls. Why is this the case? The main reason involves what each is studying. Gallup and Harris must predict election results for their newspaper customers. Newspapers want to publish interesting stories, and predictions of election outcomes are certainly that. Gallup and Harris do very well in this prediction game. However, political scientists are typically studying the last election rather than the next. This is because they don't want to predict *who* will win a particular election so much as they want to understand *why* someone won. Some forms of prediction may eventually be possible (see chapter 15), but they must be firmly based on an explanation of past elections. Explaining election outcomes requires asking people many more questions than Gallup and Harris do. Voters can't just be asked who they will vote for. They must be asked their feelings about each candidate, each party, each issue, how they obtained information on the election, how they voted in the past, and so on. This requires separate polls.

Some academic polling was done as long ago as the 1920's, but the first real academic surveys about politics were done in 1940 and thereafter. And it was not until 1948 that continuous national surveys began with the formation of the University of Michigan's well-known Institute for Social Research. The Survey Research Center (and more recently the Center for Political Studies) section of this Institute has continued surveying up to the present day. The CPS/SRC studies are among the most important voting surveys and provide the basis for most of the articles in this book. However, many elections have been studied by additional polls from other survey organizations. Also, while the Michigan CPS/SRC studies collect most of the data, the studies are made available for others (including students—ask your professor) to analyze. Hence, a number of the articles in this book are based on "secondary" analyses of the CPS/SRC data conducted by scholars who are neither involved with the original data collection nor committed to the views of the Michigan authors. A convenient list of the major studies is found in table 1.1, with the citation of the report by the principal investigators. Additionally, hundreds of books and articles have been based on these surveys, including several which cover a series of elections.

In the typical survey, from 1,500 to 2,000 people are interviewed prior to the election and then reinterviewed after the election. An important variation is repeated pre-election interviews with the same person to analyze changes in vote intentions. The other important variant is that the 1956, 1958, and 1960 Michigan studies interviewed the same people so they could examine voting change between elections. That "panel" design was repeated in the early 1970's, with the same people being interviewed by Michigan in 1972 and 1974 (and possibly 1976), again to examine voting change between elections. The more recent Michigan studies have also moved the number of interviews closer to 3,000.

This is not the place for a detailed statistical explanation of how nationwide voting can be studied with as few as 1,500 interviews, but some preliminary insights are possible. When you sample from a population, accuracy depends more on the size of the sample than on the size of the population. Whether you take a sample of 1,500 or 15,000, it is still well below 1 percent of the American electorate. How you select the sample is critical. The best samples don't involve interviews with "typical" voters, since there is no way of gauging how typical a person's attitudes are before everyone is interviewed. Instead, everyone is given an equal (or, at least, known) chance

Table 1.1 Major Electoral Behavior Surveys and Major Reports on Them

Year	Study	Report
1940	Columbia University, Bureau of Applied Social Research, sample of, Erie County, Ohio	P. Lazarsfeld, B. Berelson, and H. Gaudet, *The People's Choice,* Duell, Sloan & Pearce, 1944
1944	National Opinion Research Center, national sample	
1948	Columbia University, Bureau of Applied Social Research, sample of Elmira, N.Y.	B. Berelson, P. Lazarsfeld, and W. McPhee, *Voting,* University of Chicago Press, 1954
1948	University of Michigan SRC, national sample	A. Campbell and R. Kahn, *The People Elect a President,* SRC, University of Michigan, 1952
1950	Columbia University, Bureau of Applied Social Research, four state samples	W. McPhee and W. Glaser, *Public Opinion and Congressional Elections,* Free Press, 1962
1952	University of Michigan SRC, national sample	A. Campbell, G. Gurin, and W. Miller, *The Voter Decides,* Row, Peterson, 1954. *See also* 1956 listing
1954	University of Michigan SRC, pre-election national sample	A. Campbell and H. Cooper, *Group Differences in Attitudes and Votes,* SRC, University of Michigan, 1956
1956	University of Michigan SRC, national sample	A. Campbell, P. Converse, W. Miller, and D. Stokes, *The American Voter,* Wiley, 1960
1958	University of Michigan SRC, national sample, representation study	D. Stokes and W. Miller, "Party Government and the Saliency of Congress," *POQ,*[1] Winter, 1962 W. Miller and D. Stokes, "Constituency Influence in Congress," *APSR,*[2] March, 1963 A. Campbell, "Surge and Decline," *POQ,* Fall, 1960
1960	University of Michigan SRC, national sample	P. Converse, A. Campbell, W. Miller, and D. Stokes, "Stability and Change in 1960; A Reinstating Election," *APSR,* June, 1961. *See also* A. Campbell, P. Converse, W. Miller, and D. Stokes, *Elections and the Political Order,* Wiley, 1966

(continued)

NOTE: All of above studies involve post-election interviews, except for the 1954 pre-election study, the 1961 study of the South, and the 1967 study of participation. Most also involve one or more pre-election interviews.   [1] *Public Opinion Quarterly*   [2] *American Political Science Review*

Table 1.1 (cont.)

Year	Study	Report
1956–58–60	University of Michigan SRC, national sample, panel study	P. Converse, "The Nature of Belief Systems in Mass Publics," in D. Apter, *Ideology and Discontent,* Free Press, 1964
1961	University of North Carolina, sample of South	D. Matthews and J. Prothro, *Negroes and the New Southern Politics,* Harcourt, 1966
1962	University of Michigan SRC, national sample	
1964	University of Michigan SRC, national sample	P. Converse, A. Clausen, and W. Miller, "Electoral Myth and Reality: The 1964 Election," *APSR,* June, 1965
1966	University of Michigan SRC, national sample	
1967	NORC, University of Chicago, national sample	S. Verba and N. Nie, *Participation in America,* Harper & Row, 1972
1968	University of Michigan SRC, national sample	P. Converse, W. Miller, J. Rusk, and A. Wolfe, "Continuity and Change in American Politics: Parties and Issues in the 1968 Election," *APSR,* December, 1969
1968	Opinion Research Corp., national sample	B. Page and R. Brody, "Policy Voting and the Electoral Process," *APSR,* September, 1972
1968	University of North Carolina, thirteen state samples	D. Kovenock, J. Prothro, and Associates, *Explaining the Vote,* Institute for Research in Social Science, University of North Carolina, 1973
1970	University of Michigan CPS, national sample	
1972	University of Michigan CPS, national sample	A. Miller, W. Miller, A. Raine, and T. Brown, "A Majority Party in Disarray," *APSR,* 1976
1972	National Analysts, national sample	C. R. Hofstetter, *Television and Civic Education,* forthcoming
1972	Syracuse University, Onondaga County, N.Y.	T. Patterson and R. McClure, *Picture Politics,* Putnam, 1976
1974	University of Michigan CPS, national sample	

of being included in the sample. Statistical theory can then be used to estimate how closely sample results will come to true population results. With common sampling procedures, a sample of size 1,500 generally leads to a "sampling error" of about 3 percent, which means that most of the time (95 percent of the time, actually) the result from the sample will not be more than 3 percent off the true result. A survey may find 74 percent of the public favoring some policy, but it should be read as saying that from 71 to 77 percent of the public favor the policy when the 3 percent margin for error is taken into account. The error could be cut in half by quadrupling the size of the sample, but that would be very expensive and would only cut the margin of error to about 1.5 percent. There are many sources of error in surveys, such as the exact wording of questions, which can affect results a few percentage points either way, so a gain of 1.5 percent accuracy at the expense of 4,500 more interviews would not be worth it. Thus 1,500 interviews are adequate for many purposes—a major exception being when Gallup tries to call a very close election—and most of the studies reported here are based on about that number of respondents. [2]

Up to this point we have been suggesting why the scientific study of public opinion and voting is useful. Agreement on this point, however, does not automatically lead to agreement on just how to conceptualize voting or how to interpret results of voting surveys. Hence, the final sections of this introduction consider just how we are to understand voting behavior and why there are controversies about voting.

How to Understand Voting

How Has Voting Been Interpreted?

There are countless ways of understanding voting. The 1940 Columbia study initially employed a consumer preference model. The researchers assumed that each party presented a product to the public and that people considered these competing products throughout the advertising campaign, carefully considering each alternative, and then stepped into the booth on election day to record their final choices. The problem with this model was that most people knew how they would vote even before the national conventions were held. President Roosevelt was running for a third term in office, and, by 1940, people knew whether they were going to vote for or against Roosevelt without listening attentively to the whole campaign. The consumer preference model of voting was of little use in that election and has never since been seriously suggested in its simplest form.

The Columbia researchers instead explained the 1940 election with a sociological model. They found that a person's socio-economic status (education, income, and class), religion, and place of residence (rural or urban) were strongly related to the person's vote. They combined these into an "index of political predisposition" (IPP). For example, Protestants from rural areas and with high socio-economic status were most likely to vote Republican. The

---

[2] Sampling error can still be a problem for almost any sample size if small subsets of the population are compared. A national sample of 1,500 would contain only about 150 blacks, and an estimate of their responses would be subject to much more than 3 percent error. Oversampling of selected groups is sometimes used to overcome this problem.

social group factors accounted for most of the differences in voting. Yet this model doesn't try to explain *why* more Protestants voted Republican than did Catholics. It doesn't consider the political aspects of an election. And it is not useful in explaining change across elections, since different parties are elected in different years even if these social characteristics don't change much. Moreover, it doesn't always work. In 1948, the Michigan researchers replicated the IPP on their national sample. They found that 61 percent voted according to the IPP prediction, while 50 percent accuracy could have been obtain by flipping a coin. Thus, the sociological model may have been useful in 1940 for Erie County, but it didn't hold up nationally in 1948. The 1948 Columbia survey was also based on a sociological model, with emphasis on the group context of voting and the community context of voting and with more emphasis on issues, but the time had come for a sharp break with the sociological model.

The Survey Research Center analyzed the 1952 election using a social-psychological model. Group characteristics of the vote received less attention, with major emphasis instead on three psychological aspects—the person's attachment to a party, the person's orientation toward the issues, and the person's orientation toward the candidates. People predisposed toward the Democratic party, the Democratic issue positions, and the Democratic candidates were particularly likely to vote Democratic. Parties, candidates, and issues—finally the political variables were explicitly incorporated into the voting model.

A theory as to how these variables interrelate in their effect on the vote came in the landmark Michigan report on the 1952 and 1956 elections, *The American Voter.* A person's identification with a party became the core of the model. It in turn affected the person's attitudes toward candidates and issues. The authors describe this in terms of a "funnel of causality." The phenomenon to be explained—voting—is at the tip of the funnel. But it depends on many factors that occur earlier. The funnel's axis is time. Events follow one another, converging in a series of causal chains and moving from the mouth to the stem of the funnel. Thus a multitude of causes narrow into the voting act. At the mouth of the funnel are sociological background characteristics (ethnicity, race, region, religion, and the like), social status characteristics (education, occupation, class), and parental characteristics (class, partisanship). All affect the person's choice of party identification, the next item in the funnel. Party identification in turn influences the person's evaluation of the candidates and the issues, which takes us further into the funnel. The next part of the funnel includes incidents from the campaign itself, as these events are reported by the media. Even closer to the tip are the conversations which the voter has with family and friends about the election. Then comes the vote itself. Each of the prior factors affects the vote, though the Michigan group has concentrated on party, candidates, and issues, rather than on the very early social characteristics or the communications networks near the tip of the funnel.

This remains the basic Michigan model, with a more explicit division today between what are termed long-term and short-term factors. Party identification is an important long-term factor affecting the vote. Issues and especially candidates are short-term factors specific to the election. Using this approach the Michigan group has reported on each presidential election since 1956, but the reports are article-length rather than book-length. Their social-psychological model of the vote has affected virtually all later research, serving as the prime paradigm of the vote decision. They have also extended their work by studying elections in numerous other countries, though we shall not report on those results in this book. Finally, they have now studied parental influence directly in much greater detail (see chapter 19).

Yet there are additional ways in which the vote can be understood. One is to emphasize more the social-historical context of the vote. Elections can be analyzed within the framework of social movements and elite theories. A given election occurs at a particular moment of time, but it is the result of a set of historical forces which shape the voting. From this point of view, the emphasis on individuals' reasons for voting misses an important aspect of the electoral process. For example, to understand the voting of the American South it is necessary to understand the social structure, class, and racial situation of the past century. The solid Democratic South resulted from the post-Civil War tensions. The Wallace movement of the 1960's can be traced back to class and race conflicts in the South of the end of the last century. Similarly, while the black vote can be studied in terms of issue voting, it might be more appropriate to understand it in terms of the social cleavages and group consciousness that led to its rapid mobilization. This political sociology model of voting underlies the work of several writers, though it cannot be identified with a particular school or study as easily as can be the sociological and social-psychological approaches. It is most obvious in studies of particular groups—such as in studies of black voting, ethnic voting, southern voting—and in studies which adopt an historical approach.

The other model of voting which has become popular is a rational voter model. According to this model, voters decide whether or not to vote and for which candidate to vote on some rational basis—usually on the basis of which action gives them greater expected benefits. They vote only if they perceive greater gains from voting than the cost (mainly in time) of voting (see chapter 3). In the usual formulation, they vote for the candidate closest to them on the issues. A major contribution of this approach is that it provides a more explicit, precise theoretical basis for voting decisions and for their analysis than do other approaches. If voters are rational in this sense, then we can expect certain types of behavior in specified circumstances. In addition, this model lends itself more than others to predictions of the effects of changes in external conditions. But because the model is so much more precise (i.e., more mathematical), and because it is newer, it has not yet been developed too far. Some of the propositions from it are very nearly tautological. Increasingly, however, it is being realized that survey research provides a mechanism for testing some of the conclusions of the rational voter model. If people with particular attitudes do not behave as predicted, then the assumptions of the theory might have to be revised. If their behavior is correctly predicted, then we can extend the theory further. Substantively, the major contribution of the rational voter approach has been to emphasize the role of issues, which sometimes were submerged in other approaches.

What Are the Major Controversies?

Along with the development of a number of different models of voting has come the growth of several major controversies. Perhaps these will be settled in a few years, but in the near future, at least, the opposite seems more likely: a further expansion in the number of diverse views. Hence, we have organized this book around the major controversies that presently dominate the field. At the same time, our selection of topics is meant to assure coverage of the most important topics regarding voting behavior.

The first half of the book is organized around themes relating to voters and elections. We begin with the nature of participation in a democracy, including a consideration of the unusual proposition that it may be irrational for citizens to vote in a democracy. We next turn to the question of how ideological is the electorate, considering evidence that the electorate is intellectually incapable of operating at an ideological level.

Why do voters vote as they do? Are votes cast blindly on the basis of party? Of what value is the election if votes do not depend on issues? These questions form the basis of our discussion of vote determinants. Then we inquire whether in congressional elections a noncandidate (the President) is of greater importance than the actual candidates. What set of voting determinants leads to greatest control of government by voters? The study of voters and elections thus combines the questions, What are the empirical facts? and How should the existing state of affairs be evaluated normatively?

The second half of the book turns to topics related to electoral change. The time element is fundamental to elections, and there is a constant fascination with the extent of change in politics. Initially, we consider the question, Is party identification as fixed as a person's religion? The debate has direct implications for the potential for change in the political system. The next section examines the extent of actual change in the partisan balance. Has the party balance been changing, and, if so, what does the change mean? Are we moving toward a new party system?

The last sections turn to the question of whether the role of parties is declining in the United States, both in recent years and/or historically. Are the parties dying? What would politics be like without parties? Have the parties declined because of an elite conspiracy to take over the electoral system? As the analysis becomes historical, fascinating problems arise regarding the interpretations of voting change and the universality of our knowledge about voting.

The various topics represented in these sections are among the most important themes on voting. They raise fundamental questions regarding the why of voting, the motivations behind voting decisions, and the processes which are most desirable for the operation of a vital democracy. The current disputes involve alternative ways of looking at the political world as well as alternative views as to what might be normatively desirable. This begins to suggest that solutions may ultimately be unattainable in these several controversies. First, however, some further statement of why there are disputes is appropriate.

Why Are There Controversies?

The systematic study of public opinion and electoral behavior is not very old. It only began in 1940, and until 1960, or even later, it was a quite limited enterprise. Techniques for measuring and analyzing opinions are relatively new. Some of the methods used in this book (e.g., multidimensional scaling, used by Rusk and Weisberg) were nonexistent ten or fifteen years ago. Rational choice models were extremely scarce prior to the late 60's. Even public opinion polling is not that old; it wasn't until the mid-60's that data about several presidential elections were widely disseminated.

From this perspective, what we know about voters and elections is perhaps more surprising than what we don't know. Nonetheless, it is obvious why controversies have developed. Analyses which differ in the questions used, the techniques employed, the election(s) studied, and the model considered may quite reasonably reach different conclusions. At this level it is probably only a matter of time until the differences are resolved. To take a simple but real example, results based on only one congressional election may be accepted unquestioningly until they fail to be substantiated by studies of other elections. While such discrepancies are ultimately resolvable, they currently exist and will continue to do so for some time. Thus the readings of this book will reveal numerous disagreements—including some cases in which evidence can be marshalled for diametrically opposed points of view. In light of all this, in the section introductions we will try to highlight both the controversies and the conclusive results that emerge from past work, and wherever possible, to give some indication of the direction that work is now taking.

Controversies of a more enduring nature also exist. One reason for controversies without resolution is that there is more than one "truth." "Truth" depends on how you look at things; what is true from one perspective is not true from another, and there are very different perspectives from which to view voting. People with different perspectives will interpret the same facts in very different ways. And no one point of view is necessarily correct.

An example is provided by what has come to be known as the "spatial model" (see pp. 171–174). At least as presently developed, this model tends to ignore party identification and indeed any long-term forces in voting. If one's purpose is to advise candidates on how to win a given election, this point of view might be wholly appropriate. One can't, for example, rewrite history, so the best approach might simply be to work in the given context and to ignore questions about how that context came into being. On the other hand, if one's concern goes beyond a particular election—to explain the effects of an increase in the number of independents, for example—then an approach might be called for which focuses directly on partisanship (or its absence).

Another reason for enduring controversies is disagreement over goals. The work in this book is primarily descriptive in nature, as it should be. Hence, disputes about goals are not so apparent. But many of the results are closely related to normative concerns. Whether or not voters are knowledgeable about issues is a descriptive question, but many normative questions—including whether voters *should* know about, or know more about, issues—hinge on the answer. Perhaps the major debate which has grown directly out of voting studies is the question of whether people should be interested and involved in politics. A related question of interpretation is whether lack of political interest is evidence of satisfaction with the way things are going or of despair of being able to do anything about them. This controversy is discussed at length in the next section of the book.

Perhaps in the end elections serve one more function, in addition to those mentioned in the beginning of this introduction. Elections provide ammunition for arguments. They are fun because they can be viewed in alternative ways. Scientific analysis is able to disprove some interpretations, but to expect a single scientific interpretation of elections is as foolhardy as to expect a millennium in which political conflict disappears. Controversy is at the heart of human existence. Election contests provide the grist for debates over their interpretation. Such debates insure that elections and election analysis will retain interest well into the future.

Further Readings

Interpretations of Politics

Murray J. Edelman, *The Symbolic Uses of Politics* (Urbana: University of Illinois Press, 1964. Argument for the symbolic interpretation of politics in general and by inference the symbolic interpretation of elections.

Summary Statements of the Michigan SRC/CPS Theory of Voting

Angus Campbell, Philip E. Converse, Warren E. Miller, and Donald E. Stokes, *The American Voter* (New York: Wiley, 1960), chap. 2 (*not* in abridged version). Statement of the "funnel of causality" analogy.

Angus Campbell, "Voters and Elections: Past and Present," *Journal of Politics*, 26(1964):747–57. Summary of basic theory regarding turnout and vote choice.

Philip E. Converse, "Public Opinion and Voting Behavior," in Fred I. Greenstein and Nelson W. Polsby, eds., *The Handbook of Political Science*, Vol. 4 (Reading, Mass: Addison Wesley, 1975). Reactions to more recent work that challenges *The American Voter* interpretations.

Review Articles on Voting Studies

Peter H. Rossi, "Four Landmarks in Voting Research," in Eugene Burdick and Arthur J. Brodbeck, eds., *American Voting Behavior* (New York: Free Press, 1959). Summary of trends before publication of *The American Voter*.

Kenneth Prewitt and Norman H. Nie, "Election Studies of the Survey Research Center," *British Journal of Political Science*, 1(1971):479–502. Critical evaluation of the Michigan electoral surveys and the theory developed by the Michigan researchers.

Books Studying Voting Across a Series of Elections

Herbert B. Asher, *Presidential Elections in American Politics* (Homewood, Ill.: Dorsey, 1976).

William H. Flanigan and Nancy H. Zingale, *Political Behavior of the American Electorate*, 3d ed. (Boston: Allyn & Bacon, 1975).

Gerald M. Pomper, *Voter's Choice* (New York: Dodd, Mead, 1975).

Norman H. Nie, Sidney Verba, and John R. Petrocik, *The Changing American Voter* (Cambridge: Harvard University Press, 1976).

Books on Voting Behavior in Other Countries

Seymour M. Lipset and Stein Rokkan, *Party Systems and Voter Alignments* (New York: Free Press, 1967). Discussion of voting cleavages in several countries set in a theoretical perspective.

David Butler and Donald E. Stokes, *Political Change in Britain* (New York: St. Martin's Press, 1969). Approach and conclusions often parallel *The American Voter*.

Scandinavian Political Studies (Beverly Hills, Calif.: Sage Publications, 1966–present). A yearbook devoted to article-length studies of parties and voting in the Nordic countries.

VOTERS AND ELECTIONS

I. DEMOCRATIC PARTICIPATION

2.   Is It Rational to Vote?

In theory, democracy rests on several principles. It assumes that citizens are interested in political affairs, discuss their government, and are motivated to participate in politics. It assumes that the citizens are well-informed about government and decide how to vote on a rational basis. It assumes that voters have some meaningful choice between competing candidates. Perhaps the most basic of all aspects of democracy is the very act of voting. Without voting, democracy would have no existence.

Clearly, these assumptions are not all correct. Some people don't vote or are actually prevented from voting. Lack of informed voting has often been a problem. And frequently people have not found the choice among candidates very meaningful. Yet all of these observations did little to affect democratic theory until quite recently. It was maintained that at least democracy *should* work this way, even if in reality it didn't always do so. In theory, democracy was still thought to rest on lofty principles.

Nonvoting Is Sensible and Acceptable

The proverbial monkey wrench was thrown into this thinking in the 1950's. One influential work was Anthony Downs's book, *An Economic Theory of*

Democracy,[1] from which we have taken our first reading. Downs's entire approach differed from that conventionally used in political science. He emphasized a concept of political behavior based on a rational calculation of self-interest. This point of view is similar to that used in economic analysis, where the assumption is that individuals act so as to maximize their expected utility, which usually means minimizing dollar costs and maximizing dollar returns. Analyzing politics from a rational perspective, Downs argued, might provide a considerable degree of insight into some aspects of political behavior. It should be emphasized that Downs was not necessarily advocating rational calculations. And more important, if individuals in fact do act in this manner, it is not necessarily bad, even though the word *rational* sometimes implies this.[2] Rather, just as the economic system works well (with some controls) when everyone maximizes his or her own utility, so the political system might work best when each individual acts primarily in his or her own interest. In any event, such a model—even if descriptively wrong in some respects—might aid our understanding of political behavior.

Using a rational decision-making approach, Downs reached conclusions which conflicted sharply with those of normative democratic theory. Downs's major conclusion in the chapter reprinted here is that it might indeed be irrational for people to vote because the costs of voting outweigh the benefits derived from it. Moreover, many individuals who do vote do not find it in their self-interest to become well informed before voting. Once Downs pointed this out, the results seemed eminently sound. There are individual costs attached to voting—costs primarily in terms of time during which people could be doing other things. And the benefit from voting might be negligible. For example, if an individual sees almost no difference between the candidates in an election, it makes little difference which one wins. Moreover, since many individuals are voting, the chance that one person's vote will change the result is quite small, though calculating the exact value is perhaps impossible. The costs of becoming informed are quite large, since paying attention to campaign issues takes much time, and it is often difficult to find out precisely what the candidates are saying anyway.

Though Downs's results may seem relatively straightforward when put in this form, they ran directly counter to traditional democratic theory and opened up a new approach to the study of politics. But Downs's chief contributions with regard to voter turnout itself are the two conclusions noted above: both nonvoting and voting without being informed are often sensible from the perspective of particular individuals. Perhaps individuals *should*

---

[1] New York: Harper, 1957.

[2] Students sometimes think that "rational behavior" means a person acts like a devious, calculating Scrooge. It may mean that. But it may also mean simply that a person knows what he or she wants (e.g., a particular policy goal) and acts in a perfectly acceptable way to achieve that goal (e.g., votes for a candidate who supports that goal). Political scientists usually seem to mean the latter.

vote and *should be* informed, but we can no longer construct political theories which assume that everyone will necessarily be an informed voter.

Another perspective on voting, provided by Verba and Nie in chapter 4, suggests that for many purposes voting is less useful than other kinds of political activity. Verba and Nie do not go so far as to say that voting is useless—in fact, they make a fairly strong case for voting—but they emphasize the rationality of other kinds of participation. Most important are what they call citizen-initiated contacts. These include contacts with governmental officials about particular problems faced by individuals and their families, as well as contacts involving broader matters such as a school or a whole community. The key points are that the individual citizen chooses what the contact is about and that the nature of the problem and the solution are relatively specific. In contrast, in elections individuals don't choose what issues are involved, don't decide whom the choice is between, and often don't see that much of a choice actually exists. Given this difference, people are likely to find greater rewards in contacts they initiate than in voting.

Other types of activities (which Verba and Nie label "communal" and "campaign activity") lie between citizen-initiated contacts and voting in terms of direct, identifiable returns. These differences lead us to expect a variety of kinds of participation, with many individuals participating in one or two ways rather than in every way. That this is the case is shown by the summary of Verba and Nie's empirical study provided at the end of their chapter. But the important point from our perspective here is that the individualistic approach initiated by Downs implies that voting is typically one of the least useful ways of resolving private problems or of influencing specific governmental policies.

The arguments provided by Downs and by Verba and Nie mean that nonvoting might be rational from each individual's point of view, though it does not necessarily suggest that this is the way citizens should behave. A natural question is what implication nonvoting has for the political system. Is a nation better off when large numbers of individuals fail to vote? Some authors have taken exactly that position. They suggest that low turnout is not only individually rational, but is desirable. The best-known statement of this point of view was given by Berelson after one of the earliest empirical studies of voting. Berelson points out the dangers of high interest (and, by implication, of high voting turnout):[3]

> How could a mass democracy work if all the people were deeply involved in politics? Lack of interest by some people is not without its benefits. . . . Extreme interest goes with extreme partisanship and might culminate in rigid fanaticism that could destroy democratic processes if generalized throughout the community. Low affect toward the election—not caring much—underlies the resolution of many political problems. . . . Only the

---

[3] Bernard R. Berelson, Paul F. Lazarsfeld, and William N. McPhee, *Voting* (Chicago: University of Chicago Press, 1954), pp. 314–15.

doctrinaire could deprecate the moderate indifference that facilitates compromise.

Berelson's statement was actually part of a larger theory about the role of the mass public in a democracy. According to what became known as the "elitist" point of view, the responsibility for democracy's survival is in the hands of the political leadership. The individual citizen is not critical (in this view) so long as the elite acts responsibly. Berelson contrasted the normative theory of democracy with empirical findings and concluded that democratic theory was defective in emphasizing the citizen's role. Leadership characteristics are important. For nonleaders, he concludes that a range of behavior, including nonparticipation by many, is required.

Taken together, these articles provide an entirely new perspective on political participation and voting in particular. Instead of arguing that every citizen should be an informed voter, the question now shifts to why anyone becomes informed and why anyone votes. Is voting actually useful in terms of some individuals' self-interest? And does voting actually make democracy work? Moreover, once having raised these questions, we should also ask whether voting should be encouraged. If nonvoting serves to facilitate compromise—or if most citizens' attitudes are irrelevant—perhaps citizens should be discouraged from voting rather than encouraged to vote.

Though we have not followed an exact chronology of studies, this stand was taken by several publications on voting and nonvoting. More recently, there have been reactions to these views, and it is to these responses that we now turn. But the ideas that we have discussed so far cannot be wholly dismissed, and we shall return to them at the end of this chapter.

Voting Is Rational and Essential

If Downs's analysis is carried to its logical conclusion, it suggests the possibility that no one will vote. The main components in Downs's analysis are C, the cost of voting; P, the probability that a citizen will, by voting, affect the election outcome; and B, the extent to which an individual feels that one candidate will benefit him or her more than another ("the perceived candidate differential" or "differential benefit"). Gordon Tullock first formalized the notion that a person will vote if the expected gain (PB), that is, the benefit from one's preferred candidate winning multiplied by the probability of affecting the election by one's single vote, exceeds the cost of voting. But he argued that if each citizen has one vote, then the individual vote will have very little probability of affecting the total outcome. Thus, the probability (P) of affecting the outcome is very small, so PB will be very small, probably less than the cost (C) for most individuals. [4] It would seem as if it is irrational for most people to vote.

---

[4] Gordon Tullock, *Toward a Mathematics of Politics* (Ann Arbor: University of Michigan Press, 1968), chap. 7.

Riker and Ordeshook suggested that a different interpretation of the probability term P is required.[5] What matters is the individual's perception of his or her chance of affecting the outcome of the election, and that in turn depends on how close the election is perceived to be. Individuals may consider the election close even if in some objective sense it is not. Riker and Ordeshook tested the notion that people will be more likely to vote if the election is perceived to be close. Using data from the SRC 1952–1960 election studies, they found that perceived closeness does have an effect on the turnout. In addition, they suggested that another term must be considered, which they labeled civic duty (D). This is analogous to Downs's suggestion that individuals sometimes vote because they consider it in their long-term interest to help maintain democracy even if their short-run calculation suggests not voting. Thus the complete formula is that the gains from voting are the expected benefit plus the sense of duty minus the costs: PB + D − C. A person would vote *only* if this quantity is greater than zero (i.e., if the gains, including the sense of duty, outweigh the costs).

The suggestion of adding a duty term (D) is important, for in one sense it salvages voting for the rational individual. Citizens may conclude that their votes are unlikely to affect the outcome, that there is little advantage in one candidate over the other, and that the cost of voting is relatively high, and yet they may vote because it will help to preserve democracy for a later time in which their votes may be more critical. But this formula is not satisfactory to everyone. It seems to suggest that individuals almost never find it rational to vote in the short run, but vote only in order to preserve democracy. In other words, democracy is useful only for preserving itself. Moreover, if many individuals vote, then each individual can rationalize nonvoting. If it is in my self-interest not to vote in the short run, and if enough other individuals will vote so that democracy will be preserved, then there is no need for me to vote at all. But, of course, if everyone thought this way, then no one would vote. And yet people do.

One way out of this dilemma is to argue that P, the probability of affecting the election outcome, is irrelevant. Ferejohn and Fiorina suggest that individuals may not ask themselves how likely they are to influence the outcome, but instead ask, "My God, what if I didn't vote and my preferred candidate lost by one vote? I'd feel like killing myself."[6] If individuals decide on this basis, what is important is the relative sizes of the benefits (B) and the costs (C). Clearly, the benefits are greater than the costs for some individuals, and for these people voting is rational. Thus, voting can be consid-

[5] William H. Riker and Peter C. Ordeshook, "A Theory of the Calculus of Voting," *American Political Science Review,* 62(1968):25–42.

[6] John A. Ferejohn and Morris P. Fiorina, "The Paradox of Not Voting: A Decision Theoretic Analysis," *American Political Science Review,* 67(1974):525–36, at p. 535.

ered rational for some people, and democracy serves a purpose other than just preserving itself.

Niemi has suggested that the difficulty with the rational voter approach is that the cost of voting has been tremendously exaggerated.[7] Particularly in presidential elections, the cost of voting is likely to be very small. Even the cost of becoming informed—at least informed enough to make a decision—is quite small. Moreover, there are costs attached to not voting, such as guilt feelings when others ask whether or not you have voted. Thus, even if the expected gain (PB) is quite small, this together with the costs of not voting may easily outweigh the relatively small cost of going to the polls. This point of view has the added advantage of emphasizing the variability of the cost term in different elections, a factor which has been largely ignored.

The value of these studies has been the emphasis they have placed on the cost term. Even moderate voting costs in combination with a low expected gain *may* make voting irrational from the perspective of each individual. Or, to put it another way, small variations in cost may lead to sizable variations in the number of people who vote. While considerable progress has been made in reducing the legal barriers which have stood in the way of people voting in presidential elections, the importance of this cost factor has still been all but ignored in the context of other elections. Factors such as registration by mail, more uniform voting dates throughout the nation, more polling places, longer hours for voting, and so on, should result in a considerable increase in turnout, particularly in elections that usually draw a small number of voters.

This raises the second point made earlier: Should voting be encouraged or discouraged? Berelson's point of view suggested that it should be discouraged, or at least that low turnout has its advantages as well as its disadvantages. This elitist point of view was directly confronted by Walker, who argues that low turnout, lack of interest, and apathy are not as benign as Berelson would have us believe.[8] Drawing particularly on the experience of blacks in the United States, he argues that low turnout is not necessarily due to acceptance of the status quo, but may instead indicate complete alienation from the political system. The resulting frustration can lead to unconventional forms of political participation, including violence. Moreover, Walker reminds us that for the classical democrat, political apathy is an object of intense concern because voting is supposed to do more than accept or reject the status quo. Rather, the very act of participation in the affairs of government is supposed to be an act of pride and self-respect for citizens. Accept-

---

[7] Richard G. Niemi, "A Note on Models of Voting and Nonvoting," *Public Choice,* forthcoming.

[8] Jack L. Walker, "A Critique of the Elitist Theory of Democracy," *American Political Science Review,* 60(1966):285–95.

ance of nonvoting would, from this point of view, totally corrode the very basis of democracy.[9]

Increasingly, efforts have been made to determine empirically whether alienation is a prime cause of nonvoting. Converse with Niemi reported that all attitudinal factors for nonvoting were less frequent than legal (nonregistration) or personal (ill health, flat tire, etc.) reasons during the 1950's,[10] but this depends on the respondent's own explanation of not voting and does not explain why he or she was not motivated to register. The increased cynicism in recent years makes alienation a likely explanation of decreased turnout, and the popular press has already suggested as much.

Two recent tests, however, would suggest that cynicism is not a powerful explanatory factor in presidential voting. Brody and Page considered the impact of two psychological factors on turnout in 1968—voter alienation, defined as liking none of the candidates, and voter indifference, defined as liking all of the candidates equally.[11] The 1968 national election survey included a "thermometer question" in which respondents were asked to indicate how warm they felt toward several presidential contenders. A temperature of 50 was the neutral response, 100 indicated very warm feelings, 0, cold feelings. Brody and Page operationalize alienation in terms of the score a person gives to the presidential nominee he or she likes the most—a person whose favorite candidate has a score of 50 or less is termed alienated. A respondent who gives the three nominees the same score is termed indifferent. Alienation and indifference have definite effects on voting, but indifference accounts for a 17 percent drop, while alienation leads to only a 10 percent drop in turnout. Moreover, only one-eighth of the sample is either alienated or indifferent by their measure; so neither effect has a large impact on turnout.

---

[9] An interesting middle ground in the debate between Berelson and Walker is provided by Converse. From Converse's point of view, nonvoting itself may not be objectionable, but the sporadic participation of chronic nonvoters is. This point of view is most clearly expressed in an attempt to explain the mass support of the Nazi Party in Germany in the 30's. Converse argues that chronic nonvoters, who were uninformed and unsophisticated but not necessarily pro-Nazi as such, were major contributors to the upsurge in Nazi voting. Thus the rise in Nazi voting was due not just to an increase in turnout, but to increased turnout among those who had previously been nonvoters out of apathy and ignorance. [Philip E. Converse, "The Nature of Belief Systems in Mass Publics," in David Apter, ed., *Ideology and Discontent* (New York: Free Press, 1964), pp. 252–54.] The soundness of this argument has been disputed in W. Phillips Shively, "Party Identification, Party Choice, and Voting Stability: The Weimar Case," *American Political Science Review*, 66(1972):1203–25. Precise interpretation is difficult because conclusions must be based on an analysis of aggregate data.

[10] Philip E. Converse with Richard G. Niemi, "Non-Voting Among Young Adults in the United States" in William J. Crotty, Donald M. Freeman, and Douglas S. Gatlin, eds., *Political Parties and Political Behavior*, 2d ed. (Boston: Allyn & Bacon, 1971). Even as late as 1968, after passage of the Voting Rights Act of 1965 cut down on southern disenfranchisement of blacks, 56 percent of the nonvoting respondents (including southern blacks) cited legal reasons as the cause (CPS/SRC 1968 American National Election Study).

[11] Richard A. Brody and Benjamin I. Page, "Indifference, Alienation, and Rational Decisions," *Public Choice*, 15(1973):1–17.

A Center for Political Studies report on the 1972 election survey similarly analyzes the impact of two psychological factors on turnout.[12] Political efficacy—the feeling that one can have an influence on governmental behavior—had a substantial impact, with a 26 percent difference between high and low efficacy groups. By contrast, political trust had only a small impact, with cynics voting 9 percent less than those who trusted the government.

If these results are accepted, then current low turnout figures represent more than alienation and cynicism. On a more theoretical plane, they would suggest that Walker's view of low turnout is empirically invalid at the present time, and by inference, is at least a questionable explanation of low turnout in the past. On the other hand, these two analyses are far from definitive, and numerous further studies of the impact of cynicism are to be expected.

Conclusions

Our view of voting has come almost full circle from where it began prior to the introduction of sample surveys and of rational political theory. What have we learned on the way? First, we have learned that nonvoting may mean several things—apathy, satisfaction with the status quo, cynicism—and should not be interpreted exclusively in terms of one of these causes. No doubt the importance of each of these factors varies, and it is an empirical question as to what impact each factor has in different times and places. To arbitrarily attribute nonvoting to one cause—and therefore to conclude that nonvoting is necessarily good or bad—is misleading. While we, like most Americans, lean toward the view that high rates of nonvoting are unsatisfactory, this view should not be accepted uncritically. Depending on the times, the circumstances, and the individuals, nonvoting can conceivably be an acceptable state of affairs.

Along with this viewpoint goes the finding that nonvoting may be individually rational, as Downs suggested. This view emphasizes the costs of voting and of participating generally. It suggests that, if we want to increase participation, we should reduce the costs of participation as much as possible. While in a sense this has always been known, the point takes on added significance when it is suggested that individuals may rationally decide that it is not in their self-interest to vote given the costs that are imposed. Consistent with this point of view would be an attempt to make voting virtually costless, which includes making registration automatic and thereby effortless. Though the location of voting booths may seem like a mundane problem, all of the factors that enter into the cost of voting, taken together, are a crucial factor in individual decisions about whether to vote. Manipulation of

[12] Arthur H. Miller and Warren E. Miller, "Issues, Candidates, and Partisan Divisions in the 1972 American Presidential Election," *British Journal of Political Science*, 5(1975):393–434.

these costs is an important ingredient in the size of the turnout on our many election days.

A final conclusion to be drawn from studies of turnout and voting involves a more accurate understanding of the role of voting in democratic government. As Verba and Nie indicate, other forms of participation than voting may be more rational for many purposes. Yet they also point out that what voting lacks in the ability to convey information to leaders, it makes up for in the pressure put on the leadership. Voting cannot and should not be expected to decide particular policy alternatives, both because of the characteristics of individual voters that we shall observe later in the book, and because of the nature of the voting choice, as discussed by Verba and Nie. And yet in determining the general direction of governmental behavior, voting is a powerful means of control.[13] But the nature of that control can be known only through a better understanding of the individuals that make up the electorate—their political knowledge, their political attitudes, and the way in which they make political decisions. It is these factors that we consider in the remainder of this book.

Further Readings

Empirical Studies of Nonvoting

Angus Campbell, Philip E. Converse, Warren E. Miller, and Donald E. Stokes, *The American Voter* (New York: Wiley, 1960), chap. 5, unabridged, chap. 4, abridged. One of the most complete analyses of the correlates of turnout.
Philip E. Converse with Richard G. Niemi, "Non-Voting Among Young Adults in the United States," in William J. Crotty, Donald M. Freeman, and Douglas S. Gatlin, eds., *Political Parties and Political Behavior,* 2d ed. (Boston: Allyn & Bacon, 1971). Analysis of reasons given by respondents for not voting in the 1950s.
Richard A. Brody and Benjamin I. Page, "Indifference, Alienation and Rational Decisions," *Public Choice,* 15(1973):1-17. Analysis of attitudinal correlates of nonvoting in 1968.

Aggregate Analysis of Turnout

Stanley Kelley, Jr., Richard E. Ayres, and William G. Bowen, "Registration and Voting: Putting First Things First," *American Political Science Review,* 61(1967):359-79. Analysis of turnout figures in various cities in terms of differences in registration.

---

[13] This is also the message of the last chapter of Angus Campbell, Philip E. Converse, Warren E. Miller, and Donald E. Stokes, *The American Voter* (New York: Wiley, 1960), especially pp. 541-48. All references are to the unabridged edition unless otherwise specified.

Jae-On Kim, John R. Petrocik, and Stephen N. Enokson, "Voter Turnout Among the American States: Systemic and Individual Components," *American Political Science Review*, 69(1975):107-23. Aggregate analysis of socio-demographic, electoral competitiveness, and legal correlates of turnout in 1960.

Empirical Analysis of Political Participation

Robert A. Dahl, *Who Governs?* (New Haven: Yale University Press, 1961). Classical analysis of participation in local politics which has provoked much reaction.

Norval D. Glenn and Michael Grimes, "Aging, Voting, and Political Interest," *American Sociological Review*, 33(1968):563-75. Voting remains steady into advanced maturity; political interest actually increases.

Lester W. Milbrath, *Political Participation* (Chicago: Rand McNally, 1965). Classification of participation types and summary of literature.

Sidney Verba and Norman H. Nie, *Participation in America* (New York: Harper & Row, 1972). Analysis of modes of participation, correlates of participation, and effects of participation in a national sample.

Comparative Analysis of Political Participation

Norman H. Nie, G. Bingham Powell, and Kenneth Prewitt, "Social Structure and Political Participation: Developmental Realtionships," *American Political Science Review*, 63(1969):361-78, 808-32. Causal analysis of social experiences that explain growth of political participation in economically advanced nations.

Sidney Verba, Norman H. Nie, and Jae-On Kim, *The Modes of Democratic Participation* (Beverly Hills: Sage Publications, 1971). Cross-national study of participation modes.

Rationality of Voting

Gordon Tullock, *Toward a Mathematics of Politics* (Ann Arbor: University of Michigan Press, 1968), chap. 7. Emphasis on lack of expected gain from voting for the citizen.

William H. Riker and Peter C. Ordeshook, "A Theory of the Calculus of Voting," *American Political Science Review*, 62(1968):25-42. Importance of perceptions of how close the vote in an election will be.

John A. Ferejohn and Morris P. Fiorina, "The Paradox of Not Voting: A Decision Theoretic Analysis," *American Political Science Review*, 67(1974):525-36. Voting in order to not regret not voting.

Richard G. Niemi, "A Note on Models of Voting and Nonvoting," *Public Choice*, forthcoming. Reconsideration of the costs of voting.

A. Bruce Cyr, "The Calculus of Voting Reconsidered," *Public Opinion Quarterly*, 39(1975):19-38. Retest of the Riker-Ordeshook model.

3. The Causes and Effects of Rational Abstention

ANTHONY DOWNS

Introduction

Citizens who are eligible to vote in democratic elections often fail to do so. In fact, some citizens never vote, and in some elections abstainers outnumber voters. In this chapter we examine the conditions under which abstention is rational and attempt to appraise its impact upon the distribution of political power.

Throughout this analysis, we assume that every rational man decides whether to vote just as he makes all other decisions: if the returns outweigh the costs, he votes; if not, he abstains.

Objectives

In this chapter we attempt to prove the following propositions:

1. When voting is costless, every citizen who is indifferent abstains and every citizen who has any preference whatsoever votes.
2. If voting is costly, it is rational for some indifferent citizens to vote and for some citizens with preferences to abstain.

SOURCE: *An Economic Theory of Democracy,* by Anthony Downs, chap. 14. Copyright © 1957 by Harper & Row, Publishers. Reprinted with permission of the publisher.

3. When voting costs exist, small changes in their size may radically affect the distribution of political power.
4. The cost of information acts in effect to disenfranchise low-income groups relative to high-income groups when voting is costly.
5. Voting costs may also disenfranchise low-income citizens relative to wealthier citizens.
6. It is sometimes rational for a citizen to vote even when his short run costs exceed his short-run returns, because social responsibility produces a long-run return.

Participation in
Elections When Voting Is Costless

When the cost of voting is zero, any return whatsoever, no matter how small, makes it rational to vote and irrational to abstain. Therefore, whether abstention is rational depends entirely on the nature of the returns from voting.

Why Only Those Citizens Who Are Indifferent Abstain

. . . We pointed out [in Downs, chapter 13] that a citizen's reward for voting correctly consists of his vote value, i.e, his party differential discounted to allow for the influence of other voters upon the election's outcome. If the citizen is indifferent among parties, his party differential is zero, so his vote value must also be zero. It appears that he obtains no return from voting unless he prefers one party over the others; hence indifferent citizens always abstain.

However, this conclusion is false, because the return from voting *per se* is not the same thing as the return from voting correctly. The alternative to voting *per se* is abstaining; whereas the alternative to voting correctly is voting incorrectly—at least so we have viewed it in our analysis. But an incorrect vote is still a vote; so if there is any gain from voting *per se,* a man who votes incorrectly procures it, though a man who abstains does not.

The advantage of voting *per se* is that it makes democracy possible. If no one votes, then the system collapses because no government is chosen. We assume that the citizens of a democracy subscribe to its principles and there-fore derive benefits from its continuance; hence they do not want it to collapse.[1] For this reason they attach value to the act of voting *per se* and receive a return from it.

Paradoxically, the size of this return depends upon the cost of voting.

---

[1] This assumption does not mean that all citizens receive the same benefits from democ-racy, nor does it preclude their opposing the majority on any or all issues. Rather it implies that (1) every citizen receives some benefits and therefore (2) the loss he sustains when the majority cause something he dislikes to be done is partly offset by the benefit he receives from operation of majority rule *per se.*

When voting costs are zero, the return from voting *per se* is also zero, but when voting is costly, the return from voting *per se* is positive. The second of these assertions we discuss later; now let us examine the first one. [2]

Democracy cannot operate rationally if everyone is indifferent about who wins each election. Of course, not everyone has to have a party preference, but someone must if the election is to be a meaningful act of choice. Therefore we assume throughout this chapter that (1) at least one citizen is not indifferent, (2) no tie votes occur, and (3) indifference does not reflect equal disgust with the candidates but rather equal satisfaction with them. [3]

When the cost of voting is zero, everyone who is not indifferent votes, because his return from doing so, though small, is larger than zero. Therefore citizens who are indifferent know that the election will work and democracy will continue to function even if they abstain. This conclusion holds even when the vast majority of the electorate is indifferent; in fact, only one man need vote. The parties running still must cater to the interests of the whole electorate, because (1) they do not know in advance who will be indifferent and (2) once elected, they know that the citizens who were indifferent may vote in the future. Thus parties compete with each other to attract the potential votes of men who previously abstained as well as the actual votes of those who voted.

As a result, men who are indifferent about who wins have nothing to gain from voting, so they abstain. Hence when the cost of voting is zero, every citizen who is perfectly indifferent abstains. However, the above reasoning does not apply when voting is costly, as we shall see later.

The Nature of Indifference

In our model, indifferent voters never influence the outcome of elections. [4] Yet their interests are still catered to by each party, because competition forces parties to seek potential as well as actual votes. This fact raises the question of whether indifference has any political significance at all.

Indifferent voters are those who cannot see any net difference in the utility incomes they expect from each party if it is elected. Therefore it seems reasonable a priori that they should have no influence on who wins. However, this conclusion can be questioned on two counts.

First, are indifferent voters equally pleased by all parties or equally repelled by them? When a large portion of the electorate is indifferent—as often seems to be the case in reality—the rationality of elections as government-selectors depends upon the answer to this question. If indifference reflects equal disgust with all candidates and a strong preference for some

---

[2] Since voting costs in reality are never zero, this discussion is merely a preliminary to our later analysis.

[3] The third assumption is discussed in detail later.

[4] This conclusion holds even though some indifferent voters cast ballots when voting is costly, since they do so at random and their ballots therefore cancel each other. [See the next] section of this chapter.

noncandidate, the election is bound to produce a government repugnant to many citizens. On the other hand, if indifference indicates high but equal satisfaction with those running, only the citizens who vote against the winner will be displeased by the outcome.

Essentially, this argument raises an issue with which we dealt briefly in [Downs,] chapter 8: How are the candidates for each election chosen? To avoid discussing it further here, we assume that every political viewpoint which has a significant number of supporters is represented by some party running in the election. Thus indifference in our model is not caused by equal loathing for all the candidates but reflects ambivalence of a less pejorative nature.

The second question raised by indifference is whether indifferent voters really have zero party differentials or merely lack information. In the last chapter [of Downs] we saw that most voters do not acquire enough information to discover their true preferences, since each knows his vote is of small significance. Perhaps a great many voters who are now indifferent would cease to be so if they found out their true views. However, the cost of information makes further research irrational. Since this cost is harder to bear for low-income citizens than for high-income ones, the incidence of falsely indifferent voters may be higher among the former than among the latter. If so, uncertainty imposes a bias on the distribution of political power. It causes a disproportionate number of low-income citizens to refrain from influencing election outcomes.

The validity of this argument rests upon the following proposition: the more information a citizen receives about the policies of each party, the less likely he is to be indifferent. Unless this proposition is true, there is no reason to believe that men who know their true preferences are less likely to be indifferent than those who do not.

In our opinion, the proposition is false. The amount of information a man has necessarily affects the confidence with which he holds his decisions, but it does not necessarily affect their nature. If everyone had 100 percent information, some citizens might still be indifferent. [5] Therefore indifference is not merely an illusion caused by lack of data; so we cannot argue a priori that increases in data will tend to eliminate it. However, more information does raise the confidence of each citizen in his decision, ceteris paribus, because it moves him closer to being 100 percent informed. For this reason, the more data a man has, the less he must discount his estimated return from voting correctly.

---

[5] It is conceivable that indifference might not exist in a perfectly informed world, but only if preferences are discontinuous. Therefore most economists assume indifference is a real state of mind, even though it cannot easily be detected in behavior. To show the reasoning behind this view, let us assume that a rational consumer faces three bundles of goods: A, B, and C. He prefers A to B and B to C. Now assume that bundle A is continuously varied in composition so that it gradually comes to resemble bundle C, though in such a way that it is never identical to B. Since the consumer prefers it to B at the start and B to it at the end, somewhere between, he must be precisely indifferent between it and B, so runs the argument. We accept it.

When the cost of voting is zero, it makes no difference how much each citizen discounts his estimated party differential as long as the rate is less than 100 percent, since even a tiny net return causes him to vote. Thus information costs do not increase abstention among low-income groups relative to high-income groups. But when voting is costly, the fact that poorer citizens cannot afford as much information as their wealthier neighbors does create a bias. For example, assume that the distribution of voting costs and of real voting returns is the same for both groups.[6] Because less affluent citizens discount their returns more, fewer of them will vote. Thus lower confidence among low-income groups has no political repercussions when voting is costless but becomes quite important when voting costs are introduced into the model.

Participation in Elections When Voting Is Costly

Voting Costs and Their Behavioral Effects

Heretofore we have assumed that voting is a costless act, but this assumption is self-contradictory because every act takes time. In fact, time is the principal cost of voting: time to register, to discover what parties are running, to deliberate, to go to the polls, and to mark the ballot. Since time is a scarce resource, voting is inherently costly.

This fact alters our previous conclusion that everyone votes if he has any party preference at all. When there are costs to voting, they may outweigh the returns thereof; hence rational abstention becomes possible even for citizens who want a particular party to win. In fact, since the returns from voting are often miniscule, even low voting costs may cause many partisan citizens to abstain.

The importance of their abstention depends on the effects it has upon the distribution of political power. Such effects can stem from two sources: (1) biases in the distribution of ability to bear the costs of voting, and (2) biases in the distribution of high returns from voting.

The only direct money costs connected with registering to vote and voting are any poll taxes extant and the cost of transportation. Ability to bear these costs varies inversely with income, so upper-income citizens have an advantage. Where poll taxes do not exist, the principal cost of voting is usually the utility income lost by devoting time to it rather than something else. If the time must be taken out of working hours, this cost can be quite high, in which case high-income groups again have an advantage. But if the time comes during leisure hours, there is no reason to suppose any such income-correlated disparity exists.

---

[6] By *real* returns, we mean those which each citizen would perceive in a perfectly informed world.

At first glance, all of these costs may appear trivial, and biases in ability to bear them seem irrelevant. However, the returns from voting are usually so low that tiny variations in its cost may have tremendous effects on the distribution of political power. This fact explains why such simple practices as holding elections on holidays, keeping polls open late, repealing small poll taxes, and providing free rides to the polls may strikingly affect election results.

The Nature, Size, and Impact of the Returns From Voting

The return a citizen receives from voting is compounded of several factors. The first is the strength of his desire to see one party win instead of the others, i.e., the size of his party differential. As we pointed out in [Downs,] chapter 3, party policies determine this factor. A second factor is the degree to which he discounts his party differential to allow for the influence of other voters. In [Downs, chapter 13], we showed that this depends upon how close he thinks the election will be. These two factors together constitute his vote value.

The third factor is independent of the other two; it is the value of voting *per se*. Although we discussed it briefly earlier in the chapter, we must examine it more carefully here because of the vital role it plays when voting is costly.

We assume that everyone in our model world derives utility from living in a democracy, as stated previously. When the cost of voting is zero, receipt of this utility is not jeopardized by abstention, because only those who are indifferent abstain. But positive voting costs alter this situation by causing some men who have definite preferences to abstain also. In fact, since each citizen's vote value is usually quite small, any cost at all may threaten the political system with collapse through lack of participation.

Further analysis is complicated by an oligopoly problem similar to that described in chapter 9 [of Downs]. If each partisan voter expects many others to vote, his own vote value is tiny; hence it is outweighed by a very small cost of voting. The more voters there are who feel this way, the smaller is the total vote. But a small total vote raises the probability that any one ballot will be decisive; hence the vote value of each citizen may rise to a point where it outweighs the cost of voting. Therefore citizens who think others expect many to vote will themselves expect few to vote, and they will want to be among those few.

Each citizen is thus trapped in a maze of conjectural variation. The importance of his own vote depends upon how important other people think their votes are, which in turn depends on how important he thinks his vote is. He can conclude either that (1) since so many others are going to vote, his ballot is not worth casting or (2) since most others reason this way, they will abstain and therefore he should vote. If everyone arrives at the first conclusion, no one votes; whereas if everyone arrives at the second conclusion, every citizen votes unless he is indifferent.

Both these outcomes are self-defeating. When no one votes, democracy collapses. Yet if everyone who is not indifferent votes, in the next election each will abstain, since his ballot had so little effect previously (i.e., when everyone voted). Thus if we assume all men think alike, democracy seems unable to function rationally. What rule can we posit within the framework of our model to show how rational men can arrive at different conclusions through viewing the same situation?

The answer consists of two parts:

1. Rational men in a democracy are motivated to some extent by a sense of social responsibility relatively independent of their own short-run gains and losses.
2. If we view such responsibility as one part of the return from voting, it is possible that the cost of voting is outweighed by its returns for some but not all rational men.

Let us examine these propositions in order.

One thing that all citizens in our model have in common is the desire to see democracy work. Yet if voting costs exist, pursuit of short-run rationality can conceivably cause democracy to break down. However improbable this outcome may seem, it is so disastrous that every citizen is willing to bear at least some cost in order to insure himself against it. The more probable it appears, the more cost he is willing to bear.

Since voting is one form of insurance against this catastrophe, every rational citizen receives some return from voting *per se* when voting is costly. Its magnitude (1) is never zero, (2) varies directly with the benefits he gains from democracy, and (3) varies inversely with the number of others he expects to vote. The last of these factors depends upon the cost of voting and the returns he thinks others get from it. Thus we have not completely eliminated the oligopoly problem, but we have introduced another factor which tends to offset its importance.

To show how this factor works, let us approach it from another angle. Implicit throughout our study is the following assumption: rational men accept limitations on their ability to make short-run gains in order to procure greater gains in the long run. This assumption appears in many of the provisions of the constitution stated in [Downs,] chapter 1, and also in the solution to the indivisibility problem stated in [Downs,] chapter 10. The limitations men accept are usually "rules of the game" without which no game can be played. Each individual knows he can gain at some moments by violating the rules of the game, but he also knows that consistent violation by many citizens will destroy the game and introduce social chaos. Since he himself would be a loser if chaos prevailed, he resists the momentary temptation to let short-run individual rationality triumph over long-run individual rationality. Surely, such resistance is rational.

However, it is not uniform for three reasons: (1) the connection between a particular violation of the rules and eventual chaos is not equally obvious in all cases, (2) some violations lead to disorders worse than those caused by other violations, and (3) the immediate gains from violation are not always the same. For example, the deleterious effects of universal failure to vote are both clearer and worse than those of universal failure to become well-informed before voting. Similarly, the cost avoided by not paying income tax is much larger than that avoided by not voting. For these reasons, men can rely on each other to abide by the rules voluntarily to different degrees for different rules. In some cases, they have to back up the rules with force in order to insure observance.

Participation in elections is one of the rules of the game in a democracy, because without it democracy cannot work. Since the consequences of universal failure to vote are both obvious and disastrous, and since the cost of voting is small, at least some men can rationally be motivated to vote even when their personal gains in the short run are outweighed by their personal costs. However, this conclusion raises two problems.

The first is the arbitrary nature of assuming that such motivation operates in regard to voting but not in regard to other political actions. Why, for instance, are rational men not willing to find their true preferences before voting, since they will benefit in the long run from doing so? We can only answer by pointing to the factors mentioned previously: (1) the potential ill effects of not voting are worse than those of not becoming informed, (2) the connection between failure to vote and its ill effects is much clearer than that between failure to become informed and its ill effects, and (3) the cost of voting is lower than the cost of becoming informed.[7] Some or all of these arguments apply to all other cases of indivisible benefits where we have assumed short-run rationality dominant (e.g., paying taxes).

A second difficulty is explaining why some men vote and some abstain even though all favor democracy and benefit from its continuance. Solving this problem requires the second proposition mentioned earlier: the returns in fact outweigh the costs for some but not for all.

Although the benefits each citizen derives from living in a democracy actually accrue to him continuously over time, he can view them as a capital sum which pays interest at each election. This procedure is rational because voting is a necessary prerequisite for democracy; hence democracy is in one sense a reward for voting. We call the part of this reward the citizen receives at each election his *long-run participation value*.

Of course, he will actually get this reward even if he himself does not vote as long as a sufficient number of other citizens do. But we have already shown that he is willing to bear certain short-run costs he could avoid in order to do his share in providing long-run benefits. The maximum cost he will bear for this reason in any given election is that which just offsets his long-run participation value.

Thus the total return which a rational citizen receives from voting in a

---

[7] In this case, another fact is relevant: voting is a discrete and clearly identifiable act; whereas "being well-informed" is a vague state of mind which even the individual himself has a hard time recognizing.

given election consists of his long-run participation value plus his vote value. In other words, the reward a man obtains for voting depends upon (1) how much he values living in a democracy, (2) how much he cares which party wins, (3) how close he thinks the election will be, and (4) how many other citizens he thinks will vote.[8] These four variables insure a relatively wide range of possible returns from voting for different individuals. The range of possible costs is also wide, as we saw before. Therefore a matching of returns and costs can easily result in a mixed outcome—i.e., a large number of voters whose returns exceed their costs and a large number of abstainers whose costs exceed their returns.

Without abandoning our assumption that all men are rational, we can thus explain the following phenomena by means of our model:

1. Some men abstain all the time, others abstain sometimes, and others never abstain.
2. The percentage of the electorate abstaining varies from election to election.
3. Many men who vote do not become well-informed before voting.
4. Only a few men who become well-informed do not vote.

Furthermore, our analysis has isolated several factors upon which the incidence of rational abstention depends. Hence it may be useful in designing methods of predicting how many voters will abstain in a given election.[9]

A Revised Summary of
How Rational Citizens Decide How to Vote

The introduction of voting costs into our model forces us to revise again the behavior rule first formulated in [Downs,] chapter 3. In an uncertain world, each rational citizen makes his voting decision in the following manner:

1. He makes preliminary estimates of his expected party differential, the cost of voting, his long-run participation value, and the number of other citizens he believes will vote.
2. If his party differential is zero because all party policies and platforms appear identical to him, he weighs his long-run participation value plus the expected value of "change" as opposed to "no change" (or vice versa) against the cost of voting.[10]
   a. If returns outweigh costs and he favors "change," he votes for the opposition party. (In a multiparty system, he chooses one of the opposition parties at random and votes for it.)

---

[8] This list shows clearly the reason why the motive for voting is stronger than the motive for becoming well-informed. The former encompasses all four factors mentioned, while the latter is comprised of only factors (2) and (3).

[9] Needless to say, other authors have pointed out the same factors. For a summary analysis of their views and findings, see V. O. Key Jr., *Politics, Parties, and Pressure Groups* (New York: Thomas Y. Crowell Company, 1953), chap. 19.

[10] For an explanation of why he considers "change" as opposed to "no change" in this instance, see [Downs,] chapter 3, part II, c.

b. If returns outweigh costs and he favors "no change," he votes for the incumbent party. (If a coalition is in power, he votes for one of the parties in it chosen at random.)

c. If costs outweigh returns, he abstains.

3. If his party differential is zero because he expects identical utility incomes from all parties even though their policies and platforms differ, he weighs only his long-run participation value against the cost of voting.

   a. If returns outweigh costs, he votes for a party chosen at random.

   b. If costs outweigh returns, he abstains.

4. If his party differential is not zero, he estimates how close the election will be and discounts his party differential accordingly. (In a multiparty system he also must decide whether his favorite party is hopeless, as described in [Downs,] chapter 3.)

   a. If the discounted party differential plus the long-run participation value exceed the cost of voting, he votes for his favorite party (or some other party in certain cases—see [Downs,] chapter 3).

   b. If the sum of these quantities is smaller than the cost of voting, he abstains.

5. Throughout the above processes he procures more information about all the entities involved whenever its expected payoff exceeds its cost. Since this information may alter his estimate of any entity, he may shift from one category to another in the midst of his deliberations. He votes according to the rules applicable to the category he is in on election day.[11]

The Relation Between
Voting Behavior and the Distribution of Power

If we translate the results of the above deliberations into possible types of behavior, we discover that citizens in our model can react to an election by doing the following things:

1. Voting for their favorite party.
2. Voting for some other party chosen for strategic reasons because their favorite party is hopeless.
3. Voting for a party chosen at random.
4. Abstaining.

These four types of action do not result in equal influence for the citizens who carry them out. Seen as a group, the citizens who vote by preference determine the immediate outcome of the election and have a strong effect on the long-run development of party policies. Citizens who vote randomly

[11] This exceedingly complicated method of deciding how to vote seems to bear little resemblance to how men act in the real world. However, except for one step, the entire process is necessarily implicit in the behavior of any rational voter, even if casual observation fails to confirm this fact. The one step which is not necessary is the use of a random mechanism to "break ties" by citizens who are indifferent but wish to vote, as in 2a, 2b, and 3a above. The implications of this step are discussed in the Appendix to this chapter.

exercise only the latter effect, since their votes cancel insofar as the immediate outcome is concerned. Citizens who abstain also have no influence on who wins the election. Thus voting behavior is a crucial determinant of the distribution of political power.

There are two reasons to suspect that the proportion of low-income citizens who abstain is usually higher than the proportion of high-income citizens who do so. First, the cost of voting is harder for low-income citizens to bear; therefore, even if returns among high- and low-income groups are the same, fewer of the latter vote. Second, the cost of information is harder for low-income citizens to bear; hence more of them are likely to be uncertain because they lack information. Since uncertainty reduces the returns from voting, a lower proportion of low-income groups would vote even if voting costs were equally difficult for everyone to bear.

Because citizens who abstain exercise less influence than those who vote, low-income groups in society are likely to have less political power than their numbers warrant, and high-income groups more. Once again we see that the necessity of bearing economic costs in order to act politically biases the distribution of power against citizens with low incomes. However, we cannot tell a priori just how significant this bias really is.

Summary

When voting is costless, any return whatsoever makes abstention irrational, so everyone who has even a slight party preference votes. On the other hand, abstention does not harm those who are indifferent because (1) democracy works even if they do not vote and (2) parties still cater to their interests so as to get their votes next time. Thus there is no return from voting *per se*, and all indifferent citizens abstain.

When voting is costly, its costs may outweigh its returns, so abstention can be rational even for citizens with party preferences. In fact, the returns from voting are usually so low that even small costs may cause many voters to abstain; hence tiny variations in cost can sharply redistribute political power.

One of the returns from voting stems from each citizen's realization that democracy cannot function unless many people vote. This return is independent of his short-run gains and losses, but it is not very large because the benefits of democracy are indivisible. Nevertheless, it helps solve the oligopoly problem voters face, thereby preventing universal abstention from paralyzing democracy.

The total return each citizen receives from voting depends upon (1) the benefits he gets from democracy, (2) how much he wants a particular party to win, (3) how close he thinks the election will be, and (4) how many other citizens he thinks will vote. These variables insure a relatively wide range of possible returns similar to the range of voting costs. Thus when citizens balance their costs and returns, some vote and others abstain.

However, the abstention rate is higher among low-income citizens than among high-income citizens for two reasons. Since the former have a harder time paying the cost of voting, it takes higher returns to get them to vote. And since they can less easily bear the cost of information, they have fewer data and are more uncertain; therefore they discount the returns from voting more heavily.

Appendix:
The Possible Existence of Irrationality in the Model

Throughout this study, we have avoided making arbitrary assumptions without presenting at least some reasons why they are plausible. Therefore we offer this appendix as an *apologia* for an assumption made in this chapter which is arbitrary, but for which we have so far given no explanation.

The postulate we are referring to is the following: every citizen who wishes to vote but is indifferent about who wins chooses a party at random and votes for it. From the point of view of the individual, there is no reason why random selection is preferable to certain other methods of choice. Since he cannot distinguish between the parties on the basis of their policies, he might as well use any other basis which pleases him. For instance, he might vote for the party whose leader has the most charming personality, or the one whose historic heroes appeal to him most, or the one his father voted for. Thus a rational man may employ politically irrational mechanisms to decide for whom to vote.

Though use of such devices is individually rational, it is socially irrational. If indifferent voters do not make voting choices randomly, their votes fail to cancel each other; hence men who are indifferent about who wins affect the outcome of each election. Not only is this arrangement inefficient *per se,* but also it may have drastic effects on party behavior. If the number of indifferent voters is large, parties will plan their actions and statements to influence the nonrational mechanisms they think these voters are using. As a result, parties will cease devoting all their energies to carrying out their social function, which is formulating policies relevant to citizens' political desires.

Obviously, we have made the assumption of random selection in order to avoid this outcome. However, we believe that irrationality would not occur to a significant extent in the model even if this assumption were dropped. In our opinion, those citizens who are interested enough in politics to vote at all almost always have some party preference. If this is true, so small a number of rational voters are in a position to be influenced by politically irrational factors that parties do not exert much energy wooing them. Admittedly, this view is merely an opinion.

There are other parts of the analysis where irrational factors might conceivably exercise influence, though none are as unequivocal as the above. For example, if we count the time it takes to go to the polls as a cost of voting, why not count the social prestige received for voting as a return?

Clearly, society bestows this prestige upon men in order to get them to vote; it is not therefore rational for men to seek this reward? [12]

As we pointed out in [Downs,] chapter 1, the difficulty with such arguments is that they rationalize everything. If it is rational to vote for prestige, why is it not rational to vote so as to please one's employer or one's sweetheart? Soon all behavior whatsoever becomes rational because every act is a means to some end the actor values. To avoid this sterile conclusion, we have regarded only actions leading to strictly political or economic ends as rational.

---

[12] Actually, the social prestige connected with voting in the real world is analogous to the long-run participation value in our model. We may reasonably assume that citizens of the real world are not as calculating as those in the model. Therefore the leaders of society arrange to have them perceive social responsibility in the form of guilt feelings for wrong actions (e.g., not voting) and reward feelings for right actions (e.g., voting). These feelings function on an unconscious level to achieve the same end that the return for voting *per se* achieves consciously in our model. In a certain sense, therefore, we have already accounted for the operation of social prestige in the structure of the model.

4. The Rationality of Political Activity: A Reconsideration

SIDNEY VERBA
NORMAN H. NIE

The alternative modes of political activity, we have argued, represent different ways by which the citizen influences his government. This argument is supported by the findings reported in chapter 5 [of Verba and Nie] that different sets of orientations accompany the various types of activity. We can carry this argument a step further by considering more closely what it is that citizens expect to obtain—or can reasonably expect to obtain—from their participation; and how this differs from one mode to another. Participation is, to us, most importantly an instrumental activity through which citizens attempt to influence the government to act in ways the citizens prefer. But the alternative modes can produce different types of governmental response. In this chapter we look beyond our data to other studies to see how this is the case.

The problem relates to the current debate about the rationality of political

Source: *Participation in America,* by Sidney Verba and Norman H. Nie, chap. 7. Copyright © 1972 by Sidney Verba and Norman H. Nie. Reprinted with permission of Harper & Row, Publishers.

Editor's note: The data summarized in this chapter are based on a representative national sample of 2,549 respondents interviewed by the National Opinion Research Center in March 1967.

activity. [1] It is not our purpose to enter the complexities of that debate, but some of the considerations involved highlight differences among our various modes of activity. And, in turn, the problem of rationality looks somewhat different when one has expanded one's notion of political activity beyond the electoral context. In particular, we can go beyond the question of whether it is rational to vote and whether citizens choose candidates rationally to the question of how the choice among alternative political activities relates to citizen needs and preferences.

The debate centers around the question: When citizens participate, do they do so rationally? For a citizen to do so, he must know what he wants in terms of a governmental response (i.e., know what policy he wishes the government to pursue or know what benefit he wishes the government to provide), he must know what action is likely to increase the chances of the government providing what he wants, and he must act accordingly, taking into account the cost of that activity in relation to other uses of his time and effort. The citizen "inputs" some act of participation in the expectation that the government will "output" what he wants. If the former is appropriate to the latter—i.e., his participation increases the likelihood that the government will perform as he desires—the citizen is behaving rationally.

The clarity of the citizen's expectation is important. If one is really talking of governmental response to a citizen, the citizen's action must carry a message about his desires precise enough for the government to know how to respond to it. The citizen, in turn, must be able to tell, at least to some minimal degree, if the action of the government is responsive. To put it another way, an act of participation involves an hypothesis on the part of the participant that his act will lead to a desired response by the government. But for the act to be rationally instrumental, it must involve a *testable* hypothesis—i.e., the participant must be able to tell whether he has had any success. This suggests that the citizen's ability to act rationally in politics may depend on the nature of the political act, particularly on two of the dimensions we used to characterize political acts—the type of influence they exert (pressure or informational) and the scope of the outcome they can influence.

Most of the debate on the citizen as rational actor has dealt with him in his role as voter. And voters in general do not much measure up to the standards of rationality.

For one thing, the public has little information on which candidate takes

---

[1] There is a wide literature on this subject. Some of the most important works are: Angus Campbell, et al., *The American Voter* (New York: Wiley, 1960), chap. 10; Philip E. Converse, "The Nature of Belief Systems in Mass Publics," in David E. Apter, ed., *Ideology and Discontent* (New York: Free Press, 1964), pp. 206–61; Herbert McClosky, "Consensus and Ideology in American Politics," *American Political Science Review,* 58(June 1964): 361–82; V. O. Key, Jr., *The Responsible Electorate* (Cambridge, Mass.: Harvard University Press, 1966); Michael J. Shapiro, "Rational Political-Man: A Synthesis of Economic and Social-Psychological Perspectives," *American Political Science Review,* 63(December 1969): 1106–19; and William H. Riker and Peter C. Ordeshook, "A Theory of the Calculus of Voting," *American Political Science Review,* 62(March 1968):25–42.

which position during an election. In fact, they may know almost nothing about candidates. Miller and Stokes indicate that about half of their sample had heard or read nothing about either congressional candidate in their district and that only 25 percent had read anything at all about both candidates, still probably putting them a long way from having the information needed to make the kind of rational choice we have been discussing.[2] And in an earlier study, it was found that less than half the public knew which party controlled the Congress—certainly a useful bit of information if one is to evaluate a candidate's potential performance.[3]

In addition, it appears that few citizens know what they want. They do not have clear and consistent positions on the important issues of the day. Attitudes on public issues are lightly held, and answers to survey questions on specific issues facing the nation often appear to have a random quality.[4] Nor do citizens have clear and consistent sets of issue positions. The absence of clear structure in citizen attitudes on the issues of elections is confirmed by Campbell et al. in their analysis in *The American Voter* of the "level of conceptualization" of voters.[5] Very few respondents (3.5 percent of voters) could be considered to have a political ideology of a clear sort (and even these people provide fairly vague notions of their political ideology if one reads the examples of answers). The kind of abstract conceptualization that could give structure to the electoral choice is almost completely missing. When citizens vote, they are more likely to be influenced by candidate images or by their traditional party affiliation than they are by the issue positions of the candidates or parties.

More recent attempts to find issue-voting (behavior consistent with our definition of rational participation) have found only a trace more of it than the authors of the classic analysis in *The American Voter* did. In some elections one finds more issue-voting than was found in 1956 by Campbell et al., in *The American Voter,* but still not much.[6] If respondents self-select the issues upon which to evaluate the parties, issue-partisanship (the perception of which party will more likely take the action you want on the issues most salient to you) predicts the vote better than when the issue is presented to the respondent by the researcher. But it still predicts the vote less well than does candidate image or party affiliation. And, as we shall argue, the procedure of allowing the respondent to choose the issue is quite unrealistic.[7]

[2] Warren Miller and Donald E. Stokes, "Constituency Influences on Congress," in Angus Campbell et al., *Elections and the Political Order* (New York: Wiley, 1966), p. 366.

[3] See Robert E. Lane and David O. Sears, *Public Opinion* (Englewood Cliffs, N.J.: Prentice-Hall, 1964), p. 61.

[4] Converse, "The Nature of Belief Systems in Mass Publics."

[5] Campbell et al., *The American Voter,* chap. 10.

[6] Key, *The Responsible Electorate,* and Philip E. Converse, Warren E. Miller, Jerrold G. Rusk, and Arthur C. Wolfe, "Continuity and Change in American Politics: Parties and Issues in the 1968 Election," *American Political Science Review,* 63(December 1969):1083–105.

[7] See David E. RePass, "Issue Salience and Party Choice," *American Political Science Review,* 65(June 1971):389–400.

But voting is only one mode of activity. These data on the relative lack of instrumental orientation toward the vote contrast sharply with our data on citizen-initiated contacts. Our respondents were asked about contacts that they initiated with government officials within and/or outside of the community. If they had initiated a contact, they were asked to identify the official and also to tell us the nature of the problem.

As one reads the answers to these questions one is struck by how relatively precise and instrumental the responses are. About one-third of all contacts, as we have noted, were on problems particularized to the individual or his family; the rest are more general in referent. As one could expect, the former type of contact involves requests for specific benefits and is clearly instrumental activity: the citizen knows what he wants and acts to obtain it. But even when the subject matter of the contact is a broader problem involving the entire community or the entire society, the problems tend to be fairly clear and specific. Citizens specify a problem area and a solution. And the choice of official to contact usually is quite appropriate: citizen-initiated contacts about school matters go to school officials or other relevant local officials, contacts about more general legislative matters go to state legislators or congressmen, contacts about the war in Vietnam go to one's senator, congressmen, or perhaps the President. This is not to argue a fantastically high level of sophistication about channels of influence among the citizenry. Rather, the data simply illustrate a circumstance in which citizens act politically with specific goals in mind and in ways that are quite appropriate for the achievement of those goals.

The main reason for this, we believe, is that in contacting, the citizen takes the initiative: he decides when to contact, whom to contact, and the subject matter of that contact. This is not to imply that the situation is totally unstructured for him and that he simply acts as he wants when the spirit moves him. He is constrained to act in certain ways by the channels available for contacting the government and he may be motivated to raise one particular problem or issue rather than another by governmental action or inaction in particular areas. But the agenda is set by the individual and quite freely chosen by him. Of the vast number of programs in which the government is engaged, he chooses one about which to complain; of the vast number of ways in which government activity impinges on his own life, he focuses on one for attention; of the vast number of things the government is not doing that might affect the individual, he brings up one for discussion. This choosing of the agenda by the individual is the main characteristic that differentiates citizen-initiated contacts from other modes of participation.

This choice guarantees that the issue of the participatory act is salient and important to the respondent. As many have pointed out, the personal "agendas" of citizens are fantastically varied. Each citizen has his own particular set of problems and concerns. These are usually close to his own life space, involving job, family, house. Or, if what concerns him is more general—war, high prices, the quality of schools, traffic problems, property taxes—there remains an almost infinite variety of personal sets of public issues.

A contact initiated by the citizen can be tailored to his specific set of problems. That this indeed seems to happen can be illustrated by one small piece of data. In addition to the questions on the subject matter of their contacts to officials, our respondents were asked to tell us the most important problems they faced in their personal and family lives and the most important problems that they saw facing the community. There were no constraints on the problems that could be mentioned, and the answers range widely. The answers to the question on the citizen's contact and the problems he perceived were coded into several hundred categories. Almost as many categories were necessary for coding the "contact" questions as for coding the "perceived problems" questions, despite the fact that many fewer respondents were answering contact questions. (About a third of our respondents had contacted an official, while almost everyone could name a personal or community problem.) What this indicates is that citizen-initiated contacting brings into the political system a set of concerns roughly as wide as the set of concerns that the citizenry faces.

Rationality and Voting

The situation facing the voter is sharply different. He does not choose the occasion to vote, nor does he choose the agenda; he doesn't choose the issues that divide the candidates, nor does he usually have much voice in choosing the candidates themselves. And given the fact that his own agenda is quite individual and may contain many and varied issues, it is unreasonable to expect that there will be a voting choice tailored to his own particular policy preferences at the moment. It is even more unreasonable to expect that the questions posed to him by interviewers about his views on the issues—issues he has not chosen—will elicit responses that will then clearly predict the vote.[8] His vote can only be a rather blunt instrument under these circumstances; it cannot have the sharpness and precision of the statements that accompany citizen-initiated contacts.

Given the lack of fit between the concerns of the individual and issues of the election, it is not surprising that issue-oriented voting is rare. Even if the citizen were motivated to vote on issues, the election usually offers an uncongenial setting. Given the multiplicity of issues in an election, there must be some way for the individual to simplify the choice situation into a mean-

---

[8] RePass, "Issue Salience and Party Choice," shows that one can better predict the vote if one uses attitude position on the issue that the respondent chooses as most salient to him. But, though this removes some artificiality in political science research on voting by giving freer rein to the problems the respondent himself considers important, it adds a new artificiality. Our contention is that it is unrealistic for the individual to be allowed to choose the agenda of the election, for indeed the issues are not posed by him but by the parties and the candidates.

ingful dichotomy so that he can vote with a clear outcome in mind. This simplification of the choice situation can come about in one of two ways: the individual must have a clear and well-structured ideology and the parties must offer him a choice congruent with the ideology, or there must be some "overriding" issue in the election, and the parties must offer a clear alternative on that issue. An ideology allows a clear choice in a multi-issue situation, since such a belief system places individual issues into some overall structure. One then chooses a party in terms of its agreement with that ideology. But there is no need to spend time on this possibility, for there is little evidence that voters think in such ideological terms. Even if they did, the American parties would not offer them clear alternatives in those terms.

In the absence of an ideology that clearly sums up all issues and provides a general choice for the individual between the two political parties, the election can allow instrumental voting of a precise sort if there is an overriding issue. In this case, the individual believes that there is a single issue in the campaign compared with which other issues are minor and that one of the voting alternatives clearly is preferable to the others in relation to that issue. Under these circumstances, an individual can vote with the hope that his vote will increase the likelihood of a direct instrumental gratification— i.e., that his favorite party or candidate will win and carry out the policy he prefers in connection with the overriding issue.

But is this possible in the voting choice? It is certainly possible but unlikely. For one thing, such overriding issues do not often appear, and, second, the choice on the issue may not be clear. Actually, at the time we were conducting our study, there was an issue that seemed to be overriding—this was the issue of Vietnam. Our questionnaire contained a number of questions on it. In response to a completely open-ended question 66 percent of our sample said that the war in Vietnam was the most important problem facing the nation (74 percent if one takes into account the first and second most important problems), and many others simply referred to war. Ninety-one percent said that they worried about Vietnam. [9]

It would be hard to find a national issue upon which there was a greater focus of attention. But does this issue fit our criteria of an overriding one? Are individuals willing to vote on that issue alone and do they perceive a clear choice? In two additional surveys conducted closer to the 1968 election, respondents were asked how much importance they would give to a candidate's stand on Vietnam. In February 1968, 18 percent of a sample said that

---

[9] The data on Vietnam are from a series of studies of attitudes on that issue conducted by Richard A. Brody, Jerome Laulicht, Benjamin I. Page, and Sidney Verba. For some reports on these data see, Brody, Page, Verba, and Laulicht, "Vietnam, the Urban Crisis and the 1968 Election," paper delivered at the annual meeting of the American Sociological Association, San Francisco, September, 1969; Brody and Page, "Policy Voting and the Electoral Process: The Vietnam War Issue," *American Political Science Review,* 66(September, 1972):979–95; and Milton J. Rosenberg, Sidney Verba, and Philip Converse, *Vietnam and the Silent Majority* (New York: Harper & Row, 1970).

Vietnam would be more important than any other issue in making up their minds, and an additional 72 percent said that Vietnam would be important but that other issues would be important too. Only 4 percent said that the stand of the candidate on Vietnam would not be important. (Parallel data in June 1968, are 12 percent, 83 percent, and 6 percent respectively.) [10] At least for the group that says it will be the most important issue for them, the war in Vietnam fulfilled the first criterion for an overriding issue. But they are still a small part of our sample.

And what of the second criterion: that the individual is offered a choice on the issues by the political parties? Whether the parties did offer a choice on the issue is a question that can be answered in many ways. Let us look at the question from the point of view of the voter: Did *he* see a choice? A few survey results are relevant. In our survey in 1967 (in which 65 percent said that Vietnam was the most important issue facing the country), 66 percent agreed with the statement that it would make no difference which party was in power as far as Vietnam was concerned. (Eleven percent disagreed slightly with that statement, and 11 percent disagreed strongly.)

More telling, perhaps, is the public's perception of the position of the candidates on the issue. In a study of the 1968 election (by Brody, Page, Lauchlicht, and Verba), respondents were asked to place various candidates on a seven-position "hawk-dove" scale based on where they thought the candidate stood on the Vietnam issue. Most citizens saw little or no difference between the candidates. The average perception of the position of the candidates placed Nixon at 4.4 on the scale, Humphrey at 4.1 (i.e., on the average, Humphrey was seen as a touch more dovish than Nixon, but only a touch). In contrast, citizens placed George Wallace at 6.5. Looked at another way, over half (57 percent) of the citizens who assigned a place to both major party candidates placed them in the same position or within one scale point of each other. [11]

The data strongly suggest that the candidates were not perceived by the public as offering widely divergent alternatives on the subject of Vietnam. In addition, there is evidence that as the election campaign progressed, the issue became less and less important, perhaps because the two candidates most similar on Vietnam were chosen. [12] And an intensive analysis (by Brody and Page) of the public speeches of the two candidates shows a combination of convergence and vagueness—both of which make issue-voting difficult. [13] The specific case of Vietnam does not demonstrate that an overriding issue might not emerge in some election. But the relatively stringent criteria that would have to be met before one could say that the individual was voting with a specific policy outcome in mind suggest that the situation will be rare.

[10] See Brody, Page, Verba and Laulicht, "Vietnam, the Urban Crisis and the 1968 Election."

[11] Brody and Page, "Policy Voting and the Electoral Process."

[12] Brody, Page, Verba and Laulicht, "Vietnam, the Urban Crisis and the 1968 Election."

[13] Brody and Page, "Policy Voting and the Electoral Process."

And, of course, we are familiar with the general tendency of election campaigns to blur political issues. [14]

This is not to argue that voting on the basis of ideology or clear issue-perception is impossible. Quite the contrary. In our view, the reason why such voting is rare lies within the nature of the collective decision made during an election, not in the incompetence or "irrationality" of the voter. Given a candidate who makes a strong ideological appeal—that is, takes a strong and consistent position on a large number of issues—one might find more voters responding in those terms. Or given a candidate who taps some deeply felt and widely shared issue, one might find more voters voting instrumentally with a fairly precise goal in mind. Thus, Field and Anderson, in their comparison of the 1964 election with the data reported on the 1956 election in *The American Voter,* find that there is more reference to ideological terms in the 1964 Johnson-Goldwater race. References to explicit ideology rise from 9 percent in 1956 (they use a somewhat different definition of this than do the authors of *The American Voter*) to 16 percent in the 1960 to 24 percent in the 1964 election. [15] The rise in frequency of ideological references in 1960 suggests that the base year of 1956 in *The American Voter* may have been a year of abnormally low levels of political controversy. But even the level of ideological reference found in 1964—and we are really dealing here with such general political terms as *liberal* and *conservative*—is hardly impressive given the type of political appeal made by Goldwater. Nevertheless, the difference between 1964 and 1956 does suggest that the nature of the choice situation—as exemplified by the two presidential candidates—structures the type of response available.

More relevant to our argument is the 1968 election, in which the Survey Research Center found, among those who voted for George Wallace, clear goal orientation consistent with the appeal that Wallace had been making. [16] In contrast to the appeal of Goldwater in 1964, in which there was some

---

[14] That individuals do not approach the vote with a clear perception of alternatives ought not to be taken to imply that citizens are somehow failing in their obligations to have such clear perceptions. The obvious point is that they receive precious little help from the parties or candidates for this. See Stanley Kelley, Jr., *Political Campaigning: Problems in Creating an Informed Electorate,* (Washington, D.C.: Brookings Institution, 1960). As he puts it:

Contemporary campaign discussion is often of such a character that it is unlikely to help voters much in their efforts to arrive at a wise choice of public officials. It may, in fact, have quite the reverse effect. Campaign propagandists obscure the real differences between candidates and parties by distortion, by evasiveness, and by talking generalities (p. 80).

Anyone who examines the course of discussion in campaigns can hardly fail to conclude that it is often as well designed to subvert as to facilitate rational voting behavior. What candidates say frequently lacks relevance to any decision voters face, exposes differences in the views of candidates imperfectly, and is filled with evasions, ambiguities and distortions (p. 51).

On this general subject, see also Anthony Downs, *An Economic Theory of Democracy* (New York: Harper & Row, 1957).

[15] John O. Field and Ronald E. Anderson, "Ideology and the Public's Conceptualization of the 1964 Election," *Public Opinion Quarterly,* 33(Fall 1969):380-98.

[16] Converse et al., "Continuity and Change in American Politics."

response in general ideological terms, Wallace's appeal was in terms of a specific set of overriding issues (race, crime, the urban crisis) of great salience to a group of voters and on which the candidate was taking a strong and clear position. As the Survey Research Center analysts correctly point out, this example indicates that issue-oriented voting is possible, given the right set of issues that are deeply felt and salient to a group, as were the race and urban issues in 1968. But the fact that this type of instrumental voting appears in relation to a third-party candidate and for only a small segment of the population indicates that this is not yet the mainstream orientation of the American public to the voting choice.

The difficulty in using the vote to satisfy the specific desires of citizens can be seen quite clearly if we compare the responses reported in *The American Voter* where respondents favored a party or candidate because of some expectation of a specific beneficial outcome with the responses we received on the subject matter of citizen contacts.

Two differences seem to stand out. In relation to contacts, the individual seems to be looking forward: He is asking for some future benefit from the government. In relation to the vote, he is likely to be looking backward, even when he is focused on a specific instrumental goal. Thus *The American Voter* authors refer to the frequent appearance among "nature of the times" respondents of comments about promises that have not been kept. And the one woman quoted who mentions a specific particularized reason for favoring one party over another refers to "the good wages my husband makes." [17] V. O. Key, Jr., who makes the strongest argument for the rationality of the voter (in our terms, for his ability to make choices with a specific political outcome in mind) makes that argument in terms of the ability of the voter to make rational evaluations of past performance rather than clear demands for future performance. [18]

The second reason why expectations of specific gratification in response to one's vote differ from such expectations in response to citizen-initiated contacts is that, in some sense, such expectations are appropriate in the latter case and inappropriate in the former. The individual who contacts the government with a salient and specific outcome in mind engages in more reasonable behavior than does the individual who sees the election as related to the particular specific problem that is most salient to him at the time. (Though, as the Wallace campaign reminds us, candidates—probably third-party candidates—can sometimes tap such issues.)

This may explain why the type of answers we quote as to the subject matter of citizen-initiated contacts—answers we consider to indicate some precise understanding of political needs—are the type that, when they appeared in answer to the question of what one likes about the parties or candidates in *The American Voter*, were coded in one of the lowest categories in terms of conceptualization; the "nature of our times" category. The point

---

[17] Campbell et al., *The American Voter*, p. 244.
[18] Key, *The Responsible Electorate*, p. 61.

is that the individual can select the agenda of a contact, and he does so in the context of the specific problems that are troubling him at the time. However, in relation to the vote, one of two things may happen: on the one hand, he may respond to the agenda as offered to him in the election, but he will do so in vague terms (as when he gives general or group-oriented answers to open-ended questions) or in inconsistent and changeable terms (as when he answers questions on specific issues) because the agenda presented to him is not of his choosing and does not reflect the problems he faces most immediately. On the other hand, if he does respond to the election in terms of his own salient and specific problem, his response is inappropriate because the election rarely revolves around that problem at all or, if it does, it will certainly not revolve around that problem alone. Or one can look at this from the point of view of our distinction between pressure and information as means of influencing the government. The voting situation is an uncongenial one for conveying specific citizen preferences because there is no way to cram that information into the vote, whereas one can express precise information when one contacts a leader.

In the light of these considerations, it is no wonder that issue orientations have no larger role in the voting choice. Nor is it any wonder that those who attempt to develop a calculus from which one can infer that it is reasonable for a citizen to bother to vote—given the small impact he can have on the election—have had to turn to variables such as the gratification one receives from fulfilling a civic duty. [19] This preserves the rationality of the vote—if it makes you feel good, it's rational to do it—but it hardly makes voting an instrumental act aimed at obtaining some beneficial governmental action. And mere habit may play a role in voting turnout. As our data in chapter 5 [of Verba and Nie] indicated, voting specialists are characterized by habitual attachment to a political party and relatively little emotional concern with the issues. As we shall show later, the likelihood of voting can be partially explained simply by the length of time one has been an eligible voter, a fact consistent with an habitual basis of voting. Last, one of the prime characteristics of voting—the ease of the act and the lack of initiative required—makes it likelier that citizens will vote even if they see no specific gain from the outcome.

The difference between citizen-initiated contacts and voting support our contention that contact mechanisms and electoral mechanisms represent different systems for relating citizens to the government. Both elections and citizen-initiated contacts represent simplifying mechanisms whereby individual preferences are converted into social choice, i.e., mechanisms whereby the vast multiplicity of demands and needs that citizens have can be communicated to the government and allocations of societal resources can be made relevant to these needs and demands. But the voting and contact mechanisms work in different ways. In the election, we are dealing with social choice for the entire society. The preferences of citizens are simplified

---

[19] Riker and Ordeshook, "A Theory of the Calculus of Voting."

by being channeled into a limited number of choices: a choice among a few parties, or between those parties and abstention. Under such circumstances, the individual is unlikely to find a voting choice that allows him to make an instrumental decision relevant to the specific set of salient problems that face him at the time of the election—problems that our data (and the data of others) tell us are likely to be highly particularized, involving the health of the individual, his economic situation, and the condition of his neighborhood, as well as more public issues.[20] It is unlikely that a candidate will stand for the specific set of goals the individual has or even that the set of problems that concern him most will become the subject of the election.

The problem is not specific to the American two-party system. The fact that electoral choice in the United States is often reduced to that between two political parties intensifies both the simplification of the choice and its incongruence with the specific set of problems facing the individual. If there were more parties offering more specific programs, the individual could tailor his voting choice somewhat more to his own specific salient needs and problems. (And it is not accidental that the best example of issue-oriented voting—Wallace in 1968—involves a third-party candidate.) But that does not solve the problem of social choice. The more parties, the more an individual may find one party that comes close to his particular set of preferences. But the choice means less in terms of influencing governmental policy, because the party elected will be a minority party and will have to form some coalition with other parties to enter a government.[21] It is not the number of parties, but the making of a social choice for the whole society that leads to the distance between the vote and the particular salient preferences of the individual.

Citizen-initiated contacts represent an alternative way of simplifying social choice. This is done by decomposing the choice to the individual level. These contacts often deal with particularized problems; in many cases the response to a contact would have major impact on the individual without affecting the overall allocation of societal benefits in more than marginal ways. But the sum total of all such contacts and the myriad responses to them do represent a mechanism for social allocation without the clear necessity of general social choice. By decomposing social choice to a vast number of specific interactions with the government, the structure of citizen-initiated contacts may represent an important means of achieving instrumental goals from the government, goals that are close to the most salient problems felt by the individual.

The contrast between the vote and citizen-initiated contacts leads to further comment on the American public. Research on political beliefs has led

---

[20] See Hadley Cantril, *The Pattern of Human Concerns* (New Brunswick, N.J.: Rutgers University Press, 1965).

[21] The classic political science debate over forms of electoral system, particularly the choice between proportional representation and single-member district systems, is relevant here. See also Downs, *An Economic Theory of Democracy.*

to the conclusions that the American public rarely approaches political matters with a clear and well-defined perception of the issues, that the public is ill-informed, its political beliefs lightly held and quickly changeable, its view of political matters vague and distant, and that politics and political controversy lack salience, i.e., the individual is more likely to be concerned with his own narrow day-to-day problems than with the issues that excite the few politically involved and sophisticated citizens. This view of the American public has usually been derived from studies of political matters in which, to use our phraseology, the agenda has been set for the individual by others. (Sometimes the agenda is set by the researcher who comes to the respondent with fixed alternative questions about political matters the researcher considers important.) This view also derives from studies of electoral choice, in which individuals are not found to have a clear issue-oriented view of the meaning of the election. It derives from studies of attitudes on foreign policy, in which the individual is found to know and care little about the foreign-policy choices of the government; and it derives from studies of the consistency and stability of attitudes on major public issues when the individual is asked to take sides on some such issue.[22] For this realm of politics, the view of the public is accurate and relevant.

Our only objection is to a tendency to consider such a position representative of the sum of the citizen's relations with the government. Our data on the content of citizen-initiated contacts show a citizenry involved with the government in ways that are highly salient to them, on issues that they define, and through channels that seem appropriate. What we are suggesting is that on matters of the politics of everyday life, citizens know what they want.[23]

Furthermore, we ought to make clear that in contrasting voting and citizen-initiated contacts, we do not intend to praise the latter as a means of participation and criticize the former. Quite the contrary. A system based on individual contacts would allow adequate citizen control over the government only if access to those contacts were equally available for all and, more important, if there were no significant "macro" policy issues that had to be decided. As some data to be presented later will show, the former condition does not hold. Access to contacting is not as widespread as access to the vote. And the latter condition does not hold either. Social policy has to be made. Particularized contacts can be effective for the individual contactor but they are inadequate as a guide to more general social policy.

The point is that if one wants to maximize popular control over govern-

---

[22] See Converse, "The Nature of Belief Systems in Mass Publics"; Campbell et. al., *The American Voter*; McClosky, "Consensus and Ideology in American Politics"; and Gabriel A. Almond, *The American People and Foreign Policy* (New York: Harcourt, 1950).

[23] This is consistent with the finding that individuals manifest issue positions with more consistency on local issues and on specific issues than on general political issues. Luttbeg finds that the mass-elite distinction in terms of consistency of attitudes found on national issues does not apply to more local ones. See Norman Luttbeg, "The Structure of Beliefs among Leaders and the Public," *Public Opinion Quarterly*, 32(Fall 1968):398–410.

mental activities that affect the lives of citizens, both types of mechanisms—
the contacting and the electoral—are needed. Because governmental policies
are almost always quite general, their application to a specific individual in a
specific situation involves particular adjustments or decisions made by low-
level government officials. Insofar as this is the case, the ability of the citizen
to make himself heard on such a matter—by contacting the officials—represents an important aspect of citizen control. Though such contacts may be
important in filling the policy gaps and in adjusting policy to the individual,
effective citizen control over governmental policy would be limited indeed if
citizens related to their government only as isolated individuals concerned
with their narrow parochial problems. The larger political questions would
remain outside popular control. Therefore, though electoral mechanisms remain crude, they are the most effective for these purposes.

Thus, despite much of what we have said, the vote remains probably a
most effective means for citizen control over leaders. Even if the individual
voter has little power over the election outcome, the set of all voters is
powerful indeed. But the comparison of voting with citizen-initiated contacting helps us comprehend why it remains such an inadequate mechanism for
citizen control, an inadequacy that may lie less in the incapacities of the
citizenry than in the nature of the electoral mechanism itself.

Indeed, as we shall demonstrate in Chapter 19 [of Verba and Nie], voting
in combination with other acts is a most potent political force. Other acts have,
as we suggested, more information-carrying capacity. On the other hand,
votes are most powerful in applying pressure on leaders. When the two
coexist—pressure plus information—participation is, as we shall see, most
effective. Even if the vote can carry little information, voting can make governmental leaders more sensitive to other more informative messages coming from citizens.

The Rationality of Communal and Campaign Activity

For the purposes of illustrating the differences in the ways the modes of
activity relate the citizen to his government, the contrast between voting and
citizen-initiated contacts is the most important and illuminating. We can fill
out the picture by looking briefly at communal and campaign activity.

Much of what has been said about contacting can also be said about
communal activity. Indeed, one of the component acts of the communal
mode of participation involves contacting officials on a social issue. In these
cases, the citizen acts, as we have suggested, with fairly specific goals and
with fairly good selectivity in terms of the officials chosen for contact. The
other component of communal participation involves activity in cooperation
with others—informal cooperation with friends, neighbors, fellow-workers
or other citizens of similar interest—or activity through formally organized
groups. Such activity is particularly widespread in America. Over a century
ago, Tocqueville commented on the distinctive amount of such activity in

the United States. And recent data on participation in a variety of nations suggest that participation through cooperation with others is the mode of activity for which the rate in the United States far exceeds rates found elsewhere. [24]

Insofar as citizens are cooperating with others in attempting to influence governmental policy, one would not expect that the average citizen can set the agenda as freely as he can when he is contacting on his own, for he has to consider the views of the others with whom he cooperates. Nevertheless, such group-oriented activity should resemble contacting more than it does activity in the electoral process in terms of its ability to satisfy the most direct instrumental needs of the citizen. Citizens tend to become involved in groups that deal with problems salient to them. The problems are not as particular as the problems brought by those who contact on personal and family matters; they may indeed be general social problems of the community. But the citizen will choose to become involved in relation to problems that touch him. Parents become active in school groups; sportsmen in groups concerned with recreational facilities. The cooperation may involve informal relations among like-minded citizens, but the very term *like-minded* makes clear that the participants will be those for whom the problem is salient. Or the cooperation may involve activity through formal organizations, but citizens tend to join organizations that relate to things they consider important.

In this sense, communal activity (and, in particular, those activities carried on in cooperation with others) may combine some of the advantages of contacting with those of voting. Communal activity engaged in concert with one's fellows can deal with fairly specific problems that are high on the agenda of citizens—problems that affect some specific group to which they belong or problems that affect the community as a whole. In this sense they have the specificity and information-carrying capacity of contacting. On the other hand, the fact that citizens are joining together to act politically increases the potential influence that they can have, especially when the issue involved is broader than those associated with particularized contacting. [25] Whether these activities are those of formally organized interest groups or of informal groupings of citizens coming together for a specific purpose, they form an important part of the participatory system in the United States.

Last, we can consider campaign activity. The campaign activist is, in some sense, in the same position as the voter. He may have somewhat more control over the agenda of the election—he may be active in nominations

---

[24] Gabriel A. Almond and Sidney Verba, *The Civic Culture* (Princeton: Princeton University Press, 1963), chap. 7; and Sidney Verba, Norman H. Nie, and Jae-On Kim, *The Modes of Democratic Participation* (Beverly Hills: Sage, 1971), p. 36.

[25] The vast literature on pressure groups in America is relevant here. Stein Rokkan makes one of the best and most explicit cases for the importance of group activity as a means of filling in the gaps left by electoral competition. See his chapter on Norway in Robert A. Dahl, ed., *Political Oppositions in Western Democracies* (New Haven: Yale University Press, 1966).

and in issue selection—but it is unlikely that the average campaign activist has much voice in these matters either. But because campaign participation requires more time, effort, and initiative than voting, it is hard to see it as motivated solely by habit or sense of civic obligation.

How then does the campaign activist get instrumental benefits? Is it rational for him to be active? Several answers are possible. In the first place, campaign activists do differ from ordinary voters in having clearer issue orientations. As our data in chapter 5 [of Verba and Nie] made clear, campaign activists score higher on the scale of issue extremity than any other type of political actor, except the complete activists. [26] In addition to their stronger and more consistent issue positions, they tend to have a better developed ideological view of the differences between the parties than do ordinary citizens. [27] Thus, in terms of their own orientations to politics, campaign activists may be better equipped than the average citizen to vote "instrumentally." They are more likely to have clear and consistent policy views and to see policy differences between the parties. Yet, these activists may also be blocked from successfully pursuing instrumental goals within the electoral process by the same thing that blocks voters: They do not control the agenda of the election and therefore that agenda is unlikely to match their own.

What happens under such circumstances? There are no national data on this subject, but Eldersveld's data on party workers in Detroit are most revealing in the light of our discussion of elections and instrumental gratification. He finds that for lower-echelon party workers (which is what most of our campaign activists are), one must distinguish between the motivations for initial involvement in partisan activity and the motives for remaining active.

> . . . while grass roots workers may have been recruited under the guise of the "voluntaristic-idealistic-impersonal task-oriented" concept of party work, . . . these precinct leaders in large numbers change motivational direction during their careers. Many become disillusioned; the majority articulated personal demands, needs, and satisfactions to be derived from party activity. In reality this means that the majority of precinct leaders changed their motivational relationship to the party. . . . They either became disillusioned, or they conceptualized their relationship in terms of social friendship satisfactions (66 percent of the Democrats, 49 percent of the Republicans), a desire to be "in the know" and gain prestige in the neighborhood (4 percent of the Democrats, 6 percent of the Republicans),

---

[26] See [Verba and Nie,] chap. 5, Figure 5-2. See also Herbert McClosky, Paul J. Hoffmann, and Rosemary O'Hara, "Issue Conflict and Consensus among Party Leaders and Followers," *American Political Science Review,* 54(June 1960):406-427.

[27] Dwaine Marvick and Charles R. Nixon, "Recruitment Contrasts in Rival Campaign Groups," in Marvick, ed., *Political Decision Makers: Recruitment and Performance* (New York: Free Press, 1961), pp. 193-217.

or they saw other personalized satisfaction such as the enjoyment of the "fun and excitement" of a campaign (6 percent of the Democrats, 4 percent of the Republicans). [28]

In short, then, party activists may join parties because of some instrumental goal, a belief that they can influence governmental policy in some desired direction. However, over time, these goals become less important and side benefits become more important. On the lower levels, these side benefits tend to be social in nature (one enjoys party work, meets others, etc.), while on the upper level they are both social and material (one makes business connections, etc.). This finding is consistent with our findings on the high issue orientation of partisan activists and with our view of the electoral process as a relatively uncongenial setting for participation oriented toward dealing with issues one considers important. It may be that the ineffectiveness of the electoral mechanism for satisfying specific policy goals means that activists either adopt alternative goals that do not depend on governmental responsiveness, or drop out. We will return to this subject in chapter 12 [of Verba and Nie], where we will present contrasting data on the two parties.

The Participation Input: A Summary

In Part I [of Verba and Nie] we have attempted to analyze and describe the participation input: How much participation is there, of what kind, and from what people? In this chapter we have attempted to demonstrate that the alternative modes of participation do in fact differ in the kinds of benefits that citizens can reasonably expect from them. For some modes of participation, means-ends calculations are more difficult than for others, but when one looks across the range of alternative activities open to the citizen one may find a greater degree of instrumental and rational activity than is sometimes assumed. And where one finds rather ill-developed means-ends calculations—as in relation to voting—the source may lie in the nature of the electoral system itself at least as much as it lies in the incapacity of the average voter.

It may be useful now to tie together what we have found about the par-

---

[28] See Samuel J. Eldersveld, *Political Parties: A Behavioral Analysis* (Chicago: Rand McNally, 1964) pp. 290-92. A study of the incentives for the maintenance of activism among precinct party officials in North Carolina and Massachusetts found a similar stress on personal satisfactions. See Lewis Bowman, Dennis Ippolito, and William Donaldson, "Incentives for the Maintenance of Grassroots Political Activism," *Midwest Journal of Political Science,* 13(February 1969):126-39. Marvick and Nixon, "Recruitment Contrasts in Rival Campaign Groups," find a greater stress on concern for public issues as a reason for party activism among their sample in Los Angeles, but their question may be such as to engender "official justifications." However, they also find a heavy stress on social gains from party activity. On this subject, see also Robert Salisbury, "The Urban Party Organization Member," *Public Opinion Quarterly,* 29(Winter 1965-66):550-64.

ticipation input. Table 4.1 summarizes a good deal of what we have found. In column A we list the six types of participants that we have found to fit the patterns of activity of American citizens, and we give the proportion of the population that falls into each of these types. In column B we characterize their respective patterns of activity, and in column C we indicate how these activities fit our theoretical dimensions of participation. In column D we give the main characteristics of each group in terms of political orientations, a pattern of orientations that, we believe, confirms the meaningfulness of the distinctions we make among the types of political actors. In column E we indicate the social composition of the various activist groups. In short, one can tell from table 4.1 how many people are active in America, the ways in which they are active (and in particular, the all-important question of the types of outcome their activity can influence), and their social characteristics.

The participation input summarized in table 4.1 suggests a quite variegated pattern of participation in the United States, not a mere division of the population into several different activity levels. This is not simply to say that there are many different kinds of activities open to citizens. Rather the data reported in Part I [of Verba and Nie] support a stronger conclusion: that there are several different *systems* of participation in the United States.

There are several justifications for this stronger conclusion. In the first place, we have found that the various political acts in which citizens can engage form meaningful patterns and constitute particular modes of activity. Second, we have found that there are groups of citizens who "specialize" in one mode of activity or another. It is true that there are some citizens who engage in all modes of activity and some who do nothing, but substantial numbers of citizens limit their activity fairly closely to one mode or another. Third, we found that the alternative types of activists have distinct patterns of orientation to politics that that are consistent with our analysis of the implications of the various ways citizens can participate. And, last and probably most important, we have shown that the alternative patterns of activity relate the citizen to his government in different ways: They can influence different kinds of governmental decisions, and they allow the participant to exercise more or less influence over the result of his participatory attempt.

What Are the Alternative Systems of Participation?

First, there is the system of particularized contacting, a channel of participation that permits citizens to seek a variety of decomposable benefits from the government—benefits that aid only them. Through this system of participation, the individual citizen may seek some government service or may seek to stop some government activity that is impinging on his life. This system of participation does not touch on the great issues of policy, and perhaps for that reason little attention has been paid to it. But the government affects our lives in so many small ways that this would appear to be a critical channel, and if it were closed to some groups, they would be severely

Table 4.1   The Participation Input: A Summary

A Type of Participant	B Pattern of Activity	C Theoretical Dimensions of Activity Pattern	D Leading Orientations	E Main Social Characteristics
The inactives (22%)	No activity		Totally uninvolved, no interest, skill, sense of competence, or concern with conflict.	Lower socioeconomic levels and blacks are overrepresented, as are older and younger citizens (but not middle-aged ones) and women.
The voting specialists (21%)	They vote regularly, but do nothing else.	Broad collective outcomes, counterparticipants, and low initiative.	Strong partisan identity but otherwise relatively uninvolved and with low skills and competence.	Lower socioeconomic levels are overrepresented. Older citizens are overrepresented, as are those in big cities. Underrepresented in rural areas.
The parochial participants (4%)	They contact officials on particularized problems and are otherwise inactive.	Particularized outcomes, no conflict, and high initiative.	Some political skill (information) but otherwise no political involvement.	Lower socioeconomic groups are overrepresented, but blacks are underrepresented. Catholic rather than Protestant. Big cities rather than small towns.

The communalists (20%)	They contact officials on broad social issues and engage in cooperative activity. Vote fairly regularly, but avoid election campaigns.	Collective outcomes (but may be narrower than those of elections), high initiative, and relatively no conflict.	High sense of community contribution, involvement in politics, skill and competence. Nonpartisan and avoid conflict.	Upper socioeconomic levels very overrepresented, blacks underrepresented. Protestant rather than Catholic. Overrepresented in rural areas and small towns; underrepresented in big cities.
The campaigners (15%)	Heavily active in campaigns and vote regularly.	Broad collective outcomes, moderate to high initiative, and relatively conflictual.	Politically involved, relatively skilled and competent, partisan and involved in conflict, but little sense of community contribution.	Overrepresentation of upper-status groups. Blacks and particularly Catholics overrepresented. Big-city and suburbs rather than small towns and rural areas.
The complete activists (11%)	Active in all ways.	All characteristics of all acts.	Involved in politics in all ways, highly skilled and competent.	Heavy overrepresentation of upper-status groups. Old and young underrepresented.
Unclassified (7%)				

deprived. Indeed, life would be much more difficult even in the most democratic society if there were no means available to obtain minor adjustments and dispensations from general government policy, especially when that policy is made on such a grand scale and at places so distant from the lives it affects.

Particularized contacting is an activity carried on by all sorts of citizens—by some who are active in other ways, by some who are not. This reflects the fact that such activity deals with myriad specific problems affecting all sorts of people. Those citizens who limit their activity to particularized contacting are a special type. We have labeled them *parochial participants,* for though they have the skill and initiative to engage in fairly difficult activity, they show no involvement in political life in the broader sense.

Next we have uncovered the communalist system of participation, whereby citizens alone or, more often with others, attempt to deal with the more general problems of their communities or of particular groups. The problems are not so narrow as those dealt with via particularized contacting, but they are nevertheless problems that are specifically pertinent to the individuals or groups active in this way. The activity also seems to be relatively nonconflictual, either because the goal is some general benefit to the community or because it is some benefit to the specific group of activists but is not seen by others as affecting them negatively. Much of this activity seems to consist of mobilizing community resources or one's follow citizens to deal directly with community problems or to induce the government to do so.

The communalists' attitudes fit their activity: They have a high sense of contribution to the community and a general involvement in politics, but they seem to avoid conflict. As we have suggested, activity of this sort is found more frequently in the United States than in a variety of other countries—a fifth of the U.S. citizenry concentrate on this form of participation. However, data presented in chapter 13 [of Verba and Nie], suggest that such activity flourishes under conditions that may be disappearing in America. If so, the system of political participation in the United States will lose an important and distinctive component.

The third and fourth modes of participation with which we have dealt involve the electoral system. One way citizens take part is via an active role in the campaign process. Our data show that almost a third of the citizenry participate in some way in this process, and that over 15 percent concentrate on this form of political involvement. When we add this 15 percent to the even larger number of communalists, we see two vigorous, yet separate, systems whereby private citizens can and do attempt to influence the direction of our political life. But campaign activity differs from communal activity because the issues of the former are less specific to the participants and because they involve more conflict.

The last mode of activity is voting. We find a substantial proportion of citizens (21 percent) who limit their activity to this—but it is not nearly so large a group as other studies have suggested. And although we have found the vote to be a rather limited mode of engagement, there would appear to be few other available mechanisms whereby the preferences of all citizens can simultaneously be taken into account, giving them some control over the selection of leadership. Furthermore, some data to be presented in chapter 19 [of Verba and Nie] will indicate that although voting may have minimal effectiveness as a channel for communicating the specific needs and desires of a particular participant, when aggregated across all citizens and especially when combined with other activities conveying more information, it remains a most powerful system for insuring the responsiveness of elites.

Each of the modes of participation is distinctive and each, therefore, forms an important component of the overall system of participation in the United States. It is a rich and complex system. But it is also a system for which all the components are not equally accessible to all citizens.

II. THE IDEOLOGICAL LEVEL OF THE ELECTORATE

5. Do Voters Think Ideologically?

Liberals and conservatives. Most college students—and certainly all who have had a course or two in political science—are familiar with these terms. In fact, they are such common words in political discourse that most voters must certainly be familiar with them.

This was probably the view of most political scientists in the 1950's. But both here and on the matter of issues taken up in the next section, things became much less clear as systematic interviews of cross-sections of the American population were undertaken. In fact, in both of these areas political scientists have come almost full circle in their characterization of American voters. With regard to ideology, they have moved from the initial assumption that "everyone knows about liberals and conservatives," through a period in which there appeared to be overwhelming evidence that voters were ignorant of the meaning of such terms and that they held illogical and inconsistent political beliefs, to a current view that is at least somewhat more sanguine in its opinion of the ideological level of ordinary citizens.

But can we realistically expect voters to be ideological? One critical viewpoint—often associated with "radical" or "leftist" writings—is that the political system is so unresponsive that it makes little difference what or how people think about politics. Why should people even think about politics— much less organize their thoughts into a coherent pattern—if their opinions make little difference in what happens anyway? From this standpoint, the "system" is at fault for failing to arouse interest and invite realistic participation, rather than citizens being at fault for failing to develop coherent political views. Implicit in this point of view is the feeling that people would develop ideological positions if and when they had some realistic chance of affecting political behavior. Yet if their ideas are illogical, inconsistent, and generally incoherent, does it make any sense for political leaders to attempt to provide meaningful ways for them to express their views? We have here something of a "chicken-and-egg" problem. Voters' attitudes may be nonideological because of a failure of the political system, but the failure may be due precisely to the voters' lack of ideology.

One possible way around this problem is to look for evidence of ideological thinking in the electorate. If voters show extraordinarily little capacity for organized political thought, we might infer that they are unlikely to change even if the political system changes. If, on the other hand, they have definite and consistent opinions at some times, or on some topics, the absence of an integrated system of ideas might reasonably be attributed to the political system. There is no absolute proof for either statement, but it may be possible to determine whether the lack of ideology is due more to individual limitations or to system faults.

An Unsophisticated Electorate

The original view—that "everyone" knows about things like liberals and conservatives—was of course developed prior to research on cross-sections of the population. But such information was indeed widespread among politicians, journalists, fellow academicians, and others with whom political scientists regularly talked. Thus, when *The American Voter* was published in 1960, it was a rude shock to read the authors' conclusion that only a tiny fraction of the American electorate held an ideological view of politics.

The American Voter[1] began by analyzing the ideological structure of people's issue positions, basing the analysis on specific questions regarding foreign and domestic policy. The authors reasoned that, if voters' attitudes did have an underlying structure, their responses would fall into specified patterns. For example, in the area of foreign policy, a person who supported an extreme form of intervention abroad would also support less extreme forms.[2] It turned out, however, that responses to many questions did not fit this pattern, an immediate indication that people's attitudes tended to be inconsistent and unstructured. Moreover, there was no relationship between opinions on foreign and domestic policy—interventionists in foreign affairs were no more activist on social welfare policy than were isolationists. Thus

---

[1] Angus Campbell, Philip E. Converse, Warren E. Miller, and Donald E. Stokes, *The American Voter* (New York: Wiley, 1960), chap. 9; abridged edition, chap. 8.

[2] As will be clear from the Stimson reading (chapter 8), this is not the only way in which attitudes might be structured. We will discuss this point more fully below.

the two types of policy were being considered separately rather than fitted into an all-embracing structure. Furthermore, the responses to domestic policy questions seemed essentially to express the voters' self-interests rather than any ideology. Most people simply supported issues that would help them personally rather than adopting attitudes based on a predetermined system of ideas. In short, ideology was found to be irrelevant to the understanding of people's views on issues.

But this was only the beginning. *The American Voter* then proceeded to examine how people discuss politics. Do they actually conceive of politics in ideological terms, or are their ways of thinking about politics totally nonideological? The respondents were asked what they liked or disliked about each of the major parties and whether there was anything about each of the presidential candidates that would make the person want to vote for or against him. This series of eight questions often took ten to fifteen minutes of the interview, and it allowed individuals to express in their own words how they felt about the parties and the presidential candidates. The painstaking analysis of the responses provided *The American Voter*'s most important view of ideology in the American public.[3]

Responses to the questions were categorized into one of four "levels of conceptualization." In the top group are those characterized by ideological views or by views that at least hinted at an ideological framework of thought. Truly ideological statements consisted almost entirely of references to liberalism and conservatism. But it should not be thought that this accounts for the small number of respondents ultimately included in this group, for the authors took pains to look for abstract conceptualizations which were formulated in terms other than standard political coinage. There appeared to be a few such responses, and they were dutifully categorized as ideological.[4] Moreover, an effort was made to classify as ideologues those respondents who showed some evidence of ideological thinking even though it was less than thoroughly spelled out in response to these particular questions. The result of all this effort was that a grand total of 11½ percent of the sample showed some form of ideological thinking.

The remainder of the sample was not without some thoughts on the subjects of parties and candidates. A large portion, some 42 percent of the respondents, associated a party or candidate with benefits to some group or groups within the population. Democrats, for example, were said to benefit poor people or working people, while Republicans were said to be good for the rich or for business. Another large group, 24 percent of the sample, associated the "goodness" or "badness" of the times with a party or candidate. These were generally associations of war with one party and of good or bad times economically with a particular party. The remaining 22½ percent of the responses were devoid of any issue content, the comments being restricted to platitudes about parties or candidates and frequently some am-

---

[3] Campbell et al., *The American Voter*, chap. 10.
[4] *Ibid.*, pp. 222–23, 227–28.

biguous remarks about "dirty politics"; this fourth group also included 5 percent of the sample that had absolutely no views on politics.

The major point to be drawn from these results is the small proportion of respondents categorized as ideologues. Even in its broadest interpretation, only about one in every nine respondents deserved this label.[5] This was a far cry from the view that "everyone" thought about politics in the same way that politicians and journalists do. Moreover, even among college-educated people, only a third were classified as ideologues. Thus it could not even be said that lack of ideology was solely due to low levels of education. Rather, it seemed as if a large majority of educated respondents, and nearly all voters with little education, viewed politics in a radically different way from what had previously been thought. Though responses emphasizing benefits to social groups might be quite sensible for many voters—and we will return to this later—they were so different from what was expected that even these responses seemed to indicate that voters were extraordinarily unsophisticated in their political views. Thus was laid the foundation for the view that ideological thinking was extremely rare among American voters.

The two types of evidence marshalled in *The American Voter* are the results of complementary approaches to studying the ideological level of the public. One question is whether voters discuss politics in ideological terms, using the liberal and conservative concepts or at least recognizing and understanding their use. Another question is whether there is an underlying structure to the public's attitudes on separate issue questions. Logically, one could have one type of ideological thinking without the other, so both must be investigated. The basic conclusion of *The American Voter* was that the electorate displayed little thinking of either type.

Several years after *The American Voter* was published, Philip Converse published a brilliant article which extended and elaborated on this conclusion.[6] For Converse, the central idea of an ideology or a "belief system" is a constraint of an individual's ideas and attitudes. The most obvious source of constraint—although perhaps the least useful for organizing political ideas—is logic. As Converse notes, it would be rather inconsistent to "believe that government expenditures should be increased, that government revenues should be decreased, and that a more favorable balance of the budget should be achieved all at the same time."[7] More relevant for the organization of political views are psychological and social sources of constraint. That is, certain ideas are associated with one another even though there is no logical connection between them. For example, it is often thought that a person who is opposed to gun control is a conservative, and that he or she is

---

[5] Actually, only 2½ percent of the respondents could fully classify as ideologues, the remaining 9 percent being categorized as "near ideologues" since they gave less clear-cut evidence of ideological thinking.

[6] "The Nature of Belief Systems in Mass Publics," in David Apter, ed., *Ideology and Discontent* (New York: Free Press, 1964).

[7] *Ibid.*, p. 209.

II. THE IDEOLOGICAL LEVEL OF THE ELECTORATE

probably also opposed to busing to achieve racial integration, abortion on demand, and so on. There is obviously no reason why an individual *has to* believe in all of these things if he or she believes one of them, and certainly we can find individuals who endorse only a few of them. But most political discourse assumes that there is some relationship between a person's views on different subjects so that people who hold one view can be expected to hold certain other views. Among other things, such constraints among ideas allow a concise description of individuals' attitudes. If certain opinions are associated, then labels such as conservative, liberal, radical, socialist, and so on have a good deal of meaning. The liberal-conservative distinction is the most widely used, so that distinction is most frequently emphasized, as previously noted in discussing *The American Voter.*

Having discussed the notion of constraint among ideas and the relationship of constraint to the liberal-conservative dimension, Converse's results represent something like a logical *tour de force*. First, he considers the "active" use of ideological terms. That is, without any assistance or hints from the interviewer, do individuals spontaneously think of politics in terms of liberals and conservatives? This, of course, takes him back to the results in *The American Voter,* and the answer is a decisive "no" for most of the electorate. Converse realizes, however, that this may be too stringent a test. People understand many more ideas and concepts than they actively use in their normal thinking. Hence, he raises the question of whether voters recognize and understand the terms "liberal" and "conservative" when they are used by someone else.

To answer this question, the interviews conducted during the 1960 presidential campaign introduced questions which explicitly used the terms "liberal" and "conservative".[8] With these data, Converse stratified the population into five levels of "recognition and understanding." The results are fascinating—it is interesting to see how many respondents said things like, "The Democrats are more conservative because they spend more than the Republicans" or "The Republicans are more conservative in that they believe in conservation of our natural resources"— but it is not necessary to go into them here. Two things stand out. First, as one would expect, more people were found in the top strata in terms of recognizing and understanding liberal-conservative terms than when the respondents themselves were required to introduce the terms. Just over half of the respondents showed some recognition of the terms and properly matched the label, meaning, and party. Second, many of the respondents defined the terms very narrowly,

---

[8] Respondents were asked whether they would consider either one of the parties more conservative or more liberal than the other. If so, they were asked which party was more conservative and what they had in mind in saying this party was more conservative. To carry the matter still further, individuals who failed to see either party as more conservative were asked whether people generally consider the Democrats or the Republicans more conservative or whether they "wouldn't want to guess about that?" If they admitted or "guessed" that there was a difference, they were asked the same question about the meaning of conservatism.

mostly in "spend-save" terms, with liberals seen as spending more money and conservatives as saving more.[9] Only 16 percent of the respondents showed a broad understanding of the terms. This is somewhat more than the number of ideologues estimated by *The American Voter*, as it logically should be. But it indicates that most Americans either do not understand the terms at all or have at most a rather narrow understanding of them even when the terms are presented to them.

Both in terms of active and passive understanding of ideological terms, then, American voters have not shown any great sophistication. Converse, however, does not stop here. It may simply be that many respondents cannot articulate the ways in which their political beliefs are organized, but that the organization is still there. Or it may be that the general population organizes its beliefs in some way that is different from the way political scientists view them. If this is true, we should be able to observe that certain attitudes on specific issues would fit with others. Those favoring federal action on housing would also tend to favor federal aid on employment, and so on. However, analysis of the correlations between attitudes on separate issues found little such consistency for the general public. Not only were the correlations low in absolute terms,[10] but they were low by comparison with the correlations for an elite group—congressional candidates who had been interviewed about the same time. Converse concludes, "It cannot therefore be claimed that the mass public shares ideological patterns of belief with relevant elites at a specific level anymore than it shares the abstract conceptual frames of reference."[11]

But the most devastating blow of all is yet to come. Voters' attitudes on various questions are not interrelated to the degree found among political elites, but they do have attitudes on public issues nonetheless. Or do they? They answer questions posed to them by interviewers, but are these real attitudes or just answers supplied on the spur of the moment to make the interviewer happy? Respondents are encouraged to indicate when they have not thought much about a question and have no opinion, but the social pressure of the interview situation makes it difficult for people to admit that. Even if a person has an opinion, it might be the most fleeting reaction based on the week's news rather than an expression of a true attitude. In short, many of the survey responses may be "nonattitudes" rather than "attitudes." Nonattitudes on basic ideological questions would mean that ideology was totally absent.

The best way to test the reality of people's attitudes is to ask them the

---

[9] This may suggest what is meant when a majority of Americans call themselves conservative in Gallup polls. It also implies that a conservative party would not do as well as some conservative leaders might assume.

[10] See, for example, the average correlations for 1956–60, given by Nie, p. 109 in this volume.

[11] Converse, "Belief Systems," p. 231. Note that because of Converse's choice of correlation coefficient for this analysis, this search for structure is very similar to the Guttman scale analysis in *The American Voter*.

same questions at several different times and then examine the stability of their answers. If responses are based on an ideology, one would expect high stability, *and* change would occur in only certain specific ways. The same respondents were interviewed by the Survey Research Center in 1956, 1958, and 1960. Respondents in this "panel study" were asked the same issue questions each time. In the selection from his article included here (chapter 6), Converse analyzes the similarity of responses from each individual in all three interviews. The correlations were quite low, particularly on the most ideological questions. [12] Moreover, the pattern of correlations failed to conform to normal expectations. Specifically, one would expect that, if respondents were meaningfully changing their attitudes over time, one could predict their attitudes best (the correlations would be highest) between adjacent surveys. Hence, the correlations between attitudes expressed in 1956 and 1960 should be markedly lower than the correlations observed between 1956 and 1958 or between 1958 and 1960. Yet they were not. How was this possible? Such results were conceivable if there were two groups within the population—one group which was perfectly stable (gave the same response at all three times) and one group which answered wholly at random, with no third group whose attitudes really changed. Converse shows that if one took the most remote issue treated in the survey (which happened to be the most purely ideological question), the evidence suggested that perhaps as many as 70 percent of the respondents either confessed themselves ignorant or gave responses which suggested that their answers might be changing at random over the years. Converse makes it very clear that this was an extreme issue and that for most issues even in the late 50's, a smaller proportion had "nonattitudes," but it was impossible to calculate precise proportions. Therefore, the dominant impression left with many readers seems to have been that most voters had no opinion at all on issues that had been of long-standing public concern.

The view of the American voter had fallen to a new low. Voters did not use ideological terms such as liberalism and conservatism; they did not even understand these terms when presented with them; their opinions on various issues were not related to one another; and in many cases they did not really have attitudes at all. Obviously, neither Converse nor anyone would apply this description to all voters, and surely one could imagine situations in which most voters would have strong opinions and some information. Yet the dominant impression remained that voters were very often ignorant when it came to political matters and that they would most likely remain so.

Other studies in the 50's and early to mid-60's further strengthened this point of view by seemingly indicating that the naïveté of voters was not

---

[12] Although not reported in this selection, Converse has since indicated that the responses over time for those people with more education were no more stable than those for people with less education, and, if anything, the differences ran in the opposite direction. His interpretation of this will be discussed further on. Philip E. Converse, "Public Opinion and Voting Behavior," in Fred I. Greenstein and Nelson W. Polsby, eds., *The Handbook of Political Science* (Reading, Mass: Addison Wesley, 1975), vol. 4, pp. 103–4.

limited to issues of current public policy nor to American voters. Such a result has already been mentioned in the introduction to this book. In an article which, like *The American Voter,* was published in 1960, Prothro and Grigg reported that upwards of 95 percent of their respondents professed agreement with such statements as "the minority should be free to criticize majority decisions" and "public officials should be chosen by majority rule." [13] Yet in specific terms far fewer agreed with statements that seemed to be almost logical expressions of these principles. For example, 54 percent of the respondents agreed with the statement, "if a Communist were legally elected mayor of this city, the people should not allow him to take office." Thirty-seven percent disagreed with the statement, "if a person wanted to make a speech in this city against churches and religion, he should be allowed to speak." Though such data are subject to many interpretations, one must wonder whether citizens can be considered to have ideologies, or be informed, intelligent, or even alert if they fail to recognize or at least try to reconcile contradictory beliefs.

Evidence from both France and Great Britain bolstered this view of the lack of ideology in the electorate. France's multiparty kaleidoscope is a good example, because, as Converse and Dupeux noted, many Americans have vague impressions of "a particular intensity in the tenor of French political life," [14] which surely must manifest itself in higher levels of political knowledge and ideology than are found among American voters. And yet, Converse and Dupeux argue persuasively that these are impressions based on French political elites and that there is no reason to expect that "the shipyard worker in Nantes has political reflexes which differ from those of the shipyard worker in Norfolk." [15] Indeed, when they examine correlations over time for opinions obtained from the French general electorate, their conclusion is that many French respondents, like their American counterparts, fail to have well-formed opinions in regard to political controversies that have been the subject of basic political disagreements for decades or generations.

Great Britain is also a good case to consider because it has usually been thought that British parties are more distinctive than American ones and that this ought to be reflected in more lucidly organized attitudes among British voters. Yet when Butler and Stokes searched for the same kind of constraint among ideas and the same awareness of ideological concepts that Converse had sought in the American electorate, the results were equally disconcerting. [16] Sixty percent of the respondents, for example, were said to have no recognition of left-right concepts, and only 2 percent of the popula-

---

[13] James W. Prothro and Charles M. Grigg, "Fundamental Principles of Democracy: Bases of Agreement and Disagreement," *Journal of Politics,* 22(1960):276-94.

[14] Philip E. Converse and Georges Dupeux, "Politicization of the Electorate in France and the United States," *Public Opinion Quarterly,* 26(1962):1-23, at p. 1.

[15] *Ibid.,* p. 1.

[16] David Butler and Donald Stokes, *Political Change in Britain* (New York: St. Martin's Press, 1969), chaps. 8 and 9.

tion were said to have "fully elaborated dynamic" interpretations.[17] The same finding of lack of constraint among ideas characterized British political attitudes. The inter-item correlations were low even after the authors had sought to limit the test to about 30 percent of the sample that appeared to hold political attitudes on each of the issues. And in panel comparisons, the same pattern of correlations found by Converse was also characteristic of Britain.

Throughout the mid-60's, then, the evidence seemed incontrovertible that mass populations simply did not have ideological views on political matters. Though the data typically came from surveys covering a restricted time period, the fact that this generalization held for different countries, that the results included what were almost logical inconsistencies, and that the results withstood efforts to find *any* ideological awareness in the electorate all contributed to the view that the lack of ideology was probably endemic to mass populations. No doubt this was an overinterpretation of the results that were actually found, but many political scientists and journalists at the beginning of the 1970's firmly embraced the conclusion that general electorates were largely nonideological.

It would be possible, but entirely misleading, to dismiss these results as simply showing that the terms liberal and conservative are meaningless. The terms do have multiple meanings, often it is difficult to label even a politician as totally liberal or conservative. Yet these terms do possess important meanings. They refer to the relationship of the government to the individual (as in regard to civil liberties), to the power of the federal government, to the economic system (including the concepts of welfare state and free enterprise), and, perhaps most of all, to differences in tolerance of change, liberals being more receptive to change and conservatives more protective of the status quo. The question initially addressed was not whether a respondent would supply all of these meanings, but whether he or she would give any of these philosophical meanings or any meaningful but more narrow interpretation. Few respondents passed even this test. The later tests involved the consistency of a person's answers to the same question over a period of time, which is certainly not a matter of the significance of the terms "liberal" and "conservative." Furthermore, Converse's study of ideology in the general public also reports strikingly different results for a political elite: congressional candidates structured their attitudes with greater constraint than did the public. So the difficulty is with the level of ideology in the public, and not with an inherent flaw in the notion of ideological constraint. Political debate at elite levels is largely structured in ideological terms, and ideology

---

[17] One of the more interesting respondents, who fell among the 40 percent having some interpretation of left-right concepts, gave the explanation that, "when I was in the Army you had to put your right foot forward, but in fighting you lead with your left. So I always think that the Tories are the right party for me and that the Labour party are fighters. I know that this isn't really right, but I can't explain it properly, and it does for me." *Ibid.*, p. 209.

could serve as a critical simplification scheme for a public trying to cope with large numbers of political issues. But the research we have just reviewed argues that the general public does not make use of ideologies.

An Increasingly Sophisticated Electorate?

Things have a way of changing rapidly in the real world. The 60's were unlike the 50's in many respects. Issues like race and the Vietnam war became prominent, and events made it nearly impossible to avoid being aware of, if not taking a stand on, these issues. Presidential candidates differed from those in the 50's. Barry Goldwater deliberately called himself a conservative in 1964, and he tried to convey to the public some indication of what this meant. In 1968, George Wallace deliberately brought ideology to the fore when he indicated that the two major parties differed very little but that his views were substantially different from those expressed by Humphrey and Nixon. In 1970, Vice President Agnew led the Republican campaign for Congress by stressing the need to remove radical liberal Democrats from Congress. In 1972, McGovern was prominently labeled in the press as being more liberal than many voters and even as being radical in some respects. Frequent use of ideological terms in describing political contests could only increase the proportion of Americans who were aware of those words. Along with these developments, the level of education in the country was rising dramatically, as Nie with Andersen show in their contribution here. [18] This increased the potential for political sophistication in the electorate.

Because of these changes, researchers began to question whether the level of ideology might be rising above its apparent low point of the 50's. Field and Anderson, as well as Pierce, examined the proportion of individuals who could be classified as ideologues in 1956, 1960, and 1964. [19] Both reported an increase in the number of ideologues during this period. Their results cannot be compared directly with those of Converse or *The American Voter* because they used different definitions of ideology, but they do show that ideological expression was higher in 1960 than in 1956, and still higher in 1964. Hans Klingemann and William Wright coded 1968 responses to what people like and dislike about the parties and candidates in a manner identical to *The American Voter*'s coding of levels of conceptualization in 1956. The results (table 5.1) show an increase in the ideologue category, though it still contains less than a quarter of the population. At the same time, there is no decrease in the proportion of the population in the two lowest categories; the shift is

---

[18] See figure 7.5.

[19] John Osgood Field and Ronald E. Anderson, "Ideology in the Public's Conceptualization of the 1964 Presidential Election," *Public Opinion Quarterly*, 33(1969):380-98; John C. Pierce, "Party Identification and the Changing Role of Ideology in American Politics," *Midwest Journal of Political Science*, 14(1970):25-42.

Table 5.1 Levels of Conceptualization in the United States (Percent)

Category	1956	1968
A. Ideology		
I. Ideology	3	6
II. Near-ideology	10	17
B. Group benefits		
I. Perception of conflict	15	9
Single-group interest	18	19
II. Shallow group benefit responses	11	5
C. Nature of the times	25	25
D. No issue content		
I. Party orientation	4	8
II. Candidate orientation	9	7
III. No content	5	5
	100	100
Unclassified (excluded from percentiles)	4.5	12

NOTE: 1956 data are from *The American Voter*, p. 249; 1968 data are from Hans D. Klingemann, "Dimensions of Political Belief Systems: 'Levels of Conceptualization' as a Variable. Some Results for USA and FRG 1968/69," preliminary handout prepared for the E.C.P.R. Workshop on Political Behavior, Dissatisfaction and Protest, 12-18 April 1973, Universitat Mannheim. This table is given in Philip E. Converse, "Public Opinion and Voting Behavior," in Fred I. Greenstein and Nelson W. Polsby, eds., *The Handbook of Political Science* (Reading, Mass.: Addison Wesley, 1975), vol. 4, chap. 2, table 1, p. 102, reprinted with the permission of Addison Wesley Publishing Co.

only from the group benefits to the ideologue category. A definite increase in ideological thinking has occurred, but it is not as sharp as one might have expected. [20]

Converse has also indicated that the public's recognition of the terms "liberal" and "conservative," and its use of them did not improve after 1960. [21] The actual proportion of the public regarding the Democrats as the more conservative party was higher in 1964 than in 1960 (or 1968), notwithstanding Barry Goldwater's conservative pitch. Pierce's results also show that the proportion of the public recognizing the liberal and conservative terms held steady from 1960 to 1964. [22] Thus the evidence suggests that popular use of the terms changed little in the 1960's, increasing mainly for the moderately ideological group which already was acquainted with them.

Analysis of changes over the years is best seen in the article by Nie with Andersen included here. Their article benefits from an increase in scope,

---

[20] Note that simply using the term "radical," "liberal," or "conservative" is not automatically considered an ideological reference, just as describing Stevenson as a communist was not automatically considered ideological in 1956. Thus the increased use of the terms is not inflating the results.

[21] Converse, "Public Opinion and Voting Behavior," p. 91.

[22] Pierce, "Party Identification."

covering the whole period from 1956 to 1972 and from the fact that the methods used are identical to those used by Converse (though the questions in the surveys have changed somewhat over the years). These results show a striking increase in attitudinal consistency, with the greatest shift coming between the 1960 and 1964 elections. By 1972, the public showed more consistency in its attitudes on different issues than Converse had reported for 1958 congressional candidates. Intriguingly, Nie and Andersen find the greatest increase in ideological consistency to be among those with the least education, so that the overall increase in consistency cannot simply be attributed to rising educational levels. The reason for the change and its significance for our interpretation of electoral behavior is discussed in chapter 7.[23]

These results suggest an increase in the extent to which attitudes on separate issues are structured, which is one form of ideological thinking, but they indicate only a moderate increase in the proportion of the public that discusses politics in ideological terms, the other form of ideological thinking.

Why this mixed pattern? In a recent review of the research on the 1960's, Converse provides an explanation in terms of the different forces required to modify the level of each type of thinking.[24] Discussion of politics in ideological terms requires a certain type of educational background. People who did not learn the basic concepts in school are unlikely to pick them up later and use them in any meaningful way. Thus, the use of ideological terms is likely to increase only gradually as the level of public education rises. On the other hand, the degree to which opinions are structured depends considerably on how much thinking is done about the issues. As the political situation heats up, people pay more attention to the different issues and their opinions tend to be more consistent. As indicated in footnote 12 above, education is actually unrelated to this type of ideological thinking (see also the results of Nie with Andersen, p. 118). Converse finds that only measures of political activity, involvement, interest, and attentiveness explain differences in structuring. This accords with findings of Nie with Andersen; increased education does not explain the greater ideological structure they report. It also agrees with an analysis by Aberbach and Walker of the racial ideology of blacks, who were found to have a high ideological structure, presumably because their high motivational level more than compensated for educational deficiencies.[25]

Thus different components of ideological thinking seem to have increased at different rates in the 1960's in response to two distinct causes: increased

---

[23] Ideological constraint is also discussed by Miller et al. (chapter 10). Their correlations appear to be lower than Nie and Andersen's, although different items make exact comparisons meaningless. The lower values are probably due to the use of Pearson rather than gamma correlations.

[24] Converse, "Public Opinion and Voting Behavior," pp. 98–107.

[25] Joel D. Aberbach and Jack L. Walker, *Race in the City* (Boston: Little, Brown, 1975), pp. 130–44.

education, causing a small increase in explicit ideological awareness, and higher political interest, resulting in considerably greater attitude structure. The corollary of Converse's argument is that one of these changes may be more permanent than the other. [26] The gains due to education cannot recede, so the increase in explicit ideological awareness should not falter. Yet political interest can fall considerably, depending in part on whether the parties continue to differ. So attitude structuring might in the future fall below the levels of the 1960's, even if it does not return to the levels of the 1950's.

Measurement Questions:
Is the Foregoing Analysis Correct?

Recent analysis has not simply been limited to pointing out changes over time in ideological thinking. Rather, recent work has questioned how ideological thinking should be defined and measured. Alternative definitions and measurements suggest that the thinking of the American electorate is now, and perhaps was even in the 1950's, much more ideological than we had begun to believe.

Consider again The American Voter's coding of levels of conceptualization. Many would consider the "group benefits" references as ideological. Karl Marx's writings, for example, stressed the group concept very heavily, and no one has ever accused Marx of not being ideological. Even The American Voter discusses this category as a sort of "ideology by proxy" in which following the leadership of a group is a means of accepting their ideology. The American Voter argues that individuals in this category would cope with political change in a manner different from that of the true ideologue, [27] but there is a tacit admission that the "group benefits" category (or at least the top rung of it, category B-I in table 5.1) is somewhat ideological. This suggests a need for greater qualification when trying to state how ideological the American electorate is.

Another argument is that individual citizens may have extremely well developed ideologies that are unique to them and thus defy conventional analysis procedures. In-depth interviews are necessary to permit individuals to explain their personal belief systems. Different people could have very different belief structures, so correlations of attitudes across issues would be low. The ideologies which would be found from such in-depth interviews might seem crude by conventional academic standards, but they would suffice for the people who have them. [28] The difficulty with this view is that the

---

[26] Converse, "Public Opinion and Voting Behavior."

[27] Campbell et al., The American Voter, p. 220.

[28] Robert E. Lane, Political Ideology (New York: Free Press, 1962); Lane, "Patterns of Political Belief," in Jeanne N. Knutson, ed., Handbook of Political Psychology (San Francisco: Jossey-Bass, 1973).

concept of ideology becomes all but tautological when each person has his or her own. Moreover, ideology cannot play an important part in political communication when it is not shared, so the importance of ideological thinking is greatly diminished when it is used in this sense. Also, as Converse has noted, if the majority of the population does have personal ideologies, the correlations on issues over a period of time would be high. [29] However, Converse's selection here demonstrates considerable instability in individual attitudes over time, arguing that such personal ideologies have limited impact, except possibly on group-related (particularly racial) matters.

The article by Stimson included in this section examines another measurement question—constraint versus complexity as a measure of ideology. Marcus, Tabb, and Sullivan have argued that complexity of belief systems— the ability to understand and articulate multiple dimensions—is a better measure of ideology, and that with such a measure most, if not all, individuals have ideological views. [30] Stimson argues persuasively that for analysis of electoral behavior the notion of constraint is a more useful concept. But most striking is his empirical discovery that the two measures are correlated: "Those who have the most complex view of the political world develop the most parsimonious structure of beliefs" (p. 153). Or to put it another way, constraint is the more useful concept because "those who are capable of articulating the most dimensions actually use the fewest" (p. 153).

More generally, Stimson examines ideological thinking in the 1972 election, contrasting groups with different "cognitive ability." Those with greater cognitive ability are found to have more constrained belief systems, using fewer attitude dimensions (as determined by factor analysis) to structure their beliefs. Stimson concludes that the top half of the population has belief structuring that is consistent with a left-right dimension, though clearly there is a continuum involved and one cannot rigidly separate the two halves. Stimson carefully limits his interpretations to 1972, but it is possible that his approach would have yielded similar conclusions for earlier years, even the 1950's. [31]

A final question is whether measurement error has properly been taken into account in the analyses conducted so far. Any survey item is likely to contain some random error due to ambiguity of the question, and in this sense it may be an unreliable gauge. Psychologists often calculate the reliabilities of their items from repeated measurements and then correct their correlations for the unreliability observed. Since the reliabilities are typically

---

[29] Converse, "Public Opinion and Voting Behavior."

[30] See the references cited by Stimson, chapter 8.

[31] One question this raises is how to resolve Stimson's finding with the absence of a relationship between education and constraint reported by Converse and by Nie with Andersen. Stimson's "cognitive ability" is a combination of education and political knowledge. It is possible that political knowledge is creating most of the differences noted by Stimson.

less than one (which just means that the reliability is less than perfect), correction for unreliability typically raises the correlations above their observed values. The lower the reliability of the measures, the greater the correction. Achen has used such a procedure to reanalyze Converse's data (see chapter 6), reaching conclusions almost diametrically opposed to Converse's.[32] Achen concludes that the reliabilities of the items used in 1956-60 were very low and that the observed correlations were small as a direct result of this. When the observed correlations are "corrected," the correlations become quite large, often approaching 1.00.

A straightforward interpretation of Achen's results is that the low correlations originally observed were due to poor questions, and that better questions would have shown individuals to have stable opinions even in the 50's. However, the estimation of the reliabilities depends on a set of assumptions. If those assumptions are incorrect, then the reliabilities may be underestimated and Achen is overcorrecting Converse's correlations. It seems certain that this is the case to some extent, as Achen indicated. Unfortunately, just how much of a correction should be made in the original correlations is unclear. Our intuition says that Achen's corrections are much too great, and that nonattitudes are frequently present.[33] But better evidence is not currently attainable, and perhaps never will be for a past era. Hence, while our conclusions must be partly based on our intuition, Achen's analysis at the very least cautions us to be much more careful in the future about the problem of measurement error and suggests that political scientists might devote more effort to estimating the reliabilities of items they use.

Conclusions

These several studies illustrate the current debate about the presence of ideology in the thinking of the electorate. There seems to be general, though not unanimous, agreement both that the electorate is more ideological in the 1970's than in the 1950's and that ideological thinking even in the 1970's is far from universal by *The American Voter* definitions. Thus the real controversy involves how to define ideology, how to measure ideology, and the relative importance of nonattitudes and measurement error. As a consequence, some see greater use of ideological concepts and greater belief structuring than others. This is a debate that will probably never be resolved.

Where does all this leave us? How sophisticated is the electorate? Are the

---

[32] Christopher H. Achen, "Mass Political Attitudes and the Survey Response," *American Political Science Review*, 69(1975):1218-231.

[33] Our reason is identical to that which motivated Converse's original work on nonattitudes. Anyone who has conducted actual interviews with a cross-section sample of the public realizes that many expressed attitudes are nonattitudes. People feel they can't admit ignorance, so they choose a response to help the interviewer, they pick an answer but are embarrassed by follow-up probes, and so on.

1950's or the 1960's the more typical? There will never be consensus on the exact meaning of ideology, and so we shall not try to decide questions of definition. But we can focus on whether the 1950's or the 1960's should be considered representative, given a constant definition of ideology. When Converse turned his attention back to this subject in the mid-1970's, he concluded that with regard to constraint among ideas the 1950's are the more typical. [34] Since there is no clear way to estimate norms from American data alone, he based his evaluation on comparison with other countries of a similar developmental level. He reports that French, German, and British data for the 1960's are uniformly like the American data of the 1950's. Thus the American 1960's results may be the atypical ones, rather than those of the 1950's. Yet, Converse quickly admits that this depends considerably on how large party differences are and that this is highly changeable.

Yet we wonder whether it is worth estimating which is more typical. Party differences are inevitably going to increase and decrease over the years just as political tensions rise and fall. Consistency of belief structures may therefore vary from the lows of the calm 50's to the highs of the polarized 60's. Belief structuring will depend on the prominence of the issues, and that, rather than a "typical" level, is what is important.

What is of still greater importance is that explicit use of ideology is low no matter how we define ideology. Even the most generous estimates (combining type B-I group benefits to level A ideologues in Klingemann's coding) find only half of the electorate operating at an ideological level. Explicit ideological awareness should continue to increase as education advances, but there is vast room for improvement. Many individuals do not share the common ideological terms and concepts so freely used by political scientists, politicians, and journalists. Politicians are fond of saying they don't like to be stereotyped or placed in categories; even if they were categorized, however, it would have little meaning for many people.

In the same vein, it seems clear that the general public may combine and constrain ideas in different ways than the elites. Whereas for many individuals it seems illogical to believe in free speech while opposing the right of a communist to speak, for other individuals it seems illogical to profess anti-communism and yet permit a self-confessed communist to speak. There is no reason why all voters must combine and compare ideas in precisely the same way as leading political figures do. Thus we can continue to expect some lack of constraint among ideas even when issues are salient and individuals informed.

Finally, the differences in ideology over the years indicate that the apparent absence of ideological thinking in the 50's was not solely due to serious deficiencies in voters. Rather, given the proper circumstances, voters as a whole indicate considerable sensibility in the way they organize their political ideas. They are often uninformed and, as the results of Stimson and of Nie with Andersen show, even in times like the 70's some reveal a genuine

---

[34] Converse, "Public Opinion and Voting Behavior."

lack of constraint among their various attitudes. But the unqualified charge that voters are nonideological—or worse yet that voters are dumb—simply is not true.

An important ingredient in the level of voter sophistication appears to be elite behavior. If elites consciously use ideological terms in election campaigns, if they interpret issues in terms of larger questions and in terms of the relationships between various political matters, and if presidential candidates take stands that are reasonably clear and differentiated, then the voters will react by making the appropriate ideological distinctions. If these conditions are absent, the voters will appear to be—and may in fact be—disorganized and nonideological in their approach to politics. Elites, then, play a role not only in determining which particular issues attract attention at a given time, but in determining the way in which voters organize and structure their political thinking.

Further Readings

Survey Evidence on Ideology

James W. Prothro and Charles M. Grigg, "Fundamental Principles of Democracy: Bases of Agreement and Disagreement," *Journal of Politics,* 22(1960):276-94. Report of study that concludes that public acceptance of democratic ideology does not extend to the specifics of democracy.

Angus Campbell, Philip E. Converse, Warren E. Miller, and Donald E. Stokes, *The American Voter* (New York: Wiley, 1960), chap. 10, unabridged, chap. 9, abridged. Analysis of "level of conceptualization" of politics by the electorate.

Philip E. Converse, "The Nature of Belief Systems in Mass Publics," in David E. Apter, ed., *Ideology and Discontent* (New York: Free Press, 1964). Full statement of results about ideology.

Chistopher H. Achen, "Mass Political Attitudes and the Survey Response," *American Political Science Review,* 69(1975):1218-231. Emphasis on low question reliability causing apparent lack of ideology.

Philip E. Converse, "Public Opinion and Voting Behavior," in Fred I. Greenstein and Nelson W. Polsby, eds., *The Handbook of Political Science,* vol. 4 (Reading, Mass.: Addison Wesley, 1975). Responses to critics about ideological level of the electorate.

Nonsurvey Studies of Ideology

Robert E. Lane, *Political Ideology* (New York: Free Press, 1962). Statement of the existence of personal rather than shared ideologies.

Steven R. Brown, "Consistency and the Persistence of Ideology: Some Experimental Results," *Public Opinion Quarterly,* 34(1970-71):60-68. Experimental study arguing that attitudes are stable even among political "inarticulates."

84   George E. Marcus, David Tabb, and John L. Sullivan, "The Application of Individual Differences Scaling Analysis to the Measurement of Political Ideology," *American Journal of Political Science,* 18(1974):405–20. Finds individual ideologies for single subjects.

Comparative Studies on Ideology

Philip E. Converse, "The Problem of Party Distances in Models of Voting Change," in M. Kent Jennings and Harmon Zeigler, eds., *The Electoral Process* (Englewood Cliffs, N.J.: Prentice-Hall, 1966). Study of dimensions of party competition in France and Finland.

David Butler and Donald E. Stokes, *Political Change in Britain* (New York: St. Martin's Press, 1969), chap. 9. Finds that voter reactions to parties are not satisfied by a single left-right continuum.

Samuel H. Barnes, "Left, Right, and the Italian Voter," *Comparative Political Studies,* 4(1971):157–76. Studies the role of the left-right dimension for Italian voters.

Giacomo Sani, "A Test of the Least-Distance Model of Voting Choice," *Comparative Political Studes,* 7(1974):193–208. Test of ability to predict vote from left-right placement of voters with respect to the parties in Italy.

6. The Stability of Belief Elements over Time

PHILIP E. CONVERSE

.... All of our data up to this point have used correlations calculated on aggregates as evidence of greater or lesser constraint among elements in belief systems. While we believe these correlations to be informative indicators, they do depend for their form upon cumulations among individuals and therefore can never be seen as commenting incisively upon the belief structures of individuals.

It might then be argued that we are mistaken in saying that constraint among comparable "distant" belief elements declines generally as we move from the more to the less politically sophisticated. Instead, the configuration of political beliefs held by individuals simply becomes increasingly idiosyncratic as we move to less sophisticated people. While an equally broad range of belief elements might function as an interdependent whole for an unsophisticated person, we would find little aggregative patterning of belief combinations in populations of unsophisticated people, for they would be out of the stream of cultural information about "what goes with what" and would therefore put belief elements together in a great variety of ways.

For the types of belief that interest us here, this conclusion in itself would

SOURCE: "The Nature of Belief Systems in Mass Publics," in David Apter, ed., *Ideology and Discontent*. Copyright © 1964 by The Free Press of Glencoe, a Division of The Macmillan Company. Reprinted with permission of Macmillan Publishing Co., Inc..

be significant. We believe however, that we have evidence that permits us to reject it rather categorically, in favor of our original formulation. A fair test of this counterhypothesis would seem to lie in the measurement of the same belief elements for the same individuals over time. For if we are indeed involved here in idiosyncratic patterns of belief, each meaningful to the individual in his own way, then we could expect that individual responses to the same set of items at different points in time should show some fundamental stability. They do not.

A longitudinal study of the American electorate over a four-year period has permitted us to ask the same questions of the same people a number of times, usually separated by close to two-year intervals. Analysis of the stability of responses to . . . "basic" policy questions . . . yields remarkable results. Faced with the typical item of this kind, only about thirteen people out of twenty manage to locate themselves even on the same *side* of the controversy in successive interrogations, when ten out of twenty could have done so by chance alone.

While we have no comparable longitudinal data for an elite sample, the degree of fit between answers to our issue items and congressional roll calls is strong enough to suggest that time correlations for individual congressmen in roll-call choice on comparable bills would provide a fair estimate of the stability of an elite population in beliefs of this sort. It is probably no exaggeration to deduce that, in sharp contrast to a mass sample, eighteen out of twenty congressmen would be likely to take the same positions on the same attitude items after a two-year interval. In short, then, we feel very confident that elite-mass differences in levels of constraint among beliefs are mirrored in elite-mass differences in the temporal stability of belief elements for individuals.

We observed much earlier that the centrality of a specific belief in a larger belief system and the relative stability of that belief over time should be highly related. From our other propositions about the role of groups as central objects in the belief systems of the mass public, we can therefore arrive at two further predictions. The first is simply that pure affect toward visible population groupings should be highly stable over time, even in a mass public, much more so in fact than beliefs on policy matters that more or less explicitly bear on the fortunes of these groupings. Second, policy items that do bear more rather than less explicitly upon their fortunes should show less stability than affect towards the group *qua* group but more than those items for which contextual information is required.

Figure 6.1 gives strong confirmation of these hypotheses.[1] First, the only question applied longitudinally that touches on pure affect toward a visible population grouping is the one about party loyalties or identifications. As

---

[1] The items portrayed in figure 6.1 are the same as those in table VII [in Converse] and are described at that point.

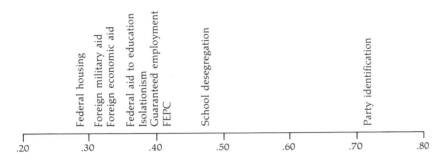

Figure 6.1 Temporal stability of different belief elements for individuals, 1958-60. The measure of stability is a rank-order correlation (tau-beta) between individuals' positions in 1958 and in 1960 on the same items.

the figure indicates, the stability of these group feelings for individuals over time (measured by the correlation between individual positions in two successive readings) registers in a completely different range from that characterizing even the most stable of the issue items employed.[2] This contrast is particularly ironic, for in theory of course the party usually has little rationale for its existence save as an instrument to further particular policy preferences of the sort that show less stability in figure 6.1. The policy is the end, and the party is the means, and ends are conceived to be more stable and central in belief systems than means. The reversal for the mass public is of course a rather dramatic special case of one of our primary generalizations: The party and the affect toward it are more central within the political belief systems of the mass public than are the policy ends that the parties are designed to pursue.

Figure 6.1 also shows that, within the set of issues, the items that stand out as most stable are those that have obvious bearing on the welfare of a population grouping—the Negroes—although the item concerning federal job guarantees is very nearly as stable. In general, we may say that stability declines as the referents of the attitude items become increasingly remote, from jobs, which are significant objects to all, and Negroes, who are attitude objects for most, to items involving ways and means of handling foreign policy.

Although most of the less stable items involve foreign policy, the greatest instability is shown for a domestic issue concerning the relative role of government and private enterprise in areas like those of housing and utilities. Interestingly enough, this issue would probably be chosen by sophisticated

[2] We regret that we did not get measures of pure affect for other groupings in the population, for all population members. A copious literature on intergroup attitudes in social psychology contains, however, much presumptive evidence of extreme stability in these attitudes over time.

judges as the classically "ideological" item in the set, and indeed table VII [in Converse] shows that the counterpart for this question in the elite sample is central to the primary organizing dimension visible in the matrix. Since the item refers to visible population groupings—"government" and "private business"—we might ask why it is not geared into more stable affect toward these groups. We do believe that measures of affect toward something like "private business" (or better, perhaps, "big business") as an object would show reasonable stability for a mass public, although probably less than those for more clearly bounded and visible groups like Negroes and Catholics. The question, however, is not worded in a way that makes clear which party—government or private business—will profit from which arrangement. Lacking such cues, the citizen innocent of "ideology" is likely to make rather capricious constructions, since the issue is probably one that he has never thought about before and will never think about again except when being interviewed.

In short, all these longitudinal data offer eloquent proof that signs of low constraint among belief elements in the mass public are not products of well knit but highly idiosyncratic belief systems, for these beliefs are extremely labile for individuals over time. Great instability in itself is *prima facie* evidence that the belief has extremely low centrality for the believer. Furthermore, it is apparent that any instability characterizing one belief sets an upper limit on the degree of orderly constraint that could be expected to emerge in static measurement between this unstable belief and another, even a perfectly stable one. While an aggregate might thus show high stability despite low constraint, the fact of low stability virtually ensures that constraint must also be low. This kind of relationship between stability and constraint means that an understanding of what underlies high instability is at the same time an understanding of what underlies low constraint.

The fact that we have asked these questions at more than two points in time provides a good deal of leverage in analyzing the processes of change that generate aggregate instability and helps us to illuminate the character of this instability.[3] For example, in figure 6.2 we discover, in comparing our indicators of the degree of instability associated with any particular belief as they register between t_2 and t_3 with the same figures for t_1 and t_2, that estimates are essentially the same. This result is an important one, for it assures us that within a medium time range (four years), differences among issues in degree of response stability are highly reliable.

Far more fascinating, however, is another property that emerges. Quite

---

[3] Unfortunately we lack the longitudinal data for elites that would permit the following analysis to be comparative. Let us keep in mind, however, that the relatively high constraint among belief elements already demonstrated for elites is almost certain proof of high stability of these elements over time as well. The phenomenon we are analyzing is thus a mass not an elite phenomenon.

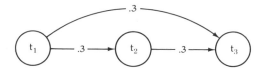

Figure 6.2 Pattern of turnover correlations between different time points.

generally, we can predict t_3 issue positions of individuals fully as well from a knowledge of their t_1 positions alone as we can from a knowledge of their t_2 positions alone. In other words, the turnover correlations between different time points for these issues tend to fit the scheme shown in figure 6.2.

It can be shown that there is no single meaningful process of change shared by all respondents that would generate this configuration of data.[4] In fact, even if we assume that there is a relatively limited number of change processes present in the population, we find that only two such models could generate these observations. The first of these models posits that some of the respondents managed in a deliberate way to locate themselves from one measurement to another on the opposite side of an issue from the one they had selected at the preceding measurement. It would have to be assumed that a person who chose a leftish alternative on a certain issue in the first measure would be motivated to remember to seek out the rightish alternative two years later, the leftish again two years after that, and so on. Naturally, an assumption that this behavior characterizes one member of the population is sufficiently nonsensical for us to reject it out of hand.

Once this possibility is set aside, however, there is only one other model involving a mixture of two types of process of change that fits the observed data. This model is somewhat surprising but not totally implausible. It posits a very sharp dichotomy within the population according to processes of change that are polar opposites. There is first a "hard core" of opinion on a given issue, which is well crystallized and perfectly stable over time. For the remainder of the population, response sequences over time are statistically random. The model does not specify what proportions of the population fall into these two categories: This matter is empirically independent, and it is clear that the size of the turnover correlations between any two points in time is a simple function of these relative proportions.[5]

---

[4] More technically, such a configuration is mathematically incompatible with the assumption based on simple Markov chain theory that a single matrix of transition probabilities can account for the change process. For the benefit of the nontechnical reader, we use the phrase "change process" in the singular to denote a single specified matrix of transition probabilities.

[5] This model has been discussed as a hypothetical case in Lee M. Wiggins, "Mathemical Models for the Interpretation of Attitude and Behavior Change: The Analysis of Multi-Wave Panels" (Unpublished doctoral dissertation, Columbia University, 1955).

In view of our earlier remarks, this "black and white" model is credible in its assumption that a mass public contains significant proportions of people who, for lack of information about a particular dimension of controversy, offer meaningless opinions that vary randomly in direction during repeated trials over time. We may be uncomfortable, however, at using a model that suggests such a rigid and polar division of the population, leaving no room for the "gray" area of meaningful change of opinion or "conversion." In this respect, while the randomness posited by the model is a discouraging property substantively, it is an empowering property mathematically, for aggregate randomness has certain predictable consequences. For example, if the model were to fit the data, we would know that some people who are responding to the items as though flipping a coin could, by chance alone, supply the same responses at three trials in a row and would therefore have response paths indistinguishable from those of perfectly stable respondents but for entirely different reasons. While we could not enter the stable group and "tag" such random people, we would at least have an excellent estimate of the number of them that lingers after three trials to pollute the set of genuinely stable respondents. Most important, however, is the fact that the very character of the model makes it possible to test quite rigorously the goodness of fit of the data to the model.

For our initial test, we singled out the issue that seemed on a priori grounds most likely to fit the model. It was the most "ideological" item in the battery yet the one that had shown the highest degree of temporal instability: the question about the respective roles of private enterprise and government in areas like housing and electrical power. It is important to understand in detail the grounds on which this item was chosen. The model requires that some people have unswerving beliefs on the subject and that other people have no beliefs at all. It also requires that there be no middle ground, no set of people whose beliefs on the subject are in the process of evolution. For these requirements, the "government vs. private enterprise issue," more than any of the others, seemed "sheltered" from meaningful change. This isolation was true in two senses. First, it involved a very basic area of political controversy, and people understanding the stakes involved in a more ideological way would not be readily dissuaded from their respective positions. Secondly, while events like the crisis at Little Rock and exposés of waste in foreign aid were occurring in this period to touch off meaningful evolutions of opinion, little was occurring that might intuitively be expected to shake true beliefs on one side or the other. At the same time, of course, the relationships to be judged in the item were sufficiently remote and abstract from the experience of most people to make many meaningless responses likely.

The fit between the data collected at three time points on this issue and our black and white model was virtually perfect.[6] This result lends remarkable assurance that our understanding of the "change" processes affecting the issue responses was accurate: The only change that occurred was random change. We naturally went on to apply this test of fit to the other issues, for which the black and white model had seemed less credible. And indeed, these other items showed a somewhat poorer fit with the model. None strays a great distance, but it is unlikely that any would survive significant tests of goodness of fit.[7] What, then, can we say about the character of beliefs touched by these other items?

Strictly speaking, as soon as we encounter data that depart in any significant measure from the black and white model, we lose all mathematical anchors, in the sense that, unless we insert a variety of restrictive assumptions, the number of models (even simple ones) that could *logically* account for the data becomes very large indeed. Despite this loss of power, the existence of one issue that does fit the black and white model perfectly provides at least an intuitive argument that those that depart from it in modest degrees do not require a totally different class of model. In other words, we come to suppose that these other items depart from the model only because of the presence of a "third force" of people, who are undergoing meaningful conversion from one genuine opinion at t_1 to an opposing but equally genuine opinion at t_2. This "third force" is small, and the dominant phenomenon remains the two segments of the population, within one of which opinions are random and within the other of which opinions have perfect stability. Nevertheless, the presence of any third force suffices to disrupt the fit between the data and the black and white model, and the degree of departure is a function of the size of the third force.

It should be reiterated that this view cannot be subjected to any unequivocal mathematical test but rather depends for its reasonableness upon the excellence of the fit shown by one issue and the approaches to fit shown by the others. It seems likely that responses to other issues of a similar type

---

[6] The logic of the test is rather simple. If the model pertains, then any respondents who change sides of an issue between t_1 and t_2 are from the random part of the population, while those who do not change sides are a mixture in known proportions of perfectly stable people and random people who happened to have chosen the same side twice by chance. If we divide the population into these two parts on the basis of their t_1-t_2 patterns and if the model is appropriate to the situation, then the turnover correlations between t_2 and t_3 for each of the two divisions of the population are determinate. The purely random group should show a correlation of .00 between t_2 and t_3; the adulterated stable group should show a correlation that falls short of unity as a direct function of the known proportions of random people still in the group. For our critical test, the original total-population turnover correlation (1956–1958) was .24. With the population properly subdivided as suggested by the model, this over-all correlation could be expected to fork into two correlations between t_2 and t_3 of .00 and .47, *if the model was applicable*. The empirical values turned out to be .004 and .49.

[7] For instance, in terms parallel to the expectations of the final sentence of footnote 6, the correlations may fork into a pair that are .07 and .35, rather than .00 and .47.

are generated in similar fashion. And while it is true that competing attitude models could be applied to describe most of these data, their assumptions simply lose all plausible ring when confronted with the results from the private-enterprise issue. [8]

Or, in another vein, the discouragingly large turnover of opinion on these issues in the total mass public might be taken as evidence that the questions were poorly written and thus extremely unreliable—that the main lesson is that they should be rewritten. Yet the issues posed are those posed by political controversy, and citizens' difficulties in responding to them in meaningful fashion seem to proffer important insights into their understanding of the same political debates in real life. More crucial still, what does it mean to say that an instrument is perfectly reliable *vis-à-vis* one class of people and totally unreliable *vis-à-vis* another, which is the proper description of the black and white model? The property of reliability is certainly not inherent *solely* in the instrument of measurement, contrary to what is commonly supposed.

As another check on the question of reliability, we decided to examine the temporal stability of belief elements of this sort among very limited sets of people whose broader interviews gave us independent reasons to believe they had particular interest in narrower belief areas (like the Negro question). We took advantage once again of interviews with a good deal of open-ended material, sifting through this voluntary commentary to find people who had shown "self-starting" concern about particular controversies. Then we went back to the relevant structured issue questions to examine the stability of these belief elements for these people over time. The turnover correlations for these limited subpopulations did increase substantially, beginning to approach the levels of stability shown for party identification (see

---

[8] For example, a random path of responses would be laid down over time by a set of people for whom the content of the item was very meaningful, yet put each individual in such a quandary that his pro-con response potential balanced exactly at .50-.50. In such cases, it could be assumed that slight rewording of the item, making it "harder" or "easier" in a Guttman sense, would shift the response potentials away from this .50-.50 balance and would thus begin to produce correlations between individual responses over time. This view cannot be challenged in any decisive way for issues generating responses that depart from our black and white model, since, in these cases, a distribution of the population continuously across the total range of response probabilities is entirely compatible with the data. It is even possible to describe the empirical situation surrounding the private-enterprise item in these terms. The problem is that such a description seems patently absurd, for it implies that the question was somehow constructed so that the content drew highly unequivocal responses from one class of people but left all the rest in perfect and exquisite conflict. Intermediate classes—people with probabilities of responding to the content positively at a level of .6, .7, .8 or .9—are simply not necessary to account for the data. Such a description lacks verisimilitude. Our assumption is rather that, had the private-enterprise item been rendered "harder" or "easier" in a Guttman sense, the respondents we call "random" would have *continued* to respond randomly, at least across a zone of items so broad as to bracket any plausible political alternatives. In other words, the problem is not one of specific wording that puts the respondent in particularly delicate conflict; it is rather that the whole area from which this item is drawn is so remote to the respondent that he has not been stimulated to any real opinion formation within it.

figure 6.1). Once again, the evidence seemed clear that extreme instability is associated with absence of information, or at least of interest, and that item reliability is adequate for people with pre-existing concern about any given matter.[9]

The substantive conclusion imposed by these technical maneuvers is simply that large portions of an electorate do not have meaningful beliefs, even on issues that have formed the basis for intense political controversy among elites for substantial periods of time. If this conclusion seems self-evident, it is worth reflecting on the constancy with which it is ignored and on the fact that virtually none of the common modes of dealing empirically with public beliefs attempts to take it into account. Instead, it is assumed that a location must be found for all members of a population on all dimensions of controversy that are measured. Our data argue that, where any single dimension is concerned, very substantial portions of the public simply do not belong on the dimension at all. They should be set aside as not forming any part of that particular *issue public*. And since it is only among "members" of any given issue public that the political effects of a controversy are felt (where such "effects" include activated public opinion expressed in the writing of letters to the editor, the changing of votes, and the like), we come a step closer to reality when we recognize the fragmentation of the mass public into a plethora of narrower issue publics.

---

[9] Results of this sort lend considerable weight to Scott's proposals for assessing cultural values through analysis of responses to open-ended questions. William A. Scott, "Empirical Assessment of Values and Ideologies," *American Sociological Review*, 24(June 1959):299–310.

7. Mass Belief Systems Revisited: Political Change and Attitude Structure

NORMAN H. NIE
with KRISTI ANDERSEN

Modern survey techniques have often been most fruitful in under-cutting common wisdom about politics. These techniques—more precise than the impressionistic techniques of earlier observers—have shown that some common understandings of the nature of mass political beliefs have been wrong. But one must approach survey-based findings with caution. Surveys too can distort, particularly if one assumes that a pattern that is found at one point in time represents a general, long-term tendency extending beyond the specific time period in which the research was conducted. We must be careful that we do not replace a common wisdom of impres-

SOURCE: *Journal of Politics,* 36(1974):540–87. Reprinted with permission of the publisher. AUTHOR'S NOTE: This paper owes a great debt to my students in the National Opinion Research Center Training program, who did much to rekindle my interest in ideology. I would also like to thank Sidney Verba and Kenneth Prewitt for their intellectual contributions at various stages. The first draft of the paper was written while I was a research Fulbright Fellow at the University of Leiden, the Netherlands. I would like to express my appreciation to the Fulbright Foundation for support during this period and to the University of Leiden for supporting the research. Additional support for myself and for the research was provided by the National Science Foundation under Grant GS 3155 and the Twentieth Century Fund. The data reported in this article come from seven separate surveys and the organization and presentation was a mammoth job in data management. This task could not have been accomplished without the efforts of Carol Ann Lugtigheid, Eric Lugtigheid, John R. Petrocik, Jaap Rozema, and Jaap van Poelgeest.

sionistic political science by a common wisdom based on a precise, but time-bound, research technique.

One of the newer "common wisdoms" derived from survey techniques has to do with the absence of ideology in the American public. Ideology has many meanings, but one of its components is usually a high degree of consistency among political attitudes—attitudes on a wide range of issues falling into clear liberal and conservative tendencies. [1] And this component has been found to be particularly lacking in the American mass public.

The mass public has usually been contrasted with more elite publics—for example, politicians, journalists, and academics. In elite publics, attitudes on a wide variety of issues are bound together in highly predictable ways. Attitudes on welfare measures, government spending, and taxation are usually highly intercorrelated, reflecting a general position on the proper scope of government activity. Furthermore, attitudes on issues such as race, civil liberties, and foreign policy also tend to be related to each other as well as to attitudes on domestic economic policies. This relationship across a wide range of issues enables us to identify many members of political elite groups as liberals or conservatives.

Studies of the interrelationship of opinions among mass publics, on the other hand, have found little evidence for this kind of ideological structuring. The citizenry at large has not organized its political beliefs along liberal/conservative lines. Within a given issue-domain there is some evidence of

---

[1] The empirical study of ideology in the mass public has proceeded along three lines. First, researchers have investigated the degree to which citizens conceptualize politics in ideological terms, either by deciding whether their spontaneous evaluations of political objects have ideological content or by directly determining their knowledge of ideological terms. (Cf. Angus Campbell et al., *The American Voter* [New York: Wiley, 1960]; and Philip Converse, "The Nature of Belief Systems in Mass Publics," in *Ideology and Discontent,* David Apter, ed. [New York: Free Press, 1964] chap. 6.) Second, students of mass opinion have looked for a coherent structure among citizens' attitudes on political issues which would suggest that they organize their political beliefs on a broad ideological continuum such as liberalism/conservatism. Finally, other students of ideology—operating on a somewhat different level and with a completely different methodology—have attempted to probe for deeper and more personal ways in which citizens make order of the political world around them. (Cf. especially Robert Lane, *Political Ideology* [New York: Free Press, 1962]).

While all three techniques have been useful in elucidating various aspects of the nature of belief systems in mass publics, the degree to which the citizenry holds consistent liberal or conservative attitudes on a wide variety of issues is perhaps the best single indicator of the political relevance of ideology. This is true, we believe, for several reasons. First, consistent views are not subject to the changing fashions in political terminology; they measure more than the facility with which people are able to bring rhetorical labels to mind. Secondly, examining attitude constraint is an economical and reliable way of studying mass ideology, whereas techniques such as those used by Lane require such intensive analysis of individuals that generalizations about national populations are difficult if not impossible. Moreover, even if techniques like Lane's can uncover some deeper structuring of an individual's political beliefs, in most of a citizen's interactions with the political world, he is presented with and asked to assume rather narrowly conceived alternative positions on political issues.

attitude consistency—for example, positions on governmental responsibility for providing employment are related to those on governmental responsibility in the areas of medicine and housing. However, attitudes in separate issue-spheres appear to bear little or no relationship to each other. Attitudes on welfare, taxation, government spending, as well as those on other domestic economic policies show only minor relationships to each other. And attitudes on the more remote issues of race, civil liberties, and foreign policy have virtually no relationship to each other or to positions on welfare or economic liberalism. In short, available studies indicate that there is little or no interdependence or opinion constraint, to use Converse's term, in mass attitudes. [2]

The explanation usually given for the difference in the structure of beliefs between elite and mass emphasizes certain critical limitations inherent in mass publics. The mass public has neither the educational background, the contextual knowledge, nor the capacity to deal with abstract concepts that sustain an organized set of beliefs over a wide range of political issues. [3]

There is, however, one major problem with these descriptions of the state of mass belief systems: the studies on which they are based are all from a single historical period some 15 to 20 years ago. V. O. Key's major work on attitude consistency is based on data gathered during the 1956 presidential election. Philip Converse's seminal article on "The Nature of Belief Systems in Mass Publics," though published somewhat later, uses data collected in 1958 and 1960. Most of the other studies which contribute to our knowledge of mass ideology, such as *The American Voter* and McClosky's study of party elites and regulars, are also based on data gathered around 1960.

Why so few follow-up investigations were made in such an important area can probably only be accounted for by the character of the findings themselves and the theory which evolved to explain them. These early studies were convincing, and they were consistent with each other. Furthermore, the theoretical argument put forward to explain the absence of ideological organization convincingly stressed inherent and thus enduring limitations of mass publics. The initial questions about the nature of mass political beliefs

---

[2] This discussion of the difference between the organization of attitudes in elites and mass publics has drawn heavily on the following works: Converse, "Belief Systems," 227–31 particularly; Herbert McClosky, "Consensus and Ideology in American Politics," *American Political Science Review*, 58 (June 1964):361–82; McClosky, Paul J. Hoffman, and Rosemary O'Hara, "Issue Conflict and Consensus among Leaders and Followers," *American Political Science Review*, 54(June 1960):419; James W. Prothro and C. W. Grigg, "Fundamental Principles of Democracy: Basis of Agreement and Disagreement," *Journal of Politics*, 22(May 1969): 276–94. The specific description of the relationship among opinions in the mass public relies upon the analysis of V. O. Key, Jr., in *Public Opinion in American Democracy* (New York: Alfred A. Knopf, 1961), chap. 7, 153–81.

[3] This explanation for the structure of mass beliefs is most coherently stated by Converse, "Belief Systems." However, it is explicit or implicit in most of the other studies cited.

had been answered in a way which foreclosed continued research on the question. [4]

But American politics in the 60's and early 70's were not the same as those of the 1950's. The quiescent Eisenhower years were followed by turmoil on many fronts: the civil-rights movement, black militancy and urban violence, a protracted and divisive war, campus unrest, changing morals and life-styles—all interspersed with a tragic series of political assassinations. This change in the nature of American politics provides a crucial test of the analysis of mass-belief systems. If the lack of organization of mass political attitudes is based on enduring characteristics of the mass public, it should be relatively insensitive to such changes in the world of politics. But if we find that the structure of mass attitudes has been affected by the political up-heavals of the 1960's, we may have to reconsider the character of mass attitudes and the factors which affect their structure.

In this paper we propose to examine the structure of mass attitudes over the past 16 years. We will show that there have been major increases in the levels of attitude consistency within the mass public. [5] Not only has the constraint among traditional issues such as those examined by Converse and Key increased substantially, but new issues as they have emerged in the 60's have been incorporated by the mass public into what now appears to be a broad liberal/conservative ideology.

In our analysis we will attempt to determine what attitudes are involved in this increasing consistency on the part of the mass public. We will also be concerned with precisely when these changes have taken place. We will try to search out the factors which produced the increases in attitude consis-tency, showing that the inherent characteristics of the mass public are less important as determinants of mass ideology than are variations in the nature and salience of political stimuli. Finally, we will review these various find-ings in order to see what they suggest about the validity of the current theory of mass beliefs and about the general determinants of belief-systems in mass publics. In the conclusion of the paper we will consider briefly how

---

[4] There are a few notable exceptions. Field and Anderson have replicated the analysis of levels of ideological conceptualization from Campbell, *The American Voter* and they find a significant increase in the proportions of the public thinking in ideological terms in 1964. This work, however, does not deal directly with attitude consistency. J. O. Field and R. E. Anderson, "Ideology in the Public's Conceptualization of the 1964 Election," *Public Opin-ion Quarterly,* 33(Fall 1969):389–98. Two recent articles have examined attitude consis-tency, but each deals with either a special public or local issue. See Norman Luttbeg, "The Structure of Beliefs Among Leaders and the Public," *Public Opinion Quarterly,* 32(Fall 1969):398–409; and Jack L. Walker and Joel D. Aberbach, "The Meanings of Black Power: A Comparison of White and Black Interpretations of a Political Slogan," *American Political Science Review,* 64(June 1970):367–88. Both of these articles in one way or another chal-lenge some of the findings of the earlier studies.

[5] Throughout this paper we use the terms attitude consistency and attitude constraint interchangeably. For us, both terms simply imply predictability of liberal/conservative attitudes across issue areas.

increased coherence of the mass political beliefs may be affecting American electoral politics—ranging from its growing effect on national elections to its deeper role in what may be a period of realignment.

We should note here that our definition of liberal/conservative consistency is not based on a priori logical relationships between political attitudes; in fact, none of the issues with which we are concerned, though they may share common symbols, bear any strictly logical relationship to one another.[6] Instead, our definition of consistency is based upon the political context in which attitudes are formed. Regardless of whether issues are logically connected, liberal and conservative positions on a wide variety of issues are established over a period of time and come to constitute the ideological "cues" of the political system. It is in this way that on such logically distant issues as the conduct of the Vietnam War and attitudes toward school integration, "liberal" and "conservative" stances are clearly defined and accepted.

The Data

The analysis is based on data gathered by the Survey Research Center at the University of Michigan in conjunction with its national election studies. Between 1952 and 1972, the Survey Research Center (SRC) has interviewed a representative sample of some 1,500 to 2,700 adult Americans in each of the presidential elections and in several of the off-year congressional elections. The respondents in each of these surveys were asked questions about their attitudes on a wide variety of political issues. Many of these opinion questions appear in only one or two of the surveys, but a set of questions covering five basic issue-areas is available for each of the presidential election years from 1956 through 1972 and for the 1958 congressional election. Similar questions were asked of a national sample in a survey which was administered by the National Opinion Research Center (NORC) in the spring of 1971.

The five issue-areas for which we have comparable data over the entire time period are:

1. *Social Welfare.* The questions elicit the respondent's attitudes on the federal government's responsibility to provide welfare programs in the areas of employment, of education, and of medical care.

---

[6] For example, respondents were asked whether they thought the federal government ought to play an active role in seeing to it that black and white children go to the same schools. They were also asked whether they thought the government should devise special programs to help blacks economically. While both questions share the symbol of blacks, it would not be illogical for a respondent to be against government enforcement of integration, but at the same time favor economic assistance to blacks. The issues may be symbolically related, but there is no formal logical connection between them.

2. *Welfare Measures Specific for Blacks.* Respondents were asked whether they thought the federal government should provide special welfare programs for blacks in the areas of jobs and housing.
3. *The Size of Government.* From 1956 through 1960 respondents were asked whether they thought it best that the federal government be kept out of areas such as housing and electric power generation that were traditionally handled by private industry. From 1964 through 1972, respondents were asked a slightly more general question concerning whether they thought the federal government was already too big and involved in too many areas. (This question is not asked in the 1971 NORC study.)
4. *Racial Integration in the Schools.* The questions asked whether the federal government ought to enforce school integration or stay completely out of that problem.
5. *The Cold War.* These questions vary from period to period as the nature of the cold war changed, but they are all concerned with the toughness of the United States toward communism and the desirability of military intervention. In 1956, 1958, and 1960, respondents were asked whether they thought the government ought to send soldiers abroad to aid countries fighting communism. The 1964 and '68 surveys asked whether the United States government should sit down and talk to Communist leaders to settle differences. In 1968, '71, and '72, the questions asked whether we should pursue a military victory against the Communists in Vietnam or withdraw our forces.

With the exceptions mentioned above, the questions to be used in the analysis are, with minor variations in wording and coding, identical at all points in time. To make interpretation easier, coding categories were reordered wherever necessary to range from conservative to liberal. For purposes of statistical comparability, answers to questions which originally permitted more than three codes were collapsed so that responses to all questions conformed to a unified trichotomous format of: (1) conservative; (2) centrist; (3) liberal. [7] Refusals, those with no opinions, and those giving "don't know" responses were always excluded from the analysis.

---

[7] Because gamma is used as our basic measure of association and because it is somewhat sensitive to the number of degrees of freedom in a table, recoding was required in order to get an unbiased estimation of the relationship between the various attitudes and between the same attitudes across time. In the recoding of the data, two guidelines were followed: (1) to make as even as possible the proportions of the population in each of the three categories, while (2) not permitting the first guideline to place respondents on the agree and disagree side of an issue in the same category. The rationale for the second recoding guideline is obvious in any attempt to classify responses as basically liberal or conservative. The rationale for the first guideline again relates to the use of gamma as the measure of association because it is highly sensitive and unreliable when there are extreme marginals.

The Emergence of Mass Ideology:
Over-Time Comparisons of Attitude Consistency

Figure 7.1 presents a comparison of levels of attitude consistency among the five issue-areas in 1956, 1964, and 1972—the beginning, middle and end points of the period under investigation. Since we will be using the basic presentational format of figure 7.1 throughout our analysis, it may be worthwhile to explicate its contents before proceeding to the substantive interpretation. The indicators of attitude constraint in 1956 are presented on the left-hand vertical line; those for 1964 on the vertical line in the middle, and those for 1972 on the line to the right. The data points represent the relationship of attitudes (measured by gammas)[8] across pairs of issues—there being ten such paired relationships for the five issues.

The coefficients tell us how much of a relationship there is between the questions in any two issue-areas. Positive correlations indicate the presence of at least some liberal/conservative opinion consistency. Zero or low correlations indicate an absence of liberal/conservative consistency, while negative coefficients signify that those giving liberal responses to questions within one issue-area are more likely to give conservative responses to questions in the other.

For those issue-areas where more than one question is available—namely social welfare and the cold war—the correlations presented are an average of the gammas between each of the questions in that issue-area and the question or questions in the other area. In those cases where there is only one question for each of the two issue-areas the simple correlation between those two questions is presented.[9]

The relatively low level of liberal/conservative attitude consistency in 1956 is quite apparent in the data presented in figure 7.1. All but three of the coefficients in this year are below .25 and two of the ten are slightly negative. None of the correlations for domestic and foreign policy attitudes is greater than .15; two are negative. Even in the domestic sphere, the average correlation is quite low; attitudes on only two pairs of issues indicate even

---

[8] Gamma was chosen as the measure of association because it is sensitive to attitude consistency of the scalar as well as the correlational type. Further, of the ordinal measures with this property it is the one most widely understood, and therefore the one most easy to interpret.

[9] The alternative to this procedure would have been to construct multiple-item indices in those areas where more than one question was available. This alternative was rejected, however, because indices tend to be more powerful measures than individual items and would have thus artificially increased consistency in all pairs of relationships involving the scales, while the relationships involving the single items would have been denied this advantage. Furthermore, this presented us with a particularly knotty problem because the number of items in a given issue-area varies from one point in time to the next. Employing averages of the gammas preserves as much information as possible without introducing the bias that would result from having some measures composed of multiple items and others not. Correlation matrices for the individual items for each year are available on request from the authors.

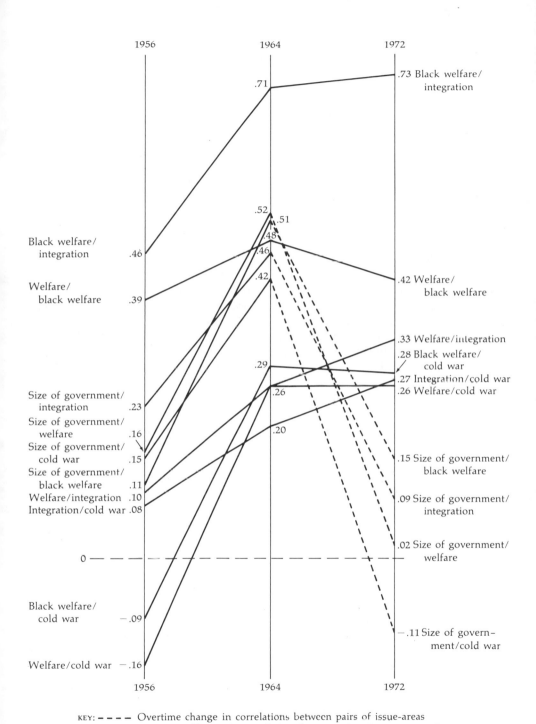

Figure 7.1 Comparison of attitude consistency in 1956, 1964, and 1972: average gammas between five issue areas.

moderately high levels of consistency in 1956. Blacks are the key referent in both questions for one of these pairs (that is, black welfare/integration) while government responsibility for welfare is mentioned in all of the questions involved in the other pair (welfare/black welfare).

Thus our findings closely parallel those reported in the earlier studies. As of 1956, there is little evidence of any unified liberal/conservative attitude continuum, and with only two exceptions—involving questions which share common symbols—there appears to be little or no opinion structure.

A quick glance at the parallel figures for 1964 reveals a dramatic change in levels of attitude consistency. The degree of association between attitudes on each of the five issues has increased, and in almost all cases the increases are quite substantial. There are no longer any negative correlations, and in contrast to 1956 where only two of the ten coefficients were greater than .25, we now find just the opposite—only one of the ten is less than .25. What is truly impressive about the pattern of consistency in 1964 is not only the magnitude of the overall increase in consistency, but also the number of different issue-domains which have come to be bound together. In 1956, moderate to high levels of attitude consistency were encountered on only two pairs of domestic issues. In 1964, on the other hand, not only has the relationship between attitudes on these increased substantially but attitudes on *all* of the domestic issues are highly intercorrelated and appear to reflect the kind of over-arching liberal/conservative ideology which is, the theory of mass beliefs suggests, beyond the capacity of the mass public. Furthermore, in 1964, there is considerable consistency between attitudes on domestic issues and positions on the conduct of the cold war.

The pattern for 1972 is more complicated. At first glance, there appears to be a substantial decline in the level of attitude constraint compared to 1964, but on closer inspection of the data, we can see that all relationships not involving size of government have (within the range of sampling error) maintained themselves or increased. Correlations among all issue-areas, both domestic and foreign, with the exception of size of government are above .25 in 1972. [10]

---

[10] Given that the major shifts in levels of attitude constraint take place between 1960 and 1964, coinciding with some subtle and perhaps important shifts in the question format used by the SRC, the issue arises as to whether or not any of the observed increase in attitude consistency is an artifact of questionnaire design. A number of different types of evidence suggest that this is not the case. (1) While the '64 question format utilizes a stronger screener to deter those who "have not thought about the issue" from responding than was used in the '56, '58, and '60 studies, there is no appreciable increase in the average number of "no opinion" responses between the pre- and post-1964 periods. Increased attitude consistency is therefore not simply a function of screening out a larger proportion of the less interested and articulate segment of the population. (2) While the timing of changes in levels of constraint and question format coincide between '60 and '64, there have been two subsequent question format changes of equal significance since 1968, and neither of these seems to have had any bearing on the level of attitude consistency.

The comparison of levels of attitude constraint across these three time points raises several questions. When did such vast changes in the organization of mass beliefs come about? Has the increase in ideological constraint been a gradual one or did the shift occur suddenly? Or is it possible that the presence or absence of ideological constraint in the mass public is a much more ephemeral characteristic than has been thought, varying in response to relatively short-term forces? All three of the surveys that we have been using were, after all, conducted in the middle of presidential election campaigns, and it is possible that the nature of particular campaigns and the kinds of candidates who are running have a significant impact on whether or not the mass public sees connections between the issues in general and between specific sets of issues in particular. Finally, while attitude constraint across all domestic and foreign issue-areas seems to be on the rise, why should attitude toward the size of government have, between 1964 and 1972, fallen off the liberal/conservative continuum?

The NORC '71 study utilizes a seven-point liberal to conservative scale much closer in format to the SRC pre-1964 Likert-type questions than to the dichotomous choices used by the SRC in '64 and '68. Furthermore, the questions in the NORC study make no explicit attempt to screen out those who had "perhaps not thought enough about the issues" to have an opinion. In 1972, the SRC itself adopted a seven-point scale, similar to that used in the NORC '71 study, for a number of the opinion questions we use. However, the SRC continued to follow its practice of attempting to deter from responding those who claimed to have thought little about individual issues. There has, in other words, been a continuous modification of question format from '68 onward, yet levels of attitude constraint have remained more or less constant in that period. In short, we have one instance—that is, between '60 and '64—where a significant shift in attitude constraint coincided with a basic change in question format. But from '64 onward we find a virtually constant level of attitude consistency in the face of two equally dramatic variations in question format. (3) Finally, it has long been a tenet of survey research that changes in question wording and format are most likely to affect the response of those who are least interested and concerned with the subject matter and thus who are least likely to have strong positions. Conversely, respondents who are highly interested and concerned, and who are most likely to take intense positions, have been found to be much less affected by the types of question changes described above. In order to provide a further test of the artifact hypothesis, we created a pool of respondents whose attitude structure should have been least susceptible to changes in question wording and format. This subset of the population was composed of those in each year who claimed to be: (a) strong partisan identifiers; (b) highly concerned with the election outcome; and (c) greatly interested in the campaign. Our findings about the levels of attitude constraint in this group are unambiguous. The largest increase in levels of attitude consistency within the population are found within this group, which is least likely to be affected by changes in the wording and coding of questions.

The arguments countering the artifact hypothesis briefly discussed above are presented in greater depth in a document entitled, "Levels of Attitude Consistency and Changes in Question Format: An Analysis of the Problem of Artifact," which can be obtained upon request from the authors. This document more fully elaborates the changes in the question formats and their significance and presents, as well, the supporting data alluded to in points 1 and 3 above.

Finally, NORC has a study currently in the field containing a full methodological experiment which should provide more definitive data on the actual impact of questionnaire wording and format on the intercorrelation among political attitudes of the type under investigation.

Table 7.1 Levels of Attitude Constraint, 1956–72

Issues	1956	1958	1960	1964	1968	1971[a]	1972
Welfare/black welfare	.39	.34	.38	.48	.51	.49	.42
Welfare/integration	.11	.16	.19	.26	.49	.42	.33
Welfare/size of government	.16	.05	.14	.52	.47	—	.02
Welfare/cold war	−.16	−.16	−.12	.26	.18	.25	.26
Black welfare/integration	.46	.64	.53	.71	.73	.63	.73
Black welfare/size of government	.11	.03	.05	.51	.40	—	.15
Black welfare/cold war	−.09	−.14	−.15	.29	.26	.24	.28
Integration/size of government	.23	.16	.17	.46	.44	—	.09
Integration/cold war	.08	−.01	.05	.20	.27	.24	.27
Size of government/cold war	.15	.04	.08	.42	.20	—	.11

[a] Data for 1971 come from the NORC National Survey. No question on size of government is available in that survey.

We have the data and can begin to address ourselves to these problems. The questions on the five policy areas posed to samples of the citizenry in the presidential elections of 1956, 1964, and 1972 were also included on surveys conducted in the 1960 and 1968 presidential elections as well as on a survey conducted during the 1958 off-year congressional elections. These data should permit us to learn more about the timing of the changes in attitude consistency.[11]

In addition to these data, a similar though not identical set of questions (providing parallel information on four of the five issue-areas) was included in the 1971 NORC survey. The 1971 NORC data and the data from the 1958 congressional elections provide us with two data points, widely separated in time, which are free from the potentially contaminating short-term forces at work in presidential campaigns. These two data sets, then, should be particularly useful in determining whether individual presidential elections have significant short-term effects on levels of opinion constraint.[12]

Using the data from these studies we can examine levels of attitude constraint on a common set of issues at seven separate points in time over a sixteen-year period beginning in 1956 and ending in 1972. These data are presented in table 7.1. The table presents the gammas among the attitudes in the five issue-areas at each of the seven points in time. The correlation coefficients displayed in the table were arrived at in a manner identical to those presented in figure 7.1. Changes over time in the level of attitude

---

[11] Readers familiar with the Michigan election studies might be curious as to why we did not use the 1970 off-year election study. The answer lies in the design of the study; a decision was made to use shorter questionnaires with varying sets of questions so that at least some information could be collected in a wide variety of areas. The result, for our purposes, is to reduce so drastically the number of cases on which we could base correlations between issue-areas that the reliability of the correlation was doubtful.

[12] The exact questions from the NORC study are presented, along with the questions from the SRC studies, in the Appendix [to this chapter].

constraint between any given pair of issues can be seen by scanning the appropriate row of the table. Comparisons of the overall levels of constraint from one year to the next (our main interest) can be made by comparing the columns in the table.

The answers to several of the questions we have raised are contained in the pattern of correlations found in table 7.1. First, the different levels of attitude constraint we encountered in 1956, 1964, and 1972 do not appear to be the result of either short-term fluctuations or of a gradual trend-like increase throughout the period. Rather, a very sharp shift appears to have occurred in levels of ideological constraint between 1960 and 1964. Similar low levels of ideological constraint are found in 1956, 1958, and 1960. There is a major shift upward in levels of constraint in 1964, involving substantial increases in the correlation between attitudes in almost all of the issue domains. More specifically, the cold-war issues have, from 1964 onward, become increasingly tied to the attitudes on domestic policies. Integration and black welfare, the only issues which were substantially related to each other prior to 1964, are now related at an even higher level. [13] In general, issues involving race began to be strongly related both to other domestic and to cold-war issues in 1964 and were even more strongly related in 1968, falling off slightly thereafter.

Though there are small fluctuations observed in the correlations (some perhaps due to sampling error, others reflecting short-term electoral forces acting on specific issues), with the exception of the disintegration of the relationship between size of government and all other issues between 1968 and 1972, we can observe two periods. There was a very low level of attitude consistency in 1956 through 1960, and constraint grew rapidly at some point between 1960 and 1964, moving the correlation among attitudes to a new level which remains at each subsequent point through 1972.

Second, there is very little evidence to suggest that individual presidential elections or any other specific events exert significant *short-term* influences over general levels of constraint. If, for example, the Goldwater-Johnson presidential election played some special role in the emergence of ideological constraint within the mass public—a hypothesis which would not be inconsistent with the timing of the changes—the changes it helped bring about persisted.

The Growth and Decline of the
Size of Government Issue: An Explanation

The description we have given of the emergence of a clear liberal/conservative structuring of attitudes among the mass public is supported by all of the data except that which shows the virtual disappearance, between 1968 and

---

[13] The small drop-off in 1971 is most likely caused by differences in question wording between the NORC and SRC studies.

1972, of the relationship between the issue of size of government and all of the domestic and foreign issues. Is the decline in relationship between size of government and other issues evidence of a weakening of constraint, or does it indicate instead that changing political cues have produced a different, perhaps more sophisticated, attitude structure?

It is true that for many years "that government is best which governs least" has been a central tenet of the American conservative position, and that at least from the time of the New Deal, American liberalism has held equally strongly that the desirable role of government is to enter as many areas of social life as necessary to rectify social and economic injustices. However, sometime in the late 1960's, a sense began to emerge among the leadership of the liberal community that big government was merely acting to reinforce existing injustices.

The data below clearly indicate that the core of these ideas has indeed taken hold in the mass public. We can demonstrate this by examining the redefinition, over the past eight years, of the liberal and conservative positions on the size of government issue. From 1964 onward, the SRC asked respondents to place several groups, including liberals and conservatives, on a "feeling thermometer" which reflected their degree of affect toward the groups. On the basis of how respondents placed liberals and conservatives on these feeling thermometers, we were able to classify the population in 1964, '68, and '72 into liberals, moderates, and conservatives.[14] Figure 7.2 presents the proportion of each of these groups, at the three points in time, who state that the government is too big and too powerful and involved in too many areas.

As of 1964, the data show that the size-of-government issue split the population along classical liberal/conservative lines. Only 25 percent of the liberals said that government was too big, while 40 percent of the moderates and fully 71 percent of the conservatives took this position. Although the direction of the relationship remained the same in 1968, the relationship had clearly begun to decline, with a substantial increase in the proportion of liberals agreeing with the conservatives that government had become too big. By 1972, as shown in figure 7.2, a monotonic relationship no longer existed between liberalism and conservatism and attitudes towards the size of government. Rather, we now find a majority of both liberals and conservatives responding that government is too big, with the moderates least opposed to big government.

Figure 7.3 further clarifies the nature of this relationship in 1972. For the first time the SRC asked respondents to identify themselves as liberals, moderates, or conservatives. It is clear that using this somewhat more direct indicator, the U-shaped relationship between liberalism and conservatism and attitude on size of government persists. Virtually identical proportions

---

[14] For each respondent his rating of conservatives (0 to 97) was subtracted from his rating of liberals (0 to 97). The resulting scores, ranging from −97 to 97, were recoded to obtain the categories of "liberal," "moderate," and "conservative."

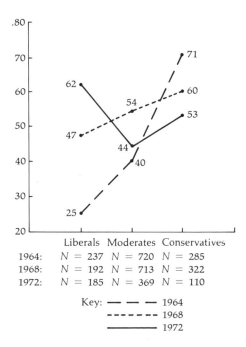

Figure 7.2 Proportion saying the government is too big among liberals, moderates, and conservatives in 1964, 1968, and 1972. (The categories in this figure were constructed by subtracting the respondents' ratings of conservatives from their ratings of liberals. The small *N*'s in 1972 result from the fact that over three times as many respondents as in 1968 refused to rank these groups.)

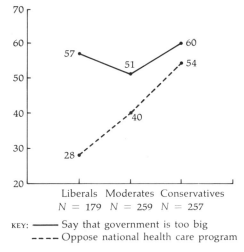

Figure 7.3 Proportion of self-identified liberals, moderates, and conservatives saying government is too big and opposing national health care program, 1972.

of liberals and conservatives agree that the government is too big and too powerful. For comparative purposes we have presented additionally in 1972, the relationship between the liberalism/conservativism scale and attitude on government-subsidized health care, an attitude which remains monotonically related to self-identification as liberal, moderate, or conservative. What is more, attitudes on each of the four issue-areas we have been discussing show a similar, monotonic relationship to self-placement on this scale. Statistically, however, there is almost as strong a relationship between liberal and conservative identification and position on size of government. The relationship, however, is not linear. With measures sensitive to curvilinear relationships, liberal/conservative position would show a considerable association with attitude on size of government.

The important point for the purposes of our analysis is that the data indicate an absence of linear correlation in 1972 which nevertheless does not represent a decline in the consistency of attitude structure but the redefinition of the liberal and conservative positions on this issue on the part of the mass public. What we find now is that there still exists, among those who identify themselves as conservatives, a substantial majority to whom big government has always been and continues to be an anathema. In addition, among self-identified liberals, a group which once accepted large government as a solution to social problems, a similar majority has emerged who are equally skeptical of big government. Given Vietnam, the failure of the New Deal and Great Society welfare programs, and the resurgence of the notion of "returning the government to the people," such a finding is only surprising in terms of *extent* to which this ideological redefinition has penetrated to the mass public.

Unfortunately, we are left with the problem of how to analyze relationships involving this variable in 1972. Inasmuch as we have no way to compare the magnitude of a curvilinear relationship to the type of linear measures of association we are utilizing, throughout the remaining analysis, the issue of size of government is not included with the 1972 data.

Summarizing the Growth of Ideological Consistency

The timing as well as the scope and magnitude of the growth of attitude consistency can be seen most clearly in the summary measures presented in figure 7.4. Plotted through time in this figure are three measures of attitude consistency. The solid line presents the overall index of constraint—a simple average of the ten correlations in each column of table 7.1. The line composed of dashes is the index of domestic attitude consistency and is computed by taking the average for each year of the correlations among the four domestic issue-areas. The dotted line is the average correlation of the four domestic issues with attitudes on the cold war.

The difference between the two periods—1956 to 1960 and after 1964—is quite striking. In the earlier period the overall index hovers around .15, but in 1964 and each year thereafter it is at about .40. The overall index of constraint has therefore increased by over two and one-half times. The index of domestic attitude constraint shows the same basic patterns. Through 1960, the index is slightly below .25, but in 1964 it climbs to about .50 and stays there in all subsequent years.

The pattern with regard to the index of the relationship between attitudes on domestic issues and positions on the cold war indicates an equally dramatic and similarly timed increase in ideological constraint. In 1956, just a few years after the end of the Korean War, the average relationship between liberal/conservative attitude on the domestic issues and the desirability of a tough stand on the international Communist threat (including attitudes on the desirability of sending American soldiers abroad to fight communism) was almost zero. In 1964 and thereafter, on the other hand, the correlation between domestic attitudes and keeping American soldiers abroad (in Vietnam specifically in 1968, '71, and '72) and otherwise taking a tough or conciliatory stand on the cold war rose to around .25. In other words, in contrast to the situation in the mid-fifties and early sixties, foreign policy attitudes, at least as measured by position on the cold war, have increasingly become part of the public's general stance on the issues.

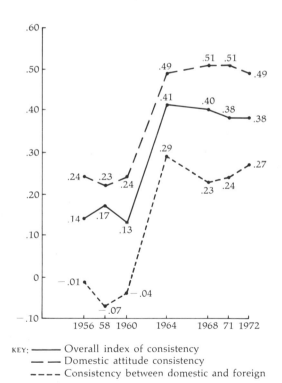

KEY: ———— Overall index of consistency
— — Domestic attitude consistency
- - - - Consistency between domestic and foreign

Figure 7.4 Changes in attitude consistency, 1956–72.

To summarize our findings thus far: the existing description of low levels of attitude consistency in the mass public and the absence of an over-arching liberal/conservative ideology indicated by this lack of consistency no longer appears accurate. From 1964 onward, attitudes in the mass public on the issues of social welfare, welfare measures specific for blacks, racial integration in the schools, and positions on the cold war are substantially intercorrelated. That is, those who are liberal in one of these issue-areas tend to take liberal positions on the others, and the same is true for those at the conservative end of the attitude continuum. The relationship of the issue of the proper size of government to the other four issue-areas has undergone more complex changes. Like attitudes in the other issue-areas, it was part of no clear ideological structure in the mid 1950's and early 60's. In the middle 60's, when ideological constraint become more pronounced, attitudes on size of government correlated highly with liberal/conservative positions on both domestic and foreign issues. Between 1968 and 1972, it appears that the ideological meaning of this issue shifted; for different reasons, both liberals and conservatives found themselves opponents of big government, while those in the center appeared less apprehensive about it. Though the linear relationship between this issue and the others has disappeared, the curvilinear relationship is clear and pronounced, and what is more, makes sense given the ideological redefinition of this issue which we demonstrated above. In regard to these five issue-areas, at least, evidence of the emergence of ideological constraints appears quite convincing.

Scope and Magnitude of the Emerging Mass Ideology

But the question of whether or not the increased attitude constraint we have been examining actually constitutes a comprehensive liberal/conservative ideology in the mass public is not a simple one. How high must correlations be before one can safely assume that something approaching a generalized ideology exists? And perhaps even more important—how many different kinds of attitudes ranging over what types of issues must be found to interrelate before we can reach such a conclusion? Questions like these must always be given relativistic answers, for a glass half full to some people will be one-half empty to others. Much, that is, depends upon one's expectations. However, a number of additional types of evidence can be examined and other comparisons can be made in order to help us estimate the current prevalence of ideology in the mass public.

In order to approach the question of changes in the scope of ideology, we will examine attitudes about the civil liberties of political dissenters as they related to our five issue-areas at the end of the McCarthy era and when this issue emerged again in the late 1960's. In addition, we will examine the extent to which the "social issues" which emerged in the 1960's have been incorporated into the overall liberal/conservative attitude structure. Finally, in order to obtain a better basis for assessing the absolute amount of mass ideology, we will compare levels of ideological constraint within mass and elite populations.

Liberal/Conservative Constraint and Attitudes on the Civil Liberties of Dissenters

Among its many components a comprehensive liberal ideology has traditionally involved not only liberal attitudes on social welfare, minority rights, and governmental control over the economy, but a concern about civil liberties and the rights of political dissenters as well. One of the key pieces of data often cited as evidence of the absence of a generalized liberal/conservative ideology in the mass public has been the lack of any relationship between positions on issues such as welfare, race, and foreign policy on the one hand, and attitudes toward civil liberties on the other. [15]

If we are now to argue that a comprehensive liberal/conservative ideology has recently emerged in the mass public, we must attempt to address ourselves to this issue. Although comparable data for attitudes on civil liberties do not exist for the entire period we are examining, several questions on attitudes toward political dissent and the treatment of dissenters are available in the beginning and towards the end of the time period.

In the 1956 election study—at the conclusion of the McCarthy era—the Survey Research Center asked the citizenry whether they thought government workers suspected of being Communists ought to be fired even though their Communist affiliation had not been proven. The 1971 NORC study included equivalent questions on the rights of political dissenters. Specifically the questions were: (1) whether the government had the right to spy on radicals and radical groups even though they may not have violated any law; (2) whether the government should have the right to enter and search the meeting places of such groups without the possession of a warrant; and (3) whether the government has the right to hold without bail individuals who stand accused of incitement to riot. In 1972, a related question is that of amnesty for those who dissented from government policy by refusing to participate in the war in Vietnam. In addition, we have in the NORC 1971 and SRC 1968 and 1972 studies a common set of questions on attitudes toward civil protest and demonstrations, specifically on whether or not there are any circumstances in which sit-ins and peaceful demonstrations should be tolerated.

Table 7.2 presents the relationship of these civil-liberties attitudes to attitudes on our basic set of issues at these three points in time. The pattern in 1956 substantiates findings reported by others and once again confirms the

---

[15] For a particularly good discussion of this point, see V. O. Key, *Public Opinion*, 171-72.

Table 7.2 Relationship Between Attitudes on Civil Liberties of Dissenters and Attitudes on Domestic and Cold-War Issues

Domestic and Cold War Issues	Firing Government Workers Suspected of Communist Affiliation	Rights of Radicals	Amnesty for Those Who Refused the Draft	Acceptability of Protests and Peaceful Demonstrations		
	1956	1971	1972	1968	1971	1972
Welfare	−.14	.22	.43	.28	.25	.25
Black welfare	.07	.33	.41	.38	.31	.33
Integration	.14	.32	.50	.29	.21	.29
Size of government	−.04	—a	—b	.23	—a	—b
Cold war	.04	.23	.70	.28	.18	.27
Average gammas	.01	.28	.51	.29	.26	.29

a Not available
b Not used in calculations

general absence of attitude constraint in the mid-50's. All of the correlations are low, and there is no discernible pattern.

In contrast, the data in 1971, perhaps the best comparison with the 1956 data, indicate considerable attitude consistency between positions on the protection of civil liberties of radical activists and attitudes in the four other issue areas. In 1972, the relationships between all four issue-areas and whether or not to grant amnesty to those who refused to serve in the military during the Vietnam War were even stronger than the substantial relationships observed in 1971. The average gammas between the issues and firing government workers in 1956 was .01; in 1971, the average correlation between the four issues and position on rights of radicals had risen to .28. And by 1972, the average correlation with attitudes on amnesty was a striking .51.

With regard to the tolerance for sit-ins and protest demonstrations, the average correlation with the domestic and cold-war issues is also substantial. Those who believed in 1968, 1971, and 1972 that under certain circumstances individuals "have the right to stop the government from engaging in its usual activities through protest and demonstration" also tend to be those giving the most liberal responses in each of the other five issue-areas. All of the correlations are consistent on this point, and they range from moderate to moderately high in comparison to others we have viewed.

If a generalized liberal/conservative ideology requires evidence not only of a highly consistent set of beliefs in the areas of race, welfare, economics, and foreign policy, but also consistency between these areas and attitudes toward civil liberties, our data indicate that although this condition did not exist in 1956, it had come into being by 1968 and has persisted through 1972.

Liberal/Conservative
Constraint and Attitudes on the Social Issue

Whether or not a pervasive liberal/conservative ideology exists depends, as we have noted, on its scope, that is, on the number of different issue spheres included within its structure, as well as upon the degree to which the attitudes are bound together. Another test of the scope of the emerging attitude structure we have described is provided by the emergence of the "social issue" in the late 1960's. This term has been used to refer to some of the civil-liberties issues we discussed in the previous section, particularly attitudes about political radicals; to the growing concern with violence and safety; and to changes in morals and values among the young. Scammon and Wattenberg and others have argued that these issues form a new political dimension, completely independent of positions on a traditional liberal/conservative continuum. [16]

Table 7.3 contains data in two areas which come under the rubric of the social issue. The first three columns of the table present the average gammas between attitudes on the issues used throughout this paper and positions on the proper way to deal with urban unrest and crime (1968, 1971, and 1972). The alternatives were employing force versus solving the problems which produced urban unrest, and being concerned with the rights of criminals versus the safety of society. The other two columns in table 7.3 present similar relationships to the life-style component of the social issue (attitudes toward hippies, asked only in 1971, and attitudes towards the use of marijuana, asked in both 1971 and 1972). Though the relationships are most modest here, particularly in 1972, all are significant and positive.

Table 7.3 Relationship Between Attitudes on "Social Issues" and Attitudes on Domestic and Cold-War Issues, 1968–72

Domestic and Cold-War Issues	Urban Unrest	Urban Unrest and Rights of Criminals		Hippies, Marijuana	Use of Marijuana
	1968	1971	1972	1971	1972
Welfare	.32	.32	.24	.21	.09
Black welfare	.31	.41	.24	.34	.15
Integration	.38	.37	.29	.36	.19
Size of government	.22	—[a]	—[b]	—[a]	—[b]
Cold war	.32	.29	.26	.25	.27
Average gammas	.31	.35	.26	.29	.18

[a] Not available
[b] Not used in calculations

---

[16] R. M. Scammon and B. J. Wattenberg, *The Real Majority* (3d ed., New York: G. P. Putnam's Sons, 1970).

The data in table 7.3 clearly indicate—in contrast to the Scammon and Wattenberg interpretation—that from the birth of these issues in the late 1960's, they were at least moderately related to the issues of integration and cold war as well as welfare and black welfare.

In short, by 1972 we find substantial correlations between domestic and cold-war issues, strong relationships between positions on these issues and attitudes on the civil liberties of dissenters, and a moderate to strong relationship between all these issues and the new social issues—indicating clearly a striking growth in the scope of the mass public's ideology as well as in its magnitude.

Attitude Consistency in the Mass and Elite

Do these data allow us to talk of the emergence of "ideology" among the mass public? Clearly not, if by that we mean a totally consistent and logically ordered political world view. The attitude consistency we have uncovered is a weaker phenomenon. But we can obtain some notion of the extent to which the correlations we find after 1964 represent meaningful consistency by comparing the mass public with a more elite group among whom one has found consistent attitudes.

We have no data over time on elite attitude consistency, but we do have it for one point in time. In conjunction with the Survey Research Center study of the 1958 congressional election, a sample of congressional candidates was interviewed and each of the candidates was asked about his attitudes on a set of questions parallel to the five main issues which we have been examining. [17] When Converse compared the elite groups to the mass public, with data collected in 1956 and 1960, the mass came off quite badly. [18] In table 7.4 we compare the attitude consistency among the congressional candidates in 1958 with that found in the mass public at each of the seven points in time. The top line of table 7.4 summarizes the level of constraint on the issues for the sample of congressional candidates. The subsequent lines of the table repeat from figure 7.4 the three parallel measures for the representative samples of the American population at each of the points in time.

---

[17] Specifically, questions in four major issue-areas were utilized—social welfare, size of government, government role in aiding blacks, and attitudes toward the cold war. The responses to the questions in each of these areas were trichotomized to conform to the specifications developed for handling the mass public surveys. The computational procedures were also identical to those employed in the cross-section analysis.

[18] Converse, "Belief Systems," 228-29. The figures presented in table 7.3 of this paper and those presented in his article are somewhat different. There are a few differences in the items employed (particularly in the foreign policy sphere) but the biggest differences stem from the fact that he includes the correlations among attitudes within issue-spheres as well as across issue-spheres, while our analysis concentrates exclusively on the latter relationships.

Table 7.4   Comparison of Levels of Attitude Consistency Between Elites and
             Mass Public

Group	Index of Attitude Consistency Within Domestic Issues	Index of Consistency Between Domestic and Foreign	Overall Index of Attitude Consistency
Congressional candidates 1958[a]	.38	.25	.31
Mass public 1956	.24	− .01	.14
Mass public 1958	.23	− .07	.17
Mass public 1960	.24	− .04	.13
Mass public 1964	.49	.29	.41
Mass public 1968	.51	.23	.40
Mass public 1971	.51	.24	.38
Mass public 1972	.49	.27	.38

[a] Exact questions posed to congressional candidates are to be found in the Appendix [at the end of this chapter].

Given the enormous differences between the two contrasting populations in levels of education, political sophistication, and contextual knowledge about politics and public affairs, the extent of attitude consistency which has come to characterize the mass public in the later period is impressive. Levels of consistency among the congressional candidates in 1958 are much higher than those encountered in the mass public in 1956, 1958, and 1960. In the 1964–72 era, however, liberal/conservative constraint across the issues, both domestic and foreign, equals or exceeds that found among congressional candidates in earlier periods. This is not to say that the mass citizenry now displays patterns of attitude consistency equal to that of their leaders, for we do not have data on the interrelationship of attitudes among a comparable elite population during the later period. What we can say, however, is that the average American citizen from 1964 onward displays a level of attitude consistency similar to and in some areas exceeding that of congressional candidates just a few years earlier. If we use the level of attitude consistency of these candidates as a criterion for a generalized liberal/conservative political ideology, it would seem that we must conclude that a similar level of ideology now exists among the citizenry at large.

Changing Levels of Education in the Mass Public: A Possible Explanation

What has been responsible for the changes in the structure of mass beliefs in so short a period of time? The question is critical for the social scientist generally interested in the nature and determinants of belief systems in mass publics. The argument put forward to explain the low level of issue consistency encountered earlier in the American public is one which emphasizes certain fundamental limitations *inherent* in mass publics. Mass publics, this argument asserts, simply do not have the ideational sophistication or the contextual knowledge required to organize opinions on diverse issues into inclusive ideologies.

This view of the mass public has little place for the kind of change we have encountered. Given the size of the increases in attitude consistency that have taken place, such a line of argument can continue to stand *only if* the increasing consistency can be shown to be associated with equally large *decreases* in the inherent limitations of the mass populations.

The first place to look for the source of the growth of attitude consistency, therefore, is in an increase within the mass public in the "ideological capacities" stressed by the theory. Capacities such as the ability to understand and manipulate highly abstract concepts and to absorb and utilize contextual knowledge have been seen (in general and within the argument itself) to be highly associated with levels of education. How much change in the educational composition of the population has there actually been in this period, and have these changes been substantial enough to have played any significant role in the growth of attitude consistency? As indicated by the data in figure 7.5, this period has indeed been one of significant changes in educational attainment. In the 16 years from 1956 to 1972 that portion of the population most likely to have the capacities stressed in the argument—those with at least some college training—has increased from less than 20 percent to almost 30 percent of the population. At the same time, those with less than a complete high school education have decreased from 52 percent of the population in 1956 to 38 percent in 1972. There has been, in other words, a 24 percent point shift in the educational composition of the population in 16 years.

It is interesting to note that the most substantial changes at both ends of the educational ladder have taken place after 1960, precisely when levels of attitude constraint shifted most significantly. [19] In short, in terms of both magnitude and timing, it seems possible that the growth of ideological constraint within the mass public has been in part, at least, the consequence of an increasingly educated and thus more knowledgeable and sophisticated public.

However, increases in levels of educational attainment, no matter how large, are not in themselves evidence that the growth of ideological constraint is in any way related to these changes. In order to determine whether

---

[19] There are two related reasons why the educational shifts become so much more pronounced after 1960. First, 1964 is the first year in which large numbers of the war-baby-boom population became old enough to be interviewed in the surveys. Second, this group is not only very large, but has received an unprecedented amount of educational training. In short, because these young adults represent a big portion of the population who are highly educated, they have a major effect on the overall proportions of the population at various levels of educational attainment.

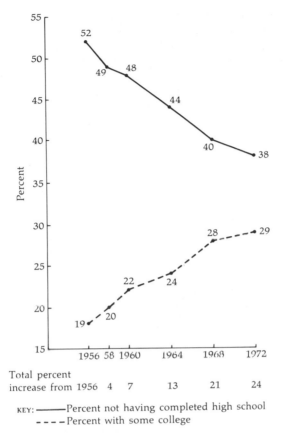

Figure 7.5 Changes in levels of educational achievement, 1956–72.

and to what degree increased educational attainment is responsible for the emergence of consistent liberal/conservative attitudes in the masses we must examine, over time, the levels of consistency of those at different levels of educational attainment.

Figure 7.6 presents over-time data on levels of attitude consistency for two educational groups—those with less than a complete high school education and those who have at least some college training. We present two separate summary measures of the degree of ideological constraint. The [upper] graph in figure 7.6 contains the overall summary measure (average gammas) that takes into account the relationship among all the core issues, both domestic and foreign. The [lower] graph presents the average degrees of constraint considering only the relationships among the domestic issues.

Let us concentrate for the moment on the [upper] graph which indexes overall levels of attitude consistency across both domestic and foreign issues. The data in this graph make it quite clear that educational shifts have had little if any impact on the changes in the structure of mass beliefs that we have encountered. While those with some college education manifest higher levels of consistency throughout the period, both the educated and less-educated groups have shown increases in consistency which are far greater than the differences between the groups at any point in time. More important, those with less than a high school education have shown increases in consistency almost equal in magnitude to the increases shown for the college educated.

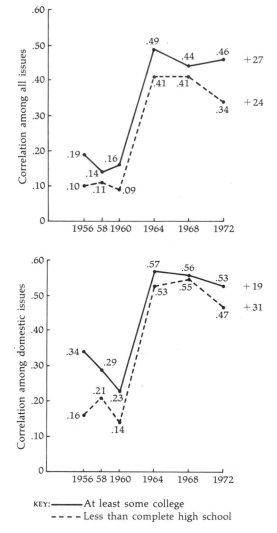

Figure 7.6 Comparison of levels of attitude consistency through time for two educational groups. [The numbers to the right of the graphs (+27, +24, +19, +31) show the growth of consistency between 1956 and 1972.]

When we concentrate on the core domestic issues, which, after all, have been the major focus for liberal/conservative divisions throughout the era, we find that there has been a decline in the disparity in levels of attitude consistency between the less- and the better-educated. Moreover, though consistency on these issues has increased for those at both levels of educational achievement, increases in consistency have been greater for the low educational group—those, according to the theory of mass beliefs, who are the least capable of maintaining a highly organized liberal/conservative ideology. The level of attitude consistency among those with less than a high school education has increased by 31 points, while the comparable figure for those with at least some college is only 19 points.

Most important, with regard to both overall and domestic attitude consistency, is the fact that the sharp increases in levels of attitude constraint which occurred between 1960 and 1964 took place among both the highly educated and those with little formal education.

The implication of the findings in figure 7.6 can be easily summarized. The growth of attitude consistency within the mass public is clearly not the result of increases in the population's "ideological capacities" brought about by gains in educational attainment. These findings seem to have major implications for the theory of mass beliefs, for they seriously question the importance of permanent personal characteristics such as ideational sophistication or the ability to obtain and utilize contextual knowledge as determinants of levels of attitude consistency in mass publics. Those with the lowest educational attainment have experienced the largest increases in consistency on the core domestic issues; and little significant difference appears to be present between the two educational groups in comparison to the dramatic increases in consistency which both groups have experienced. It would be hard to argue that those who have not completed high school are as capable of manipulating abstract concepts as those who have some college training. Yet if factors such as these place limits on the level of attitudinal consistency among the masses, we would not now find that those at the educational extremes display relatively equal and high levels of attitude consistency.

The Changing Salience of Politics: An Explanation

The explanation of the emerging ideological constraint among political attitudes does not appear to be related to inherent limitation in the mass public. What, then, can account for the dramatic shifts in both the breadth and the depth of liberal/conservative attitude structure which we have documented? The answer, we believe, lies in the changing nature of politics from the 1950's to the 1970's and, as a result of these changes, the growing sense on the part of the mass public that politics has a significant effect on their lives.

A repeated finding from social-psychological research on attitude change and attitude structure is that inconsistent or dissonant beliefs are frequently held in areas of people's lives distant from their daily concerns.[20] However, these studies indicate that when the salience or centrality of the psychological object is heightened, tremendous pressures are brought on individuals to force their heretofore inconsistent beliefs into harmony. We argue that the political events of the last decade, and the crisis atmosphere which has attended them, have caused citizens to perceive politics as increasingly central to their lives. If we are correct about this increased salience, then the social-psychological theories of attitude change represent a possible explanation for the observed increases in ideological constraint. However, in order to test this argument we must show first, that the level of salience of politics has increased; and second, that consistency has increased primarily among those to whom politics has become salient.

Although we have no data tapping the centrality of politics to people's lives, we do have a number of alternative measures of what one might call "positive salience," that is, the degree to which citizens report being interested or actively involved in politics. These include over time data on rates of campaign participation, frequency of following election campaigns in the media, and general interest in the campaigns. Each of these measures displays the same pattern as revealed in figure 7.7, which presents the propor-

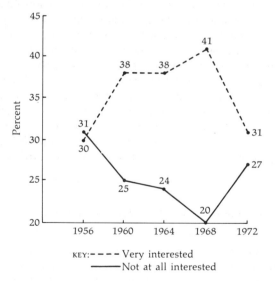

KEY: ---- Very interested
—— Not at all interested

Figure 7.7   Interest in presidential campaigns, 1956–72.

---

[20] See Leon Festinger, *A Theory of Cognitive Dissonance* (Stanford, Calif.: Stanford University Press, 1968). Various types of empirical evidence confirming the proposition that increased salience leads to increased attitude constraint can be found in Milton J. Rosenberg et al., *Attitude Organization and Change,* Yale Studies in Attitude Communication, vol. 3 (New Haven: Yale University Press, 1960).

tion of the population who are "very much interested" and "not at all interested" in each of the presidential elections between 1956 and 1972.[21]

As the data in this figure show, citizen interest in presidential elections
rose steadily from 1956 through 1968. The percentage who report being very
interested in the campaigns grew from 30 percent in 1956 to 41 percent in
1968. Conversely, the proportion reporting no interest at all in the campaigns registered an equally sharp decline—from 31 percent to 20 percent.
There was, in other words, a 22 percentage-point increase in campaign interest between 1956 and 1968. However, in 1972, levels of campaign interest in
the mass public fell precipitously, with the proportion reporting high interest declining almost to the 1956 level and the proportion reporting no interest rising sharply from 20 to 27 percent.[22]

If attitude consistency is a function of the salience of politics, and if the
level of campaign interest taps the salience of politics, consistency should
show a concomitant decline in 1972. The data, however, indicate that the
level of attitude consistency remained constant between 1968 and 1972.
Thus, while the salience hypothesis seems plausible up until 1968, the pattern after this point casts some doubt on the argument.

But simply examining marginal shifts in interest does not enable us to
come to any conclusion; as was the case with the hypothesis involving education, we need to examine the levels of attitude consistency over time
among the interested and uninterested. This we do in figure 7.8, where we
plot the levels of attitude consistency for those who are highly interested in
the campaigns and for those who report no interest at all. Once again we
present two separate graphs: the first displays the level of consistency for the
two groups taking into account positions on all of the issues, domestic and
foreign. The second graph presents the average levels of consistency for the
core domestic issues.

We can see that the growth of interest does not alone account for the rise
of liberal/conservative ideology because consistency has gone up among the
interested and uninterested alike, just as it has gone up among both the
educated and less educated. However, while increased educational attainment appeared to play almost no role in the growth of attitude consistency,
increases in political interest (or the salience of politics), as these data indicate, have played a very significant role.

---

[21] The precise question asked in each year was: "Some people don't pay much attention
to the political campaigns. How about you, would you say that you were very much
interested, somewhat interested, or not much interested in following the political campaigns this year?" Responses to this question are not affected by the spread of television as
are the media questions, and they provide more variance than campaign participation.

[22] The total percentage point increase from 1956 to 1968 in interest in presidential elections (as computed in figure 7.7) is 19 percentage points for those with at least some college
training and 17 percentage points for those who have not completed high school. Furthermore, sizable increases are also found among blacks and whites, young and old, and those
residing in both North and South.

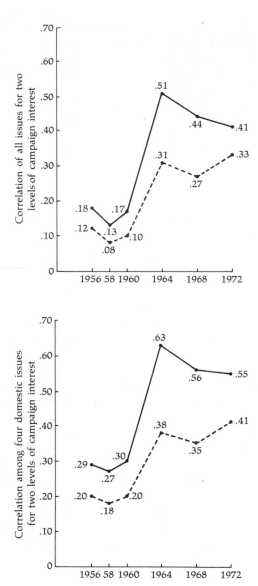

Figure 7.8 Comparison of levels of attitude consistency for the interested and uninterested in presidental campaigns, 1956–72. [Upper graph] shows correlation of all issues for two levels of campaign interest; [lower graph] shows correlation among four domestic issues for two levels of campaign interest.

Between 1960 and 1968, it was among the growing group of citizens interested in politics that one found the largest increase in attitude consistency. Furthermore, unlike the data on education—where there tended to be less difference in the degree of ideological consistency between the better and lesser educated at the end of the time period than at the beginning—we find in relation to political interest that there was a much greater gap in constraint between the more and less interested in 1964 and 1968 than in the pre-1964 period. By 1968, overall consistency (including domestic and foreign issues) among those with no interest had increased only 15 percentage points from 1956, while for the highly interested the average gammas among the same issues had grown 26 points. The pattern is the same for the average correlations among the core domestic issues.

Remember also that the relative size of the interested group had undergone a steady increase, from 30 to 40 percent of the population, while the uninterested declined from 30 percent to 20 percent of the population. The combined impact of the rise in attitude consistency among those interested in politics and the increase in the numbers of such citizens accounts for a major proportion of the observed growth of ideological constraint in the population as a whole.

By 1968 and 1972, however, the interest-based explanation seems to fall apart. While the group of highly interested citizens displays levels of consistency comparable to, or only slightly less than, those found in 1968, consistency among those reporting no interest in the campaign unexpectedly rises rather sharply. What is more, as we saw in figure 7.7, the highly interested group has significantly diminished in size from its 1968 level, while those claiming no interest have increased in number.

If the rise of constraint among the manifestly uninterested is responsible for the maintenance of high levels of consistency in the face of a sharp decline in campaign interest, how can this pattern be reconciled with the salience hypothesis? The answer, we believe, is that the nature of salience has changed: events of recent years have rendered campaign interest inadequate as a measure of the salience of politics. As we pointed out earlier, indicators such as levels of campaign interest or campaign participation are not direct measures of salience but measure it only insofar as *positive* involvement captures the major part of salience. In fact, it is both possible and, in circumstances such as those of the late 1960's and early 1970's, likely that there are citizens for whom politics is quite salient in terms of its perceived ability to affect their lives, but whose frustration with governmental policies or political processes has led them to withdraw from or express disinterest in specific political events such as elections. Thus among the recently expanded segment of the population that reports no interest in the presidential campaign, the group which is crucial to understanding the patterns we have found in the 1972 data, at least two kinds of citizens may be present. There are those who are simply quiescent; their attitude toward politics is one of apathy toward a remote phenomenon. Others who claim to be uninterested may do so out of a sense of frustration or disenchantment—they are dissatisfied with the choices they must make or feel that government and politics are corrupt and unresponsive. For this latter group, lack of interest may indicate anything but a lack of salience.

While we do not have data to differentiate between these two groups throughout the time period, we do have a comprehensive battery of questions on cynicism toward political and governmental processes which precisely tap this dimension from 1964 onward.[23] By combining these items into a summary index we can examine two types of citizens who profess disinterest in election campaigns—the disenchanted (those who are distrustful or cynical towards government) and the quiescent (those who basically trust the government). The proportion of "uninterested" citizens who respond in a predominantly disenchanted manner to these questions has grown steadily since 1964. In that year, only 40 percent of those who reported no interest in the campaign could be categorized as disenchanted, with the remainder quiescent. This proportion had risen to 50 percent in 1968 and by 1972 the disenchanted had come to constitute almost 65 percent of those who claimed to be uninterested. In fact, we have some reason to believe that it is this very growth of disenchantment which is largely responsible for driving down levels of interest.

If we examine levels of attitude consistency for those two types of citizens—the quiescent and the disenchanted—alongside the citizens who report high levels of political interest, perhaps we can begin to solve the puzzle presented by the patterns of consistency in the 1972 data.[24] The two graphs in figure 7.9 present the levels of overall consistency and inconsistency on domestic issues for three groups: the interested, the disenchanted, and the quiescent.

---

[23] The questions are as follows: "Do you think that people in government waste a lot of the money we pay in taxes, waste some of it, or don't waste very much of it?" "How much of the time do you think you can trust the government in Washington to do what is right?" "Would you say the government is pretty much run by a few big interests looking out for themselves or that it is run for the benefit of all the people?" "Do you feel that almost all of the people running the government are smart people who usually know what they are doing or do you think that quite a lot of them don't seem to know what they are doing?" "Do you think that quite a few of the people running the government are a little crooked, not very many are, or do you think hardly any of them are crooked at all?" These questions were entered into a factor analysis; the scale based on the first principal component was dichotomized at the overall (that is, for all years) mean. Our interest in the relationship between political trust and ideology was initially stimulated by Arthur H. Miller, "Political Issues and Trust in Government 1964–1970" (paper delivered at the 68th annual meeting of the American Political Science Association, Washington, D.C., 5–9 September 1972).

[24] Of course the highly interested population can also be broken into two groups according to their level of distrust. If this division is made, we find that the proportion of distrustful citizens among the interested has also been rising since 1964, and that these people show higher levels of consistency in all three years than do those who trust the government.

What has happened to maintain high levels of attitude consistency despite the drastic decline in campaign interest, or what we term "positive salience," is quite clear. First, in 1964 and 1968, only the positively involved were characterized by high levels of consistency; both the disenchanted and the quiescent displayed modest levels of constraint, relative to the interested population. In 1972, on the other hand, we can discern two markedly different groups among those who claim to be uninterested in the presidential campaign, with the disenchanted now approaching the levels of ideological constraint shown by the highly interested. The levels of consistency shown by the quiescent group, on the other hand, remain at a low level. Furthermore, the disenchanted are the only group to show, between 1964 and 1972, a marked increase in their liberal/conservative consistency on the core domestic issues. The modest levels of consistency manifested in 1964 and 1968 by both the quiescent and the disenchanted suggest that politics was salient for neither group.

Several factors lead us to believe, however, that the nature of the disenchanted group underwent a fundamental change between 1968 and 1972. While the proportion of the population reporting no interest in the election campaign rose sharply from '68 to '72 and the proportion reporting high interest declined even more steeply, the percentage of the population classified by our measures as quiescent remained virtually constant. Given this

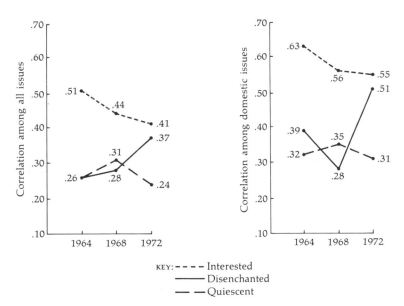

Figure 7.9 Attitude consistency for three groups, 1964–72. Graph on left shows correlation among all issues; graph on right shows correlation among domestic issues.

constancy in the proportion of quiescent in 1968 and 1972, the growth of the disenchanted in '72 must have resulted from the withdrawal of citizens who were previously among the interested—that is, among those for whom politics was highly salient. The high levels of ideological constraint displayed by the disenchanted in 1972 suggest that politics has remained central to these individuals but has turned from a politics of positive salience to one of negative salience. Whether or not this interpretation is precisely correct there can be little doubt about the empirical facts: the disenchanted have become a significant portion of the population in 1972; and it is this group alone which has caused the level of ideological constraint to remain high despite a decline in positive political interest.

Summary

Once again we want to stress that the data in the preceding section are by no means a definitive test of the hypothesis that heightened salience of politics has produced higher levels of attitude constraint among the mass public. Without a direct measure of centrality of politics to people's lives, the argument is tentative at best. And, even with a direct measure of salience we would be without a data-based explanation for the causes of the rise in salience. But, after all, this is the crux of our argument. The problem with the classical theory of mass beliefs is that it is built around notions of enduring characteristics of the mass public, of the sort which are relatively impervious to changes in the nature of the political world. Linking changes in attitude structure instead to events in the real world, which are not measurable characteristics of individuals, is a much more difficult task.

But let us think for a moment about American politics during the period we are investigating. The year 1956 was the middle of the Eisenhower era; the Korean War and the McCarthy hearings were in the past, and in a very real sense, not very much was happening politically. Not only were there no visible social problems which threw into question the system's ability to cope, but the administration's policy was one of de-emphasizing Washington and the federal government as the focal point of politics. It is not surprising that the modal attitude toward government was one of acceptance and noninvolvement. Politics was indeed, as Robert Dahl described it at the time, merely a sideshow in the circus of life.

The first big change in this picture occurred in 1960 with the advent of a deliberately activist administration, a new focus on the problems of race and poverty, and perhaps most important, a Kennedy-inspired conviction, on the part of many citizens, that involvement in politics could actually bring about desired changes. Available data on participation support the claim that one of the most significant accomplishments of the Kennedy administration was an increased positive interest and involvement in politics.

The tremendous media focus on Kennedy's assassination brought politics even more into the forefront of national life, and within a year all of this heightened positive involvement was channeled into a highly ideological election. As we have seen, issue positions in 1964 displayed a consistency and a polarization which was in stark contrast to the situation found in 1956, '58, and '60. But the 1964 election, and the impetus it provided to citizens to structure their political beliefs into a coherent liberal/conservative ideology, was not merely a transient phenomenon. In the middle and late 1960's, Americans were bombarded with one social and political crisis after another: urban rioting, increased militancy within the civil-rights movement, campus demonstrations, political assassinations, deeper involvement in the quag-mire of a distant war. Even though our data are essentially pre-Watergate, by the late 1960's the positive involvement of the early and mid-60's had turned decidedly sour. The war lingered on, the Great Society programs appeared to have failed, and it seemed as if the government was incapable of dealing with new problems such as crime, pollution, and inflation. The cyni-cism which arose from government's failure to deal with the society's prob-lems by no means decreased the salience of politics—the feeling that what happens in Washington affects one's life persists—but, we believe, did cause many people to withdraw from politics in frustration.

The important point is that the pattern of attitudes found among Ameri-cans in the 1950's was a transient phenomenon and not an inevitable char-acteristic of mass politics. Of course, the pattern that emerged in the 1960's may be transient as well, but that does not change our argument about the lack of inevitability of the earlier pattern. Indeed, our data suggest that not only specific political attitudes but the *structure* of mass attitudes may be affected by politics in the real world. The average citizen may not be as apolitical as has been thought.

Ideology and Electoral Behavior: Some Political Implications

We have located a substantial and widespread increase in the consistency of political attitudes in the post-1960 era and we have argued that this finding is indicative of the growth of a more ideologically-oriented mass public. However, the analysis thus far has dealt exclusively with the interrelation-ships among attitudes, and the question remains as to whether or not such attitudes have actually come to play a more significant role in American politics. In the concluding section of the paper we will endeavor to provide an answer to one aspect of this question by determining whether positions on the issues have come to have a greater impact on the way citizens vote and thereby on the outcome of elections.

In the last several years there has been a surge of interest in voter ration-ality and issue voting; there are now a number of studies which show an increase in the degree to which citizens are voting in accordance with their attitudes on political issues. [25] An extensive over-time analysis of issue voting and its relationships to increased ideological consistency obviously is a mammoth undertaking in its own right and is beyond the scope of this paper. However, without some evidence as to whether the emergent mass ideology is having an impact on electoral behavior, the analysis presented here becomes more an exercise in social psychology than a piece of political analysis. If heightened attitude consistency is indicative of an increased ideological orientation with the electorate, then the types of attitudes with which we have been dealing should have become more consistent with voting preferences, as well as with each other. Furthermore, if there has been a substantial increase in issue-oriented voting, this would seem to be a good indication that the changes in attitude structure we have observed are having significant political consequences. [26] In each presidential election between 1956 and 1972 we will examine the relationship between left-right attitudes on our comparable issues and voting choice (that is, whether the respondent voted for the Democratic or Republican candidate). In addition, we will present the relationships between attitudes on civil liberties of dissenters and presidential vote for 1956, 1968, and 1972. The relevant data are presented in figure 7.10. The measures of association are once again average gammas.

The light solid line in the figure presents the average gammas at each point in time between liberal/conservative positions on the standard set of issues and the direction of the presidential vote. The broken line displays parallel information but takes into account only the attitudes on the domestic issues. The dotted line gives the average correlation between the presidential vote and left-right positions on the conduct of the cold war. Finally, the heavy line displays for 1956, 1968, and 1972 the average gamma between attitudes on civil liberties and the vote.

All of these measures indicate that the relationship between liberal/conservative attitudes and the presidential vote has increased rather dramati-

---

[25] The increase in issue-oriented voting is becoming well-documented. In fact, a recent edition of the *American Political Science Review* contained two articles, several comments, and several rejoinders making this argument. While the authors often disagreed on the meaning and on many of the implications of issue-oriented voting, they all clearly pointed out a recent increase in the relationship between issue positions and partisan choice. See in *American Political Science Review,* 66(June 1972), the following: Gerald M. Pomper, "From Confusion to Clarity: Issues and American Voters, 1956-1968," 415-28; Richard W. Boyd, "Popular Control of Public Policy: A Normal Vote Analysis of the 1968 Election," 429-49; Richard A. Brody and B. I. Page, "Comment: The Assessment of Policy Voting," 450-58; John H. Kessel, "Comment: The Issues in Issue Voting," 459-65; Pomper, "Rejoinder to 'Comments' by Richard A. Brody and B. I. Page and John Kessel," 466-67; Boyd, "Rejoinder to 'Comments' by Richard A. Brody and Benjamin I. Page and John H. Kessel," 468-70.

[26] Consistency between attitudes and voting choice however, is not wholly dependent on the mass public. A strong relationship requires not only an ideological orientation on the part of the public but also depends upon whether or not the parties and candidates offer the kinds of choices that enable citizens to act upon their preferences.

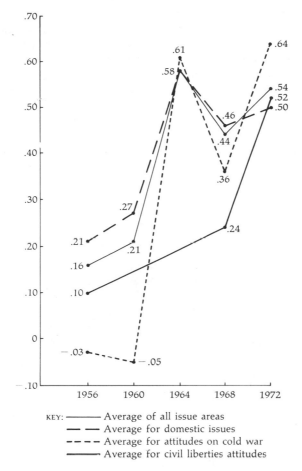

Figure 7.10 Average correlation (gammas) between liberal/conservative attitudes and presidential vote choice (Democratic vs. Republican) 1956–72.

cally during the 1956–72 period. Furthermore, as can be seen, the increased relationship between attitudes and voting pertains to positions on civil liberties as well as both foreign and domestic issues; and a more detailed analysis of these data reveal that the correlations for each of the individual attitudes on which the averages in the figure are based have increased significantly. Finally, we note that the increased association between voting and attitudes has occurred at approximately the same point in time at which we earlier found increases in attitude consistency. Once again, the distinction between the pre- and post-1964 era is apparent. However, as one would expect, there appears to be more election-specific fluctuation in these relations than in the levels of consistency themselves. No matter how the Wallace voters are treated, in the 1968 election, issues bore less relation to the vote than in either 1964 or 1972. [27] More important, however, is the fact that all three of the presidential elections since 1964 are on a new, higher plateau than those in 1956 and 1960. To this extent at least the growth of ideology appears to be having a significant impact on presidential elections.

The increased importance of ideology in the voting behavior of the mass public as well as its heightened importance in presidential elections is

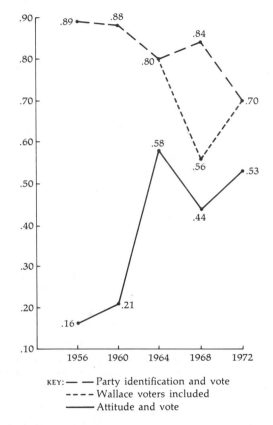

KEY: — — Party identification and vote
---- Wallace voters included
——— Attitude and vote

Figure 7.11 Correlations between attitudes and presidential vote and between party identification and presidential vote, 1956–72.

---

[27] There are, of course, special problems in dealing with the three-candidate 1968 election. When the Wallace voters are excluded from the analysis, party identification and presidential vote are quite highly correlated, but excluding them distorts reality by ignoring 12 percent of the population who defected in their vote from the normal party identification. When the Wallace voters are included, placed to the right of the Nixon voters, the gamma between party and the vote falls to .56. However, this figure probably represents a distortion in the opposite direction, and we have presented both relationships. Reality undoubtedly lies somewhere in between, revealing a steady decline in the impact of party identification throughout the period.

brought into even starker relief when we compare the changing impact of political attitudes with more habitual determinants of the vote such as partisan identification. An over-time comparison of the importance of attitudes versus that of partisan identification as alternative explanations of the presidential vote appears in figure 7.11.[28]

The solid line in figure 7.11 simply displays once again the average gammas between the comparable attitudes and presidential vote. The dashed line represents the gamma between party identification and presidential vote for each year. In 1956 and 1960 political attitudes appear to have had only a small impact on presidential voting while standing partisan affiliation played a predominant if not exclusive role in explaining the direction of the presidential vote. In 1964, 1968, and 1972, the situation changes substantially; in these elections, position on the issues has come to have a much greater impact on the vote, while the role of party identification declines concomitantly. In 1956, the average gamma between attitudes and presidential vote was .16. By 1972, it had grown to .53 and in each of the elections after 1964 it hovered around .50. In contrast, the relationship between party identification and the vote has steadily declined throughout the period, from .89 to 1956 to .70 in 1972. In short, in the last three presidential elections, political attitudes have come to be an increasingly significant force in determining the direction of the presidential vote while the impact of partisan identification, once predominant, has become much less significant. Perhaps voter rationality, like attitude consistency, is also more a function of the political context than a consequence of innate limitations of the mass public.

Some of our findings are also relevant to another change in American politics which has lately come to be of much concern—the possibility that the United States may be in a period of major party realignment. Our data show that greater potentiality exists now for the division of the American public into ideological camps than was the case just a few years ago.[29] In this connection it is interesting to note the evolving relationship between the political attitudes on the one hand and presidential voting and party identification on the other. Table 7.5 presents the data.

At the beginning of the period under investigation, political attitudes had little relationship to either presidential voting or partisan identification. As

---

[28] On the basis of the same questions asked in each survey the respondents were coded into three categories of partisan identification from left to right: (1) Democratic; (2) independent; and (3) Republican. Those sometimes classified as Democrat or Republican leaners as well as those who maintained their independent stance throughout the battery of questions were classified as independents for our analysis.

[29] Critical election periods heralding major realignments have been long thought to depend upon the emergence of a deep and enduring cleavage in the electorate, precisely of the sort we have located. See Key, "A Theory of Critical Elections," *Journal of Politics*, 17(February 1955):3–18. The phenomenon of critical elections, as well as the role of policy questions and group divisions in such realignments are discussed at some length in W. D. Burham, *Critical Elections and the Mainsprings of American Politics* (New York: Norton, 1970).

Table 7.5 Comparison of Correlations (Gammas) with Attitudes 1956-72

	1956	1960	1964	1968	1972
Presidential voting and attitudes	.16	.21	.57	.43	.53
Party identification and attitudes	.12	.15	.32	.26	.16
Difference	.04	.06	.25	.17	.37

we have shown, the relationship between attitudes and presidential voting has risen dramatically from the pre- to the post-1964 period. The relationship between these attitudes and more permanent party allegiance has undergone a more complex pattern of change. In 1956 attitudes on political issues bore little or no relationship to party identification. In 1964 and to a lesser degree in 1968, this picture appeared to have changed somewhat: while rising less rapidly and dramatically than the relationship between attitudes and presidential voting, that between attitudes and party allegiance had increased substantially over the 1956 level.[30] As Pomper argues, in 1964 and 1968 it appeared that the parties were capturing the heightened ideological consistency and polarization and effecting a realignment which reinforced existing party divisions: a liberal Democratic party and a conservative Republican one. In 1972, however, while attitude consistency in the mass public remained at the same high level as in 1968 and the impact of attitudes on the vote had increased somewhat, the parties in 1972 no longer appeared to be reflecting attitudes which are increasingly aligned on a left-right continuum. In fact, the average gamma falls almost to the 1956 level. This drop raises the spectre of a very different kind of realignment than that suggested by Pomper, one in which new partisan attachments may form that are not based on an increasingly liberal Democratic party versus an increasingly conservative Republican party. We are obviously in the midst of rapid social and political change, and it is very difficult given the possible election-specific nature of many of the shifting relationships, to see any clear long-term trends with regard to realignment. Whether the growth of political ideology in America results in any type of ideologically opposed political parties will turn upon whether the more consistent and polarized attitude structure persists among citizens and upon the evolving party positions and the candidates they nominate. The persistence of attitude consistency among the mass public will depend—as we have demonstrated—on the character of the American political experience in the 1970's.

---

[30] In his recent article, "Confusion to Clarity," Pomper has demonstrated increases in the relationship between political attitudes (of the kind we have been looking at) and partisan identification. Pomper argues that this may be evidence of a party realignment.

Part I.   Questions From the Main Five Issue Areas

A.   *Social Welfare*
1.   *Employment:*
(*1956, 1958, 1960*) "The government in Washington ought to see to it that everybody who wants to work can find a job. Do you have an opinion on this or not?"

(Agree strongly—disagree strongly.)

(*1964, 1968*) "In general, some people feel that the government in Washington should see to it that every person has a job and a good standard of living. Others think the government should just let each person get ahead on his own. Have you been interested enough in this to favor one side over the other?"

(*1972*) Same as 1964 and 1968. "Where would you place yourself on this scale?"

2.   *School Aid:*
(*1956, 1958, 1960*) "If cities and towns around the country need help to build more schools, the government in Washington ought to give them the money they need. Do you have an opinion on this or not?"

(Agree strongly—disagree strongly.)

(*1964, 1968*) "Some people think the government in Washington should help towns and cities provide education for grade and high school children; others think that this should be handled by the states and local communities. Have you been interested enough in this to favor one side over the other?"

(*1972*) Not asked.

3.   *Medicare:*
(*1956, 1960,* No question asked in 1958) "The government ought to help people get doctors and hospital care at low cost. Do you have an opinion on this or not?"

(Agree strongly—disagree strongly.)

(*1964, 1968*) "Some say the government in Washington ought to help people get doctors and hospital care at low cost, others say the government should not get into this. Have you been interested enough in this to favor one side over the other?"

(*1972*) "There is much concern about the rapid rise in medical and hospital costs. Some feel there should be a government insurance plan which would cover all medical and hospital expenses. Others feel that medical expenses should be paid by individuals, and through private insurance like Blue Cross. Where would you place yourself on this scale, or haven't you thought much about this?"

4. *NORC 1971 Welfare Questions:* "Now about welfare. Some people think that the government should support any family that doesn't have enough money to live on, even if the father is working. Look at Card F. They would be at point 1. Other people think that, no matter how poor a family is, they should take care of themselves. They would be at point 7. Still other people have an opinion that falls somewhere in between. Where would you place yourself?"

"Some people think that the government should use all its resources to eliminate poverty in this country. Look at Card K. They would be at point 1. Others think the government has already done too much about poverty. They would be at point 7. And others have opinions that fall somewhere in between 1 and 7. Where would you place yourself?"

B. *Black Welfare*
(1956, 1958, 1960) "If Negroes are not getting fair treatment in jobs and housing, the government should see to it that they do. Do you have an opinion on this or not?"

(Agree strongly—disagree strongly.)

(1964 and 1968) "Some people feel that if Negroes (colored people) are not getting fair treatment in jobs the government in Washington ought to see to it that they do. Others feel that this is not the federal government's business. Have you had enough interest in this question to favor one side over the other?"

(NORC 1971) "Some people think that the recent attempts to improve conditions for blacks in America should be speeded up. Look at Card E. They would be at point 1. Others think that these efforts should be slowed down; they would be at point 7. And those who have other opinions would be somewhere between 1 and 7. Where would you place yourself?"

(1972) "Some people feel that if black people are not getting fair treatment in jobs the government in Washington ought to see to it that they do. Others feel that this is not the federal government's business. Have you had enough interest in this question to favor one side over the other?"

C. *School Integration*
(1956, 1958, 1960) "The government in Washington should stay out of the question of whether white and colored children go to the same school. Do you have an opinion on this or not?"

(Agree strongly—disagree strongly.)

(1964, 1968, and 1972) "Some people say that the government in Washington should see to it that white and Negro children are allowed to go to the same schools. Others claim this is not the government's business.

Have you been concerned enough about this question to favor one side over the other?"

(NORC 1971) "Some people believe that the government should do whatever is necessary to see to it that blacks can buy homes in white neighborhoods. Look at Card I. They would be at point 1. Others feel that the government should stay out of it altogether. They would be at point 7. While others have opinions somewhere in between. Where would you place yourself?"

D. *Size of Government*
(1956, 1958) "The government should leave things like electric power and housing for private businessmen to handle."

(Agree strongly—disagree strongly.)

(1960) "The government should leave things like electric power and housing for private business to handle. Do you have an opinion on this or not?"

(If Yes) "Do you think the government should leave things like this to private business?"

(1964, 1968, and 1972) "Some people are afraid the government in Washington is getting too powerful for the good of the country and the individual person. Others feel that the government in Washington is not getting too strong for the good of the country. Have you been interested enough in this to favor one side over the other?"

(NORC 1971—no parallel question)

E. *Cold War*
(1956, 1958, 1960) "The United States should keep soldiers overseas where they can help countries that are against Communism. Do you have an opinion on this or not?"

(Agree strongly—disagree strongly.)

(1964, 1968) "Some people think our government should sit down and talk to the leaders of the Communist countries and try to settle our differences, while others think we should refuse to have anything to do with them. Have you been interested enough in this to favor one side over the other?"

(1968 and 1972) "There is much talk about 'hawks' and 'doves' in connection with Vietnam, and considerable disagreement as to what action the United States should take in Vietnam. Some people think we should do everything possible to win a complete military victory, no matter what results. Some people think we should withdraw completely from Vietnam right now, no matter what results. And, of course, other people have opinions somewhere between these two extreme positions. Suppose the people who support an immediate withdrawal are at one end of this scale at point number 1 and suppose the people who support a

complete military victory are at the other end of the scale at point number 7. At what point on the scale would you place yourself?"

(NORC 1971) "About the war in Vietnam. Some people think we should withdraw completely from Vietnam right now; other people think we should do everything necessary to win a complete military victory; and others have opinions somewhere in between. Look at this card. If you think of the people who support an immediate withdrawal at point 1, and the people who support complete military victory at point 7, and those who have other opinions as somewhere between 1 and 7, where would you place yourself?"

Part II. Elite Attitude Questions

A. *Welfare*
   1. *Education:*
   "Do you think the government should provide grants to the states for the construction and operation of public schools, or do you think the support of public education should be left entirely to the state and local governments?"

   2. *Jobs:*
   "Do you think that the federal government ought to sponsor programs such as large public works in order to maintain full employment, or do you think that problems of economic readjustment ought to be left more to private industry or state and local government?"

B. *Size of Government*
   "How about the controversy over the development of atomic power. Do you think the government should develop power from atomic energy, or do you think this should be left to private industry?"

C. *Race*
   1. *Voting:*
   "Now, in the area of civil rights. Do you think the question of the voting rights of Negroes should generally be left to state and local authorities, or should the federal government take action in this field?"

   2. *Jobs:*
   "Do you think the federal government should establish a fair employment practices commission to prevent discrimination in employment?"

   3. *Schools:*
   "If Congress were to vote to give federal aid to public schools, do you think this aid should be given to schools which are segregated?"

D. *Cold War*

"What do you feel about aid for underdeveloped countries that take a neutral position between the United States and the Soviet Union? Do you think we should give them aid only if they support the West?"

8. Belief Systems: Constraint, Complexity, and the 1972 Election

JAMES A. STIMSON

When the authors of *The American Voter* first concluded that "the concepts important to ideological analysis are useful only for that small segment of the population that is equipped to approach political decisions at a rarefied level," they set off a debate about the structure of belief systems in the American electorate that is as lively today as when *The American Voter* was first published.[1] It is a fruitful debate because both sides are increasingly asking the sort of questions amenable to empirical answers. It is unresolved because both sides are finding evidence in support of their position. It is vital because the answer has direct implications for democratic theory.

This article brings new evidence to bear on the belief systems question.

SOURCE: *American Journal of Political Science,* 19(1975):393–417. Reprinted with permission of The Wayne State University Press.

AUTHOR'S NOTE: Funds for this study were provided by the Research Foundation of the State University of New York. The Center for Political Studies 1972 Election Study data were provided by the Inter-University Consortium for Political Research. I have been aided in this work by the assistance of Elizabeth Plumb and Alan Negin, and have been the beneficiary of the ideas and critical scrutiny of Edward Carmines, John Sinclair, Richard Zeller, and John L. Sullivan. Data included in an earlier version of this paper were generously provided by George Marcus, David Tabb, and John Sullivan.

[1] Angus Campbell, Philip E. Converse, Warren E. Miller, and Donald E. Stokes, *The American Voter* (New York: Wiley, 1960), p. 250.

The Debate About Belief Systems

A brief examination of the belief systems debate is in order to set the stage
for the analysis to come. If *The American Voter* started the rumblings of
controversy, Philip Converse articulated what will here be called the "em-
piricist" position so precisely that it remains ten years later the most influential statement. [2] Converse spelled out what a political belief system worthy of
the name "ideology" would look like; it would have abstract *objects of centrality,* wide *scope,* and would be *constrained.* The constraint concept refers to
internal consistency, and the way Converse uses the concept implies consistency along a single powerful underlying dimension. Consistency itself does
not *imply* unidimensional structure, Converse argues (Politics being the ambiguous world that it is, nothing seems to be implied in the logical sense.);
but since the American political elite structures its beliefs along this dimension, both psychological (What is perceived as consistent with what?) and
social (What is learned along with what?) forces define consistency. Hence,
the culturally prevalent dimension (left-right) is the base against which consistency is measured. Constraint, then, for Converse implies unidimensional
constraint.

The Converse school will be called "empiricists" from their scientific
world view. [3] They tend toward building theory out of small-scale testable
hypotheses. They might also be called "elitist" (because they find the mass
public wanting in comparison with political elites), but that term has broad
normative implications that are probably inaccurate. They are also "unidimensionalists," but that tag fails to capture much of the scope of their position.

The opposing school will be denoted as "rationalists," because their common denominator is the assertion that the electorate has the cognitive appa-
ratus necessary for rational choice. A more normative characterization is
"populist," because they find great virtue in the common man. With some
significant exceptions, [4] their implicit ontology is formalist. [5] They build theory deductively; starting with formal models, they make inferences about
what the electorate would look like if their models "fit," delimit the scope of

---

[2] "The Nature of Belief Systems in Mass Publics," in David Apter, ed., *Ideology and
Discontent* (New York: The Free Press, 1964).

[3] The usage is borrowed from Paul Diesing, *Patterns of Discovery in the Social Sciences*
(Chicago: Aldine-Atherton, 1971).

[4] George Marcus, David Tabb, and John Sullivan, "The Application of Individual Differences Scaling Analysis to the Measurement of Political Ideology," *American Journal of
Political Science,* 18(1974):405-20.

[5] It is no accident that "rationalism" is associated with formalism. Some form of rationality postulate is ordinarily necessary for deductive inference from the formal models of
electoral choice.

confirming evidence, and test. A significant new trend in rationalist approaches is the postulation of multidimensional belief systems.[6]

Why, if both sides appeal to empirical evidence in support of their theories, does the debate continue? Part of the answer is that they are interpreting the same "facts" differently. The rationalists are searching for *some* evidence of rational choice in the electorate and finding it. The empiricists look for belief structuring and find it only in a minority of the electorate. The two findings are not inconsistent (as indeed they ought not to be, since both sides frequently exploit the same data!). It is, in part, the classic, "The glass is half full." "No, it is half empty," interpretation problem.

A second barrier to agreement is differing emphasis. The empiricists look for belief structuring and are only secondarily concerned with rationality. The rationalists look for evidence of rational choice and are only secondarily concerned with its proximate causes. Thus, the two sides never address exactly the same phenomenon.

A last, and more speculative, explanation for the less than total convergence of the two sides is that the rationalists believe they have time on their side. The major election studies may provide slim support for the rationalist position; but they might as well support an assertion that the electorate is changing, becoming more rational (and more ideological) every four years. Why strike an unfavorable bargain with the empiricists, the rationalists might say, if the voters are moving toward our position? If this is the case, the 1972 election study is not just new data, another case, but an important indicator of the future.

Ideological Choice in 1972

If ever a good case of ideological choice in American presidential elections could be found, it would be 1972. From the first Democratic primary of March through the postmortems of November, contrasting candidate ideologies were a constant focus of media and (presumably) popular attention. The New Hampshire contest was described as "left" versus "center"; Florida, "left" versus "center" versus "right"; California and New York, "left" versus "center," and so on. Only extraordinary inattention to politics could have left a voter unaware that George McGovern represented the "left" segment of the Democratic Party and was indeed widely regarded as a "radical" in his own party.

It may well be that the candidate whose ideology was less well known was Richard Nixon, the incumbent president. Nonetheless, the less visible Republican primaries included ideological challenges from both "left" (McCloskey) and "right" (Ashbrook). If the lines were as sharply drawn, they

---

[6] See Herbert F. Weisberg and Jerrold G. Rusk, "Dimensions of Candidate Evaluation," *American Political Science Review*, 64(1970):1167–85; Marcus et al., "Individual Differences."

were probably not as salient to the electorate, since few apparently regarded the Republican challengers as serious threats to the Nixon candidacy.

Issue positions were unusually sharply defined in 1972. In most cases, the McGovern position was a clear challenge to the status quo. The Democratic candidate called for radical alterations in taxes and welfare, for peace in Vietnam with something less than Nixon's "honor," and for massive government spending to reduce joblessness. He was publicly associated with groups who pushed for the legalization of marijuana and the radical restructuring of the role of women in American society. His most prominent status quo position, on busing school children, was unfortunately for him an immensely unpopular status quo, ably exploited by Nixon from the right.

McGovern, a "prairie populist" to those in the press who liked him, simply a "radical" to those who didn't, was widely regarded a captive of the small and intensely ideological constituency he molded to achieve the Democratic nomination. That tiny constituency, compensating for lack of numbers by extraordinary organizational skill and hard work, was just barely enough to impress in some states and to win in others, aided by the low turnout and rampant chaos of presidential primaries. It was not enough to seriously contest the presidency.

McGovern could not win in November without compromising his issue positions, but could not compromise without relinquishing his only strategic advantage, his zealous army of volunteer campaign workers—most apparently more concerned with McGovern being right than president. In the end, he did attempt some small and tentative compromises, but appeared to have gained only alienation of some of his workers and a new reputation for indecisiveness for his effort.

It is often argued that voters fail to discriminate on ideological grounds because "Tweedledum-Tweedledee" candidates and parties in the American system offer no perceptible choice. It is arguable whether this contention is accurate even for the contests normally cited as illustrations, the Eisenhower-Stevenson elections of the placid fifties. Few but the most extreme ideologues could deny that the 1972 contest presented ideological cues of unprecedented clarity and consistency.[7] As a high water mark in the clarity of ideological choice, the Nixon-McGovern contest allows the examination of belief-structuring hypotheses under conditions which do not allow the attribution of ambiguous responses to ambiguous stimuli.

The Data

To examine questions of belief structuring, we will employ the Center for Political Studies' 1972 American National Election Study. The 1972 sample

---

[7] The Johnson-Goldwater contest of 1964 runs a close second in this regard and might have been more ideological had not the salience of Goldwater's "itchy trigger finger" vastly exceeded that of his conservative domestic program. See Philip E. Converse, Aage Clausen, and Warren E. Miller, "Electoral Myth and Reality: The 1964 Election," *American Political Science Review*, 61(1965):321–26.

of 2,705 respondents was divided into sets who responded to partially over-lapping interview schedules. Primary emphasis here will be on the subsample of 1,119 respondents who responded to pre- and postelection versions of the "Form 1" interview. The Form 1 respondents were asked to position themselves on ten issue dimension scales and a similar liberal-conservative scale. In each case, questions defined the poles of the scale and asked respondents to place themselves at one of seven points along it (see Appendix [to this chapter]). These scales are somewhat more abstract than conventional Likert items, which ask respondents to agree or disagree with a specific statement. They also seem to more closely approximate equal interval data. We shall treat them as if they were such.

Ideology in the 1972 Electorate

For a first approximation of the impact of ideological thinking on the 1972 electorate, we examine the simple relationship between position on the seven-point liberal-conservative scale and 1972 vote. Table 8.1 reveals a strong and consistent relationship between position on the scale and reported vote. Moving across the scale from "most liberal" to "most conservative," the Nixon proportion of the two-party vote rises in steps from a low of 8 percent to a high of 92 percent. Arbitrarily coding the vote (0, 1 for McGovern and Nixon, respectively), the data of table 8.1 produce a healthy product moment correlation of .51, substantially higher than would be expected from earlier voting studies.

Before the impact of unidimensional ideology on the 1972 electorate is confirmed, some selection biases of table 8.1 should be noted. Its 607 respondents are only 54 percent of the 1,119-member (Form 1) sample. Its more evident (and perhaps admirable) bias is that it, of course, includes only those who reported casting a presidential vote in 1972. A more serious bias is that nearly one-third of the sample did not place themselves on the liberal-conservative scale. Thus, a more limited conclusion is in order: *Of those*

Table 8.1   1972 Two-Party Vote by Ideology (Liberal-Conservative)

Vote	Ideology							Total
	Most Liberal ←					→ Most Conservative		
	1	2	3	4	5	6	7	
McGovern	92%	88%	61%	29%	14%	10%	8%*	34%
Nixon	8*	12	39	71	86	90	92	66
Total	100%	100%	100%	100%	100%	100%	100%	100%
N	13	66	72	218	139	87	12	607

* Only one case in cell.

voters for whom the liberal-conservative dimension seems meaningful, there is a strong and consistent relationship between scale position and 1972 vote.

Enduring party loyalty may account for part of the relationship between ideology and vote of table 8.1. Party loyalists might be presumed to be closely anchored to their party's position and cast votes which give the appearance of ideology, but are, in fact, caused by partisanship. Table 8.2 decomposes the responses of table 8.1 into party loyalists (strong or weak identifiers of each party who voted for their party's candidate) and others (independents and defectors from party) to examine this hypothesis.

An examination of table 8.2 leads to further caution about the relationship between ideology and vote. The relationship is actually much stronger among the party faithful ($r = .59$) than among the more dynamic element of the electorate ($r = .43$), leading to some doubt about the degree to which ideology may be used to account for electoral *change*. Not only is the relationship between ideology and vote weaker for the independents and defectors, but it is different. Table 8.2A shows the expected break between liberals and conservatives, McGovern garnering most liberal votes and Nixon winning most conservative votes and more than his share of the neutrals. In table 8.2B we expect McGovern to do badly, since defection in 1972 is overwhelmingly defection to Nixon; but what is unexpected is that McGovern

Table 8.2 Nixon-McGovern Vote by Ideology (Liberal-Conservative) for Party Loyalists and Others

A. Party Loyalists: Weak and Strong Identifiers Who Voted for Their Party's Candidate

Vote	Most Liberal ←	2	3	4	5	6	→ Most Conservative 7	Total
	1	2	3	4	5	6	7	
McGovern	88%	98%	85%	42%	16%	14%	0%	44%
Nixon	13*	2*	15	58	84	86	100	56
Total	101%	100%	100%	100%	100%	100%	100%	100%
N	8	41	34	104	64	56	6	313

B. Others: Defectors and Independents

Vote	Most Liberal ←	2	3	4	5	6	→ Most Conservative 7	Total
	1	2	3	4	5	6	7	
McGovern	100%	72%	39%	17%	12%	3%*	17%*	23%
Nixon	0	28	61	83	88	97	83	77
Total	100%	100%	100%	100%	100%	100%	100%	100%
N	5	25	38	114	75	31	6	294

* Only one case in cell.

does not do well even among the minority who class themselves "liberals." Of the 68 liberal respondents in the nonloyalist sample, only 38 (56 percent) report a McGovern vote. If the 1972 contest had been decided by ideology, without the restraining effects of party loyalty, these data suggest that the McGovern landslide defeat would have been unmitigated disaster. McGovern would have won majority support only from the two most leftist positions, which together account for slightly more than 10 percent of the electorate.

What of the nearly one-third of the 1972 sample who could not place themselves on the liberal-conservative scale? There is widespread agreement that the liberal-conservative dimension is not common to all voters.[8] Large numbers of voters fail to refer to it when asked to explain their partisan preferences,[9] to define it in a way that captures much of its breadth,[10] or even to associate it with the two parties.[11]

Converse has found the use of the concept of a liberal-conservative ordering dimension to be associated with level of formal education (as well as levels of political activity and information).[12] Presumably, the skills required to associate an abstract ordering dimension with the concrete issues of day-to-day politics are nurtured in formal education. Others have argued that not lack of perceptual skills, but the use of *alternative* dimensions differentiates those of higher and lower educational backgrounds.[13]

Because differences in the use of the liberal-conservative ordering continuum by voter cognitive ability are expected, a simple index of cognitive ability is developed which, in the ensuing analysis, will be used to stratify the 1972 electorate. The index is a linear combination of two variables presumed to be related to cognitive skills, *education* and *political information*.[14] The former is expected to be related to ability to manipulate abstract concepts. The latter, based on the number of correct answers to six objective questions about basic features of American politics (e.g., How many years in a senator's term?), measures command of factual information. Cognitive

---

[8] See Converse, "Belief Systems"; Marcus, et al., "Individual Differences"; and Harry Wilker and Lester Milbrath, "Political Belief Systems and Political Behavior," *Social Science Quarterly*, (1970):447-93.

[9] Campbell et al., *The American Voter.*

[10] Converse, "Belief Systems."

[11] *Ibid.*

[12] *Ibid.*

[13] Marcus et al., "Individual Differences"; Wilker and Milbrath, "Political Behavior."

 [14] Each variable was standardized to contribute equal variance to the index. Marquette notes the hazards of this technique, and Levine its safety. See Jesse F. Marquette, "Standard Scores as Indices: The Pitfalls of Doing Things the Easy Way," *Midwest Journal of Political Science*, 16(1972):278-86; Mark S. Levine, "Standard Scores as Indices: The Pitfalls of Not Thinking It Through," *American Journal of Political Science*, 17(1973):431-40.

Table 8.3 Liberal-Conservative Ideology and the 1972
Vote, Stratified by Level of Cognitive Ability ✳

Cognitive Ability Group	Product-Moment Correlation Between Ideology and Vote	Explained Variance (r^2)	Number of Voters in Group
Group 1 (Lowest) (N = 295)*	.31	.10	69
Group 2 (N = 292)	.43	.19	144
Group 3 (N = 267)	.55	.30	178
Group 4 (Highest) (N = 264)	.61	.37	215
Sample	.51	.26	606

* Unevenness in group size is due to the discontinuous distribution of the ability index. The between-group cut points on the index approximate the quartiles.

ability rests in perceiving "facts" and integrating them into a larger framework. The index taps both facets of this process.[15]

Table 8.3 displays the simple correlations between ideology and vote, stratified (approximately at the quartiles) by the cognitive ability index. It shows that the obtained correlation between ideology and vote is based upon very uneven levels of correlation for the four ability strata and a dramatic selection bias that effectively weights the behavior of respondents from the higher ability levels out of proportion to their numbers in the sample.

Thus, we introduce a further note of caution. When we examine the ideology of the mass public, we are quite likely to overstate its impact because the evidence of impact is most slight for that part of the electorate that systematically selects itself out of such analyses by not voting and not responding to measures of ideology. Table 8.4 illustrates the point.

The Structure of Beliefs

Having seen that position on a liberal-conservative scale was a potent predictor of voting for many respondents in 1972, the question is raised here of what respondents *meant* when they classified themselves on the scale. More

---

[15] Neither measure is, however, optimal. Years of formal education is not as good a measure of the ability to manipulate concepts as, for example, I.Q. And the need for objectively "right" answers makes the political information items constitutional and legalistic rather than attuned to current and controversial issues in the political sphere.

Table 8.4   Reported Voting Turnout and Response to Liberal-Conservative Scale, by Cognitive Ability Strata

Cognitive Ability Group	N	Percent of Sample	Percent Reporting Vote	Percent of All Voters	Percent Responding to Liberal-Conservative Scale	Percent of All Scale Respondents
1 (Lowest)	295	26	44	17	43	16
2	292	26	72	27	65	24
3	267	24	80	27	83	28
4 (Highest)	264	24	87	29	93	31
Total	1118	100		100		99

specifically, we raise the question: What are the attitudinal correlates of the liberal-conservative dimension? It is a question often asked and often answered. The answers are, unfortunately, various.

Form 1 of the 1972 election study includes ten respondent attitude scales in the same seven-point format as the liberal-conservative scale. Nine of these are employed here to locate the issue correlates of the liberal-conservative scale. [16] The correlations between these scales and the liberal-conservative scale begin to tell the meaning of the presumed liberal-conservative dimension for the 1972 respondents. The nine issues were a mixture of economic (on government action to control inflation, to guarantee jobs, to provide health insurance), foreign (on ending the war in Vietnam), racial (on protection of minority rights and "busing"), civil liberties (on the rights of accused criminal suspects), and social (on legalization of marijuana and the role of women in American society). They are a good selection of issues, new and old, hypothesized to be relevant to wide-ranging conceptions of political life.

Table 8.5 presents correlations of the nine issues with the liberal-conservative scale, first for the whole sample and then for each ability stratum. As the slightest glance at the table will tell, the liberal-conservative dimension has more meaning for the higher ability respondents than for their lower ability counterparts. More issues are related to the liberal-conservative di-

---

[16] A tenth item, a tax reform scale, was not used because it suffers from ambiguity—the same kind of ambiguity that stifles popular discussion of the issue. The item (see Appendix [to this chapter]) refers to tax rates, ignoring important controversies about what constitutes taxable income. Respondents could choose between "have the same tax rate for everyone" (i.e., lower total tax payments for the wealthy than the current progressive rate system) or "increase the tax rate for high income." The question does not address what is likely to have been on respondents' minds: who should pay more tax and who less. It seems likely that the 30 percent who responded on the "same tax rate" pole of the scale meant something like everyone should pay his fair share—meaning that the wealthy should pay more—which was just the opposite of the change they were apparently endorsing.

mension (and those more strongly) for those high in cognitive ability. Because many issue positions are related to these respondents' location on the liberal-conservative scale, their conception of the meaning of the dimension may be said to be broad and abstract—at least relative to lower ability respondents.

It is much more difficult to say what the liberal-conservative dimension means for the two low ability groups, or even if it exists as anything more than an item in a survey interview. Low correlations could result from lack of constraint between the abstract (liberal-conservative scale) and the concrete (the issue scales), from a concrete interpretation of the liberal-conservative scale (as something other than the nine issues), from concrete, but nonconsensual definitions of the scale, or from some combination of the three. We can say that the liberal-conservative dimension does not seem to be used as a structuring principle by many lower ability respondents, nor does it seem powerful for those who do employ it. For the electorate as a whole, the evidence suggests that these widely used concepts have no shared connotations. What is "liberal" to one citizen may not be "conservative" to another, but it is quite likely irrelevant to his conception of "liberalism."

It is at this point that we begin to encounter the objections of the various "rationalist" positions. All these objections speak to the problems arising from the use of the notion of a liberal-conservative continuum to assess the mass public's conception of the political world. The objections are taken up here in order of severity.

The mass public may use the liberal-conservative continuum, it is argued, but be unable to *articulate* responses to survey questions on it. The argument here is that *use, recognition of use,* and *articulation of position* may be a good deal less than perfectly correlated. Large numbers of people might have reasonably accurate "gut" impressions of the ordering of candidates and parties in American elections, but be unable to say so. The articulation of subtle concepts is clearly related to cognitive ability, but the implication of this first rationalist argument is that *use of the liberal-conservative dimension to structure the political world is not related to cognitive ability.*

The notion of a liberal-conservative ordering dimension has wide currency among the American political elite. It is widely held to be "central" to the belief systems of political activists. That it is central to the beliefs of political scientists may explain, according to a second rationalist objection, why we look for it in the mass public. Might it not be the case that members of the mass public have belief systems equally constrained along some abstract dimension other than the liberal-conservative dimension? The implication of this argument is that *at various cognitive ability levels we should expect to see perhaps different ordering dimensions, but dimensions that are equally abstract and powerful in all groups.*

The final objection holds that voters do not structure their beliefs along any single dimension but use several; and more important, it holds that multiple-dimension belief systems show more "cognitive complexity" than

Table 8.5 Correlations of Issue Dimensions with the Liberal-Conservative Scale, by Cognitive Ability Group

		Cognitive Ability Group			
	Whole Sample	1 (Lowest)	2	3	4 (Highest)
49					
48					
47					Busing .47
46					Minority .46
45				Jobs .45	Health ins. .45
44					
43				Minority .42	Vietnam .43
42				Busing .42	
41				Vietnam .41	Jobs .41
40					Marijuana .40
39				Marijuana .39	
38	Minority .38				
37	Busing .38			Rights of acc. .37	Rights of acc. .37
36					
35	Vietnam .35				
34				Health ins. .34	
33					
32	Jobs .31				
31	Rights of acc. .31				
30			Minority .30		
29	Marijuana .29	Minority .29	Busing .29		
28	Health ins. .29				
27					
26					

	695–786	110–128	165–191	201–221	224–245
25		Vietnam .25	Vietnam .25		Women .25
24			Jobs .24		
23			Rights of acc. .23		
22	Women .22	Women .22		Women .22	
21		Rights of acc. .21			
20		Busing .20	Women .2C		
19					
18					
17				Inflation .17	
16					
15		Marijuana .15			
14		Health ins. .15			
13					
12			Marijuana .12		
11					
10					
9					
8		Jobs .08			
7			Health ins. .07		Inflation .07
6	Inflation .06				
5					
4					
3					
2			Inflation .C2		
1					
00		Inflation −.06			
N	695–786	110–128	165–191	201–221	224–245

the unidimensional. [17] By implication, multidimensional and complex are more appropriate to rational choice than unidimensional and simple. This objection, preferring complexity, rejects constraint as a desirable property of belief systems. The multidimensional argument implies that *those of higher cognitive ability use more dimensions to structure their political perceptions.*

All three rationalist arguments lead to testable propositions. The first holds that people at all ability levels employ the liberal-conservative continuum, although they may not articulate it. The second holds that people at all ability levels use a single abstract dimension, but it may not be the liberal-conservative dimension. The third holds that the number of dimensions used increases with cognitive ability.

As a means of simplifying some rather substantial correlation matrices to bring summary data to bear upon each of the three propositions, we have performed a principal components factor analysis. Factor analysis is not an ideal method for examining belief systems. The number of dimensions "found" is quite clearly in part a function of the number and centrality of issues chosen for analysis. Factor analysis may also overstate the number of real dimensions. And interpretation of rotated factors is always hazardous.

None of these deficiencies of factor analysis is particularly severe for our purpose. The "number of factors" problem is more problematic for inferences about the whole electorate than for comparisons between respondents. The number and substance of items do affect the number and substance of resulting factors, but here all respondents are subject to the same items. [18] Interpretation, too, is sometimes problematic, particularly for residual factors, but on the whole requires few leaps of faith. Factor analysis does speak to central questions—"How many dimensions?" and "What are they?"—without forcing either particular dimensions or levels of articulation on respondents.

The factor analysis is based on the intercorrelations of the nine issue scales of table 8.5 and the liberal-conservative scale. The liberal-conservative scale was included to ease factor interpretation after ascertaining that its inclusion did not materially affect the factor structure. [19]

The first question to be approached is: How many dimensions? In more operational terms: How many of the factors explain how much variance? Figure 8.1 diagrams, for each ability group, the amount of variance explained by each factor with an eigenvalue greater than 1.0. It speaks clearly

---

[17] Marcus et al., "Individual Differences."

[18] The one exception is that the lowest ability group actually responded to fewer items on the average. Some inflation of the appearance of structure in their responses is to be expected.

[19] The inclusion of the liberal-conservative scale does affect the factor structure derived for the lowest ability group (but not the number of factors or their explanatory power). This structure is so unstable that virtually any small change affects it dramatically. Since the instability itself is the most salient characteristic of the derived "structure" of beliefs for this group, we are not particularly concerned about those changes.

to the argument that number of dimensions used increases with cognitive ability. Exactly the opposite is the case. Moving from those of low cognitive ability upward on the scale, the number of dimensions used declines (from 4 to 3 to 2 for the highest two groups), and the variance explained by each increases. The evidence of figure 8.1 suggests that for those of lowest cognitive ability, structure—if it exists at all—is multidimensional. The upper strata of the sample show evidence of a tendency toward attitude constraint and *perhaps* unidimensional constraint. Both upper strata groups show impressive differences between the proportions of variance explained by the first and second factors, suggesting that the latter are unimportant residual dimensions.

We have yet to deal with the *meaning* of structuring dimensions. Is the structure of the lower ability groups the structure of higher ability groups writ small? Or do different dimensions structure the beliefs of different ability strata? In table 8.6, we examine the content of the factors derived for each group. Question marks indicate skepticism about the inherent interpretability of some factors.

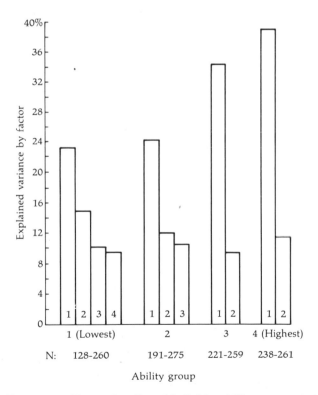

Figure 8.1 Dimensionality of belief by ability group, 1972.

Table 8.6   The Derived Factor Structure by Cognitive Ability Group

Factor	Eigenvalue	Interpretation	Defining Variables
		Group 1 (Lowest)	
1	2.39	Race	Minority, Busing
2*	1.47	Social issues	Vietnam, Rights of accused, Marijuana
3*	1.03	Economic issues	Inflation, Jobs, Health insurance
4	1.01	Women	Women
		Group 2	
1	2.42	Social: Crime, Race, Vietnam	Rights of accused, Minority, Vietnam, Liberal-Conservative
2	1.25	Economic issues	Health insurance, Jobs
3	1.13	?	Marijuana, Women, (Inflation −)
		Group 3	
1	3.45	Left-Right	Liberal-Conservative, Jobs, Health insurance, Minority, Vietnam, Rights of accused, Busing
2	1.01	New social issues	Women, Marijuana
		Group 4 (Highest)	
1	3.90	Left-Right	Jobs, Busing, Minority, Health insurance, Liberal-Conservative, Vietnam, Inflation
2	1.21	Social issues	Marijuana, Women, Rights of accused

* Factors 2 and 3 are reversed when the liberal-conservative scale is not included in the analysis.

It is a good deal more problematic to tell what factors mean than to tell how many of them there are and how much variance each explains. It is particularly difficult for the lower ability respondents, because it is not clear that the presumed dimensions are real.

Despite these difficulties, some clear patterns are to be observed from table 8.6. One is a clear separation of issue types at the lowest cognitive ability level. For the most part, the issues that load together on any given factor are high in superficial similarity. Racial issues load with other racial issues, economic issues with other economic issues, and social issues with other social issues (except the role-of-women item, which loads on a minor factor all by itself). Perhaps most conspicuously, the liberal-conservative scale loads highly on none of the factors. [20] Beginning in the second group, and increasing in the third and fourth, the first factor cuts across issue types. In both of the higher strata, seven of the ten items load highly on the first factor, including all of the issue types except the new issues of 1972, the role of women and the legalization of marijuana. In sum, the *scope* of particular

[20] Its best loadings are .40 and .41 on factors 1 and 2, respectively.

dimensions is narrow for lower ability respondents and broad for those from the upper strata of cognitive ability.)

(Scope of belief systems is broader for higher ability respondents because the objects of centrality—the fundamentals—are far more abstract.)Dimensions for the upper level respondents that correlate with attitudes toward race, economics, and the Vietnam War are evidently approaching the kind of abstract structuring principles implied by the concept of Ideology. Those in the lowest ability groups just as clearly lack such abstract structuring principles. If dimensions cannot be derived that cut across policy types, then ordering may be no more abstract than the policies themselves.

(How *constrained* are respondent beliefs? Before answering that question, we note the implicit bias of the constraint concept. It is a parsimony concept, clearly implying that few structuring dimensions are better than many) By extension, one structuring dimension (e.g., left-right) is better than multiple dimensions. This constraint notion is specifically rejected by scholars who look to multiple structuring dimensions as evidence of belief complexity, persumably more appropriate to rational choice. [21]

What evidence would demonstrate belief constraint? Converse[22] and more recent studies[23] employ correlations of specific attitude scales. The 1972 election study has similar evidence, but the unwieldiness of analysis of four 10-by-10 correlation matrices leads to factor analysis as a summary device.

A number of similar indicators from the factor analysis are operational measures of belief constraint. All point to the same conclusion. The higher ability groups have fewer factors (according to the arbitrary 1.0 eigenvalue cut off). The first factor explains more variance for the higher ability respondents, and more variables load on it. (See table 8.7.) The average variance explained by each factor increases with cognitive ability; and, finally, the

---

[21] Marcus et al., "Individual Differences," used INDSCAL analysis of paired comparisons of abstract political concepts to show that those of higher cognitive ability (by indicators analogous to ours) used more dimensions to structure their responses than those of lesser ability, and that the number of dimensions used, called cognitive complexity, was an indicator of sophistication of political beliefs. Our analysis (available on request) of responses to political slogans—another data set from the same study—finds patterns similar to the 1972 sample; those of higher ability use fewer dimensions to structure their responses to the slogans than their low ability counterparts. The INDSCAL analysis of responses to abstract stimuli seems to measure respondents' capability of articulating relational concepts or dimensions, while the correlational and factor analytic techniques tap the number of dimensions used to structure responses to more concrete stimuli. The joint finding: those who are capable of articulating the most dimensions actually use the fewest. "Complexity" and "constraint," which seem logically to be polar opposites, empirically are found together. Those who have the most complex view of the political world develop the most parsimonious structure of beliefs.

[22] Converse, "Belief Systems."

[23] Steve Bennett, "Consistency among the Public's Social Welfare Policy Attitudes in the 1960's," *American Journal of Political Science,* 17(1973):544–70; Norman H. Nie with Kristi Andersen, "Mass Belief Systems Revisited: Political Change and Attitude Structure," *Journal of Politics,* 36(1974):540–91.

Table 8.7   The Factor Structure as Evidence of Belief Constraint, by Cognitive Ability Group

Cognitive Ability Group	Number of Factors	Number of Variables with Highest Load on First Factor	Variance Explained by First Factor (Percent)	Mean Variance Explained (Percent)	Item Content Sensitivity
1 (Lowest)	4	2	23.9	14.7	High
2	3	4	24.2	16.0	Moderate
3	2	8	34.5	22.3	Low
4 (Highest)	2	7	39.0	25.6	Low

obtained factor structure is insensitive to marginal changes (addition or deletion of items) for the higher ability groups, but extremely sensitive for the lowest group. In sum: *those of higher cognitive ability have more constrained belief systems.*

What then were the dimensions of belief current in the 1972 electorate? It is a question which appears not to be answerable *for the electorate.* We can say that roughly the upper half in cognitive ability seem to have structured their beliefs, at least on traditional political issues, around the left-right continuum. For the lower half, belief dimensions are more complicated, more issue-specific, less stable and less powerful.

We have shown that the number of belief dimensions used by the 1972 respondents to structure responses to issue dimensions declines as level of formal education and political information increase. If any element of the electorate can be expected to choose rationally among political alternatives, most would concur that the expectation of rationality would be highest among the educated and informed. Since those most likely to be rational use the fewest dimensions, the evidence then suggests that few dimensions, rather than many, are linked with rational choice.

If the number and content of belief dimensions extracted by factor analysis are more than testimony to the power of computers to undertake the creative manipulation of nonsense, they should predict attitudes and behavior. To say that a belief dimension is meaningful is to say, in a most important sense, that it is related to real political choices. Two such choices are candidate evaluation and vote.

Candidate evaluations, as Stokes[24] has noted, are the most variable elements in American presidential elections; but it is not clear to what degree they are composed of more than fluff—reactions to projected images of sincerity, piousness, and the like—rather than more genuinely political content. A candidate's character is undoubtedly important, but it fails to convey important information about what he will do if elected. Knowing only char-

---

[24] Donald Stokes, "Some Dynamic Elements in Contests for the Presidency," *American Political Science Review*, 60(1966):19–28.

acter is not to know the shrines of a candidate's political faith, the groups he will appease and those he will ignore, or the programs he will sponsor.

Table 8.8 examines the degree to which candidate evaluation may be predicted by the dimensions of political belief previously isolated for the four ability groups. Dependent variables are McGovern and Nixon "feeling thermometers," measures of affect toward the two candidates. Independent variables are factor scores representing the dimensions of belief derived for each ability group. These dimensions are derived from items that make no reference to either party or candidate, but only issue dimensions, and hence may be thought of as relatively pure indicators of enduring beliefs, little affected by the fluff of campaign and candidates. Candidate evaluations heavily influenced by fundamental beliefs about politics would seem to be *prima facie* evidence of rational choice. The lack of such influence indicates either nonrational evaluation or some form of policy-irrelevant rationality.

The message of table 8.8 is clear: Even though more dimensions of belief are allowed to contribute to the predicted evaluations of lower ability groups, higher ability groups are substantially more predictable. In the highest ability group, a mere two dimensions of belief account for about 37 percent and 43 percent of the variance in evaluation of McGovern and Nixon respectively. In the lowest group, four dimensions account for 20 percent and 8 percent respectively. Those who use fewer dimensions appear more to evaluate candidates on the basis of rational considerations. This is true both relatively (variance explained per dimension) and absolutely (total variance explained).

Another message of table 8.8 is that McGovern evaluations are more uniformly predictable among ability groups than Nixon evaluations. It seems

Table 8.8 Affect Toward Candidates: Multiple Correlations of Belief Dimensions With Candidate Feeling Thermometers, by Cognitive Ability Group

Cognitive Ability Group	McGovern Feeling Thermometer			Nixon Feeling Thermometer		
	Multiple Correlation (R)	Variance Explained (Percent)	N	Multiple Correlation (R)	Variance Explained (Percent)	N
1 (Lowest) Four dimensions	.448	20.1	262	.290	8.4	272
2 Three dimensions	.456	20.8	287	.402	16.2	288
3 Two dimensions	.515	26.5	266	.514	26.4	267
4 (Highest) Two dimensions	.605	36.6	263	.655	42.9	264

reasonable to postulate that the frequent public reference to McGovern as "radical" made him uncommonly easy to evaluate by ideological criteria. Nixon's less ideological appeal seems to have captured many voters of lower cognitive ability in spite of—not because of—their benefits.

Table 8.9 takes us to the final question about belief structure: What impact does it have on the vote? To answer that question, we introduce party identification both as a baseline and as a control. As a baseline it allows comparisons between the impacts of structures of belief on the one hand and simple party loyalty on the other. Since it may interact with belief structure, we also examine party identification jointly with belief dimensions.

Those of higher cognitive ability, which is to say those who use few dimensions to structure their political beliefs, cast votes which are far more predictable from their beliefs than do those of lower ability. The range of multiple correlation coefficients is from about .38 for the lowest ability group to .68 for the highest. These levels of predictability are remarkably similar to the predictability of voting gained by examination of party identification for each group. For both belief dimensions and party identification, predictability increases with cognitive ability, the only significant deviation occurring among those of highest ability, where belief predictability increases and party predictability declines.

The combination of belief dimensions and party identification to predict vote shows that both factors have substantial independent predictive power. The impact of party is not so neatly related to cognitive ability as is the case with belief dimensions, and indeed there is no reason to expect that it

Table 8.9 **Belief Dimensions and 1972 Vote: Multiple Correlations of Belief Dimensions with Reported Vote, by Cognitive Ability Group**

Cognitive Ability Group	N	Multiple Correlation: Belief Dimensions and Vote	Simple Correlation: Party Identification and Vote	Multiple Correlation: Party, Belief Dimensions, and Vote
1 (Lowest) Four dimensions	131	.378	.384	.509
2 Three dimensions	211	.466	.420	.559
3 Two dimensions	213	.588	.622	.743
4 (Highest) Two dimensions	230	.675	.599	.741

should be. Differences between the first two and second two groups are, however, substantial.

We may infer from table 8.9 that few voter defections from party identification occur among those of high cognitive ability (and constrained beliefs), *and* that those defections which do occur are more predictable from fundamental voter beliefs. The lower ability groups, on the other hand, are less tied to party *and* less predictable when they depart from party loyalty. Those of high cognitive ability structure their beliefs simply and behave in a manner consistent with theories of rational choice. Those of low ability do not show evidence of simple and powerful belief structuring, and their more complex derived belief structures are far less predictive of their behavior at the polls.

A Concluding Irony

A picture has been sketched here of a conflict between unidimensional and multidimensional approaches to belief structuring, between simple structures and complex structures. We have found simple structures more associated with high levels of cognitive ability, more powerful in predicting attitudes, and more predictive of two important political choices, candidate evaluation and vote. All of this would seem to suggest simply enough that the Converse approach to measuring belief structure has been fundamentally correct all along.

But the conflict about the proper way to conceptualize belief systems was part of a larger debate about the level of belief structuring present in the American electorate. Differing conceptualizations led to differing conclusions; unidimensionalists found little structure, multidimensionalists found it widespread. A strange thing has happened on our way to a conclusion. The same data that shore up the validity of the unidimensional approach lead to a conclusion about the level of belief structuring that is strikingly different from Converse's. They show that at least half of the eligible electorate (and more of the actual electorate) displays evidence of belief structuring that is consistent with the standards originally laid down by Converse; that is, the upper two ability groups show evidence of using the left-right dimension in a manner which is sufficiently abstract to encompass a wide scope of more specific political attitudes, and which is demonstrably important in predicting their responses to the choices offered by the political system.

How can Converse be both right and wrong? The 1972 data do not speak directly to the point, but a recent article by Norman Nie and Kristi Andersen [25] demonstrates what many have long suggested: that a very substantial change has occurred in American politics since 1960 and that the presiden-

[25] Nie with Andersen, "Belief Systems Revisited."

tial elections which were the subject of Converse's analysis were vastly less ideological in the minds of voters than all those which have occurred since then. The 1972 data would seem to confirm the Nie et al. hypothesis. It remains to be seen whether this change is a prelude to future quiescence or a lasting rearrangement of the shape of American politics.

Appendix

1972 Election Study Issue Dimension Scales

The same format is followed for each scale; a descriptive lead-in is followed by the question: "Where would you place yourself on this scale, or haven't you thought much about this?" Only the lead-ins are listed here.

G1. Suppose people who believe that the government should see to it that every person has a job and a good standard of living are at one end of this scale—at point number 1. And suppose that the people who believe that the government should let each person get ahead on his own are at the other end—at point number 7.

G2. As you know, in our tax system people who earn a lot of money already have to pay higher rates of income tax than those who earn less. Some people think that those with high incomes should pay even more of their income into taxes than they do now. Others think that the rates shouldn't be different at all—that everyone should pay the same portion of their income, no matter how much they make.

G3. Some people think that the use of marijuana should be made legal. Others think that the penalties for using marijuana should be set higher than they are now.

G4. There is much discussion about the best way to deal with racial problems. Some people think achieving racial integration of schools is so important that it justifies busing children to schools out of their own neighborhoods. Others think letting children go to their neighborhood schools is so important that they oppose busing.

G5. There is much concern about the rapid rise in medical and hospital costs. Some feel there should be a government insurance plan which would cover all medical and hospital expenses. Others feel that medical expenses should be paid by individuals, and through private insurance like Blue Cross.

G9. Recently there has been a lot of talk about women's rights. Some people feel that women should have an equal role with men in running business, industry, and government. Others feel that women's place is in the home.

J3. With regard to Vietnam, some people think we should do everything necessary to win a complete military victory, no matter what results. Some people think we should withdraw completely from Vietnam right now, no matter what results. And, of course, other people have opinions somewhere between these two extreme positions.

J4. There is a great deal of talk these days about rising prices and the cost of living in general. Some feel that the government must do everything possible to combat the problem of inflation immediately or it will get worse. Others say the problem of inflation is temporary and that no government action is necessary.

J5. Some people are primarily concerned with doing everything possible to protect the legal rights of those accused of committing crimes. Others feel that it is more important to stop criminal activity even at the risk of reducing the rights of the accused.

J6. Some people feel that the government in Washington should make every possible effort to improve the social and economic position of blacks and other minority groups. Others feel that the government should not make any special effort to help minorities because they should help themselves.

J8. We hear a lot of talk these days about liberals and conservatives. I'm going to show you a seven-point scale on which the political views that people hold are arranged from extremely liberal to extremely conservative.

III. DETERMINANTS
OF THE VOTE

9. Parties, Candidates, or Issues?

Why do people vote as they do? What determines election outcomes? These are the basic questions about voting and elections that have been asked ever since voting behavior studies began. If politicians knew the answers, they would know exactly how to attract votes and exactly how to interpret the election mandate when they won office. If historians knew the answers, they would be able to offer solid interpretations of streams of thought in American politics and of America's electoral history. If political scientists knew the answers, they would have a more thorough understanding of the role of elections in our society.

The simple answer to both questions—why people vote as they do and what determines election outcomes—is "issues." Voters follow the presidential campaign, they vote on the basis of the issues raised in that campaign, and consequently elections can be interpreted as popular mandates on those issues. This was in fact the classical image of the rational voter. Up to twenty or thirty years ago, such a view made a great deal of sense. It fit the assumption that voters thought in liberal-conservative ideological terms. And the importance of issues seemed obvious to politicians, journalists, and academicians whose world revolved around issue politics.

It is possible, however, that factors such as parties and candidates are more critical than issues in affecting individual votes and election results. If so, this would imply certain things about the nature of American democracy.

If the bulk of voters blindly followed one party or the other, voting would become more a matter of habit than of reasoning. If candidate factors predominated, voting would follow fads as different types of candidate personalities became more attractive to the public. In either case, elections would be less a matter of great issues than of how to market party and candidate images effectively. The election would lose much of its importance in classical democratic theory, since voting would appear to be little more serious than selection of a favorite sports star. Effective campaign strategies, interpretations of electoral history, and the role of elections themselves all depend on the quality of the American electorate. At a minimum, reinterpretation of the nature of elections would be required.

Absence of Issue Voting

The original view may have been that issues were all-important, but, as with the matter of ideology, things became more complicated when researchers began interviewing actual voters. The very first studies—the Columbia studies in the 1940's—began to suggest that a reconsideration was in order. They found that individual vote decisions were often made prior to the campaign, in other words, before issues were even raised. Voters often misperceived the candidates' positions on issues, simply assuming that the candidate they favored agreed with them and that the other candidate disagreed with them. Under such circumstances, issues could only play a very limited role.

But it was *The American Voter* which finally shattered the classical image. A careful analysis of a series of issues strongly suggested that none of them could have had much impact on the election of 1956.[1] If an issue is to affect a person's vote, the authors reasoned, three conditions must be fulfilled: the person must be familiar enough with the issue to have an opinion, know what the government is doing on the issue, and believe that the parties differ in their positions on the issue. Respondents were asked about sixteen specific issues in 1956, and only 18–36 percent of the sample passed all three tests. A typical finding was that 12 percent of the public had no opinions on school desegregation, an additional 34 percent had an opinion but did not know what the government was doing, and another 23 percent had an opinion and knew what the government was doing, but did not perceive any difference between the parties on this issue. In other words, only 31 percent of the public met the required conditions. And even these figures were inflated in some ways. For example, further analysis showed that often the "informed" individuals disagreed about which party advocated which policy. Given these results, it seemed clear that issue voting could not be very frequent.

---

[1] Angus Campbell, Philip E. Converse, Warren E. Miller, and Donald E. Stokes, *The American Voter* (New York: Wiley, 1960), chap. 8; abridged version, chap. 7.

The view that issues are important for only a few voters was reinforced by a number of subsequent studies. One of the most important was Converse's analysis of "The Nature of Belief Systems in Mass Publics."[2] We have already noted (pp. 70–73) Converse's conclusion that "nonattitudes" exist on some matters of public policy. He noted that there were "issue publics" on each issue which did not have real attitudes, but those issue publics tended to be small (less than a majority of the public on any single issue). Only for selected segments of the population could issue voting have any reality.

Butler and Stokes's study of Great Britain in the middle 1960's was also important, because many Americans regarded Britain as an example of "responsible parties"—a system in which each party took well-defined and clearly differentiated stands so that the public could readily vote on the basis of its policy preferences. Butler and Stokes pointed out that for an issue to have maximum impact on an election (a slightly different perspective than the one employed in *The American Voter*) there had to be a high degree of attitude formation among the public, a skewed opinion distribution (since otherwise contrary attitudes would balance out to the benefit of neither party), and public perceptions of different stands by the parties on the issue.[3] Only social services issues were of this type in Britain. Such issues as immigration and the death penalty might have had great impact, but party differences on them were not perceived. Opinions on such questions as nationalization of industry and British nuclear weapons were so unstable over a period of time (measured by correlating attitudes in different waves of a panel study, as Converse had done) as to indicate little genuine attitude formation. Views on joining the Common Market were balanced in 1963 and 1964, and a third of the sample had no opinion. Thus, even in countries such as Britain, the impact of issues seemed slight.

How is the vote to be interpreted if it is not based on issues? *The American Voter* emphasized the importance of party identification, as discussed in greater detail in a later section of this book. Most of the public will indicate that they generally consider themselves Republicans or Democrats, and even most of those who think of themselves as independents will say that they consider themselves closer to one party or the other. Party identification was found to be closely related to the vote (see the correlations in figure 7.11 of Nie with Andersen, p. 130), with strong Republicans much more likely to vote Republican than strong Democrats.

The effects of party identification are actually embedded in a far richer theory. It is not only that party identification is a direct cause of the vote but that party identification affects how people evaluate candidates and issues, and these short-term evaluations, in turn, have some effect on the vote decision. Thus *The American Voter* reports an analysis of a set of questions

---

[2] In David Apter, ed., *Ideology and Discontent* (New York: Free Press, 1964).

[3] David Butler and Donald Stokes, *Political Change in Britain* (New York: St. Martin's Press, 1969), chaps. 8–9.

asking people what they liked and disliked about each party and each presidential nominee. The responses were categorized in terms of six attitudes: feelings about the Republican candidate, the Democratic candidate, foreign issues, domestic issues, parties as managers of government, and group-related attitudes. A given respondent might be pro-Republican on foreign issues, pro-Democrat on domestic issues, neutral on the Democratic candidate, and so on. Republican identifiers were found to be more likely to give pro-Republican comments on each of these themes, while Democratic identifiers were more likely to give pro-Democratic views. Thus, although the Eisenhower victories of the 1950's could be partly explained in terms of public feelings about Eisenhower and foreign issues (plus the managers-of-government theme in 1952), these attitudes were themselves partly determined by party identification.

How does this theory explain the sizable shifts in the vote from one election to another? Party identification is very stable and issues have limited importance, so candidates must be the reason for the change (which means that party identification does not *completely* determine candidate evaluation). This is indeed the result which Stokes obtained when analyzing the six partisan attitudes from *The American Voter* over the period from 1952 to 1964.[4] He found that domestic issues and group-related attitudes consistently favored the Democrats, while party performance and foreign issues favored the Republicans, at least until Goldwater's 1964 candidacy. But the great variation was with regard to the candidates, with the candidate effects being so strongly pro-Republican in 1956 that they created a landslide for Eisenhower, not sufficiently pro-Republican in 1960 to overcome the Democratic advantage in party identification, and very strongly pro-Democrat (or actually anti-Goldwater) in 1964. Thus Stokes concludes that the dynamism of election outcomes is largely dependent on the emergence of new candidates for the presidency.

This conception—especially the irrelevance of issues—formed perhaps the major theme of voting studies in the mid-1960's. While a careful rereading of these studies makes it clear that the authors realized that issues *could be* more important at other points in history and that issues can be important in ways other than directly influencing the vote, the usual impression is that voters always followed the irrational appeals of party and candidates rather than rationally considering the issues. In short, voters were fools.

Before bringing this theme up to date, two significant points should be made about the complete theory. First, if the theory emphasized candidates, and especially party identification, more than issues, it is partly because partisanship could serve as a surrogate for the latter. Presumably, people choose to identify with a party with which they generally agree. (They also form attitudes on the basis of their party identification as noted above—i.e., there is two-way causation.) As a result they need not concern themselves

[4] Donald E. Stokes, "Some Dynamic Elements of Contests for the Presidency," *American Political Science Review,* 60(1966):19–28.

with every issue that comes along, but can generally rely on their party identification to guide them. Party identification becomes a short cut for deciding how to vote without investing the time at each election to research issue differences between the parties. Yet it gives voters some assurance that they are voting for the party they would agree with anyway.

Moreover, this theory, which de-emphasizes the role of issues in specific elections, gives issues an especially important role in the shifting of party allegiances over several elections. A person's party identification can change because of issues. If people become dissatisfied with their party's positions on very important issues for a long enough time, they may change their partisanship. There is relatively little evidence of such change occurring in the 1950's, but analyses of the late 1960's and 1970's are finding more. And issues are increasingly being viewed as the most important determinant of that change (see our discussion below, pp. 170–71). This theme will be revisited in the realignment section below. However, the important point here is that even in the original theory issues could not be ignored if a longer period of time was being considered.

The Prevalence of Issue Voting

But are voters fools in any one election? The first attempt to contradict that view was by the leading political scientist, V. O. Key, Jr. in his posthumously published book, _The Responsible Electorate._ [5] (He argued that issues were important in a very particular sense: that vote change _between_ elections was due to satisfaction or dissatisfaction with the performance of the incumbent administration.) Those who vote for the administration but become dissatisfied with its performance switch their votes to the opposition party in the next election, while those who vote for the opposition party but are satisfied by government policies switch their votes to the party in power. For example, Key reports from Gallup data that 60 percent of 1956 Eisenhower voters who disapproved his performance in office switched to vote for Kennedy in 1960, while 22 percent of 1956 Stevenson voters who were satisfied with Eisenhower's performance switched to vote for Nixon in 1960.

Unfortunately, Key's analysis suffers from severe methodological problems. It is based on "recall data," where respondents must recall how they voted four years earlier. Next, many voters have no opinion on the issues or agree with both sides. Many of those who expressed opinions voted against their own policy positions, a fact that Key's theory can't explain. But most important, as Key admits, a voter may "improvise policy views that seem to be consistent with the way he planned to vote for other reasons entirely." [6] Furthermore, the question of satisfaction with the administration comes

---

[5] (Cambridge, Mass.: Harvard University Press, 1966).
[6] _Ibid.,_ p. 45.

very close to being a candidate evaluation rather than a real issue question. Yet regardless of the difficulties with Key's analysis, his book served to reopen the question of the importance of issues to voting.

Another challenge to the supposed irrelevance of issues came from Re-Pass, who made a simple but crucial methodological point.[7] The surveys for the 1950's asked voters for their likes and dislikes about the parties and candidates, but the issue items were closed-ended questions about issues selected by the researchers. The logic of Converse's discussion of issue publics is that different issues may determine the votes of different voters, so it is essential to permit the respondents to identify the important issues. The SRC/CPS surveys of the 1960's included a question asking voters to name the problems facing the government in Washington which they deemed most important. In analyzing these data, RePass showed that the public did list problems, did perceive party differences, and did recognize party positions reasonably accurately.

Overall, RePass's analysis shows that issues have a substantial effect, almost equal to the effect of partisanship in 1964. By implication, had *The American Voter* been able to analyze similar questions for the 1950's, it *could* have come to very different conclusions about issue importance. Unfortunately, the 60's were sufficiently different from the 50's that there is no way of telling how important issues would have appeared had such questions been asked earlier. But RePass's analysis of the 60's does emphasize the importance of the questions asked, suggesting that it may be best to obtain voters' views of the issues they think are important (see also p. 173). Even so, RePass's results would not mean that elections can be interpreted as a mandate on any single issue because only small portions of the electorate (one-fifth for 1964) agree as to what is the major problem facing the government.

Beyond the question of how to measure issue voting, the importance of issues had to be reconsidered because the times were changing. Conflict over issues was violent in the 60's. Civil rights disputes moved from the halls of Congress to marches in the streets of cities across the nation and then to riots in many of those cities. Later, the Vietnam War divided the nation. It would have been hard for voters to ignore these issues, in contrast to the issues of the 50's, which had little direct impact on the electorate. The "issueless 50's" had passed, and the 60's were dominated by issues. The issues still could not affect voting if the candidates took similar stands on them, as Nixon and Humphrey did on the Vietnam War in 1968,[8] but the general trend was toward clearer party positions.

This "nature of the times" theme underlines still another argument against the irrelevance of issues. Pomper demonstrates dramatic changes

---

[7] David RePass, "Issue Salience and Party Choice," *American Political Science Review*, 65(1971):389–400.

[8] Benjamin I. Page and Richard A. Brody, "Policy Voting and the Electoral Process," *American Political Science Review*, 66(1972):979–95.

with regard to issues from 1956 to 1968.[9] By 1964, the role of issues had changed considerably from that of the 1956 election reported in *The American Voter*. There were now sharp differences in the proportions of Democrats and Republicans supporting liberal issue positions; large proportions of the public perceived party differences, and most perceived the Democrats as more liberal on the issues. Pomper's analysis shows that this change cannot easily be "explained away" by such things as the increasing education of the electorate. Instead it seems likely that once the parties adopted differing issue positions, the voters quickly recognized the differences. The preconditions of issue voting were then met—at least to a much greater degree than previously. Importantly, this showed that voters *could* surpass such "hurdles" even if they had failed to do so in the 1950's.

But how much issue voting was actually occurring even in the 1960's and 1970's? Chapters 10 through 13 all provide insight into this question. The Center for Political Studies' report on the 1972 election concludes that issues were vital in that election in a way they had not been in any of the previous elections they studied.[10] The 1972 election was marked by perceptions of sharp policy differences between Nixon and McGovern. Issues were found to have a considerable impact on the vote, even when controlling for party identification. Partisanship did have a substantial influence when its effect on how people evaluate issues was taken into full account, but the impact of the issues themselves was no less sizable. The authors conclude that 1972 constituted an issue contest.[11]

Even this interpretation is open to debate. Popkin, Gorman, Phillips, and Smith have argued that candidate factors were more important even in 1972.[12] Extending Stokes's analysis of the relative importance of the various partisan attitudes over time,[13] they find issues were no more important in 1972 than in recent elections while candidate factors increased in importance. Additionally, their own surveys show that perceptions of McGovern's qualifications to be president fell sharply as the 1972 campaign progressed, so that his bad loss was due to voters seeing him as incompetent. McGovern's issue positions hurt him less than doubts as to his competence.

The article by Schulman and Pomper (chapter 11) carefully contrasts the determinants of the vote in all three eras. Few studies use the same variables

---

[9] Gerald M. Pomper, "From Confusion to Clarity: Issues and American Voters, 1956-1968," *American Political Science Review*, 62(1972):415-28.

[10] This study relies heavily on assessments of how differently groups vote from what might be expected, given their long-term partisanship. The measures are based on a "normal vote analysis" which is explained in chapter 17 below.

[11] Chapter 10 also deals with ideology in 1972 and with intraparty differences among Democrats. These aspects of the paper should not be ignored, though we feel that its primary emphasis is on issue voting.

[12] Samuel L. Popkin, John W. Gorman, Charles Phillips, and Jeffrey A. Smith, "What Have You Done for Me Lately?" *American Political Science Review* 70(1976), in press.

[13] See above, p. 164.

in studying more than one election, but Schulman and Pomper are able to do so in analyzing the impact of candidates, issues, and party on the vote in 1956, 1964, and 1972. They employ "causal modeling" techniques to trace the importance of each predictor with the others statistically controlled. Instead of relying on the correlation of candidate evaluation with vote, for example, they adjust that correlation for the effects of issues and parties on the vote and the fact that candidate evaluations are themselves related to issues and parties in a specifiable manner. Their findings reveal considerable change from the 1950's, a change which becomes fully evident by 1972 but which had started by 1964. The force of the issues has become much more substantial, while the party impact has correspondingly decreased.

Perhaps significantly, Schulman and Pomper have not included 1968 in their analysis. The Center for Political Studies' report on the 1968 election (chapter 12), while using a different methodology, suggests that only Wallace was an issue candidate in that year, while the Nixon and Humphrey candidacies were essentially party contests. [14] The explanation for this result is very likely found in the similarity of the major party candidates, an explanation which emphasizes the role of parties and candidates in providing the conditions under which issue voting can occur. Voters *can* take stands, perceive party differences, and vote on the basis of them. But whether they do or not depends heavily on the candidate and the parties.

Another report on the 1968 election arrives at different conclusions. While agreeing that the issues had a stronger, and partisanship had a weaker, effect on the Wallace vote compared to the major party nominees, Kovenock, Beardsley, and Prothro find issues to be slightly more important than party for Humphrey and only slightly less important than party for Nixon. [15] Their major conclusion is that party need not be the basic vote determinant; issues can also play that role. The difference between these and the CPS results is largely due to the very different measurements used in the Comparative State Election Project, which broaden the definition of issues to include some candidate effects. [16] The two reports agree as to the great importance of issues in Wallace voting, but their disagreement on the major party candida-

---

[14] Rusk and Weisberg reach the same conclusion from an analysis of evaluations of the presidential contenders in 1968. See p. 383 in this volume.

[15] David M. Kovenock, Philip L. Beardsley, and James W. Prothro, "Status, Party, Ideology, Issues, and Candidate Choice: A Preliminary Theory-Relevant Analysis of the 1968 American Presidential Election," paper presented at the Eighth World Congress of the International Political Science Association, Munich, West Germany, August 1970.

[16] Respondents placed themselves, the candidates, and the parties on eleven policy items and four "group benefits" items about the parties and evaluated the presidential and vice-presidential candidates according to four criteria involving personal characteristics. These variables were combined to form the issue rating. While, in a sense, the influences of candidates can often be interpreted in terms of issues (and vice versa), it seems useful to distinguish them as much as possible. Similarly, group benefits, while clearly related to issues, are conceptually distinct from specific policies.

cies suggests the importance of more careful models to separate issue positions from the personal aspects of candidates.

Where are we now in the study of determinants of the vote? In one sense, the question must remain unanswered for the moment because of a basic methodological problem. As Brody and Page show in chapter 13, three different processes can explain results such as those reported for 1972. An analysis of issue importance generally assumes that a person's issue position and his or her perceptions of the candidates' positions are independent, but that together they determine the person's evaluation of the candidates and subsequent vote. But what if the voter were persuaded to adopt the candidate's ideas? The voter's issue positions would reflect his/her candidate evaluations rather than vice versa. Alternatively, voters may misperceive candidate issue positions, projecting their own attitudes onto the candidates. (Brody and Page call this process projection; others have called it rationalization.) This process also inhibits true issue voting. The Brody and Page article discusses the difficulty of disentangling these three processes. They offer no conclusions as to the real extent of issue voting, but instead show how the question can be properly attacked through the use of "simultaneous equation models" in which issues and party identification are recognized as influencing *each other*. Such models are more difficult to test since they do not assume unidirectional causation (that partisanship determines issue position but not vice versa). Ironically, to estimate such equations would probably require us to obtain panel data from a single election year, just as was done in the 1940 Columbia study. [17]

We can actually carry Brody and Page's point one step further. Party identification and issue positions may be related to one another via the same three processes discussed by Brody and Page for issues and voting. Ideally, a simultaneous equation approach should also be used to estimate the effects of these variables on each other. When party identification, issue positions, and the vote are all brought together, the situation becomes even more complex. Thus Schulman and Pomper and Miller et al., specifically address the question of the causal ordering of the variables, noting that the effect of partisanship should be gauged not only by its direct impact on the vote, but also by its indirect impact via its effect on issue positions (i.e., partisanship affects issue positions which in turn affect the vote). Even then, as we have suggested (and as Schulman and Pomper note, p. 205), the indirect linkages which they specify do not fully represent the interconnections between partisanship, issues, and the vote.

---

[17] It should be noted that Schulman and Pomper and Miller et al., are not oblivious to the problems raised by Brody and Page. Schulman and Pomper avoid using proximity measures—i.e., a judgment about the distance between a voter and a candidate—because they feel that such measures "do not gauge if the voter has any information about the issue or if he perceives candidate or party differences correctly" (p. 200 below). Miller et al., use proximity measures, though they also report in a footnote their use of self-placement scores.

Conclusions

While a complete answer to the question of parties, candidates, or issues cannot, therefore, be given presently, the debate has been productive. First of all, it is clear that we cannot return to the classical image of voters who are fully aware of the issues involved in the campaign and who vote solely on the basis of issues. Though the results may not often be as extreme as those reported for the 1950's in *The American Voter*, there is often a large proportion of voters who cannot pass the elementary tests necessary for issue voting. [18] (One of our favorites is a lady who in 1965 could think of no difference between the parties except that in her opinion one party had supported Prohibition while the other had not.) Moreover, voters may adopt issue positions because their favorite candidate has those positions, and not because of an independent evaluation of the issues. Moreover, candidate evaluation—including such intangible things as leadership ability and such "irrelevant" things as the candidate's appearance—is very important, especially if there is more variation in candidate evaluations over a given time period than there is in the issue positions adopted by the candidates.

Similarly, it has been shown that issues rarely dominate an election sufficiently to provide a real mandate. In no case studied to date has an issue public been found which is large enough to supply an effective mandate on any issue. For example, Kirkpatrick and Jones found that the largest issue public in 1968 was Vietnam. But that was only 29 percent of the sample, and half of these people had no preferred policy, did not feel strongly, or saw no party difference. [19] In 1960 and 1964, RePass found only 16 percent and 21 percent, respectively, who cited any one issue as most important. [20] Hence any description of voters going to the polls to give their verdict on a specific issue would be considerably exaggerated. Such elections might occur, but it would clearly be incorrect to interpret the average election that way.

Neither of these conclusions, however, at all implies that the electorate is irresponsible or that issues are unimportant. If issues are not of *overwhelming* importance in elections, that is because the voters rarely need to consider them. The original choice of a party can satisfy most peoples' feelings on the issues most of the time. At least in normal times it becomes rational for citizens not to take the time to research the issues. Even when the times are not normal, party differences on issues are often so slight that people cannot be expected to notice them. Or to put it in a way still more favorable to voters, party differences may be so small that it is irrational to try to understand those slight variations.

---

[18] This point is extremely well made in an article which challenges recent interpretations of a more enlightened electorate. Michael Margolis, "From Confusion to Confusion: Issues and The American Voter (1956-1972), *American Political Science Review*, 71(1977), in press.

[19] Samuel Kirkpatrick and Melvin E. Jones, "Issue Publics and the Electoral System," in Allen R. Wilcox, ed., *Public Opinion and Political Attitudes* (New York: Wiley, 1974), p. 546.

[20] RePass, "Issue Salience."

But in a still stronger sense, issues have been found to be very important. First of all, they are directly related to the vote. In fact, as was found for 1972 by Miller, et al., the direct link between issues and the vote may be considerably stronger than that between party identification and the vote. Secondly, the link which has not yet been explored, by which issues alter party identification over a period of time, can only add to the importance of the issues. Just as we cannot return to the classical view of the voter skillfully weighing all issues, so we cannot any longer take the view that issues are unimportant. Their importance—and the way in which they are important—will vary from one election to another, but they cannot be ignored as irrelevant.

A final point is the importance of parties and elites in determining the role played by issues in specific elections. Voters can perceive differences between parties and can relate their preferences to their voting behavior. Whether they do so, however, depends in large part on the stands taken by the candidates and other party leaders. While it is perhaps a truism that the voters cannot choose on the basis of issues if the candidates do not differ, the significance of this point has often been overlooked. Ironically, it may be the candidates who cause the most passionate feelings—those such as Goldwater, Wallace, and McGovern—who contribute the most to issue voting by taking positions clearly different from those taken by the majority of voters. Whether this is good or not, and in what respects, is something which the reader might wish to consider.

It is unfortunate, perhaps, that the world is not so simple. It would be much easier if we could say that issues are totally unimportant or that issues—or even single issues—determine electoral outcomes. Unfortunately, the world is extraordinarily complex, and electoral analyses will become more complicated as we learn more about elections.

Vote Prediction

Up to this point in our discussion we have said little about vote prediction models. If issues are important, it should be possible to accurately predict a person's vote from his or her issue positions. Actually, one could predict a person's vote solely on the basis of party identification (with 81–86 percent accuracy from 1956 to 1964 and 75 percent accuracy in the three-candidate race of 1968, excluding pure independents),[21] the partisan attitudes as reported in *The American Voter* (with 86 percent accuracy for 1956),[22] or by candidate preferences (90 percent accuracy in 1968 when using party identification to break ties).[23] But for some purposes these prediction models are

---

[21] Stanley Kelley, Jr. and Thad W. Mirer, "The Simple Act of Voting," *American Political Science Review*, 68(1974):572–91, tables 2 and 9.

[22] Campbell et al., *The American Voter*, p. 74.

[23] Richard A. Brody and Benjamin I. Page, "Indifference, Alienation and Rational Decisions," *Public Choice*, 15(1973):1–17, at p. 15.

not as useful as one would like. Therefore, those who have studied voting from a formal (rather than empirical) perspective have constructed their own model, usually referred to as a rational voter model or a spatial model. [24] In this model, the voter determines his or her distance from a candidate on each issue, squares that distance (since the multidimensional issue space is seen as Euclidean) and weighs that squared distance by the importance he or she attributes to the issue, sums up the weighted squared distance from the candidate on each issue, and then votes for the candidate for whom the sum of weighted squared distances is least. The two basic elements in this formulation are the proximity to the candidate on the issue and the salience of the issue.

The value of such a model, if it works, is that it could actually be used in directing political campaigns. If one can adequately specify the relationship between voter preferences, candidate positions, and the vote, one can theoretically predict the consequences of changes in a candidate's stands. It is usually a very difficult and risky business to try to predict the effect of candidate actions on the electoral outcome because issues are interrelated in complicated ways. However, if one has fully specified these relationships, then a candidate could be given extremely specific and knowledgeable advice about how to win the election—or at least on how to come as close as he or she can to winning. The model cannot yet (and perhaps never will be able to) predict change in *all* the relevant variables, such as voter preferences, but the model should be extremely valuable.

This model has been tested most directly in an article by Shapiro. [25] Voters were asked to specify the issues important to them, the salience of those issues, and their estimates of candidate proximity to them on those issues. On this basis Shapiro was able to predict 85.5 percent of individual votes correctly for a special sample of voters in Hawaii in 1968. Only 77.5 percent could be correctly predicted without taking issue salience into account, so the salience term proved important in this case.

A study by Kelley and Mirer employed a simpler prediction scheme. [26] They examined the Survey Research Center questions on likes and dislikes about parties and candidates. In essence these questions permit the respondent to indicate the issues important to him or her. Kelley and Mirer's prediction was simply that a person whose net comments favor a party would vote for that party; a person would vote in accord with party identification when his or her attitudes were exactly balanced. This method yielded

---

[24] The most readable introductions to this literature are Otto A. Davis, Melvin J. Hinich, and Peter C. Ordeshook, "An Expository Development of a Mathematical Model of the Electoral Process," *American Political Science Review,* 64(1970):426-48, and William H. Riker and Peter C. Ordeshook, *Introduction to Positive Political Theory* (Englewood Cliffs, N. J.: Prentice-Hall, 1973), chaps. 11-12.

[25] Michael J. Shapiro, "Rational Political Man: A Synthesis of Economic and Social-Psychological Perspectives," *American Political Science Review,* 63(1969):1106-19.

[26] Kelley and Mirer, "Simple Act of Voting."

predictions that were 85–90 percent correct in the 1952 to 1964 surveys, and 82 percent correct in the three-candidate 1968 race.

Results presented by RePass can be examined from a similar point of view.[27] He examined the problems which voters mentioned as most important along with their perceptions of which party could handle these issues better. If one predicted that people would vote according to their issue partisanship, with party identification being used to break ties, 83 percent successful prediction could be obtained for 1964.

What is intriguing about these several results is, first of all, that very high predictive accuracy can be obtained using issue measures.[28] Advising a candidate on the basis of some type of a spatial model may be a reality in the future. Equally interesting is the fact that highly accurate predictions have been obtained whether or not a salience measure was employed and whether or not a proximity measure of agreement with the candidate was used. Kelley and Mirer do an excellent job with an issue model without a separate salience measure, where the only weighting occurs by whether or not a voter mentions an issue. On the other hand, Shapiro uses individuals' estimates of the salience of an issue, ranging from 0 (totally irrelevant) to 5 (extremely important). Similarly, Kelley and Mirer measure only a dichotomy—which candidate is closer and which is further from the individual's preference—while Shapiro uses a seven-point proximity measure.

At this juncture it appears to us that the common component of all three of these vote prediction models is the use of voters' own statements about which issues are important in the campaign as opposed to using a researcher's judgments. It may well be that this feature is more crucial than the matter of relative distances and perhaps even the matter of salience.[29]

We can note in concluding that these vote prediction models add to our contention that we have made considerable progress even if we cannot yet specify the precise role played by parties, candidates, and issues. Models

---

[27] RePass, "Issue Salience." The success rate was calculated by us from table 6.

[28] These articles do not use purely issue measures and do not necessarily measure the variables exactly as is specified in the spatial model literature. Nonetheless, we think they quite adequately show that votes can be predicted solely on the basis of issues. Actually, one might debate about exactly what to include in an "issue" model. Candidate leadership ability is not a matter of public policy in the usual sense, but it may be an "issue" in the campaign. The decision about what constitutes an issue should probably depend on what one wants to do with the model.

[29] However, see also a study by Fishbein and Coombs in which they have respondents evaluate twenty-four political items (ranging from the parties to medicare) and give their beliefs as to the candidates' attitudes on those items. In accord with Fishbein's attitude theory, they multiply the person's view by his/her evaluation of a candidate's position on the same subject, sum this over the twenty-four items, and predict the respondent will vote for the candidate for whom this sum is largest. Their predictions for a sample of a midwestern city in the 1964 election give correlations of .73 with the vote. Martin Fishbein and Fred S. Coombs, "Basis for Decision: An Attitudinal Approach Toward an Understanding of Voting Behavior," paper delivered at the annual meeting of the American Political Science Association, Chicago, 1971.

based on any or all of these components can be highly predictive of voter behavior. And, though we indicated that none of the components can be considered irrelevant, models based on one component—such as a spatial model based solely on issues—might be highly useful for specific purposes. We expect that there will be a variety of such models in the future.

Further Readings

The Role of Issues

V. O. Key, Jr., *The Responsible Electorate* (Cambridge, Mass.: Harvard University Press, 1966). Began the reconsideration of the role of issues.

David E. RePass, "Issue Salience and Party Choice," *American Political Science Review*, 65(1971):389–400. Issue importance depends on how questions are asked.

Richard W. Boyd, "Popular Control of Public Policy: A Normal Vote Analysis of the 1968 Election," *American Political Science Review*, 66(1972):429–49. Normal vote analysis of issue impact.

John H. Kessel, "The Issues in Issue Importance," *American Political Science Review*, 66(1972):459–65. Alternative interpretations of findings showing increased issue importance.

Benjamin I. Page and Richard A. Brody, "Policy Voting and the Electoral Process: The Vietnam War Issue," *American Political Science Review*, 66(1972):979–95. Importance of issues depends on positions taken by candidates.

John E. Jackson, "Issues, Party Choices, and Presidential Votes," *American Journal of Political Science*, 19(1975):161–85. Issue positions influence both the vote decision and party identification.

Gerald M. Pomper, "From Confusion to Clarity: Issues and American Voters, 1956–1968," *American Political Science Review*, 62(1972):415–28. Voters increasingly perceive consistency between parties and issue positions.

Michael Margolis, "From Confusion to Confusion: Issues and the American Voter (1956–1972)," *American Political Science Review*, 71(1977), in press. Challenges recent interpretations of a more issue-oriented electorate.

The Role of Candidates

Donald E. Stokes, "Some Dynamic Elements of Contests for the Presidency," *American Political Science Review*, 60(1966):19–28. Candidates provide the main reason for voting change between elections.

Herbert F. Weisberg and Jerrold G. Rusk, "Dimensions of Candidate Evaluation," *American Political Science Review*, 64(1970):1167–85. Analysis of the candidate competition space.

Vote Determinants

Arthur S. Goldberg, "Discerning a Causal Pattern among Data on Voting Behavior," *American Political Science Review*, 60(1966):913–22. Causal model of voting.

David M. Kovenock, James W. Prothro, and Associates, *Explaining the Vote,* Vols. 1
and 2 (Chapel Hill, N.C.: Institute for Research in Social Science). Alternative
models of the vote, applied to 1968 data.

Vote Prediction

Stanley Kelley, Jr. and Thad W. Mirer, "The Simple Act of Voting," *American Political Science Review,* 68(1974):572–91. Develops simple predictor of the vote and compares it against other predictors.

Spatial Modeling of Political Competition

Anthony Downs, *An Economic Theory of Democracy* (New York: Harper & Row, 1957), especially chap. 8. This was the first work on spatial modeling.

Donald E. Stokes, "Spatial Models of Party Competition," *American Political Science Review,* 57(1963):368–77. Leading critique of Downs's analysis.

Otto A. Davis, Melvin J. Hinich, and Peter C. Ordeshook, "An Expository Development of a Mathematical Model of the Electoral Process," *American Political Science Review,* 64(1970):426–48. Nonmathematical statement of the more recent theories.

William H. Riker and Peter C. Ordeshook, *An Introduction to Positive Political Theory* (Englewood Cliffs, N.J.: Prentice Hall, 1973), chaps. 11, 12. A summary of work on spatial modeling.

10. A Majority Party in Disarray: Policy Polarization in the 1972 Election

ARTHUR H. MILLER
WARREN E. MILLER
ALDEN S. RAINE
THAD A. BROWN

The 1972 election marked the third time running that one of the major parties failed to cope with the polarization of policy demands among its supporters in the contest for the presidency. McGovern's defeat was the most notable of the three, but Humphrey and Goldwater before him also lost numerically significant and ideologically distinct segments of their parties' supporters to opponents whose policy positions were sufficiently more attractive to outweigh normal considerations of party loyalty and candidate preference at the polls. Indeed, even in the face of the Nixon landslide there are indications that the Republican party in 1972 confronted the same dilemma that faced a Democratic party whose internal disagreements had remained unresolved since the rebirth of the party under Franklin Roosevelt's leadership. This is the more significant precisely because policy disagreements strong enough to cause massive defections among rank and file party supporters had not been characteristic of postwar American national politics. Apparently it took twelve years of national leadership focused on

Source: Adapted from *American Political Science Review,* 70(1976), forthcoming. Reprinted with permission of the publisher.

Note: This paper is based on the Center for Political Studies' 1972 election study which was made possible by grants from the National Science Foundation (GS-33956, GI-29904, GS-3322) and the National Institute for Mental Health (MHI9516-03).

national problems and policy alternatives to begin to reshape the American electorate and overlay the traditional politics of the 1950's—rooted in the Great Depression and the social cleavages made deep by economic distress—with a new issue politics. And it was the 1972 election that exposed the pervasive consequences that follow from dislodging party loyalty and candidate appeal from positions of dominance in mass electoral politics and complementing them with a widespread concern over policies intended to resolve very real national problems.

Contemporary electoral research came into being at the end of the era of Roosevelt and the New Deal and following a war that had been a total national preoccupation for five years or more. The seven years of the Truman presidency during postwar relocation served largely to revive the issues and alignments of the Roosevelt era. The "issueless 50's" were so for a variety of reasons. The Cold War threatened to engage the electorate in a new and dire concern with foreign policy, but the Eisenhower presidency ended that threat, or opportunity. In the election of 1952, party lines were as sharply drawn on the broad dimensions of internationalism-nationalism or interventionism-withdrawal in foreign affairs as they were on controversies over the policies of the New Deal and the Fair Deal. But Eisenhower's leadership moved enough Republicans into the internationalist-interventionist camp to obliterate foreign policy as an arena for national partisan dispute for a decade or more.

During the eight years of the Eisenhower presidency, the de facto national Democratic leadership of Johnson and Rayburn thwarted the attempts of such organizations as the Democratic Policy Council to define new domestic policy goals for the Democratic party and to engage the president in open confrontation over national policy directions. The nation was led by a popular, largely nonpartisan president and a government only dimly perceived to be divided. "Mr. Republican," Senator Robert Taft, died before the end of Eisenhower's first term, and the rerun of the Eisenhower-Stevenson competition in 1956 produced a second election in which the only real contest was between persistent Democratic loyalties and the popular folk hero, General Ike. Whatever the "real problems" of the nation, the national leadership of both parties deprived its followers of any great sense of urgency to define the problems and argue over alternative solutions.

John F. Kennedy's call to get the nation moving again in an assault on the New Frontiers marked the beginning of a change in the posture of national party leadership toward questions of public policy. Although Quemoy and Matsu, the Great Debates, and Kennedy's Catholicism were prominent features of the Kennedy-Nixon contest, it was the subsequent Kennedy presidential legislative program that defined the enduring themes of national presidential politics for the next eight years. In 1964 the Republicans and Senator Goldwater did their part to sustain the decision to make American politics issue politics. Whatever the short-run costs to his candidacy and his party, the Goldwater decision to offer "a choice not an echo" reaffirmed the primacy of issues in presidential politics. And as President Johnson was applying his insider's skills to the achievement of national public purpose, the very real problems of the society were being publicized by word and deed through the dramatic medium of national television. In 1968, Governor Wallace, with virtually nothing in the way of personal appeal as a candidate and little more in the way of major party support, was an important national candidate solely because he articulated policy alternatives favored by one out of every seven or eight voters. Political scientists' long-standing pleas for the elevation of issue politics and the creation of conditions that would permit or force responsible party government into existence were being answered.

At the same time that national leaders were injecting a large element of policy-based controversy in American politics, a widening stream of research was documenting a spectacular change in the quality of mass attitudes toward questions of public policy. Both within and across broad policy domains, the structuring of popular attitudes in ways that make sense to the politician and to the student of mass ideology was replacing the ideological formlessness noted in comparable evidence from the 1950's. The universe of policy questions came to be reasonably well ordered by the electorate, with apparently sophisticated structuring. The change in level of inter-item and inter-domain constraint was so great, in contrast to the earlier period, that an intense search was launched to locate the cause of what appeared to be a basic discontinuity in the partisan concerns of the electorate.

Unhappily, research on mass behavior has seldom seriously grappled with—indeed has seldom even recognized—the problem of incorporating the conditioning and causing events of the real world in the design of the research. In the electoral realm we have been too prone to try to assemble disembodied data to map the "natural history of an issue" with little regard for the likely fact that leadership decisions to promote, to modify, to resist, or to surrender in a policy fight are major factors in determining that "natural" history. Systematic electoral research has largely ignored a major source of the observed change in the quality of mass attitudes on questions of public policy: leadership behavior that brings the substance of issue politics into the public domain.

The 1972 election provided a unique opportunity to investigate the consequence of change in leadership focus on policy and the responses of an electorate mobilized by policy considerations. A detailed inspection of the electoral outcome illuminates some of the systemic problems which flow not only from the changes in the quality of electoral response to the contests for the presidency, but also from the increased impact of policy preference on partisan defection, the increased importance of issues as predictors of the vote decision, and the transformed nature of contemporary public involvement in policy issues. Each of these facets of the 1972 election makes it very different from the presidential elections of the 50's. This contrast is most clearly revealed by analyses which compare the relative importance of policy voting with alternative and complementary explanations for the particular outcome of the 1972 presidential contest. Ideology and issue voting in that election provide a means for better explaining the unique elements of the contest than do the voters' social characteristics, the nature of candidates, the events of the campaign, political alienation, cultural orientations, or partisan identification. A consideration of the relative balance of these factors on the forces under the particular social and political conditions of 1972 helps us to recognize the problems facing political parties and political leaders whose constituents have been aroused to a high concern over questions of governmental policy. The mass recognition of the enduring existence of salient social problems uncovered by the analyses of the 1972 election suggests that subsequent electoral contests may be fought along lines of deepening policy cleavages.

The Political Setting

During the period just prior to the 1972 presidential primaries numerous factors suggested a Democratic victory in the upcoming elections. Foremost among these was the war in Southeast Asia. Despite Richard Nixon's 1968 campaign pledge of a rapid end to U.S. involvement, the war continued, and it came to be seen as Nixon's war. American bombings of Vietnam and Cambodia continued even as the 1972 election approached. Although Nixon had run on a "law and order" platform in 1968, with promises of a reduction in the crime rate, violent crimes were still on the increase in 1972. The Administration itself was beset by a series of scandals involving possible criminal activity by well-placed members of the Administration. Moreover, the economic situation appeared bleak: unemployment was higher throughout the Nixon Administration than it had been under Lyndon Johnson; inflation increased substantially; government deficits grew, and the imbalance in foreign trade increased. All of these factors created a situation that seemed certain to benefit the Democrats. By early 1972 the Gallup poll reported a significant shift from 1968, with the Democratic party once more popularly perceived to be the party best able to cope with the important problems facing the nation. And the Democratic lead in basic partisan loyalties showed little or no decline over 1970, a year in which the long string of Democratic national victories at the polls was continued with the re-election of a Democratic Congress.

While the advantages and strengths of the Democrats prior to the campaign were substantial, some factors could be expected to benefit the minority party candidate, particularly the fact that Richard Nixon was an incumbent president in a position to exploit the ample political advantages of the highest office in the nation. Moreover, Nixon had achieved impressive gains in foreign affairs, including a historic Peking summit meeting and a growing détente with Moscow. By establishing price controls, he had reduced criticism on the economic front. He could, further, rebut criticism relating to the war in Southeast Asia by reference to the peace negotiations then in progress which eventually led to the pre-election pronouncement that "peace was at hand."

Throughout the campaign and almost up to the time of the election, more than half of the population expected to vote for Richard Nixon. The ultimate margin of victory (approximately 61 percent voting Republican)[1] was, nevertheless, somewhat unexpected since among the eligible electorate, self-proclaimed Democrats[2] continued by almost 2 to 1 to outnumber Republicans.[3] The degree of ticket splitting which reinstated a heavily Democratic Congress was likewise not widely forecast. Most surprising, however (and perhaps equally alarming), was the lack of citizen concern about the outcome of the election. The percentage of the electorate expressing a personal concern about the outcome was lower than it had been for any previous presidential election during the past twenty years.[4] On election day, only 55 percent of the eligible electorate participated in the presidential election—the lowest turnout since 1948.

Policy Preference and the Vote

Following the election, politicians and political observers offered many explanations for the outcome, for the substantial defection among Democrats, for the high degree of ticket-splitting, and for the low turnout. Most often, these accounts speculated on the effects of various political incidents of the previous months, including such early events as the California Democratic primary debates, the selection of Democratic convention delegates on the

---

[1] Data for this report are primarily from the Center for Political Studies' 1972 national election survey, the twelfth in a series, which was based on a standard University of Michigan Survey Research Center national stratified probability sample of 2705 cases. The data are derived from personal interviews with eligible voters (citizens 18 years and older) taken before the election (September 1 to November 6) and reinterviews with the same respondents taken immediately after the election. The data and relevant codebooks for the 1972 study are available to any interested scholars upon request through the Inter-university Consortium for Political Research, The University of Michigan, Ann Arbor, Mich. 48106.

[2] Party identification is based on the standard measure which asks the respondent: "Generally speaking, do you usually think of yourself as a Republican, a Democrat, an independent, or what? Would you call yourself a strong Republican/Democrat or a not very strong Republican/Democrat?" If independent—"Do you think of yourself as closer to the Republican or the Democratic party?" The question gives rise to a measure with seven categories that range from strong Democrat to strong Republican. For the purpose of this paper whenever Democrats, independents and Republicans are referred to, the leaning independents have been collapsed with the independent-independents.

[3] The most extensive analysis of the concept of party identification is provided in Angus Cambell, Philip E. Converse, Warren E. Miller, Donald E. Stokes, *The American Voter* (New York: Wiley, 1960). See especially p. 124 for the distribution of party identification in the 1950s.

[4] In response to the question, "Generally speaking, would you say that *you personally* care a good deal which party wins the presidential election this fall, or that you don't care very much which party wins?", the percentage personally caring about the outcome of the election in 1952 was 68 percent; in 1956, 65 percent; 1960, 67 percent; 1964, 69 percent; 1968, 64 percent; 1972, 62 percent.

basis of quotas rather than meritorious party service, the acerbity of the Illinois and California seating fights at the Democratic Convention, and the inability of McGovern campaign workers to cooperate with Democratic party regulars. The role of Nixon-McGovern disagreements over national policy, on the other hand, was frequently minimized by assertions that no real policy differences existed among the voters, or that McGovern wavered so much on the issues that he did not project a consistent, tenable policy position and hence was not perceived in terms of basic issues. Lipset and Raab, for example, argued the unimportance of issues. They concluded that "there was no real gap on political issues separating the body of McGovern voters and the body of Nixon voters. The voters, in fact, were on the same side of *all* political issues. . . ."[5] The same report went on to contend, moreover, that with respect to the issues the voters perceived little difference between the candidates. More generally, however, the treatment of issues in postelection analyses varied from the view that the issues were relatively unimportant to assertions that they entirely explained the 1972 presidential election outcome. Some analyses emphasized the importance of only a few issues, such as the "cultural" or the "racial" issues. Kirkpatrick, for instance, declared that "at every campaign stop he [McGovern] was hounded by questions about the 'three A's': amnesty, acid, and abortion. . .,"[6] and Rosenthal alleged that the election outcome was determined by the "hidden issue" of race.[7] At the other extreme, some claimed that McGovern supporters constituted an ideological or issue elite who shaped the election outcome by taking an extremely liberal position on all the important issues of the day.[8]

It is understandable that many interpretations of the election placed little emphasis on the issues. Nixon had undertaken to neutralize the war in Vietnam, one of the most potent issues of the 1968 election, and the October announcement that "peace was at hand" seemed to guarantee peace with honor. At home, the college campuses were peaceful, and with the anticipated end to the military draft, they could be expected to remain so. The racial situation had quieted, and "crime in the streets" no longer captured headlines. Indeed, the only heated issues before the election appeared to be issues that had only recently become salient in the McGovern campaign: abortion, amnesty, busing, and the legalization of marijuana. On all these issues Nixon had taken a public stand which reflected the position of a large popular majority.

Nevertheless, there was reason to believe that issues had been important in the election, and that there had been sharp issue differences between the supporters of the two candidates. At the time of the election, the Vietnam

---

[5] Seymour Martin Lipset and Earl Raab, "The Election and the National Mood," *Commentary*, 55(1973): 43. Emphasis in the original.

[6] Jeane Kirkpatrick, "The Revolt of the Masses," *Commentary*, 55(1973):60.

[7] Jack Rosenthal, "The Secret Key Issue: Study of Polls Shows Racial Attitudes to be Critical with Nixon Gainer," *The New York Times* (7 November 1972).

[8] Kevin Phillips, "How Nixon Will Win," *The New York Times Magazine* (6 August 1972), pp. 8, 34, 35-37.

War was still a position issue with the debate revolving around immediate American withdrawal from Vietnam versus a protracted military engagement while a peace settlement was negotiated. Despite the growing support for peace, even through unilateral American withdrawal, Nixon's supporters favored an escalation of the war and a renewed national commitment to achieve a military victory. Furthermore, McGovern's position on immediate withdrawal from Vietnam, his pro-amnesty sentiments, and his supposed special appeal to youth were intended to mobilize support along lines reflecting alternative ways of dealing with the nation's continuing social problems. While the racial situation had quieted, widespread social discrimination still existed in America, and there was little reason to expect much change in attitudes toward government assistance aimed at improving the social and economic condition of minority groups. Nixon's praise of the work ethic and his denigration of welfare were clearly at odds with McGovern's statements on welfare, including his early promise of a minimum $1,000 personal income for every person in the nation.

In analyzing the role of policy preferences in the 1972 election, one must first ask whether the composition of McGovern's support changed during the campaign. Since much of McGovern's eventual success in attaining his party's nomination was based on his primary victories, it is useful to determine how different the policy preferences of his early and later supporters were. If they were different, this would illustrate the process by which a candidate is chosen as the presidential nominee of a party and then must broaden his base to include a national electorate as well as the fellow partisans who opposed his nomination.

The intraparty divisions within the Democratic ranks were already evident at the time of the primaries. On each of several issues, and especially with respect to Vietnam, amnesty, and government aid to minorities, McGovern's primary supporters were far more "liberal" than were those who voted for the other candidates in the Democratic primaries. As table 10.1 reveals,[9] McGovern captured most of the primary vote of the liberal

---

[9] The issue scales used in table 10.1 ranged from 1 to 7 with the extremes indicating designated policy alternatives. The respondents were asked to place themselves on the issue scale. The scales were trichotomized for ease of tabular presentation: categories 1 to 3 were combined into the "left" category, number 4 formed the "center," and categories 5 to 7 were designated as "right." On all the issue scales the left position identifies the liberal position. This is most clearly identified on the last scale in the table which ranged from "liberal" to "conservative" without any specific issue content.

The five-issue policy orientation index is different in that it combined responses to five of the specific issue scales. To form this index an average score was obtained from self-placement on the issues of the Vietnam War, urban unrest, campus demonstrations, protecting the rights of the accused, and government aid to minorities. Scores ranging from 1 to 3 were considered as pro-social change while scores of 5 to 7 were designated as pro-social control. Placement at 4 on the scale was labeled "center." The distribution for this trichotomized index is 41 percent pro-social change, 29 percent at center, and 30 percent pro-social control. For a more complete discussion of this concept, see Arthur H. Miller, "Political Issues and Trust in Government," *American Political Science Review*, 68(1974):951–72.

Table 10.1 Issue Composition of the Candidates' Support

Issue and Position	McGovern Primary Voters (N:78)	Other Primary Voters (104)	Democrats Voting for McGovern (377)	Democrats Voting for Nixon (271)	All Democrats (1092)	McGovern Voters (566)	Nixon Voters (1021)
Vietnam							
Left	79%	34%	69%	30%	52%	69%	29%
Center	17	26	19	31	24	19	29
Right	5	40	12	39	24	12	42
Amnesty							
Left	52%	17%	49%	18%	34%	54%	15%
Right	48	83	51	82	66	46	85
Marijuana							
Left	41%	19%	30%	10%	20%	37%	17%
Center	19	6	11	7	8	11	11
Right	41	75	59	83	72	52	72
Campus unrest							
Left	*	*	40%	12%	31%	43%	11%
Center	*	*	18	24	22	20	23
Right	*	*	42	64	47	37	66
Minorities							
Left	49%	18%	50%	25%	39%	52%	25%
Center	25	35	24	24	22	23	27
Right	26	47	26	51	39	25	48
Standard of living							
Left	53%	28%	53%	21%	39%	50%	18%
Center	16	22	23	24	23	24	25
Right	31	50	24	55	38	26	57
Busing							
Left	19%	4%	23%	2%	14%	22%	3%
Center	10	2	8	2	5	8	4
Right	70	94	69	96	81	70	93
Five issues							
Left	51%	18%	45%	15%	34%	50%	16%
Center	30	42	30	33	31	29	34
Right	18	40	25	52	35	21	50
Liberal-Conservative							
Left	48%	24%	50%	14%	33%	54%	13%
Center	38	33	36	44	41	32	37
Right	14	43	14	42	26	14	50

NOTE: The format for the amnesty question was suitable for collapsing into two categories only.

*Data unavailable because primary voting and campus unrest questions were on opposite half-samples in the study design.

Democrats while the conservative faction went to the several other contenders. Yet it should also be noted that the *total* set of Democratic primary voters was biased in a direction that might benefit a candidate espousing McGovern's policies. Even those who voted for some Democrat other than McGovern in the primaries were generally slightly more liberal than Democrats who were later to vote for Nixon in the general election.

The depth of the split within the Democratic ranks was fully exposed in the general election. There were only minor differences between McGovern's primary supporters and the much larger set of Democrats who voted for him in November. The differences that do appear, such as the slightly more liberal complexion of the primary supporters with regard to Vietnam and marijuana, largely reflect age differences between the two groups of voters. However, a deep policy schism among the Democrats is sharply defined when Democrats voting for McGovern in the general election are compared with the Democrats who voted for Nixon. The defecting Democrats were much less in favor of immediate withdrawal from Vietnam; they were much more likely to support the use of police force as the means of ending campus demonstrations; and they strongly opposed an active role for government in maintaining or improving the quality of life experienced by minority groups. On each of the specific issues, as well as on a more general policy orientation index and a liberal-conservative scale, Democrats as a whole were a very heterogeneous collection of citizens. This lack of cohesion reflected long-standing regional differences between southern and non-southern Democrats, but, even within regional subgroups, a substantial degree of intraparty polarization was exposed by the general election.

The Republicans, on the other hand, exhibited a substantial degree of consensus on each issue except Vietnam, where the intraparty division found 31 percent preferring immediate withdrawal, 30 percent favoring a complete military victory and 30 percent in the center. The Republican positions on the liberal-conservative scale also revealed substantial differences of ideological position within the party: 41 percent saw themselves as "conservative" but 28 percent labeled themselves as "liberal." On other more specific issues, the dominant Republican position was, more often than not, an overwhelming majority supporting a conservative preference against the minority made up of liberals and neutrals combined.

The stark issue differences that separated the total group of McGovern voters from the Nixon voters are also revealed by the data of table 10.1. McGovern supporters were consistently more liberal than Nixon supporters. Even on the highly one sided issues—busing, amnesty and the legalization of marijuana where 86, 72, and 68 percent of the total sample, respectively, expressed a very conservative policy preference—McGovern voters were more liberal than Nixon voters. [10] On the question of Vietnam, which specif-

---

[10] It should be noted, though, that of these three issues only on the question of amnesty did a majority of McGovern voters take a liberal position; 70 percent were against busing and 52 percent favored increasing the penalties for the use of marijuana.

ically referred to immediate withdrawal versus a complete military victory, 40 percent more McGovern voters than Nixon voters preferred an immediate end to the fighting. Even with "peace at hand," a military victory in Vietnam was the Nixon supporters' preferred way to end the war. Using a trichotomized five-issue policy orientation index (see table 10.1), we find that half of McGovern's voters exhibited a social-change policy orientation, whereas an equal fraction of Nixon voters displayed a diametrically opposed social-control orientation. Similarly, on the liberal-to-conservative scale a full 54 percent of McGovern's voters identified themselves as clearly "liberal," while half of Nixon's voters saw themselves as strongly "conservative." These are large differences between the candidates' support groups since the total population was divided almost equally among three categories including a "middle of the road" option in both the policy orientation index and the liberal-conservative scale. These differences are even greater than those between the Democratic factions because of the distinctive appeal of the two candidates to different groups of independents. McGovern clearly captured the votes of the more liberal independents, and therefore his total vote support group was generally more liberal than were the Democrats who voted for him. The more conservative independents, on the other hand, voted for Nixon, joining conservative Republicans in a group slightly more conservative than the subset of Democrats voting for Nixon.

In general, McGovern supporters were sharply distinct from Nixon voters in their policy preferences, but they were also a distinct subset among Democrats. Since McGovern's supporters formed 58 percent of all Democrats, however, it cannot be argued that they were just a splinter faction within the party; it can more reasonably be argued that they were the vanguard of a liberalizing trend occurring in the population as a whole and centered in the ranks of the Democrats. If so, McGovern's principal error in adopting his policy positions for the campaign may have been in overestimating the speed and the magnitude of the national liberal trend on questions of public policy. . . .

Ideological Politics in 1972

With more than a dozen specific issue items available for analysis, a simplification of the data pertaining to issues is obviously desirable. The search for a parsimonious assessment of policy voting led to a factor analysis of the numerous issue questions included in the study. This analysis disclosed four general issue dimensions defined by policies concerning the *war*, and *economic*, *social*, and *cultural* issues.[11] The war domain included the issues of Vietnam withdrawal, amnesty for draft dodgers, and reducing military

---

[11] A factor analysis of some twenty issues was employed to ascertain the dimensional structure of the issue space. The loadings of the items on their respective common factors were all above .6.

spending. The issues of government health insurance and a government guaranteed standard of living were the best representatives of the economic dimension. Attitudes toward urban unrest, campus unrest, protecting the rights of those accused of crime, and government aid to minorities formed the social issue domain. Finally, the issues of equal rights for women, abortion, and the legalization of marijuana composed the cultural issue dimension. A normal vote analysis of the proximity measures for these four issue domains is presented in figure 10.1 and reveals an exceptionally strong short-term component for each issue domain. The data of figure 10.1 show that by aggregating issues into general domains and employing the proximity format, the objectives of analytic parsimony and predictive power are maximized.

The normal vote analysis of the four issue domains documents a substantial relationship between issues and the vote. [12] The implications of the factor analysis four factor solution, however, go well beyond the simple relationship of the four issue domains to the vote. In addition to the structuring of attitudes implied by the solution, the voter's self-location on the liberal-conservative scale was clearly relevant to all four factors. This suggests a degree of consistency in issue attitudes that has traditionally been associated with an ideological interpretation of politics. [13] Indeed, a multivariate analysis of the role of issues in determining vote preference with the liberal-conservative proximity measure included as an "issue" demonstrates that the liberal-conservative measure is as strong a predictor of the vote as the most potent issue proximity measure based on any one of the four issue domains. This relative importance of the liberal-conservative measure implies that a broad segment of the population in 1972 was reacting to politics in a fairly ideological manner. As Converse points out,

> . . . the use of such basic dimensions of judgment as the liberal-conservative continuum betokens a contextual grasp of politics that permits a wide range of more specific idea-elements to be organized into more tightly constrained wholes . . . . There are many crucial consequences of such organization: With it, for example, new political events have more mean-

---

[12] The results of a multivariate analysis with the two-party vote as the dependent variable and the several individual issue proximities excluding the liberal-conservative scale but including party identification revealed the seven most important single issues. These were, in order of importance as determined by a step-wise regression: Vietnam, a government guarantee of a job and good standard of living, dealing with campus unrest, protecting the rights of individuals accused of crimes, legalization of marijuana, the use of busing to achieve racial integration of schools, and urban unrest. These seven issue proximities explained roughly 60 percent of the variance in the vote. The last four mentioned issues, however, each added only 1 percent of explained variance and only 2 percent more explained variance is achieved after adding eight other issues to the regression analysis.

[13] Philip E. Converse, "The Nature of Belief Systems in Mass Publics," chap. 6 in David Apter, ed., *Ideology and Discontent*, (New York: Free Press, 1964).

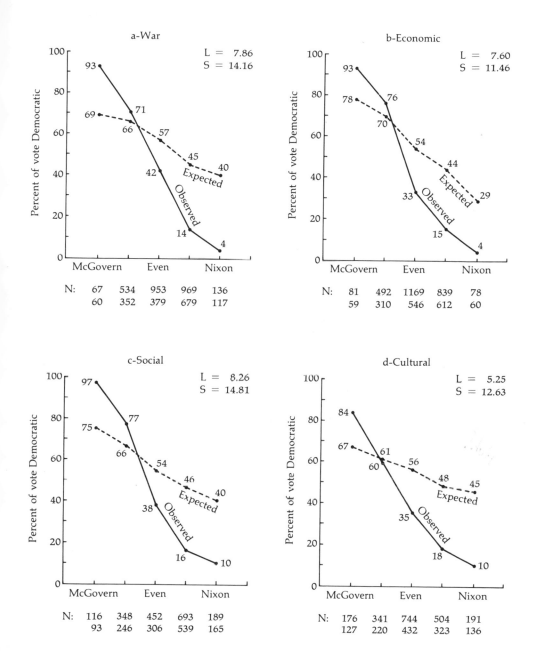

Figure 10.1 Normal vote analysis of issue proximity measures for major issue domains. (1) The Republican vote is always 100 percent minus the Democratic vote; (2) the category N's below each figure are for expected vote (top row) and the observed vote (bottom row), respectively.

ing, retention of political information from the past is far more adequate, and political behavior increasingly approximates that of sophisticated "rational" models, which assume relatively full information.[14]

The relationship between the liberal-conservative proximity measure and the vote in 1972 is, of course, only inferential evidence of the tightly constrained attitude sets that Converse has equated with ideology. What must be added to authenticate a role for "ideology" in the 1972 election is a direct investigation of the interrelatedness of preferences on public policy questions and of the consistency between the respondents' self-location on specific issue questions and the respondents' self-location on the liberal-conservative continuum.

Table 10.2 provides data on such interrelatedness of attitudes. The interrelatedness of attitudes on issues can be inspected in terms of correlations both within the clusters of issues that constitute the four issue domains and between the several items forming the separate clusters.

The entries in table 10.2 show within-domain and between-domain correlations that are quite high for mass public survey data. These data are consistent with findings reported in previous studies[15] that show relatively higher levels of attitude constraint than were found prior to 1964. This temporal change in the level of ideology has paralleled, if not produced, the change in issue polarization in the population. Furthermore, the change in indicators of ideological structuring of political attitudes coincides with the upgrading in the quality of political rhetoric and debate that has occurred since the 1960 presidential campaign. It doubtless reflects the fact that the past twelve years have witnessed an increased articulation of the ideological differences between the parties, as well as political interpretations of the pervasive social and cultural turbulence that has been so widely transmitted by the mass media. In short, the increase in the ideological nature of public opinion can be understood to be the consequence of spokesmen and movements utilizing public—and often out-of-the-ordinary—channels for airing their grievances.

The increased clarity of both policy disagreements and ideological constraint is particularly well documented by the apparently consistent meanings associated with the liberal-conservative scale. Studies investigating the meaning of liberal-conservative differences in mass populations have often found contradictory, confused, and unclear images associated with those two terms. The rather substantial correlations in the bottom line of table 10.2 suggest that there is much less confusion today in translating certain political issues and events into a liberal-conservative framework.

---

[14] *Ibid.,* p. 227.

[15] Norman H. Nie and Kristi Andersen, "Mass Belief Systems Revisited: Political Change and Attitude Structure," *Journal of Politics,* 36(1974):540–91; Gerald M. Pomper, "From Confusion to Clarity: Issues and American Voters, 1956–1968," *American Political Science Review,* 66(1972):415–28.

Table 10.2 Ideological Constraint. Inter-Item Correlations for Issues and Liberal/Conservative.

Issues	Vietnam	Amnesty	Military	Standard of Living	Insurance	Urban	Campus	Accused	Minorities	Women	Abortion	Marijuana	Busing
War													
Vietnam													
Amnesty	.42												
Military	.38	.30											
Economic													
Standard of Living	.22	.27	.15										
Insurance	.22	.23	.14	.33									
Social													
Urban	.14	a	a	.25	a								
Campus	.22	a	a	.26	a	.39							
Accused	.20	.28	.16	.18	.12	.37	.41						
Minorities	.23	.30	.22	.38	.23	.39	.42	.35					
Cultural													
Women	.12	.08	.09	.04	.08	.08	.17	.17	.18				
Abortion	.09	.17	.18	.02	.06	.10	.16	.11	.10	.24			
Marijuana	.22	.27	.24	.06	.16	.19	.40	.29	.25	.28	.37		
Busing													
Busing	.26	.30	.23	.30	.16	.25	.34	.25	.35	.13	.10	.25	
Ideology													
Liberal/Conservative	.31	.42	.31	.32	.31	.27	.41	.32	.38	.19	.12	.32	.37

NOTE: *Average correlations:*   *Within-domain: .36*   *Between-domains: .18*   *With Lib/Con: .31*   *Total matrix: .24*

ᵃ Correlations between Insurance, Amnesty, and Military Spending on the one hand, and Urban and Campus Unrest on the other, are unattainable, since these sets of questions were on opposite half-samples on the study design.

Richard Nixon won a truly impressive electoral victory on November 7, 1972. Not only did he obtain 94 percent of the vote among self-proclaimed Republicans and 66 percent among independents, but he also captured 42 percent of the vote among self-identified Democrats. This feat seems even more impressive when it is recalled that in 1952 Dwight Eisenhower, perhaps the most popular and personally appealing candidate since Franklin D. Roosevelt, attracted only 28 percent of the votes cast by Democrats.

By the simplest of logic, party identification, which has traditionally been seen as the most important determinant of American voting behavior, must have been seriously challenged by other causal factors in 1972. For several years, voting researchers have argued that issue concerns have escaped the low levels of saliency in which they languished during the "issueless" 50's. The evidence we have just reviewed supports that argument. But how does one measure the relative weight of issue concerns and partisan predispositions in deciding an election? Even the most naive test must compare the direct effects of the various explanatory factors in a single multivariate analysis.

The results of one such multivariate analysis demonstrate that the liberal-conservative and war indices were by far the most important of the "issue proximity" measures, while the economic and cultural issues showed relatively weaker independent effects. Most crucially, however, the proximity measures, when taken together as reflecting ideology and policy voting, were substantially more important as direct explanations of the vote than was party identification. At the same time it must be noted that party identification has been theoretically interpreted as a perceptual screen or predisposing attitude that is much further removed, in a causal sense, from the actual vote decision than are either candidate assessments or attitudes on issues as measured with proximity indices. [16] For many respondents, this implies that party identification has a predisposing effect that forces images of candidates and attitudes or issues to be consistent with party attitudes which, in turn, are the factors that directly affect the vote decision. Therefore, since party identification is not coordinate in a causal sense with candidate assessments and issue attitudes, its total effect on the vote cannot be ascertained from a simple regression analysis based on one point in time.

---

[16] It might be suggested that if self-placement on the issues were used in place of the proximities, party identification might appear to be relatively more potent because these measures are more coordinate in the causal sense in which they are treated by Angus Campbell et al., *The American Voter*, p. 128. A multiple regression was therefore performed using the 1972 self-placement issue measures instead of proximities. The calculations show that some of the issues were still as important as party identification in predicting the vote. But as Kessel has pointed out, comparisons of the relative magnitude of relations using different types of question formats are fraught with methodological difficulties. The relationship between these different types of issue questions and party identification along with possible shifts in the relationship over time is quite difficult to discern. See John H. Kessel, "Comment: The Issues in Issue Voting," *American Political Science Review,* 66(1972):460–61.

Following this argument, however, the total effects of partisan attachment may be better estimated and compared with those of the proximity measures through stagewise regression analysis or from a limited causal modeling analysis using path coefficients.

In a stagewise regression [17] analysis, party identification was the first entered predictor of vote. Other variables were allowed to operate only on the remaining unexplained variance. This procedure maintains the theoretical notion that party attitudes are long-term central attitudes that heavily influence reactions to specific issues and candidates. This analysis revealed that 31 percent of the variance in the vote was explained by party identification as the first variable in the equation. After party identification, the issue proximity measures were entered into the equation and they explained an *additional* 31 percent of the variance in the vote. The beta coefficient for party identification in the equation that included the proximity measures was .19, whereas the largest single beta among the policy indices was .21—for the social index. Thus, the proximity measures of issue attitudes were exceptionally potent predictors of the vote even after controlling for party identification.

This conclusion was further strengthened with the computations of a path analysis. [18] Using a simple three-variable model with the vote, party identification, and a single composite proximity measure based on fifteen specific issues (but excluding the liberal-conservative item), we found the total effect of party identification to be .51, whereas the issue effect was .55. *As an*

---

[17] The stagewise regression employed here operated on a "case deletion" procedure; that is, a case was excluded from the analysis if missing data were encountered for any single variable used. The order of the variables entered and the beta coefficients for each variable in the final equation were as follows: party identification (.13), the liberal-conservative proximity (.11), war (.08), social (.16), economic (.03), and radical indices (.01), a measure of reaction to McGovern's campaign performance (.06), McGovern ($-$.26), and Nixon (.25) thermometer ratings. The multiple R was .82 and R² equaled .68.

[18] For a concise statement of path analysis see Donald E. Stokes, "Compound Paths in Political Analysis," in *Mathematical Applications in Political Science V*, edited by James F. Herndon and Joseph L. Bernd, (Charlottesville, Va.: University Press of Virginia, 1971), pp. 70–92.

A four-variable, multiple equation, path analysis including party identification, a single composite issue proximity measure, a composite candidate thermometer, and the vote confirms the results of the stagewise regression and the limited causal analysis presented in the text. The path coefficients and total effects summed from the several equations for the three independent variables are presented below.

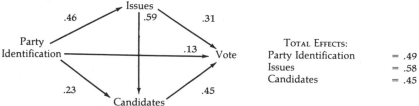

TOTAL EFFECTS:
Party Identification = .49
Issues = .58
Candidates = .45

It should be noted that the total effects are only for the model presented. This model assumes that issue attitudes are not determined by candidate ratings; thus it corresponds to the requirements for policy voting as stated in the text.

explanation of the vote in 1972, issues were at least equally as important as party identification.[19] Of course, since party identification is a preconditioning factor influencing political behavior over a long period of time, it is still somewhat inappropriate to gauge its total effect on national electoral behavior with a single cross-sectional survey. This problem simply cannot be circumvented with the present data. Nevertheless, the comparison of the party identification and issue effects clearly demonstrates the significance of policy-related evaluations as an explanation of the 1972 election outcome.

This finding is consonant with the issue polarization so clearly found, particularly among Democrats. During a period of issue consensus or strong alignment between issue orientation and traditional partisan divisions, party ties can be expected to have a significant impact, both directly and as a predisposing agent, on the vote decision. However, during periods when questions of policy attain new levels of public salience and divide the population in a fashion that is orthogonal to traditional partisan differences, other political stimuli, such as new candidates and especially candidates associated with the new issues, may become relatively more important in explaining voting behavior. If a series of new issues endure and develop a profundity and centrality that compete with the predisposing potential of party identification, a good deal of inconsistency between traditional partisan attitudes and behavior will be observed. This inconsistency may simply endure until (1) either the attitudinal differences are resolved through the disappearance of the new issues, or (2) the new issue attitudes gain ascendancy and erode the previously central partisan attitude so that it may be changed to coincide with the new issue orientation, or (3) party leaders reorient the parties and resolve the conflict. Under any circumstance other than the last, partisan realignment may occur at an ideological or cultural attitudinal level, rather than as change originating in the sociological bases of party support. Of course, the degree to which realignment could possibly occur at only the attitudinal level depends on the strength of association between new issue alignments and sociological cleavages. Furthermore, such a realignment would occur only to the extent that new partisan cues emanating from leaders and policies correspond with the new issue cleavages. A systematic investigation of the realignment question will not be entertained in this paper, but the point to be made here is that the 1972 data indicate that the direct results of the inertial, or predisposing, effects of party identification are for the first time in at least twenty years slightly less potent in determining voting behavior than are issue attitudes.

---

[19] A preliminary attempt to determine the effects of issues on the vote was made by D. M. Kovenock, P. L. Beardsley and J. W. Prothro, "Status, Party, Ideology, Issues, and Candidate Choice: A Preliminary Theory-Relevant Analysis of the 1968 American Presidential Election," paper delivered at Specialist Meeting B:XI ("New Approaches to the Study of Social Structure and Voting Behavior"), Eighth World Congress of the International Political Science Association, Munich, West Germany, 31 August—5 September 1970. It should be pointed out that contrary to what we treat as issues Kovenock et al. included reactions to individuals such as the vice-presidential candidates as an issue.

Without exploring the topic of sociocultural cleavages, it should be noted that the relative importance of party identification in the 1972 vote varied among different demographic subgroups. Comparisons across education levels are particularly interesting, for they help to explain the predominance of ideology and issues in this election. As the focus of analysis moves across educational levels from grade school to college, the bulk of the explanatory power shifts from candidate image to issues and ideology. Voters with college educations are better informed politically, generally more cognizant of policy differences between the candidates and, therefore, more likely to make a vote decision on the basis of policy preferences than are less well educated individuals. It is apparently far easier for college-educated individuals to translate issue attitudes into a vote decision than for the relatively less well educated who use the candidate as an intervening focus for their ideology. The relatively greater importance of issues as an explanation of the 1972 election may, therefore, be partially a delayed reflection of the changing composition of the electorate. This hypothesis is supported by the finding that since 1964 turnout rates among the relatively less well educated have been declining, while turnout for the college educated group has remained rather stable and, indeed, actually *increased* between 1968 and 1972. [20]

The net result of these turnout trends was a voting population (that is, those who reported actually voting) in which 37 percent had at least some college education in 1972, compared to only 26 percent in 1964. Given their generally higher level of formal education, the population of actual voters in 1972 was better prepared to respond to the candidates in terms of policy preferences than were the voters in 1964.

An additional explanation for the decreased predictive power of party identification is that partisan attachment itself had declined significantly in the population by 1972 as evidenced by an increase in the percentage of self-identified independents between 1964 and 1972. In 1964, 23 percent of the eligible electorate described themselves as independents; by 1968 that figure has risen to 30 percent; and in 1972 it was 35 percent. [21] Given this increase in independents, party identification was a meaningful predisposing factor

---

[20] Turnout in presidential elections from 1964 to 1972 was as follows:

Turnout by Education, 1964-1972

	1964	1968	1972
Grade school	68%	60%	58%
High school	78	77	70
College	89	84	87

These data are from the CPS national election surveys for the indicated years.

[21] It should be noted that independents include those individuals who lean toward one of the parties as well as those who have no tendency to identify with a party. When "leaning" independents are excluded, the percent of independents increased from 8 percent in 1964 to 13 percent in 1972. Most of this increase in independents appeared, in the aggregate, to be at the expense of the Democrats since their proportion of the electorate declined from 52 percent in 1964 to 41 percent in 1972. At the same time the proportion of Republicans remained quite stable at about 25 percent.

for a much smaller proportion of the electorate in 1972 than it had been in earlier elections. With the shrinking of partisan attachment, party loyalty could, in turn, be expected to account somewhat less powerfully for the vote decision.

If these trends in turnout and partisan identification continue, issues can be expected to play an increasingly significant role in future elections. This circumstance would obviously have a long-lasting, major influence on political behavior, particularly at the level of presidential elections. . . .

In summary, there remain abiding and predictable partisan differences between the sociological groupings defined along economic, racial, religious, and residential class lines. Generally, the groups popularly associated with the Democratic and Republican parties tended to cast their vote in proportions consistent with their long-standing attachment to either of the two parties. The short-term influences in the 1972 election had relatively little differential impact by economic class; they cut across traditional socioeconomic and demographic differences. After the affective ratings of the candidates, the next most important short-term factor accounting for the voter's decision was a liberal-conservative ideology, that is, response to the candidates in terms of a single left-right dimension. This continuum provided a simple policy yardstick by which the presidential candidates were evaluated with respect to the voters' own policy orientation. For others who were less consistently liberal or conservative in their policy orientation, particular issues proved more important in explaining the vote than did the liberal-conservative summary measure. [22] The war issue—including Vietnam policy, amnesty, and cutbacks in military spending—and the social issue—incorporating policy alternatives for dealing with urban problems and unrest, government aid to minorities, protection of individual civil liberties in criminal cases, and alternative modes for dealing with student demonstrations—were the issue domains that contributed significantly to the explanation of the vote. The economic issues and the cultural issues (abortion, equality for women, and the legalization of marijuana) proved relatively less potent. The most important revelation of the foregoing analysis was the substantial impact of the polarizing effects of specific issues relevant to the election. Indeed, when the relative contributions of the three general factors explaining the vote, namely, the candidates, parties and issues, are compared to previous elections, it becomes clear not only that this was an issue election but

---

[22] That the liberal-conservative scale is a summary policy measure is evident from its relation to the issues in table 10.2. Further evidence is derived from the finding that as more and more issues are added to a composite proximity measure, the correlation between the composite index and the liberal-conservative measure increases up to a value of about .7.

One reason why certain specific issues had an important impact on the vote in addition to the liberal-conservative effect is that about a quarter of the voters could not place themselves on that continuum. The bulk of these respondents could, however, place themselves as well as the candidates on the more specific issue questions.

that it may more appropriately be labeled an ideological election. Above all else, the outcome of the election was the result of the ideological polarization within the Democratic ranks that pitted the left-wing Democrats against those on the right.

11. Variability in Electoral Behavior: Longitudinal Perspectives from Causal Modeling

MARK A. SCHULMAN

GERALD M. POMPER

Electoral studies increasingly have sought the elaboration of relationships among ever more sophisticated survey variables. A proliferation of concepts and methods have been employed to refine or reformulate hypotheses or to describe the character of specific elections. Theoretical emphasis has shifted from initial sociological and psychological models which conceived of voting almost as a "deterministic" act [1] to those which stressed the electorate's essentially "rational" predispositions. [2] Cross-tabulation

Source: *American Journal of Political Science,* 19(1975):1–18. Reprinted with permission of The Wayne State University Press.

Acknowledgements: We acknowledge financial assistance of the University of Maryland, Eastern Shore, the courtesy in obtaining data of the Inter-University Consortium for Political Research, and the research support of the Rutgers University Research Council and the Center for Computing and Informational Services.

[1] Paul Lazarsfeld, Bernard Berelson, and Helen Gaudet, *The People's Choice,* 2d edition (New York: Columbia University Press, 1948); Bernard Berelson, Paul Lazarsfeld, and William McPhee, *Voting* (Chicago: University of Chicago Press, 1954); Eugene Burdick and Arthur Brodbeck, eds., *American Voting Behavior* (New York: Free Press, 1959); Angus Campbell, Philip E. Converse, Warren E. Miller, and Donald E. Stokes, *The American Voter* (New York: Wiley, 1960).

[2] V. O. Key, Jr., *The Responsible Electorate* (Cambridge, Mass.: Harvard University Press, 1966); Gerald M. Pomper, "From Confusion to Clarity: Issues and American Voters, 1956–1968," *American Political Science Review,* 66(1972):415–28; Richard Boyd, "Popular Control of Public Policy: A Normal Vote Analysis of the 1968 Election," *American Political Science Review,* 66(1972):429–49; Norman H. Nie with Kristi Andersen, "Mass Belief Systems Revisited: Political Change and Attitude Structure," *Journal of Politics,* 36(1974):540–91.

methods have been supplemented by new techniques, such as computer simulation, multidimensional scaling, and spatial analysis.[3]

Much of this research, however, has been based upon cross-sectional survey data, limited to a single time period (i.e., "synchronic" data).[4] Reliance on survey data derived from one election presents three related dangers. The most general problem is that such analyses tend to provide a view of society "suspended at a given moment, giving the illusion of a static structure that may be quite at variance with both theory and reality."[5] Different behaviors existing in different temporal circumstances cannot be discovered. Thus, time itself is disregarded as a variable of possible explanatory power.

This problem is illustrated by contrasting findings of time series data with those of cross-sectional surveys. The former, or "diachronic," studies have indicated a high degree of voter dynamism and responsiveness, with perhaps half of American presidential elections considered "deviating."[6] Yet analyses of single surveys have cast aspersions on the ability of the electorate to think coherently and understand issues, to discern party differences on issues, and to free itself from traditional party loyalty.

These contrasting conclusions point to the second danger of reliance on synchronic data, that of overgeneralization from time-bound data. The tendency to draw longitudinal inferences from such data is evident in *The American Voter*, whose authors concluded that "the relationships in our data reflect primarily the role of enduring partisan commitments in shaping attitudes toward politics."[7] Yet, as one of these authors later mused, such conclusions may have been a product of "investigator's misfortune" in choosing campaigns in which the tides of change were weak.[8] The original finding, while accurate for 1952 and 1956, may well have been a time-bound description rather than an enduring truth. Static description inadvertently can become commingled with general explanation.[9]

A third problem is the tendency for methodological innovation to be conjoined with synchronic data. Spurred both by the late V. O. Key's normative

---

[3] William R. Shaffer, *Computer Simulations of Voting Behavior* (New York: Oxford University Press, 1972); Jerrold G. Rusk and Herbert F. Weisberg, "Perceptions of Presidential Candidates: Implications for Electoral Change," *Midwest Journal of Political Science,* 16(1972):388–410; Samuel Kirkpatrick, "Political Attitudes and Behavior: Some Consequences of Attitudinal Ordering," *Midwest Journal of Political Science,* 14(1970):1–24; Benjamin Page and Richard Brody, "Policy Voting and the Electoral Process: The Vietnam War Issue," *American Political Science Review,* 66(1972):979–95.

[4] Mathilda White Riley and Edward Nelson, "Research on Stability and Change in Political Systems," in Bernard Barber and Alex Inkeles, eds., *Stability and Social Change* (Boston: Little, Brown, 1971).

[5] *Ibid.,* p. 408.

[6] Richard Merelman, "Electoral Instability and the American Party System," *Journal of Politics,* 32(1970):115–39.

[7] Campbell et al., *The American Voter,* p. 135.

[8] Donald E. Stokes, "Some Dynamic Elements of Contests of the Presidency," *American Political Science Review,* 62(1966):19–28, at p. 19.

[9] Ronald Brunner and Klaus Liepelt, "Data Analysis, Process Analysis, and System Change," *Midwest Journal of Political Science,* 16(1972):538–69.

concerns as well as by recent political ferment, revisionists have seriously challenged notions of the mass public's "inherent limitations." [10] These recent endorsements of voter rationality have often been based on new methodologies. Thus, RePass argues that preworded, preselected issue questions used in previous studies may have depressed issue-voting relationships existing in the data. [11] However, much of this revisionist research is based on data collected since the 1964 election. The innovative findings, therefore, may reflect changed temporal circumstances, rather than improved methodologies.

With the extensive accumulation of surveys, these problems can be met. Surveys can serve, to some extent, as a diachronic data source to test hypotheses in varying empirical situations. Theory can then be focused on the analysis of stability and change in survey variable relationships over time. As the election itself becomes the unit of analysis, replication becomes a means of establishing longitudinal data.

Prerequisites for such time-series analysis are comparable techniques and comparable data sets. Methodological and conceptual changes in survey procedures and questions, in addition to inevitable changes in salient events, limit comparative survey analysis. [12] Since election data sets are never precise duplicates of one another, variables must be carefully selected and strategies must be chosen which enhance comparability or, at least, explicate possible distorting effects caused by differences in the data. In the following analysis of three recent presidential elections we seek both to promote longitudinal research and to illustrate how some specific problems of survey comparability were satisfied.

Causal Modeling of Presidential Elections

Processes of electoral continuity and change can be examined through the causal modeling of survey data. By using the same technique in three different empirical contexts, we can begin to generalize about variability in voter behavior. Comparative causal modeling provides a convenient summary of complex, linear, multivariate relationships, relating variables frequently used in electoral research. For each election, considered separately, it promotes analysis of developmental relationships in that period. By comparing

---

[10] Philip E. Converse, "The Nature of Belief Systems in Mass Publics," in David Apter, ed., *Ideology and Discontent,* (New York: Free Press, 1964).

[11] David RePass, "Issue Salience and Party Choice," *American Political Science Review,* 65(1971):389-400; John C. Pierce, "Party Identification and the Changing Role of Ideology in American Politics," *Midwest Journal of Political Science,* 14(1970):25-42; John Field and Ronald Anderson, "Ideology and the Public's Conceptualization of the 1964 Election," *Public Opinion Quarterly,* 33(1969):380-98.

[12] John H. Kessel, "Comment: The Issues in Issue Voting," *American Political Science Review,* 66(1972):459-65.

elections, the method then permits specification of the variables as relatively stable or relatively changeable in their effects over time. [13]

For this study, the presidential elections of 1956, 1964, and 1972 have been employed. The 1956 election was, in many respects, the modal election in *The American Voter* and related analyses. [14] The 1964 election has been equally important in the research of latter-day revisionists, some of whom, including Burnham, have suggested that it might be a "critical election." [15] The 1972 results provide the most recent time point, and are of intrinsic interest because of the apparent disequilibrium they reveal. By analyzing three elections with varying substantive outcomes, and which span sixteen years of intensive scholarly research, we hopefully avoid concentration on the unique characteristics of isolated events.

The variables and method employed generally parallel those of Arthur Goldberg. [16] Seven variables are included:

1. Family Socioeconomic Partisan Predispositions: Derived from a dummy variable regression analysis of five demographic variables on the party identification of that parent who is more politically interested. [17] The five demographic variables are race, religion, region of residence, place of residence, and subjective social class.
2. Family Party Identification: Using the more interested parent, Republicans were scored 1, Democrats 0, and independents 0.5.
3. Respondent's Socioeconomic Partisan Predispositions: Operationalized in a manner similar to the family index.
4. Respondent's Party Identification: Operationalized in a manner similar to the family partisanship.
5. Candidate Evaluation: An arithmetic sum of pro-Republican and anti-Democratic candidate evaluations *minus* the total of pro-Democratic and anti-Republican candidate evaluations. [18] References to issues and parties are excluded from the measure.

---

[13] It should be understood that we do not seek to compare the absolute magnitudes of the coefficients over time. Such comparisons are inappropriate when using standardized coefficients.

[14] Reliance on the 1956 data is evident in both *The American Voter* (Campbell et al.) and *Elections and the Political Order* (Campbell et al., Wiley, 1966), and the influence of these works is also evident in subsequent research. See William Flanigan, *Political Behavior of the American Electorate,* 1st and 2d ed. (Boston: Allyn & Bacon, 1968, 1972).

[15] Walter Dean Burnham, "American Voting Behavior and the 1964 Election," *Midwest Journal of Political Science,* 12(1968):1–40.

[16] Arthur S. Goldberg, "Discerning a Causal Pattern among Data on Voting Behavior," *American Political Science Review,* 60(1966):913–22.

[17] Langton has found that the more highly politicized parent tends to have relatively more "pulling power" with regard to the transmission of party identification to offspring. In "ties" between the parents, the father's party identification is employed. See Kenneth Langton, *Political Socialization* (New York: Oxford University Press, 1969), chap 3.

[18] For a similar measure, see Stanley Kelley, Jr. and Thad W. Mirer, "The Simple Act of Voting," *American Political Science Review,* 68(1974):572–91. In the 1956 election model, FPI was established on the basis of data from a second wave with the same panel, in 1958. In 1972, only "Form 1" respondents could be employed.

6. Partisan Issue Index: Derived from a dummy variable regression analysis of the five most frequently mentioned issues in each election upon the respondent's vote.

7. Respondent's Vote: The dependent variable was scored 1 for a Republican, and 0 for a Democratic, vote. [19]

The issue variable presented the greatest problem in this analysis. We sought to construct a measure which included issues salient to each election, which was comparable among elections, and which was least subject to voter rationalization. Open-ended inquiries on the salient issues were not available in all of the surveys. Similarly, scales measuring the "proximity" of respondents and the candidates are another recent innovation, and may be affected by respondent rationalization, [20] as well. Limiting ourselves to those few questions asked in all three surveys could result in the inclusion of past issues that have faded from the "zone of relevance" [21] and the exclusion of such vital, but latter-day, questions as Vietnam. To include all questions asked would be excessive, while still excluding issues not included in the interview schedule.

The approach we adopted established an issue selection criterion based upon the five issues mentioned most frequently in a series of open-ended questions, common to all three surveys, about what the respondent likes and dislikes about candidates and parties. The Partisan Issue Index was then constructed from the respondent's position on the closed-ended equivalents of those issues. The selection criterion therefore achieves comparability over time, with the issues selected being clearly salient to each election. [22] Furthermore, by use of the respondent's actual issue position, the index specifically excludes rationalization, where the voter projects his own issue stand upon the candidate he favors. An artificial inflating of the correspondence between issue position and the vote is avoided. [23]

---

[19] Four important modifications have been made in Goldberg's analysis. Mothers, as well as fathers, are included in family characteristics. Independent voters are included. The voters' evaluations of candidates and policy questions have been separated. A separate issue index has been constructed.

[20] Richard A. Brody and Benjamin I. Page, "Comment: The Assessment of Policy Voting," *American Political Science Review,* 66(1972):450–58; Page and Brody, "Policy Voting."

[21] V. O. Key, Jr. and Frank Munger, "Social Determinism and Electoral Decision: The Case of Indiana," in Eugene Burdick and Arthur Brodbeck, eds., *American Voting Behavior* (New York: Free Press, 1959).

[22] In 1964 and 1972, a comparison of the responses to the "salient issue" and "like-dislike" questions shows high correspondence in the issues selected. This result heightens our confidence in the salience of the issues employed. Cf. RePass, "Issue Salience."

[23] In contrast, see the emphasis on subjectivity rationality through the use of proximity indices by Michael Shapiro, "Rational Political Man: A Synthesis of Economic and Social-Psychological Perspectives," *American Political Science Review,* 63(1969):1106–19, and Arthur H. Miller, Warren E. Miller, Alden S. Raine, and Thad A. Brown, "A Majority Party in Disarray: Policy Polarization in the 1972 Election," paper presented at the annual meeting of the American Political Science Association, New Orleans, 1973. In our view, indices constructed from proximity measures do not gauge if the voter has any information about the issue or if he perceives candidate or party differences correctly.

The variables are ordered as follows: (1) Family Socioeconomic Political Predispositions; (2) Family Party Identification; (3) Respondent's Socioeconomic Political Predispositions; (4) Respondent's Party Identification; (5) Partisan Issues Index; (6) Candidate Evaluation; (7) Respondent's Vote. While the correct ordering of variables cannot be determined by statistical derivation,[24] the variable ordering follows established practice and theory. Party identification temporally precedes the issues and candidates of a particular election, as has been shown in past electoral research and socialization studies.[25] Issues, in turn, tend to be more long-standing than the particular candidates running in a given election.[26] In our particular cases, moreover, some of the issues are present in more than one election, while there was no overlap of candidates.

After ordering the variables, the paths in the model were solved through a series of multiple regressions, with nonsignificant relationships eliminated.[27] Each variable is treated as a dependent variable in a multiple regression, with the independent variable being all variables in the model for which there is a single direct path to that dependent variable.

From 1956 to 1972

Figure 11.1, a causal model of the 1956 election using standardized regression coefficients or beta weights, reflects the "dual mediation" model developed by Goldberg. The model has several distinctive features. First, party identification is the "pivotal encapsulator" of prior political socialization, with no direct links between background socioeconomic characteristics and the respondent's vote. As Goldberg notes, the omission of direct causal links between these variables and voting behavior, as well as the omission of such a link between childhood sociological characteristics and adult party identification "certainly justify the qualms of the authors of *The American Voter* about the sociological explanations of voting behavior."[28]

Second, Goldberg reported a "dual mediation" of the respondent's vote by party identification and a Partisan Political Attitudes index. However, the attitude index was one of the more unsatisfactory aspects of Goldberg's work because it combined both candidate evaluations and issues. In light of current interest in issue voting, the effects of these two variables were calcu-

---

[24] Hugh Forbes and Edward Tufte, "A Note of Caution in Causal Modeling," *American Political Science Review,* 62(1968):1258–64; Hubert M. Blalock, Jr., ed., *Causal Models in the Social Sciences* (Chicago: Aldine-Atherton, 1971).

[25] Campbell et al., *The American Voter,* chap. 7; Fred I. Greenstein, *Children and Politics,* (New Haven: Yale University Press, 1965), chap. 4.

[26] Stokes, "Some Dynamic Elements," pp. 20–22.

[27] The significant paths (p < .001) were the same in each of the three elections, with the exception in 1972 of FSPP/RSPP. This path is retained as a dashed line in the 1972 diagram solely for comparability.

[28] Goldberg, "Discerning a Causal Pattern," p. 919.

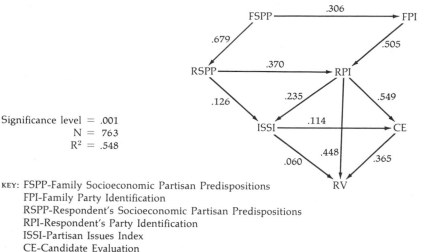

Significance level = .001
N = 763
R² = .548

KEY: FSPP-Family Socioeconomic Partisan Predispositions
FPI-Family Party Identification
RSPP-Respondent's Socioeconomic Partisan Predispositions
RPI-Respondent's Party Identification
ISSI-Partisan Issues Index
CE-Candidate Evaluation
RV-Respondent's Vote

Figure 11.1 Causal model of the 1956 presidential election (beta weights).

lated separately in figure 11.1. The result indicates that the preponderance of Goldberg's RPA path to the vote (.596 in his model) is accounted for by candidate evaluations, with both the direct and indirect (through CE) paths from the issue index to vote being very weak. [29] Reviewing the link between party identification and the vote, both RPI's direct path (.448) and its indirect path through candidate evaluations (.200) remain strong. At the same time, the path between respondent's party identification and the issue index, while significant (.235), must engender support for those researchers who have emphasized the often "nonrational" nature of party identification.

In summary, the 1956 election may still be viewed as being dominated by a dual mediation process. However, the dual mediators are party identification and candidate evaluation, with issues only weakly linked to the vote. The model seemingly comports well with *The American Voter*'s conclusion, cited previously, that "the relationships in our data reflect primarily the role of enduring partisan commitments in shaping attitudes toward politics." [30]

The 1964 model, in figure 11.2, using variables identical with those in the 1956 analysis, reveals a pattern quite distinct from 1956. For the most part, moreover, these differences continue to be evident in the 1972 model, in figure 11.3, indicating that the contest between Johnson and Goldwater was not a completely unique event. Three implications are suggested by these new patterns.

[29] In this case, the indirect path is obtained by multiplying the following:
ISSI/CE·CE/RV.
[30] Campbell et al., *The American Voter*, p. 135.

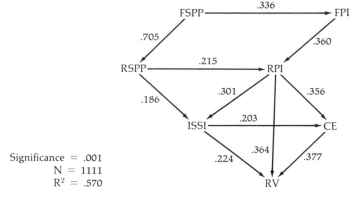

Figure 11.2 Causal model of the 1964 presidential election.

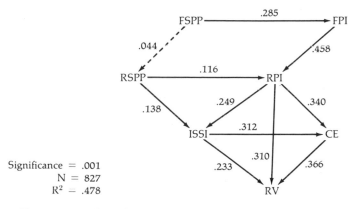

Figure 11.3 Causal model of the 1972 presidential election.

First, we see an evident breakdown in the New Deal's socioeconomic party coalitions. The older generation shows a rather stable effect of demographic characteristics on party identification, measured as the path from FSPP to FPI. However, this relationship is fast diminishing among current voters. The relationship between socioeconomic variables and partisanship weakens from one election to the next, as shown in the very low beta weight in 1972 for RSPP-RPI.

A shift in the nature of the partisan coalitions is also shown by the falling into insignificance in 1972 of the path between FSPP and RSPP. Compound path analysis reveals the same conclusions, showing that most of the transmission of partisanship between the generations now occurs through FPI, by

Table 11.1   Compound Path Coefficients to Respondent Vote

Path	1956		1964		1972	
	Coeff.	Relative Importance*	Coeff.	Relative Importance*	Coeff.	Relative Importance*
Direct: RPI/RV	.448	66.6	.364	61.8	.310	59.5
Through Candidate: RPI/CE/RV	.200	29.8	.134	22.8	.125	23.9
Through Issues: RPI/ISSI/RV	.014	2.1	.067	11.4	.058	11.1
Through Issues and Candidate: RPI/ISSI/CE/RV	.010	1.5	.023	3.9	.028	5.4
Total	.672	100.0	.588	99.9	.521	99.9

*Figures in this column are the percentages of the total relationship between RPI and RV which are explained by the given paths.

tradition itself, rather than by the replication of the relationship of demographic variables to the current electorate's loyalty. [31]

Second, the importance of issues to the vote has been enhanced considerably. This development is evident in 1964 both in terms of the direct impact of issues (.224) and their indirect path through candidate evaluation (.076). In 1972, the impact of issues was still greater, both marginally in a direct fashion (.233) and particularly as issues affect the evaluation of candidates and the resultant vote (.114).

Concurrently, there has been a decline in the impact of partisanship on the vote. This decline is evident in the simple path from party loyalty to the vote, where there is a continuous drop in weight from 1956 to 1964 and, again, from 1964 to 1972. The decline is evident as well in the complex paths. Candidate evaluations have become far more independent of party loyalty, while the controlled influence of such evaluations on the vote has remained largely unchanged. The importance of party identification remains, but it is seemingly more than a simple reflection of traditional loyalty. An increasing proportion of its impact is through the relationship with issue preferences.

---

[31] Compound path coefficients are calculated as the product of the simple path coefficients. With RPI as the dependent variable, the following compound relationships result:

	FSPP/RSPP/RPI	FSSP/FPI/RPI
1956	.251	.155
1964	.152	.121
1972	.005	.131

The relative importance of the political variables can be gauged by analysis of the compound paths between respondent's party identification and the vote. While the direct path between the two variables remains primary, as seen in table 11.1, the contribution of the indirect paths through the issue index has risen considerably. [32] Excluded from the model are those issue preferences which influence party identification itself. Therefore, the total impact of issues on the vote in these years is underestimated. [33]

Alternative Explanations

The most obvious difference in these elections is the apparently greater importance of issue preferences in 1964 and 1972. The vote has become less determined by sociological characteristics and traditional loyalties and is more affected by the electorate's position on public policy and its corresponding evaluation of the candidates. Such influences bring results as disparate as the Democratic landslide of 1964 and the overwhelming Nixon triumph eight years later.

To explain these changes in the level of issue voting since 1956, one might hypothesize that a new, issue-oriented younger generation in 1964 and 1972 replaced older, less issue-conscious cohorts. [34] To examine generational shift, the magnitudes of issue-voting paths for 1956 age cohorts were compared, in table 11.2, to those of their generational cohorts in 1964 (age in 1956 + 8 years) and in 1972 (age in 1956 + 16 years). If common generational learning experiences were responsible for low levels of issue voting in 1956, similarly low levels should be evident within the same cohorts across the three elections. Little variation would appear, then, in the rows of table 11.2. If a new issue-oriented generation is changing global voting behavior, the highest coefficients would be evident in the first entry in each column.

Data in table 11.2 soundly disconfirm the generational shift hypothesis. While new voters in 1964 and 1972 demonstrate greater issue responsiveness than the older 1956 cohorts they presumably replaced, a substantial increase in issue voting is evident across time in all generational cohorts (rows in table 11.2.) In fact, viewing each election separately, it is not necessarily the new voters who demonstrate the greatest influence of issues on their votes. Although the aged might be considered inflexible by some, they

[32] Warren E. Miller and Donald E. Stokes, "Constituency Influence in Congress," in Campbell et al., *Elections and the Political Order.*

[33] H. Daudt, *Floating Voters and the Floating Vote,* (Leiden: Stenfert Kroese, 1961).

[34] Mathilda White Riley, "Aging and Cohort Succession: Interpretations and Misinterpretations," *Public Opinion Quarterly,* 36(1973):35–49; Neal E. Cutler, "Generation, Maturation, and Party Affiliation: A Cohort Analysis," *Public Opinion Quarterly,* 23(1969–1970):583–92.

Table 11.2 Direct Paths From Partisan Issue Index to Respondent's Vote, by Generational and Maturational Cohorts

Generational Cohort	Age in 1956	Age in 1972	1956	1964	1972
		18–25			.244
		26–33		.220	.162
1	18–25	34–41	.121	.277	.323
2	26–33	42–49	.116	.279	.217
3	34–41	50–57	.074	.169	.168
4	42–49	58–65	.039	.258	.206
5	50–57	66 & older	.016	.253	.268
6	58–65		−.008	.123	
7	66 & older		.035		

show more responsiveness to issues, particularly in 1972, than do many younger cohorts.

Parenthetically, the data also permit us to draw some inferences about life-cycle or maturational effects on voting behavior. If the life cycle is a predominant influence, relatively little variation should be present along the diagonal lines of table 11.2, which indicate the same life-cycle age groupings. Furthermore, if aging reduces susceptibility to issue influences, as is implied in *The American Voter*,[35] the coefficients across the horizontal rows should diminish. Precisely the opposite conclusions must be drawn from the data. There is wide variation along the diagonals and a general increase along the horizontal rows. Maturity does not mean rigidity.[36]

The generational shift hypothesis fails to explain the heightened association between issue preferences and the vote. To pursue the subject, an analysis of variance was undertaken. Of the total variance, 74.5 percent is explained by the elections (columns in table 11.2), and the degree of explanation is even higher when we compare the 1956 cohorts to either 1964 or

[35] Campbell et al., *The American Voter*, p. 165.

[36] This conclusion is in keeping with new findings in developmental psychology, where many heretofore hypothesized "maturational" differences, such as cognitive abilities and intelligence levels, are now viewed as products of "generational" differences. See K. Warner Schaie and C. R. Crother, "A Cross-Sectional Study of Age Changes in Cognitive Behavior," *Psychological Bulletin*, (1968):671–80.

Table 11.3 Direct Paths From Partisan
Issue Index to Vote,
by Educational Levels

Educational Level	1956	1964	1972
Grades 0–8	.008	.158	.213
Grades 9–12	.094	.189	.217
College	.109	.295	.258

1972 alone. Voting behavior appears quite distinct in these latter two contests. [37]

A second possible reason for upward shifts in issue voting might be the
increasing educational achievement among the electorate from 1956 to 1972.
Table 11.3 presents the results of controlling for level of education. Substantial increases in issue voting are apparent at every level in 1964 compared to
1956, and this development generally continues in 1972. Interestingly, issue
voting was more pronounced in 1964 and 1972 among respondents in the
lowest educational categories than among college-educated voters in 1956.
The electorate in the latter two elections was responding quite differently
than in 1956, and the transformation is evident throughout the national
sample. We must therefore reject the hypothesis that educational upgrading
explains these results.

Given the inability of demographic variables to account for heightened
issue voting, the most obvious explanation must be offered, namely, politics
itself—the contrasting circumstances and styles of the three elections and
their impacts on the electorate. In 1956, according to Kelley,[38] both Eisenhower and Stevenson described their policy positions in terms so general
that "their statements lacked any clear relation to issues on which voters had
to decide."

> Both were for peace, social welfare, full justice for farmers, honest govern-
> ment, a strong national defense, the expansion of civil liberties, full em-
> ployment, the development of individual talents, a vigorous economy, a
> flourishing world trade, and a large number of other objectives of similarly
> general appeal . . . (A)t no time did either candidate declare himself to be
> opposed to any statement of fundamental belief that his opponent had
> advanced.

What major differences which may have existed did not transform themselves into affective and cognitive links with the voters.

---

[37] The correlation ratio is .770 for 1956–1964 and .784 for 1956–1972. It is a stark zero for
the comparison of 1964–1972, indicating the great similarity of results within age cohorts in
this pair.

[38] Stanley Kelley, Jr., *Political Campaigning* (Washington, D.C.: Brookings Institution,
1960).

By contrast, the 1964 and 1972 campaigns surely marked a departure from "Tweedledum-Tweedledee" politics. Offering "a choice, not an echo," the Johnson-Goldwater contest presented the electorate with two clearly different sets of domestic and foreign blueprints, with Goldwater representing a challenge to the New Deal legacy of "positive government." Sharp differences between the candidates were also evident in 1972, and were perceived as such by the voters. Regardless of their own positions on the issues, the electorate saw McGovern as quite dovish and welfare-minded, and Nixon as more aggressive in Vietnam and economically conservative.[39] With a choice available, the voters chose.

Conclusions

Using comparable survey variables and causal modeling techniques, we have sought to gain a longitudinal perspective on two divergent sets of hypotheses on voting behavior, both of which were derived largely from synchronic, cross-sectional survey analysis. The first hypotheses stress continuity and stability, with the electorate viewed as the captive of "inherent limitations." The second, which might be termed, after Key, the "voters-are-not-fools" hypotheses, find the electorate capable of acting responsibly. Three elections, spanning sixteen years, each featuring an incumbent president, were compared.

The 1956 election comported well with the continuity paradigm exemplified by *The American Voter:* (1) party identification was the "pivotal encapsulator" of prior political socialization, with a strong linkage between parents' partisan attachments and those of the voter; (2) links between party identification and issue positions were not as strong as in 1964, raising questions about the ability of political parties to aggregate issues meaningfully for purposes of electoral competition; (3) the voting decision was mediated primarily by party identification and candidate evaluations; (4) issues were only weakly associated with the voting decision, indicating the electorate's inability to discern them.

The 1964 and 1972 elections, by contrast, present portraits of the electorate which better conform to the "voters-are-not-fools" model. The findings indicate that: (1) the linkages between demographic factors and family tradition to offspring's partisanship diminished considerably; (2) while party identification was still a significant indicator of the vote, it remained so partially because of the greater weight of the paths from partisanship through issues; and (3) issues played a meaningful role in the voting decision. These changes cannot be explained by generational or educational alterations in the electorate.

---

[39] McGovern was seen as more "dovish" on the 1972 "Vietnam action scale" and more inclined to "social solutions" on the "urban unrest scale" by a majority of respondents in every response category. Cf. Miller et al., "Majority Party in Disarray."

Thus, the voters are capable of a wide range of behaviors and are not "inherently limited." In the appropriate circumstances, such as the intense contests of 1964 and 1972, the electorate will respond to issue differences between the candidates. We do not believe that the finding of increased issue voting can be explained simply by the use of new methodological and conceptual tools. The relationship of issues to the vote was not constant during this period, nor disguised by flawed techniques. Rather, actual changes in the level of issue voting may now be inferred from 1956 through 1964 and 1972.

Finally, our most general conclusion is that theory generated from any single election must, necessarily, be incomplete and static. Voters must be studied comparatively, in a variety of empirical and temporal contexts. In doing so, we have found reason to support Key's view that "the electorate behaves about as rationally and responsibly as we should expect, given the clarity of the alternatives presented to it and the character of the information available to it."[40]

---

[40] Key, *The Responsible Electorate,* p. 7.

12. The "Responsible Electorate" of 1968

PHILIP E. CONVERSE
WARREN E. MILLER
JERROLD G. RUSK
ARTHUR C. WOLFE

. . . . In describing the current of discontent that swirled around the Democratic party and the White House in 1968, we indicated that disgruntled Democrats rather indiscriminately supported McCarthy in the earliest primaries, but soon began to sort themselves into those staying with McCarthy versus those shifting to Nixon or Wallace, according to their more precise policy grievances on the major issues of Vietnam, civil rights, and the problem of "law and order." By the time of the election, the sorting had become remarkably clean: in particular, differences in issue position between Wallace supporters and what we have called the McCarthy hard core are impressive in magnitude.

Even more generally, 1968 seems to be a prototypical case of the election that does not produce many changes of policy preferences but does permit electors to sort themselves and the candidates into groups of substantial homogeneity on matters of public policy. This trend over the course of the

SOURCE: "Continuity and Change in American Politics: Parties and Issues in the 1968 Election," *American Political Science Review*, 63(1969):1095–1101. Reprinted with permission of the publisher.

EDITORS' NOTE: The following is an excerpt from the SRC report on the 1968 election. It is based on a representative national sample of 1,559 citizens of voting age, most of them interviewed both before and after election day.

campaign calls to mind the posthumous contention of V. O. Key, in *The Responsible Electorate,* that the mass electorate is a good deal less irrational, ill-informed or sheep-like than it had become fashionable to suppose. He presented empirical materials to develop a counter-image of "an electorate moved by concern about central and relevant questions of public policy, of governmental performance, and of executive personality."[1] He argued that in a general way voters behaved rationally and responsibly, or at least as rationally and responsibly as could be expected in view of the pap they were frequently fed by contending politicians, while recognizing in the same breath that contentions of this unequivocal nature were necessarily over-statements.

To our point of view, Key's general thesis represented a welcome corrective on some earlier emphases, but his findings were hardly as discontinuous with earlier work as was often presumed, and the "corrective" nature of his argument has itself become badly exaggerated at numerous points. We cannot begin to examine here the many facets of his thesis that deserve comment. However, several features of the 1968 campaign seem to us to demonstrate admirably the importance of the Key corrective, while at the very same time illustrating vividly the perspective in which that corrective must be kept.

It is obvious, as Key himself recognized, that flat assertions about the electorate being rational or not are of scant value. In New Hampshire, as we have observed earlier, Democrats exasperated at Johnson's lack of success with the Vietnam War voted for Eugene McCarthy as an alternative. The relationship between this disapproval and the vote decision is exactly the type of empirical finding that Key musters in profusion from a sequence of seven presidential elections as his main proof of voter rationality and responsibility. In the New Hampshire case, however, we might probe the data a little farther to discover that more often than not, McCarthy voters were upset that Johnson had failed to scourge Vietnam a good deal more vigorously with American military might, which is to say they took a position diametrically opposed to that of their chosen candidate. This realization might shake our confidence somewhat in the preceding "proof" of voter rationality. But then we push our analysis still another step and find that many of the New Hampshire people fuming about Vietnam in a hawkish mood voted for McCarthy without having any idea of where he stood on the matter. Hence while they may have voted directly counter to their own policy preferences, they at least did not know this was what they were doing, so the charge of irrationality may be a bit ungenerous. In the most anemic sense of "rationality," one that merely implies people have perceived reasons for their behavior, these votes perhaps remain "rational."

However, when we reflect on the rather intensive coverage given by the national mass media to Eugene McCarthy's dissenting position on Vietnam

---

[1] V. O. Key, Jr., *The Responsible Electorate: Rationality in Presidential Voting, 1936-1960* (Cambridge, Mass.: Belknap Press, 1966), pp. 7-8.

212

for many months before the New Hampshire primary, and consider how difficult it must have been to avoid knowledge of the fact, particularly if one had more than the most casual interest in the Vietnam question, we might continue to wonder how lavishly we should praise the electorate as "responsible." Here, as at so many other points, pushing beyond the expression of narrow and superficial attitudes in the mass public to the cognitive texture which underlies the attitudes is a rather disillusioning experience. It is regrettable that none of the data presented in *The Responsible Electorate* can be probed in this fashion.

Key was interested in showing that the public reacted in a vital way to central policy concerns, at least as selected by the contending political factions, and was not driven mainly by dark Freudian urges, flock instinct, or worse still, the toss of a coin. With much of this we agree wholeheartedly. In addition, to put the discussion in a slightly different light, let us imagine, in a vein not unfamiliar from the literature of the 1950's, that voting decisions in the American electorate might be seen as a function of reactions to party, issue and candidate personality factors. Let us imagine furthermore that research suggests that these determinants typically have relative weight in our presidential elections of 60 for the party factor, and 40 divided between the issue and candidate determinants. The exact figures are, of course, quite fanciful but the rough magnitudes continue to be familiar. Since classical assumptions about voting behavior have attributed overweening weight to the issue factor, it is scarcely surprising that investigative attention shifts heavily away from that factor to the less expected party and candidate influences. If the issue factor draws comment at all, the finding of greatest interest is its surprisingly diluted role.

It is at this point that the Key volume exerts its most useful influence. Key points out that there *is*, after all, an issue factor, and he develops an analytic format which dramatizes the role that issue reactions do play. This dramatic heightening is achieved by focusing attention on voters who are shifting their vote from one party to the other over a pair of elections. If we set for ourselves the explanatory chore of understanding why the change which occurs moves in the direction it did, it is patently evident that the party factor—which merely explains the abiding finding that "standpatters" persistently outnumber "changers" by factors usually greater than four—is to be set aside as irrelevant. If this in turn leaves candidate and issue factors sharing the explanatory burden, our sense of the relative importance of the issue factor is, of course, radically increased, even though it is our question that has changed, rather than anything about the empirical lay of the land. Key was quite explicit in his desire to explain movement and change in the electorate, rather than voting behavior in a more general sense, and there is no gainsaying the fact that from many points of view it is indeed the change—marginal gains and losses—which forms the critical part of the story of elections.

In our analyses of such changes in the national vote over the course of presidential elections in the 1950's and 1960's we have been impressed with the magnitude of the effects introduced as new candidates focus on different issues of public policy, and as external events give particular candidate-issue intersections greater salience for the nation.[2] However, 1968 provides an opportunity to examine relative weights of party, candidate and issue factors under more varied circumstances than United States presidential elections usually proffer. We have talked above for illustrative purposes as though there were "standard" relative weights that would pertain for these three factors in some situation-free way. This is of course not the case: we can imagine many kinds of elections which would vastly shift the weights of such factors, if indeed they can be defined at all.

The Wallace movement is a good case in point. By Key's definition nobody who voted for Wallace could have been a "standpatter": all must be classed as "changers." Therefore party identification as a motivating factor accounting for attraction to Wallace is forced back to zero, and any variance to be understood must have its roots distributed between Wallace's attraction as a personality and the appeal of the issue positions that he advocated.[3]

In point of fact, the Wallace candidacy was reacted to by the public as an *issue* candidacy, a matter which our data make clear in several ways. For example, about half of the reasons volunteered by our respondents for favorable feelings toward Wallace had to do with positions he was taking on current issues; only a little more than a quarter of the reactions supporting either of the two conventional candidates were cast in this mode. Still more noteworthy is the relative purity of the issue feelings among the Wallace clientele where the major controversies of 1968 were concerned. Among the *whites* who voted for one of the two major candidates, only 10 percent favored continued segregation rather than desegregation or "something in between"; among Wallace voters, all of whom were white, almost 40 percent wanted segregation. Where the issue of "law and order" was concerned, a substantial portion of the voters felt that Mayor Daley's police had used about the right amount of force in quelling the Chicago demonstrations.* However, among white voters for Nixon or Humphrey, the remainder of the opinion was fairly evenly split between criticizing the police for using too

---

[2] Donald E. Stokes, "Some Dynamic Elements of Contests for the Presidency," *American Political Science Review*, 60(March 1966):19–28.

[3] This is not to say that it would be inconceivable for identification with one of the two traditional parties to correlate with preference for some third-party candidate. For example, it is possible that most of the voters for Henry Wallace's Progressive Party in 1948 were identified with the Democratic Party. However, it is clear that in such an instance "party loyalty" would have been a rather spurious name for the motivating factor. In the case of George Wallace, even this kind of spurious correlation is absent, except insofar as his Democratic origins and the invisibility of his American Independent Party label made it easy for Democrats to support him. Indeed, in the context of this argument it will be fascinating to discover whether Republicans and Democrats invoked different images of Wallace's party location in order to satisfy their need for consonance while voting for a man who reflects their own issue commitments.

* [This reference is to the demonstrations at the 1968 Democratic national nominating convention.]

much force or too little, with a small majority (55 percent) favoring the latter "tough line." Among Wallace voters, the comparable ratio was 87–13 favoring a tougher policy. Or again, 36 percent of white voters for the conventional parties felt we should "take a stronger stand (in Vietnam) even if it means invading North Vietnam." Among Wallace voters, the figure was 67 percent. Much more generally speaking, it may be observed that all Wallace voters were exercised by strong discontents in at least one of these three primary domains, and most were angry about more than one. Wallace was a "backlash" candidate, and there is no question but that the positions communicated to the public and accounted for his electoral support in a very primary sense. The pattern of correlations between issue positions and the vote for these "changers" would support Key's thesis of a "rational" and "responsible" electorate even more impressively than most of the data he found for earlier elections.

Another way of organizing these preference materials helps to illuminate even more sharply the contrast between the bases of Wallace support and those of the conventional candidates. It will be recalled that all respondents were asked to give an affective evaluation of each of the three candidates taken separately, along with other aspirants. If we examine the pattern of correlations between issue positions and the ratings of Humphrey, Nixon and Wallace, we capture gradations of enthusiasm, indifference, and hostility felt toward each man instead of the mere vote threshold, and we can explore the antecedents or correlates of the variations in sentiment toward the individual candidates.

Where the ratings of Wallace given by whites are concerned, patterns vary somewhat South and non-South, but substantial correlations with issue positions appear everywhere. In the South, the most generic question of civil rights policy shows a relation of .49 (gamma) with Wallace reactions; the most generic question on "law and order" shows a .39; and the central Vietnam policy question shows a relationship of .30. Party identification, however, shows a relation of only .04. Other ancillary questions probing more specific aspects of policy feelings in these areas vary around the most generic items somewhat, but tend to show fairly similar magnitudes of relationship. Outside the South, patterns are a little less sharp but remain unequivocal. Instead of the above correlations of .49, .39 and .30 in the main issue domains, the figures are .25 (civil rights), .27 (law and order), and .25 (Vietnam). The relationship of party identification to Wallace ratings among whites, however, is .01. Thus it is true in both regions that party identification is entirely dwarfed by any of several issue positions in predicting reactions to Wallace among whites, and in terms of "variance accounted for" the differences between issues and party would best be expressed in terms of *order of magnitude*.

Differences that are almost as sharp turn up in the relationships surrounding the ratings of Nixon and Humphrey. Here, however, everything is exactly reversed: it is *party* that towers over all other predictors, and the central 1968 issues tend to give rather diminutive relationships. Thus comparable correlations (gammas) between partisanship and candidate ratings all run between .36 and .44, varying only slightly by region and man. Where Nixon is concerned, the average correlation values for issue items in the three main domains emphasized in the 1968 election never get as high as .10, and fall as low as .01, with the central tendency about .05. Where Humphrey is concerned, somewhat higher issue values are observed, varying between .05 and .25 according to the region and the domain. Moreover, there is another issue domain not hitherto cited in which average values over three items for Humphrey considerably outstrip the Wallace correlation in both North and South. Significantly, this is the domain of items concerning governmental social welfare activities that one might associate with the period running from the New Deal through the 1950's.[4] Nevertheless, averaging correlations across all of these issue domains (the obsolescing as well as the three most salient in 1968) suggests that party identification still accounts for three to five times as much variance in Humphrey ratings as does the average issue among the eighteen issues posed in the study. These correlation patterns are summarized by region in table 12.1.

Such dramatic comparisons between types of support for Wallace on one hand and the conventional candidates on the other may be perplexing to the casual reader who is keeping the thesis of V. O. Key in mind. After all, it is the pattern of Wallace support that shows the kind of strong issue orientation Key sought to demonstrate, whereas evaluations of both Humphrey and Nixon seem to show a strong factor of traditional party allegiance suffocating most issue concerns into relative obscurity. Yet the span of time Key's data covered limited him almost completely to observation of races of the routine Humphrey-Nixon type. Did these earlier two-party races look more like the Wallace patterns for some unknown reason?

The answer, of course, is very probably not. However, if we set the Wallace phenomenon in 1968 aside and limit our attention in the Key fashion to two contrasting groups of "changers" between the 1964 and 1968 election (Johnson to Nixon; Goldwater to Humphrey) we can show correlations with issue differences which look very much like those presented in cross-tabulations by Key for earlier elections: some strong, some weak, but nearly always "in the right direction." There are, to be sure, other problems of interpretation surrounding such correlations that one would need to thrash out before accepting the Key evidence fully.[5] But our principal point here is the

---

[4] Another domain of issues surrounding the "cold war" as it confronted the nation in the 1950's with controversies over foreign aid and trade with communist countries shows only modest correlations with the candidate rankings, and Nixon and Humphrey ratings show more of a parity with the Wallace correlations, although in an absolute sense the latter continue to outrun the former sharply in the South and mildly elsewhere. See table 12.1.

[5] These include such considerations as that of the causal direction underlying the observed relationships; or known and systematic biases in recollection of a presidential vote four years later; or the superficiality of the issues that show such patterns, as opposed to issues thought basic by sophisticated observers; or blatant misinformation supporting the issue positions registered; or a tendency for the less informed to "shift" more quickly than the better informed, with position on any given issue held constant, etc.

Table 12.1 Correlations Between Issue Positions, Partisanship and Affective Ratings of the Major Candidates (Whites Only)[a]

Issue Domain	Non-South			South		
	Humphrey	Nixon	Wallace	Humphrey	Nixon	Wallace
A. Civil rights (6 or 7 items)[b]	.17	.09	.27	.24	.08	.41
B. Law and order (2 items)	.25	.05	.27	.19	.01	.35
C. Vietnam (2 items)	.05	.03	.23	.14	.02	.26
D. Cold war (4 items)	.12	.11	.15	.16	.05	.28
E. Social welfare (2 or 3 items)[b]	.22	.20	.09	.26	.13	.10
F. Federal gov't too powerful? (1 item)	.37	.18	.17	.49	.13	.15
Sum: 18 issue items	.19	.10	.20	.22	.07	.31
Sum: Three major 1968 issue domains (A,B,C)	.16	.07	.26	.22	.07	.37
Partisanship (3 items)	.47	.47	.04	.39	.36	.03

[a] Cell entries are average absolute values of gamma ordinal correlations between items of the types listed in the rows and affective ratings of the candidates noted in the columns.

[b] An item having to do with the role of the federal government in aid to local education was considered a social welfare item outside the South, but a civil rights issue within that region.

simple one that even with Wallace analytically discarded from the 1968 scene, the rest of the 1968 data seem perfectly compatible with the data Key used. The only reason there may seem to be a discontinuity, then, is due to the different nature of the question being asked by Key which, by focusing on marginal change from election to election, effectively defines party loyalty out of the explanation and correspondingly opens the way for greater orienting weight for issues.

It is because the change in vote division from election to election is so critical that V. O. Key's contribution is a welcome corrective. On the other hand, the configurations of 1968 data we have summarized here help to put that contribution into perspective. The patterns of Wallace support show how empirical data *can* look when issues play a strongly orienting role. The contrasts between these patterns and those generated by routine two-party politics may help to suggest why investigators have tended to be more impressed by the feeble role of issues than by their strength.

The lessons to be drawn are several. One is a simple point of methodology. It has been suggested upon occasion in the past that relationships between issue positions and voting choice turn out to be as pallid as they usually are because investigators fail to ask the right questions or word them in confusing ways. We feel that improvement in these matters is always possible. However, we have seen that exactly the same issue items which continue to look pallid in accounting for assessments of Humphrey and Nixon blaze forth into rather robust correlations where Wallace is concerned. Hence we conclude that poor item choice scarcely accounts for past findings.

Another lesson is more substantive. Some past findings have been to our mind "overinterpreted" as implying that issues are poorly linked to voting preferences because of innate and hence incorrigible cognitive deficiencies suffered by the mass electorate in the United States.[6] Merely the Wallace data taken alone would suffice to show, exactly as Key argued, that the public can relate policy controversies to its own estimates of the world and vote accordingly. The fact that it does not display this propensity on any large scale very often invites more careful spelling out of the conditions under which it will or will not.

It seems clear from the 1968 data that one of the cardinal limiting conditions is the "drag" or inertia represented by habitual party loyalties: as soon as features of the situation limit or neutralize the relevance of such a factor, issue evaluations play a more vital role. Much research has shown that partisanship is fixed early in life and tends to endure. As the individual moves through the life cycle, old political controversies die away and new ones arise toward which at least some individuals crystallize opinions. While the parties try to lead this new opinion formation among their faithful, and probably succeed on a modest scale, there are many independent sources of such opinion for the citizen. The average citizen either does not know his party's position well enough to be influenced on many matters, or if he knows, frequently resists the influence. As a result, policy opinions are very loosely or anachronistically linked to party preference at any point in time. But in the moment of truth in the polling booth, party allegiance seems the most relevant cue for many voters *if conditions permit it to be used.*

Another type of condition which mediates the links between citizen position on issues and voting choice is the "objective" degree of difference between parties or candidates with respect to policy controversy, or the clarity with which any objective difference gets communicated to the populace. In every United States election there are accusations from one quarter or another that the two conventional parties provide no more than "Tweedledee" and "Tweedledum" candidates. However, these accusations as aired in the public media rose to something of a crescendo in 1968 from both the Wallace and the McCarthy perspectives. And even as measured a source as *The*

---

[6] We much prefer an interpretation which hinges on a general inattention which is endemic because information costs are relatively high where little information is already in hand, and the stakes are rarely seen as being very large. While such a "condition" is likely to persist in mass electorates, there is nothing about it which is immutable given the proper convergence of circumstances.

New York Times noted wrily that it would take no more than the deletion of two or three codicils to make the official 1968 campaign platforms of the Democratic and Republican parties into utterly undistinguishable documents. If the main discriminable difference between Humphrey and Nixon began and ended with the party label then it would certainly not be surprising that the public sorted itself into voting camps by party allegiance and little more, save where Wallace was concerned. In this case, the public would be limited to exactly that "echo chamber" role which Key ascribed to it.

As a matter of pure logic, nobody can deny that policy differentiation between parties is likely to be a precondition for meaningful relationships between policy feelings and partisan voting decisions. Our only problem here is to evaluate whether the party/issue data configurations surrounding Humphrey and Nixon are the obvious result of some lack of policy difference peculiar to 1968, or represent instead some more abiding feature of presidential voting in the United States. Unfortunately, there is no obvious way to arrive at an objective measurement of "degree of party difference." Perhaps the closest approximation is to ask the public how clear the differences appear to be. Nevertheless, since some people invariably feel party differences are big and others feel they are non-existent, even this approach leaves one without reference points as to "how big is big" where reports of this kind are concerned, except inasmuch as trends in such reports can be observed over periods of time. In this light, it can be said while reports of "important differences" between the Democrats and the Republicans were slightly fewer in 1968 than in 1964 (the year of Goldwater's "choice, not an echo"), they show a reasonable parity with such reports for 1952 and 1960. Hence in the public eye, at least, differences between what the major parties stand for were not lacking in unusual degree in 1968.

It may be useful to note that whereas we have labeled the Wallace effort in 1968 an "issue candidacy" from the point of view of the electorate, we have not said that it was an ideological candidacy from that same point of view. From other viewpoints of political analysis, it was of course just that: a movement of the "radical right." Moreover, with occasional exceptions, data on issue positions show Wallace voters to differ from Humphrey voters in the same "conservative" direction that Nixon voters do, only much more so. Therefore by customary definitions, not only the leadership of the radical right, but the rank-and-file espoused clearly "rightist" positions of a sort which were frequently extreme, on highly specific questions of public policy.[7]

---

[7] This was not true across every issue domain. The most notable exception was in the area of social welfare issues such as medicare and full employment guarantees, on which issues Wallace voters were significantly more "liberal" than Nixon voters, and almost matched the liberalism of Humphrey voters. This admixture was of course familiar in Wallace's frequent appeals to the underdog and the working man, in the tradition of Southern populism.

Table 12.2 Ideological Responses of White Voters for Different Presidential Candidates in 1964 and 1968[a]

Region	1964		1968		
	Johnson	Goldwater	Humphrey	Nixon	Wallace
Non-South	51.8	39.9	51.8	43.4	44.9
South	49.6	35.9	49.5	40.7	41.9

[a] The cell entry registers the mean value shown on the ideological scale described in the text for white voters for each of the candidates listed. A high value indicates that liberalism is held in relative favor; a low value means that conservatism is preferred.

Yet there was an element of ideological self-recognition present among Goldwater voters in 1964 that was simply lacking among Wallace voters in 1968. One measure of ideological location which we use involves the respondent in rating the terms "liberal" and "conservative." If the respondent gives the highest possible score to the stimulus "liberal" and the lowest possible score to "conservative," he is rated as the most extreme liberal, with a score of 100. In the reverse case, the extreme conservative receives a score of zero. At 50 are clustered individuals who either do not recognize these terms, or give the same affective rating to both.[8] In 1964 there was a rather considerable relationship between such a measure and response to Goldwater, in the expected direction. In 1968, the same scale showed only a very limited correlation with reactions toward Wallace (gammas of .13 and .09 among whites within the South and outside, respectively). Indeed, as table 12.2 shows, in both political regions of the country Wallace voters were more favorable to the "liberal" label than Nixon voters! Thus while Wallace supporters were entirely distinctive in their "backlash" feelings on public policy, they were much less ideologically attuned to a left-right spectrum than their Goldwater predecessors.

Although Wallace supporters did not seem anywhere nearly as distinctive in terms of ideological measures as they did on specific issues, they did show moderate trends in terms of other more generic political attitudes. In particular, various measures bearing on discontent with the responsiveness and probity of government show correlations with ratings given by whites to Wallace, and are related but with opposite signs to ratings of the "establishment" candidates, Humphrey and Nixon. Since Wallace was more of a mainstream candidate in the South than in the rest of the country, it might be thought that his appeal in that region might depend less strictly on this syndrome of political alienation than it would elsewhere. However, these relationships are stronger and more pervasive in the South, and seem only weakly mirrored in other parts of the nation. Within the South, white atti-

---

[8] For reasons discussed elsewhere, a rather large proportion of the American electorate— nearly half—is found at this point of ideological neutrality.

tudes toward Wallace are quite sharply associated with our scales of political efficacy and cynicism about government. People drawn to Wallace tended to feel they had little capacity to influence government, and expressed distrust of the morality and efficiency of political leadership. These correlations reach a peak on items where the referent is most explicitly "the federal government in Washington," and it is plain that Southern voters felt more or less attracted to Wallace in the degree that they responded to his complaints that Washington bureaucrats had been persistently and unjustly bullying the South with particular respect to civil rights. Since there is no methodological need for it to be true, it is of particular interest that ratings of Humphrey show as substantial correlations in the opposing direction, in the South and other regions as well: people responding warmly to Humphrey had quite sanguine views of government.

All told, then, a sense of political alienation was a rather visible correlate of a sorting of the citizenry away from the conventional candidates toward Wallace, as was certainly to be expected and necessary if terms such as "backlash" are relevant. At the same time, it is worth keeping the apparent temporal sequences clear. The data suggest that Southern whites have become alienated with government because prior attitudes, particularly racial ones, have been contradictory to national policy for nearly twenty years. Thus there is a readiness to condemn government on a much broader front, and Wallace appealed in obvious ways to this readiness in the South. Outside the South Wallace also articulated the same array of specific grievances and received a clear response. However, the evidence suggests that any resonance he might have achieved in terms of a more generic condemnation of government, while present, was relatively limited.

13. The Assessment of Policy Voting

RICHARD A. BRODY
BENJAMIN I. PAGE

The voter has the option of voting or of abstaining; if he votes, he chooses among candidates. By "policy voting" we mean the extent to which these behaviors are caused by the voter acting in accord with his policy preferences. The question with which we are here concerned is: How do we know whether and to what extent "policy voting" has taken place in a given election? The process of obtaining this knowledge is what we mean by the "assessment of policy voting."

We will argue that the assessment of policy voting depends upon the specification of necessary and sufficient conditions for the influence of policy attitudes in the voting decision. But prior to this specification and in order to justify it, we will review existing assessment techniques.

SOURCE: *American Political Science Review,* 66(1972):450–458. Reprinted with permission of the publisher.

AUTHORS' NOTE: Research drawn upon in this commentary was supported by National Science Foundation Grant GS NSF #2855. Data on the 1968 election were made available through the Inter-University Consortium for Political Research; the authors are solely responsible for analysis and interpretation.

Policy Voting as a
Resultant of Short-term Forces

The causal significance of policy preferences for the vote is generally treated as inhering in a given election. The issues that affect one election do not necessarily affect other elections past or future. Policy preferences, the voter's attitude toward the issue, are by these criteria treated as "short-term" forces.

The categories of short-term forces are conceived of by most scholars as persisting from election to election. However, the specific content of the categories and the impact of a given short-term force have been found to be highly variable.[1] Because such evidence as we have from the voting studies indicates that policy preferences are extraordinarily labile,[2] our theories of voting do not employ such concepts as "stable" foreign affairs or labor relations attitudes in the way that they employ the concept of "stable partisan attitudes."

There is a mutual reinforcement between the conception of short-term effects of issues and the cross-section or short panel sample survey design. The learning of policy satisfaction/dissatisfaction over time which hypothetically could affect the strength and eventually the direction of partisanship, cannot easily be studied with such a data-gathering procedure. It is unusual in the cross-section to see partisan identification treated as a response partly learned from the reinforcement of policy preferences. Gerald Pomper, for example, does not consider the possibility that partisan realignment would produce exactly the same correlations that he attributes to increasing "ideological clarity."[3] We are certainly not asserting that if the panel data were available, they would show a massive effect on partisan identification of the feedback of policy satisfaction. Clearly, we do not have such data available.

In our leading models of voting, partisan identification is said to be learned early as a part of primary socialization into family and class. The issue content of partisan identification, to the extent there is any, reflects these familial and class sources.[4] This content in turn affects the attraction to issues (their salience for the voter) as well as the voter's stands on new issues as they arise. David RePass's notion of "issue partisanship" exemplifies this conception.[5]

---

[1] Donald E. Stokes, "Some Dynamic Elements of Contests for the Presidency," *American Political Science Review,* 60(March 1966):19-28.

[2] See, for example, Philip E. Converse, "The Nature of Belief Systems in Mass Publics," in *Ideology and Discontent,* ed. David Apter, (New York: The Free Press, 1964), pp. 206-61 and David Butler and Donald E. Stokes, *Political Change in Britain* (New York: St. Martin's Press, 1969).

[3] Gerald Pomper, "From Confusion to Clarity: Issues and American Voters, 1956-1968," *American Political Science Review,* 66(June, 1972):415-28.

[4] V. O. Key, Jr., *Politics, Parties and Pressure Groups,* 4th ed. (New York: Crowell, 1958), p. 238.

[5] David RePass, "Issue Salience and Party Choice," *American Political Science Review,* 65(June 1971):389-400.

Our leading models, thus, conceive of partisan identification as a "standing decision" which may reflect or may have once reflected preferences for a direction of policy (perhaps still viable and rational, perhaps not) as well as a persistence of habitual behavior not related to public policy. [6] Even occupational mobility, which may bring the voter into a new relationship with the consequences of public policy, does not much affect the voter's partisanship. [7]

Thus as political attitudes go, partisan identification, as currently conceived, is an attitude that does not yield to experience. [8]

Assessing Short-term Effects

The notion of stable partisanship gives rise to techniques for assessing the extent of policy voting: V. O. Key, for example, uses votes contrary to partisanship among those who express dissatisfaction with their party's past performance or in their expectation of its performance in the future to estimate the impact of issues on the vote. [9]

Table 13.1 is constructed in the manner of those Key offers as evidence that issues are considerations in the collective electoral decision. [10] Since in this table the proportions voting for Humphrey decrease monotonically along both columns and rows, the table shows both partisanship and performance evaluation related to patterns of voting for or against the candidate of the Democratic Party. But table 13.1 does not unambiguously offer evidence of the impact of the lack of confidence in President Johnson's performance in the field of foreign affairs.

The ambiguity in such tables arises from three sources: (1) from the lack of a null model against which to compare observations; (2) from uncertainty about the direction of causality between the issue assessment by the voter and his vote; and (3) from the fact that the *same* defecting votes may be explained by other variables.

We need a null model in order to assess the strength of the effect of an issue. Suppose there were no other factors in the voting decision except

---

[6] V. O. Key, Jr. and Frank Munger, "Social Determinism and Electoral Decision: The Case of Indiana," in *Public Opinion and Politics,* William J. Crotty, ed., (New York: Holt, Rinehart and Winston, 1970), p. 253.

[7] James A. Barber, Jr., *Social Mobility and Voting Behavior* (Chicago: Rand McNally, 1970), p. 114.

[8] Not all conceptions of partisanship reflect this point of view: See, for example, Arthur Goldberg's "Model V," "Discerning a Causal Pattern among Data on Voting Behavior," *American Political Science Review,* 60(December, 1966):920-21. In this model Goldberg shows partisanship to be affected by partisan attitudes which include issue orientations. James L. Sundquist (*Politics and Policy* [Washington, D.C.: Brookings Institution, 1968]) finds the "[p]arty allegiances of some voters changing" in response to presidential performance (p. 438).

[9] *Public Opinion and American Democracy* (New York: Knopf, 1961), pp. 472 ff.

[10] See, for example, V. O. Key's tables 18.4 and 18.5. *Public Opinion,* p. 473 and p. 475.

Table 13.1   Vote for Humphrey by Party Foreign Policy Performance by Partisan Identification

Party Identification	Party Preferred on Foreign Policy[a]					
	Democrats		Same by Both		Republicans	
	%	N	%	N	%	N
Strong Democrats	92[b]	72	85	102	50	16
Medium Democrats	87	29	56	151	29	35
Independents[c]	72	24	28	144	4	78
Medium Republicans	50	6	9	74	7	68
Strong Republicans	—	0	4	27	2	85

[a] "Looking ahead, do you think the problem of keeping us out of a bigger war would be handled better in the next four years by the Democrats, by the Republicans, or about the same by both?"
[b] Entries are percent of the two-party vote going to the Democratic candidate, Humphrey; data from the SRC/ICPR 1968 American National Election Study.
[c] Those in this row responded "independent" on the first probe.

partisanship and a given issue. Under the null model, that is, under the circumstances in which the issue had no short-term effect, how would this table appear? Key's interpretations seem to imply that, for party identifiers, the six Democratic identifier cells should show a one hundred percent Democratic vote and the six cells for Republican identifiers should show a zero percent Democratic vote. It is not clear what the expected Democratic vote among independents would be. This null model cannot be the one Key intended. It denies any relevance to the strength of partisanship and Key uses this information. But how do we modify the null prediction to take account of the strength of partisanship? How much should we discount the expected vote of less than "strong" partisan identifiers?

A handy answer to our need for a null model is found with Converse's concept of the "normal vote."[11] Converse argues that the distribution of partisan loyalties among those with a given attitude or among those who subscribe to a given issue position, when weighted by the voting propensities associated with strength of partisanship, yields an expected percentage voting Democratic for the like-minded. Since this percentage reflects only the distribution of stable partisan loyalties, it is exactly the estimate of the expected vote in the absence of short-term forces that we need for the null model. The extent of the short-term effect of the issue is then estimated by the comparison of observed voting percentages with the percentages derived from the null model.

Applying this technique to the distribution of responses to the question of "which party can better handle the problem of keeping us out of a bigger

---

[11] Philip E. Converse, "The Concept of a Normal Vote," in Angus Campbell, Philip E. Converse, Warren E. Miller, and Donald E. Stokes, *Elections and the Political Order* (New York: Wiley, 1966), pp. 9–39.

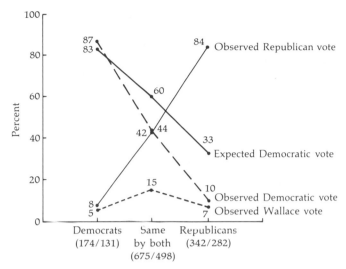

Figure 13.1 Attitudes toward war handling capabilities of the parties and presidential vote.

war," we can see more clearly the processes underlying table 13.1. Figure 13.1 displays this analysis. The distribution of partisan loyalties across positions on this issue leads us to expect a very substantial long-term effect. Compared to the fifteen issues examined in Richard Boyd's article, this policy issue with a "magnitude of long-term effect" equal to 12.9 would rank first. [12] A short-term component is also present. Those voters who did not feel positive about the past or prospective performance of the Democrats in the field of foreign affairs defect at a rate higher than that predicted by the null model. Compared with the issues Boyd examines, the short-term component is modest. With a magnitude of $S = 4.77$, this issue ranks between the twelfth and thirteenth issues. [13]

"Normal vote" analyses help us to understand the effect of a given issue in the electorate at large. But, they share with V. O. Key's technique ambiguity about the direction of causality between attitudes and behavior and the problem of the possible continued re-explanation of the same voting acts. Both techniques assume that the issue attitudes exist prior to and thus can be a cause of the vote. Clearly, however, "rationalizing" of one's vote or intention to vote contrary to one's partisanship, through finding fault with

---

[12] Richard Boyd, "Popular Control of Public Policy: A Normal Vote Analysis of the 1968 Election," *American Political Science Review,* 66(June 1972):Appendix II.

[13] It might be thought that there is a necessarily negative relationship between the magnitude of short and long-term effects. On the contrary, across the fifteen issues examined by Richard Boyd, the sizes of these two components are highly *positively* correlated ($r_s = .58$; $p < .025$). This suggests that, with some notable exceptions, previously politicized issues are the ones that get activated for and used by the voter during the campaign.

the party's performance, would produce tables that look exactly like those produced by the process in which negative views of performance caused defecting votes. In fact, if causality runs from opinion to behavior for some citizens (the "policy voters") and from behavior to opinion for other citizens (the "rationalizers") tables such as this will still look the same. If, however, voters are simply rationalizing a defection which is otherwise caused, and if we cannot distinguish them from those who switch their vote on the basis of policy considerations, we are in danger of overestimating the extent of policy voting by the number of such voters.

Exploring Rationalization

We know of no ironclad way, within a cross-section sample survey on a given issue *considered by itself*, of disentangling these substantively different processes. But if we are willing to think of rationalizing as a general response set, its effects can be examined.

Think of the repeated naming of one political party as "best able" to solve important problems or as "closer" to one's own policy position as a measure of response consistency. Suppose we are willing to assume that those who rationalize their vote on one issue, by letting their vote dictate their stand, are apt to attempt to achieve psychological balance in the same way on a set of issues; then it is clear that the rationalizers will appear among those with high consistency scores.

If rationalization is *one way* of achieving a high party/issue consistency score, we can use this knowledge to test the *implausibility* of the hypothesis that rationalization causes the findings to be attributed to policy voting. Given an index of consistency, if the rationalization hypothesis is not justified, we will not find especially pronounced "anti-Democratic" issue consistency scores among those Democrats who vote against their party's candidate. We can only assess the *absence* of rationalization as a plausible explanation for the findings in the tables of the Key and Boyd type because other processes besides rationalization can lead to high consistency scores. If Democrats who defect are not pronouncedly more anti-Democratic than those who do not, rationalization is excluded; if they are, the question of causality is left unsettled.

Based on responses to two clusters of items in the 1968 SRC/ICPR pre- and post-election surveys, we have developed indices of partisan response consistency: The "Partisan Issue Alignment Index" reflects the degree to which the respondent felt the Democratic Party is the one to handle the "most important problems faced by the government in Washington." The index mirrors David RePass's approach of permitting the voter to identify the issues he feels are important.[14] The index summarizes, on a 19-point scale—*viz.*, +9 (pro-Democratic) to −9 (anti-Democratic) the pattern of re-

---

[14] David RePass, "Issue Salience."

sponses to the "first," "second," and "third," most important problems identified by the respondent. [15]

Our second index, "Expectation of Policy Satisfaction," summarizes the pattern of response to 11 forced-choice policy items. It describes the degree on a 23-point scale—viz., +11 (pro-Democratic) to −11 (anti-Democratic) to which a voter feels the positions he prefers will be carried out by the Democratic Party. [16]

Comparing the means and distributions of the two indices in the subsamples voting for and against Humphrey (tables 13.2a and 13.2b), we find: (1) Those who vote against Humphrey are on the average less "pro-Democratic" in their assessment of the policy performance of the Democratic Party than are those who vote for him; this is true in every group of party identifiers. (2) The distributions about these means are such as to suggest that, within party identification groups, voters for and against Humphrey by virtue of their policy attitudes constitute separate and distinct subgroups. (3) These findings are true for salient issues and for those considered without regard to their salience for the voter.

These findings, of course, replicate David RePass's finding of the strong relationship between "issue partisanship (or alignment)" and voting choice in the 1964 Election. They do not, however, eliminate the ambiguity about whether attitudes are, as RePass contends, "a powerful influence . . . on voting choice" [17] or whether voting choice is a powerful influence on attitudes.

When we control the comparison of Humphrey and Nixon voters' Partisan Issue Alignment by their opinion on "which party would better handle the problem of keeping us out of a bigger war" (table 13.3), we find evidence which raises questions about the rationalization interpretation.

---

[15] In the case of each of the three most important problems, the respondent was asked which party, if either, would carry out the policy he favored. The Partisan Issue Alignment Index sums the responses to these probes with weights 5, 3, and 1 attached to the first, second, and third most important problems, respectively. Thus, if a voter named the Democrats on all three probes, his weighted score would be +9; if he named the Republicans or Wallace, his score would be −9. On each probe, the "Democrats" response was scored +1, the "Both/Either" response was scored 0, and the "Republicans" or "Wallace" response was scored −1. It is these scores which are weighted and summed to form the index.

[16] The Expectation of Policy Satisfaction Index expresses the degree to which the respondent, on eleven policy questions, saw the Democrats carrying out policies which he favored or associated the Republicans with policies of which he disapproved. The eleven policies covered: Aid to education, the growth of governmental power, federal medical programs, aid to employment, fair employment practices, integration, public accommodations, foreign aid, negotiations with Communist nations, trade with Communist nations, and Vietnam policy. On each issue, if the respondent favored a point of view and associated the Democrats with that point of view or if he expressed opposition to a policy and associated the Republicans with that policy position, he received a score of +1; if the opposite conditions obtained, he received a score of −1; if he did not respond to the policy or if he did not identify a party with one stand or the other, his score on that item was 0. The index sums these scores over the eleven issue areas.

[17] David RePass, "Issue Salience," pp. 399–400.

Table 13.2 Response Consistency, Party Identification and the Vote

Party Identification	Voters for Humphrey			Voters Against Humphrey[a]			t	Statistical Significance
	Mean	S.D.	N	Mean	S.D.	N		
a. Partisan Issue Alignment Index								
Strong Democrats	4.70	4.3	188	−0.68	5.2	34	6.52	.005
Medium Democrats	1.82	4.4	139	−2.89	4.2	102	8.31	.005
Weak Democrats	3.14	4.6	49	−3.14	3.7	44	7.14	.005
Independents	1.35	2.7	20	−3.59	3.6	65	5.62	.005
Weak Republicans	−1.50	3.1	4	−5.27	4.0	97	1.85	.025
Medium Republicans	0.00	5.2	16	−4.30	4.1	147	3.88	.005
Strong Republicans	−3.67	7.5	3	−6.24	3.1	116	1.31	ns[b]
b. Expectation of Policy Satisfaction Index								
Strong Democrats	3.44	3.5	188	0.27	4.3	34	4.62	.005
Medium Democrats	1.71	3.3	139	−1.02	2.5	102	6.99	.005
Weak Democrats	2.24	3.3	49	−0.31	3.1	44	3.81	.005
Independents	1.48	2.7	20	−0.87	2.1	65	4.02	.005
Weak Republicans	−0.88	1.4	4	−1.64	2.9	97	0.51	ns[b]
Medium Republicans	2.19	3.4	16	−1.38	3.1	147	4.33	.005
Strong Republicans	−0.17	3.9	3	−1.71	3.3	116	0.78	ns[b]

[a] Combines voters for Nixon and Wallace.
[b] $p > .05$.

Table 13.3 Response Consistency of Democratic Identifiers by Strength of Partisanship, Presidential Vote, and Beliefs About Which Party Can Better Handle the Problem of War: Partisan Issue Alignment Index

Which Party Can Handle War/ Partisan Strength	Voters for Humphrey			Voters for Nixon[a]			t	Statistical Significance
	Mean	S.D.	N	Mean	S.D.	N		
"Democrats"								
Strong Democrats	6.57	3.6	67	3.50	5.9	4	1.56	ns[b]
Medium Democrats	5.96	3.5	26	0.00	—	1	—[c]	—
Weak Democrats	6.50	2.2	14	−8.00	—	1	—[c]	—
"Same by both"								
Strong Democrats	4.06	4.0	87	−0.17	2.9	6	2.53	.01
Medium Democrats	1.26	4.1	85	−3.11	3.5	36	5.49	.005
Weak Democrats	2.11	4.4	27	−3.06	2.8	17	4.19	.005
"Republicans"								
Strong Democrats	−1.88	4.9	8	−5.17	5.4	6	1.10	ns[b]
Medium Democrats	−2.90	4.2	10	−5.70	4.1	23	1.73	.05
Weak Democrats	8.00	—	1	−3.71	4.1	7	—[c]	—

[a] Since the "Republicans" was a specific category in the item, 56 Wallace voters are not considered here.
[b] $p > .05$.
[c] Too few cases for comparison.

Strong Democrats who think the Republicans can handle the war problem better and who voted for Nixon are not significantly more prone to depreciate their party consistently than are Strong Democrats who share their foreign policy beliefs but who did not defect. These Democrats are on the average less pro-Democratic, but their scores are so variable as to make the mean an unreliable estimate of the response tendencies within the group. According to cognitive balance theories, this group of voters should have the greatest psychological incentive for rationalization; their failure to conform to its predictions is a source of doubt about the rationalization interpretation.

Our doubts increase when we consider that those Strong Democrats who do not distinguish the parties on their war-handling capability and who voted against their partisanship in this instance behaved contrary to their overall response tendency and passed up an opportunity to deprecate the performance of the Democratic Administration.

With such small N's within cells, these findings can hardly be considered conclusive. They should give pause to those who argue the rationalization of defection.

These analyses partly clear the Key and Boyd approaches of the problem of rationalization. If we are satified on this score, we have, especially in the normal vote approach, techniques for establishing whether or not there is a correlation between policy preferences and voting choices in the electorate at large. But, as Boyd explicitly acknowledges, this does not permit us to conclude "that the issue was causally related to the vote or that the issue made some net contribution to the observed Democratic vote."[18] Since it is necessary to establish precisely these facts in order to demonstrate that policy voting has taken place, we are not fully content with normal vote analysis as a technique.

While agreeing with Boyd's analysis of the shortcomings of the normal vote approach—and, incidentally, with his analysis of its strengths, as well—we have reservations about his contention that these shortcomings are inherent in survey data.[19] We believe the difficulty lies with aggregating across the electorate, rather than with modeling the individual voting decision, and with treating each policy issue in isolation from every other. Taking the issues one at a time means that the approach is continually reapportioning the same observed variation in the vote. In this way many factors can appear as indispensable in explaining the vote. Given the multifaceted nature of political reality, disciplined statements about the causes of behavior will be necessarily multivariate.

There is no way to avoid modeling the individual voting decision and still estimate policy voting. The analysis must bring the respondents by means of their own testimony into a direct relationship with the issues. The analyst

---

[18] Richard Boyd, "Popular Control," p. 432.
[19] Richard Boyd, "Popular Control," p. 432.

must determine that the voter viewed the candidates or parties in relation to the policy issues. In short, the analyst has to ascertain whether the voter has satisfied the necessary and sufficient conditions for policy voting.

The Requirements of Policy Voting

We have from diverse sources more or less consonant lists of the elements required for policy voting.[20] The elements of such lists describe a decision process which includes as independent variables: (1) The salience of the policy issue (or issue area) for the voter. Butler and Stokes term it a "link" between the issue and the self.[21] Davis, Hinich, and Ordeshook make attention to the issue and responsiveness to the candidates a requirement.[22] (2) The voter's position on the issue or his preferences for a line of policy. (3) The voter's perception of the candidates' or parties' position on the policy issue.[23]

Given these elements, an influence of policy on voting is said to be present when the voter's comparative evaluation of the candidates or his vote or both are independently affected by the relative proximity of the candidates to his position on issues that are for him salient. Figure 13.2 idealizes this decision process as a recursive arrow diagram. It reflects the assumption that *ceteris paribus* the voter will prefer (i.e., evaluate more positively), the candidate closer to him on salient issues and that he will, if he votes, vote for the preferred candidate.

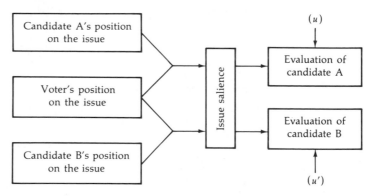

Figure 13.2 Necessary and sufficient conditions for policy voting.

[20] See Butler and Stokes, *Political Change*, "The Analysis of Issues," pp. 173–92 and Otto Davis, Melvin Hinich, and Peter Ordeshook, "An Expository Development of a Mathematical Model of the Electoral Process," *American Political Science Review*, 64(June 1970):426–28.

[21] David Butler and Donald E. Stokes, *Political Change*, p. 174.

[22] Otto Davis, Melvin Hinich, and Peter Ordeshook, "An Expository Development," p. 429.

[23] Those familiar with the Davis et al., "An Expository Development" article, will recognize that in singling out the policy or issue component of these elements, we have made policy voting a special case of their broader class of "rational voting."

From the perspective of assessment, this model gives rise to the need for
measures of the salience of issues and of the perceived position of the candidates on the issues.

"Salience," which can be measured as RePass suggests by respondents'
identification of the "most important problems the government . . . should
try to take care of,"[24] is an indication of an *affective* link between the voter
and the issue. Salience does not, however, ensure a *cognitive* link. Simply
because voters are attracted to an issue or think it an important problem is
no guarantee that they will necessarily seek or retain information about it. If
this generalization needs support, consider, for example, the fact that in 1967
more than one-third of those who thought the war in Vietnam important
enough to engage in the unusual political act of trying to change someone's
opinion on the problem could not identify Hanoi as the capital of North
Vietnam.[25]

Partly because of this lack of cognitive fidelity, we feel it is essential to
measure the voter's perception of the candidates' issue positions. Davis, Hinich, and Ordeshook assume that *"all citizens make identical estimates"* of a
candidate's issue position.[26] However expedient such an assumption may be
in modeling candidate behavior, it is not necessary in order to model voting
behavior. Singularity of perception of the candidates' stands is, of course,
counterindicated by an impressive amount of data.[27] But the assumption is
not required on analytic grounds either.

Relaxing the assumption that voters share a common perception of where
the candidates stand in "issue space" entails admitting causes of that perception beside or in addition to candidate behavior. Once it is established where
the candidates are *perceived* to stand in issue space, the voter's individual loss
function[28] or other psychological distance measure[29] can be computed and
related to his voting behavior. In other words, the basic hypothesis that the
voter will vote for the candidate most proximal to him on the issues is

---

[24] See Items 16 through 16p on the SRC/ICPR 1968 Pre-Election Questionnaire.

[25] Richard A. Brody and Sidney Verba, "Hawk and Dove: The Search for an Explanation
of Vietnam Policy Preferences," *Acta Politica,* forthcoming.

[26] Otto Davis, Melvin Hinich, and Peter Ordeshook, "An Expository Development," p.
431, emphasis in the original.

[27] See, for example, Bernard Berelson, Paul Lazarsfeld, and William McPhee, *Voting*
(Chicago: University of Chicago Press, 1954) and Benjamin I. Page and Richard A. Brody,
"Policy Voting and the Electoral Process: The Vietnam War Issue," *American Political
Science Review,* 66(September 1972):979–95.

[28] Otto Davis, Melvin Hinich, and Peter Ordeshook, "An Expository Development," p.
432.

[29] The 1968 election was the occasion for at least three independent efforts to relate
psychological distance/proximity to voting behavior. Michael Shapiro's study of voters in
Hawaii is reported in "Rational Political Man: A Synthesis of Economic and Social-Psychological Perspectives," *American Political Science Review,* 63(December 1969):1106–19. The
two based on national samples are represented in preliminary reports in convention pa-
pers: see Richard A. Brody, Benjamin I. Page, Sidney Verba, and Jerome Laulicht, "Viet-

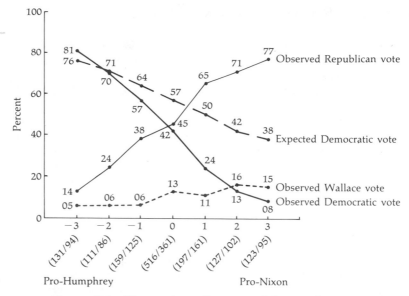

Figure 13.3 Vietnam issue distance and the vote in 1968.

common to both approaches. The hypothesis does not depend upon the candidate's being perceived at one and only one point.

As formulated, the hypothesis is undoubtedly true. It is true of the electorate on particular issues, and it is true when issues are aggregated and a composite index is generated.

Consider figure 13.3, for example: in this graph the abscissa is an attenuated version of a scale measuring the signed difference of the perceived distance from the voter to Humphrey and the voter to Nixon, on a seven-point "Vietnam policy" scale. [30] Using the "normal vote" component as our null model, we find that there is a long-term effect which reflects the correlation of the Vietnam distance comparison with partisan identification. An even larger short-term component can also be seen in these data; [31] proximity on this issue and voting behavior clearly covary.

---

nam, The Urban Crisis, and the 1968 Presidential Election: A Preliminary Analysis," paper delivered at the Annual Meeting of the American Sociological Association, San Francisco, California, September 1969; and David M. Kovenock, Philip L. Beardsley, and James W. Prothro, "Status, Party, Ideology, Issues, and Candidate Choice: A Preliminary Theory-Relevant Analysis of the 1968 American Presidential Election," paper delivered at the Eighth World Congress, International Political Science Association, Munich, Germany, 31 August–5 September 1970.

[30] See SRC/ICPR, 1968 Post-Election Questionnaire, questions 67, 67b, 67c, and 67e.

[31] Compared with the fifteen issues examined by Richard Boyd ("Popular Control," Appendix II), comparative distance on Vietnam policy, with L = 7.91 and S = 8.65, ranks fifth on long-term effect and third on its short-term component.

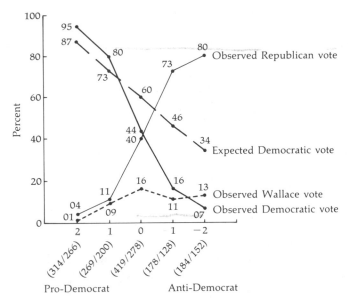

Figure 13.4 Issue alignment and the vote in 1968: salient issue distances.

Similarly, in figure 13.4, we can see that a composite measure of distances across salient issue areas[32] shows substantial long and short-term components. A long-term effect of this magnitude (L = 14.5) would rank first among the fifteen issues examined by Boyd. A short-term effect of this magnitude (S = 8.37) would rank just below the second most potent of Boyd's issues. These data unambiguously show that issue proximities covary with voting behavior.

A Question of What Causes What

If it is true, as we have shown, that voters vote for the candidates proximal to them on the issues, then the processes relevant to the perception of that proximity become pertinent in assessing the extent of policy voting. These processes are pertinent because we may wish to exclude from our definition of policy voting some behaviors which they describe.

Consider the elements of the model depicted in figure 13.2: If we relax the assumption of recursivity and permit the voter's evaluation of the candidates (or his vote) to cause his perceptions of their stands or his own policy position or both, we can distinguish three "proximity" processes. These pro-

---

[32] Our composite measure is the Partisan Issue Alignment Index (see footnote 15). We interpret the response to "which party do you think would be most likely to do what you want on this . . .?" as a dichotomous (near, not near) distance measure. In this graph, the abscissa values are a grouping of the +9 to −9 index; −9 to −6 = −2; −5 to −1 = −1; 0 = 0; 1 to 5 = 1; and 6 to 9 = 2.

cesses, singly or in combination, could produce graphs like those in figure 13.3 or 13.4.

The first process, "Policy Oriented Evaluation," is depicted in figure 13.2. It describes the cases in which the prior held policy position of the voter and his perceptions of the candidates' positions (which are presumably independent of each other) *cause* his evaluation. This, in the slice of time considered by this model or covered in a cross-sectional survey, the voter's position and perception are invariant, and evaluations vary in accord with the issue proximities.

Suppose we change the invariant elements of this model: If perceptions and evaluations were invariant and the respondent's own position yielded to or formed around the position he believed was held by the candidate he favored (or intended to vote for), we would say that the voter had been "persuaded" by the candidate. "Persuasion" may be a perfectly legitimate political process, but in the slice of time being considered here, it is an effect of, not a cause of, candidate evaluation. In these terms, we cannot say that the voter who is persuaded is evaluating or voting on the basis of policy.

The third process stems from allowing the perceived position of the candidate to vary with the voter's own position and his evaluation of the candidate. Under this model, a voter could see a candidate as close to himself on an issue because he otherwise felt positive about the candidate, and he could see other candidates as distant from him on the issue(s) because he felt negative about them for other reasons. In other words, a voter would "project" his own (or a nearby) stand onto candidates he favored. We are reluctant to call those who project "policy voters."

Both persuasion and projection have been found to operate in the American electorate. Berelson, Lazarsfeld, and McPhee found these processes operating on policy stands as clear as President Truman's position on Taft-Hartley repeal;[33] we found them operating on the less clear Vietnam policy positions of candidates Nixon and Humphrey in 1968.[34]

The presence of these two "alternate" processes in the electoral system makes it inappropriate to declare policy-oriented evaluation *the* cause of the correspondence between issue proximity and voting behavior. We need some means for examining the potential for "persuasion" and for "projection" and of estimating them as separate processes.[35]

If we confine ourselves to the "position," "perception," and "evaluation" variables in a given survey, there is no way to estimate the separate effect of

---

[33] Bernard Berelson, Paul Lazarsfeld, William McPhee, *Voting*, pp. 220-22.

[34] Benjamin I. Page and Richard A. Brody, "Policy Voting."

[35] David M. Kovenock, Philip L. Beardsley, and James W. Prothro, "Status, Party," pp. 29-31, discuss this problem and refer to reasons for believing it not to be important. Their reasoning is based on the number of issues examined, the nature of their data gathering procedures, the fact that the items most clearly associated with the several candidates are different for each of them, and the fact that on some issues those who vote for one candidate are closer to another. Such plausible evidence encourages rather than satisfies the search for estimates of the three proximity processes.

each of the three proximity processes. The solution to the problem lies with panel data within a given election year, in the manner of the Lazarsfeld studies, or with expanding the set of variables considered. This latter approach would entail finding causes of persuasion which are not also causes of projection or policy-oriented evaluation; finding causes of projection which are not causes of either persuasion or policy-oriented evaluation; and finding causes of policy-oriented evaluation which are not causes of the other proximity processes.[36] The specification of such causal factors would permit us to use a technique of causal modeling which explicitly takes account of the possibility of all three processes working and estimates the extent of each; we refer, of course, to the econometrician's simultaneous equation estimation procedures.

In the case of policy-oriented evaluation of a candidate, the simultaneous equation approach suggests a three-equation model; in this model, each of the central variables (own position, perception of candidates' positions, and evaluation of the candidate) has a single equation in which it is the dependent variable and hence a function of the other two. This would give us one equation for each proximity process. Up to this point without the independent (exogenous) causal factors, no estimates can be derived; once the independent causal factors are found, we can at last achieve an estimate of the extent of policy voting.[37]

The discovery of these independent causal factors is no easy matter. There is no statistical procedure which will uncover them. They must come from our theories of behavior and our knowledge about the act of voting. However difficult it is to specify such causal factors, that is exactly where the problem is. If the estimation of policy voting is important to the understanding of the role of the citizen in a democracy—and theorists of democracy certainly write as if it is—then any procedure which fails to control for projection and persuasion will be an undependable base upon which to build our understanding.

Research such as that of Boyd, Key, Kovenock, Jackson, Pomper, RePass, and Shapiro—and, we hope, our work, too—should unsettle those who are complacent in their belief that policy and issues play no role in the electoral decisions of the American voter. Having unsettled the complacent, let us take the steps necessary to settle the question.

---

[36] Those acquainted with econometric approaches to nonrecursive causal modeling will recognize these causal sets as the exogenous variables required to "identify" a system of simultaneous equations. See, for example, Franklin Fisher, "Statistical Identifiability," in *International Encyclopedia of the Social Sciences, Volume 15,* ed. David Sills (New York: Macmillan and Free Press, 1968), pp. 201–6.

[37] For example, see: Michael Shapiro, "Rational Political Man" and John Jackson, "The Importance of Issues and Issue Importance in Presidential Elections," Discussion Paper #3, Program of Quantitative Analysis in Political Science, Government Department, Harvard University, January, 1972.

IV. CONGRESSIONAL ELECTIONS

14. Is Congressional Voting Basically Partisan?

By far the majority of work on electoral behavior has been devoted to studying presidential voting. In a way this is ironic, since there is such a tremendous number of other elections. Some elections we might easily write off as unimportant. There was considerable controversy of the election of a drain commissioner in eastern Michigan in 1972, but we doubt that people very often get worked up over the question of who will be drain commissioner or even whether there is a drain commissioner. Similarly, we doubt that many people care much about the election of a county coroner, whose clientele are no longer in a position to complain. Yet gubernatorial and congressional elections are important, not to mention mayoral and school board elections. And while the average state bond issue may not excite most voters, there are occasionally referenda that should and do attract considerable interest.

Fortunately, this neglect of subpresidential elections is diminishing, at least with regard to congressional voting. Some of the best of this work is represented here. Much of it revolves around the problem of how to interpret congressional elections. Are the candidates important? Or is congressional voting basically partisan? Or might voting for Congress be determined by national economic and political trends other than party?

It might seem obvious that voting for Congress would depend on the candidates, and that certainly is what had always been assumed. But surveys found voters so ignorant of the candidates that there has been a search for other possible explanations. Party became the obvious contender for the role of determinant in congressional contests. More recent research is beginning to suggest a wider potpourri of determinants of the congressional vote, such as evaluations of the incumbent president.[1]

What is most intriguing about the evolving explanations is that the prime determinants of congressional voting are often beyond the control of those running for the office. Candidates may take issue positions which attract some votes, but the findings show that voters place greater stress on the candidate's party, the state of the national economy, the popularity of the president, the fact of incumbency, and similar factors. The implications are astounding. Apparently, the candidate has an amazingly wide degree of flexibility—he or she can do or say anything this side of outrageous without jeopardizing chances of victory. Once in office, the legislator's voting record may have minimal impact on re-election because so few constituents are aware of how their representative votes.

Is this desirable or undesirable? Should we want greater individual roles for our representatives? Or does the current system implicitly carry a degree of party responsibility for government actions which is itself useful? If congressional voting does not depend primarily on the candidates, then congressional elections may serve as a very effective reward or punishment for the party controlling the presidency. Although this violates the conventional image of voting for the best candidate, it may still be performing a noble function. At least, it is reasonable to consider which alternative is preferable while reading through the following analyses of congressional elections.

Congressional Elections as Partisan

The early view—that voters vote on the basis of the candidates—seemed quite reasonable at the time. After all, the candidates were running for the office, they received publicity in the media, and their names appeared on the ballot. However, all of this rests on a few not very subtle assumptions: that voters know there is a congressional election, that the local media cover the congressional elections, and that voters know who the candidates are. After what previous chapters have shown about the actual state of knowledge and ideological thinking of the American electorate, it might not come as a huge surprise (though it certainly did when the first surveys reported these results) that these assumptions simply are not justified.

The first congressional election to which a national academic survey was devoted was the 1958 congressional election. Stokes and Miller's analysis of

---

[1] Most studies actually focus on voting for the House of Representatives rather than for the Senate, and henceforth our references will be to the House except where we explicitly cite the Senate. Presumably, voting for the two chambers would differ somewhat in that senators and hence senatorial elections have far greater visibility.

the results of that study sounds quite similar to the analysis of *The American Voter* in many respects.[2] But their results bear close inspection, as they are more than a repetition of what was said about the 1956 presidential election.

Candidate orientations are important in presidential elections, but it turned out that public awareness of the candidates was minimal or completely absent in congressional races. Stokes and Miller report that fully 46 percent of the 1958 voters (this excludes those not interested enough to vote) conceded they had not read or heard *anything* about *either* candidate. Only a quarter of those who voted claimed to have read or heard anything about *both* candidates. More recent surveys provide supporting data.

Issues were seen as relatively unimportant in the 1956 presidential election, but Stokes and Miller found them to be far less important in the ensuing congressional election. The most interesting piece of evidence suggesting public ignorance of policy matters was the fact that a significant portion of the electorate simply did not know which party controlled Congress. Even excluding nonvoters, Stokes and Miller found that only 61 percent of the respondents correctly assigned control to the Democrats. When a simple correction was made for guessing, they estimate that only about half of the voters really knew which party controlled Congress. With this crucial piece of information missing, it would be difficult to maintain that the congressional election was fought over the parties' legislative records. Stokes and Miller also tested the assumption that voters would vote against their own party if they think it is in control and domestic affairs have gone badly or if they believe the other party is in control and domestic affairs have gone well, but there is no real trend in this direction.[3] Still more direct evidence was that less than 10 percent of the comments by constituents about their representatives involved legislative issues. Issue orientation was, if anything, weaker than candidate orientation.

If this lack of information about legislative candidates and issues seems unusual, two further points can be made. The 1958 election study originally sought to survey the content of newspaper stories about congressional candidates in the areas where their respondents lived, but there were so few stories (and they were usually buried somewhere between the food ads and the obituaries) that they had to abandon this effort as pointless. More recently, a survey by CBS news the week before the 1974 election found huge portions of the electorate unaware that there would be an election for representative, senator, and/or governor the following week. Thus, the absorption of information about congressional elections seems to be incredibly low. This is a basic fact about congressional elections and must guide any attempt to understand the voting.

---

[2] Donald E. Stokes and Warren E. Miller, "Party Government and the Saliency of Congress," *Public Opinion Quarterly,* 26(1962):531–46.

[3] Somewhat comparable data for 1970 is found in Stanley R. Freedman, "The Salience of Party and Candidate in Congressional Elections: A Comparison of 1958 and 1970," in Norman R. Luttbeg, *Public Opinion and Public Policy,* rev. ed. (Homewood, Ill.: Dorsey, 1974).

Regardless of the lack of information, the election occurs and many people do vote. If they don't know much about the candidates or issues, then what forms the basis for their vote? The conclusion regarding the 1958 election seemed inescapable at the time—partisanship. This is the most readily available piece of information about the congressional candidates (perhaps other than their sex), and so it is the obvious basis for the vote decision. And partisans did indeed support their own party overwhelmingly. The congressional elections were thus seen by Stokes and Miller to be essentially partisan contests.

There are two levels on which to understand voting—the decision faced by the individual voter and the decision made by the electorate as a whole. Stokes and Miller explain individual voting for Congress in essentially partisan terms. In a companion article, Campbell traces the implications of this individual result for aggregate election outcomes.[4] In particular, Campbell uses the differences in voter characteristics between presidential and congressional elections to explain why, almost without exception since 1860, the party winning the presidency has lost seats in the House of Representatives in the ensuing off-year election.

Campbell describes what he terms a "surge and decline" effect. The presidential elections are relatively high stimulus events, meaning that there is a great deal of interest in them and popular awareness of them. Consequently, people who are relatively uninterested and uninvolved in politics turn out to vote. Because of their general inattentiveness, they tend to be swayed by current trends of public opinion such as the popularity of a particular individual or an issue of momentary importance. These "short-term forces" tend to favor one candidate, so the presidential election is more one-sided than it would otherwise be. The presidential election thus involves a double surge—an increase in the electorate and in the direction of the winning candidate.

In the ensuing congressional election year, these short-term forces are nonexistent or at least considerably weakened. Two things happen as a result. First, turnout declines. But the decline is not uniform throughout the population. Rather, individuals with little interest and information and relatively weak partisanship—precisely those who were most affected by short-term forces in the presidential election—are the ones to drop out of the electorate. What remains is a more informed, more interested, more partisan set of voters. The terms "peripheral voters" and "core voters" describe this distinction nicely. The second characteristic of congressional elections is that short-term forces are relatively unimportant even for individuals who do vote. Despite their greater interest and involvement, the inconspicuousness of individual congressmen and their legislative records means that the core voters make decisions on the basis of their underlying partisan feelings to a greater degree than in presidential elections.

---

[4] Angus Campbell, "Surge and Decline: A Study of Electoral Change," *Public Opinion Quarterly*, 24(1960):397–418.

As a consequence of both of these factors, in the congressional year race there is a decline in turnout and in support for the president's party (which had benefited from the short-term effects in the previous presidential race). Because of the nature of this decline, the vote for House candidates more closely parallels the underlying partisan division of the electorate than does the presidential vote. The surge and decline rhythm, according to Campbell, explains why the president's party seems invariably to lose seats in the next congressional election. It also explains why the president's party loses fewer seats after a close presidential election than after a landslide contest. [5]

Thus, the Stokes and Miller article and the Campbell article agree that congressional elections involve low levels of public information about the specific electoral races and consequently are essentially partisan contests. However, there are other possible interpretations, particularly interpretations which give greater emphasis to the effects of incumbency and popular satisfaction with the economy and with presidential performance, and there are other possible ways of testing the importance of partisan voting in congressional elections. More recent work has adopted these approaches to challenge the essentially partisan interpretation of congressional elections.

Congressional Elections as More Than Partisan Contests

One alternative explanation of congressional elections is to see them in terms of popular reactions to the president, his performance, and the condition of the country during the preceding two years. If this emphasis on the president seems strange in an analysis of congressional voting, it actually coincides very well with the low-information character of congressional elections. The public may be unaware of which party controls Congress but it is very much aware of the president's party. The American system in which one party can control the presidency and another can control Congress is unusual and difficult for the ordinary citizen to fathom. So is the fact that the president and Congress can move in different directions even when both are controlled by the same party. Thus the simplest reaction is to assume that Congress is of the same party as the president and just does his bidding. Hence it makes sense for voters to hold Congress responsible for the performance of the government in general and of the president in particular.

One of the most important sources of satisfaction with the government is the economy and particularly improvements in the economy since the last presidential election. Kramer has successfully shown that a number of economic variables are related to the total congressional vote over the entire period from 1896 to 1964. [6] Though his model has been subject to a number

---

[5] Thus, when Kennedy was elected in 1960 with less than a normal Democratic vote, Campbell correctly predicted in advance of the 1962 election that the Democratic loss that year would be slight. See Angus Campbell, "Prospects for November: Why We Can Expect More of the Same," *New Republic,* 147(8 October 1962):13–15.

[6] Gerald H. Kramer, "Short-Term Fluctuations in U.S. Voting Behavior," *American Political Science Review,* 65(1971):131–43.

of criticisms and analyses,[7] it is clear that one can quite accurately predict the results of congressional elections on the basis of economic factors. Real personal income is a particularly powerful predictor of the vote, while, perhaps surprisingly, unemployment rates are not. Perhaps the important point about Kramer's analysis is his conclusion that "election outcomes are in substantial part responsive to objective changes occurring under the incumbent party"[8] where incumbency refers to the president. Even though voters may not know the prospective congressman's name or program, this evidence would suggest that their voting is far from being a random or "irrational" phenomenon. Nor is it solely the result of partisan loyalties.

Tufte, in a paper included here (chapter 15), extends the analysis by adding to Kramer's economic predictor a measure of satisfaction with the president's performance in office. Changes in real, disposable, per capita income are used along with Gallup's presidential approval score to predict the "standardized" vote loss by the president's party in midterm elections. It should be emphasized that what Tufte's model predicts is the *deviation* from the long-run vote for Congress. Unlike Kramer, who uses the actual congressional vote as a dependent variable, Tufte standardizes this vote by subtracting the average congressional vote for the party of the incumbent president over eight preceding elections. In simple terms, Tufte is not predicting why the vote in a particular year is, say, 46 percent, but rather why the vote is 46 percent rather than the 47.3 percent one would expect on the basis of past elections. This is not said to detract from Tufte's analysis, but it is important to realize that his results concern deviations from a normal vote rather than the actual congressional vote. Indeed it raises the question of what "causes" the long-run or normal vote. Yet in any event Tufte shows that economic variables and public approval of the president are powerful predictors of the congressional vote. The congressional election can be viewed as a popular judgment of the government's performance.

The analyses of Kramer and Tufte apply to the electorate as a whole rather than to individuals. They are more relevant to Campbell's concentration on aggregate outcomes than to Stokes and Miller's analysis of voters' motivations. Thus it remains to be seen how these factors relate to the actions of the individual voter.

Work based on sample surveys is in fact beginning to re-evaluate voter behavior in congressional elections. Arseneau and Wolfinger have produced results that are highly useful because they provide specific comparisons between congressional voting in presidential and off-year elections and because they compare many of the earlier findings with data from the 1960's

---

[7] Hermann Garbers and Bruno S. Frey, "Communication," *American Political Science Review,* 66(1972):584. George J. Stigler, "General Economic Conditions and National Elections," *American Economic Review,* 63(1973):160–67. Susan J. Lepper, "Voting Behavior and Aggregate Policy Targets," *Public Choice,* 18(1974):67–81.

[8] Kramer, "Short-Term Fluctuations," p. 140.

and 1970.[9] Arseneau and Wolfinger find congressional voting to be partisan. But they find that defection from party is related to candidate information, to issue positions, and to satisfaction with the president's performance. Individual votes are certainly not exclusively partisan or exclusively random. Rather, the individual level results agree well with Tufte's aggregate level analysis.

Another alternative explanation of congressional elections is in terms of the effects of incumbency. Voters may be poorly informed about congressional elections, but this operates to the advantage of the incumbent, who has generally been familiar to the electorate for a longer period of time and has served the constituency for many years. Consequently, one would expect incumbency to reduce the partisan character of congressional elections.

Several authors have by now investigated the effects of incumbency.[10] Cowart, for example, predicts that, holding party identification and which party is preferred on domestic issues constant, a voter is more likely to vote Democratic when the incumbent is a Democrat than when the incumbent is a Republican.[11] Analysis of the 1956, 1960, 1964, and 1968 election surveys supports this prediction. For example, 93 percent of the Democratic identifiers who were pro-Democrat on domestic issues supported Democratic incumbents for the Senate, while only 83 percent of the same group voted Democratic when there was a Republican incumbent. The fall-off is even greater when someone who identifies with one party favors the other party on domestic issues. Cowart's results suggest an incumbency effect ranging from 10 to 15 percent for Senate voting. They also show that voting a split ticket (one party for president and another for Senate or for governor) is most common when the preferred presidential candidate and the incumbent senator or governor are from different parties. This result helps explain the phenomenon of "divergent majorities" (a majority in the state favoring, say, the Republican presidential candidate but electing a Democratic governor) so frequently observed in American politics.

The studies reviewed so far all suggest that congressional elections are more than partisan contests. Satisfaction with the government and the president and incumbency are important ingredients, even if specific issue and candidate factors generally are not. However, all of these studies are deficient in that they analyze the particular factors separately rather than considering their combined impact. Even the partisan nature of congressional

[9] Robert B. Arseneau and Raymond E. Wolfinger, "Voting Behavior in Congressional Elections," paper presented at the annual meeting of the American Political Science Association, New Orleans, 1973.

[10] For example, Erikson uses aggregate vote totals to estimate a 5 percent incumbency effect in House voting since 1966 versus only 2 percent prior. Robert S. Erikson, "Malapportionment, Gerrymandering, and Party Fortunes in Congressional Elections," *American Political Science Review*, 66(1972):1234–45.

[11] Andrew T. Cowart, "Electoral Choice in the American States: Incumbency Effects, Partisan Forces, and Divergent Partisan Majorities," *American Political Science Review*, 67(1973):835–52.

elections can be fairly assessed only by an analysis which takes issue effects, candidate effects, satisfaction with the government and incumbency directly into account.

This approach has been adopted in the study of presidential, gubernatorial, and senatorial voting by Hinckley, Hofstetter, and Kessel in chapter 16. They consider most of the factors listed above, and their results are surprising. They report that party identification is of less importance for subpresidential voting than for the presidential contest, while reactions to the party and experience of the candidates are more important at the subpresidential levels. [12] Incidentally, the data base of this project is unusual—it involves a 1968 survey of a large number of voters in thirteen states and is designed specifically to permit more careful analysis of statewide elections than has previously been possible. [13]

This analysis suggests explicitly that the description of Senate elections as partisan may be incorrect. These races may actually be less partisan than the presidential contest. Certainly it seems that issues, candidate characteristics, and incumbency cannot be excluded from an explanation of subpresidential voting.

Conclusions

With the work included here we are beginning to make good progress on understanding congressional elections. Several major conclusions seem justified. First, a long-term component—whether called partisanship or something else—has considerable influence on congressional voting. The uninterrupted Democratic control of Congress since 1954 supports this idea. Hinckley, Hofstetter, and Kessel suggest that the cue that party provides about the candidate may be more important than party identification per se, but this does not disprove the importance of party in congressional elections. It would now be useful to test simultaneously the effects of long-term and short-term components on voting in presidential and congressional elections.

---

[12] Exactly how "party-as-a-cue" differs from party identification—except in an operational sense—is not as clear to us as it is to Hinckley, Hofstetter, and Kessel. Nonetheless, even the simple correlations between party identification and the vote are lower for subpresidential than for presidential voting in their study.

[13] Gerald Wright has analyzed the same data and achieved similar conclusions regarding the importance of partisanship at different election levels with a somewhat different set of predictors. He also found that much of the incumbency effect involves party identification and candidate awareness, but with that removed, incumbency helped senators by 4.1 percent while it hurt governors by 1.2 percent (presumably because governors are blamed for undesired changes in their states, particularly higher taxes). See Gerald C. Wright, Jr., *Electoral Choice in America: Image, Party and Incumbency in State and National Elections* (Chapel Hill, N.C.: Institute for Research in Social Science, University of North Carolina, 1974).

A second important point about congressional voting is that the most crucial factor in determining candidate orientation seems to be an evaluation of the incumbent president (and possibly of both presidential candidates in presidential election years). This conclusion is highly supported by Tufte's analysis for the overall election result and is suggested at the individual voter level by the analysis of Arseneau and Wolfinger.

The extent to which voters are familiar with individual congressional candidates depends on a variety of conditions. It seems important to study these conditions because familiarity with the candidates—that is, simple recognition, which may not include detailed knowledge of their careers or policies—does influence voting behavior. Incumbency, of course, is a prime aid to such recognition, and we suggest that incumbency can easily be incorporated under the general rubric of recognition. However, there are many other reasons why a candidate may be well-known, including such things as "friends and neighbors effects," [14] celebrity in another field (John Glenn or Ronald Reagan), sex of the candidate, [15] and so on.

Candidates' political records (such as reflected in roll call behavior) or positions on current issues are apparently only of minor importance. This is probably due to widespread ignorance of the identity of the majority party and individual congressmen, to say nothing of the details of congressional behavior. Occasionally, of course, a particular congressman's record is conspicuous. Miller and Stokes, for example, cite the example in the fifth district of Arkansas in 1958, in which civil rights became a dominant issue. [16] In that particular instance, every one of the individuals in their sample of that district had read or heard something about both of the congressional candidates. The result of the unusual awareness was that a majority of the voters wrote in the name of the segregationist candidate Dale Alford to unseat incumbent moderate Brooks Hays. Such awareness, however, is by far the exception and not the rule.

Are congressional elections essentially partisan? The answer is not as simple as it once seemed. Clearly, people are less informed about congressional elections than they are about presidential races, and this has a direct effect on voting. But separation of the various election influences at the level of the individual voter will require a more complex analysis than has been performed to date, with the full range of suggested predictors employed simultaneously. The analysis by Hinckley, Hofstetter, and Kessel at the Senate level suggests what must be performed at the House level, with more explicit inclusion of evaluations of the president and of government performance and more exact specification of the long-term component. If the final tallies are not yet in, we are for once satisfied that they can be obtained.

---

[14] See Stokes and Miller, "Party Government," p. 544. The phrase is from V. O. Key, Jr., Southern Politics (New York: Vintage Books, 1949), where it was used to explain localism in southern voting behavior.

[15] Stokes and Miller, "Party Government," p. 543.

[16] Warren E. Miller and Donald E. Stokes, "Constituency Influence in Congress," American Political Science Review, 57(1963):45–56.

If this is the nature of congressional elections, how should we interpret voter behavior in midterm elections? This question has frequently been raised in an attempt to discover whether or not voters behave rationally. Tufte, for example, concludes his paper with precisely this question. We would use the results to emphasize a slightly different point. Perhaps the question is not so much whether or not voters are rational, but in what sense they are rational. If midterm elections are a referendum on the performance of a president, this indeed says that voters are basing their votes on *something*—that is, they are not voting randomly or on the basis of totally irrelevant considerations such as the candidate's hair color or even on the basis of "blind partisanship." But on the other hand, voting for congressmen on the basis of the president's performance is quite different from selecting a congressional candidate on the basis of his or her own characteristics, attitudes, experience, and so on. Interpretations of midterm elections as a reaction to proposals by the party out of power, for example, would be misguided. Similarly, it may be highly "rational" to vote for a candidate because of certain characteristics related to his or her ability to perform in office—such as experience, intelligence, and so on—but it is quite another thing to vote for someone whose most salient characteristic is being a former astronaut, a former congressman's wife, or a "local boy." How the type of rationality exhibited by voters affects our interpretation and evaluation of congressional voting is a question that will have to be considered in the future.

Finally, we must admit that we have only begun to explore the question of subpresidential elections in this consideration of congressional voting. State and local elections, primaries, and referenda furnish large numbers of elections yearly. Some attract even less attention than congressional races, while some local elections and presidential primaries involve the dissemination of a great deal of information. If we have not ventured into this thicket in this essay, it is not because the subject is unimportant but that it is too vast for us to do justice to it in the available space.

Further Readings

Determinants of Voting for Congress

Angus Campbell, "Surge and Decline: A Study of Electoral Change," *Public Opinion Quarterly,* 24(1960):397–418. Theory of differences between presidential and off-year congressional elections.

Donald E. Stokes and Warren E. Miller, "Party Government and the Saliency of Congress," *Public Opinion Quarterly,* 26(1962):531–46. Emphasizes the information level of congressional elections.

Barbara Hinckley, "Interpreting House Midterm Elections: Toward a Measurement of the In-Party's 'Expected' Loss of Seats," *American Political Science Review,* 61(1967):674–700. Based on figures showing that midterm losses are heaviest where President ran ahead of ticket two years earlier.

Gerald H. Kramer, "Short-Term Fluctuations in U.S. Voting Behavior," *American Political Science Review,* 67(1971):131-43. Aggregate analysis of the importance of economic factors in congressional voting.

Francisco Arcelus and Allan H. Meltzer, "The Effect of Aggregate Economic Variables on Congressional Elections," *American Political Science Review,* 69(1975):1232-39. Further analysis of economic factors and congressional voting.

Howard S. Bloom and H. Douglas Price, "Voter Response to Short-Run Economic Conditions: The Asymmetric Effect of Prosperity and Recession," *American Political Science Review,* 69(1975):1240-54. Additional modeling of the effects of the economy on congressional voting.

John E. Mueller, "Presidential Popularity from Truman to Johnson," *American Political Science Review,* 64(1970):18-34. Study of the determinants of presidential popularity.

Andrew T. Cowart, "Electoral Choice in the American States: Incumbency Effects, Partisan Forces, and Divergent Partisan Majorities," *American Political Science Review,* 67(1973):835-52. Applies Michigan SRC/CPS voting theory to subpresidential elections.

David R. Mayhew, "Congressional Elections: The Case of the Vanishing Marginals," *Polity,* 6(1974):295-317. Discusses the increased number of safe seats in Congress.

Effects of Constituency on Congress

Warren E. Miller and Donald E. Stokes, "Constituency Influence in Congress," *American Political Science Review,* 57(1963):45-56. Impact of constituency on roll call voting by members of Congress.

Morris P. Fiorina, *Representatives and Roll Calls* (Lexington, Mass.: Lexington Books, 1974). Formal analysis of constituency electoral characteristics and their impact on voting in Congress.

Other Types of Elections

Eugene C. Lee, *The Politics of Nonpartisanship: A Study of California City Elections* (Berkeley: University of California Press, 1960). Study of voting behavior in nonpartisan elections.

Austin Ranney, "Turnout and Representation in Presidential Primary Elections," *American Political Science Review,* 66(1972):21-37. Finds voters in presidential primaries to be nonrepresentative of party identifiers in their states.

15. Determinants of the Outcomes of Midterm Congressional Elections

EDWARD R. TUFTE

The outcomes of midterm congressional elections appear as a mixture of the routine and the inexplicable. In every off-year congressional election but one since the Civil War, the political party of the incumbent President has lost seats in the House of Representatives. Yet the factors explaining the variation around the usual aggregate outcome of midterms are not well understood; indeed, in *Politics, Parties and Pressure Groups*, V. O. Key suggested that the nature of the midterm verdict lacked explanation in any theory of a rational electorate:

SOURCE: *American Political Science Review,* 69(1975):812–26. Reprinted with permission of the publisher.

AUTHOR'S NOTE: I wish to thank Marge Cruise, Jan Juran, Alice Anne Navin, Susan Spock, Michael Stoto, and Richard Sun for their help in the collection and analysis of the data. John L. McCarthy, Richard A. Brody, Gerald H. Kramer, Duane Lockard, David Seidman, and Jack Walker provided advice and encouragement. Financial support came from the Woodrow Wilson School of Public and International Affairs at Princeton University and from a fellowship at the Center for Advanced Study in the Behavioral Sciences. Early drafts of the paper were presented in seminars at the Center (October 1973); the Bay Area Political Behavior Seminar (January 1974); and Princeton University (October 1974). A partial, preliminary version of the model is reported in Edward R. Tufte, *Data Analysis for Politics and Policy* (Englewood Cliffs, N.J.: Prentice-Hall, 1974), pp. 140–45. I wish also to thank several anonymous reviewers and Dr. Ellen Y. Siegelman of the *Review* for their helpful comments. These individuals and institutions do not, of course, bear responsibility for the faults of the study.

Since the electorate cannot change administrations at midterm elections, it can only express its approval or disapproval by returning or withdrawing legislative majorities. At least such would be the rational hypothesis about what the electorate might do. In fact, no such logical explanation can completely describe what it does at midterm elections. The Founding Fathers, by the provision for midterm elections, built into the constitutional system a procedure whose strange consequences lack explanation in any theory that personifies the electorate as a rational god of vengeance and of reward. [1]

Furthermore, the central facts of midterm elections—the almost invariable loss by the President's party combined with the great stability in partisan swings compared to on-year elections [2]—both suggest an electorate returning to their normal partisan alignment after the more hectic presidential contest two years earlier, rather than an electorate responding to short-term national forces and acting as a "rational god of vengeance and of reward." In seeking to explain the sources of midterm loss, both Campbell and Key emphasized the differences in turnout in off-year compared to on-year elections—rather than short-run factors such as the electorate's evaluation of the performance of the President and his party. [3] Following up this approach, Hinckley assessed the administration's midterm loss with reference to the prior presidential election and concluded: ". . . the midterm 'referendum' appears quite derivative. It is, in part, a continuation of the verdict expressed in the preceding presidential elections and, in part, an adjustment of that verdict, an adjustment built into the midterm by the preceding presidential election." [4] Another recent analysis of midterms from 1954 to 1970 concludes that they are "non-events" and "non-elections," predictable solely from the preceding presidential election. [5] Finally, the Stokes-Miller study of the 1958 midterm found that voters were simply not responding to the parties' legislative records in casting midterm ballots.

---

[1] V. O. Key, Jr., *Politics, Parties, and Pressure Groups,* 5th ed. (New York: Thomas Y. Crowell, 1964), pp. 567-68.

[2] Donald E. Stokes and Warren E. Miller, "Party Government and the Saliency of Congress," *Public Opinion Quarterly,* 26(Winter 1962):531-46.

[3] Angus Campbell, "Voters and Elections: Past and Present," *Journal of Politics,* 26(November, 1964):745-757; Angus Campbell, "Surge and Decline: A Study of Electoral Change," *Public Opinion Quarterly,* 24(Fall 1960):397-418; and Key, pp. 568-69.

[4] Barbara Hinckley, "Interpreting House Midterm Elections: Toward a Measurement of the In-Party's 'Expected' Loss of Seats," *American Political Science Review,* 61(September 1967):700.

[5] Mark N. Franklin, "A 'Non-election' in America? Predicting the Results of the 1970 Mid-term Election for the U.S. House of Representatives," *British Journal of Political Science,* 1(October 1971):508-13. See also Anthony King, "Why All Governments Lose By-Elections," *New Society,* 21 March 1968, pp. 413-15; Nigel Lawson, "A New Theory of By-Elections," *Spectator* (November 1968):651-52; and John D. Lees, "Campaigns and Parties—The 1970 American Mid-Term Elections and Beyond," *Parliamentary Affairs,* 24(Autumn 1971):312-20. The view that midterms represent, in large measure, the electoral swing of the pendulum (or electoral surge and decline) does not seem to be held by politicians. Sam Kernell has compiled convincing evidence that a central premise among American politicians is that "the president's popularity directly affects his congressional party candidates' chances for election" in midterms: Sam Kernell, "Presidential Popularity

Nevertheless, the prevailing view of midterm outcomes as an adjustment restoring the normal partisan equilibrium unrelated to objective events in the two years prior to the midterm is incomplete, for while it explains why the President's party should almost always be operating in the loss column, it does not account for the *number* of votes and seats lost by the President's party. In statistical parlance, the adjustment model of midterm congressional elections explains the location of the mean rather than variability about the mean. But, as Key indicated, "The significance of a specific midterm result comes not from the simple fact of losses by the President's party. Some loss is to be expected. It is the magnitude of the loss that is important."[6]

In this study, we seek to explain the *magnitude of the national midterm loss* by the President's party: why do some presidents lose fewer congressional seats at midterm than other presidents? Do the outcomes of midterm congressional elections represent the electorate's evaluation of the President's performance? Do such outcomes reflect the electorate's evaluation of the administration's management of the economy? If a relatively large proportion of the electorate approves the President's handling of his job or his management of the economy, then does his party lose less in the midterm congressional elections? Or, on the other hand, is the midterm "referendum" only "derivative" and the outcomes lacking in rational explanation? Since those citizens showing up at the polls in the midterm are probably somewhat more politically sophisticated and interested than those voting in on-year elections,[7] the assertion that midterm outcomes are "irrational" provides a substantial challenge to the view that the electorate behaves in rational ways, or at least in ways somewhat responsive to the political environment.

Because there are no other targets available at the midterm, it is not unreasonable to expect that some voters opposed to the President might take out their dissatisfaction with the incumbent administration on the congressional candidates of the President's party. Arseneau and Wolfinger, using survey data, provide some evidence that ". . . the public image of Congress is rather undifferentiated and, moreover, assessments of the two parties' performance are likely to be determined predominantly by evaluations of the President rather than Congress. . . . congressional candidates are likely to suffer or benefit from voters' estimates of how well the Pres-

---

and Negative Voting: An Alternative Explanation of the Mid-Term Electoral Decline of the President's Party," paper delivered at the 1974 annual meeting of the American Political Science Association. See also the variety of interpretations of the outcome of British by-elections in Chris Cook and John Ramsden, eds., *By-Elections in British Politics* (New York: St. Martin's Press, 1973). Alternative midterm models are discussed in Richard W. Boyd and James T. Murphy, "How Many Seats Will the Republicans Lose? Changes in the House: A Prediction," *New Republic,* 24 October 1970, pp. 12–14.

[6] Key, p. 569.

[7] This conventional description of the midterm electorate has been challenged by the evidence of Robert B. Arseneau and Raymond E. Wolfinger, "Voting Behavior in Congressional Elections," paper delivered at the 1973 annual meeting of the American Political Science Association.

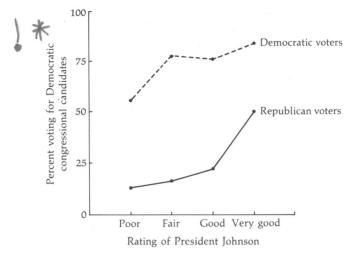

Figure 15.1 Relationship between evaluations of the President and vote for congressional candidate, 1968. (Source: Arseneau and Wolfinger, "Voting Behavior in Congressional Elections," p. 16.)

ident has been doing his job."[8] Figure 15.1 shows their analysis of the Survey Research Center data for the 1968 election; for voters of both parties, support for Democratic congressional candidates increases by about thirty percentage points as the evaluations of President Johnson go from "poor" to "very good."

Thus our first link in the model explaining midterm outcomes is the relationship between the aggregate outcome and the electorate's evaluation of the President at the time of the election: at what rate are fluctuations in presidential popularity translated into fluctuations in votes and congressional seats in off-year elections? Two kinds of evidence help assess the relationship: aggregate data for the whole nation and individual interviews in surveys of the electorate. Although this study is largely based on aggregate data, fortunately some new detailed material at the individual level also bears on the issue.

The second explanatory variable in our analysis of midterm outcomes is the performance of the economy in the year prior to the midterm. There is already available a careful study linking prevailing economic conditions to aggregate electoral outcomes, including midterms. Kramer's model explains 56 percent of the variation in the national partisan division of vote in the

---

[8] Arseneau and Wolfinger, p. 3. Several other recent studies have greatly reinforced the evidence linking evaluations of the incumbent president to electoral choices in congressional races. See Kernell, "Presidential Popularity and Negative Voting," for an extensive analysis of Gallup poll data in six midterm elections; and James E. Pierson, "Presidential Popularity and Midterm Voting at Different Electoral Levels," *American Journal of Political Science,* 19(1975):683–94, which uses data from the 1970 election study conducted by the Center for Political Studies at the University of Michigan.

midterms from 1898 to 1962.[9] Although these results have been subjected to vigorous, but not convincing, critiques by Stigler and others, it seems clear from Kramer's analysis that midterm outcomes are responsive to changes in objective economic conditions taking place between the presidential election and the midterm itself.[10]

In summary, our data analysis here will estimate the impact on midterm congressional elections of the electorate's evaluations of presidential performance and of prevailing economic conditions prior to the election. Such estimates lead to predictions of the national partisan division of the congressional vote. That vote, of course, is not the ultimate measure of the midterm outcome—it is the resulting partisan distribution of *seats* in the House of Representatives that matters politically. As we will see, the translation of votes into seats has changed considerably over the period covered in our study: comparable shifts in the midterm partisan division of the vote are now worth less than half as much in terms of congressional seats compared to 35 years ago[11]—thus significantly muting the impact of midterm elections on party alignment in the House. It is therefore not enough to explain and predict the partisan division of the vote; it is necessary also to take into account the changing political consequences of that vote resulting from the changing character of the translation of votes into congressional seats. Thus the model is:

Public approval of President at time of midterm election   Pre-election shifts in economic conditions

↘   ↙

Magnitude of national vote loss by President's party

↓

Magnitude of congressional seat loss by President's party

---

[9] Gerald H. Kramer, "Short-Term Fluctuations in U.S. Voting Behavior, 1896–1964," *American Political Science Review,* 65(March 1971):131–43. A data error in this paper is corrected in its Bobbs-Merrill reprint (PS-498); see also Saul Goodman and Gerald H. Kramer, "Comment on Arcelus and Meltzer, 'The Effect of Aggregate Economic Conditions on Congressional Elections'," *American Political Science Review,* 69(1975):1255–65; Gerald H. Kramer and Susan J. Lepper, "Congressional Elections," in *The Dimensions of Quantitative Research in History,* ed. William O. Aydelotte, Allan G. Bogue, and Robert William Fogel (Princeton: Princeton University Press, 1972), 256–84; and Susan J. Lepper, "Voting Behavior and Aggregate Policy Targets," *Public Choice,* 18(Summer 1974):67–81.

[10] George J. Stigler, "General Economic Conditions and National Elections," *American Economic Review,* 63(May 1973):160–67; and further discussion by Paul W. McCracken, Arthur M. Okun, and others, pp. 169–80. Stigler's method might best be described as a "most squares" technique: find the specification that maximizes the error variance. But the outstanding work in discovering the pessimum most squares model is Francisco Arcelus and Allen H. Meltzer, "The Effect of Aggregate Economic Conditions on Congressional Elections," *American Political Science Review,* 69(1975):1232–39; see the reply of Goodman and Kramer.

[11] On the translation of votes into seats, see Edward R. Tufte, "The Relationship Between Seats and Votes in Two-Party Systems," *American Political Science Review,* 67(June 1973):540–54.

A substantial amount of recent research has contemplated the three variables in the first stage of the model: the measurement of economic performance in relation to electoral outcomes, the meaning of the long-run Gallup
poll question on approval of the President, and the proper way to interpret
midterm congressional outcomes with respect to the vote and the seat loss
by the President's party. It is clear from Stigler's study that the results in the
aggregate analysis of congressional elections are sensitive to the particular
specification of variables in the model. The problem is further complicated
by the difficulty of choosing among alternative specifications, given the relatively small number of data points, the high intercorrelation between alternative measures of the same general concept, and difficulty in handling
idiosyncratic problems such as third party candidacies, elections that involve
unusual factors, and the like. In the face of these problems, some special
attention to the particular operationalization of each variable is necessary,
even though each seemingly has rather obvious empirical referents.

The most important variable to measure well in the dependent or response variable, the magnitude of the midterm loss by the President's party.
As most discussions evaluating midterm losses point out, the idea of "loss"
implies the question "Relative to what?"[12] The relevant comparison, it
seems, is between the normal, long-run congressional vote for the political
party of the current President and the outcome of the midterm election at
hand—that is, a standardized vote loss that takes the long-run partisan trend
into account:

Standardized vote loss by President's party in the ith midterm election

= national congressional vote for President's party in the ith election

− average national congressional vote for party of current President in
previous elections

Thus the loss is measured with respect to how well the party of the current
President has normally done, where the normal vote is computed by averaging that party's national vote over the eight preceding both on-year and off-
year congressional elections.[13] This standardization is necessary because the
Democrats have dominated postwar congressional elections; if the unstan-

---

[12] Hinckley, "Interpreting House Midterm Elections;" Harvey Zeidenstein, "Measuring
Congressional Seat Losses in Mid-Term Elections," *Journal of Politics,* 34(February
1972):272–76; and A. H. Taylor, "The Proportional Decline Hypothesis in English Elections," *Journal of the Royal Statistical Society,* Series A, 135(1972):365–69.

dardized vote won by the President's party is used as the response (dependent) variable, the Republican presidents would appear to do poorly. For example, when the Republicans win 48 percent of the national congressional vote, it is, relatively, a substantial victory for that party and should be counted as such. The eight-election standardization takes this effect into account as well as yielding a model with a bit of dynamics to it.[14] It is straightforward, furthermore, to reconstruct the actual or predicted outcome from the standardized vote, thereby permitting pre-election predictions of the partisan division of the vote. There are many alternative ways of quantitatively assessing the midterm loss.[15] The elections used in the standardization could be weighted, with the heaviest weight given to the most recent elections. On-year congressional elections might be discarded altogether. A larger or smaller number of elections might be used. In general, most of the obvious alternatives are highly correlated; in addition, experiments with a variety of methods for computing the normal vote revealed that the model performed well under most reasonable alternatives. Table 15.1 shows the computations for the midterm elections from 1938 to 1970.

---

[13] See the normalizations in William H. Flanigan and Nancy H. Zingale, "The Measurement of Electoral Change," *Political Methodology*, 1(Summer 1974):49–82; also William H. Flanigan and Nancy H. Zingale, "Electoral Competition and Partisan Realignment," paper delivered at the 1973 annual meeting of the American Political Science Association. The standard discussion is, of course, Philip E. Converse, "The Concept of a Normal Vote," in Angus Campbell et al., *Elections and the Political Order* (New York: Wiley, 1966), pp. 9–39.

[14] The Democratic loss in the 1938 midterm election is measured relative to the share of votes received by Democratic congressional candidates in the previous *three* elections (1932, 1934, and 1936), rather than the eight used for estimating the normal vote in the other midterms. The eight election normalization fails for 1938 because of the rapid and extensive realignment from 1930 to 1932; thus the averaged results of congressional elections from 1932 on gives a more reasonable estimate of the 1938 normal vote than the inclusion of several Republican dominated years prior to the realignment. The percentage share of the congressional vote received by the Democrats during that period shows the problem:

Year	Percent
1938	50.8
1936	56.2
1934	56.2
1932	56.9
1930	45.9
1928	42.8
1926	41.6
1924	42.1
1922	46.4

From this series, it seems clear that a reasonable estimate of the normal Democratic vote for the 1938 election should be based on the elections of 1932, 1934, and 1936, rather than earlier years.

[15] See Harvey M. Kabaker, "Estimating the Normal Vote in Congressional Elections," *Midwest Journal of Political Science*, 13(February 1969):58–83.

Table 15.1   Data for Midterm Elections   255

Year	V_i Nationwide Midterm Congressional Vote for Party of Incumbent President (%)	N_i^β Mean Congressional Vote for Party of Incumbent President in 8 Prior Elections (%)	$Y_i = V_i - N_i^\beta$ Standardized Vote Loss ($-$) or Gain ($+$) by President's Party in Midterm Election (%)	P_i Gallup Poll Rating of President at Time of Election (%)	ΔE_i Yearly Change in Real Disposable Income Per Capita
1938	50.82	Democratic 57.18*	-6.36	57	$-\$82$
1946	45.27	Democratic 52.57	-7.30	32	$-\$36$
1950	50.04	Democratic 52.04	-2.00	43	$\$99$
1954	47.46	Republican 49.79	-2.33	65	$-\$12$
1958	43.90	Republican 49.83	-5.93	56	$-\$13$
1962	52.42	Democratic 51.63	$+0.79$	67	$\$60$
1966	51.33	Democratic 53.06	-1.73	48	$\$96$
1970	45.68	Republican 46.66	-0.98	56	$\$69$

*For 1938, mean is based on last three elections only. See note 14, p. 254.

Let us now consider the explanatory variables, the public's approval of the President and the economic conditions prevailing at the time of midterm election.

The only long-run consistent measure of the public's evaluation of the President's general performance is the standard Gallup poll question asked in their monthly surveys: "Do you approve or disapprove of the way [the incumbent] is handling his job as President?" [16] While the Gallup poll has asked for evaluations of the President since 1935 (thereby limiting our study to the midterms since 1938), the wording of the question has shifted and it was only in 1945 that the standard wording was adopted. The wording used immediately prior to the 1938 midterm, however, differs only slightly from

---

[16] The presidential approval ratings from 1946 to 1970 are from *The Gallup Opinion Index*, 64(October 1970):16; the 1938 approval rate, 57 percent, was averaged (because of inconsistencies in question wording and survey dates) from two surveys: September, 1938—"Are you for or against Roosevelt today?" 55.2 percent; and October 1938—"In general do you approve or disapprove of Roosevelt as President?" 59.6 percent. The source for the 1938 data is George Gallup, *The Gallup Poll* (New York: Random House, 1972), pp. 118, 122. Similar, but not identical figures are reported in a fine study by Wesley C. Clark, "Economic Aspects of a President's Popularity" (Ph.D. dissertation, University of Pennsylvania, 1943), p. 47, which also contains an extensive discussion of the early years of the series. A flawed analysis of the factors affecting the ratings is given in John E. Mueller, "Presidential Popularity from Truman to Johnson," *American Political Science Review*, 64(March 1970):18–34; and in John E. Mueller, *War, Presidents and Public Opinion* (New York: Wiley, 1973). The substantive and statistical difficulties in Mueller's analysis are discussed in Richard A. Brody and Benjamin I. Page, "The Impact of Events on Presidential Popularity: The Johnson and Nixon Administrations," paper delivered at the 1972 annual meeting of the American Political Science Association; and in Douglas A. Hibbs, Jr., "Problems of Statistical Estimation and Causal Inference in Time-Series Regression Models," in *Sociological Methodology, 1973–1974*, ed. Herbert Costner (San Francisco: Jossey-Bass, 1974), pp. 252–308.

the postwar surveys and consequently our analysis includes the 1938 survey results. [17]

Table 15.1 shows the approval ratings from the surveys taken prior to each midterm election. The simple correlation between the normalized midterm loss by the party of the President and the pre-election approval rating is .50, indicating that larger losses are associated with lower popularity.

Although we have only a single relatively consistent indicator over the years of the public's evaluation of the President, there are available, on the other hand, many different possible measures for the other dependent variable, the performance of the economy. Neither theory nor data strongly suggest a good choice. The discussions of the studies of Kramer and Stigler by McCracken, Okun, Riker, and Ireland reveal many speculations and little theory—beyond the observation, agreed upon by all, that general economic conditions might somehow have an effect on some elections—that suggest specific hypotheses about which economic variables should be important or what kinds of time perspectives voters might use in evaluating the pre-election performance of the economy. [18] Kramer's empirical work has shown the political importance of inter-election shifts in real income and of inflation; both seem to have more impact on congressional elections than do shifts of ordinary magnitude in unemployment. [19] The best measure of economic conditions for our model therefore appears to be pre-election changes in real disposable income per capita. [20] This measure may reflect the economic concerns of many voters, for it assesses the short-run shift in average economic conditions, measured in terms of real purchasing power, prevail-

---

[17] The details of the shifting wording are in Clark, *Economic Aspects of a President's Popularity*, pp. 47, 55–60.

[18] Stigler's article itself, as well as the commentary, makes clear the lack of theoretical specificity found in current models correlating economic time series to electoral outcomes; see Stigler, "General Economic Conditions and National Elections," pp. 160–67; and further comments, 168–80. Stigler uses a two-year difference to compute the change in economic conditions for his model, on the view that voters compare the change in the economy in the current election year with that at the time of the previous election two years before. That model seems doubtful, attributing an excessively long time perspective to voters, especially for moderate economic changes. Another way to look at the matter is to consider the voter's problem as the generation of an estimate of the rate of real economic change immediately prior to the election—in order to estimate what can be expected with respect to the performance of the economy under the incumbent administration. If those expectations are good, the party of the incumbent President receives a vote; otherwise the out-party gets the vote. If this is a reasonable description of the problem facing the voter, then the voter would probably not use Stigler's method—a two-year difference in economic changes—to estimate expected or immediately past economic performance. A one-year different is at least slightly more realistic. Additional progress on this question can probably be made by examining survey evidence at the individual level rather than by still more specifications of aggregate models.

[19] Kramer, "Short-Term Fluctuations," p. 139; see also Goodman and Kramer, "Comment."

[20] The yearly change in real disposable personal income per capita (in 1958 dollars) was computed from data in *The Annual Report of the Council of Economic Advisers, 1973* (Washington, D.C.: U.S. Government Printing Office, 1973), p. 213; and *The Annual Report of the Council of Economic Advisers, 1971*, p. 215.

ing at the individual level—a shift in conditions for which some voters might hold the incumbent administration and the political party of the incumbent administration responsible.

In summary, our model explaining the midterm vote received by the political party of the incumbent President is:

$$Y_i = \beta_0 + \beta_1 P_i + \beta_2(\Delta E_i) + u_i \tag{1}$$

where

Y_i = standardized midterm vote for the political party of the incumbent President in the ith midterm congressional election, $Y_i = V_i - N_i^8$;

V_i = nationwide share of the two-party congressional vote received by political party of the incumbent President in the ith midterm;

N_i^8 = normal congressional vote for the political party of the incumbent President at the time of the ith midterm; computed as the average, over the preceding eight congressional elections (both on- and off-years) prior to the ith midterm, of the nationwide share of the two-party congressional vote received by the political party of the President in office at the time of the ith midterm;

P_i = percentage of sample in Gallup poll in September prior to the ith midterm who approve of the job the incumbent President is doing;

ΔE_i = yearly change in real disposable personal income per capita between the year of the midterm and the previous year; and

u_i = residual or error term.

Note that the model can be rewritten to estimate the nationwide congressional vote for the President's party:

$$V_i = \beta_0 + \beta_1 P_i + \beta_2(\Delta E_i) + \beta_3 N_i^8 + u_i. \tag{2}$$

Thus, while equation (1) leads to estimates of Y_i, the standardized vote loss by the President's party, equation (2) estimates V_i, the nationwide proportion of the congressional vote for the party of the President. The two models are identical, however, if β_3 is unity—for then N_i^8 can be moved, in equation (2), from the right-hand to the left-hand side of the equation. The data were used to fit equation (2) and β_3 was, in fact, very close to unity; and therefore equation (1) will be the model developed in the remainder of the analysis. Equation (1) estimates one less parameter than equation (2), an advantage since the model must be estimated on the basis of a very small number of cases. The small N and the potential fragility of the model also suggest that extraordinary tests of the model's explanatory and predictive capacity are necessary. Many such tests will be conducted, including an assessment of

Table 15.2 Multiple Regression Fitting Standardized Vote Loss by President's Party in Midterm Elections

Variable	Regression Coefficient and (Standard Error)	Simple Correlation with Midterm Loss
Presidential approval rating (P)	$\hat{\beta}_1 = .133^*$ (.033)	.503
Yearly change in real disposable personal income per capita (ΔE)	$\hat{\beta}_2 = .035^*$ (.006)	.795

$Y = \beta_0 + \beta_1 (P) + \beta_2 (\Delta E)$
Constant $(\hat{\beta}_0) = -11.083.$ $R^2 = 0.912.$
*Statistically significant at the .01 level.

the model in predicting the outcome of the 1974 midterm congressional elections.

We now use the data of table 15.1 to estimate the β's, the regression coefficients, in the model.[21] The estimate, $\hat{\beta}_1$, assesses the impact of presidential approval rating on the midterm vote; and $\hat{\beta}_2$, the impact of the pre-election change in real disposable personal income per capita on the midterm vote.

Fitting the Model and Confirming the Results

In order to explain the magnitude of the aggregate loss of votes by the President's party in midterm congressional elections, we estimate our multiple regression model described above (written here in more informal notation):

Standardized vote loss by President's party in the midterm
$= \beta_0 + \beta_1$ [Presidential popularity]
$+ \beta_2$ [Yearly change in economic conditions]

The idea is, of course, that the lower the approval rating of the incumbent President and the less prosperous the economy, the greater the loss of support for the President's party in the midterm congressional elections.

Table 15.2 shows the estimates of the model's coefficients. The results are statistically secure since the coefficients are at least four times their standard errors. The fitted equation indicates:

---

[21] The midterm of 1942 is omitted from the analysis because of the special effect of wartime controls on the economy and of wartime conditions on evaluations of the incumbent President. Kramer also dropped wartime years; see Kramer, p. 137.

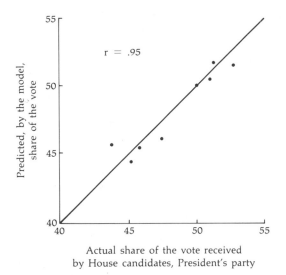

r = .95

Predicted, by the model, share of the vote

Actual share of the vote received
by House candidates, President's party

Figure 15.2 Actual and predicted share of the two-party vote received by congressional candidates of President's party, midterm elections, 1938–1970.

- A change in presidential popularity of 10 percentage points in the Gallup poll is associated with a national change of 1.3 percentage points in national midterm vote for congressional candidates of the President's party.
- A change of $100 in real disposable personal income per capita in the year prior to the midterm election is associated with a national change of 3.5 percentage points in the midterm vote for congressional candidates of the President's party.

The fitted equation explains statistically 91.2 percent of the variance in national midterm outcomes from 1938 to 1970,[22] or, to put it another way, the correlation between the actual election results and those predicted by the model is .955, as shown in figure 15.2. Since the fitted equation uses two meaningful explanatory variables, it seems reasonable to believe that in this case a successful statistical explanation is also a successful substantive explanation.

Before turning to the substantive consequences of the fitted equation, it is necessary to test the soundness of the model. Such tests are important because the model is based on a relatively short series of elections (although more than many studies of midterms)—and also because the model is apparently so successful in terms of the variance explained. Are the findings the result of some artifact?

---

[22] In regressions of this sort, involving such a small number of degrees of freedom, some prefer to use a corrected R^2 that takes into account the loss in degrees of freedom as the coefficients are estimated. In our case, the corrected R^2 is 0.88. See Carl F. Christ, *Econometric Models and Methods* (New York: Wiley, 1966), pp. 509–10.

The overall equation and the estimates of the individual regression coefficients are statistically significant at the .01 level. Let us consider four additional tests of the model: the independent replication of the estimated regression coefficients, and tests assessing the stability, postdictive quality, and predictive quality of the regression equation.

Some independent studies are consistent with estimates of the regression coefficients in this model. Kramer finds that, in congressional elections from 1896 to 1964 (including both on- and off-year congressional elections), "a 10 percent decrease in per capita real personal income would cost the incumbent administration 4 to 5 percent of the congressional vote, other things being equal." [23] Since the average real disposable personal income per capita in the period under study here is around $1800, Kramer's model estimates that a shift of approximately $180 in real disposable income would produce a shift of 4 to 5 percent in the congressional vote. Our regression indicates that a shift of $180 in income would produce a shift of about 6 percent in the congressional vote. Given the differences between the studies with respect to the period and types of elections covered, the results seem quite comparable. Our short-term (1938-1970) estimate approximately matches Kramer's long-term (1896-1964) estimate of the impact of economic conditions on congressional elections.

An independent confirmation of the estimated effect of the presidential approval level on the midterm outcome comes from a study based on survey interviews from national samples of individual voters. Kernell computed voter defection rates by analyzing responses to the interviews in the Gallup poll's samples prior to the midterms of 1946, 1950, 1954, 1958, and 1962. He finds that "for every nine point change in the percentage approving the president, his party's congressional vote will change 1.4 percentage points." [24] Our estimate, using aggregate data, is virtually identical. The two estimates—one based on individual interviews recording respondent's claimed vote choice in the midterm and the evaluation of the incumbent president, the other based on the aggregate approval rating and the actual vote result—were arrived at completely independently.

In our small data set, based on single readings taken once every four years immediately prior to each midterm, there is no relationship between the presidential approval rating and the pre-election shift in real disposable income. (Note that the approval rating is measured in absolute terms, rather than as a pre-election shift.) For example, the Eisenhower midterms of 1954 and 1958 reflect a popular President and a mediocre short-run economic performance. More generally, it appears that presidential approval ratings are a function of many different factors, including performance in foreign affairs, the President's personality, scandals, and large downward shifts in economic conditions.

---

[23] Kramer, p. 141.
[24] Kernell, "Presidential Popularity and Negative Voting," p. 32.

Table 15.3 After-the-Fact Predictive Error of the Model

Year	Actual Vote for House Candidates, President's Party	Gallup Poll Prediction*	Model Prediction	Gallup Absolute Error	Model Absolute Error
1938	50.8	54	50.8	3.2	0.0
1946	45.3	42	44.5	3.3	0.8
1950	50.0	51	50.1	1.0	0.1
1954	47.5	48.5	46.9	1.0	0.6
1958	43.9	43	45.7	0.9	1.8
1962	52.4	55.5	51.6	3.1	0.8
1966	51.3	52.5	51.7	1.2	0.4
1970	45.7	47	45.4	1.3	0.3

Average absolute error, Gallup = 1.9 percentage points.
Average absolute error, Model = 0.6 percentage points.

*National survey taken 7 to 10 days prior to the election. The question asked is "If the elections for Congress were being held today, which party would you like to see win in this congressional district, the Democratic or the Republican party?"

To check the stability of the fitted equation, the model was re-estimated after excluding one election at a time from the computations. [25] The regression coefficients remained very stable and statistically significant, and the R^2 did not go below .89 in the re-estimates. It is clear that the estimates for the overall model are not dominated by a single set of outlying values for one election.

As another check of the adequacy of model, its after-the-fact predictions of midterm outcomes were compared with the pre-election predictions made by the Gallup poll in the national survey conducted a week to ten days before each election. [26] As table 15.3 shows, the model outperforms the pre-election predictions based on surveys directly asking voters how they intend to vote. Now all this is, of course, after the fact and it would be more useful to have a genuine prediction in hand prior to the election to test the model. This leads to our strongest test of the model—for we can examine its *predictive* powers in a series of historical experiments.

Suppose the model had been estimated prior to the 1970 election, using the data from the midterm elections from 1938 to 1966. The fitted equation prior to the 1970 election was:

Standardized midterm loss = $-11.06 + .133(P) + .035 \ (\Delta E)$.

[25] The discarding of observations one at a time coupled with re-estimation is the first step in producing a "jackknife" estimate of a complex statistic along with a confidence interval; see Frederick Mosteller and John W. Tukey, "Data Analysis, Including Statistics," in Gardner Lindzey and Elliot Aronson, eds., *The Handbook of Social Psychology*, 2nd ed. (Reading, Mass.: Addison-Wesley, 1968), pp. 133-60; and Rupert G. Miller, Jr., "The Jackknife—A Review," Technical Report No. 50 (28 August 1973), Department of Statistics, Stanford University, Stanford, California.

[26] Polls reported in Gallup, *The Gallup Poll*.

Now let us use this model, generated from the experience from 1938 to 1966, to predict the outcome of the 1970 election. The September 1970 level of presidential approval was 56 percent; the 1969–1970 shift in real disposable personal income per capita was $69. Plugging those values into the pre-1970 equation leads to a pre-election forecast of the 1970 outcome:

$$\text{Predicted 1970 normalized midterm loss} = -11.06 + .133(56) + .035(69)$$
$$= -1.20 \text{ percent.}$$

Since the actual normalized loss was -0.98 percent, the model performed well in this predictive trial. To translate these results to the actual partisan division of the vote, the pre-1970 model predicted the 1970 outcome to be 45.4 percent of the vote for the party of the President, the Republicans; in fact, they won 45.7 percent of the vote in 1970.

Table 15.4 shows the outcome of this historical experiment for three other midterm elections—1958, 1962, and 1968. In each case, the predictions are based on a model estimated *prior* to the election predicted—that is, they are honest predictions. Note how stable the model is over the years, even though it is based on fewer and fewer elections as we go backwards in time. Table 15.4 shows that the model performs very well indeed in its predictions, doing even somewhat better than pre-election polls directly asking voters what party's candidate they intend to support in the upcoming midterm election. Table 15.4 thus provides a very strong test of an explanatory model based on non-experimental data—a test of predictive success. The before-the-fact predictive trials of the model show the following: in the four midterm elections from 1958 to 1970, the pre-election forecast generated by the model deviated by an average of 1.1 percentage points from the actual partisan division of the vote. In these tests, based on genuine prediction, the model performs successfully.

The model for the years 1938–1970 has performed well in all our statistical tests:

- high explanatory power, $R^2 = .91$
- statistical significance (.01 level) of all estimates

Table 15.4 Before-the-Fact Predictions of the Model

Model Based on Years	$\hat{\beta}_1$	$\hat{\beta}_2$	R^2	Predicting Election of	Vote for President's Party		Model Absolute Error	Gallup Absolute Error
					Predicted %	Actual %		
1938–1954	.12	.032	.98	1958	46.0	43.9	2.1	0.9
1938–1958	.11	.032	.85	1962	50.8	52.4	1.6	3.1
1938–1962	.13	.036	.90	1966	51.9	51.3	0.6	1.2
1938–1966	.13	.035	.90	1970	45.4	45.7	0.3	1.3
1938–1970	.13	.035	.91	1974	39.2	41.1	1.9	1.1

Average absolute error, Gallup = 1.5 percentage points.
Average absolute error, Model = 1.3 percentage points.

- independent replication, using other data or models, of parameter estimates
- no multicollinearity
- no outliers dominating estimates; stability of estimates when parts of data are discarded
- historical experiments: successful postdictions
- historical experiments: successful predictions.

This is all very nice, but how well did the model do in its predictions of the 1974 midterm congressional elections?

The Model and the 1974 Elections: A Difficult Test in a Landslide Election

In the fall of 1973, I constructed table 15.5—showing what the model would predict for the 1974 midterm, given varying levels of presidential approval ratings and performance of the economy. It was possible, then, to track the vote estimates for the huge changes in approval ratings and economic conditions as both President Nixon and the economy collapsed. Using data for approval rating and economic conditions, a pre-election prediction for the 1974 midterm was generated from the model. The calculations and the prediction were made public two weeks before the election; in addition, several other people used the model on their own to generate pre-election predictions. All in all, the election of 1974 provided a particularly stern test—both explanatory variables had undergone very large short-term shifts and had reached historical extremes in the period before the election. And Mr. Ford had only been in office for three months.

Table 15.5 Predicted Republican Congressional Vote in 1974

Percentage Approving the Job President is Doing (P)	Yearly Change in Real Disposable Personal Income Per Capita (ΔE)				
	−$100	−$50	$0	$50	$100
25	34.9	36.6	38.4	40.1	41.9
30	35.5	37.3	39.0	40.8	42.7
35	36.2	37.9	39.7	41.5	43.2
40	36.9	38.6	40.4	42.1	43.9
45	37.5	39.3	41.0	42.8	44.5
50	38.2	39.9	41.7	43.4	45.2
55	38.9	40.6	42.4	44.1	45.9
60	39.5	41.3	43.0	44.8	46.5

Predicted national congressional vote for Republicans in $1974 = 35.04 + .133P + .035 \Delta E$,
where P = percent approving the job the President is doing
ΔE = yearly change in real disposable personal income per capita

The prediction for the 1974 midterm was constructed from the model:

Standardized midterm loss in 1974 (predicted)
= predicted Republican vote in 1974
− average Republican congressional
vote in prior elections, 1958–1972
= − 11.083 + .133P + .035(ΔE).

The average Republican vote over the last eight congressional elections (from 1958 to 1972) is 46.12 percent. Substituting this value into the above equation yields the estimates shown in table 15.5. The predicted Republican share of the congressional vote in 1974 is shown for a variety of combinations of popularity levels and economic conditions and the exact prediction is determined by the approval level and economic conditions prevailing immediately before election. In the months before the 1974 elections, President Ford's popularity shifted greatly. [27]

Date	Percent
August 16	71
September 6	66
September 27	50
October 22	55

The condition of the economy also changed greatly prior to the election; real disposable income in March 1974 had declined about $45 over the preceding year, but by the time of the November elections the decline was $90. Putting the pre-election values for the approval rating and economic conditions into the equation led to the following late-October prediction for the 1974 midterm vote:

Predicted Republican congressional vote
= 35.04 + .133(55) + .035(−90)
= 39.2%

The final pre-election Gallup poll predicted 60 percent Democratic, 40 percent Republican; a national phone poll by Decision Making Information led to a 62–38 prediction; and our midterm model predicted 60.8 to 39.2 [28] The actual vote was 58.9 to 41.1 in 1974. [29] Thus the error of the mid-term model was 1.9 percentage points; of the Gallup poll, 1.1 points; and of the DMI poll, 3.1 points. Although the predictive error of the model for the 1974 election was slightly above its previous average, the model still performed very well in a most difficult election.

During 1973–74, both explanatory variables in the midterm model moved toward historical extremes, *both* high and low: presidential approval ratings ranged between 24 and 71 percent; and ΔE between + $198 and − $90; and

---

[27] "Gallup Says Poll Shows Ford Popularity on Rise," *The New York Times*, 24 October 1974.
[28] "Poll Confirms GOP Fears," *The Washington Post*, 4 November 1974, p. A5.
[29] Vote as reported in *The Gallup Opinion Index*, 118(April 1975):27.

Table 15.6 **1974 Election Projections from the Midterm Model and Polls, 1973–1974**

Date	Percentage Approving President	Change in Real Income (ΔE)	Projection of Midterm Model, % Democratic	Polls, % Democratic in Upcoming Election (G=Gallup, H=Harris, DMI=Decision-Making Information)
October, 1974	55	−$90	61	60, 62 (G, DMI)
July, 1974	24	−$91	65	63 (H)
May, 1974	27	−$78	64	60, 64 (H, G)
March, 1974	26	−$44	62	62 (H)
January, 1974	27	+$22	60	59, 65 (H, G)
October, 1973	28	+$168	55	64 (G)
September, 1973	34	+$168	54	58 (H)
May, 1973	44	+$198	51	55, 60 (H, G)

as these variables changed, the projected midterm vote shifted. These shifts can be compared with a series of polls taken during 1973–74 in which respondents were asked what party's candidate they intended to support in the upcoming congressional elections. Although the different polls themselves are not always consistent with one another, the projections of the midterm model follow rather well the shifts in the vote recorded in the polls (table 15.6). [30] The dynamics of the midterm model show how economic conditions and the electorate's changing evaluations of Nixon and Ford shaped the Democratic landslide of 1974: while Ford's replacement of Nixon helped congressional Republicans by nearly six percentage points, most of that gain was offset by a declining economy and by the fifteen-point loss in Ford's approval rating following the pardon of Nixon.

Table 15.6 also indicates that the midterm model may over-respond to very extreme values in approval ratings and particularly in economic conditions; the model's projection computed in May 1973 deviates quite substantially from the Gallup poll (although less so from the Harris survey of the same month). Nevertheless the important point is not only that the model did survive the really difficult test of the 1974 midterm, but that it also

---

[30] Data sources: Gallup approval rating for October 1974 from "Gallup Says Poll Shows Ford Popularity on Rise," *The New York Times,* 24 October 1974; other months from *The Gallup Opinion Index,* 103(January 1974):3; 108(June 1974):1; and 111(September 1974):12. The change in real disposable income per capita is available only by quarters and the monthly values are interpolated; it should also be noted that the quarterly figures are quite unstable, with provisional and final estimates often differing substantially. The computations are based on data in Bureau of Economic Analysis, *Business Conditions Digest,* January 1975 (Washington, D.C.: U.S. Government Printing Office, 1975), p. 69. The reports of polls asking people how they intended to vote in the 1974 congressional election are from "Poll Confirms GOP Fears," *The Washington Post,* 4 November 1974, p. A–5; "Poll: Democrats Will Sweep Into the House," *New York Post,* 8 August 1974, p. 24; and *The Gallup Opinion Index,* 110(August 1974):1–4. Nonresponses have been divided equally between the two parties.

helped assess the electoral effects of the political and economic earthquakes in the months prior to the election. And, of course, the experience of 1974 is clearly contrary to the textbook view of midterms—that off-year congressional elections are not much more than the electoral swing of the pendulum, mainly the consequence of differences in off-year compared to on-year turnout.

In summary, the tests of the midterm model confirm that even though the fitted equation is based on a relatively short series of elections, the quantitative results are quite secure—as indicated by the independent replications of both regression coefficients, the postdictive and predictive trials, the conventional tests of statistical significance, the pre-election predictions for the 1974 midterm, and the model's ability to move with changing events.[31] The midterm model also explains most of the variance in midterm outcomes. Few models of political behavior have passed such tests, particularly those of fairly complete statistical explanation, replication, and honest prediction.

We now consider the political significance of the midterm.

From Votes to Seats

The political consequences of a midterm election flow from the resulting partisan distribution of seats in the House of Representatives, rather than from the partisan distribution of the national congressional vote. Since, as we shall see, the character of the translation of votes into seats has shifted greatly over the years, the political meaning of the midterm has itself shifted.

For midterms from 1938 to 1970, the relationship between seats and votes is a moderately strong one—variations in votes explain 76 percent of the variation in seats. Much of the strength of that relationship comes from the more extreme outcomes of 1946 and 1958; omitting those years, the vote explains less than 4 percent of the variance in seat shares. The lack of a really strong and consistent relationship between votes and seats in midterms is a reflection of changes in the swing ratio—the rates at which votes are translated into seats—over the years. The change in the value of the midterm vote in terms of seats can be seen by comparing the gain in the nationwide congressional vote made by the out-party with their gain in

---

[31] The model appears to over-respond to very large short-run improvements in economic conditions. Such improvements have been more typical of on-years than off-years. The model performs acceptably for ups and downs of less than $150 per capita in real disposable income, which has been the case for all midterms since 1938. In addition, the model might be examined comparatively—for example, in British by-elections. Finally, the model could be extended for on-year elections (although Gallup did not ask the presidential approval question for incumbent presidents in the six months prior to on-year elections until the 1960s). On-year elections are clearly a much more complex problem; and the midterm model is best seen as an alternative to "surge and decline" and the similar approaches cited in footnotes 1–5.

House seats. In the 1938 midterm, for example, the Republicans gained 7.7 percentage points in their national congressional vote compared to their 1936 congressional vote—and the result was an 18.1 percent gain in their share of seats in the House. This yielded a swing ratio of:

$$\text{Swing ratio for 1938 midterm} = \frac{\%\ \text{change in seats, 1936 to 1938}}{\%\ \text{change in votes, 1936 to 1938}}$$

$$= \frac{18.1}{7.7} = 2.4$$

In the 1970 midterm, the Democrats gained 3.4 percentage points in their share of the congressional vote over 1968, but only 2.8 percentage points in seats:

$$\text{Swing ratio in 1970 midterm} = \frac{2.8}{3.4} = 0.8$$

Thus a comparable change in the midterm vote in the 1970 midterm was worth one-third what it was in 1938. The trend in the swing ratio over all the midterms has been:

Year	Ratio
1938	2.4
1942	2.0
1946	2.0
1950	2.1
1954	1.6
1958	2.2
1962	0.2
1966	1.8
1970	0.8
1974	1.5 (approximately)

Figure 15.3, recording the results of alternative estimates of the swing ratio, reveals the same pattern: a 'significant decline in the swing ratio over the years. The estimates of figure 15.3 are computed as the least-squares slope calculated in the region within five percentage points of the actual nation-wide congressional vote.[32] The estimates indicate that, in a normal election, shifts in the congressional vote are worth about half of what they were twenty years ago in terms of seats in the House of Representatives.

Figure 15.4 shows how the electoral systems of individual states have contributed to the nationwide change in the swing ratio in midterm congressional elections over the years. The graphs compare the translation of votes into seats for the midterm congressional elections of 1950 and 1970 in four large states. Note the difference between the seats-votes curves in the midterm of 1950 compared to 1970: a flat spot in the middle of the 1970 seats-

---

[32] This technique is described in Tufte, "Seats and Votes," pp. 549-51.

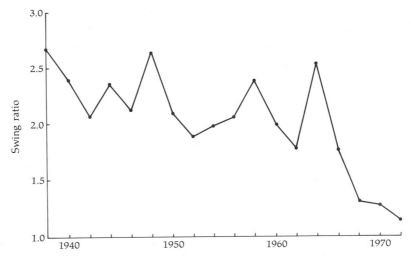

Figure 15.3 Swing ratio in congressional elections, 1938–1972. (The swing ratio is the percentage change in congressional seats associated with a one percent change in the nationwide congressional vote.)

votes curve has developed and, on that plateau, changes in the congressional vote in that state yield no changes at all in the partisan distribution of seats. Some of those flat spots are rather large; a party can gain 10 or 12 percent of the vote in every congressional district in a state and still not gain a single additional congressional seat. The swing ratio in such states is, for all practical purposes, zero: any change of ordinary magnitude in the vote results in no change in seats. The plateaus in the 1970 seats-votes curves are found in the region between 40 and 60 percent of the vote for each party—right where the statewide congressional vote falls in most relatively competitive states. That is, elections are taking place on the section of the seats-votes curve that has the lowest swing ratio. The effect of all this is to secure the tenure of incumbent representatives, since they are invulnerable to vote swings occurring in typical congressional elections.[33]

Thus the electoral system—the arrangements for the aggregation of the votes of citizens into seats in the House—does not respond consistently (and hardly responds at all in some states) to changes in the aggregate preferences of voters, even though the voters themselves are casting their ballots in a

---

[33] The causes of recent increases in congressional tenure are not yet clear; see David R. Mayhew, "Congressional Elections: The Case of the Vanishing Marginals," *Polity,* 6(Spring 1974):295–317; Walter Dean Burnham, "Communication," and Edward R. Tufte, "Communication," *American Political Science Review,* 68(March 1974):207–13; and Robert S. Erikson, "Malapportionment, Gerrymandering, and Party Fortunes in Congressional Elections," *American Political Science Review,* 66(December 1972):1234–55. Some consequences of seat changes are described in David W. Brady and Naomi B. Lynn, "Switched-Seat Congressional Districts: Their Effect on Party Voting and Public Policy," *American Journal of Political Science,* 17(August 1973):528–43.

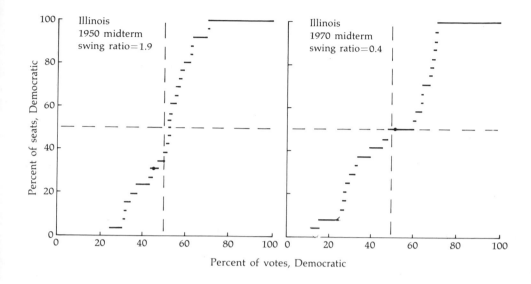

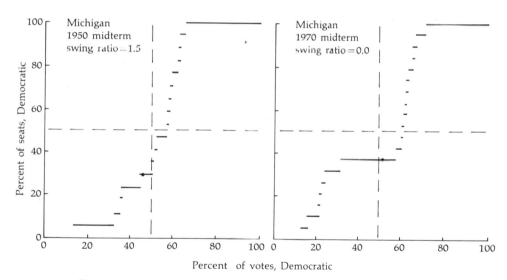

Figure 15.4 Votes-seats curves for the 1950 and 1970 midterm congressional elections: Illinois, Michigan, Ohio, and Pennsylvania. *(Continued on page 270.)*

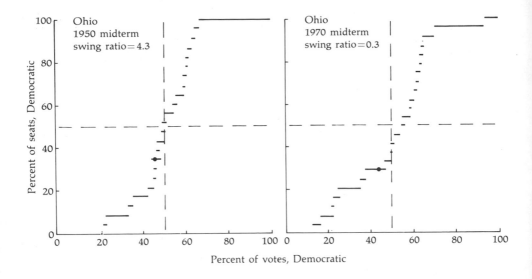

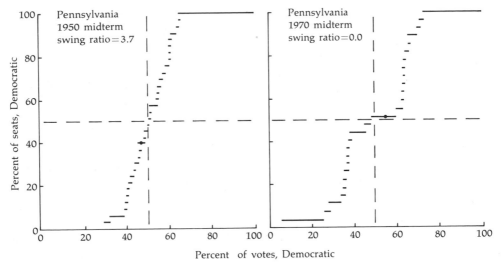

Figure 15.4 (Continued)

systematic and focused way in midterm congressional elections. No wonder midterm outcomes—especially when they were evaluated in terms of changes in seats rather than votes—appeared, in V. O. Key's words, as "a procedure whose strange consequences lack explanation in any theory that personifies the electorate as a rational god of vengeance and reward."[34]

Conclusion

Our fundamental finding is that the vote cast in midterm congressional elections is a referendum on the performance of the President and his administration's management of the economy. Although the in-party's share of the nationwide congressional vote almost invariably declines in the midterm compared to the previous on-year election, the magnitude of that loss is substantially smaller if the President has a high level of popular approval, or if the economy is performing well, or both. The fitted model indicates that the aggregate midterm outcomes from 1938 to 1970 (omitting the wartime election of 1942) are explained by—and are predictable from—the economic conditions and the level of approval of the President prevailing at the time of the election. To be specific: a change of 10 percentage points in the President's approval rating in the Gallup poll is related to a change of 1.3 percentage points in the national midterm congressional vote for the President's political party; and a change of $50 in real disposable personal income per capita in the year of the election is related to a change of 1.8 percentage points in the vote. These estimates, although based on a relatively short series of elections, appear to be very stable and are confirmed by independent replication and by genuine predictive tests. From a statistical point of view, the model constitutes a virtually complete explanation of the aggregate vote in midterm elections: the model explains 91 percent of the variation in the partisan division of the vote in midterms from 1938 to 1970; the model performed successfully in predicting the outcome of the 1974 congressional election.

Our second main finding is that the midterm referendum of the nationwide congressional *vote* is often poorly reflected in the resulting partisan distribution of *seats* in the House of Representatives. Thus even though the voters, in aggregate at least, have done their best to make the midterm a referendum on the performance of the administration, their efforts are greatly muted by the structure of the electoral system.

The finding that the midterm vote does, in fact, constitute a referendum— albeit a sometimes hidden referendum because of shifts in the votes-seats translation—on the performance of the President and his administration's management of the economy is especially significant when compared to the political science textbook view of midterms. The standard view is, of course, that the midterm outcome derives from the prior on-year election, mostly a

---

[34] Key, p. 568.

residual product of an electorate from which the short-term forces prevailing in the prior on-year have been subtracted. But our evidence indicates that the midterm is neither a mystery nor an automatic swing of the pendulum; the midterm vote is a referendum.

Along much more speculative lines, the midterm model also suggests a partial explanation of the fundamental fact of midterm elections, the loss of votes by the President's party. The model indicates that the loss occurs because the electorate's approval of the President has declined since the prior on-year election and because the economy is performing less well at the time of the midterm than it was two years earlier during the presidential election. Mueller has estimated the yearly decline of presidential approval at about six percentage points per year in office.[35] And, in general, the economy—measured here in terms of the yearly increase in real disposable income per capita—has historically performed better in on-years than in off-years.[36] At present, such an application of the midterm model is very speculative; I suspect that a satisfactory explanation of why the President's party always operates in the loss column in off-years will grow from a combination of the midterm model and a revised version of Campbell's "surge and decline" model (which, in revision, might place more emphasis on the surge and decline of coattail effects and less on turnout effects).

Let us conclude by considering the relevance of the findings for the eternal issue of voter rationality.

Stokes and Miller demonstrated that the midterm election could hardly be regarded as the electorate's evaluation of the legislative record of the two parties in Congress because an embarrassing number of voters lacked the minimal information required to cast a ballot informed by a judgment of a party's legislative performance. For example, a majority of those surveyed failed to recall which party controlled Congress. Less political information is demanded of voters, however, if they are to cast their midterm ballots as a referendum on the performance of the administration—only knowledge of what political party the President belongs to. And the link between the President's party and the congressional candidate is easy, because each congressional candidate's party is printed on the ballot along with the name of the candidate.[37] Thus the information necessary to cast an off-year congressional vote for or against the party of the President is at hand for most voters. If the information demands on voters are minimal enough (in this case, knowing the name of the President's political party), then the aggregate performance of the electorate can be consistent with objective factors prevailing at the time of the election.

The basic idea behind the model—that, in midterm congressional elections, at least some voters reward or punish the party of [the] President by

---

[35] Mueller, "Presidential Popularity," p. 25.

[36] Edward R. Tufte, "The Political Manipulation of the Economy: Influence of the Electoral Cycle on Macroeconomic Performance and Policy," manuscript, Princeton, 1974.

[37] Stokes and Miller, "Party Government," pp. 544–46.

casting their votes for representatives in line with their perceptions and evaluations of the President and economy—is a theory about the behavior of individual voters. It is important to realize, however, that all we observe in these data is the totally aggregated outcome of the individual performances of the forty million voters who turn out in midterm elections. Many different models of the underlying electorate are consistent with electoral outcomes that are collectively rational; and the observation of aggregate rationality clearly does not imply a unique specification or description of individual voters or of groups of voters making up the electorate. Aggregate studies provide evidence about aggregates. And surely for many citizens of voting age the midterm is not a referendum on the performance of the incumbent administration: some do not have the opportunity for a referendum vote since they find only one party's candidate on their ballots; others rely entirely on party affiliation, name recognition, and incumbency to guide their decisions; and a majority do not show up at the polls in the off-year.

Consequently, our highly aggregated evidence speaks only most indirectly to the central political questions concerning the rationality of voters as individuals:

- What kinds of decision rules do individual voters use?[38] Which voters use what decision rules?
- What conditions encourage voter rationality?
- How may these conditions be nurtured?

These concerns once again emphasize the theoretical interest (as well as the continuing practical interest) in ticket splitters, swing voters, and citizens who fail to vote in some elections—for it is, after all, the aggregate combination of these individual effects that leads to the striking collective rationality apparent in our findings here.

---

[38] See Stanley Kelley, Jr. and Thad Mirer, "The Simple Act of Voting," *American Political Science Review*, 68(June 1974):572–91.

16. Information and the Vote: A Comparative Election Study

BARBARA HINCKLEY
C. RICHARD HOFSTETTER
JOHN H. KESSEL

Voting studies have been the showpiece of American political science—complete with a small core of theory, sophisticated measurement techniques, and some impressive predictive and explanatory results. Yet even this array is rather tenuously grounded. Research has concentrated on the presidential race at the expense of other national, state, and local contests. This is understandable in part because of the greater interest and concern that surrounds the nation's highest office. But it may be due in larger part to the absence of survey data drawn from subnational samples. Survey research at the national level has shown the importance of attitudinal

Source: *American Politics Quarterly,* 2(1974):131-58. Reprinted with permission of the publisher, Sage Publications, Inc.

Authors' note: We should like to thank the Comparative State Election Project for their courtesy in releasing the data for this analysis. The data from the 1968 Survey Research Center study were supplied through the Inter-University Consortium for Political Research. Neither the Comparative State Election Project nor the Consortium bears any responsibility for the present analysis. We are grateful to Mr. Jerry Stacy, who analyzed the open-ended data on presidential voting, and to Mr. William Oiler, who aided in the construction of the basic data set. The Polimetrics Laboratory at Ohio State University provided facilities for the analysis reported in this paper. Professors Herbert B. Asher, Aage R. Clausen, Richard Li, and Donald F. Stokes gave helpful counsel on the appropriateness of various statistical approaches, and Professors Asher and Clausen reacted to an earlier draft of this paper in a way that led to improvements in this version.

determinants of the individual vote.[1] Without similar data, research on subpresidential elections has had to rely on aggregate election statistics[2] and a
few simulations.[3] The best-known survey of congressional voting, based on
1958 data, has become a small classic in the field.[4] The result of this single-
office concentration is that our "knowledge" of American voting behavior
may be based on a very atypical—or at best a very partial—situation.

We know that presidential voting studies have had success by assessing,
in one way or another, the effects of attitudes toward such political objects
as candidates, parties, and issues.[5] But we also know that attitudes have
different effects as a function of the information known to the voter.[6] And
we know that those voting in congressional races exhibit relatively low levels
of information when compared with the more highly publicized presidential
contest.[7] These findings suggest that information may vary from office to
office and that this variation in information may produce very different
kinds of voting behavior: specifically, differences in the relative importance
of various attitudes to the vote. Our position is that the visibility of the office
(or candidates for the office) will affect the information the voter is likely to
have in hand, and this, in turn, will affect the way he makes his decision.
Hence, we want to distinguish conditions that will make it more or less
likely that the office will be salient to the voters.

One obvious distinction would be between presidential and subpresidential voting. We already have some documentation from the late 1950's about
the low levels of information and interest characteristic of congressional

---

[1] Angus Campbell, Philip E. Converse, Warren E. Miller, and Donald E. Stokes, *The American Voter* (New York: Wiley, 1960).

[2] See, for example, Milton Cummings, *Congressmen and the Electorate* (New York: The Free Press, 1966); Charles Press, "Voting Statistics and Presidential Coattails," *American Political Science Review*, 52(December 1958):1041-50 and "Presidential Coattails and Party Cohesion," *Midwest Journal of Political Science*, 7(November 1963):320-35; and Barbara Hinckley, "Interpreting House Midterm Elections," *American Political Science Review*, 61(September 1967):694-700.

[3] Donald E. Stokes, "A Variance Component Model of Political Effects," in *Mathematical Applications in Political Science, I,* John M. Claunch, ed. (Dallas: Southern Methodist University Press, 1965); Harvey M. Kabaker, "Estimating the Normal Vote in Congressional Elections," *Midwest Journal of Political Science,* 13(February 1969):58-83; Barbara Hinckley, "Incumbency and the Presidential Vote in Senate Elections," *American Political Science Review,* 64(September 1970):836-42.

[4] Donald E. Stokes and Warren E. Miller, "Party Government and the Saliency of Congress," in Angus Campbell, et al., *Elections and the Political Order,* (New York: Wiley, 1966), 194-211.

[5] Campbell, et al., *The American Voter;* David RePass, "Issue Salience and Party Choice," *American Political Science Review,* 65(June 1971):389-400, and discussion and comments by Gerald Pomper, Richard Boyd, Richard Brody and Benjamin Page, and John Kessel in *American Political Science Review,* 66(June 1972):415-70.

[6] Philip E. Converse, "Information Flow and the Stability of Partisan Attitudes" in Angus Campbell, et al., *Elections and the Political Order,* pp. 136-57; J. Merrill Shanks, "The Quality of Electoral Change," a paper prepared for delivery at the 1969 Annual Meeting of the American Political Science Association, New York, New York, 2-6 September 1969.

[7] Stokes and Miller, "Party Government and the Saliency of Congress."

elections.[8] And this evidence is corroborated by data from the present study concerning both senatorial and gubernatorial contests. It would seem reasonable to expect, therefore, that high information cues would be more important in presidential voting while low information cues would be more important on the subpresidential level. For example, issues require a fairly complex calculus that Z issue exists, and that candidate X or candidate Y is closer to the voter's preference on this issue. Party-motivated choices, on the other hand, call for only the minimum recognition that candidate X is a Republican or Democrat. Hence, it would seem that issues ought to be a more and party a less important predictive component in presidential as opposed to subpresidential voting.

A second possible distinction would be between executive and legislative office. A governor is a single office holder. His capital office keeps him in his constituency and gives him instant access to statewide media. A senator, whatever his prestige in the state, is only one of a hundred peers in a norm-bound, relatively distant, legislative institution. It has been suggested that executive and legislative incumbents differ in accountability with only executives held responsible for government action during their tenure.[9] The greater visibility of the governor would mean that voters would be more likely to have information in hand to make this accountability possible. If this is the case, then it might be expected that issues, such as "bad times," "high taxes," and the like, would be a more important component in the vote for executive than for legislative contests.

A third distinction would be that between incumbents and nonincumbents. There is the obvious point that an incumbent, who has enjoyed some years of publicity, has an advantage, but there is also the more subtle point that the fact of incumbency may be a more important consideration in offices about which relatively little is known. Experience and incumbency, like party, require only minimum information. Recognition of the title, "Governor X" or "Senator Y," will suffice. Hence, we shall want to distinguish between personal qualifications of the candidates (e.g., honesty, intelligence, personality, background) and those concerned with experience and incumbency. It is possible that the traditional "candidate" component in attitudinal models is masking two very different kinds of orientations, and that incumbency effects are more important in voting for low-visibility offices about which the voter has relatively little other information. This reasoning would be consistent with aggregate analysis, which has shown incumbency to be particularly important in voting for senator.[10]

In short, our expectations are that greater information will be available to the voter in the case of presidential rather than subpresidential offices, executive rather than legislative offices, and in the case of incumbents rather

---

[8] Stokes and Miller, "Party Government and the Saliency of Congress."

[9] Joseph A. Schlesinger, *Ambition and Politics: Political Careers in the United States* (Chicago, Rand McNally, 1966), pp. 68–69.

[10] Barbara Hinckley, "Incumbency and the Presidential Vote in Senate Elections."

than nonincumbents. In high information situations, we expect issues to be relatively more important in voting decisions; in low information situations, we look for the cues of party and incumbency to be of relatively greater consequence.

Methodological Considerations

For the first time, extensive survey data are available which make it possible to compare presidential, gubernatorial, and senatorial voting. Open-ended answers stating why respondents thought they would vote for or against presidential candidates come from the 1968 Election Study of the University of Michigan Survey Research Center. All other data come from the Comparative State Election Project of the same year. The S.R.C. studies are well known, and the methodology and presidential analyses of the Comparative State Election Project [11] are being reported elsewhere. But perhaps a few words would be in order about the samples and data we have used.

We had three samples. There is first the national sample of the Survey Research Center. This contains 1,673 cases of which 969 were classified as having voted for either Nixon or Humphrey. The second is a sample of the set of states having senatorial elections in which each state is weighted proportionally to the state's population. The weighted n for these 31 states is 5,573, including 4,156 voters. The third is a sample of the set of states having gubernatorial elections, again with each state weighted proportionally to the state's population. The weighted n for the gubernatorial states is 2,388, including 1,821 voters. [12] There is a partial overlap, some 1,725 cases, between the senatorial and gubernatorial samples. [13]

The critical attitudinal measure taken from the surveys is the series of open-ended questions about what respondents "like" or "dislike" about the

---

[11] Comparative State Election Project, *Explaining the Vote: Presidential Choices in the Nation and the State, 1968,* (Chapel Hill, N.C., Institute for Research in Social Science, 1973).

[12] There were two weighting procedures employed. The first, which might be called a technical correction, was used to weight the sample back to the original design specifications because some of the sample estimates did not correspond to known population parameters. The second weights each state's cases proportionally to the state's population. The original design called for representative samples of 500 in each of thirteen states with enough additional cases from other states so one could also obtain representative regional samples or a representative national sample. To obtain a sample of one of the C.S.E.P. states, one used "s weight." To obtain a regional or national sample, one uses "n weight." For example, by using "s weight," one obtains 498 cases in Illinois which was one of the C.S.E.P. states, and forty-seven cases in Indiana which was not. By using "n weight," the Illinois cases are weighted down to 426, and the Indiana cases are weighted up to 195. The weighted n we are using comes from "n weight." If one used "s weight" with the samples, one would have 6286 cases in the senatorial states, and 2736 cases in the gubernatorial states. Therefore the actual number of cases is somewhat higher than the weighted n's we shall be reporting, and, incidentally, much higher than the number of cases in most national samples used to analyze presidential voting.

[13] Since the senatorial sample was larger, this means that 72.7 percent of the gubernatorial respondents are contained within the senatorial sample, but only 30.1 percent of the senatorial respondents are contained within the gubernatorial sample.

two major party candidates for president,[14] governor, and senator. Two positive comments and two negative comments were coded for each open-ended question. The pro-Democratic comments were scored positively (that is, assigned a +1 for each positive comment about a Democratic candidate and for each negative comment about a Republican candidate) and the pro-Republican comments negatively. These scores, which could range from +4 to −4, were combined into attitudinal categories which served as the independent variables in a multicomponent model. There are two versions of this model. The short version had four components dealing with references to the parties, the candidates' experience or incumbency, the candidates' personal qualifications, and issues. In an expanded version, the latter three components were decomposed into more specific categories to permit more detailed comparisons.

The effect of these independent variables on the reported vote was measured by linear regression. In all cases, the dependent variable used was a dichotomous choice with a positive value (+4) assigned to a Democratic vote and a negative value (−4) assigned to a Republican vote to correspond to the maximum and minimum values that could be attained by the independent variables. Using vote as a dichotomous choice had the effect of excluding third-party candidates—most importantly, George Wallace on the presidential level and New York's James Buckley on the senatorial level. However, most of the subpresidential races were two-man contests, and we thought it important to maintain comparability across offices.[15]

In the subsequent analysis and discussion, standardized regression coefficients (betas) are used to compare the relative importance of the response categories. (The reasons for this are discussed in Appendix II.) We cannot, of course, discuss effects when there are multiple races involved.[16] This could

---

[14] In 1968, the Survey Research Center asked open-ended questions about the Republican and Democratic parties, Richard Nixon, Hubert Humphrey, and George Wallace. To maximize comparability with our data, we used only the answers to the candidate questions about Nixon and Humphrey.

[15] Using a dichotomous dependent variable also raises a methodological problem, specifically that independent and dependent variables are assumed to be continuous. When a dependent variable can take on only two values, this represents a severe violation of these assumptions. Therefore, we also analyzed our presidential data by means of probit analysis, a technique developed in biometrics to handle the case of a two value dependent variable. The results were substantially the same as those obtained with linear regression. We could not make an analogous test for the gubernatorial and senatorial data because these data had non-integral weights (which restricted us to software available in the S.P.S.S. package), but we were satisfied that this check justified our use of regression. On probit analysis, see William Zavoina and Richard McKelvey, "A Statistical Model for the Analysis of Legislative Voting Behavior," a paper prepared for delivery at the 1969 Annual Meeting of the American Political Science Association, New York, New York, 1-6 September, 1969.

[16] Effects are usually determined by multiplying some measure of the importance of the attitude (such as a regression coefficient) by a measure of the extent to which one party or the other is favored by the attitude (such as a mean attitudinal score). In the case of multiple races, favorable comments about a strong candidate in state A will be offset by unfavorable comments about a weak candidate in state B. Since the party means tend toward zero, it would be pointless to use these means to calculate a measure of effects.

Table 16.1 Frequency of Responses: "Like" or "Dislike" About Two Candidates (% of Respondents)

Office	0 Comments	1 Comment	2 or More Comments	Total
President	7	6	87	(100)
Governor	14	22	64	(100)
Senator	16	33	52	(100)

be done for individual races, but our present goal is to make general comparisons of the information levels and the importance of the attitudinal categories related to voting for the three offices.

Analysis

Information Level

Comparison of the information known to the voters is quite revealing. When respondents were asked what they liked or disliked about *both* candidates, fully 49 percent (for senators) and 36 percent (for governors) had at most *one* comment to make. By contrast, only 13 percent of the respondents for the presidential contest had no more than one comment to make. The response frequencies are given in table 16.1. The most striking difference in frequency is found between presidential and subpresidential voting, but within the subpresidential category, races for governor provoke more comments than races for senator. Barely one-half the respondents could make two or more comments about the candidates running for the U.S. Senate in their states. Incidentally, of the zero-comment respondents for senator and governor, 34 percent and 36 percent, respectively, still managed to vote in the contest. Of the one-comment respondents, 74 percent and 73 percent managed a vote, and of the two-or-more-comment respondents, 86 percent and 87 percent voted.

Information is not only low, it is affected by incumbency, as table 16.2 makes clear. When one controls for incumbency, many more positive references for incumbents are revealed. This pattern is consistent for both Republican and Democratic and senatorial and gubernatorial situations. Negative references do not seem similarly affected. What seems to be happening is that in a generally low information context, incumbency provides one item of positive information.[17] (One should, of course, recognize that the

[17] Cf. the similar finding from the 1958 study that of the two candidates, incumbents were far the better known: "Party Government and the Saliency of Congress."

Table 16.2   Incumbency and Information About Candidates

Office	% Nonresponses[a] in Races With:		
	Democratic Incumbent	Republican Incumbent	No Incumbent
Senator			
1st positive reference			
Democratic	41.4	61.5	47.5
Republican	60.3	38.2	57.8
1st negative reference			
Democratic	67.1	67.1	65.3
Republican	72.5	62.2	64.9
n states/races	15/1,994	5/1,333	9/1,996
Governor			
1st positive reference			
Democratic	47.9	54.2	54.1
Republican	63.4	45.3	58.1
1st negative references			
Democratic	71.1	55.4	68.6
Republican	64.9	55.7	76.6
n states/races	6/1,036	8/639	7/844

[a] A "nonresponse" includes these coded as "don't know," "no answer," and "nothing"—i.e., nothing liked or disliked about the candidate.

extremely high nonresponse rates of table 16.2 are partially due to the breakdown into the four possible combinations of positive and negative responses to Democratic and Republican candidates. Thus, respondents having one or two comments to make would be recorded for nonresponses in all remaining categories.)

Some detail on the kind of information offered about subpresidential candidates can be seen by the most frequent category of responses given (see table 16.3). Reference to the "political record" of incumbents is the most frequent positive response given for Democratic and Republican, senatorial and gubernatorial incumbents. Where incumbency is mentioned specifically, it tends to be a negative reference. Respondents like the political record of Democratic and Republican Senate incumbents (in 15–16 percent rates) and dislike their incumbency and older age (in 5–10 percent rates). They like the political record of gubernatorial incumbents (in 10–16 percent rates) more than they dislike their party or tax policy (4–14 percent rates). For incumbent governors, held responsible for "tax policy," the positive edge has been considerably narrowed. Note also the frequent reference to the "lesser of evils" in Senate responses reported *against* the challenger. In other words, the known evil of the incumbent appears a "lesser evil" than the unknown.

Table 16.3 Incumbency and Most Frequent Responses Given

	Most Frequent Response Given		
Office	Races With Democratic Incumbent	Races With Republican Incumbent	Races With No Incumbent
Senator			
1st positive reference			
Democratic	Political record (15%)	General party (7%)	Political record (7%)
Republican	General party (5%)	Political record (16%)	General ability (6%)
1st negative reference			
Democratic	Incumbency (4%)	Lesser of evils (4%)	General party (7%)
Republican	Lesser of evils (5%)	Older (10%)	General party (7%)
Governor			
1st positive reference			
Democratic	Political record (10%)	General party (7%)	General party (12%)
Republican	General party (4%)	Political record (16%)	General party (7%)
1st negative reference			
Democratic	General party (4%)	General party (5%)	General party (7%)
Republican	General party (8%)	Tax policy (14%)	General party (8%)

NOTE: Percentages refer to the percentage of total responses (including non-responses) falling within the category.

For a second point, consider the generality of the most frequent responses. Some eighty categories were coded—including specific references to issues (Vietnam, tax policy, natural resources), to groups (business, labor, blacks), to personal qualifications (honesty, campaign ability, intelligence). But with only a few exceptions in table 16.3, the most frequent responses tend to be very general: a general reference to the party, to the candidate's ability or political record, or to the "lesser evil" of the known incumbent. A general party reference is overwhelmingly the most frequent response in gubernatorial contests, whereas party shares the honors with general candidate ability for the Senate contests.

In the second-most frequent responses (not reported in the table), more specific references appear. There is a positive reference to "natural resource policy" (5 percent) for Senate Democratic incumbents and a negative reference (3 percent) on their older age. There is a positive reference to youth (3 percent) for Democratic challengers to Republican Senate incumbents, and a negative reference to "liberalism" (3 percent) for Democratic candidates in nonincumbent contests. Republican gubernatorial challengers receive a negative reference (3 percent) on their campaign ability and their opponents receive a negative reference (3 percent) on their associates. Information may be predominantly low and general, but in a number of cases specific kinds of information can become salient.

The foregoing gives some sense of the level and kind of information offered in the year 1968—a year marked by political upheaval, assassinations, an exceptional third-party contest for the presidency, and the unusual case of a president declining to run for renomination. But there is little stimulation from these events apparent in the subpresidential voting. Nevertheless, these respondents voted for senator and governor, and some 85 percent of them had at least one comment to make about the candidates. The subsequent analysis will show how these comments are related to the vote.

Attitudes and the Vote

Statements about (1) the parties, (2) the candidate's experience or incumbency, (3) personal qualifications, and (4) issues were related to the vote, as reported in table 16.4. The table gives the zero-order correlation (r) between each attitude and the vote, and the standardized regression coefficients of the attitude in its effect on the vote when the other attitudes are controlled. The total power of the model, combining all four attitudes, is given by the R^2 at the bottom of the table, which reports the percentage of the variance in the vote that is explained.

Overall, the model is reasonably satisfactory. We are able to explain 59 percent, 69 percent, and 57 percent of the variance in senatorial, gubernatorial, and presidential voting, respectively. Each of the attitudinal components is related to vote for all three offices. Indeed, the regression coefficients in

Table 16.4   Attitudes and the Vote: Races for Senator, Governor and President Compared

| Attitude Component | Relationship With the Vote | | | | | |
| | Senator | | Governor | | President | |
	r	Beta	r	Beta	r	Beta
Parties	.40	.34	.46	.36	.33	.24
Experience and incumbency	.41	.33	.46	.28	.33	.22
Personal qualifications	.48	.40	.55	.38	.55	.45
Issues	.40	.33	.50	.38	.47	.37
n	4,156		1,821		970	
R^2	.59		.69		.57	

NOTE: All components are significant at the .01 level.

this four-component version of the model suggest that the attitudinal categories are of almost equal importance. This certainly would be a fair reading of the senatorial results, although the low information experience category is less important for the governor, and both the parties and experience categories are less important for president. It should also be reported that the intercorrelations between these attitudinal categories are quite low.[18] By creating categories on theoretical grounds—that each of these components appeared to refer to a different class of attitudinal objects—we have achieved components that are empirically separate. This means that each of the components is exercising an independent effect on the vote and that the regression coefficient is a fair measure of its importance.[19]

While the four components are significant in the voting for all offices, there are some differences between offices which require attention. It was suggested earlier that party and experience may be "low-information" cues, requiring only the information of the candidate's party and title, and so might be more important in subpresidential compared to presidential voting. Support for this reasoning is given by the results in table 16.4. Party and experience show higher beta weights for the two subpresidential contests compared to the presidential results and are more strongly correlated with the vote.

A second difference can be observed in issue references for executive versus legislative voting. Contests for governor and President show a stronger correlation between issues and the vote than the contests for senator and somewhat higher standardized regression weights. In fact, races for governor show issues as important as races for President—suggesting that responsibility for issues does indeed follow more of an executive-legislative than a presidential-subpresidential distinction. Voting for governor, then, appears to share some of the characteristics of both senate and presidential voting: it

---

[18] The intercorrelation matrices are as follows:

Office	Party	Experience	Personal Qualifications	Issues
Senator				
Party	(1.00)	.08	.02	.06
Experience	.08	(1.00)	.11	.05
Personal qualifications	.02	.11	(1.00)	.10
Issues	.06	.05	.10	(1.00)
Governor				
Party	(1.00)	.12	.08	.11
Experience	.12	(1.00)	.27	.07
Personal qualifications	.08	.27	(1.00)	.17
Issues	.11	.07	.17	(1.00)
President				
Party	(1.00)	.08	.10	.07
Experience	.08	(1.00)	.10	.13
Personal qualifications	.10	.10	(1.00)	.13
Issues	.07	.13	.13	(1.00)

[19] Hayward R. Alker, Jr., "Statistics and Politics" in S. M. Lipset, ed., *Politics and the Social Sciences* (New York: Oxford University Press, 1969), pp. 253–55.

Table 16.5 Attitude and the Vote: Races for Senator, Governor, and President Compared

Attitude Component	Relationship With the Vote					
	Senator		Governor		President	
	r	Beta	r	Beta	r	Beta
Party statements	.40	.34	.46	.35	.33	.23
Experience	.38	.31	.39	.24	.22	.11
Incumbency-challenger	.15	.12	.25	.15	.24	.19
Youth-age	.05	.08	.08	.04	.06	.05
General qualifications	.38	.26	.43	.23	.42	.24
Honesty-integrity	.25	.18	.33	.15	.36	.23
Intelligence	.14	.08	.18	.07	.17	.08
Personality and background	.20	.17	.26	.16	.20	.17
Campaigning ability	.08	.06	.13	.06	.17	.12
General issue references	.30	.20	.33	.16	.33	.20
Education	.11	.08	.10	.03	.01	.01
Civil rights-law and order	.13	.12	.20	.12	.24	.13
Natural resources	.07	.06	−.08	−.09	.05	.01
Spending and taxes	.07	.07	.32	.19	.16	.09
Vietnam	.12	.10	−.05	−.01	.20	.14
Welfare	.21	.13	.34	.19	.23	.14
R^2	.61		.72		.57	

is like the former in the greater importance of party and like the latter in the greater importance of issues.[20]

The effect of personal qualifications is less clear. While it is by far the strongest component in the presidential solution, it is also the strongest for the Senate and at least equally as strong as issues in gubernatorial voting. Considering all three offices together, it appears to be the most important attitude component in its effect on the vote. However, this finding may be in part a function of the question, which directs the respondents' attention to what is liked or disliked about the candidates. Answers in terms of personal qualifications may seem most appropriate.

A more detailed analysis can be supplied by the solutions to the sixteen-component version of the model as reported in table 16.5. The very slight increase in R^2s suggests there is little to be gained in explanatory power by

---

[20] We considered the possibility that the greater importance of issues in gubernatorial voting was not related to a legislative-executive distinction, but was caused by the increased information presumably available to gubernatorial voters. We tested this by running the gubernatorial and senatorial regressions with the high-information (two or more comments) subsample. The betas for issues were higher for both offices, but the issue component for governor remained more important than that for senator (.44 compared with .37). The other standardized regression coefficients were virtually identical with those reported in table 16.4.

Table 16.6 Attitudes and the Vote: The Added Effect of Party Identification

Attitude Component	Senator		Governor		President	
	r	Beta	r	Beta	r	Beta
Parties	.40	.22	.46	.26	.33	.14
Experience and incumbency	.41	.27	.46	.24	.33	.15
Personal qualifications	.48	.32	.55	.34	.55	.32
Issues and groups	.40	.27	.50	.34	.47	.26
Party identification	.60	.31	.58	.23	.70	.35
n	4,156		1,821		969	
R^2	.67		.74		.64	

using the expanded rather than the compressed version of this model. Nevertheless, some interesting differences between offices can be observed. Despite our independent knowledge that incumbents have a much higher success rate for the Senate than for gubernatorial contests,[21] the beta weights in the table show the incumbent-challenger variable lowest of all three offices for Senate races. The explanation may be that, when incumbency is mentioned specifically, it tends to be a negative reference.[22] Moreover, the experience component,[23] which includes the positive references to the "political record" of the incumbent, shows the Senate beta by far the highest of the three offices. There are also some noticeable interoffice differences within the issue categories. "Spending and taxing" is clearly a gubernatorial issue, and "Vietnam" a senatorial and presidential issue. The amalgam of "civil rights, law and order, and gun control" affected all three offices in 1968. So while issues generally are more important in executive than legislative voting, the electorate does seem to be distinguishing to some extent between national and state issues.

One curiosity of American voting behavior remains to be recognized. Comparing betas among specific personal qualifications, we see that "honesty-integrity-trust" leads for all three offices with "personality and background" second. "Intelligence," although only in third place, is at least more important than "campaigning ability" on the subpresidential level. It is not more important than campaigning ability, however, for the presidency.

Party Identification

The central organizing attitude of party identification was not included in the original model. The model was more parsimonious and quite robust without it.[24] But when party identification was added, the resulting changes

[21] Hinckley, "Incumbency and the Presidential Vote in Senate Elections," p. 839.
[22] For example, "I thought Joe Clark had had it and we could use a change."
[23] A typical comment was: "I like Clark's experience. He's had experience."
[24] Inclusion of party identification explains an additional 8 percent, 5 percent, and 7

were quite interesting—and quite unexpected. As the data in table 16.6 reveal, party identification is more strongly associated with presidential than with subpresidential voting. The importance of party identification is inversely related to the importance of party-as-a-cue-about-the-candidate, the party attitude we have been discussing up to this point. The betas for party identification are .35, .31, and .23 for presidential voting, senatorial voting, and gubernatorial voting, respectively. The betas for party-as-a-cue-about-the-candidate are .14, .22, and .26 for the same offices. The same kind of inverse relationship also exists between the importance of party identification and the explanatory power of the model. Why so?

Without party identification, we have a very simple model: four (or sixteen) independent variables acting on one dependent variable. The links are simple and direct. But when party identification is added, it becomes the independent variable, and the specific attitudes become intervening variables. Thus, one must consider the direct effects of party identification on vote, the indirect effects of party identification acting through the four specific categories, and the direct effects of the four attitudinal categories. It might be supposed that the data reported in table 16.6 are statistical artifacts created by the more complex model. This is plausible, but seems not to be the case. When the indirect effects of party identification are traced out, the sums for the three offices are quite similar. [25]

---

percent of the variance for senator, governor, and president, respectively. The explanatory power of the original model appears to depend on the association between the affect of the comments generated by the open-ended questions and the respondent's voting behavior rather than any particular arrangement of the components. We also tested the familiar six-component model devised by Donald Stokes. This proved to have more explanatory power at the sub-presential level than with the presidential data reported in *The American Voter.* It was slightly stronger than our sixteen-component model with respect to senatorial voting; and the sixteen-component model was just a shade better than the Stokes model with respect to gubernatorial voting.

The Stokes solution is as follows, with all components significant at the .01 level except foreign policy for governors, which is not significant.

Attitude Component	Senator		Governor	
	r	Beta	r	Beta
Republican candidate	−.60	−.37	−.64	−.35
Democratic candidate	.58	.36	.60	.36
Parties as managers of government	.41	.25	.44	.25
Groups and group interest	.27	.14	.33	.17
Foreign policy	.14	.10	−.05	.00
Domestic policy	.28	.19	.38	.26

[25] The compound path coefficients for party identification acting through the other attitudinal categories are:

Attitude Component	Senator	Governor	President
Parties	.09	.12	.05
Experience-Incumbency	.06	.06	.04
Personal qualifications	.07	.09	.15
Issues	.06	.08	.11
Total indirect effects for party identification	.28	.35	.35

The important consideration is the difference between party identification and party-as-a-cue-about-the-candidate. It is unfortunate that their names are so similar. They are very different kinds of attitudes. The objects of party identification include the self, a reference group, and the perceived relationship between the self and the reference group. The object of party-as-a-cue-about-the-candidate is a bit of information about the candidate. The attitudinal consequences of the differences between "I think of myself as a Democrat" and "Hubert Humphrey is a Democrat" are vast. The former is a central attitude that plays a crucial role in organizing much of one's information;[26] the latter is a fragment that is likely to be organized by other, more central attitudes.

Consider now the probable differences in the role of a central anchoring attitude in the three kinds of information situations. Gubernatorial voters have a moderate amount of information. A few things are known about the candidates, and one or two policy differences are likely to be sharply drawn. These salient fragments are likely to be strongly related to vote, and not much affected by the way they are tied to a central attitude. (Note that the gubernatorial betas for personal qualifications and issues are those least reduced when party identification is added.) Senatorial voters know less. The incumbent has the greatest advantage in simply being known as "the Senator." In this vague situation, party identification becomes a little more important. Finally, presidential voters have the most information. Those with a moderate degree of interest are likely to know favorable and unfavorable things about both candidates and to have conflicting feelings about different issues. In this situation, the way conflicting cues are related to each other, and particularly to party information, may be quite important.

Party identification, in other words, does not play a simple role in voting choice. Its importance appears to have a curvilinear relationship to the amount of information available. When there is enough information available for there to be both positive and negative affective forces toward the candidates (as for president), an arbiter is needed. Party identification is important here because it plays a balancing role between positive and negative attitudes. When a moderate amount of information is available, and it points in the same direction (as tends to be the case for governor), no arbiter is needed, and party identification effects are reduced. When very little other political information is available (as for senator), party identification becomes a little more important again, but this time to provide a partisan context for whatever the voter does bring to bear on his choice.

Age, Education, Partisanship, and Incumbency

Finally, we also tested the four-component solution for senator and governor with subelectorates whose characteristics were likely to affect the amount of

---

[26] On centrality, see Theodore Newcomb, Ralph H. Turner, and Philip E. Converse, *Social Psychology* (New York: Holt, Rinehart and Winston, 1965), pp. 58-65, 138-49.

information that bore on their electoral choices. We wanted to see if the relative importance of the attitudinal categories were affected by differences in age, education, partisanship, or incumbency. Consider first the effects of age and education as reported in table 16.7.

The results for age would seem quite important. Considering the proposition that a younger electorate would give rise to an increase in issue voting and a declining importance for party, one can see that there is virtually no difference in attitude structure as it relates to the vote between young

Table 16.7 Attitude and the Vote: The Effects of Age and Education

	Age					
	Young		Middle		Old	
Attitude Component	r	Beta	r	Beta	r	Beta
Senatorial candidates						
Parties	.37	.32	.38	.33	.44	.38
Experience and incumbency	.45	.32	.39	.34	.43	.30
Personal qualifications	.47	.39	.46	.39	.51	.42
Issues	.42	.33	.42	.35	.38	.28
n	629		2,363		1,163	
Gubernatorial candidates						
Parties	.44	.38	.49	.37	.43	.32
Experience and incumbency	.45	.30	.49	.29	.42	.26
Personal qualifications	.51	.39	.55	.37	.61	.41
Issues	.47	.40	.49	.37	.55	.36
n	290		1,024		499	

	Education			
	High		Low	
Attitude Component	r	Beta	r	Beta
Senatorial candidates				
Parties	.33	.28	.42	.37
Experience and incumbency	.43	.35	.40	.32
Personal qualifications	.47	.39	.48	.40
Issues	.43	.35	.40	.32
n	1,344		2,775	
Gubernatorial candidates				
Parties	.40	.32	.48	.37
Experience and incumbency	.45	.30	.45	.27
Personal qualifications	.48	.36	.58	.40
Issues	.54	.45	.48	.34
n	527		1,275	

NOTE: For age, "young" is defined as between 18 and 29 years, "middle" from 30 to 59, and "old" as 60 and over. For education, "high" includes some college or more, "low" high school graduate or less. All components are significant at the .01 level.

(18-29) and middle-aged (30-59) respondents. For the Senate, the results are almost identical. For governors, issue voting shows no difference, and although middle-aged respondents are stronger than the young in party voting, they are less strong than the older respondents. The only difference by age observable in the results is that older Senate respondents (60 and above) show a stronger tendency to vote by party than do other respondents. On balance, age appears to have little clear effect on attitude structure in subpresidential voting.

The results for education are more in the expected direction. Respondents with more education (at least some college) show somewhat stronger issue voting and somewhat weaker party voting for both senate and gubernatorial contests than respondents with a high school education or less.

Differences in partisanship, set forth in table 16.8, yield the expected result that party voting increases from independent to weak partisan to strong partisan. Compare the beta weights of .24, .30, and .42, respectively, for the Senate results and .28, .32, and .42, respectively, for governors. Moreover, issues are a somewhat stronger component in the solutions for independents than they are for strong or weak partisans. But perhaps the most intriguing finding from table 16.8 is the interparty difference in preference for partisan cues. [27] The beta weights for party statements among Republicans are lower compared not only to Democrats, but even to independents. While Democrats are more likely to rely on party, Republicans give greater emphasis to such other informational cues as experience and personal qualifications for senator and issues for governor. This finding may help explain the difference in "coattails" between the 1964 Democratic and 1972 Republican presidential landslides. If Democrats find party more salient than Republicans in subpresidential voting, they may be expected to stick more closely with their party's candidates even when deserting the top of the ticket.

One last point deserves attention. Earlier, it was seen that both the amount and the kind of information given varied with conditions of incumbency. One can now see the effect on the vote. As table 16.9 reports, in voting for both senator and governor, the party component is stronger in nonincumbent than in incumbent contests. This adds some further support to the speculation that incumbency may substitute for party as a low-information cue. For, if voters with low information may use *either* party *or* incumbency to decide their vote, then in the absence of the incumbency cue

---

[27] This is one of a series of findings that suggests important differences that are empirically related to identification with one party rather than logically derivative from the concept of a single party identification dimension. In general, these reflect more information, more emphasis on ideology, and higher activity among Republicans. Cf. John C. Pierce, "Party Identification and the Changing Role of Ideology in American Politics," *Midwest Journal of Political Science*, 14(February 1970):25-42; Sidney Verba and Norman H. Nie, *Participation in America: Political Democracy and Social Equality* (New York, Harper & Row, 1972), chaps. 12, 16; David Nexon, "Asymmetry in the Political System: Occasional Activists in the Republican and Democratic Parties, 1956-1964," *American Political Science Review*, 65(September 1971):716-30.

Table 16.8 Attitudes and the Vote: Partisanship and Party Identification

| | Partisanship | | | | | |
| | Strong | | Weak | | None | |
Attitude Component	r	Beta	r	Beta	r	Beta
Senatorial candidates						
Parties	.49	.42	.34	.30	.27	.24
Experience and incumbency	.45	.34	.35	.31	.42	.33
Personal qualifications	.44	.34	.50	.47	.51	.40
Issues	.39	.31	.37	.34	.46	.36
n	1,778		1,285		1,058	
Gubernatorial candidates						
Parties	.55	42	.38	.32	.34	.28
Experience and incumbency	.49	.30	.38	.24	.49	.34
Personal qualifications	.57	.35	.56	.42	.51	.37
Issues	.52	.35	.50	.34	.46	.44
n	778		545		482	

| | Party Identification | | | | | |
| | Democrat | | Independent | | Republican | |
Attitude Component	r	Beta	r	Beta	r	Beta
Senatorial candidates						
Parties	.26	.30	.27	.24	.17	.19
Experience and incumbency	.33	.30	.42	.33	.37	.38
Personal qualifications	.41	.39	.51	.40	.42	.45
Issues	.29	.29	.46	.36	.20	.25
n	1,813		1,058		1,250	
Gubernatorial candidates						
Parties	.28	.30	.34	.28	.23	.25
Experience and incumbency	.33	.23	.49	.34	.19	.20
Personal qualifications	.53	.45	.51	.37	.38	.23
Issues	.43	.35	.46	.44	.62	.56
n	827		482		497	

NOTE: All components are significant at the .01 level.

(i.e., in nonincumbent contests), party voting would become more important.

The interesting difference between offices involves issue voting. In Senate contests, the issue component is weaker in incumbent compared to nonincumbent races. In gubernatorial contests, it is stronger, supporting the proposition that executives are more likely than legislators to be held responsible for the issues of their administration. Those seeking a "more responsible Congress" might ponder the implications of senate-gubernatorial differences in table 16.9.

Table 16.9 Attitudes and the Vote: The Effects of Incumbency

Attitude Components	Races With Democratic Incumbent		Races With Republican Incumbent		Races With No Incumbent	
	r	Beta	r	Beta	r	Beta
Senatorial candidates						
Parties	.38	.33	.39	.36	.47	.38
Experience and incumbency	.40	.33	.43	.36	.37	.25
Personal qualifications	.47	.39	.42	.36	.50	.42
Issues	.40	.33	.37	.30	.46	.36
n	1,559		981		1,527	
Gubernatorial candidates						
Parties	.42	.34	.41	.27	.54	.43
Experience and incumbency	.39	.27	.58	.33	.40	.24
Personal qualifications	.56	.44	.59	.34	.50	.32
Issues	.50	.36	.66	.50	.37	.27
n	719		513		589	

NOTE: All components are significant at the .01 level.

Conclusions

Our initial suspicions were that the information known to the voters could be classified three ways—presidential-subpresidential, executive-legislative, and incumbent-nonincumbent—with more known about the former in each case. We also suspected that the fact of party or the fact that a man was in office would be more important cues when information was limited, and that issues would be more important when relatively more information was in hand. In the main, these expectations have been substantiated. Voters know more about presidential candidates than about gubernatorial candidates, and more about gubernatorial candidates than about senatorial candidates. Personal qualifications are important in voting decisions about all three offices, but issues are relatively more important in presidential and gubernatorial voting, parties are relatively more important in gubernatorial and senatorial voting, and the vague reference to experience becomes most important in senatorial voting. Further, we found that the executive-legislative distinctions—issues more important for governors and experience more important for senators—held up when comparison was limited to voters with high information or to incumbents.

Along the way, we found that young voters are not more likely to be motivated by issues, that Democrats are more likely to rely on partisan cues, that Republicans are more likely to rely on experience in voting for Senators and issues in voting for governor, that party identification did not have the same effects as party-as-a-cue-about-the-candidate, and that the effects of party identification were related to the voter's information in a very complex way.

More generally, the four-component solution has been shown to have reasonable explanatory power. Alternative arrangements of the independent variables, as in the sixteen-component solution or the six-component model from *The American Voter* yield essentially the same explanatory power. The R^2s are increased noticeably, however, when there is a better-informed electorate or when the election produces sharply defined issues that are closely associated with candidate choice.[28] This suggests the upper limits of predictive power may well lie in the amount and kind of information used by the electorate in voting for particular offices.

The major finding, of course, is that voting does vary by office. At the very least, this suggests that we should be cautious about generalizing about American voting habits without further investigation of other-than-presidential contests. As we noted at the outset, the study of presidential candidate choice had been a spectacular first cut into the field of voting behavior. But as we have also seen, things are very different in that wide world of voting decisions beyond the presidential contest.

Appendix I. Proximity Models

Another data source in the Comparative State Election Project made it possible to construct models based on the attitudinal proximity between each respondent and his perception of the two major parties. This was a series of parallel, precoded questions on some fifteen issue and group relationships. On cost of living, for example, parallel stimulus items asserted: "The government ought to hold down the cost of living." "When in office the Republican party holds down the cost of living," and "When in office the Democratic party holds down the cost of living." The respondent indicated his own attitude and his perceptions of the two parties by placing a card in one of seven locations (strongly agree, agree, slightly agree, not sure, slightly disagree, disagree, strongly disagree) along a sort board. Three similar items ascertained the respondent's perceptions of the three presidential candidates, and, elsewhere in the interview schedule, each person was asked whether he regarded "what happens to the cost of living" as "very important, important, not very important, or not important at all." We could not use the candidate items to compare voting across offices, but to the extent that the voter saw the various candidates as representative of the positions of their parties, the distances between each respondent and his perception of

---

[28] The multiple coefficients of determination for the sixteen component gubernatorial solution are .78 for those expressing high concern over the outcome, .81 for those able to make at least two statements about the candidates, and .90 when a Republican incumbent is running for re-election.

the parties provided measures for independent variables in a model applicable to voting for president, senator, and governor.

We worked with five issues—open housing, cost of living, jobs and wages, peace in Vietnam, and increasing police authority—selected because they had low correlations with each other, and because each could serve as an examplar of a cluster of related attitudes. ("Jobs and wages," for instance, was correlated with attitudes about social security, helping the common man, and helping labor unions.) Data on the respondent's positions and his perceptions of the Democratic and Republican parties on these five issues were combined into two types of proximity scores. Calculation of a straight proximity score began by taking the absolute difference between the position of the voter and that of each party as a measure of attitudinal distance. Next, these were converted into proximity measures for each party by subtracting the observed attitudinal distance from the maximum possible distance. Finally, the difference between the proximity measures for the two parties gave proximity scores ranging from $+6$ (where the voter's position coincided with his perception of the Democrats and was as far as possible from the Republicans) to -6 (where the opposite was the case). A step-function score was calculated in much the same way except that the maximum positive score was assigned to the party closest to the voter, and the maximum negative score was assigned to the other party. A score of zero was assigned to both parties if the voter perceived them as being equally distant from his own attitude. These step-function scores, in other words, were based simply on which party was most proximate, and neglected distance.

Using both types of proximity scores with and without salience weighting (from the question on the importance of each issue) gave us four different kinds of proximity solutions: an unweighted straight proximity solution, an unweighted step-function solution, a weighted proximity solution, and a weighted step-function solution. It turned out that these variations did not make much difference in explanatory power. The multiple Rs for senator and governor for all four solutions lay between .44 and .52, with the weighted solutions not quite as strong as the unweighted solutions. The

Table IA Issue Proximity and The Vote: Races for Senator, Governor and President Compared

Issue	Standardized Regression Coefficients		
	Senator	Governor	President
Prox. open housing	.03	.10	.03
Prox. cost of living	.13	.13	.21
Prox. jobs and wages	.19	.18	.25
Prox. peace in Vietnam	.16	.15	.28
Prox. more police authority	.12	.13	.19
R^2	.24	.24	.54

straight proximity solution was the best for senatorial voting, and the step-function was the best for gubernatorial voting. Since there were no clear empirical grounds for preferring one or the other, we chose the straight proximity solution because it seemed to be the simplest.

When the proximity solutions are compared across offices, we see clear differences between presidential and subpresidential levels. At the presidential level, this proximity solution is nearly as strong as those based on open-ended data, while at the subpresidential level, the proximity solutions do not account for as much variance as does party identification alone. When party identification is added, the subpresidential solutions collapse (that is, the betas become quite low, and most of them lose statistical significance) whereas the presidential solution in fact becomes stronger ($R^2 = .68$) than the multicomponent solutions discussed in the paper.

The differences in performance at the presidential and subpresidential levels add further support to the evidence that information and voting varies by office. There are at least three reasons why the proximity models are better at the presidential level. First, issues are more important in executive than legislative voting, and the issues in this model tend to be national rather than state issues. Second, the presidential candidates are far more important in providing cues to the voter about the party's position on an issue than are subpresidential candidates. A comparison between our mean proximity scores based on "party alone" and those used in the Comparative State Election Project which included perceptions of the candidates' positions as well shows a very strong relationship. Finally, since presidential voting is characterized by a relatively high information level, the respondent's issue preferences are often multidimensional. The virtue of the proximity solution is that it is designed to test the effects of conflict between issue preferences. In short, it works at the presidential level simply because the assumptions of the model seem to be reasonably consistent with the cognitive processes of voters in making their choices between presidential candidates.

Appendix II.
Use of Standardized Regression Coefficients

Our conclusions about the relative importance of the attitudinal categories have been based on comparisons among standardized regression coefficients (betas) rather than unstandardized regression coefficients. Since some might question this decision, we thought it wise to explain the rationale for following this procedure.

Multiple regression is a technique for assessing the relative importance of independent variables in explaining variation in a dependent variable. Regression coefficients give the extent of change in the dependent variable that is associated with a unit change in the independent variable. (In the simple equation, $y = a + .5x$, an increase of 1.0 in x will produce an increase of .5 in y.) Thus, the larger the regression coefficient, the more important we deem the independent variable to be.

In order to compare several independent variables in a regression analysis, it is necessary for the variables to be measured in the same units. If the independent variables do not have the same metric, inferences about the relative importance of each variable will be confounded. To avoid this problem, one can use standardized data in which the independent variables have identical metrics and distributions ($\bar{x} = 0$, $s^2 = 1$). The standardized regression coefficients thus produced can be compared to one another in spite of differences in the original metric. *However,* one obtains standardized coefficients by multiplying the unstandardized coefficient by the ratio of the standard deviation of the dependent variable. Therefore, differences in the standard deviations will affect the magnitude of the standardized coefficients. This leads to the problem suggested by data in table IIA.

When the standard deviations are similar (as in the experience category between senatorial, gubernatorial, or presidential elections, or between the experience, honesty-integrity, and general qualifications categories in the expanded gubernatorial solution), it does not make any difference whether we use b's or betas. When the standard deviations differ, selection of unstandardized or standardized coefficients for use in an analysis could lead to different substantive conclusions. Therefore a choice was made based on what we considered the source of the variance to be and on how the variance was assumed to be related to the theoretical question in the study.

As inspection of table IIA will show, greater differences in standard deviations occur within the single equations analyzing voting in one type of election rather than across the comparable variables in different equations. The largest difference between equations is for the standard deviations for the personal qualifications variable in the compressed solution, .78 between the presidential and senatorial figures. Larger differences occur within single equations—for example, 1.30 between personal qualifications and party statements in the compressed presidential solution or 1.15 between party statements and spending and taxes in the expanded senatorial solution. We therefore believe that sharply different frequencies of response are largely responsible for the very different variances for the variables within a single equation for each election.

The comparative statements we wish to make depend on the relative ordering of categories within each type of election. Thus, when we say that welfare is more important in gubernatorial voting, we mean that the coefficient associated with the welfare variable is relatively high when compared with the coefficients associated with other issue variables in the gubernatorial column. Since we wanted to make this kind of comparison, and since differences in response frequencies are the source of the differences in variance, we decided to use standardized coefficients. This allowed us to "force" identical variances for each variable for a given election and enabled us to compare the importance of each variable for a given election. Stated another way, we avoided assigning exaggerated significance to variables that were

Table IIA Regression Statistics for Ad Hoc Solutions by Type of Election

Solution	Senatorial			Gubernatorial			Presidential		
	b	Beta	Std. Dev.	b	Beta	Std. Dev.	b	Beta	Std. Dev.
Compressed									
Party statements	1.06	.34	1.30	1.78	.35	.80	1.79	.24	.53
Experience and incumbency	1.76	.33	.74	1.65	.28	.68	1.30	.22	.67
Personal qualifications	1.51	.40	1.05	1.39	.38	1.08	.99	.45	1.83
Issue references	1.50	.33	.87	1.32	.38	1.14	1.19	.37	1.24
Expanded									
Party statements	1.05	.34	1.30	1.74	.34	.80	1.77	.23	.53
Experience	1.95	.31	.64	1.75	.24	.56	.95	.11	.45
Incumbency—challenger	1.63	.12	.29	1.82	.14	.33	1.52	.19	.50
Youth-age	.99	.08	.31	.83	.03	.19	2.39	.05	.08
General qualifications	1.78	.26	.59	1.15	.15	.55	.94	.23	.97
Honesty-integrity	1.16	.18	.64	1.71	.23	.55	1.11	.24	.88
Intelligence	1.50	.08	.22	1.21	.07	.21	1.13	.08	.29
Personality and background	1.37	.17	.49	1.30	.16	.50	.94	.17	.72
Campaigning ability	1.00	.06	.22	1.12	.06	.23	.98	.12	.49
General issue references	1.58	.20	.52	1.08	.16	.59	1.26	.20	.63
Education	1.74	.08	.26	.56	.03	.28	.51	.01	.10
Civil rights law and order	1.83	.12	.18	1.64	.12	.21	1.27	.13	.42
Natural resources	1.33	.06	.17	−4.02	−.09	.09	1.10	.01	.04
Spending and taxes	1.95	.07	.15	1.59	.19	.47	1.30	.09	.27
Vietnam	1.53	.10	.26	−.55	−.01	.09	.96	.14	.60
Welfare	1.19	.13	.44	1.62	.19	.48	1.18	.14	.47

strongly associated with vote, but which were mentioned very infrequently. [29]

---

[29] In making this choice, we followed the lead of Stokes, et al. who used standardized coefficients to make judgments about the importance of attitudes on voting choices. Donald E. Stokes, et al., "Components of Electoral Decision," *American Political Science Review*, 52(June 1958):367–87. A much more sophisticated procedure, though equivalent with respect to the problem being discussed here, was used in Stokes's comparison of four elections. Donald E. Stokes, "Some Dynamic Elements of Contests for the Presidency," *American Political Science Review*, 60(March 1966):19–28.

ELECTORAL CHANGE

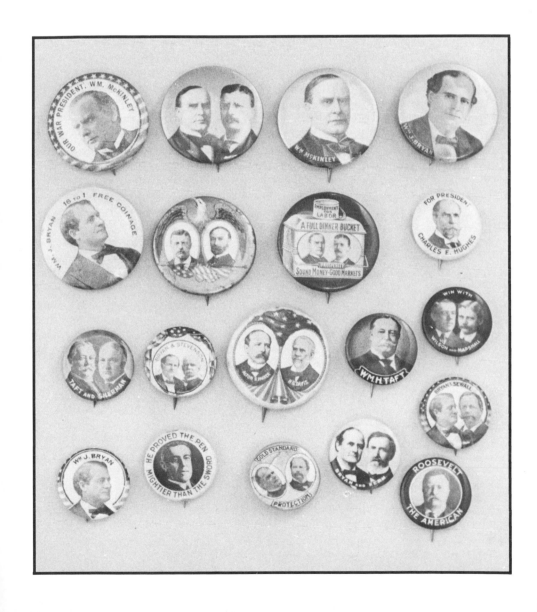

I. INDIVIDUAL PARTISANSHIP

17. Is Party Identification Stable?

An election presents the voter with a set of alternatives, and the voter chooses from the alternatives presented in that election. That statement seems tautological, and yet it misses an important part of reality. It implies that voters make a fresh choice in each election from the alternatives available at that time. But voters may base their decisions on a past experience, or on a whole series of past experiences, with minimal attention to the current election. This possibility requires us to move away from single election analysis into a consideration of the elements of continuity between elections.

Each election is not an isolated event, totally separated from all previous elections. Many of the same issues are raised in successive elections, and candidates have usually been involved in politics before—perhaps even as candidates for the same office. Most importantly, the national parties remain the same between elections and have been so for the past century. Although the parties may stand for different things at different times, they clearly have some continuity in the minds of voters. For example, many voters view the Democratic party as being generally favorable to working people and to minority groups, while others associate it with mistakes in foreign policy, and at least a few see it as the more liberal party. These associations are not created anew for each election, but are based on a long-range view of the parties.

How strong is this sense of long-term continuity? Though early theories made no allowance at all for such influences, cross-section surveys pointed to partisanship as a key element of continuity between elections. Partisanship provided this continuity by being itself highly stable. Party identification seemed to be passed on from parent to child, and, once received, to be consistently maintained. The only important change seemed to be a strengthening of the party association as the person reached middle and old age.

Such impressive stability has numerous implications for individual behavior and for the life of the political system. For example, it suggests that parties ordinarily need not pay much attention to the ideas of their followers, since support changes significantly only in the face of catastrophic events.

What if partisanship were more flexible than this? Most obviously, it would mean that the parties would have to be continually concerned with keeping the support of their identifiers. Not only would catastrophic events alter party support, but minor grievances could turn people away. Similarly, parties could not count on support from the children of their followers. Each generation of new adults would have to be wooed—but not so much so as to lose support of older adults.

All of this leads inevitably to the question of the importance of partisanship for a political system. Is it desirable to have voting largely determined by a stable characteristic such as party? It does simplify the choice for the individual voter. If there were no parties to provide cues for voters, there might be confusion about the candidates, and, consequently, reduced participation. On the other hand, the absence of parties might lead to greater emphasis on issues, with less emphasis on party allegiance. Partisanship also helps keep the political system stable by making it more difficult for new parties and minor parties to win. Yet too much stability may be dangerous. Total stability of partisanship could effectively mean suppression of the minority, which could never win political arguments, just as total instability could mean chaos.

Now, as we accumulate more surveys, it is possible to take a critical look at the concept of stable partisanship. Recent studies have begun to suggest that partisanship, though still relatively stable, is much less so than was first believed. The difference may merely be between very high stability and moderately high stability, but that difference may have tremendous implications for the potential of the system to respond to change.

Recent studies have gone much further by suggesting that partisanship has become meaningless. Typically, the argument is that the number of partisans is declining and that partisanship no longer determines voting behavior anyway. This notion of the declining relevance of party is important enough for us to deal with it briefly at the end of this chapter as well as devoting a whole section to it (chapters 24–26). In this chapter we are assuming, we think correctly, that partisanship will continue to be an important concept.

V. O. Key had written of the "standing decision" of communities to support one party or the other,[1] but it was The American Voter that popularized the importance of party identification of voters.[2] In 1952, the Survey Research Center began asking respondents, "Generally speaking, do you think of yourself as a Republican, a Democrat, an independent, or what?" Most voters responded in terms of one of the parties. Those who called themselves independents were pushed, "Do you think of yourself as closer to the Republican or Democratic Party?" With that added question, less than 10 percent of the sample in the 1950's (and only a bit more than 10 percent in the 1970's) declined to associate themselves with one party or the other.[3] Finally, those who did identify with a party were asked, "Would you call yourself a strong (Republican, Democrat) or a not very strong (Republican, Democrat)?" The result is a sevenfold classification of party identification: strong Republican, weak Republican, independent leaning Republican, pure independent, independent leaning Democratic, weak Democrat, and strong Democrat.[4]

The American Voter found party identification a critical variable for the understanding of voting. Most strong party identifiers reported generally voting for the same party while most independents reported voting for different parties; most strong Democrats voted Democratic while most strong Republicans voted Republican. Overall, party identification showed a stronger relationship with the vote than any other single question. More important, party identification affected people's attitudes toward the short-term candidates and issues. Democrats were more apt to like the Democratic candidate and to prefer the Democrats on issues than were Republicans—presumably, in many cases, because they were Democrats and not because of a searching analysis of current candidates and issues.[5]

Since The American Voter found party identification to be so important, it devoted some attention to development of partisanship. People were found

---

[1] V. O. Key, Jr., and Frank Munger, "Social Determinism and Electoral Decision: The Case of Indiana," in Eugene Burdick and Arthur Brodbeck, eds., American Voting Behavior (Glencoe, Ill.: Free Press, 1959), pp. 281–99.

[2] Angus Campbell, Philip E. Converse, Warren E. Miller, and Donald E. Stokes, The American Voter (New York: Wiley, 1960).

[3] An additional few percent in the 1950's were classified as "apoliticals" since they were so unaware of politics as to not understand the question. This group consisted mainly of southern blacks who were not permitted to vote. Apoliticals have now virtually disappeared.

[4] Note that psychological identification is being measured by this set of questions rather than legal membership in the party. Party membership is rare in the United States, few Americans "join" a party, and party registration (in those states that have such a system) is not necessarily identical with a person's current partisan identification.

[5] The importance of party identification is currently under fire, though the point is typically that issues as well as partisanship determine political attitudes and behavior. Stated this way, we agree completely. See also our discussion of vote determinants in chapter 9 and of the "end of parties" in chapter 24.

to generally adopt the party of their parents, particularly when their parents had been politically active. Most voters still identified with the party they voted for when first eligible to vote, and few respondents indicated they had ever changed partisanship. Perhaps the most important change in partisanship reported by *The American Voter* was the tendency of party loyalty to strengthen with time. Older people were more strongly identified with parties than younger people, but not because of their age as much as the length of time they had thought of themselves as part of the party. Indeed, age was unrelated to strength of party identification when duration of party identification was held constant.

These results were the foundation of the view that partisanship was highly stable. They had one major defect, however, in that data about parents, past behavior, and so on, were necessarily based on recall information. This defect was corrected by a number of subsequent studies, beginning a few years later when Converse reported actual rates of change observed in a panel study (the same respondents interviewed more than once) conducted from 1956 to 1960. That data showed that a mere 2 percent of the white population changed from Republicans to Democrats or vice versa over this four-year period.[6] Similarly, when Converse (chapter 6) presented correlations over time for partisanship and issues, the correlation for partisanship was much higher than the comparable figures for issue positions. The data on continuity between generations were a little later in coming, but evidence from 1965 (presented here on p. 334) showed that only 7 percent of the nation's high school seniors deviated from the partisanship of their parents. These results seemed to put the lid on the case. Recall data, data gathered from a panel study, and data gathered independently from parents and youths showed a high degree of partisan stability.

Thus *The American Voter* and related work created an image of partisan stability, both between generations and within generations. Partisanship was modified mainly in the sense of partisanship increasing with longer partisan attachment. This gives rise to a "life cycle" view of partisan development. Psychological attachment to a party begins very early, and with the exception of a small number of individuals who do change, it strengthens with age.

The applicability of party identification outside the United States has always been questionable, but results from a number of countries seemed to permit broad generalization of *The American Voter* conclusions. In Great Britain, for example, Butler and Stokes found a strong relationship between party preferences of parent and offspring and a strengthening of partisanship with age and length of association.[7] A study in France highlighted the

---

[6] Philip E. Converse, "On the Possibility of Major Political Realignment in the South," in Angus Campbell, Philip E. Converse, Warren E. Miller, and Donald E. Stokes, *Elections and the Political Order* (New York: Wiley, 1966), p. 225.

[7] David Butler and Donald Stokes, *Political Change in Britain* (New York: St. Martin's Press, 1969), chap. 3.

importance of parents' partisanship.[8] The strengthening of partisanship with the length of its duration was further supported by analysis of additional data from the United States and Great Britain, as well as data from Germany, Italy, and Mexico.[9] Thus the patterns of stability, intergenerational transmission, and strengthening of partisanship with age seemed to be general processes extending well beyond American findings.

If party identification is indeed stable, as seemed to be the case, and if it is an important determinant of the vote, then it can be of considerable use in sorting out long- and short-term components of electoral change. This notion led Converse to develop the "normal vote" concept.[10] Short-term forces specific to an election have a greater effect on those with weaker party identification and lower political involvement levels. Converse developed estimates for each party identification category of turnout in the North and South and of the expected Democratic proportion of the two-party vote for a hypothetical "normal election" in which these short-term forces are balanced between the parties and are moderate in size. These were used to obtain an estimate of the "normal vote" in the nation. Given the greater Democratic identification, but also given the lower turnout among Democrats, Converse estimated the normal vote to be roughly 54 percent Democratic in the 1950's. The estimate for the 1960's is very similar.

The importance of the normal vote concept is not simply the estimation of its national value. The normal vote represents the long-term component of a group's vote. Thus its actual vote can be compared to its normal vote to show the effect of short-term forces on that group. For example, Converse reports that the Catholic vote was more Democratic than the Protestant vote in 1952, but that that is wholly due to the greater Democratic normal vote among Catholics.[11] Catholics and Protestants differed in their partisanship sufficiently for the normal vote among Catholics to be 20 percent more Democratic than among Protestants. Yet for both groups, the 1952 actual vote was 13 percent less Democratic than their normal vote. In other words, the short-term forces of 1952 affected the two groups in identical ways. The difference in their vote was due solely to long-term party identification differences. Group vote differences could now be broken down into long-term partisan differences and short-term differences due to the particular election conditions.

---

[8] In particular, Converse and Dupeux find that a similar transmission process holds in the United States and France, with 80 percent of those who could recall a party identification for their father having a partisan identification themselves, while only half of these not recalling their father's partisanship did themselves identify with a party. Philip E. Converse and George Dupeux, "Politicization of the Electorate in France and the United States," *Public Opinion Quarterly*, 26(1962):1–23.

[9] Philip E. Converse, "Of Time and Partisan Stability," *Comparative Political Studies*, 2(1969):139–71.

[10] Philip E. Converse, "The Concept of a Normal Vote," in Campbell et al., *Elections and the Political Order*.

[11] *Ibid.*, p. 31.

Boyd has developed explicit measures of the long-term and short-term components of an issue based on the normal vote concept.[12] The normal ("expected") vote and the actual vote are computed for each opinion category. For example, the category of people who feel that civil rights programs are moving too fast might be calculated to have an expected Democratic vote of 54 percent though their actual Democratic vote is 33 percent. The long-term component of the issue is based on the differences in the expected Democratic vote of those with different issue positions. The issue would have no long-term component if people who have different positions on it have the same expected Democratic vote, but the issue would have a substantial long-term component if those with diametrically opposed opinions differ sharply in their partisanship and normal vote. The short-term component of an issue is based on the differences between the actual and expected Democratic votes. If the individuals in each category have identical expected and actual Democratic votes, then the issue has no short-term effect on the election. It would have a substantial short-term effect if those with one position voted much more Democratic than expected while those with the opposite position voted much less Democratic than expected. Boyd's measures are employed extensively in the Center for Political Studies report on the 1972 election (see chapter 10).[13]

What we have at this point is a picture of an electorate whose very stable partisanship has a significant effect on the vote. According to this view, partisanship is so stable that it can be used to permit estimates of the short-term contributions of other factors to election outcomes. The only significant change in partisanship is related to life cycle development.

Partisanship as Flexible

But is the idea of stable partisanship fully justified? Or is it perhaps applicable to the 1950's and early 1960's but not to more recent years? If the latter is true, then we might ask whether party identification is actually still useful as a concept or whether it was primarily useful in the quiescent 50's.

One set of challenges to the idea of party stability comes from several authors who have analyzed aggregate changes in partisanship using cohort analyses. (This is the method used by Abramson in chapter 18.) This method relies on repeated cross-sectional surveys. While the same individuals are not interviewed more than once, one can compare, say, a sample of individuals who were twenty in 1960 and another sample who were thirty in 1970.

[12] Richard W. Boyd, "Popular Control of Public Policy: A Normal Vote Analysis of the 1968 Election," *American Political Science Review,* 66(1972):429–49.

[13] As Boyd himself pointed out (*Ibid.,* p. 432), the normal vote results do not tell us whether an issue contributed in a causal sense to the observed vote. The actual causal flow could be quite complex, with the effect attributed to one issue actually due to some cause with which it is highly correlated. See also the critique of the normal vote and the Boyd approach by Brody and Page (chapter 13).

In each year this represents a sample of those born in 1940, so some inferences can be made about individual changes of this "cohort" from the pattern of aggregate changes. These overall changes have been sufficient for Glenn and Hefner to conclude that "aging adults seem to have a rather high potential for participation in political change, which apparently does not have to depend very largely upon the sole process of the population turnover in the electorate through maturation and death."[14] As these authors point out, this evidence shows no wholesale conversions from one major party to the other, but it does suggest that individuals are loosely enough identified with a party that substantial numbers can be jarred loose from their associations, becoming independents.

These results apply primarily to recent times. However, reanalysis and reinterpretation of data from the 50's and 60's suggest that we were perhaps too quick in judging partisanship to be extremely stable at that time. Here a crucial matter of definition intrudes. A move from one party to the other clearly shows a change, but what about a move from one party to independence or vice versa? Should a move from weak Democrat to independent leaning to the Democratic side be considered a shift in partisanship? What about a shift to pure independence? Using correlations to measure partisan stability overcomes this problem to some extent, though problems such as the type of correlation to use, intervals between categories, corrections for measurement error, and the appropriate standard of comparison (how high a correlation represents "stability") remain.

The whole question of intergenerational change in 1965—just before the proportion of independents began to rise—is considered in the selection reprinted here from the Jennings and Niemi survey of high school seniors and their parents (see chapter 19). It shows that the intergenerational transmission of partisanship is weaker than one might have expected. Only 7 percent of the students differed from their parents when only Republican/Democratic change is considered, but 41 percent showed a deviation if movement into and out of the independent classification is included. The intergenerational correlation (tau-b) is 0.47, indicating that considerable change occurred along with some underlying stability. Jennings and Niemi consider the conditions governing intergenerational stability and discuss why student partisanship might correlate better with parents' vote than with parents' partisanship.

Within generations, reconsideration of data from the 50's indicates at least a degree of ambiguity. Dreyer, for example, has noted that change over a two-month period in 1960 was approximately as high as the change shown by Converse over the entire 1956-60 period.[15] This suggests a lesser degree of stability than is suggested by only the 1956-60 comparison. The matter of

---

[14] Norval D. Glenn and Ted Hefner, "Further Evidence on Aging and Party Identification," *Public Opinion Quarterly*, 36(1972):31–47, at p. 47.

[15] Edward C. Dreyer, "Change and Stability in Party Identification," *Journal of Politics*, 35(1973):712–22.

independents is also relevant here. In the same study in which Converse reported a 2 percent shift between the parties, he also found an additional 20 percent of the respondents shifting from an independent to a partisan category or vice versa. If this kind of shift is important, and if the single comparison of 1956 with 1960 underestimates the true extent of shifting during that period, then partisanship might be regarded as quite variable even during the 50's.[16] On the other hand, the correlation between 1956 and 1960 reports is high—approximately 0.72 (see p. 87) to 0.93, depending on the type of correlation used and the correction for unreliability.[17] In any event, results from a new panel study covering the period from 1965 to 1973 suggest that partisan stability definitely declined after the mid-60's. Jennings and Niemi found that, of the parents interviewed in 1965, only 4 percent transferred from one party to the other. But 24 percent shifted between the Republican, independent, and Democratic categories, with a (tau-b) correlation of 0.67.[18] Change was considerably greater among young people (age 17–18 in 1965) during this period, with a correlation of only 0.39 (see table 17.1). A study of children in fourth through eighth grades in 1968–1969 also reports a fair degree of instability, though no comparable data from the 50's exists.[19]

Not only does it appear that change within and between generations is greater than was originally thought, but the notion of voters becoming more partisan with age has been challenged on the basis of cohort analysis. It remains the case in the 1970's that older voters are stronger partisans than young ones. The "life cycle" interpretation mentioned earlier presumes that something about the aging process (or duration of partisanship) makes people change their political views. Another possible explanation is that older voters grew up under considerably different circumstances from younger voters and differ as a result of these conditions. The result would be a "generational" difference rather than a "life cycle" difference. The authors of *The American Voter* attempted to test which explanation was correct, but a lengthy series of surveys is required to provide complete proof. Evidence from both Gallup polls[20] and from the SRC/CPS studies has been used to suggest a generational interpretation.

---

[16] Similarly, while *The American Voter* (p. 148) shows that only 10 percent of the population claimed to have ever identified with a different party if only Republican/Democratic switches are considered, this figure jumps to 19 percent if the independent category is included.

[17] Herbert B. Asher, "Some Consequences of Measurement Error on Survey Data," *American Journal of Political Science* 18(1974):469-85.

[18] We would like to thank M. Kent Jennings for allowing us to use these data.

[19] Over 40 percent of the white children in the sample and considerably more of the black children switched their partisan responses over a period of only six months. Most of the changes involved the independent category. See Pauline Marie Vaillancourt and Richard G. Niemi, "Children's Party Choice," in Richard G. Niemi and Associates, *The Politics of Future Citizens* (San Francisco: Jossey-Bass, 1974).

[20] Glenn and Hefner, "Aging and Party Identification." However, this paper deals primarily with the possibility of increased Republicanism with age.

The article by Abramson (chapter 18) presents the strongest argument for the idea that partisanship differences are basically due to differences between generations. He interprets the cohort data as showing that individuals do not become stronger partisans as they age and that the increase in the number of independents in recent years is a result of generational differences. Interestingly, the generations affected include not only the very young, but also individuals who were born in the mid- to late 20's and therefore reached adulthood shortly after World War II.

Table 17.1 Party Identification Circulation (in Percentages), 1965–1973

Filial Generation (N = 1321)

1973

		Demo.	Indep.	Repub.	
	Demo.	24.2	14.0	2.7	40.9
1965	Indep.	6.7	23.8	5.9	36.4
	Repub.	3.4	8.9	10.5	22.8
		34.3	46.7	19.1	100.1

$Tau_b = .42$

Parental Generation (N = 1140)

1973

		Demo.	Indep.	Repub.	
	Demo.	38.9	5.8	2.5	47.2
1965	Indep.	5.2	15.8	4.9	25.9
	Repub.	1.3	3.9	21.8	27.0
		45.4	25.5	29.2	100.1

$Tau_b = .67$

SOURCE: Printed with the kind permission of M. Kent Jennings.

Yet it is difficult to separate life cycle and generational effects, particularly if there is an important change in the political system during the time under study. Say, for example, that the life cycle effect described by *The American Voter* was a slow one, amounting to an increase in the number of strong partisans of under 1 percent for each age group in each year. And say that in the mid-1960's events caused an upheaval which shook the party loyalties of many people. Overlay the latter "period effect" on a small life cycle effect, and the result may look a lot like a generational effect, since older people's normally heightened partisanship would be offset by the across-the-board weakening of partisanship.

Abramson responds that this interpretation fails to take into account the changing composition of the electorate and that, in any event, the life cycle explanation strongly suggests absolute increases in identification (i.e., not increases offset by other factors).[21] At the very least, it seems clear from Abramson's work that both period effects and generational differences were involved in the changes observed in the American electorate in the late 60's and into the 70's. To what extent life cycle effects really do exist remains open to debate, though the argument for them has been considerably weakened.

According to these studies, partisanship is more flexible than was once thought. How changeable it is remains somewhat unclear—partly because of the question of defining what change of party means and partly because of alternative interpretations of age-related data. But the potential for change in partisanship is now recognized to be much greater than it seemed.

Conclusions

How important is partisanship? On the one hand, many voters decide how to vote solely on the basis of long-term considerations. Even before the candidates are nominated, the votes of many people are decided. Barring the most unusual development, the majority of large businessmen are already inclined to vote Republican in the next election, for example. Yet these initial inclinations can be upset. If the Democrats nominate George Wallace for President, most black voters would find it distasteful to vote Democratic despite their usual inclinations. Short-term forces can deflect the long-term considerations.

Still, except in extreme circumstances, we can be sure than many individuals will find their initial inclinations are reinforced by the parties' choices of candidates. Indeed we can be almost certain this has happened in the past, for if it were not the case we would not find the familiar long-term associations of particular groups with a specific party. Nor would we expect from

---

[21] Paul R. Abramson, "Generation Change and the Decline of Party Identification," *American Political Science Review*, forthcoming.

30 to 40 percent or more of the voters to make up their minds about the presidential vote before the nominating conventions. [22]

The question then is how to characterize the long-term component of voting behavior. We could ignore it, analyzing each election only in terms of the issues and candidates involved in that particular campaign. Since one can't change the past, candidates might rationally act as if they each had a fifty-fifty chance of winning the election. For purposes of explanation, however, it is highly likely that we will want to have some measure of a long-term component in our theories. If our theories are to be dynamic, capable of explaining behavior over an extended period of time, some kind of long-term component is essential. Party identification has become the most common measure of this component, though some other measures might be better suited for particular purposes.

But is the partisanship concept outmoded? Many feel that partisanship is no longer important. The "Dealignment" section which follows focuses on the recent decline in party identification. Without fully restating that discussion, it is fair to emphasize that most people still identify themselves with a major party and few indicate that they do not lean toward either party. An increase in split-ticket voting or defection from party does not mean that people necessarily will ignore party in future settings when current short-term forces vanish.

Furthermore, partisanship plays a critical role in dynamic theories of electoral behavior. Certain aspects of future voting behavior might in fact best be explained in terms of party identification—and its decline. If the decline in partisanship is of major significance, then the concept itself is important. The extent of partisanship is a key parameter that varies over time, but the variation does not mean that it is insignificant theoretically.

Similarly, we would argue that lack of complete stability of individual partisanship does not reduce the meaningfulness of the concept. The stability remains high enough to make the concept important theoretically and practically. Yet if partisanship is more flexible than was previously believed, we must turn our attention more to the causes of change in partisanship. Jennings and Niemi (chapter 19) show some of the factors that relate to intergenerational stability. More attention to factors causing change within an individual is required. Perhaps of greatest interest would be the connection between issues and partisanship. With the recent recognition of greater variations in partisanship, along with increased emphasis on issues, it becomes important to examine the link between issues and party shift. The apparent decrease in the stability of partisanship suggests that we should alter our understanding of it and should redirect our research efforts toward discovering the bonds between issues, candidates, and partisanship.

---

[22] William H. Flanigan and Nancy H. Zingale, *Political Behavior of the American Electorate,* 3d ed. (Boston: Allyn & Bacon, 1975), p. 158.

The Measurement of Partisanship

Philip E. Converse, "The Concept of a Normal Vote," in Angus Campbell, Philip E.
    Converse, Warren E. Miller, and Donald E. Stokes, *Elections and the Political
    Order* (New York: Wiley, 1966). Development of the normal vote concept.
Richard W. Boyd, "Popular Control of Public Policy: A Normal Vote Analysis of the
    1968 Election," *American Political Science Review,* 66(1972):429-49. Develops
    summary statistics of the effect of issue beyond the expected normal vote.
Everett C. Ladd, Jr. and Charles D. Hadley, "Party Definition and Party Differentia-
    tion," *Public Opinion Quarterly,* 37(1973-74):21-34. Analyzes alternative defini-
    tions of partisanship and how they relate to political behavior.
John R. Petrocik, "An Analysis of Intransitivities in the Index of Party Identification,"
    Political Methodology, 1(1974):31-47. Discusses the lack of monotonicity in re-
    lating party identification to participation.

Age Effects on Partisanship

Philip E. Converse, "Of Time and Partisan Stability," *Comparative Political Studies,*
    2(1969):139-71. Discusses strength of partisanship as a function of its duration.
Norval D. Glenn and Ted Hefner, "Further Evidence on Aging and Party Identifica-
    tion," *Public Opinion Quarterly,* 36(1972):31-47. Finds through cohort analysis
    of Gallup poll data that aging does not make people more partisan or more
    Republican.

Stability of Partisanship

Donald E. Stokes and Gudmund R. Iversen, "On the Existence of Forces Restoring
    Party Competition," *Public Opinion Quarterly,* 26(1962):159-71. Analyzes stabil-
    ity of American two-party system.
M. Kent Jennings and Richard G. Niemi, "Party Identification at Multiple Levels of
    Government," *American Journal of Sociology,* 72(1966):86-101. Federalism con-
    tributes to shifting party affiliations.
Arthur S. Goldberg, "Social Determinism and Rationality as Bases of Party Identifica-
    tion," *American Political Science Review,* 63(1969):5-25. Model of determinants
    of party identification.
Pauline Marie Vaillancourt and Richard G. Niemi, "Children's Party Choice," in Rich-
    ard G. Niemi and Associates, *The Politics of Future Citizens* (San Francisco:
    Jossey-Bass, 1974). Studies stability of partisanship among grade-school children.
Paul Allen Beck and M. Kent Jennings, "Parent as 'Middlepersons' in Political Social-
    ization," *Journal of Politics,* 37(1975):83-107. Considers transmission of partisan-
    ship from grandparents to parents to children.

Cross-National Studies

Angus Campbell and Henry Valen, "Party Identification in Norway and the United
    States," *Public Opinion Quarterly,* 25(1961):505-25. Contrasts partisanship in
    two countries with different degrees of ideological and class orientation.

Philip E. Converse and Georges Dupeux, "Politicization of the Electorate in France and the United States," *Public Opinion Quarterly,* 26(1962):1–23. Finds that effects of parental partisanship on offspring are similar across countries.

Jack Dennis and Donald J. McCrone, "Preadult Development of Political Party Identification in Western Democracies," *Comparative Political Studies,* 3(1970): 243–63. Comparative study of socialization of partisanship.

Ronald Inglehart, "The Silent Revolution in Europe: Intergenerational Change in Post-industrial Societies," *American Political Science Review,* 65(1971):991–1017. Transformation of basic political priorities in current generations of Western Europeans.

18. Generational Change and the Decline of Party Identification

PAUL R. ABRAMSON

The relationship of social class to presidential voting behavior has declined dramatically during the postwar years. Yet, some would argue that there will be no new partisan alignments until there are changes not only of behavior, but of underlying voter attachments to the political parties. Voters may make, in V. O. Key's words, a "standing decision" to support a party, and that decision may remain unaltered even though they may vote for the opposition in a given election.

Since 1952 the Survey Research Center (SRC) has monitored basic feelings toward the political parties by asking questions that measure partisan loyalties on a continuum, ranging from strong attachment to the Democratic party to strong attachment to the Republicans. . . . [1] Whether or not large numbers of citizens hold strong party loyalties may have important behavioral consequences. Campbell and his colleagues long have argued that high

SOURCE: *Generational Change in American Politics,* by Paul R. Abramson. Lexington, Mass.: Lexington Books, D. C. Heath and Co., 1975, pp. 51-70. Reprinted with permission of the publisher.

[1] Respondents are asked, "Generally speaking, do you usually think of yourself as a Republican, a Democrat, an independent, or what?" Persons who call themselves Republicans or Democrats are asked, "Would you call yourself a strong (Republican, Democrat) or a not very strong (Republican, Democrat)?" Persons who call themselves independents are asked, "Do you think of yourself as closer to the Republican or Democratic Party?"

levels of partisan support among mass electorates contribute to the stability of democratic political systems. Persons with strong partisan feelings, they argue, are more likely to participate in politics; they possess a conceptual framework that helps them interpret new and complex issues; and, perhaps most important, they are more likely to resist the appeals of new parties and of leaders outside the traditional party system.[2] While some of these conclusions have been challenged in recent years,[3] the development of party identification remains a central research concern.[4] And the erosion of American party loyalties during the past decade concerns not only political scientists, but others interested in the future of American politics.

Table 18.1 presents the party loyalties of whites between 1952 and 1972.[5] A large and growing proportion of Americans claims to be neither Republican nor Democratic. Regardless how we define attachment to a party, the proportion of identifiers has declined markedly since 1964. In all the surveys from 1952 through 1964, the proportion of whites who were strong party identifiers never fell below 35 percent. By 1970 only 27 percent were strong identifiers; by 1972, when the percentage of strong Democrats dropped sharply, strong partisans were only 24 percent of the total. Through 1964 about three out of four whites were either strong or weak identifiers, but this proportion declined in each subsequent election; by 1972 only 62 percent were strong or weak identifiers. The percentage of pure independents, that is those who leaned toward neither major party, rose from eight percent in 1964 to 13 percent in 1972.

Is the trend toward weakening party attachments likely to continue? [One can gain greater confidence about the direction of a trend by studying subgroups that may provide a guide about future relationships. One promising method is to examine age-group differences, for the behavior of the young is more likely to point to future relationships than that of their elders.] By examining the relationship of age to strength of party identification, we replicate a well-established finding—Young persons have weaker partisan attachments than their elders. The problem is to explain that relationship, and, as I am using data originally analyzed by Campbell and his colleagues, I will use their discussion as a point of departure.

---

[2] These arguments are advanced by Angus Campbell et al., *The American Voter* (New York: Wiley, 1960), pp. 120-45, and in several essays in the volume by the same authors, *Elections and the Political Order* (New York: Wiley, 1966).

[3] For example, see Donald D. Searing, Joel J. Schwartz, and Alden E. Lind, "The Structuring Principle: Political Socialization and Belief Systems," *American Political Science Review*, 67(June 1973):415-32; and W. Phillips Shively, "Party Identification, Party Choice, and Voting Stability: The Weimar Case," *American Political Science Review*, 66(December 1972):1203-25.

[4] For example, see the extensive discussion of this research literature in David O. Sears, "Political Socialization," in *Handbook of Political Science. Volume 2: Theoretical Aspects of Micropolitics*, ed. Fred I. Greenstein and Nelson W. Polsby (Reading, Mass.: Addison-Wesley, 1975).

[5] Although party identification was measured in 1954, the SRC survey for that year used arbitrary age categories, and the survey cannot be used in my time-series cohort analysis.

Table 18.1 Party Identification Among Whites from 1952 Through 1972 (Percentages)

Party Identification	1952	1956	1958	1960	1962	1964	1966	1968	1970	1972
Strong Democrat	21	20	26	20	22	24	17	16	17	12
Weak Democrat	25	23	22	25	23	25	27	25	22	25
Independent, leans Democratic	10	6	7	6	8	9	9	10	11	12
Independent	6	9	8	9	8	8	12	11	13	13
Independent, leans Republican	7	9	5	7	7	6	8	10	9	11
Weak Republican	14	14	17	14	17	14	16	16	16	14
Strong Republican	14	16	12	17	13	12	11	11	10	11
Other party	†	†	†	1	†	1	†	†	†	†
Apolitical	2	2	3	1	3	†	1	1	1	1
Total percent	99	99	100	101	101	99	101	100	99	99
(Number)	(1615)	(1610)	(1638)ᵃ	(1739)ᵃ	(1168)	(1394)	(1131)	(1387)	(1395)	(2397)
Strong party identifiers	35	36	38	36	35	36	27	27	27	24
Strong and weak party identifiers	75	73	77	76	75	75	71	68	66	62

ᵃ Weighted N.   †Less than one percent.

The authors of *The American Voter* clearly demonstrated that young persons have weaker partisan attachments than their elders.[6] Combining data collected in seven surveys from 1952 through 1957, they show the percentage of strong party identifiers increased steadily with age; the percentage of independents (including independents who leaned toward one of the major parties[7]) decreased. But Campbell and his colleagues not only presented their findings; they also recognized, and attempted to test, alternative explanations for them.

Age differences could result from generational effects, for "age may mark an historical epoch in which the person has matured or undergone some special variety of experience that has left an imprint on his attitudes and behaviors."[8] On the other hand, differences between age groups could result from the differing position of people in the life cycle, for "age may serve as an index of the length of time that the individual has lived in a specified state or engaged in a specified behavior."[9] "The historical interpretation of our data," they continued, "would suggest that partisan feeling was more intense several decades ago than now. If older persons have more intense party loyalties than younger, it is a reflection of the politics of an earlier American period."[10]

Campbell and his colleagues attempted to discriminate between explanations, and their findings supported a life-cycle explanation. As their test used cross-sectional data, however, they could not examine the political attitudes of persons as they moved through the life cycle. Among persons who remain attached to the same party throughout their life, one cannot distinguish age, length of attachment to a party, or the period in which persons entered the electorate. But for persons who have switched their partisanship, duration of attachment can be distinguished from age and era of maturation. If the life-cycle explanation were valid, Campbell and his colleagues reasoned, the tendency of the old to have stronger partisan loyalties than the young would be eliminated once duration of attachment were controlled. Campbell et al. tested the relationship between age and strength of party loyalties while controlling for the length of time the respondents identified with their party. When length of attachment was held constant, the young had somewhat stronger party attachments than their elders. "This pattern of relationships," they concluded, "fits very well a more general thesis that group identification is a function of the proportion of a person's life he has been associated

---

[6] Campbell et al., *The American Voter,* p. 161.

[7] In this analysis, the Michigan authors did not differentiate between independents who lean toward a party and those who did not.

[8] *Ibid.,* p. 161.

[9] *Ibid.*

[10] *Ibid.*

with the group. The longer a person thinks of himself as belonging to a party, the stronger his sense of loyalty to it will become." [11]

But Campbell's test is scarcely definitive, for few old persons had short-term party attachments, and only the simplest controls were applied. [12] More important, although older persons who had recently acquired their current party attachments were likely to have weak party loyalties, the causality of this relationship could be the opposite of that suggested by the Michigan authors. Rather than weak party identifications resulting from the brief attachment to a party, the brief duration might result from weak partisan loyalties. Indeed, panel data suggest that weak partisans are more likely to convert to another party than strong partisans, and they are more likely to become weak partisans of the opposite party than to become strong partisans of their new party. [13]

Even without panel data, however, one can discriminate between alternative explanations of the relationship of age to strength of partisanship by comparing similar cohorts sampled at different times. Campbell and his colleagues did not find this kind of analysis attractive, for they had collected data over only five years. By combining the results of surveys conducted at different times, they precluded any tentative effort at examining the effects of aging upon young adults who, even over five years, might have developed stronger party attachments. Now, we can examine age groups over two decades.

Age and Party Identification Between 1952 and 1972

Table 18.2 presents the percentage of whites who were strong party identifiers between 1952 and 1972, table 18.3 the percentage of party identifiers (combining strong and weak identifiers), and table 18.4 the percentage of pure independents. [14] The data are presented according to age cohorts. [15] Let

---

[11] *Ibid.*, p. 163. For a similar analysis examining the relationship between age and strength of partisanship in Britain, see Butler and Stokes, *Political Change in Britain: Forces Shaping Electoral Choice* (New York: St. Martin's Press, 1969), pp. 56–57.

[12] The basic procedure was to compare persons 44 years or younger with those 45 years or older. But the authors found only twenty-seven persons 45 years old and older who held their current attachments for less than four years, and only forty who had held their current attachments for between four and seven years.

[13] See Edward C. Dreyer, "Change and Stability in Party Identifications," *Journal of Politics,* 35(August 1973):712–22.

[14] I am following the procedures used by the Michigan authors by "folding" the party identification measure to combine strong partisans and to combine strong and weak partisans.

[15] With all these surveys, year of birth or actual age was recorded, and one can use any cohort divisions. To maintain comparability with the analysis in chapter 3 [of Abramson], I continued to use the same cohort divisions employed in that chapter. However, I also conducted this analysis dividing persons born before 1924 into eight-year cohorts. The alternative procedure yields similar results, although the consistency in levels of identification from survey to survey among older cohorts is reduced somewhat when smaller cohorts are used.

Table 18.2 Percentage of Whites Who Were Strong Party Identifiers from 1952 Through 1972, by Years of Birth[a]

Year of Survey	Years of Birth								X̄ for Total White Electorate
	1884-1893	1894-1903	1904-1913	1914-1923	1924-1931	1932-1939	1940-1947	1948-1954	
1952	43 (193)[b]	43 (267)	34 (342)	24 (395)	30 (249)	28 (98)			35
1956	48 (157)	40 (225)	36 (313)	33 (435)	27 (293)	31 (155)			36
1958[c]	47 (155)	43 (236)	35 (316)	36 (419)	32 (275)	34 (194)			38
1960[c]	43 (162)	43 (239)	35 (341)	32 (435)	34 (307)	21 (183)			36
1962	50 (94)	47 (157)	42 (212)	30 (257)	30 (194)	28 (229)	†		35
1964	50 (96)	46 (177)	42 (243)	34 (299)	32 (220)	19 (156)	25 (104)		36
1966	44 (73)	38 (148)	32 (169)	26 (239)	23 (195)	22 (189)	17 (138)		27
1968	44 (68)	44 (163)	36 (204)	22 (283)	26 (240)	19 (186)	11 (225)		27
1970	44 (52)	36 (142)	33 (216)	32 (226)	23 (199)	19 (186)	21 (236)	18 (124)	27
1972	41 (68)	42 (195)	33 (344)	29 (366)	24 (330)	15 (313)	14 (420)	12 (342)	24

a Percentage who are strong Democrats or strong Republicans.
b Numbers in parentheses are the totals upon which percentages are based.
c Weighted Ns.
† Because of the small Ns, the percentage of strong partisans has not been presented.

Table 18.3 Percentage of Whites Who Were Strong or Weak Party Identifiers from 1952 Through 1972, by Years of Birth[a]

Year of Survey	Years of Birth								X̄ for Total White Electorate
	1884–1893	1894–1903	1904–1913	1914–1923	1924–1931	1932–1939	1940–1947	1948–1954	
1952	77[b]	81	75	72	68				75
1956	82	71	77	73	68	55			73
1958	83	79	81	78	69	70			77
1960	81	82	76	72	72	74			76
1962	84	83	81	75	67	65	†		75
1964	83	84	81	74	71	69	65		75
1966	81	77	75	72	67	67	59		71
1968	91	78	75	71	66	67	44		68
1970	87	73	77	73	62	61	55	48	66
1972	85	80	73	73	65	56	49	45	62

[a] Percentage who are strong Democrats, weak Democrats, strong Republicans, or weak Republicans.
[b] For the totals upon which these percentages are based, see table 18.2.
† Because of the small Ns, the percentage of strong and weak partisan identifiers has not been presented.

us begin by examining the relationship between age and strength of party identification in 1952. The percentage of strong party identifiers was lowest among persons born between 1914 and 1923 (ages 29 through 38), and was next lowest among those born between 1924 and 1931 (ages 21–28) (see table 18.2); these 21- to 28-year-olds also had the lowest percentage of strong and weak identifiers (see table 18.3). Only a small percentage were pure independents, and there was no relationship between age and being a pure independent (see table 18.4). As Campbell's discussion suggests, there are two plausible explanations for the weakness of party loyalties among these young adults. A life-cycle explanation suggests that their weak partisan loyalties result from their political inexperience, whereas a generational explanation suggests that differences exist between the formative socialization of these young adults and that of their elders.

If a life-cycle explanation for the weak party loyalties of the young were valid, their feelings of party identification should grow stronger as they aged. The cohort born between 1914 and 1923, which had the largest percentage of weak partisans, should develop stronger partisanship as it aged. So, too, the cohort born between 1924 and 1931 should develop stronger partisanship as persons in that age group gain more experience and more opportunities to grow attached to the party of their choice; this cohort had the largest percentage of independents who leaned toward one of the major parties and many of them might become loyal partisans as they aged. Even pure independents might develop partisan attachments. [16] Thus the percentage of strong and weak party identifiers among the 1924 to 1931 cohort should grow during the subsequent two decades.

A generational explanation is based upon different assumptions and predicts different relationships. The basic assumption . . . is that there is a formative socialization period during which fairly enduring attitudes are learned; after that, attitudes tend to become relatively stable. . . . [T]he most important experiences in changing a person's party loyalties probably occur between the time he enters the work force and the first few elections in which he participates. If social and political conditions contribute to the formation of strong party loyalties during this period, the relative level of partisan identification among the cohort will continue to be high. But if conditions during this formative period contribute to the development of weak party loyalties, party loyalties are likely to remain weak.

If the assumptions that constitute the generational explanation are correct, most persons in the 1914 to 1923 cohort had their formative socialization experiences during the 1930's and World War II, and by 1952 would be relatively resistant to partisan change. Low levels of partisan identification among this cohort might well continue as they aged. Persons born between 1924 and 1931 had their formative socialization experiences during or after

---

[16] On the other hand, independence might be a form of loyalty in and of itself. Pure independents might become more committed to independence as they gained greater political experience.

Table 18.4 Percentage of Whites Who Were Independents with No Party Leanings from 1952 Through 1972, by Years of Birth[a]

Year of Survey	Years of Birth								X̄ for Total White Electorate
	1884-1893	1894-1903	1904-1913	1914-1923	1924-1931	1932-1939	1940-1947	1948-1954	
1952	8[b]	4	7	6	6				6
1956	6	12	8	9	9	13			9
1958	5	6	9	5	9	12			8
1960	11	5	12	9	7	12			9
1962	4	5	5	9	14	8	†		8
1964	5	8	6	8	7	10	12		8
1966	10	11	11	13	9	13	15		12
1968	3	9	11	11	12	10	18		11
1970	10	9	12	11	13	14	14	22	13
1972	3	7	9	9	13	17	17	19	13

[a] Percentage of independents who lean toward neither the Democratic nor Republican party.
[b] For the totals upon which these percentages are based, see table 18.2.
† Because of the small Ns, the percentage of pure independents has not been presented.

World War II, and in 1952 many would still be relatively open to partisan change. A generational explanation would not necessarily predict either a rise or decline in levels of partisan identification. But, given the political and social conditions following 1952, party loyalties might remain low. Party leadership was weak. [17] The division of party responsibility between the president and Congress for much of this period may have dampened the development of strong party loyalties. Candidates, especially Republicans, played down their party and ran highly individualized campaigns. Television, by stressing candidates at the expense of parties, may have further weakened party loyalties. And, although there was rapid social change, neither party seemed capable of capitalizing upon that change by offering programs to reinforce party loyalties. Given these conditions, it is plausible that, in spite of the expectations of the life-cycle explanation, party loyalties might fail to develop among the young as they gained more political experience.

These explanations can be tested by a time-series cohort analysis. [18] A life-cycle explanation predicts that the overall level of party identification will increase among the 1914 to 1923 and 1924 to 1931 cohorts as their mean age increases; a generational explanation predicts that the overall level of party identification should remain low. To the extent that the youngest cohorts are still relatively flexible in their partisan loyalties, the level of party identification might, indeed, decline.

By tracing cohorts over the next two decades, we find virtually no support for the life-cycle explanation. The percentage of strong partisans among the 1914 to 1923 cohort increased by 1956, but after 1964 it declined; in 1972 the percentage of strong partisans was only five percent greater than it had been two decades earlier (see table 18.2). The percentage of strong party identifiers among the 1924 to 1931 cohort increased slightly by 1960, but after 1964 the percentage of strong partisans among this age group remained consistently *below* the level achieved in 1952. The 1932 to 1939 cohort attained its highest level of identification in 1960, when it was between the ages of 21

---

[17] See David S. Broder, *The Party's Over: The Failure of Politics in America* (New York: Harper & Row, 1972). For another provocative discussion, see Walter Dean Burnham, "The End of American Party Politics," *Trans-action,* 7(December 1969):12-22.

[18] All these surveys are based upon national random samples, and as the Ns have been reported, the reader can evaluate the probability that the differences between age groups are likely to result from sampling error. (As weighted Ns were used for 1958 and 1960, tests of significance are not valid for those years.) However, the best assurance that differences between cohorts are meaningful is the replication of age differences in numerous surveys based upon separately conducted samples. In this respect, too, the data for 1958 and 1960 are less satisfactory, for over half the persons interviewed in those years were originally sampled as part of a panel study begun in 1956. Thus, the consistency in levels of identification in 1956, 1958, and 1960 partly results from sampling procedures.

One can also gain greater confidence that age-group differences are meaningful by replicating this analysis with other data sets. To this end, I report upon a study by Norval D. Glenn who used Gallup data to conduct a similar analysis.

and 28,[19] but the percentage of strong identifiers fell thereafter, and by 1972 it was markedly less than it had been when that cohort first entered the electorate. In 1964, when adult members of the 1940 to 1947 cohort were between the ages of 21 and 24, a fourth were strong partisans; by 1966 this percentage dropped and in 1972 only one in seven was a strong partisan. The youngest cohort sampled in 1970, which included 18-, 19-, and 20-year-olds who had not yet been enfranchised, had the lowest percentage of strong party identifiers. By 1972 the proportion of strong identifiers among this age group had declined to only one person in eight. Among the entire cohort born in 1940 and after, which entered the electorate after Eisenhower's presidency, only 13 percent were strong partisans. Among the entire postwar electorate born in 1924 and after, only 16 percent were. While the very low level of strong identifiers might result partly from the special circumstances of the 1972 election, this analysis provides virtually no evidence that the proportion of strong partisans rises as cohorts age.

The data in table 18.3 offer no support for a life-cycle explanation. The 1924 to 1931 cohort had the lowest percentage of party identifiers in 1952. That percentage increased marginally by 1964, but declined after that, and by 1972 the percentage of identifiers was somewhat lower than it had been when that cohort first entered the electorate. A relatively small number of persons in the 1932 to 1939 cohort were sampled in 1956, and they had a much lower percentage of identifiers than their elders. This percentage increased by 1958, and reached its highest level in 1960. The proportion declined after 1964, and by 1972 the percentage of identifiers reverted to the 1956 identification level. In 1964 nearly two out of three persons in the 1940 to 1947 cohort were party identifiers; after that this proportion declined, and by 1972 just less than half were. The youngest cohort sampled in 1970 was the only age group in that year among which less than half were identifiers; the percentage declined marginally by 1972. By 1972, among the entire post-Eisenhower cohort, less than half were party identifiers, and among the entire postwar cohort only 53 percent were.

The changing percentage of pure independents (see table 18.4) has not been as dramatic, but there is no evidence that persons become less independent as they age. In 1952 the 1924 to 1931 cohort did not differ from its elders, but the proportion of independents among this age group increased over a 20-year period such that by 1972 the percentage was twice that of 1952. The 1932 to 1939 cohort, when first sampled in 1956, had the largest percentage of pure independents of any age group. That percentage fluctuated from survey to survey, but by 1972 it was somewhat higher than it had

---

[19] Although I report levels of partisanship among the 1932 to 1939 cohort in 1956 and 1958, the full eight-year cohort was not sampled until 1960. Likewise, the full eight-year cohort born between 1940 and 1947 was not sampled until 1968. In 1970 the SRC began to sample 18-, 19-, and 20-year-olds. The 1948 to 1954 cohort sampled in 1970 includes persons born during a five-year period, and in 1972 includes persons born during a seven-year period.

been sixteen years earlier. The 1940 to 1947 cohort, when first sampled in 1964, had the highest percentage of independents of any age group, and that percentage rose five percent during the next eight years. And the 1948 to 1954 cohort, when sampled in 1970, was the first age group in which over one person in five was a pure independent, although that proportion dropped to just under one in five in 1972. By 1972, among the entire post-Eisenhower cohort, some 18 percent were pure independents; among the entire postwar electorate, some 17 percent were.

This analysis strongly suggests that the weak party identifications among the young result from fundamental differences between their socialization and that of their elders. It provides virtually no evidence that the low level of identification among the young is a temporary phenomenon that will change as they age. Moreover, two additional analyses, based upon totally independent data sets, also convincingly refute the life-cycle explanation.

One study includes Norval D. Glenn's and Ted Hefner's excellent cohort analysis of Gallup data collected from 1945 through 1969, and Glenn's updated analysis of surveys conducted in 1971.[20] As the Gallup surveys do not distinguish between strong and weak partisans, or between independents who lean toward a party and those who do not,[21] these data are roughly comparable to my analysis of the proportion who are strong or weak partisans.[22] Glenn reported a decline in party identification over the twenty-six-year period, from 78 percent in 1945 to 70 percent in 1971, almost all of which occurred after 1965. Glenn's analysis provided virtually no evidence that young adults become more partisan as they age. Based upon their analyses, Glenn and Hefner concluded that "the widely cited finding of Campbell, Converse, Miller, and Stokes that older people have stronger party identification on the average than young adults reflects, largely or entirely, an intercohort rather than a life-stage difference."[23]

In addition to Glenn's analyses, a panel study by M. Kent Jennings and Richard G. Niemi demonstrates conclusively that in recent years young

---

[20] See Norval D. Glenn and Ted Hefner, "Further Evidence on Aging and Party Identification," *Public Opinion Quarterly*, 36(Spring 1972):31-47; and Norval D. Glenn, "Sources of Shift to Political Independence: Some Evidence from a Cohort Analysis," *Social Science Quarterly*, 53(December 1972):494-519.

In these analyses, Glenn employed a weighting procedure to compensate for the tendency of [the proportion of women in the cohorts to increase]. As he reports, sex differences in levels of party identification were small, and his weighting procedures had little effect on his results. In my own analysis, I consistently controlled for sex, but as sex differences were small I did not use a weighting factor to compensate for the tendency of women to outlive men.

[21] Since 1940 the Gallup surveys have asked, "In politics, as of today, do you consider yourself a Republican, Democrat, or independent?"

[22] Glenn usually reports a slightly higher proportion of identifiers than I discovered using the Michigan data. Glenn's analyses include nonwhites, but this difference does not account for his tendency to find a larger proportion of identifiers than I did. When I include blacks, the overall percentage of party identifiers is affected only marginally.

[23] Glenn and Hefner, "Further Evidence on Aging," p. 44.

adults have not become more partisan as they aged.[24] In 1965 Jennings and Niemi began with a sample of high school seniors and a sample of their parents; the second wave of their study was carried out early in 1973, and over 1,300 youths and 1,100 parents were interviewed in both waves.[25] In 1965, 25 percent of the youths had been strong party identifiers; by 1973 only 13 percent were. In 1965, 65 percent were strong or weak identifiers; by 1973, 51 percent were. Even the percentage of pure independents rose slightly, from 13 percent in 1965 to 16 percent in 1973.

These changes, Jennings and Niemi concluded, were "startling." Because a life-cycle explanation clearly would lead us to expect the proportion of identifiers to rise among a cohort that had matured from its late teens into its mid-twenties, the decline of partisan identification, they concluded, "provides a compelling argument for a generation effects interpretation."[26] They then speculated that, "Although there may be a decline in the proportion of independents [including independents who lean toward one of the major parties] in the future, it seems likely that the rate of decline will not bring this proportion down to levels observed in previous generations for some years, if ever."[27]

Both the Glenn and the Jennings and Niemi studies lead us to reject a life-cycle explanation for the low level of partisan identification among the young. Both studies support my conclusion that the low level of identification among the young results from generational differences. But none of these authors adequately emphasizes that the overall decline in the proportion of identifiers during the postwar years results largely from new persons entering the electorate. Yet, a close inspection of both my results and theirs shows that the proportion of party identifiers has declined very little among older persons. With few exceptions, the older cohorts have been relatively stable in their levels of partisanship (see tables 18.2 through 18.4).[28] Moreover, the overall level of party identification among the entire prewar electorate has changed very little.

Among whites born before 1924, 36 percent were strong partisans in 1952, and by 1964, 41 percent were; after 1964 the percentage dropped, and in 1972, 34 percent were strong party identifiers.[29] While the overall proportion

---

[24] M. Kent Jennings and Richard G. Niemi, "Continuity and Change in Political Orientations: A Longitudinal Study of Two Generations," *American Political Science Review,* 69 (1975): 1316-35.

[25] Although Jennings and Niemi have panel data, they present only total distributions for each sample. [EDITORS' NOTE: The turnover tables are presented in chapter 17.]

[26] *Ibid.*

[27] *Ibid.*

[28] As I report above, these results are somewhat less stable when persons born before 1924 are divided into eight-year cohorts.

[29] These figures include persons born before 1884.

The changes between 1952 and 1972 partly result from the changing composition of the prewar cohort. The cohorts born before 1894, who had high levels of identification, had higher death rates than the younger prewar cohorts. These older cohorts made up 25 percent of the prewar electorate in 1952, but only 8 percent in 1972.

of strong partisans had declined 12 percent between 1952 and 1972, the percentage of strong party identifiers among the prewar electorate dropped a mere two percent. The overall decline resulted almost totally from the ever-increasing number of persons who entered the electorate after World War II. The percentage of strong and weak party identifiers among the prewar electorate has remained even more constant. In 1972, 76 percent of the prewar whites were party identifiers; the proportion rose to 80 percent in 1958, and remained at that level in 1964; by 1972 it had declined to 75 percent. While the proportion of party identifiers among the entire elector- ate declined 13 percent during the postwar years, the proportion among the prewar electorate declined a negligible one percent. Again, the overall de- cline came from cohorts born after 1923. The proportion of pure indepen- dents among the prewar electorate was only six percent in 1952, and reached 12 percent in 1966; by 1972 it had dropped to eight percent. Among the entire white electorate, the proportion of pure independents rose seven per- cent during the two decades studied, but among the prewar electorate, it rose only two percent. Once again, the overall change largely resulted from persons who had entered the electorate after World War II.

Glenn's cohort divisions allow us to approximate closely the prewar, post- war dichotomy. [30] Among persons born before 1925, 78 percent were party identifiers in 1945, and that percentage was unchanged 26 years later. The percentage of party identifiers among the entire electorate had dropped eight percent, entirely as a result of persons born after 1924 entering the electorate. Jennings and Niemi do not present data on the overall decline of party identification among the electorate, but their data show considerable stability in the identifications of the parental generation. In 1965, 34 percent of the parents were strong partisans; in 1973, 30 percent were. In their first wave, 73 percent were strong or weak identifiers, in the second, 75 percent were. Ten percent were pure independents in 1965, as was an identical proportion eight years later.

The relative stability of partisan predispositions among older respondents accounts for the importance of generational change. If partisan loyalties were highly malleable, older cohorts would be influenced by the same forces that have impeded the development of strong party loyalties among new cohorts. Generational change is most likely to be an important process in explaining attitudes and predispositions that are relatively stable. Yet, even among older persons partisan loyalties can change. To demonstrate this fact, we could turn to cross-national comparisons and examine countries where

---

[30] Glenn reports the ages of his cohorts during the year they were surveyed. My reports about the year of birth of his cohorts are based upon my approximations.

As all persons sampled in 1945 were born before 1925, I reported the overall level of identification for that year; with the 1971 data I reported the partisanship of persons born between 1885 and 1924.

partisan change has been far more dramatic than in America. [31] But no cross-national comparisons are needed to demonstrate this point, for one need only examine the partisan loyalties of black Americans.

Party Identification Among Blacks

Table 18.5 presents the partisan identification of blacks between 1952 and 1972. Among blacks, as among whites, partisan loyalties have weakened in recent years, for there has been a 20 percent drop in the percentage of strong Democrats between 1968 and 1972. Moreover, when we examine the partisanship of blacks over the last two decades we find other sudden changes. Through 1962, about one black in seven was a Republican; in 1964, with Goldwater's nomination, the proportion of black Republicans dropped to one in 14. Through 1962, about one black in seven was classed as "apolitical," that is to say, someone who could not relate himself to the questions used to measure party identification. In 1964, presumably because of the controversies surrounding the Civil Rights Act, as well as efforts by civil rights leaders to mobilize southern blacks, the proportion of apoliticals suddenly dropped to less than one in twenty, and remained less than one in twenty in all four subsequent surveys. [32] Such sudden shifts cannot result from generational change, but are caused by political conditions affecting persons of all ages. This fact can be demonstrated by a cohort analysis, but because the number of blacks sampled is small, we must use more broadly defined cohorts than in our analysis of whites.

Table 18.6 presents the percentage of strong and weak Republicans among blacks born before 1914 and among blacks born in 1914 and after. [33]

---

[31] For example, in France there was a sharp rise in the percentage of party identifiers between 1958 and 1968, even among older cohorts. See Ronald Inglehart and Avram Hochstein, "Alignment and Dealignment of the Electorate in France and the United States," *Comparative Political Studies*, 5(October 1972):343–72. Inglehart and Hochstein also used SRC data collected in 1958 and 1968 to conduct a cohort analysis of partisan change in the United States.

[32] Philip E. Converse discusses the changing proportion of apoliticals in "Change in the American Electorate," in Angus Campbell and Philip E. Converse, eds., *The Human Meaning of Social Change* (New York: Russell Sage, 1972), p. 306. As Converse notes, most black apoliticals live in the South.

[33] Whereas a prewar-postwar cohort dichotomy often has proved useful in analyzing change among whites, a different cohort division was used to examine change among blacks. Blacks have had fundamentally different political experiences, and cohort divisions that are meaningful for whites may not be meaningful for blacks. This is suggested by Donald R. Matthews and James W. Prothro who found that the relationship between age and political participation usually found among whites was not present among blacks. They found that among southern whites, participation increased with age (except for whites 80 and above), whereas among southern blacks participation was highest among those between the ages of 40 and 49. They interpret this difference by arguing that specific generational effects account for high levels of participation among blacks who were in their twenties and thirties when the Supreme Court ruled the white primary unconstitutional. See *Negroes and the New Southern Politics* (New York: Harcourt, 1966), pp. 71–72.

Table 18.5 Party Identification Among Blacks from 1952 Through 1972 (Percentages)

Party Identification	Year of Survey										
	1952	1956	1958	1960	1962	1964	1966	1968	1970	1972
Strong Democrat	30	27	32	25	35	52	30	56	41	36
Weak Democrat	22	23	19	19	25	22	31	29	34	31
Independent, leans Democratic	10	5	7	7	4	8	11	7	7	8
Independent	4	7	4	16	6	6	14	3	12	12
Independent, leans Republican	4	1	4	4	2	1	2	1	1	3
Weak Republican	8	12	11	9	7	5	7	1	4	4
Strong Republican	5	7	7	7	6	2	2	1	0	4
Other party	1	1	0	0	1	0	0	0	0	†
Apolitical	17	18	16	14	15	4	3	3	1	2
Total percent	101	101	100	101	101	100	100	101	100	100
(Number)	(171)	(146)	(161)ª	(171)ª	(110)	(156)	(132)	(149)	(157)	(267)
Strong party identifiers	35	34	39	32	41	54	32	57	41	40
Strong and weak party identifiers	65	68	69	59	73	81	70	87	79	75

ª Weighted N.   †Less than one percent.

Table 18.6   Percentage of Blacks Who Identified as Strong or Weak
Republicans from 1952 Through 1972, by Years of Birth

Year of Survey	Years of Birth	
	Before 1914	1914 and After
1952	16 (92)[a]	9 (77)
1956	21 (62)	17 (83)
1958[b]	17 (70)	18 (91)
1960[b]	25 (72)	9 (99)
1962	26 (47)	5 (62)
1964	6 (52)	8 (103)
1966	19 (37)	5 (92)
1968	4 (45)	1 (103)
1970	3 (35)	3 (118)
1972	10 (52)	7 (210)

[a] Numbers in parentheses are the totals upon which percentages are based.
[b] Weighted Ns.

Blacks born before 1914 entered the electorate no later than 1934 (although if they lived in the South they probably were not able to vote). Those born in 1914 and after entered the electorate either during a period when Roosevelt rapidly was winning the loyalties of black voters or during a period when the Democrats already had won the loyalties of most blacks. Through 1962, older blacks tended to be Republican more often than younger blacks.[34] Presumably this difference reflects the residual Republican loyalties that had developed before the New Deal, although even older blacks were about twice as likely to be Democrats as to be Republicans. But in 1964 the Republicanism among older blacks virtually disappeared. Likewise, the proportion of apoliticals declined among blacks of all ages, and by 1966 older blacks were no more likely to be apolitical than younger blacks.

The rapid change in party identification among older blacks demonstrates that even mature adults may discard established loyalties.[35] In spite of the

---

[34] The 1958 survey provides the only exception to this generalization.

[35] Although these rapid changes in party loyalties demonstrate that partisanship can change even among mature adults, blacks are atypical because their party loyalties seldom were reinforced by political behavior. In the South, blacks often were disfranchised and thus had no opportunity to reinforce whatever party loyalties they may have had, and even in the North, blacks participated less often than whites. Thus, even those blacks who claimed to identify with a party may have had weaker party loyalties than their answers to the party identification questions might indicate. This is suggested by Converse who found that southern blacks sampled in a panel survey conducted in 1956 and 1960 often switched their party loyalties over this period. (See "On the Possibility of Major Political Realignment in the South," in Campbell et al., *Elections and the Political Order,* pp. 212-42, at pp. 233-35.)

recent erosion of party loyalties following the Watergate relevations,[36] the long-term decline in party loyalties among whites largely resulted from generational change. Although the current low level of party loyalties may be temporary, we have no basis for projecting that levels of party loyalty will return to those of the late 1950's and the mid-1960's. Rather, there are likely to be few strong partisans and many Americans who identify with neither political party.

Concluding Comments

Although this analysis provided no support for the life-cycle explanation for the weak party loyalties of young adults, that explanation may have been valid for earlier periods in American history or for other societies today. But the life-cycle explanation, as developed by Campbell and his colleagues, does not take politics adequately into account. Partisan loyalties may grow stronger throughout the life cycle, if political conditions reinforce party ties. Apparently, conditions in postwar America did not. Yet, this analysis does not allow us to specify those conditions that contribute to developing strong party loyalties. Although it strongly suggests that conditions in the 1920's and 1930's were far more conducive to developing party loyalties than those during the postwar years, we do not know what it was about those earlier conditions that encouraged partisan ties. I strongly suspect that the differences between these eras are largely political, but television—the long-term effects of which are difficult to measure—also may have contributed to the decline of partisanship. Such questions may be answered best through cross-national research that allows us to discriminate between alternative explanations.

If political conditions did erode party loyalties, future conditions might strengthen partisanship. If such conditions occurred during the next decade, we would expect partisan loyalties to grow stronger, especially among younger cohorts relatively open to partisan change. A generational explanation suggests that the strength of partisan loyalties would then no longer increase directly with age, for partisanship would be strongest among the oldest and youngest cohorts. But this proposition can be tested only if political conditions that strengthen party loyalties do, in fact, occur.

---

[36] In late 1973 and early 1974 party identification levels reached all-time lows. A survey conducted by the University of Michigan Center for Political Studies in October and November of 1973 found that the proportion of party identifiers had declined 6 percent from the already low levels of late 1972. (See *ISR Newsletter,* 1[Winter 1974]:6.) The Gallup polls also report a decline in party identification. In the period between June and October 1972, 71 percent were identifiers; during September 1973 through January 1974, 66 percent were. (See *The Gallup Opinion Index,* 105[March 1974]:22). Although no detailed analyses were reported, a sudden decline in partisanship during a single year cannot result from generational change alone, for the demographic composition of the electorate changes little during that time.

It seems far more likely that future American party loyalties will be weak. The prewar electorate, which still has strong party ties, is being replaced continuously by voters who have weak party loyalties, and we have no evidence that the young will become more partisan as they age. But regardless of future partisan loyalties, these findings are important because they shed light on one process through which party loyalties among mass electorates gradually are transformed: a process of generational change in which the partisan loyalties among older generations tend to persist, although older generations gradually are replaced by new generations that have attitudes different from their elders.

19. Attachments to the Political Parties

M. KENT JENNINGS
RICHARD G. NIEMI

The nature of parties and of the party system have come to be recognized as critical features of the adult political world. Attachments of the electorate to the parties have been related to events at the micro level of the individual voter and to events at the macro level of the functioning of political systems.[1] Comparative studies have shown that partisanship is an important phenomenon in many countries[2] and historical studies have be-

SOURCE: *The Political Character of Adolescence: The Influence of Families and Schools,* by M. Kent Jennings and Richard G. Niemi, Copyright © 1974 by Princeton University Press, pp. 37-62. Reprinted with permission of Princeton University Press.

EDITORS' NOTE: The following excerpt is based on interviews in the spring of 1965 with a representative national sample of 1,669 high school seniors. In addition, 1,992 of their parents were independently interviewed. Most of the analysis is based on student-parent pairs, in which each student was matched with his or her mother or father. Parental homogeneity was studied by using student-mother-father triads for a subset of the respondents for whom both parents were interviewed. Numbers of cases in tables are greater than the number of student interviews because of weighting of cases to take account of unavoidable lack of complete information at the time of sampling.

[1] See Angus Campbell, Philip E. Converse, Warren E. Miller and Donald E. Stokes, *The American Voter* (New York: Wiley, 1966), and *Elections and the Political Order* (New York: Wiley, 1966), and numerous other writings using this concept.

[2] Campbell et al., *Elections and the Political Order;* Gabriel Almond and Sidney Verba, *The Civic Culture* (Princeton: Princeton University Press, 1963).

gun to outline the impact of party affiliations in earlier years.[3] At the adult level, then, there is little doubt that partisanship is a singularly important political orientation.

At the pre-adult level partisanship is important, first of all, because it begins to develop early in life. By the age of ten or twelve most children recognize the terms Republican and Democrat, and they respond in a partisan or consciously independent fashion to a question about voting preferences.[4] Party loyalties take shape before children acquire much knowledge about the parties themselves and before much is learned about political and social issues.[5] In fact, it is likely that partisanship itself affects the later acquisition of political knowledge and attitudes.

Party affiliations are also important because it has been shown that children often take on the partisan character of their parents. Especially when compared with other political orientations, the similarity of children's and parents' partisanship stands out as particularly strong.[6] Moreover, differentiation in the rate of parent-child transmission is associated with differences in the functioning of political systems.[7]

With high school seniors there are at least two added reasons for paying attention to party identification. At the end of their senior year, high school students are at or very close to voting age. Therefore, it is of interest to observe the relationship of partisan loyalties to the candidate preferences of youth. The aim is to see whether partisanship "works" for the student in the same way that it functions for the adult. At the same time, candidate preferences are important in their own right and can be viewed in relation to parents' preferences.

Second, with children at the age when many begin to leave the family, it seems relevant to get a parents'-eye view of the partisanship of their children. With younger children we might presume that most parents are unaware of their budding party feelings. For high school seniors, however, parents may well be cognizant of these developing orientations. By observing the extent to which this is true, insight may be gained into the nature of the transmission of party identification.

---

[3] Walter Dean Burnham, "The Changing Shape of the American Political Universe," *American Political Science Review,* 59(March 1965):7-28, especially pp. 22 ff; *Critical Elections and the Mainsprings of American Politics* (New York: Norton, 1970).

[4] Robert D. Hess and Judith V. Torney, *The Development of Political Attitudes in Children* (Chicago: Aldine, 1967), p. 90.

[5] Fred I. Greenstein, *Children and Politics* (New Haven: Yale University Press, 1965), chap. 4.

[6] M. Kent Jennings and Richard G. Niemi, "The Transmission of Political Values from Parent to Child," *American Political Science Review,* 62(March 1968):169-84; Herbert H. Hyman, *Political Socialization* (Glencoe, Ill.: Free Press, 1959), chap. 4; Herbert McClosky and Harold E. Dahlgren, "Primary Group Influence on Party Loyalty," *American Political Science Review,* 53(September 1959):757-76; Campbell et al., *The American Voter,* pp. 146-48.

[7] Philip E. Converse and Georges Dupeux, "Politicization of the Electorate in France and the United States," *Public Opinion Quarterly,* 26(Spring 1962):1-23.

Table 19.1   Student-Parent Party Identification   (N = 1852)

Students	Parents (Percentages)							
	Strong Dem.	Weak Dem.	Ind. Dem.	Ind.	Ind. Rep.	Weak Rep.	Strong Rep.	Total
Strong Dem.	9.7	5.8	1.6	1.1	.1	.3	.2	18.8
Weak Dem.	8.0	9.0	2.1	1.6	.5	2.1	.9	24.2
	(32.6)[a]			(7.0)		(3.4)		(43.0)
Ind. Dem.	3.4	4.2	2.1	1.6	.8	1.6	.8	14.5
Ind.	1.8	2.6	1.7	2.7	.9	2.3	.8	12.8
Ind. Rep.	.5	.7	.8	1.2	.9	1.9	2.4	8.4
	(13.2)			(12.7)		(9.7)		(35.7)
Weak Rep.	.9	1.6	.7	.9	1.3	5.0	3.3	13.6
Strong Rep.	.5	.7	.2	.5	.5	1.9	3.5	7.7
	(3.6)			(4.1)		(13.6)		(21.3)
Total	24.7	24.7	9.3	9.7	4.9	15.0	11.7	100.0
	(49.4)			(23.9)		(26.7)		

$$\tau_b = .47$$

[a] The full 7 × 7 table is provided because of the considerable interest in party identification. However, for some purposes, reading ease among them, the 3 × 3 table is useful. It is given by the figures in parentheses; these figures are (within rounding error) the sum of the group of numbers below which they are centered.

It should be pointed out that historical changes, such as the increase in the proportion of independents after about 1966, mean that some of the parameters we cite would be different today. This is inevitable in any study made in a dynamic historical period. Nevertheless, the analysis should provide much needed insight into youthful partisanship, and especially its intergenerational sources, at a crucial juncture in our recent past.

Student-Parent Partisanship

Much needs to be said about student-parent partisanship at both the levels of aggregate distributions and individual student-parent pairs. As a beginning let us observe the overall similarity of students and parents. The substantial agreement between parent and student party affiliations is indicated by a correlation of .47,[8] a statistic nearly unaffected by the use of three, five, or all seven categories of the party identification spectrum generated by the

---

[8] The figure is based on parent-student pairs in which both respondents have a party identification; eliminated are the two percent of the pairs in which one or both respondents are apolitical or undecided. The product-moment correlation for these data is .59.

question sequence.[9] The magnitude of this statistic reflects the twin facts of the presence of a large amount of exact agreement and the absence of many wide differences between students and parents. When the full 7×7 matrix of parent-student party loyalties is arranged as in table 19.1, the cells in which parents and students are in unison account for a third of the cases. The cells representing maximum disagreement are very nearly empty. If we consider only the broad categories of Democrat, independent, and Republican, 59 percent of the students fall under the same heading as their parents, and only seven percent bridge the wide gap between Republicans and Democrats.

Surely this degree of student-parent similarity is significant, especially when compared with the correlations for other types of political orientations. Still, it is substantially less than perfect agreement, and one may wonder why it is not even higher. Part of the answer lies in the fact that we are dealing here with parental partisanship as reported by parents themselves. Intervening between this partisanship and the students' own orientations are the students' perceptions of their parents' position. Since these perceptions are sometimes inaccurate, students may adopt what they think are their parents' attitudes without really becoming like their parents. That misperceptions do affect the degree of student-parent similarity is indicated by the fact that the student-"parent" (i.e., the student's report of the parent) correlation is .58. This is .11 higher than the true student-parent correlation reported above. Thus part of the reason that students and parents are not even more like each other is that some students adopt what are in fact incorrect perceptions of parental attitudes.[10]

The similarity between parents and students suggests that transmission of party preferences from one generation to the next is carried out rather successfully in the American context. However, there are also indications that other factors have temporarily weakened the party affiliations of the younger generation. This is most obvious if we compare the marginal totals for parents and students in table 19.1. The student sample contains almost 12 percent more independents than the parent sample, drawing almost equally on the Republican and Democratic proportions of the sample. Similarly, among party identifiers a somewhat larger segment of the students is but weakly inclined toward their chosen party. Nor are these configurations simply an artifact of the restricted nature of the parent sample, since the

---

[9] The standard SRC question was used: "Generally speaking, do you usually think of yourself as a Republican, a Democrat, an independent, or what?" (If Republican or Democrat) "Would you call yourself a strong (R)(D) or not very strong (R)(D)?" (If independent or other) "Do you think of yourself as closer to the Republican or Democratic party?"

[10] From a methodological point of view this finding is important because most studies rely on children's reports of parents' attitudes. In general this procedure overestimates the true student-parent correlation by about .10. See Richard G. Niemi, "Collecting Information about the Family: A Problem in Survey Methodology," in Jack Dennis, (ed.), *Political Socialization: A Reader in Theory and Research* (New York: Wiley, 1973), chap. 19.

Table 19.2   Student Party Identification by Parent Party Identification

Students	Parents (Percentages)		
	Democrat	Independent	Republican
Democrat	66	29	13
Independent	27	53	36
Republican	7	17	51
Total	100	99	100
Number	(914)	(442)	(495)

distribution of party identification among the parents closely resembles that of the entire adult electorate as observed in November 1964 (SRC 1964 election study). [11]

This greater independence of students is clearly a result of the development of partisanship over the life cycle. Data from the Chicago study show that the proportion of independents grows steadily throughout the elementary years. By eighth grade, according to that study, about 37 percent of the students who have made any decision are independents. [12] This coincides almost exactly with the 36 percent of the seniors claiming to be independents. Since we know from adult studies that partisanship increases steadily over the adult years, [13] it appears that the maximum proportion of independents is reached some time during the adolescent years. It is at this age of maximum independence that we have captured our student respondents.

Turning to the party identifiers, we find that the ratio of Democrats to Republicans is almost the same in both the student (67 percent) and parent (65 percent) samples. In the transmission process some changes in party loyalties have occurred, but the net balance does not favor either party. The balance between new Republicans and new Democrats, however, is not a result of two equally attractive alternatives. The Democratic party has a visibly greater retaining and drawing power among the students. The data in table 19.2 demonstrate this. Among students with a Democratic parent, almost two-thirds retain the parental party preference; the same is true of only half of the children of Republican parents. Among students who do not follow their parents' preference, a slightly larger percentage of the Republican offspring shift to the opposing party rather than to an independent position. Similarly, children of independent parents who adopt a party preference move disproportionately into the Democratic column. In short, the

---

[11] Obviously the differences in the distributions of students and parents lower the student-parent correlation. Since these distributions vary over the life cycle (see below in the text), the correlation itself may vary slightly with age of the respondents.

[12] Hess and Torney, *Development of Political Attitudes in Children*, p. 90. We have equated their "sometimes Democrat, sometimes Republican" category with independents. The SRC question probably results in a slightly smaller number of independents.

[13] Campbell, et al., *The American Voter*, pp. 161–65.

influences other than parental party identification acting on pre-adults in 1965—such as Democratic majorities in nation and states, and the aftermath of the Goldwater campaign (see below)—were significantly stronger in the direction of Democratism than of Republicanism.

The observation that defection rates from Democratic and Republican parents vary and yet the net balance of student Democrats and Republicans was virtually unchanged is noteworthy. The reason, of course, is not hard to find. A small *proportion* of students was attracted to the Republicans from a large *number* of Democratic parents (7 percent of 914 is 64 students). In contrast, a larger *proportion* of students was drawn off the smaller pool of Republican parents, resulting in an identical number of defectors (13 percent of 495 is 64 students). Similarly, if one analyzes defections from independent parents, and from partisan parents to an independent student position, the gains and losses to each party are nearly equal. [14]

These kinds of "transition probabilities" have been observed in other contexts, and the consequences of them (assuming they remain unchanged over a long period of time) have been worked out. [15] For present purposes two main points stand out. The first point is simply to emphasize that one cannot facilely generalize from defection rates to subsequent states of affairs. The greater defection rates from Republican parents observed in table 19.2 would not in the short run result in massive Republican losses in the new generation—even if these defection rates remained unchanged.

The second point follows closely from the first. Under different distributions of parents, similar defection rates could lead to short-run changes in the overall distribution of party identifiers. A case in point is the contemporary South. The defection rates in the South are much like those observed in table 19.2. The Democratic party clearly has greater holding and pulling power among Southern youth. Yet the pool of Democratic parents is so much larger than the number of Republican parents, that the student distribution shifts in a Republican direction! Among party identifiers 78 percent of the parents are Democratic. This figure drops to 73 percent among the students. [16] This is a small change, but it is significant when the Democrats nationally and in the South have a greater attractiveness for young people. Put another way, the Democratic party is not sufficiently more attractive to Southern youth to maintain the enormous edge in popularity found among the older generation.

Owing to variations in the distribution of parental partisanship and to varying defection rates (although always with a Democratic advantage), a number of other distributional differences occur. The Northeast and Mid-

[14] For the Democrats, $-27\% \ (914) + 29\% \ (442) = -247 + 128$ for a net loss of 119 students. For the Republicans, $-36\% \ (495) + 17\% \ (442) = -178 + 75$ or a net loss of 103 students.

[15] John G. Kemeny, Hazleton Mirkil, J. Laurie Snell, and Gerald L. Thompson, *Finite Mathematical Structures* (Englewood Cliffs: Prentice-Hall, 1959), chap. 6.

[16] Among Southern whites the change is even greater, from 75 percent Democratic among the parents to 66 percent among the students.

west, like the South, are areas in which parent and student partisanship are dissimilar. In both areas the advantage redounds to the Democrats. In the Northeast, 56 percent of parent identifiers and 61 percent of the student identifiers support the Democrats. The respective figures among Midwesterners are 58 percent and 68 percent. Only in the West are the proportions of Democrats and Republicans nearly identical in both generations (66 percent among parents and 64 percent among students).

Parent-student differences also occur along racial and religious lines, but the direction of the differences reveals the enormous pull of the post-Goldwater Democratic party on minority group members. Blacks[17] and Jews are among the most Democratic groups in the electorate. Ninety percent of the black parents and 89 percent of the Jewish parents who identified with a party chose the Democrats. Nonetheless the attraction of the party among the seniors was so great that even higher proportions of students called themselves Democrats. The exact figures are 96 percent among the black students and 91 percent among Jewish seniors. Catholics in 1965 were also heavily Democratic, gaining the support of 77 percent of the parental party identifiers. Among this group as well the lure of the Democrats was sufficient to raise their level of support among the younger generation. Of the Catholic seniors who identified with a party, 86 percent of them were Democrats. The Protestants, by far the largest religious group in the electorate, contain equal proportions of student and parent Democrats.

Turning to social strata, we still find the lure of the Democrats rather constant across all groups, but when this fact is combined with the distribution of party identifiers among the parents, an interesting result occurs. Among parents, as one would expect, there is a strong and nearly monotonic relationship between social class and the proportion of Democratic identifiers. If we take occupation of the head of the household as a measure of class (and using whites only, since blacks have already been discussed), some 75 percent of the partisans in the lowest stratum are Democrats; in the highest stratum this proportion falls to 51 percent.[18] However, due to the concentration of Democrats in the lowest stratum, the net shift in this segment of the student sample is in the *Republican* direction. At the same time, the nearly even division of partisans in the upper stratum allows the Democrats to take advantage of their attractiveness and manage a net gain. The proportion of Democrats in the lowest stratum thus drops to 69 percent, and in the highest

---

[17] Throughout the book the category "black" includes a small percentage of other non-whites—chiefly Puerto Rican—and Mexican Americans. This group makes up only about 6 percent of the "black" group. While every racial group or subgroup is to some extent distinctive, our judgment is that in many politically relevant circumstances, Puerto-Rican and Mexican Americans share many of the characteristics ordinarily associated with the black population. In the absence of a large enough number for separate analysis, the decision was made to include them with blacks.

[18] Both samples were divided into five strata according to the decile scale of the Duncan code. For the construction of this code, see the chapters by Otis Dudley Duncan in Albert J. Reiss, Jr., *Occupations and Social Values* (New York: Free Press, 1961).

stratum increases to 56 percent. Moreover, among the students the proportion of Democrats is more nearly curvilinear, with the highest figure in the middle status group. Hence a strong, nearly monotonic relationship between social class and party identification among the parents becomes a weaker, curvilinear pattern among the students. Remaining as a matter for speculation is whether the unusual pattern and relative lack of differentiation by class will be a permanent feature of the younger generation.

It should be noted that in all of these comparisons of regional, racial, religious and class differences, we have concentrated on the relative proportion of Democrats and Republicans in each sample. In every case a substantial number of students and parents are independents. The proportion of independents as well as the difference between students and parents remain fairly constant across these groups. The strongest exception to this statement is among blacks. For both black students and parents the proportion of independents is about ten percent below the figures for the entire samples. This also slightly lowers the proportion of independents in the South.

Variations in Student-Parent Similarity

Widespread variations are observable in the degree of similarity between student and parent partisanship. We will take up these variations in several stages. First, differences along demographic lines will be noted. While such variations are certainly temporally bounded, they do reveal some of the reasons for deviations from familial attitudes. Secondly, family characteristics per se will be considered, where one of the chief considerations is the role of children's perceptions in the transmission process. Finally, we will observe the impact on student-parent similarity of two rather specific influences—the parents' voting behavior in 1964 and the partisanship of the students' friends.

The most noticeable feature of student-parent correspondence among demographic groups is the reduction in the correlations when one party has a special attraction. Blacks provide the most striking example. Offhand one would think that black students are very much like their parents, since there existed in 1965 such widespread agreement on which party better served their interests. Yet the student-parent correlation is an abysmal .12. The reason for this extraordinary low correspondence lies in the attractiveness of the Democrats to all young blacks regardless of parental preferences. Thus when the parent was a Democrat, as in most cases, the student followed suit more often than in the population as a whole (table 19.2). In the few cases, however, in which the parent was an independent or a Republican, the student remained just as likely to be a Democrat. Nor is this simply a matter of misperceptions by the students. Even when black seniors thought that their parents were independents or Republicans, the same high proportion were themselves Democrats.

For Southern whites the same kind of attraction of one party kept the student-parent similarity slightly below that in other parts of the country: .43 versus .48 for the Northeast, .49 for the Midwest, and .52 for the West. In this case it was the Republicans who were *relatively* more attractive, even though the Democrats still had greater pulling power. Combined with the large number of blacks in the South, the overall transmission process is substantially weaker in this region (.39) than elsewhere.

Among religious groups we noted that the Democrats were particularly attractive to young Catholics. Correspondingly, the student-parent correlation among Catholic families (.41) is below the national norm. Jews may be an exception to our generalization, since the correlation is almost identical to the national figure despite the pull of the Democratic party. However, there are so few Jewish independents or Republicans that the estimate of the correlation is unreliable. Among Protestants the student-parent correlation is a perfect match of the national figure.

Major variations in student-parent similarity are also found when the population is divided into a social status hierarchy. Using either the parents' occupation or education as a measure of status, there is a sizable decrease in student-parent correspondence as one moves down the status ladder. Grouping the sample into five strata by occupation, the correlations fall monotonically from .53 in the highest status group to .33 in the lowest. Using parental education, the correlation is .53 among families where the parent had at least some college training; this figure drops to .49 among high school graduates and to .36 for those with some high school or with an education of eight grades or less. Of course one important implication of these findings is that the overall correlation reported at the beginning of this chapter (table 19.1) probably overestimates slightly the true correlation for the entire cohort of seventeen and eighteen-year-olds. Similarly, studies relying on homogeneous populations, such as college students, are likely to discover considerable variation in the degree of student-parent correspondence.

One of the reasons for this relationship between social class and the amount of parent-student similarity is the heavy concentration of blacks in the lower strata. We have already seen that black students resemble their parents less closely than whites for reasons most likely unrelated to their family life. However, taking whites only, the relationship between social class and parent-student similarity still exists, although the differences are somewhat smaller. Among whites the explanation of variations by social class is probably found in the varying degrees of political interest in different social strata. Below it will be shown that students' knowledge of parents' partisanship varies directly with expressions of political interest, and that these more accurate perceptions of partisanship result in greater student-parent correspondence. Similarly, parental knowledge of students' feelings is more accurate where political interest is high, suggesting that parents in politically involved families are more likely to influence consciously the political ideas of their children. In any case, the findings reveal that the transmission of partisan loyalties from parent to child is affected significantly by the social status of the family.[19]

Characteristics of individual family members and relationships within the family are the second type of variable that may inhibit or facilitate the transmission of political partisanship from one generation to the next. A number of social and psychological studies, for example, have reported that power and affective relationships in the family are related to the acceptance of parents as role models.[20] Studies of specifically political orientations have suggested that acceptance of parental political values is similarly affected.[21] Still others have suggested that the level of politicization in the household is a prime determinant of the rate of parent-student transmission. Finally, sex roles are said to have an effect because of the presumed dominance of the male in political life.

Of these three kinds of characteristics—affectivity and control relationships, politicization, and sex roles—one revealed rather unexpected findings, one showed no impact on transmission rates at all, and only one conformed to our initial expectations. The unexpected conclusions result from an analysis of sex roles, where mothers appeared at least as influential as fathers. Because of the unexpected nature of the findings, a separate chapter [in Jennings and Niemi] is partly devoted to examining the relative contribution of mothers and fathers in the transmission of political orientations generally.

Affectivity and control relationships are the characteristics which proved to be unrelated to the degree of parent-student similarity, a finding which presages the negative results of subsequent chapters [in Jennings and Niemi]. These relationships were operationalized in a number of ways in order to measure interaction regarding politics; general interaction; relationships

---

[19] Expected social mobility of the student was also considered as a possible concomitant of variations in student-parent similarity. The occupation the student expected to enter was compared with the occupation of the head of the household to generate a mobility measure. Neither the overall student-parent similarity nor the defection rate in one direction (Democratic or Republican) varied as one would predict. The absence of any effect of social mobility is consistent with recent findings on parent-student partisanship and on defection from partisanship in voting behavior. See Campbell et al., *The American Voter,* pp. 458-59; Arthur S. Goldberg, "Social Determinism and Rationality as Bases of Party Identification," *American Political Science Review,* 63(March 1969):5-25; Richard W. Boyd, "Presidential Elections: An Explanation of Voting Defections," *American Political Science Review,* 63(June 1969):498-514.

[20] William H. Sewell, "Some Recent Developments in Socialization Theory and Research," *The Annals,* 349(September 1963):163-81; Glen H. Elder, Jr., "Parental Power Legitimation and Its Effects on the Adolescent," *Sociometry,* 26(March 1963):50-65; Elizabeth Douvan and Martin Gold, "Modal Patterns in American Adolescence," in Lois and Martin Hoffman, eds., *Review of Child Development* (New York: Russell Sage Foundation, 1966), vol. 2, pp. 469-528.

[21] Russell Middleton and Snell Putney, "Political Expression of Adolescent Rebellion," *American Journal of Sociology,* 68(March 1963):527-35; Robert E. Lane, "Fathers and Sons: Foundations of Political Belief," *American Sociological Review,* 24(August 1958):502-11; Eleanor E. Maccoby, Richard E. Matthews, and Anton S. Morton, "Youth and Political Change," *Public Opinion Quarterly,* 17(Spring 1954):23-39.

Table 19.3 Levels of Politicization and Similarity of Student
and Parent Partisanship

Politicization Level	Student-Parent Correlation		Student-"Perceived Parent" Correlation[a]		"Perceived Parent"-Parent Correlation[b]	
Interest in public affairs						
Low	.38	(301)[c]	.58	(279)	.51	(274)
Medium	.48	(778)	.57	(693)	.60	(680)
High	.49	(771)	.58	(718)	.61	(708)
Husband-wife political conversations						
Not at all	.32	(310)	.46	(284)	.48	(275)
Not very often	.45	(429)	.56	(395)	.55	(394)
Pretty often	.49	(526)	.60	(475)	.62	(470)
Very often	.54	(349)	.61	(334)	.64	(330)

[a] The correlation between the student's partisanship and the perception of the parent's partisanship.

[b] The correlation between what the student perceives to be the parent's partisanship and the parent's own reported partisanship; i.e., this is a measure of the accuracy of students' perceptions.

[c] Number of respondents given in parentheses.

between the mother and father as well as between the parents and children; evaluation of parental control; the current student-parent closeness and whether this feeling had changed over the past several years. Moreover, in line with some earlier findings, we considered the possibility of interaction between these characteristics and levels of politicization.[22] But even among highly politicized families affection and the location of power do not consistently alter the level of congruency between student and parent partisanship. An implication of this is that differences in the modes of interaction among families of higher and lower strata or of different races or religions do not in general affect the transmission of partisan orientations. The source of the variations observed earlier among demographic groups must be sought elsewhere.

The saliency of politics for family members has a predictable and rather hardy impact on the similarity of parents' and students' partisanship. The more interested and involved the family members are, the greater the congruency of student and parent attitudes. Examples based on two different measures are found in the first . . . column of table 19.3. In the first column [top part] we show that the students' own reported levels of interest[23] help

---

[22] Middleton and Putney, "Political Expression of Adolescent Rebellion."

[23] As a measure of political interest we will use a question which asks respondents how often they "follow what is going on in government and public affairs—most of the time, some of the time, only now and then, or hardly at all." Often we will refer to these responses as indicating High, Medium, and for the last two categories combined, Low interest.

determine their similarity with their parents. The figures in the first column [bottom part] show that the frequency of husband-wife conversations about politics[24] has the same effect. In each case the effect is most noticeable among the lowest group.

Since we have available to us the seniors' perceptions of their parents' partisanship, it behooves us to probe into these findings somewhat further. Specifically, the explanation for the findings just reported may be in the accuracy of perceptions of students in varying environments. That is, where political interest is high or conversations are frequent, students may perceive their parents' partisanship more accurately. The politically interested students readily pick up or perhaps seek out cues about their parents' feelings, and in a home where politics is discussed freely, cues are likely to be made more obvious and more often. If perceptual accuracy varies in this fashion, it alone may explain the decrease in the student-parent correlation among less politicized families. Children may adopt their "perceived parents' " partisanship equally at all levels of politicization, but the poorer accuracy of some students leads to a reduction in the true student-parent correlation.

In part this intricate process is just what happens. This is most obvious when the students' own political interest is the control variable. The student-"perceived parent" correlations given in the second column of table 19.3 [top part] show that students at all levels of interest mirror their parents to the same degree. However, the third column of figures reveals the decreasing accuracy of the less interested students. These two properties, the steady reflection of perceived partisanship and the declining accuracy of the perceptions, combine to give the results, already noted, in the first column of the table.

The data in the [lower] part of the table show that perceptual distortion is not the sole explanation of varying rates of parent-student transmission. The correlations in column [two] do show a steady decline, so that where parental political conversations are less frequent, students are less likely to take on what they believe to be their parents' views. Still, the differences in the student-"perceived parent" correlations are not as great as the true differences. The extremes in the former case differ by .15, while in the latter case they differ by .22. Thus the declining accuracy of perceptions observed in column [three] does not create, but rather magnifies the variations in student-parent similarity.

In general the pattern observed for husband-wife political conversations is probably more frequent than that using the students' political interest. It is at least true that inaccuracy is usually accompanied by a large decline in the

---

[24] We will make frequent use of the question on husband-wife political conversations and a similar one on student-parent conversations. They come from the parent and student questionnaires respectively. The exact wordings are: "Do you and your (wife)(husband) ever talk about any kind of public affairs and politics, that is, anything having to do with local, state, national, or international affairs? (If Yes) Is this very often, pretty often, or not very often?" "Do you ever talk about public affairs and politics with any of the following people: First with members of your family? (If Yes) How often would you say that is— several times a week, a few times a month, or once or twice a year?"

student-"perceived parent" correlation. In the case of mothers, for example, in which the accuracy of student reports was rated from one (perfect accuracy) to four (three or more steps off the diagonal of the 7×7 matrix), the correlations between student and "parent" partisanship are .69, .57, .47, and .24 respectively. For fathers the correlations are very similar—.68, .61, .51, .29. Whichever pattern is more frequent, however, it is instructive to know that patterns like those in table 19.3 do occur. In either case the variations in family transmission patterns are in large part due to declining accuracy of perceptions among less politicized families. Such students are rebelling against or unintentionally straying from their parents' orientations less often than meets the eye, and in some cases no more than children in highly politicized families.

Having now dealt with demographic variables and characteristics of individual family members and the interaction among them, we consider briefly the effects of two other factors. The first of these is the parents' vote in the 1964 presidential election between Lyndon Johnson and Barry Goldwater. The impact of the parents' vote may be particularly important if one focuses on the way in which partisanship develops. For young children, the presidential vote along with other behavior around election time may be taken as the best indicators of the parents' partisan attitudes. Other indicators, such as expressions of partisan opinions, may be much less salient or meaningful to children. Moreover a youngster has not accumulated a set of experiences from which to judge the normality or frequency of one kind of vote or other partisan act. This lack of relevant experiences may be especially important for independent parents, for independence is not easily conveyed in a single election. [25] If this reasoning is correct, parental voting has its greatest impact on young children. Still, high school seniors do not have the strong partisan ties that will develop later, so that some residual impact of the parents' voting should be observed.

In this context the force exerted by the parents' voting behavior seems quite significant. Relevant data are presented in table 19.4. Although there are no data from other years with which to make a comparison, the retention rate, say, of 57 percent among Republicans who voted for Goldwater seems very much greater than the 38 percent rate among Republicans voting for Johnson. The effect of the vote is particularly large among Democratic parents who voted for Goldwater, where the retention rate drops to only 24 percent. There were very few such Democrats, of course, as the N's at the bottom of the table indicate. But it seems as if a parental vote contrary to a strong national trend has particular potency for changing the partisan loyalties of children. Among independent parents the impact of a Democratic vote was slightly greater than that of a Republican vote. Overall, however,

---

[25] Even among the seniors, the identification of independent parents was less accurately perceived than that of partisan parents. See Niemi, "Collecting Information about the Family," p. 478.

Table 19.4   Student Party Identification by Parent Party Identification, by Parent's 1964 Presidential Vote

Students	Parents (Percentages)					
	Voted Dem.[a] Party ID			Voted Rep. Party ID		
	Dem.	Ind.	Rep.	Dem.	Ind.	Rep.
Democrat	70	37	21	24	13	10
Independent	25	52	42	42	56	33
Republican	5	11	38	34	31	57
Total	100	100	100	100	100	100
Number	(808)	(277)	(151)	(75)	(130)	(325)

[a] Thirteen percent of the parents are nonvoters who are grouped by the preference they expressed for Johnson or Goldwater. Separate analysis of nonvoters and voters showed no major difference in the impact on students.

the effect among independent parents fell in between the impact on the two partisan groups.

The net effect of parental voting should not, of course, be overestimated, and it may be salutary to compare table 19.4 with table 19.2. Since most Democrats voted for Johnson, the left-most column of the earlier table is very similar to the left-most column in table 19.4. And even though many Republicans also voted for Johnson, the right-most columns of the two tables are quite similar. Also the overall retention rate among independent parents is almost identical to both the figures in table 19.4. These similarities suggest that current voting behavior is a marginal rather than major determinant of the seniors' partisan ties. This same conclusion is reached if one calculates the net contribution of parents' voting behavior to rates of defection from parental partisanship. A very generous estimate suggests that voting behavior resulted in the defection of about an additional nine percent of the students (out of 41 percent who defected).[26]

At the same time that one minimizes the net effect, it should be emphasized that when conflict between partisanship and voting does occur, the seniors prove to be quite malleable. When parents preferred one party but voted for the other, only about a third of the students followed the parents'

---

[26] Referring to table 19.4, one might reasonably assume that of the 63 percent defectors from Republican parents who voted Democratic, *at least* 43 percent would have defected anyway (since 43 percent defected even when the parent voted Republican). Thus voting behavior may have contributed to the defection of 20 percent of the children of these 151 parents. Making similar calculations for the other groups, we find the following figure for the net contribution of parental voting: $[.20(151) + .46(75) + .24(277) + .20(130)]/1766 = 157/1766 = .089$. This calculation is very liberal since it takes no account of defections prevented when voting reinforces parental partisanship.

partisanship. Moreover, when the students defected, fully a quarter went all the way over to the other party rather than adopting an independent stance. It seems likely that if seniors are this malleable, younger students are even more susceptible to the shifting influence of voting behavior and other partisan cues. For young children, relatively high partisan instability in the face of conflict is a predictable result.

A second specific influence on students' partisanship is the perceived partisan position of their friends. In many cases, of course, reinforcement or at least no conflict exists; 37 percent of the students felt that their friends' partisanship was the same as their parents', and another 30 percent of the students described their friends as about evenly split between Republicans and Democrats. Nevertheless, this leaves a third of the students for whom there was a conflict between the parents' and friends' loyalties. Almost half of these conflicts—15 percent of all students—were a combination of Republican and Democratic loyalties, while the remainder were a mixture of independents and partisan forces.

That friends' partisanship has a considerable effect on students' own loyalties can be observed in table 19.5. To interpret this table it is helpful to use as a standard of comparison the situation in which respondents perceived their friends to be about equally split ("half and half"). Presumably the friends exerted little pull on these students. Note, incidentally, that these entries are very similar to the overall figures in table 19.2. If every other column is compared to the relevant column of the "half and half" portion of the table, it shows that the perceived friends' partisanship does exert a force over the partisan tendencies of students. Retention rates go up and defection rates go down when the friends' identification is consistent with parental partisanship. Just the opposite is true when a conflict exists. The force exerted by independent friends appears to be the greatest, for vastly increased proportions of students emerge when friends are perceived as non-partisan. This may be due to the fact that few students perceived their friends as mostly independents, since it was a volunteered response. Probably only those who felt relatively sure about their perceptions gave this answer.

Here, in contrast to the parents' voting behavior, we have a better way of estimating the net effects of the friends' partisanship on deviations from parental loyalties, and the results are enlightening. By assuming that the figures in the "half and half" portion of table 19.5 represent the absence of friends' influence, we can estimate both the additional defection arising from conflict situations and the reduced defection resulting from reinforcement of parental loyalties. When this is done, the net impact of friends' loyalties is judged to be a nearly two percent *decrease* in overall defection. [27] Our results here thus underscore the twin points made in connection with parents' voting behavior. The overall effect of friends' partisanship is small, and it perhaps even contributes to less defection than would otherwise oc-

---

[27] The calculation involved is: $[-.10 \ (478) + .07 \ (175) + .01 \ (155) + .17 \ (121) - .02 \ (69) - .21 \ (157) + .42 \ (38) - .38 \ (34) + .46 \ (25)]/1794 = 33/1794 = .018$.

Table 19.5 Student Party Identification by Parent Party Identification, Controlling for Partisanship of Students' Friends

Students' Friends (Percentages)[a]

Students	Democrat Parents			Republican Parents			Independent Parents			Half & Half Parents		
	Dem.	Ind.	Rep.	Dem.	Ind.	Rep.	Dem.	Ind.	Rep.	Dem.	Ind.	Rep.
Dem.	75	39	18	48	25	7	24	6	6	65	28	12
Ind.	21	45	35	30	54	24	75	91	92	27	53	40
Rep.	4	16	47	22	21	69	2	4	2	8	20	48
Total	100	100	100	100	100	100	101	101	100	100	101	100
Number	(478)	(175)	(155)	(121)	(69)	(157)	(38)	(34)	(25)	(254)	(146)	(142)

[a] Includes students who said they were sure of their friends' partisanship and those who were unsure but "guessed." Separate analysis of the sure and unsure respondents revealed no major discrepancies.

cur. This is due to the fact that these forces most often reinforce parental partisanship. However, when the forces do conflict, there is a considerable pull away from the partisan attitudes of parents.

Parental Homogeneity

The effects of parental agreement across a wide array of issues will be considered in chapter 6 [of Jennings and Niemi]. In addition, a detailed analysis of partisanship can be found elsewhere. [28] For present purposes suffice it to say that the effect of parental homogeneity on student-parent similarity is definitely in the expected direction, but the correlation with homogeneous parents (.57) is not as much above the figure for the total population (.47) as might be anticipated. When parents are homogeneous, [29] one's predictive ability is not vastly increased over the predictive power gained by relying on data from a single parent. The explanation for this, while perhaps not obvious, is simple and involves us again with distributional matters. It is simply the case that with seven-tenths of the parents being homogeneous, one is most often dealing with a family in which the parents agree. Thus overall comparisons are largely made up of homogeneous cases, and measures of student-parent similarity based on the total sample or on the homogeneous portion differ by only a moderate amount. In any event, both the student-mother correlation (.40) and the student-father statistic (.35) are decidedly lower when the parents differ.

Student-Parent Candidate Preferences

Many of the seniors whom we interviewed were eligible to vote in the subsequent presidential election of 1968. By inquiring into student preferences in the election preceding the interviews, and by ascertaining parental voting behavior, something can be learned about the sources of incipient voters' candidate preferences. In particular, we are concerned with the similarity of student and parent candidate preferences and with the impact of partisanship on student preferences. The interplay of parental preferences and student partisanship will also be noted.

The correlation between student preferences and parental voting behavior is .59, indicating a rather high degree of correspondence between the parents' behavior and student voting intentions. [30] There are two chief reasons

---

[28] M. Kent Jennings and Kenneth P. Langton, "Mothers versus Fathers: The Formation of Political Orientations among Young Americans," *Journal of Politics,* 31(May 1969): 329–58.

[29] Operationally, parents are considered homogeneous if the values for the mother and father fall along the main diagonal of a square matrix representing a cross-tabulation of mother and father values on a given variable. Otherwise they are heterogeneous. Pairs are eliminated if there is missing data for either parent.

[30] Student-parent correlations are based on pairs in which the parent voted. However, use of parental preferences for the nonvoters barely affects the statistics. No attempt was made to determine which students would actually vote.

why this correlation is not even higher. One is again the matter of perceptions. On the basis of the students' perceptions of their parents' voting behavior, the correlation is raised to .68, so that students are somewhat more similar to how they *think* their parents voted. The second factor tending to reduce the overall correlation is that students, compared to parents, leaned in a Democratic direction. As a result, when the parent voted for Johnson, students followed suit almost all of the time (93 percent); but when the parent favored Goldwater, many fewer students followed this lead (64 percent).[31] Here, unlike the case of party identification, the differential pull of the Democrats led to an overall edge for them in the aggregate distribution. Seventy-four percent of the students reportedly would have voted for Johnson, whereas 68 percent of the parents claimed to have done so.

The deviation of students from a Goldwater preference can be explained in part by the weaker partisan ties of the students. It has been convincingly shown that the longer one identifies with a party, the stronger the ties to the party become.[32] A slight extension of this reasoning would lead one to expect that at the same expressed level of partisanship students are actually less tied to their party loyalties and can more readily express a preference for the expected winner. This is in fact what happens. Among all partisan and independent groups (except for strong Democrats, where the difference is .5 percent), a higher percentage of students than parents "voted" for Johnson. In a Republican year, of course, we would expect students to swing in a Republican direction to a greater extent than parents.[33] In spite of this constant shift in favor of the Democratic candidate, the correlation between partisanship and voting preference is roughly the same for students (.45) and parents (.52). For both samples partisanship works the same way, sharply differentiating respondents according to their propensity to vote in one direction or the other.

One interesting implication of these findings is that the eighteen-year-old vote is likely to increase the amount of electoral swing, contributing disproportionately to the winning side, especially in landslide elections.[34] Another consequence might be to make it easier for a third party to pull voters away from the major parties. However, the eighteen- to twenty-year-old group is small enough compared to the rest of the electorate that the effects will be very small.

Significantly, student voting preferences among parts of the population are related to parents' votes in much the same way as party identification. One of the chief findings regarding partisanship was the relationship of family politicization to actual and perceived student-parent similarity. Those

---

[31] Overall, 83 percent of the students preferred the candidate for whom their parent voted.

[32] Campbell et al, *The American Voter*, pp. 161–65.

[33] A similar finding is reported in Philip E. Converse, "Of Time and Partisan Stability," *Comparative Political Studies*, 2(July 1969):139–71, at footnote 4.

[34] However, this did not happen in 1972, since young voters were slightly more in favor of McGovern than were older voters.

findings are reproduced almost exactly in the expressions of candidate preference. When the students' political interest is controlled as in the [top part] of table 19.6, the actual student-parent correlation dips convincingly as interest decreases. The student-"perceived parent" correlation, however, is nearly constant, and the drop in the true figures is due to the increasingly poorer perceptions among the less interested. Also shown in the table is that the frequency of husband-wife political conversations has the same complex effect that it had on partisanship. The student-"perceived parent" correlation does decrease as conversations become less frequent, but the drop is much less than the decrease in the true correlation. This difference is a result, of course, of the less accurate perceptions among less politicized families.

From the analysis of party identification, we would also expect more or less deviation from parents' behavior depending on the degree of conflict in the student's environment. One obvious way in which conflict can arise is when the students' own partisanship tends in a direction opposite that of the parents' voting behavior. When this occurs, we would expect greater deviation from parental voting behavior than when student partisanship and parental voting are consistent. A test of this hypothesis bears out our reasoning. If one uses the independent students as a baseline, it is apparent both that consistency increases student-parent similarity and that inconsistency decreases it. For example, only 16 percent of the Republican students deviated from a parental preference for Goldwater compared to 49 percent of the independent students and 68 percent of the Democratic students.

Table 19.6 Levels of Politicization and Similarity of Student and Parent Candidate Preferences

Politicization Level	Student- Parent Correlation		Student- "Perceived Parent" Correlation[a]		"Perceived Parent"- Parent Correlation[b]	
Interest in public affairs						
Low	.49	(240)[c]	.70	(207)	.70	(198)
Medium	.56	(646)	.65	(569)	.83	(532)
High	.65	(626)	.70	(559)	.84	(535)
Husband-wife political conversations						
Not at all	.45	(240)	.59	(212)	.74	(196)
Not very often	.54	(342)	.65	(298)	.77	(280)
Pretty often	.59	(456)	.66	(394)	.82	(383)
Very often	.72	(295)	.78	(273)	.86	(262)

[a] The correlation between the student's candidate preference and the perception of the parent's preference.

[b] The correlation between what the student perceives to be the parent's candidate preference and the parent's own reported preference.

[c] Number of respondents given in parentheses.

Similarly, barely three percent of the Democratic students deviated from a parental vote for Johnson, while 12 percent of the independents and 26 percent of the Republican students did so. Along with the greater attraction for the students of Johnson over Goldwater, these figures show clearly the effects of consistency and conflict.

A second way in which conflict can develop for students is when the mother and father vote for different candidates. We have come to expect this sort of conflict to be infrequent, but when it occurs, to lower dramatically the degree of correspondence between adolescents and parents. In voting behavior the nature of the variable in a sense compels such a reduction in student-parent similarity. The variable we are working with is dichotomous, so that if parents acted differently, a student must agree completely with one parent and disagree with the other. Hence, unless one parent consistently has greater influence, both the student-mother and student-father correlations will be quite low. Also, the correlations with each parent will have the same value but different signs. That each parent does have some influence (positive or negative) over the student is indicated by the low value of the correlations: $+.09$ for students and their mothers and $-.09$ for students and fathers. In percentage terms, the students in these heterogeneous homes preferred Johnson less than students in homogeneous "Johnson families" but more than those in purely "Goldwater families." Where the parents were homogeneous, the student-parent correlation (.63) is about the same as for the sample as a whole.

In sum, students' candidate preferences are much like their parents'. Deviations from parental behavior occur for the same reasons that departures from the parents' partisan attitudes arise. These reasons are chiefly the poorer perceptions that accompany lower degrees of political interest, various kinds of environmental conflict, and the temporal advantage accruing to one party or the other in a particular year.

Parental Awareness of Student Partisanship

An interesting and hitherto unconsidered aspect of socialization in the family is parental awareness of children's developing political orientations. Though much has been written about the role of the family in political socialization, there has been virtually no attempt to obtain a parent's-eye view of the process. Do parents know what their children's political views are? Or more basically, do they even know that their children are developing political ideas? Such questions have not been explored even though they may tell us a great deal about the amount of and type of family influence on pre-adult political attitudes.

These questions are very broad, of course, and consideration of their full breadth is well beyond the scope of the present analysis. We can, however, dip into a narrow aspect of the whole topic. The parents in our sample were

352

asked about the partisanship of their high school senior. From this we can determine the extent to which parents report awareness of the partisan coloration of their children. This will allow us to infer the degree of manifest attempts at partisan socialization.[35]

A large minority of the parents cannot identify their children's partisan preferences. Altogether 37 percent of the parents were unable to locate their child along the partisan spectrum, even though the question was designed so that parents had to volunteer this response.[36] Parents expressed their lack of awareness in different terms. Twenty-six percent simply said that they did not know how the student felt, while another 11 percent said the student "hasn't decided yet."[37] The wording is suggestive. The "hasn't decided" response, if taken literally, suggests that parents know something about the student's feelings. They know either that the student has simply not thought about partisan politics enough to judge the parties or that he or she has consciously considered the merits of the parties but has been unable to arrive at any decision (including the decision that the parties are about the same). The "don't know" or DK response suggests a genuine lack of awareness on the part of the parent. Whatever partisan attitude, if any, the student has, the parent is ignorant of it.

Despite the plausibility of these interpretations, no distinction between "hasn't decided" and DK responses will be made below. Although further investigation is clearly warranted, with follow-up questions or interviewer probes to clarify parents' responses, we are not yet convinced that the phrasing of the answer implies different levels of parental awareness. On the one hand, it is possible that for some parents a DK response really indicates that the parent thinks the student has not made any partisan choice. On the other hand, some parents may use the "hasn't decided" response because it is less embarrassing than saying "I don't know." In any event, comparison of the relative frequency of the two responses in numerous subgroups of the population did not reveal any meaningful differences. The ratio of one response to the other is usually quite stable, and the rest of the time fluctuates in an inconsistent pattern.[38]

The relationships between a number of socio-political traits and the proportion of parents unable to identify their children's partisan feelings are

---

[35] A more extensive analysis of parents' reports, with a methodological emphasis, is found in Richard G. Niemi, *How Family Members Perceive Each Other* (New Haven: Yale University Press, 1974), chap. 4.

[36] The question also included a preface to discourage the response that "he isn't old enough to worry about politics yet." The question was: "Although your (son)(daughter) isn't old enough to participate in politics much, do you think (he)(she) would consider (himself)(herself) a Republican, a Democrat, an independent or what?"

[37] By their own reports, only one percent of the students are undecided about their loyalties. Less than one-half of one percent said they were uninterested in politics or apolitical.

[38] In the remainder of the chapter "don't know" or "DK" responses refer to parents who said they do not know their children's partisan attitudes and those who said that the students had not made up their minds.

given in table 19.7. As expected, parents are most often unable to classify independent students, but the pattern of DK's within categories of the students' party identification is less regular and not as strong as supposed. Parents label independent Democrats just as often as weak Democrats, and both of those nearly as often as strong Democrats. On the Republican side the variations are monotonic and sharper, but even then over a third of the weak identifiers were not labeled by parents. The erratic pattern of DK's within party identification categories is partially due to the effects of other variables given in the table. Blacks, for example, who are labeled by parents less often than whites, tend to raise the proportion of DK's among strong Democratic identifiers but not among other students. Among white strong Democrats, the proportion of DK's drops to 31 percent. Parent and student political interest also contribute to the erratic pattern. In particular, it helps account for the small number of DK responses among parents of strong Republican identifiers. Strong Republicans are considerably more politicized than any other group, which makes their partisan attachments more salient. It ought to be observed, however, that a rather uneven pattern of DK's within party identification categories is maintained for all levels of political interest.

The level of political interest of family members is itself significantly related to the proportion of parents who do not know their children's party identification. Fully a third of the parents are unable to label their children

Table 19.7 Proportion of Parents Who Do Not Know Their Offspring's Party Identification, Within Control Categories

Control Category	Proportion Don't Know[a] %	(N)	Control Category	Proportion Don't Know[a] %	(N)
Offspring's party identification			Interest in public affairs (parent)		
Strong Dem.	34	(359)	Very low	50	(138)
Weak Dem.	38	(457)	Low	44	(251)
Ind. Dem.	37	(274)	Medium	37	(586)
Ind.	51	(242)	High	34	(936)
Ind. Rep.	45	(158)	Interest in public affairs (student)		
Weak Rep.	36	(258)			
Strong Rep.	18	(143)			
Region			Very low	48	(47)
Northeast	40	(464)	Low	42	(267)
Midwest	38	(581)	Medium	38	(804)
South	38	(542)	High	35	(795)
West	36	(328)	Race		
			White	37	(1717)
			Black	44	(199)

[a] Includes parents who responded "don't know" and "hasn't decided yet."

when either the parent or student is highly interested, but this is much less than the 50 percent DK rate among the least interested respondents. It should also be noted that the frequency of student-parent political conversations and of husband-wife political conversations were also related to the proportion of DK responses. As the frequency of either type of conversation increased, the proportion of DK's decreased steadily. One other measure of parental involvement, the campaign activity index, was not monotonically related to the proportion of DK's but it did show that parents who were very inactive were able to label their children's feelings much less often than parents who were more highly involved.

Of the other variables examined, none reveals the expected relationship to parents' claims of knowledge. There is a difference in the proportion of DK's between whites and blacks, for example, but the direction is mildly surprising. It might have been expected that black parents would say that their children were Democratic (as 96 percent of them are) even if they really did not know. The tendency to assume that students are Democrats might also have been expected to lower the proportion of DK's in the South, but regional differences are minimal. Almost no differences at all are observed among parent and student sex combinations. Parents are no less likely to know their daughters' than their sons' partisan feelings and mothers label their children as often as fathers. Finally, there are no meaningful differences in the proportion of DK responses for families of various sizes and for younger or older parents.

Conclusion

The findings just reported on parents' perceptions of students' partisanship offer an interesting and in some ways ironic conclusion to our analysis of party identification. As we have stressed so many times, partisanship is unlike other political stimuli in the degree to which it is a permanent, salient, generalized posture toward the political world. As such, students should and probably do know more about their parents' party ties than about most other aspects of parental political attitudes and behavior. Parents should and do know something about their children's partisanship, whereas it is likely that they know very little about their children's other political orientations. Partly owing to these perceptions, we should also expect the similarity of students and parents to be greater for partisanship than for most other political matters. And we know that this is true.

In spite of all this, the findings regarding parents' reports of their students' partisanship lead us to conclude, first of all, that the process of socialization into partisan orientations is often carried on at a nearby subconscious level. It is not much of an exaggeration to say that parents socialize their children despite themselves. Certainly the parents who do not know their children's party identification and those who think that their children have not yet made up their minds are not intentionally directing the development of their children's political ideas. If they were attempting to exercise deliberate influence, the children's current feelings would be the first information they would seek. For the two-thirds of the parents who do attribute a party identification to their sons or daughters, the possibility that they are consciously directing their children's learning cannot be ruled out entirely. However, this possibility can be discounted on other grounds. The fact that parents do not often accurately perceive their children's preferences suggests that they have a very shaky basis for attempting to influence them.[39] That parents have not always conveyed their own preferences to their children also suggests a lack of effort on their part. Among most parents the process of political socialization is not a pressing concern.

Secondly, and perhaps more surprisingly, we conclude that parents by and large do not care what their children's partisan orientations are.[40] This seems to follow directly from the first conclusion. If their children's partisan attitudes were important to parents, they would make a greater attempt to influence their development in desired directions. But if parents are mostly indifferent to the party loyalties of their children there is no particular reason for them to be even aware of what they think. It might be argued that parents *seem* unconcerned because they assume that children simply follow in parents' footsteps. There is some validity in this argument since parents did bias their views of students' attitudes toward their own feelings. But the proportion of DK's and the extent of the bias hardly support the conclusion that parents assume children accept their views unquestioningly. Hence, many parents must be relatively indifferent to the partisan orientations of their children.

We hasten to add that the lack of deliberate efforts to direct the socialization of youths in partisan directions does not mean that such efforts are lacking on all political and social matters. Parents are concerned about their children's attitudes regarding basic societal rules, such as obeying the law or being loyal to one's country. At times there are also less consensual topics on which parents try to influence children's views. One thinks, for example, of civil rights, which for some is a moral or religious as well as a social concern. When contemporary events bring such an emotionally charged issue to the fore, parents may feel called upon to guide their children's views as much as possible.

An additional qualification of the present conclusion is that parents' lack of concern about children's partisan attitudes, as well as political attitudes more generally, is not unlimited. Parents may be totally indifferent about their children's political views—so long as they do not become_____ (Socialists, Communists, John Birchers, Ku Klux Klansmen, SDSers, pacifists,

---

[39] Among parents who gave a partisan or independent preference for the students, the correlation with the students' own reports of their party identification was .57.

[40] This is similar to the conclusion reached by Almond and Verba, *The Civic Culture,* p. 135, that "overwhelming majorities of the respondents of both parties [in the United States but not in other countries] expressed indifference regarding the partisan affiliations of the future mates of their children."

etc.). The blank is filled in variously by different people. For some the bounds of political acceptibility may be very narrow and for others rather wide. But for most parents we suggest that there are limits between which they attempt to guide their children. The limits may be fuzzy, of course, and they certainly change over periods of history. Moreover, in many and perhaps most cases, parents have to provide little explicit direction to guide their children along the desired paths; the efforts of other socialization agencies and the example of parents' own attitudes and actions are a sufficient force. Nevertheless, parents do try to insure that their children develop within certain bounds.

Within these bounds, however, the development of children's partisanship is frequently a laissez-faire operation. That the correspondence between students' and parents' partisanship is as high as it is under these conditions attests to the strength of family socialization in this area of pre-adult political development.

II. PARTISAN REALIGNMENT

20. Is the Party Balance Shifting?

Politics is fun to observe partly because of its ever-present potential for change. Most political changes are small, but there is always a lurking possibility of radical transformation. New issues may arise which will crack the dominant political coalition apart. Groups long associated with one party may move *en masse* to the opposition party (or even form a new one), causing drastic shifts in the nature of electoral coalitions. The emergence of new or significantly modified political coalitions is likely to have a number of consequences. For one thing, the benefits obtained by various social groups may be altered because some groups can, for the first time, lay claim to political benefits while others lose access to them. Huge alterations in public policy may also occur: the massive growth of the power of the federal government beginning in the 1930's is one example. There is also the possibility that these trends may be checked or even reversed as the politically dominant groups again shift.

Lasswell defined politics in terms of the questions: "Who gets what? When? How?" When major realignments in party support occur, there is a fundamental shift in who is able to get the benefits, what policy is enacted, and possibly even in how the political system operates. Evolution in American politics and in our public policies is usually slow, but this potential for sudden change excites interest because of the inherent unpredictability with which it strikes.

How does partisan change occur? When political scientists began to regard partisanship as generally stable both across and within generations, they developed the notion of "party realignment" to account for the significant changes which can and do occur. As suggested by the phrase itself, party realignment means that something has happened to change the previous party alignment. The result is usually a shift in the balance between the parties; sometimes even the identity of the major parties is transformed.

No sooner was the realignment concept suggested than political scientists began to examine survey data in detail for any clues that a realignment was at hand. It did not take long for most researchers to realize that it was much easier to detect realignments from historical perspective than from current happenings. At present, there is no consensus that a realignment has occurred in recent years, though some political scientists do see some evidence of one. Before considering this evidence and discussing the possibilities, however, some greater attention to the concept of realignment is necessary.

The Realignment Concept

Originally, scholars simply assumed that each time control of the presidency changed from one party to another there had been a meaningful change in American partisan politics. It became apparent, however, that this approach overemphasized minor shifts which lacked historical significance while not giving sufficient emphasis to those changes which had lasting effects. The historian Arthur Schlesinger sought to remedy this by proposing a cyclical theory in which there was a shift from the liberal direction to the conservative side or back again every sixteen years.[1] Yet even the sixteen-year change was on the short-term side, and Schlesinger's theory did not relate such change to the behavior of the electorate.

The type of change which was of greater significance was the kind which occurred in the 1930's. For several decades prior to that time, the Democrats usually had a minority of congressional seats and were able to elect a president only in 1912 when the Republicans were divided and in the following election year when the incumbent, Wilson, was running. But from the 1930's into the 1950's and beyond, the Democrats were the dominant party, and the Republicans had a difficult time winning congressional majorities. Indeed, up to this writing in early 1976, the last times the Republicans won a majority in Congress were 1952, 1946, and 1930. Just what happened at the individual voter's level in the 1930's is unclear because public opinion surveys of a reliable kind were only beginning by the middle of that decade. But, clearly, there was a massive shift in party alignment, and any theory of partisanship had to allow for such a phenomenon.

---

[1] Arthur M. Schlesinger, "Tides of American Politics," *Yale Review,* 29(1939):217-30.

A way of explaining this kind of change was suggested by V. O. Key, Jr., in a classic article entitled, "A Theory of Critical Elections."[2] Key indicated that certain elections result in a realignment in the electorate which is "both sharp and durable."[3] Using aggregate voting data for counties to show when such critical elections had occurred, Key observed that the Depression era (he actually identified the change as beginning in the late 1920's) was not the only period of major electoral shifts; the mid-1890's were also such a period. By upsetting a nearly even balance between the parties in the last quarter of the nineteenth century, the McKinley election in 1896 began an era of Republican dominance. Since both of these periods saw a change in the party balance which lasted for a considerable length of time, Key appropriately dubbed them critical elections. This provided a link with data on individual partisanship that was being collected about the time that Key was writing. Partisanship was presumed stable for long periods of time for most individuals. However, at times of critical elections, major changes in partisanship would occur.

The American Voter extended Key's notion of the critical election into a typology of elections.[4] The book was written about the Eisenhower victories of the 1950's, and it had to determine whether these victories signified a realignment. The authors concluded that they did not, since partisanship was not changing in the 1950's. Instead, they formulated a new classification of elections. If a realigning (critical) election signaled partisan change, a "maintaining" election meant that the majority party was unchanged and won the presidency, while a "deviating" election meant that the majority party was unchanged even though the minority party won the presidency. Thus, large numbers of Democrats might have been inclined to vote for a Republican war hero in the 1950's, but they maintained the Democratic allegiance and would return to the Democratic fold once Eisenhower was no longer running for president. The elections of the 1950's could be explained as deviations rather than realignments. Confirmation of this conclusion came in the 1960 election when the Democrats regained the White House in what the authors of *The American Voter* later dubbed a "reinstating" election.[5]

The realigning election has the greatest importance in voting-behavior theory because it establishes the basis of political competition for the next several decades and, even more importantly, it seems to establish the issues over which political competition occurs. Thus, for example, the Depression of the 1930's made economic questions the basic source of party conflict as well as making the Democrats the dominant party. Even as late as 1968,

---

[2] *Journal of Politics,* 17(1955):3–18.

[3] *Ibid.,* p. 11.

[4] A revised version appears in Angus Campbell, Philip E. Converse, Warren E. Miller, and Donald E. Stokes, *Elections and the Political Order* (New York: Wiley, 1966), chap. 4.

[5] *Ibid.,* chap. 5.

Humphrey revived some of these traditional issues in the closing stages of his campaign.

Issues thus seem to be critical to realignment, but how do issues lead to realignment? Sundquist depicts five possible scenarios resulting from the introduction of a new polarizing issue. [6] The issue may be quickly resolved, so there is no permanent system change. If not, realignment of the two parties may occur in a variety of ways. The parties might take opposite stands on the issue, each gaining some adherents from the other party and losing some of its own. A third party might form, with realignment occurring when it is eventually absorbed by one of the major parties. A third party might actually displace one of the major parties. Finally, two new parties might form on opposite sides of the new issue, and, if the issue remains important long enough, the new parties might displace both major parties. We have grown so accustomed to Republican-Democratic competition that the last two scenarios seem unlikely, but it is important to remember the fall of the Federalist party at the end of our first party system and the fall of the Whig party at the end of our second party system.

As the astute reader has no doubt realized, political history cannot be quite so neatly divided up as we have suggested. Nor it is as simple as we have implied to determine just which elections are critical. Part of the difficulty is methodological. Prior to the 1940's or 1950's, good data on individual partisanship did not exist. Hence, if realignment is measured by a major change in the partisan distribution, it is impossible to indicate when critical elections occurred throughout most of our history. Even more important, the lack of survey data for the 1930's means that we do not really know how individual partisanship changes during a realignment. Do people actually change their partisanship ("convert"), do they just vote for the opposite party without changing their affiliation ("defect"), or do they continue to vote for the same party? In the latter case, the real change would come from older voters dying and being replaced by new ones who identify with different parties ("population replacement"). It is possible to account for most of the change in the 1930's by hypothesizing population replacement and some defection with minimal amounts of conversion, [7] though we will never have the survey data necessary to test this interpretation. If one assumes that partisanship can remain very stable during a realignment—the change resulting from large amounts of population replacement and defection—then it is even difficult to interpret contemporary survey data on partisan realignment.

---

[6] James L. Sundquist, *Dynamics of the Party System* (Washington, D.C.: Brookings Institution, 1973), chap. 2.

[7] Philip E. Converse, "Public Opinion and Voting Behavior," in Fred I. Greenstein and Nelson W. Polsby, eds., *Handbook of Political Science* (Reading, Mass.: Addison-Wesley, 1975): vol. 4, pp. 139–44.

Methods have been developed which use aggregate data,[8] but no single method has thus far proved definitive. Depending on which measurements are used, elections in or about 1796, 1812, 1824, 1852, 1888, 1932;[9] 1854, 1874, 1894, 1930;[10] 1896 and 1928;[11] and even 1952,[12] and 1964,[13] have been regarded as critical elections. At the very least, it seems as if we need to think of realignment in terms of periods as opposed to single critical elections. And, in general, we need to refine our notion of critical elections so that we can more positively identify them in the future even if we cannot do so for the past. Fortunately, it is very likely that we will continue to have frequent surveys of party identification, so the degree and type of change in this important parameter can be monitored.

Despite the ambiguity in the precise identification of critical elections, one conclusion stands out. The generally-agreed-upon critical election periods of the past hundred years have occurred in fairly regular intervals of three or three and a half decades. The political conflicts over slavery and the Civil War, the urban-rural and East-West conflicts of the 1890's, and the class conflicts of the 1930's stand out as eras of major changes in party alignment. Though the periods have been less well researched, it is evident that major changes also occurred in the late 1790's, with the introduction of a party system and in the 1820's, with the ascendancy of the Jacksonians.[14]

Given the periodic nature of past critical elections, another realigning era was expected in the late 1960's and early 1970's. What is the evidence for realignment at present? And why do critical elections occur in the first place? We now turn directly to those questions.

A Realigning Party System?

If realignment is periodic, so is speculation about realignment—it follows every presidential election! In 1952, there was speculation that a Republican majority was forming and in 1956, a "modern Republican" party and majority was predicted. The 1960 election re-established Democratic dominance,

---

[8] Walter Dean Burnham, *Critical Elections and the Mainsprings of American Politics* (New York: Norton, 1970), chaps. 1 and 2; William H. Flanigan and Nancy H. Zingale, "The Measurement of Electoral Change," *Political Methodology*, 1(1974):49–82; Key, "Critical Elections;" Charles Sellers, "The Equilibrium Cycle in Two-Party Politics," *Public Opinion Quarterly*, 29(1965):16–37.

[9] All from Sellers.

[10] All from Burnham.

[11] Both from Key.

[12] Flanigan and Zingale.

[13] Gerald M. Pomper, "From Confusion to Clarity: Issues and American Voters, 1956-1968," *American Political Science Review*, 66(1972):415–28.

[14] These earlier periods clearly differ from the other three realignments, and, indeed, the three alignments themselves differ in some important ways. This by itself does nothing to upset the notion of critical election periods.

and Johnson's landslide in 1964 had journalists seriously considering the possibility of the Republican party's dying out.

The 1968 election renewed interest in an "emerging Republican majority." [15] As Kevin Phillips saw it, adding the Wallace vote to the Nixon vote would yield a new conservative electoral majority. Nixon's southern strategy had this as its goal, and Nixon's re-election landslide in 1972 seemed to have accomplished that goal. Yet even the 1972 election was a personal victory rather than a party victory, with Democratic control of Congress undiminished. By now, the Watergate scandals together with economic difficulties have combined to end speculation about a Republican majority and have instead caused many to wonder whether the Republican party is dying.

How do we gauge whether a realignment is occurring? Historical comparisons would be useful, but the data on them are not yet available. The ratio of the Republicans to Democrats has remained relatively stable, with little change in the basic Democratic dominance over twenty years. Yet, in a realignment, numbers of party identifiers might be the last thing to change.

There has been a considerable increase in the number of independents. Some authors imply that there could not be a critical election period unless the ratio of Democrats to Republicans was changing considerably. Our view is that there is nothing inherent in the concept of a critical election which requires a change in the proportions of the two major parties. A critical election period may be the result of a growth in independents. The real test is whether the change proves durable. There remains the possibility that these independents will be heavily swayed in the direction of one of the major parties or in the direction of a new party, but it may also happen that the number of independents will remain high for a considerable period of time.

What about the matter of issues? If there has been a critical election period, we should be able to identify those issues over which party battles will be fought for a long time to come. Moreover, the future history of the party system—the questions of relative strength of existing parties, the possibility of a third party, and a continuing high proportion of independents—will depend on what issues are dominant in this critical election period. Two themes predominate.

First is the matter of race. This issue has been a source of tension since Franklin Delano Roosevelt's New Deal coalition of the solid Democratic South with the northern urban black. Realignment could occur as a result of a black exodus from the Democratic fold if George Wallace, or someone of his persuasion, won the Democratic presidential nomination. At the same time, as racial troubles now confront the North as well as the South, the nomination of a strong pro-civil-rights candidate by the Democrats could alienate many of its white voters. The South itself seems to have become the

---

[15] Kevin Phillips, *The Emerging Republican Majority* (Garden City, N.Y.: Anchor, 1970).

solid Republican South in presidential politics as a response to recent Democratic presidential nominees. Currently, the question of busing to achieve school integration seems to be the most salient concern. This is the type of emotional issue that could completely galvanize a race-related realignment. However, at the time of this writing the busing controversy seems to be declining rather than increasing.

The second subject of speculation has been what Scammon and Wattenberg dubbed the "social issue," a mélange of law and order, disruption and reactions to it, pornography and permissiveness generally, welfare, and a host of related problems. Although they are prominent, it is questionable whether these issues could form the basis for a realignment because they do not always have two sides. Neither party is in favor of crime, and few people favor disruptive demonstrations. While a party might cautiously favor an extreme interpretation of the right of free speech, none would want to be identified as pro-pornography.

In the mid-1970's two additional issues have arisen. One is the problem of government corruption, associated with Watergate. Again, this is not likely to form the basis for a new alignment since no party would take a pro-corruption stand. The other is the economy. Economic issues have traditionally divided the Democrats and Republicans, but it is unlikely that the argument will continue in the same fashion as before. The argument is no longer over whether social security should be provided or whether the government has a large role to play in the economy, but over the means of fighting inflation and recession in a world with limited energy resources.

No one can precisely predict what the future holds, and hence only time will tell whether the new racial, social, or economic questions will be the basis for a realigned party system. Nonetheless, contemporary analysis of evaluations of candidates, parties, and issues can tell us something about the changing shape of the space in which the party battle is fought. To what extent do candidates reflect different positions on the issue? To what extent are the viewpoints on various issues correlated with one another? That is, to what extent is there something that might be labeled a "social issue," as opposed to a whole set of issues that are unrelated to one another? These kinds of questions are discussed in the Rusk and Weisberg paper in chapter 21. While we cannot automatically apply their conclusions beyond 1970, their discussion of the way in which candidates try to accommodate new issues in their campaigns and the ways in which voters structure their perceptions of old candidates on new issues is very informative because it attempts to develop dynamic theories of electoral behavior. Their approach permits identification of change in the dimensions of political conflict, as when a liberal-conservative economic dimension is supplanted by a new dimension of political cleavage.

In a realignment, we would also expect the group bases of the parties to change. Axelrod has provided a very useful gauge of change in the group basis of the parties (see tables 20.1 and 20.2). Note first the columns showing "percentage deviation in loyalty" of various groups to the parties, representing the difference between the percentage of the group's vote cast for a party and the percentage of the national vote won by that party. The clearest shift is the movement away from the Democrats by Southerners and by members of union families. Yet, as the absolute "loyalty" columns show, less than a majority of the poor and Catholics, as well as of Southerners and union family members supported McGovern in 1972. In addition, as the voting rate ("turnout") and number of people in each group ("size") change, the contribution of each group to the party's vote total (columns 1-6) also changes. Thus, as the contributions of the poor and the central cities to the Democratic vote decline, an increasing contribution has been made by blacks and, as Axelrod has noted,[16] by the young, who in 1972 contributed 32 percent of the Democratic vote.

Axelrod's analysis is also useful in evaluating Scammon and Wattenberg's widely quoted discussion of the importance of appealing to the "unyoung, unpoor, and unblack."[17] Axelrod finds that group to consist of 62 percent of the electorate in 1968 with a turnout of 70 percent. But he still calculates that a party getting 55 percent of the vote of the "unyoung, unpoor, and unblack" would require at least 39 percent of the vote of the "young, poor, or black" in order to win a majority of the popular vote.[18] This suggests that it would be unwise for any party to write off the "young, poor, or black," just as Scammon and Wattenberg warn the Democrats against writing off the "unyoung, unpoor, and unblack."

Finally, even if we cannot predict the exact shape of the political future, could we have predicted that the late 1960's would see the beginning of a critical election period? Why do party realignments seem to occur at intervals of thirty to thirty-five years? An ingenious answer is provided by Beck in chapter 23. This paper helps tie together the matter of issues, of stability and change in individual partisanship, and the role of long-term components in electoral behavior. The argument revolves around the way in which people learn about political conflicts and the length of time that it takes for a new generation (which does not think of politics in the same way as those who lived through an earlier realigning era) to come of age. Although the specific details concerning generation lengths are imprecise, the concept is seminal because it suggests new ways to tie together notions of political socialization and realignment.

---

[16] Robert Axelrod, "Communication," *American Political Science Review,* 68(1974): 717-20. Axelrod defines the young as voters under 30. The increased contribution to the Democrats was a result of relative increases in all three factors—size, turnout, and loyalty. A more complete explanation of the table is given in Robert Axelrod, "Where the Votes Come From: An Analysis of Electoral Coalitions," *American Political Science Review,* 66(1972):11-20.

[17] Richard M. Scammon and Ben J. Wattenberg, *The Real Majority* (New York: Coward, McCann & Geoghegan, 1970), chap. 4.

[18] Axelrod, "Where the Votes Come From," p. 20.

Table 20.1 The Democratic Coalition, 1952–1972

Year	Percentage Contribution						(Size ×						Turnout ×						Loyalty) +						(NT×NL)	
	P	B	U	C	S	CC	P	B	U	C	S	CC	P	B	U	C	S	CC	P	B	U	C	S	CC	NT	NL
1952	28	7	38	41	20	21	36	10	27	26	28	16	46	23	66	76	35	68	47	83	59	57	55	51	63	44.4
1956	19	5	36	38	23	19	25	9	26	25	29	14	40	23	64	72	39	63	47	68	55	53	52	55	60	42.0
1960	16	7	31	47	27	19	23	10	25	25	34	13	46	31	60	74	50	74	48	72	66	82	52	65	64	49.7
1964	15	12	32	36	21	15	19	11	23	26	28	12	45	42	69	72	49	65	69	99	80	75	58	74	63	61.1
1968	12	19	28	40	24	14	16	11	24	26	31	10	44	51	61	68	53	63	44	92	51	61	39	58	62	42.7
1972	10	22	32	34	25	14	12	11	25	25	34	8	37	47	58	65	44	60	45	86	45	43	36	61	56	37.5
Column	1	2	3	4	5	6	7	8	9	10	11	12	13	14	15	16	17	18	19	20	21	22	23	24	25	26

Percentage deviation in loyalty to Democrats

Year	P	B	U	C	S	CC
1952	+2	+38	+14	+12	+10	+6
1956	+5	+26	+13	+11	+10	+13
1960	−2	+22	+16	+32	+2	+15
1964	+8	+38	+19	+14	−3	+13
1968	+1	+49	+8	+18	−4	+15
1972	+8	+49	+8	+6	−2	+24
Column	27	28	29	30	31	32

KEY: P Poor (income under $3,000/yr.)
B Black (and other nonwhite)
U Union member (or union member in family)
C Catholic (and other non-Protestant)
S South (including border states)
CC Central cities (of 12 largest metropolitan areas)
NT National turnout
NL National loyalty to Democrats

SOURCE: Reprinted with permission from Robert Axelrod, "Communication," *American Political Science Review*, 68(1974):718–19.

Table 20.2 The Republican Coalition, 1952–1972

Year	Percentage Contribution =						(Size ×						Turnout ×						Loyalty) +						(NT×NL)	
	NP	W	NU	P	N	NCC	NP	W	NU	P	N	NCC	NP	W	NU	P	N	NCC	NP	W	NU	P	N	NCC	NT	NL
1952	75	99	79	75	87	84	64	90	73	74	72	84	72	67	61	58	73	61	56	57	61	61	57	57	63	55.1
1956	84	98	78	75	84	89	75	91	74	75	71	86	67	64	58	56	69	60	59	59	63	62	60	60	60	57.4
1960	83	97	84	90	75	90	77	90	75	75	66	87	70	68	65	61	71	63	50	51	55	63	50	52	64	49.5
1964	89	100	87	80	76	91	81	89	77	74	72	88	67	66	61	60	68	63	40	42	45	44	38	40	63	38.5
1968	90	99	81	80	80	92	84	89	76	74	69	90	65	63	62	60	66	62	44	47	46	49	47	45	62	43.4
1972	93	98	77	74	73	95	88	89	75	75	66	92	58	57	55	52	62	55	61	66	63	64	60	63	56	60.7
Column	1	2	3	4	5	6	7	8	9	10	11	12	13	14	15	16	17	18	19	20	21	22	23	24	25	26

Percentage deviation in loyalty to Republicans

Year	NP	W	NU	P	N	NCC
1952	+1	+2	+6	+6	+6	+2
1956	+1	+1	+5	+4	+2	+2
1960	0	+1	+5	+13	0	+2
1964	+1	+3	+6	+5	−1	+1
1968	0	+3	+2	+5	+3	+1
1972	+1	+5	+3	+3	−1	+2
Column	27	28	29	30	31	32

KEY:
NP Nonpoor (income over $3,000/yr.)
W White
NU Nonunion
P Protestant
N Northern (excluding border states)
NCC Not in central cities of 12 largest metropolitan areas
NT National turnout
NL National loyalty to Republicans

SOURCE: Reprinted with permission from Robert Axelrod, "Communication," American Political Science Review, 68(1974): 718–19.

If we are in a critical election period, the question is what direction will political changes finally take? As many answers have been offered as are logically possible: an emerging Republican majority, a new Democratic majority, a new majority behind a conservative party, a new majority behind a liberal party, a birth of multiparty politics, or a decline of all parties. On the one hand, it is possible to imagine a continuation of the present political situation without change, though, on the other hand, there is the possibility that by the 1980 election the present party system will have expired with the death of the Republican party, the birth of a conservative party, and possibly even a four- or five-party race for the presidency. In the end, what happens may depend most on the actions of the political elite—whether strong presidential contenders decide they must move beyond the familiar party system in order to establish viable candidacies.

A parallel question involves what electoral coalitions are forming to shape politics in future years. Again, the analysts have sharply differing perspectives. Hamilton writes of a continuation and possible intensification of the class basis of party politics. [19] Burnham sees the possibility of a "top and bottom" coalition of the advantaged and disadvantaged against the middle class. [20] And in another interpretation, Sundquist claims that the New Deal coalition might be revitalized. [21] The fact that such different positions can be maintained indicates the considerable potential for change at the present time.

We moved to a discussion of realignment to shift attention away from short-term electoral change and focus instead on long-term changes. Yet the speculation on party realignment pulls us inevitably into an interpretation (and possibly overinterpretation) of every short-term fluctuation in terms of its potential for long-term change. Perhaps this irony has important implications of its own; perhaps the difficulty is not the prediction of realignment, but the concept itself. The realignment concept may overemphasize the long-term type of change so much that it distracts attention from short-term changes which have meaningful implications for party conflict. Whether or not there has been realignment, technology and the nature of current events mean that party conflict today is very different from that of 1932 or even 1952. If there is danger in overemphasizing the degree of change, there is equal fallacy in overstating the amount of constancy. The period since 1932 has seen a complex evolution of partisan change. The long-heralded realignment may or may not be here; the change is undebatable.

---

[19] Richard F. Hamilton, *Class and Politics in the United States* (New York: Wiley, 1972).
[20] Walter Dean Burnham, *Critical Elections,* chap. 6.
[21] Sundquist, *Dynamics,* chap. 17.

The Concept of Realignment

V. O. Key, Jr., "A Theory of Critical Elections," *Journal of Politics*, 17(1955):3-18. Early statement of the critical election idea, based on analysis of aggregate election data.

Angus Campbell, "A Classification of the Presidential Elections," in Angus Campbell, Philip E. Converse, Warren E. Miller, and Donald E. Stokes, *Elections and the Political Order* (New York: Wiley, 1966). Expands a classification of the types of presidential elections.

James L. Sundquist, *Dynamics of the Party System* (Washington, D.C.: Brookings Institution, 1973). Explanation of why realignments occur.

The Electoral Coalition Base of Parties

Robert Axelrod, "Where the Votes Come From: An Analysis of Electoral Coalitions, 1952-1968," *American Political Science Review*, 66(1972): 11-20. Considers the contribution of a group to a party's vote total.

Richard F. Hamilton, *Class and Politics in the United States* (New York: Wiley, 1972). Discussion of changing class bases of politics.

Paul R. Abramson, *Generational Change in American Politics* (Lexington, Mass.: Lexington Books, 1975). Analysis of generational effects on political change.

Realignment Possibilities

Philip E. Converse, "On the Possibility of a Major Realignment in the South," in Angus Campbell, Philip E. Converse, Warren E. Miller, and Donald E. Stokes, *Elections and the Political Order* (New York: Wiley, 1966). Convergence of politics in the South and other areas of the country.

Richard M. Scammon and Ben J. Wattenberg, *The Real Majority* (New York: Coward-McCann, 1970). Advises parties how to maintain their support.

Paul T. David, *Party Strength in the United States, 1872-1970* (Charlottesville: University Press of Virginia, 1972). Develops index numbers of party strength, which reveal changing state and regional partisanship patterns.

21. Perceptions of Presidential Candidates: Implications for Electoral Change

JERROLD G. RUSK
HERBERT F. WEISBERG

Presidential elections invariably raise questions regarding system change. Frequently, the short-term policy mandate which can be imputed to an election is unclear, but more often the long-term implications of an election for system change are misinterpreted. The classic case is the widespread discussion of the possible demise of the Republican Party after 1964, a topic which seemed irrelevant once a Republican president was elected in 1968. Yet a presidential election often can have important systemic implications which we would not want to overlook. The 1968 election spawned its own discussion of electoral change, with particular interest expressed in the possibility of a party realignment leading to a Republican majority. Our own analysis of 1968 survey data suggested the potential for system change, while emphasizing our lack of suitable longitudinal data for the evaluation of our results. [1]

SOURCE: *Midwest Journal of Political Science,* 16(1972):388–410. Reprinted with permission of the publisher.
ACKNOWLEDGEMENTS: Thanks are due Warren E. Miller, who read and criticized an earlier version of this paper, and Mary Lee Muhlenkort Luskin who assisted in the data analysis. Professor Weisberg acknowledges the support of the Horace H. Rackham School of Graduate Studies of The University of Michigan for the research reported here.

[1] A report on the 1968 results is given in Herbert F. Weisberg and Jerrold G. Rusk, "Dimensions of Candidate Evaluation," *American Political Science Review,* 64(December 1970):1167–85.

The mid-term congressional election affords another opportunity for students of voting behavior to assess the relative degree of electoral constancy and change. It lacks the intensity of a presidential election, but it permits replication of previous work to determine which results were more than ephemeral. Therefore, we have employed data from the 1970 national election study of the University of Michigan's Center for Political Studies in order to test the validity of our previous work, as well as to examine whatever change may have occurred between 1968 and 1970.

Our approach is one of analyzing the factional lines of American politics. Presidential contenders in this country represent the various party factions. We examine the extent to which these contenders are perceived along traditional party lines, and the extent to which perceptions are molded by a new issue factor. The group context of candidate perceptions will be explored to see whether the candidates fit into the fabric of the new vocal social groups which are emerging, or if they are instead cast in the scenario of older group conflicts. The implications of the present panorama of candidate perceptions for possible changes in party structures will be emphasized—whether increased electoral volatility and eventually realignment will be the pattern of the future, or if such "surface" perceptions merely mask an increasing stability and constancy of the party system. The final section of this report places the results into a theoretical framework of the components of electoral change.

The Thermometer Question

Perceptions of possible contenders for the presidency were measured on a *feeling thermometer* in the 1970 election study. This measuring instrument is a 0-to-100 degree scale on which respondents indicated how they felt toward each candidate. Scores above 50 degrees corresponded to warm feelings, those below 50 degrees represented cold feelings, and 50 degrees signified that the respondent had no feelings about the candidate. The question also sought to obtain "don't know" respondents to individual candidates when appropriate. [2] Our ability to compare perceptions across time is enhanced by the availability of similar data collected after the 1968 election.

The selection of names for the study was restricted to those who seemed likely to be contenders in 1972, or who were fairly well-known figures within their parties. Such candidates included President Nixon, Vice-President Agnew, Ronald Reagan, John Lindsay, George Wallace, and a series of Democratic hopefuls—Edmund Muskie, Hubert Humphrey, Ted Kennedy,

---

[2] The full wording of the question is given in the Appendix of Weisberg and Rusk, "Dimensions of Candidate Evaluation," p. 1185. The thermometer card handed to the respondent is also shown in this article, although it was inadvertently placed on page 1175.

Eugene McCarthy, and George McGovern.[3] The scores received by the candidates inevitably reflect the post-election timing of the study, those most active in the congressional campaign being most affected in this regard. Another aspect of the timing of this research is the fact that we describe public reactions two years before the 1972 election, well before the media campaigns increase the salience of the actual candidates. This means that our 1970 measurements were obtained at a less intense point in time than our 1968 data, so that some of the differences between the two sets of observations represent only the necessary differences, particularly in salience, between presidential and mid-term election settings.

A Spatial Mapping of Candidate Perceptions

Perceptual data on the candidates can tell us much about how the public views the factional structure of politics—the basic conflicts and cleavages which exist in the political world today. Candidates both initiate and represent such conflicts, their nature and intensity most often become apparent in the presidential race, and the differences people perceive between the candidates center on the underlying structure of political conflict.

Inter-Candidate Correlations

An analysis of this underlying structure of political conflict must first start with an examination of which candidates are perceived as similar to one another and which are not. Clusters of candidates viewed as similar to one another and the relationships between these clusters provide a rough guideline to ascertain the underlying factional bases of perceptions of candidates. Correlation values will be used to summarize the perceptual similarity or dissimilarity of pairs of candidates. Candidates being perceived in a similar fashion should have substantial positive correlations and fall into the same cluster; those seen as quite dissimilar from one another should have sizable negative values and fall into different clusters. Correlations near zero indicate an absence of shared perceptions between given pairings of candidates.

Using this logic in 1968, we found that the set of candidate correlations revealed four basic clusters—the members within each cluster being viewed by the public as similar in certain ways, while candidates residing in different clusters were perceived as dissimilar to each other. The four clusters consisted of (a) mainstream Democrats (Humphrey, Muskie, Johnson, and Kennedy), (b) mainstream Republicans (Nixon, Agnew, and Reagan), (c) American Independent Party candidates (Wallace and LeMay), and (d) bi-

---

[3] The comparable candidate list for the 1968 election study included seven candidates listed in the 1970 study (President Nixon, Vice-President Agnew, Ronald Reagan, George Wallace, Edmund Muskie, Hubert Humphrey, and Eugene McCarthy), plus Robert Kennedy, Lyndon Johnson, Nelson Rockefeller, George Romney, and Curtis LeMay.

partisan liberals (McCarthy, Rockefeller, and Romney). Shades of both partisan and issue cleavages were evident in such candidate perceptions—representing the major elements of political competition.

The candidate clusters visible in the 1970 data were similar but not identical to those found in 1968. A mainstream Republican cluster was again evident, since the correlations between Nixon, Agnew, and Reagan ranged from .51 to .58. Humphrey, Muskie, Kennedy, McCarthy, McGovern, and Lindsay formed a second cluster (correlations ranged from .21 to .60) which could be decomposed into two more familiar sub-clusters—the Democratic mainstream group of Humphrey, Muskie, and Kennedy (correlations between .43 and .50) and the Democratic and Republican liberal group of McCarthy, McGovern, and Lindsay (correlations between .34 and .60). Wallace, as in 1968, tended to be isolated from the other clusters.

Greater change was evident in the relationships between the clusters. Wallace's correlations with the mainstream Republican cluster in 1970 were all positive and larger than before. This could have resulted from less concentration on the unique aspects of Wallace's candidacy in the off-year, from policy convergence between the administration and Wallace, or both. Whatever the exact cause, one side effect of this was that the strongest negative correlations in 1970 were between the partisan clusters, whereas in 1968 the strongest negative correlations had been between the Democrats and Wallace. Hence, Wallace was both seen as closer to the Republican position (or vice-versa), and not as the polar object to the Democrats, the Republicans being polar to the Democrats in 1970.

These elements of continuity and divergence suggest the possibility once again of mapping the American competitive space into partisan and issue terms, while at the same time, implying that the partisan factor had a greater weight in 1970 than in 1968 (as might be expected in an off-year election). But at this stage such projections of candidate perceptions along these factional lines are mainly conjectural. Based on our experience in 1968, the correlations do not present a ready or systematic comprehension of the underlying competitive structure from simple inspection alone. What is needed is to transform such correlational information into a geometric representation of the perceived differences between the candidates. By use of the Shepard-Kruskal scaling technique, we can arrive at a *candidate space* based on the correlational data; such a technique places the candidates in a space so that those with the highest correlations are closest together, while those with the most negative values are furthest apart. This monotonic rule may not provide a perfect solution within a space of small dimensionality, but the technique seeks a solution for any given number of dimensions, attempting to come as close as possible to satisfying the rule of monotonicity between correlation values and candidate distances. [4]

---

[4] Shepard-Kruskal scaling is a nonmetric, multidimensional scaling algorithm. A nonmetric technique has been employed because the order of the correlations is more invari-

By using this technique, we get a "physical picture" of the candidates—how close together or far apart they are from one another. Such a space gives us a better grasp of what competitive dimensions the public views as pulling some candidates together and others apart. Figure 21.1 shows the two-dimensional representation of the correlation coefficients.[5] The Republican and Democratic clusters suggested in the discussion of the correlations are evident here, with Lindsay being closest to the Democratic cluster. Wallace is seen to be separated from the two main clusters, but closer to the Republican one. The vertical axis, running from Nixon and Agnew to Humphrey and Kennedy, corresponds to a partisan factor. The Republicans are separated from the Democrats in the public's mind—certainly the essential basis of all political competition—with Wallace and Lindsay occupying the middle

---

ant under the vagaries affecting the measurement than are the exact correlation values. Multidimensional scaling is preferable to factor analysis in that the latter overestimates the dimensionality of the data. See Weisberg and Rusk, "Dimensions of Candidate Evaluation," footnote 12, pp. 1173–1174.

Of more fundamental importance is our decision to analyze correlation coefficients rather than directly analyzing the individual preference orders. Since the correlations measure the covariation in the ratings of candidate pairs while controlling for idiosyncratic variation unique to each given candidate, the resultant spatial representation is particularly suitable for determining the common dimensions of conflict. Yet a space based directly on the individual preference orders would be better suited for describing the distribution of voters in the candidate space and discussing candidate strategies in competing in that space. Each approach has its own utility and limitations; we consider the correlational space appropriate for present purposes, but we expect future work to give more emphasis to the preference space. See George B. Rabinowitz, *Spatial Models of Electoral Choice: An Empirical Analysis* (Chapel Hill, N.C.: Institute for Research in Social Science, 1973). Also see Hans Daalder and Jerrold G. Rusk, "Perceptions of Party in the Dutch Parliament," in Samuel C. Patterson and John C. Wahlke, eds., *Comparative Legislative Behavior: Frontiers of Research* (New York: Wiley, 1972), pp. 143–98, for a comparison of the two methods on Dutch elite data. In this latter report, the correlation approach revealed traditional dimensions of conflict, while the focus on individual preference order data highlighted a party coalition strategy space (analogous to the voter-candidate strategy space on the mass level).

[5] This solution was obtained from Kruskal's MDSCAL program (version 5). See Joseph B. Kruskal, "Multidimensional Scaling by Optimizing Goodness of Fit to a Nonmetric Hypothesis," *Psychometrika*, 29(March 1964):1–27. The extent of monotonicity between the correlations and spatial distances is summarized by a measure known as stress, ranging in value from 0 for a perfect solution to a maximum value of 1. The solution shown in figure 21.1 has a stress of .060 which Kruskal would term "excellent." A "good" one-dimensional representation (stress = .177) could be obtained with the mainstream Republicans and Wallace on one end of the dimension and the other candidates at the opposite end (Nixon and Kennedy being at the respective extremes). However, such a solution places Wallace too close to the Republican mainstream candidates and Lindsay too far from them, problems remedied by the two-dimensional solution given in figure 21.1. The stress values cited here are larger than those in our previous article because we have switched to Kruskal's second stress formula which leads to values about twice as large as those given by his first formula. The axes are arbitrary in multidimensional scaling; we have chosen a varimax rotation around the centroid of the space for the figures presented in this paper.

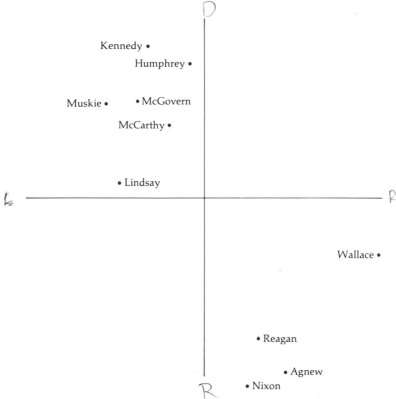

Figure 21.1 1970 candidate space.

positions as a reflection of their ambiguous party positions. The horizontal axis places Wallace at one end and Lindsay and Muskie at the other. This second dimension has left-right overtones, but its exact meaning cannot be specified from figure 21.1 alone.

This spatial representation is basically similar to the candidate space we obtained from the 1968 data. To illustrate this point, we have rotated the 1970 solution to obtain the best fit with the 1968 space. [6] This result is shown in figure 21.2; the two solutions being superimposed on one another. The general structures of the two spaces resemble each other in the overall clustering and in the relations between the clusters. It is evident that the two partisan clusters remain largely intact over the two year period, the 1968 and 1970 clusters for each party adhering closely to one another while the main

---

[6] Schönemann and Carroll's least squares matrix comparison procedure has been used on configurations of the candidates common to both thermometer measurements. This procedure is described in Peter H. Schönemann and Robert M. Carroll, "Fitting One Matrix to Another Under Choice of a Central Dilation and a Rigid Motion," *Psychometrika,* 35(June 1970):245-55.

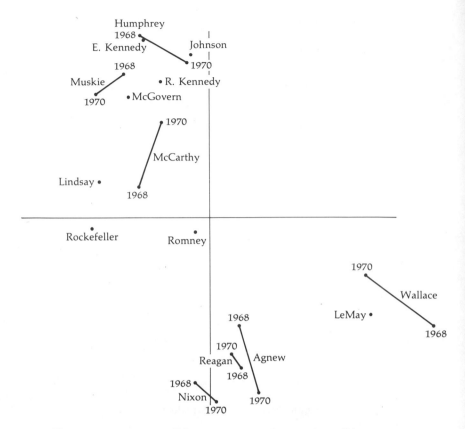

Figure 21.2 1970 candidate space rotated to 1968 candidate space.

clusters of the two parties reside in opposite parts of the space. Also, Wallace is separate from the partisan clusters in both measurements.

While the overall reading is one of stability in candidate perceptions, figure 21.2 also calls attention to some elements of movement and change. The fourth cluster evident in our 1968 space—McCarthy, Rockefeller, and Romney—does not exist in 1970. In part this reflects the omission of the latter two candidates from our 1970 measurement, but it also denotes a movement of McCarthy toward the mainstream Democratic cluster, something that is more noticeable here than in our earlier discussion of the correlations taken alone. Essentially, McCarthy is not viewed as distinct from his party as he was in 1968. Lindsay seems to occupy a position similar to McCarthy's in 1968, but he does not form a separate cluster entirely by himself, his ties to the Democrats putting him in a middle position.

The largest movements between the two years involve Wallace, McCarthy, and Agnew. Wallace is viewed as less extreme than in 1968, due presumably to the lower intensity of the 1970 election and its lessened focus on

Wallace *per se*. McCarthy's move toward the Democratic cluster has resulted as circumstances causing him to deviate from his party have receded in the public memory. Agnew's move toward the end of the Republican scale reflects his greater embodiment of the Republican partisan position in 1970. His increasing salience and intense partisan rhetoric over the two year period undoubtedly explain this movement. Such movements add the flavor of change to perceptions of the candidates these past two years, but they are perhaps even more noteworthy because they stand against a backdrop of remarkable stability between the two candidate configurations. The basic notions of the vertical axis being a partisan factor and the horizontal one representing some type of left-right stance on the issues (or at least a Wallace versus non-Wallace position on the issues) remain unchallenged, the movement of Wallace, McCarthy, and Agnew only bolstering these interpretations by providing further reference points in such a discussion.

Societal Mappings

The essence of our interpretation thus far centers on the idea that a conflict space of the kind we have described mirrors people's perceptions of the candidates. A further test of this contention would be to relate the public's perceptions of various social groups associated with these conflicts to how people view the candidates. If there is a firm relationship between the two sets of perceptions, then we have additional evidence that political conflict, whether partisan or issue-oriented is the underlying basis for perceptions and evaluations of the candidates.

Our measurement of people's group perceptions is again based on the feeling thermometer, enhancing the comparability between these perceptions and those of the candidates. In the 1970 election study, we had respondents score some seventeen groups on the thermometer, ranging from standard partisan and racial groups to such new social groups as urban rioters and marijuana users. While the average popularities of candidates varied between 32 and 59 on the thermometer scale, the means for the seventeen groups used ranged from 8 (for urban rioters) to 80 (for police). The mean scores for most of the groups were more extreme than those of the candidates. In short, the groups clearly evoked strong feelings, making the evaluations of the candidates look pallid by comparison.

Figure 21.3 portrays the scaling of the candidates with the groups. While it essentially retains the structure of the earlier candidate space (see figure 21.1), some of the candidate positions have moved somewhat in order to satisfy the additional constraints imposed by the inclusion of the new data set on groups. To satisfy these additional constraints, a three-dimensional solution was required. The vertical dimension in this solution is partisan, as before—the Republican and Democratic candidates loading high on opposite ends of the dimension, with Wallace being the only candidate not having his highest loading here. The vertical dimension poses President Nixon at one end of the axis to the Democratic candidates at the other.

Figure 21.3 1970 candidate–group space.

Other items which loaded highly on this dimension include the Republican and Democratic partisan groups and the "conservative" and "liberal" groups. We would expect the Republicans and Democrats to be located on this dimension, lending further validation to its being a partisan factor, but why the conservative and liberal groupings? The answer lies in the fact that such terms have a very restricted meaning to the public—referring mainly to "government spending," a referent first attached to these terms in the social welfare, New Deal days, and one which became closely associated with people's party identification over the years (a point evident in the 1968 data and one which will again be demonstrated below for the 1970 materials). [7] Suffice it to say that such terms or groupings basically are not identified by the public with general ideological belief systems or left-right positions on the new political issues of the 1960's, but instead are associated with the partisan

[7] See Philip E. Converse, "The Nature of Belief Systems in a Mass Public," in David E. Apter, ed., *Ideology and Discontent* (New York: Free Press, 1964), pp. 206-56.

conflicts centering on "government spending" that originally arose in the New Deal days of the 1930's.

The horizontal dimension involves the left-right distinctions associated with some of the new issues and groups which have dominated political headlines in the past few years. The police and military seem posed at one end of the dimension, contrasted with the marijuana users, urban rioters, black militants, radical students, rock festival followers, protest march ministers, and women liberators at the other. Implications of a social or moral issue factor come to mind. Wallace, Agnew, Nixon, and Reagan are viewed on the *traditional* side of the dimension, while McGovern, Kennedy, McCarthy, and Lindsay tend toward the *change* side. This political-social dichotomy remains when we place specific issues into the space with the candidates. The third dimension has a special character of its own. It is concerned primarily with the racial question, pitting the blacks and civil rights leaders against Wallace. However, the John Birch Society also loads highly on the conservative side of this dimension, indicating that its meaning may be somewhat broader than a strictly civil rights interpretation. Both the second and third dimensions highlight a conflict structure underlying candidate perceptions which involves left-right cleavages over the new political issues of the day, and the groups associated with them.

The spaces displayed thus far point to the fact that no one dimension alone shapes perceptions of the candidates. However, the vertical dimension—the partisan factor—has the strongest explanatory power, although it cannot account for perceptions of some of the candidates and most of the social groups. Ideological and life style considerations can begin to account for some of the differences we have shown, but these are matters best confronted when we add issues to our universe, a point to which we now turn.

Issues of Contemporary Society

In the 1968 election study, the public gave notice that a new issue area was an object of their concern, one that centered on such problems as the plight of the cities, civil rights, Vietnam, protest, and law and order. In 1970, the public was still very much concerned with these issues. About 63 percent of the respondents in the 1970 election study continued to mention these issues as the major problems facing the country, compared to 75 percent two years earlier. Vietnam was still the specific issue most mentioned though its salience as a problem fell from 42 percent to 30 percent in the two year span as Nixon began winding down the war. There were other changes in emphasis within the new issue context, such as less concern with urban riots and more concern with campus disorder. But, the overall concern with the new issues remained central as before. While there was much discussion in the media about the effect of economic issues on the 1970 election, we found that public concern over economic questions was still minimal, only increasing from 3 percent mentioning such problems in 1968 to 12 percent doing so in 1970.

We have mentioned this new set of problems as if it were a coherent issue area. The relationships among these issues are, however, far from perfect, a situation which is typical of attitudinal survey data. This limitation aside, we do find a tendency for attitudes on these issues to cohere. The 1970 study included attitude questions concerning possible solutions to eight problems: urban unrest, campus unrest, rights of accused criminals, government aid to minorities, Vietnam, inflation, pollution, and government health insurance. The first five of these issues formed a distinct cluster, as one would expect if a new issue area really existed. The correlation values ranged from .20 to .50. The remaining items showed very little relationship to one another or to the new issue cluster.

The relationship between these issues and party tells us much about the direction of partisan competition. The new issues had very small correlations with party in 1968, correlations ranging from .02 to .15 but with an average of only .07. The new issues were correlated somewhat more with party in 1970, although the correlations remained low. The average 1970 correlation with party was .12, ranging from .09 to .17. Two of the items were asked in both years: attitudes on urban unrest became less partisan as a Republican president had to face responsibility for such problems (.15 to .11), while attitudes on Vietnam became more partisan as leading Democratic candidates moved to a more dovish position on the war (.02 to .08). Of the remaining items, government health insurance had the highest correlation with party (.23), coming closest to tapping the social welfare concerns out of which present partisan divisions developing during the New Deal.

The Candidate-Issue Space

We have shown a spatial representation of the candidate perceptions. Now we can add issue items to that space, to show the relationship between the candidates and these issues. We employed four attitudinal items for this purpose: party identification and government health insurance as representative of traditional concerns, and urban unrest and Vietnam as representative of the new issue concerns. If our contention is correct that a conflict structure underlies candidate perceptions, we should be able to use these . . . items as validation, much as we did with the earlier social group items.

Adding these items to the space results in the solution shown in figure 21.4.[8] The familiar partisan element seems to be the dimensional basis for

---

[8] We should emphasize that issues are being added to the space to facilitate interpretation of the two-dimensional candidate space, and not as a separate test of the dimensionality of the space. We include in figure 21.4 both the liberal and conservative poles of the issue items to draw attention to the placement of the issues with respect to the full set of candidates within the confines of the two dimensions of figure 21.1. Additional issues could have resulted in added dimensions, as in figure 21.3 where the dimensionality of the 17 groups predominates over that of the 10 candidates. However, our choice of issue areas is based on the analysis of the major problems cited by the respondents in the 1970 election study, with the cluster analysis testifying to the integrity of the issue areas. In particular, the racial problem is part of the new issue cluster and is implicit in the urban unrest item.

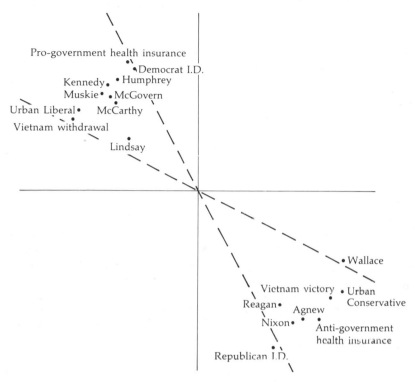

Figure 21.4 1970 candidate–issue space.

candidate perceptions along the vertical axis. The array of candidates here resembles the cast of contenders in 1968, with Nixon and Humphrey occupying the polar positions on the continuum and Wallace, the third party candidate, found relatively near the middle. Buttressing the partisan interpretation is the fact that the Republican and Democratic codings of party identification load very highly on this dimension. These party items are also located close in space to their respective clusters of candidates. The government health insurance item is found near these clusters and the party items, and this finding fits well with the partisan interpretation since social welfare was the major issue of government spending arising out of the Roosevelt period, during which present party loyalties were molded.

The second dimension pits Wallace against Muskie, and among issue items, the conservative ends of the urban unrest and Vietnam issues with their liberal counterparts. The position of these issue items indicates the effect which new issue and political forces have had on how the public perceives the candidates. Also, it indicates some breaking away from the traditional partisan conflicts of the past, from a total reliance on party to screen and color one's perceptions of the other forces in the political environment. The separation of the new issues and some of the candidates from party is hardly complete, but it begins to give indications of what might develop as a major force in the future.

We found a similar two-dimensional solution in 1968, but one important difference exists between the two years. In 1968, the two dimensions of candidate perception, party, and the new issue factor, were largely independent of one another; in 1970, they were not. One can see readily that many of the candidates in the 1970 space have moderate loadings on both dimensions. The dotted lines in figure 21.4 indicate this fact of correlated dimensions in 1970, while the solid lines show how the solution would look within the confines of an orthogonal structure. The correlation of these oblique axes in 1970 was a high .81, whereas a similar set of axes for the 1968 solution yielded a correlation of only .24 between the dimensions.

A fundamental question is, "Why were the two dimensions uncorrelated in 1968 but correlated in 1970?" Several possible answers can be given, answers which are not necessarily mutually exclusive and which cannot be completely verified with the data at hand. One obvious explanation would be the fact that an off-year election, without the presidential race, is relatively issue-less, with a stronger emphasis on party loyalties. Basically, congressional races are partisan campaigns, the contestants hewing to party appeals and the party line. What is all the more remarkable is that, despite this partisan climate in an off-year election, the issue dimension still was clearly visible in the electorate's mind. Even in an off-year election, there are enough tensions in the system to preclude total reliance on party.

A second explanation is that the parties and their leading presidential candidates have moved closer to the new issue dimension. With Johnson removed from the scene, Democratic candidates have more flexibility to deal with the new issues, particularly more ability to assume a dovish stand on the war. A Republican administration inevitably has the effect of forcing its party to take positions on these issues, and thereby associate Republican candidates with those positions, as when Nixon had to act on the Vietnam War and hence identify his party with his position on that issue. This process is not only partly inevitable, given a change of administration following on the heels of wide dissension in the previous administration's party concerning its policies, but also it may be the result of a more conscious effort on the part of one or both parties to merge the new issues with traditional party appeals. Viewed in this light, the consolidation process has gone far, but still remains incomplete.

All told, the issue space, just as the social group space above, has presented the picture of both partisan and issue cleavages underlying perceptions of the candidates. While a tendency existed in 1970, unlike 1968, for the partisan and issue factors to merge, the circle has by no means been closed. Some candidates are still seen more in partisan than in issue terms, and others reflect the opposite pattern. Our next question will be to assess the relative explanatory weights these two factors have for each of the candidates.

A discussion of the results portrayed in figure 21.4 has given some initial idea of the relative influences of party and issue factors on candidate perceptions. How close a candidate is to the extremity of a dimension obviously indicates the extent to which the public identifies him with the content of that dimension. A further and more direct aid to understanding the relative influence of these two factors is to partial out the effects of one factor in order to ascertain the independent explanatory power the other factor possesses when related to the public's perceptions of the candidates.

Table 21.1 presents partial regression statistics which summarize the relative importance of party identification and two of the new issue items in determining candidate ratings.[9] For example, the values in the party identification columns indicate the effect of partisan loyalty on candidate perceptions after the impact of attitudes on urban unrest and Vietnam have been controlled. Data for both 1968 and 1970 are given in the table to facilitate comparisons between the two years.

Party is the major determinant of candidate ratings for a large majority of the candidates. The only instances in which one of the new issues is more important than party are with Wallace and Lindsay in 1970 and Wallace, LeMay, McCarthy, Rockefeller, and Romney in 1968. The principal change between the two years is in perceptions of McCarthy; McCarthy is seen in more partisan terms than earlier, a result which fits with his changing position in the multidimensional scaling space (see figure 21.2). Since issue conflicts recede in an off-year election while partisan cleavages become intensified, it is little wonder that party is the dominant perceptual cue for candidates in 1970, maintaining a much stronger position in this regard than it did in 1968. Other factors are more important than party in 1970 only in those rare cases in which the candidate's partisan location has become blurred by having conducted campaigns for office as an independent and having, at the same time, become labelled as a party renegade.

Increases are visible in the partisan images of several of the candidates. McCarthy's turn in this direction has already been noted, reflecting the fact that the public has, to some extent, forgotten his bold and independent moves to upset his party's incumbent president in 1968. The mainstream Republicans—Nixon, Agnew, and Reagan—are also viewed as more partisan in 1970 than in 1968, due, in part, to the administration's active campaign in the partisan off-year elections. Senator Edward Kennedy is another who is seen in heavily partisan terms in 1970, the public obviously projecting its strong partisan image of his late brother to its perceptions of the senior senator from Massachusetts.

---

[9] The figures reported here are partial beta coefficients produced by Multiple Classification Analysis, a multivariate technique which assumes additive but not linear effects. See Frank Andrews, James Morgan, and John Sonquist, *Multiple Classification Analysis* (Ann Arbor, Mich.: Institute for Social Research, University of Michigan, 1967).

Table 21.1   Effects of Party Identification, Urban Unrest, and Vietnam Attitudes on Candidate Ratings, 1968 and 1970

| Candidates | Beta Coefficients | | | | | | Multiple Correlation Coefficients | |
| | Party Identification | | Urban Unrest | | Vietnam | | | |
	1968	1970	1968	1970	1968	1970	1968	1970
Muskie	.29	.28	.16	.17	.08	.14	.35	.39
Humphrey	.44	.41	.22	.15	.19	.07	.54	.46
Johnson	.42	—	.17	—	.10	—	.48	—
Kennedy, R.	.31	—	.20	—	.15	—	.43	—
Kennedy, E.	—	.41	—	.19	—	.10	—	.49
McCarthy	.09	.18	.14	.13	.17	.07	.24	.24
McGovern	—	.25	—	.12	—	.15	—	.34
Lindsay	—	.03	—	.12	—	.18	—	.22
Rockefeller	.10	—	.11	—	.10	—	.15	—
Romney	.09	—	.15	—	.10	—	.18	—
Agnew	.25	.33	.03	.16	.09	.13	.24	.42
Nixon	.42	.49	.03	.09	.09	.13	.42	.54
Reagan	.25	.36	.14	.09	.12	.09	.32	.40
LeMay	.10	—	.22	—	.20	—	.35	—
Wallace	.13	.09	.32	.27	.32	.18	.45	.38

Table 21.1 also calls attention to shifts in the issue images of many of the candidates. Nixon, Agnew, and Muskie are perceived more in new issue terms in 1970 than in 1968. This increase, even if mild, is important since it was registered in a relatively issueless partisan election year. The issue positions of the Republican administration and the Democratic front-runner have become better known over the two year period, and issue partisans correspondingly differ more in their assessments of the candidates. On Vietnam policy and urban problems, the soft-liners have become increasingly disenchanted with the administration positions, while Muskie has lost favor among Vietnam hawks.

One important qualification must be added to this discussion of the impact of public attitudes on candidate perceptions. The combined impact of party and issues is only moderate at best. Much of the variation in candidate ratings is due to individual response differences among those interviewed which have not been controlled, to unclear public images of some of these figures, and to candidate personality factors which go beyond parties and issues (such as "charisma"). Little of the variation in the responses given to Lindsay and McCarthy are explained by party or the issues in the 1970 ratings (and the same was true for Rockefeller, Romney, McCarthy, and Agnew in 1968). A similar pattern is evident for McGovern, although the public's highly superficial knowledge of the South Dakota senator may well explain why he was identified more in party than in issue terms. All three—Lindsay, McCarthy, and McGovern—have more of a potential for an issue candidacy than is evidenced here, but it is contingent on their becoming salient to the public and communicating their positions to that public.

In summary, the mixture of partisan and issue cleavages is apparent, with party being the dominant element shaping perceptions of candidates. However, the fact that the issue dimension continues to persist into 1970 logically raises the question of what its impact may be on future elections and on the party structures competing in those elections. The extent to which the issue dimension is correlated with party also raises the question of how party and issues will interact in the future in forming candidate perceptions. Will the new issue dimension merge with party, or will it break away in 1972 to achieve the same independent status it had in 1968? What will the implications of such cleavages be on an electorate that is increasingly characterized as highly volatile in nature? Implications to the broader panorama of electoral change and party realignment are evident in the way people perceive candidates for the highest office in the land.

Electoral Change: Toward Realignment or Volatility?

The study of electoral behavior is fundamentally concerned with the study of long-term and short-term electoral change. On the short-term level, the prime question is whether there will be a change in the party and administration in power. Nixon's narrow victory in 1968 makes his position unusually vulnerable. Data from the 1970 election study indicate that he has captured the advantage in the two-year interim, but the data cannot tell us how safe that lead is.

While popular interest in short-term change is well-justified, our concern must also concentrate on the implications for long-term change. One basic bundle of long-term system components is *party alignment*—the number of parties, their group bases, their issue appeals, and most fundamentally, their levels of strength. A second bundle of long-term system components centers on the level of electoral *volatility*—the adhesion of the electorate to the party system and the fidelity of individual voters to their own party. Identification of the entire public with the parties, coupled with strict party voting, results in low system volatility; large numbers of independent identifiers and sizable deviations from party voting indicate high levels of volatility. Increased volatility is inevitable as party alignments shift, with a corresponding decrease in volatility as voting patterns restabilize after a realignment period. Volatility can increase without realignment occurring, but increased volatility should heighten the potential for realignment.[10]

---

[10] For a recent clarification of the conceptual questions involved in what constitutes a realignment as well as analysis of recent survey data in this regard, see Bruce D. Merrill, *Party Realignment and Social Class: 1958-1970* (unpublished Ph.D. dissertation, University of Michigan, 1971).

Evidence from the late 1960's is unequivocal in its indication of increasing volatility of the electorate. The proportion of independent identifiers has risen, as has the extent of partisan defection.[11] The sizable vote gathered by Wallace in 1968 is further evidence of increased volatility in the system. There are those who see the end of political parties in these developments. However, the parties still have a long life remaining to them if their speed of demise remains constant. Volatility may be on the increase, but does this imply changing party alignments?

Party identification, a basic survey measure of party strength, has been astoundingly stable since the early 1950's. But party identification by itself is an imperfect measure of changes in party alignments. The party identification measure may mask a balance between the partisanships of those entering the electorate and those leaving the electorate during this period, or it may conceal changes among those who were in the electorate throughout this period which were balanced by the differences in the partisanship of those entering and leaving the electorate. The overall stability of party identification provides no clue to whether the group bases of the parties and their issue appeals have changed. Our discussion of a new issue dimension points to the possibility of changing issue appeals.

The popular press has made much of Scammon and Wattenberg's presentation of a new "Social Issue" composed of such elements as crime (safe streets and the law and order theme), race, youth (campus unrest and the drug culture), values (changing standards in the areas of sexual mores and dress), and Vietnam dissent (and the reaction to it.)[12] Yet theirs is basically a style issue—one on which there is general agreement (no one really favors unsafe streets and few members of the electorate favor disruptive demonstrations) which can damage candidates who find themselves associated with the unpopular side. Elections can turn on style issues, but the party disadvantaged by style issues usually manages to defuse them before they cause irreparable harm.

By contrast, we would emphasize the position issue aspect of our new issue cluster. There are style overtones to the problems of the cities, civil rights, and Vietnam, but they are fundamentally issues on which actors (parties, candidates, and voters) take differing stands. The emergence of an important new position issue introduces the possibility of major system realignment if that issue polarizes the electorate in a manner unrelated to existing partisan divisions. In 1968 the importance of the new issues and their virtual independence from traditional party appeals signified that the necessary conditions were met for a changing party alignment based on issue appeals.

How do parties cope with the development of a new issue dimension?

---

[11] See Philip E. Converse, "Change in the American Electorate," in Angus Campbell and Philip E. Converse, eds., The Human Meaning of Social Change (New York: Russell Sage, 1972).

[12] Richard Scammon and Ben J. Wattenberg, The Real Majority (New York: Coward-McCann, 1970).

One possibility would be to ignore the new issues with the hope that they would recede in importance. We have seen that the importance of these issues to the public decreased only slightly by 1970, and we would not expect the urban and racial problems to vanish. Party leaders could still feel that the issues are not yet intense enough to require the parties to take positions on them. Increased volatility is the likely consequence. Third and fourth party movements become more probable. Greater fluctuations between elections may occur, with the possibility of a series of one-term presidents. The question of which party is the dominant party may not change, but that dominant party would find itself losing a greater proportion of the elections. There is every evidence of these developments occurring up through 1968. If the issues were extremely intense and the parties did not respond to them, we would expect new parties to replace the major parties, but even Wallace's efforts did not seriously challenge the dominant positions of the major parties in 1968.

Alternately, the parties could directly address the new issues, taking opposite positions on them and thereby absorbing the new issue dimension. Convergence between the new issues and party would mean that the parties would remain intact but with corresponding changes in party alignment. There is evidence of such developments between 1968 and 1970. The increased correlation between party and the new issues indicates a degree of convergence, though that convergence is still far from perfect. That this convergence could be caused by the inevitable off-year concentration on partisanship rather than issues means that it may only be temporary. However, we have also argued that the polarization-convergence process (polarization of parties and convergence of dimensions) is partly inevitable. The administration must take stands which associate its party with the new issues while the out-party, freed from the associations of the previous administration, is able to move to a position of opposition to the new issue policies of the administration. The issue bases of the parties are changing, slowly but unmistakably. Leadership bolts have occurred more frequently than is often the case in major realignments, with a number of southern Democrats becoming Republican and with Mayor Lindsay becoming a Democrat. The extent to which the group basis of politics changes in the process is not yet apparent. No doubt the process is not yet finalized. The intense attitudes toward the new groups mentioned earlier suggests that the party system is not yet able to accommodate these new groups so that continuing modification is likely.

A gradual realignment process can change the balance of the parties. Phillips has seen this resulting in the emergence of a Republican majority, in large part a consequence of the administration's southern strategy.[13] We find no evidence of a new Republican majority. A high level of volatility

[13] Kevin P. Phillips, *The Emerging Republican Majority* (New Rochelle, N.Y.: Arlington House, 1969).

makes such a result possible, but it also makes possible that further solidification of the Democratic majority.

The enfranchisement of the 18–20 year olds further increases the potential for volatility. Even before that development, we argued that the coming of age of the post-war baby-boom was going to increase electoral volatility in 1972. [14] The infusion of this doubly large group is particularly significant because their attraction in sizable numbers to one party or another in their first presidential vote could give that party an advantage for a series of elections. Our data suggest that young voters would not be necessarily enthusiastic in their reactions to most of the candidates, with the exception of a strong positive reaction to Senator Kennedy. There is also some tendency for them to be enthusiastic about McCarthy, McGovern, and Lindsay, but relatively unenthusiastic about Humphrey and Republicans Agnew, Reagan, and Nixon. The minority party has accepted the enfranchisement of a set of voters which could cause that party's demise if it were attracted in large and permanent numbers to the majority party by an appealing candidate. What happens depends on the identity of the Democratic candidate, but the potential for large scale realignment resulting from the stream of new voters is unusually high.

A mid-term election does not afford a suitable setting for the resolution of questions concerning electoral change. However, it does provide an effective opportunity for sharpening our questions about future directions. We see electoral change as occurring presently, but as being incomplete. We see signs of increased volatility in the system, but we do not consider them as foreshadowing the end of parties or the emergence of long-term minor parties. We recognize the potential for a Republican majority, but we would also emphasize the possibility of the Democrats so increasing their majority as to make the Republican position untenable. We find the issue appeals of the parties to be changing, but with only limited effect to date on the group bases of these parties. The stability of indicators in the issueless 1950's desensitized analysts to the possibility that continued stability during the issue-packed 1960's could hide real change. The 1970's should witness the culmination of this process. Our mid-term assessment is one of increased volatility with some realignment of the issue bases of the parties; the scope of the realignment and its ultimate implications for the partisan balance are questions which must be put off for a later report.

---

[14] Weisberg and Rusk, "Dimensions of Candidate Evaluation," p. 1185.

22. A New Tide Observed: The Social Issue

RICHARD M. SCAMMON
BEN J. WATTENBERG

In 1964 the first unpleasant political rumblings were heard from what may be a new Voting Issue. Early in the year, Governor George C. Wallace of Alabama challenged President Lyndon Johnson in a series of Democratic state primaries. Wallace, who had made his national reputation as a "segregation now; segregation forever" politician, did surprisingly well against the stand-ins who nominally represented President Lyndon Johnson. In Wisconsin—a state with a long liberal tradition—George Wallace received 34 percent of the Democratic primary vote against Governor John Reynolds. In Indiana, Wallace received 30 percent of the party primary vote against Governor Matthew Welsh. In Maryland, Wallace got 43 percent of the Democratic vote against Senator Daniel Brewster.

In 1964 Wallace was regarded primarily as an antiblack candidate, and the term "backlash" came into the political lexicon, describing a white response to what some whites perceived as "Negroes getting too much, too fast, with too much turmoil."

Lyndon Johnson, of course, didn't see it that way. In fact, in a speech to Congress he later picked up the rallying cry of young blacks seeking equity

SOURCE: *The Real Majority,* by Richard M. Scammon and Ben J. Wattenberg, pp. 35–44. Copyright © 1970 by Richard M. Scammon and Ben J. Wattenberg. Reprinted with permission of Coward, McCann & Geoghegan, Inc., and Harold Matson Company, Inc.

in America and announced to America and the world that "we shall over-come." Lyndon Johnson did overcome in 1964. When the Wallace candidacy dropped away, the backlash vote found a haven with Barry Goldwater, and Mr. Johnson noted one day that there were many Americans who believed in "frontlash" and a fair deal for blacks. Indeed there were, as the election returns showed.

By any purely statistical standard, the election of 1964 was "tidal." Lyndon Johnson—a then popular, activist President in a prosperous, peaceful time—won with 61 percent of the vote.

But the main reason behind the vote was a strange, onetime wave in the political ocean: Barry Goldwater. One of the precepts of this book [*The Real Majority*] is that American politicians normally drive toward the center of the political spectrum. But Senator Goldwater chose instead to head for the right flank. In so doing, Senator Goldwater showed what happens when a candidate moves away from the center: A political stick of dynamite is lit. As perceived by tens of millions of Americans, Senator Goldwater was that worst of all political types: an extremist. As so perceived, he sought to wreck Social Security, to sell TVA, and to put the decision to use nuclear weapons in the hands of field commanders in Vietnam. Voters were apparently voting neither on "backlash" nor on "frontlash," but on what might be called "otherlash"—*i.e.* Goldwater himself. When the electoral dynamite blew up, Goldwater was still holding the charge, still explaining that what America really wanted was a choice, not an echo.

The Goldwater defeat, however, was a one-shot loss owing mostly to the voters' perception of the candidate as an anticentrist and radical. It was a big electoral wave, but not the sort of continuing tidal phenomenon that we have been chronicling here, such as the tides started by McKinley in 1896 and Franklin Roosevelt in 1932. As evidence, by 1968 no one was talking about junking Social Security, selling TVA, or putting nuclear weapons in the control of field commanders.

But perhaps ironically, perhaps coincidentally, and perhaps neither, it was the perception of Goldwater as an extreme candidate that masked the fact that among national major-party Presidential candidates, he was the first to touch the raw nerve ending of the Social Issue. And as he was losing votes on TVA, "nukes," and Social Security, he was in some places gaining votes on race and crime. In Leake County, Mississippi, Barry Goldwater got 96 percent of the vote whereas Richard Nixon had received only 9 percent of the vote four years earlier. Farther north, in the largely "ethnic" Ward 2 of Baltimore, Goldwater got 24 percent of the vote whereas Nixon had received 15 percent.

Listen to Barry Goldwater phrase the Social Issue as he addresses the 1964 Republican Convention in San Francisco:

> ... Tonight there is violence in our street, corruption in our highest offices, aimlessness among our youth, anxiety among our elderly, and there's a virtual despair among the many who look beyond material success toward the inner meaning of their lives. ...

The growing menace in our country tonight, to personal safety, to life, to limb and property, in homes, in churches, on the playgrounds and places of business, particularly in our great cities, is the mounting concern of every thoughtful citizen in the United States. Security from domestic violence, no less than from foreign aggression, is the most elementary and fundamental purpose of any government, and a government that cannot fulfill this purpose is one that cannot long command the loyalty of its citizens.

That Goldwater was speaking to a real issue that rather suddenly was concerning tens of millions of Americans is demonstrated from the following list published by the Gallup organization. It concerns what the American public perceives as "the most important problem" facing the nation, and it covers a full decade. The italics are ours.

1958

Feb. 2   Keeping out of war
Mar. 23   Unemployment
Nov. 16   Keeping out of war

1959

Feb. 27   Keeping world peace, high cost of living, *integration struggle*
Oct. 16   Keeping out of war, high cost of living

1960

Mar. 2   Defense "lag"
July 8   Relations with Russia

1961

Mar. 15   Keeping out of war

1962

Apr. 29   International tensions, high cost of living, unemployment

1963

July 21   *Racial problems,* Russia
Oct. 2   *Racial problems*

1964

Mar. 1   Keeping out of war
May 20   *Racial problems,* foreign affairs
June 3   *Integration,* unemployment
July 29   *Racial problems*
Aug. 21   International problems
Oct. 11   International problems
Nov. 18   Vietnam war, medical care for the aged

1965

Apr. 16	*Civil rights*
May 9	Education, *crime*
June 11	International problems
Aug. 11	Vietnam war, *civil rights*
Oct. 13	*Civil rights,* Vietnam war
Dec. 1	Vietnam war, *civil rights*

1966

May 27	Vietnam crisis, threat of war
Sept. 11	Vietnam war, *racial problems,* cost of living

1967

Oct. 18	High cost of living, taxes, health problems, cost of education, Vietnam war

1968

Feb. 28	*Crime, civil rights,* high cost of living
May 26	Vietnam war, *crime and lawlessness, race relations,* high cost of living
Aug. 4	Vietnam war, *crime and lawlessness, race relations,* high cost of living
Sept. 8	Vietnam war, *crime, civil rights* and high cost of living
Oct. 30	Vietnam war, *crime, race relations,* high cost of living

1969

March	Vietnam war, *crime and lawlessness, race relations,* high cost of living

1970

February	Vietnam war, high cost of living, *race relations, crime*

Suddenly, some time in the 1960's, "crime" and "race" and "lawlessness" and "civil rights" became the most important domestic issues in America.

The nondomestic issue of Vietnam was "more important" but as will be shown later in detail, Americans were not voting primarily on a pro-Vietnam or anti-Vietnam basis despite its "importance." An examination of public opinion polls over recent years shows an extremely ambivalent set of feeings about the Vietnam War, circling around the desire to "get out without bugging out." Insofar as both Presidents Johnson and Nixon stayed roughly close to this position, neither man was gaining or losing massive numbers of votes on the substantive hawk versus dove positions on Vietnam. This will be demonstrated. Some votes in 1968 did swing on a tangential feeling of malaise and nonaccomplishment in the field of foreign affairs generally and Vietnam specifically, but the numbers were not large. Many votes, however, did swing on the domestic side effects of the Vietnam War: disruption, dissension, demonstrations.

Generally speaking, it is the feeling of the authors that Americans vote for candidates largely on the basis of domestic issues, not international issues. The ever-potent Economic Issue always holds a high priority and in a time of economic crisis—great inflation, depression, deep and lengthy recession— the Economic Issue will likely be the crucial Voting Issue in a national election. This is as it has been, as it is, and as it will likely continue to be.

But now a new element has been added. To the authors, the italicized words above seem to herald the clear emergence of a new and major Voting Issue in America, an issue so powerful that it may rival bimetallism and depression in American political history, an issue powerful enough that under certain circumstances it can compete in political potency with the older economic issues. We call this force the Social Issue, and, as shall now be noted, it is complex, and it deals with more than just race and crime as listed above.

We can begin by recounting some of the events and circumstances of recent years that swept the Social Issue to the forefront of the American political scene. They constitute a unique set of converging factors that acted one upon the other, beating ripples into waves and perhaps moving waves into a tide that will be politically observable for decades to come.

There was, first, the "crime wave." From a professional data-gathering point of view, the FBI statistics on crime are probably the worst collection of numbers regularly put between federal covers. Still, in recent years, there can be no doubt that there *has* been a sharp increase in crime, no matter how the statistics are tended. The data concerning "offenses against persons" show a 106 percent increase from 1960 to 1968. These crimes include the ones that frighten the public the most: murder; rape; robbery; aggravated assault. It is of interest to note that a great deal of the "crime wave" can be attributed to a sharp increase in the numbers of young people in recent years. There were more than half again as many Americans aged fifteen to nineteen in 1968 as there were fifteen years earlier, and these crimes that frighten are precisely the crimes that are disproportionately committed by young people.

But citizens afraid of being mugged weren't buying statistical explanations; they were buying guns for protection. Tens of millions of Americans felt unsafe as they walked the streets of their city neighborhoods at night. That the political jugular ran through these same attitudinal neighborhoods could have been gleaned from the results of the special election in New York City in 1966 concerning the setting up of a civilian review board as a check on alleged police brutality. Almost every major politician and Establishment leader endorsed the plan. Yet the voters turned it down 2 to 1. By August, 1968, when Mr. Nixon delivered his acceptance speech in Miami, he knew full well the potency of the crime issue. He spoke of "cities enveloped in smoke and flame" and of "sirens in the night." And then he said: "Time is running out for the merchants of crime and corruption in American society. The wave of crime is not going to be the wave of the future in the United States of America. We shall reestablish freedom from fear in America. . . ."

Race is certainly a second key element of the Social Issue, and of course, the racial question has always been with America. But in the last decade there has been a sharp, yet apparently paradoxical change in the perceptions that white Americans have of black Americans.

This can perhaps best be seen as a series of three fleeting video scenes flashed upon a television screen.

The first picture shows a young, clean-cut black man seated at a lunch counter in a Southern state. In the already archaic language of the late 1950's the young black is known as a New Negro—college-educated, articulate, neat. As he is seated at the lunch counter, a wiry, slack-jawed white man comes up behind him and pours ketchup on his head. Quietly, and with great dignity, the black man remains in his seat, determined to gain for himself and his people the elementary civil rights so long denied.

The second video scene shows buildings aflame, sirens wailing, and mobs of young black youths racing across a city street. We see next a jagged plate-glass window. Through the window comes a grinning young black, excited as at a carnival. He is carrying a television set.

The third scene is at Cornell University. A group of black students emerge from a campus building they have recently "taken over." They are carrying rifles.

It would be wrong to say that these three scenes represent the facts of the recent racial situation in America, but they do represent the perceptions that many Americans had and have, and these perceptions lay at the root of changing white attitudes as the Social Issue emerged. And yet, at the same time that white fear and resentment were growing, white attitudes toward civil rights for blacks were probably *liberalizing*. This paradox is explored later in this book [*The Real Majority*].

In any event, in 1964 Harlem had a riot. In 1965 Watts had a riot. By 1966 every major city in America was asking itself, "Would it happen here?"— and major riots did erupt in Hough and Chicago. The apparent peak of a series of long hot summers was reached in 1967, when first Newark and then Detroit exploded in an orgy of violence, disorder, and looting. In April, 1968, on the night of Martin Luther King's assassination, outbreaks were reported in more than 100 cities, with Washington, Chicago, and Baltimore taking particularly heavy damage. The summers of 1968 and 1969 were quieter, but the electoral damage had been done. The electoral nerve had been rubbed raw. Voters were frightened and angry.

And then there was "kidlash." Among a highly publicized segment of young America, hair got long, skirts got short, foul language became ordinary, drugs became common, respect for elders became limited, the invasion and sacking of offices of college administrators became the initiation rite— and adults became fearful and upset. Again.

A fourth element of the Social Issue might simply be called values. Pornography blossomed with legal sanction; sexual codes became more permissive; priests were getting married; sex education was taught in the schools.

Further, the man who works hard, pays his taxes, rears his children—the man who has always been the hero of the American folk mythology—now found himself living in an era where the glorified man is the antihero: morose, introspective, unconcerned with God, country, family, or tax bill.

Finally, to this already combustible mixture, a new highly flammable element was added: the Vietnam protest movement. Suddenly American boys and girls were seen burning American flags on television; clergymen were pouring containers of blood on draft records; the President was jeered.

All these elements acted on one another and on the American voter. The Social Issue was in full flower. It may be defined as a set of public attitudes concerning the more personally frightening aspects of disruptive social change. Crime frightens. Young people, when they invade the dean's office, or destroy themselves with drugs, or destroy a corporate office with a bomb, frighten. Pornography, nudity, promiscuity are perceived to tear away the underpinnings of a moral code, and this, too, is frightening. Dissent that involves street riots frightens.

Put together, it spelled out great change. It was change that some few Americans perceived as beneficial, but measurably larger numbers did not. Most voters felt they gained little from crime, or integration, or wild kids, or new values, or dissent. Of many of the new facets of American life they were downright fearful. These voters became the core of an antidissent dissent, feeling the breath of the Social Issue hot and uncomfortable on their necks. When these voters had a chance to vote against it—in 1968 and again in 1969—they did. Other voters, approving of some of the changes but profoundly disturbed by others, felt only confusion.

Many of the political life, misreading both the issue and the popular reaction to it, feared an era of repression. Many of the political right chortled, sensing a clear turn of affairs their way. But both groups were probably premature in their judgments and very probably wrong.

As it stands now, at the beginning of the 1970's, the Social Issue appears up for grabs in the decade to come, an issue honestly and legitimately troubling tens of millions of Americans. As we shall examine it subsequently [in *The Real Majority*], the Social Issue is not a straight right/left or liberal/ conservative issue. While the economic issues of the past will continue to shape much of our politics in whatever form they may appear, the Social Issue is a new factor in the political equation—or at least it is new in terms of its present massive impact. While we know less about it than we do of its economic counterpart, it seems clear that it will have great political effect in the years to come. When voters are afraid, they will vote their fears. Accordingly, it may well be that the party and the candidates that can best and most intelligently respond to the social turbulence that is presently perceived by American voters will be known by the simple word: winners.

23. A Socialization Theory of Partisan Realignment

PAUL ALLEN BECK

Students of politics since the time of Plato have posited the existence of strong linkages between preadult political learning and the operation of political systems. For all their concern, however, there was little systematic research on preadult political learning prior to the late 1950's. Students of socialization outside the field of political science largely ignored socialization into explicitly political roles, while those few students of politics who were interested in political socialization focused narrowly and often impressionistically on civic education in the schools.

In slightly over a decade, all of that has changed. As Herbert Hyman observed in the preface to a new edition of his inventory of political socialization research:

> Now—by 1969—the study of political socialization has become a large-scale enterprise. It has become the organizing principle for scientific meetings and lengthy conferences. Journals devote special issues to the theme.

SOURCE: *The Politics of Future Citizens,* by Richard G. Niemi and Associates. Copyright © 1974 by Jossey-Bass, Inc. Reprinted with permission of the publisher.

ACKNOWLEDGEMENTS: My thinking has been stimulated greatly by the work of Walter Dean Burnham and Philip E. Converse, and I would like to take this opportunity to acknowledge my intellectual debts to them. I am also grateful to James Miller, Richard Niemi, and Bert Rockman for their useful comments on earlier versions of this chapter.

Texts and theoretical works in political science and monographs on the politics of many countries contain chapters on the topic. Scholarship has developed to the point that collections of articles are ready for the press, and the bibliography already runs to dozens of pages. . . . With this luxuriant scene before our eyes, it is hard to bring back to mind the barren vistas of the previous decade. [1]

The outpouring of socialization research in the past decade has greatly enhanced political scientists' knowledge of the preadult political world. It has provided an increasingly clear picture of what is learned and how it is learned. Yet this research has contributed little to an understanding of adult political behavior or the operations of modern political systems. The reason for this is implicit in almost all political socialization research. Researchers have been content to assume that preadult political learning has important consequences for both individuals and the political system. This assumption has allowed them to avoid coming to grips with the recalcitrant question which motivated students of politics to focus on childhood socialization in the first place: what is the relevance of preadult political learning for adult political behavior and, consequently, for political systems? [2]

If political socialization research is to continue to make important contributions to the study of politics, it must deal with these linkage questions. I take some initial steps in that direction here by outlining an explanation of a macropolitical phenomenon which seems critical to the functioning of American politics—partisan realignment. My explanation is grounded in theories of childhood partisan socialization and adult partisan change. Taken together these two theories provide a persuasive new explanation for past realignments as well as for contemporary politics.

Erosion of Childhood Partisanship

Of all the political orientations which develop in the preadult years, none promises to be more durable throughout an individual's life than partisanship. Psychological attachments to the Democratic and Republican parties emerge as early as grade two and become increasingly widespread among elementary school students with each passing year. [3] Although this partisanship appears to wane after elementary school (presumably as a result of nonpartisan influences in the school), high school seniors have been shown to be only about 10 percent less partisan than their parents. [4] While child-

---

[1] Herbert H. Hyman, *Political Socialization* (New York: Free Press, 1959; rev. ed., 1969).

[2] One suspects that this linkage question has been ignored because of the ease of collecting data from school children and the difficulty of gathering data which tied adult political behavior directly to preadult political learning.

[3] Fred I. Greenstein, *Children and Politics* (New Haven: Yale University Press, 1965), pp. 64–78; Robert D. Hess and Judith V. Torney, *The Development of Political Attitudes in Children* (Chicago: Aldine, 1967), pp. 101–04.

[4] M. Kent Jennings and Richard G. Niemi, "Patterns of Political Learning," *Harvard Educational Review*, 38(1968):443–67, at p. 453.

hood partisanship may represent little more than imitation of parental partisan orientations, there is little doubt that it typically provides a strong foundation for adult partisan behavior. [5]

Partisan orientations normally develop early in the preadult years and persist throughout the life cycle. But during certain phases in American political history, inherited partisan orientations have been noticeably eroded. These periods of sharp change in the distribution of party loyalties in the electorate are termed *partisan realignments.* In the 1820's (before the emergence of the modern two-party system), the 1860's, the 1890's, and the 1930's, partisan changes have been of such force that they destroyed the previous balance of party power and inaugurated new lines of political conflict.

The aggregate characteristics of these realignment phases in American electoral politics are relatively easy to identify. Each has been accompanied by increases in electoral participation, sharp intraparty as well as interparty conflict, extensive geographical shifts in voting patterns, and unusually severe social or economic traumas. [6] Each has been preceded by a rise in electoral support for minor parties.

But individual changes during these realignments are difficult to identify. About the only source of data on such changes is the University of Michigan presidential election series, which sheds some light, though indirectly through recall of past voting behavior, on the realignment of the 1930's. Through analysis of the past and present partisan behavior of the respondents in these voter surveys, Campbell and his colleagues have been able to piece together a picture of individual change during this political upheaval. [7] In the following pages, I elaborate upon this picture—buttressing it with data drawn from a wider temporal interval and placing it into a broader theoretical context.

The realignment of the 1930's seems in retrospect to have been wrought principally by the new voters during the New Deal realigning phase, not by those who had voted in earlier years. As is demonstrated in table 23.1, the first votes of these new voters were cast overwhelmingly in support of Franklin Delano Roosevelt. This behavior reflects the tendency for new voters to be swayed more heavily than their elders by the short-run forces in a particular election. It suggests also that the voting dispositions of these young voters were not wholly predetermined by their childhood partisan socialization. Given the likelihood that a majority of these first voters came from Republican homes (Republican identifiers were a majority prior to the 1930's), this first-time voting behavior signifies wholesale defections from inherited partisanship.

---

[5] Angus Campbell, Philip E. Converse, Warren E. Miller, and Donald E. Stokes, *The American Voter* (New York: Wiley, 1960), pp. 146–49.

[6] Walter Dean Burnham, *Critical Elections and the Mainsprings of American Politics* (New York: Norton, 1970), pp. 6–9.

[7] Campbell et al., *The American Voter.*

Table 23.1   Reported Presidential Votes, 1924–1940   399

Election	Percent Democratic of Two-Party Vote		
	All Voters	"Coming-of-Age" Voters	"Delayed" First Voters
1924	35	29	20
1928	41	38	53
1932	59	80	93
1936	62	89	77
1940	55	69	72

SOURCE: Campbell et al., *The American Voter*, p. 155.

Before moving on, table 23.1 warrants more careful examination. New voters are divided into two separate categories: those who were voting for the first time because they had just attained majority and those who were of age previously but had not voted. The behavior of these two groups of new voters is similar in all but one election—that of 1928. The nomination of a "wet" Catholic, Al Smith, by the Democrats in that year may well have attracted voters to the presidential contest who had been uninterested in presidential politics in previous years.[8] But on the whole, these two groups of new voters are virtually indistinguishable in terms of their voting behavior. The "delayed" voters were undoubtedly young adults moved by the same forces governing the "coming-of-age" voters.

Voting defections of the type portrayed in table 23.1 are hardly sufficient to spawn a realignment. Realignments occur only when either inherited or active partisan allegiances are changed, producing large-scale shifts in the partisan loyalties of the voting public.[9] While the electorate usually contains enough independents to allow some change in the distribution of partisanship, a shift of the magnitude of a realignment seems unlikely without many voters changing their partisan attachments.[10]

---

[8] One could infer from these data that Key's evidence of a realignment in 1928 in the industrial Northeast was, in reality, evidence of substantial defections only among older voters. These defections could probably not have forged a realignment by themselves without the subsequent depression of 1929. See V. O. Key, Jr., "A Theory of Critical Elections," *Journal of Politics*, 17(1955):3–18.

[9] Burnham, *Critical Elections*, p. 6.

[10] There is a possibility that a realignment could be produced without any partisan changes through the conversion of independents to a partisan disposition. This possibility was unlikely, however, as long as independents were few in number and the least knowledgeable and politically involved of all voters as was the case in the 1950's (Campbell et al, *The American Voter*, pp. 142–45). In more recent times, the characteristics of independents seem to be changing, and one can speculate that the absence of realigning forces in an electorate ripe for realignment has created a growing number of knowledgeable, involved independents—particularly among the young. This trend may well differentiate contemporary electoral politics from those of any previous era. Discussion of the implications of such a trend is left until later.

Experienced voters in the 1930's seem to have returned to relatively stable partisan loyalties. They support the theory that partisanship progressively hardens over an individual's life cycle, becoming more resistant to change with each passing year. [11] Partisan shifts in a realignment are better explained by the recent entry of new age cohorts into the electorate. These young people are probably moving away more from a *nominal* inherited partisanship than from any deep-seated partisan orientations.

This theory of individual change during realignments cannot be tested adequately until a new realignment occurs. It is based on the assumption that adult partisanship is much deeper, and hence less subject to change, than that articulated by a child or even a young adult. Support for this assumption can be found in a panel study comparing young adults and their parents. [12] Adult partisan orientations have been reinforced by voting. Childhood partisan identifications, on the other hand, have received little of this behavioral support and, as socialization research has shown, are rarely buttressed by a well-developed sense of the policy differences between the parties. Although many adults see no difference between parties and although children clearly manifest partisan orientations that are likely to be reinforced in adulthood, nonetheless the weakest link in the transgenerational partisan chain within any family lies in the preadult years.

Circumstantial evidence can be marshaled to support the notion that this weakest link is most likely to be broken during the transition years between childhood and full adulthood—the first time childhood partisanship is tested. Young voter cohorts which supported Roosevelt so overwhelmingly in 1932 and 1936 were overwhelmingly Democratic in their partisanship as well. Their break with tradition to cast a Democratic vote became a permanent rather than temporary defection. This is demonstrated in figure 23.1: the major discontinuity in the division of party identifiers is found between those who were in their twenties when the Depression of 1929 struck and those who were over thirty at that critical watershed. [13] This change in the distribution of partisanship is both sharp and durable, preordaining the emergence of a new Democratic majority as the process of population replacement worked its inexorable magic.

---

[11] Philip E. Converse, "Of Time and Partisan Stability," *Comparative Political Studies*, 2(1969):139–71.

[12] M. Kent Jennings and Richard G. Niemi, "Continuity and Change in Political Orientations: A Longitudinal Study of Two Generations," *American Political Science Review*, 69 (1975):1316–35.

[13] This figure parallels one reported in Campbell et al., *The American Voter*, p. 154, but it is based on a much wider time interval and is restricted to presidential elections to ensure equivalency. Slightly different conclusions may be drawn from these two distributions of party identification by age cohort. Generational discontinuity in figure 23.1 is not as sharp as that which appears in the figure from *The American Voter*. One reason is surely that independents have been excluded from the latter figure, but a second reason may be that the passage of time has dulled the apparent effects of the New Deal realignment.

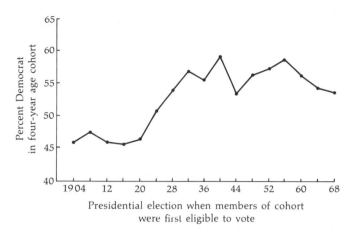

Figure 23.1 Party identification by four-year age cohort. These are the Democratic identifications of each four-year age grouping—including those who classified themselves as independents on first response but later admitted leaning toward the Democratic party—that were cumulated over every presidential election from 1952 through 1968, using the Survey Research Center election study data. The total N is approximately 9000 and the N is not less than 100 for any age cohort.

Given these data, however tentative they might seem, one must doubt that preadult political socialization fully determined the adult partisan orientations of these Depression generations. It seems much more likely that preadult orientations gave way under the impact of strong political forces for those who were in the transition years between childhood and full adulthood. Not yet habituated to a partisanship by actual electoral decision-making, these new voters were mobilized in new partisan directions. In the process, a new Democratic majority was formed.

The newest members of the electorate provide the dynamic element to American electoral politics. They are the ones most likely to break the partisan continuity between past and future and to force comprehensive changes in the policy agenda. Inherited partisan orientations are not always subjected to the intense pressures of a realigning phase, however. The excitement which pervades such a period, caused by the critical battle over agenda-setting for the future, cannot be sustained for long. Realignment phases then give way to the long periods of "normal politics," in which the party coalitions and policy agenda remain relatively stable. Normal politics promotes a high degree of intergenerational continuity in partisan orientations. Politics is simply too unexciting and too repetitious to continually subject the inheritances of new voters to severe pressures. Such pressures may be present in individual cases for idiosyncratic reasons, but they are unlikely to cumulate across an entire age cohort.

The study of political socialization has matured and prospered during a normal phase of American electoral politics. Thus it is not surprising that socialization theorists have seen more continuity than change in preadult political orientations and in the political system. It should now be obvious, though, that theories of socialization erected on a normal politics data base—especially those concerning partisanship—are misleading.

Cycles in Partisan Socialization

If it is true that the politics of realignment are intense enough to cause large numbers of voters to desert their childhood partisanship, it is also likely no other generation has more deeply entrenched partisan orientations and that, as a result, no other generation will transmit partisan orientations as successfully to its offspring as this realignment generation. These two assumptions combine to produce a new and powerful theory of preadult partisan socialization and the dynamics of realignment.

Three different groups of voters are involved in this theory. The members of group one adopt their enduring partisan orientations as emerging adult participants in a realigning phase. The partisanship of these realignment generations should have stronger intellectual underpinnings—a firmer grounding in rational responses to operative political realities—than that of any other age group. Group two includes all individuals who receive their preadult partisan socialization from members of a realignment generation. These "children of realignment," while lacking direct adult exposure to intense partisan conflict, are likely to receive much of the flavor of such conflict "across the dinner table" from their parents. Most group two individuals may be expected to carry into adulthood a partisanship which is supported by visceral if not intellectual underpinnings. Their childhood partisan orientations should be well insulated against change-inducing forces.

The third group of partisan learners is composed of the individuals of the next generation. Their childhood political experience is gained during a period of normal politics; their parents were not direct participants in a realignment. The childhood partisan learning of these "children of normal politics" should provide little insulation from the short-term political forces they encounter as young adults.

A clear similarity exists between groups one and three—the realignment generation and the children of normal politics—even if they are sharply differentiated by age. Both receive relatively weak childhood partisan socialization, but the members of group one experience strong partisan socialization during their years of transition into adulthood, while the members of group three have not passed through this transition period yet. Even though the children of normal politics have become a realignment generation in every previous instance, there also exists the possibility that no such transformation will occur. This distinction is critical: in it lies the difference between political instability (when large numbers of voters reject partisanship) and political change (when large numbers of voters accept new partisanship).

Regular cycles of partisan stability and change have dominated American politics for more than a century. Realignments have occurred at roughly three-decade intervals, and each realignment has been followed by a long period of stable normal politics. This previously puzzling regularity in partisan politics is explicable when change is conceptualized in terms of the movement through the electorate of the realignment generation, the children of realignment, and the children of normal politics. Through the process of population replacement, the relative weight of each of these groups changes continually. Furthermore, the potential for sweeping partisan change depends on which of these groups is just entering the electorate.

This explanation can be grasped more readily if accompanied by a look at the century of American politics postdating the emergence of the modern two-party system. Three realignments have been identified in this time period. The first was associated with the political conflicts over slavery and civil war, the second with the urban-rural conflict of the late 1800's, and the third with the class conflicts of the New Deal. Each of these realignments occurred at a time when the children of normal politics were entering the electorate in full force. These voters seem to have been mobilized during their early adult years and subsequently became a realignment generation.

The fundamental population replacement process which underlies this theory is represented in figure 23.2. Underlying the visible precision of this

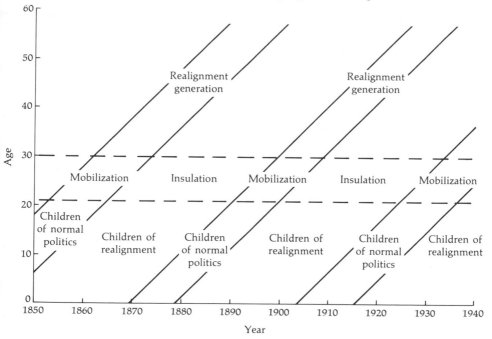

Figure 23.2 Population replacement and partisan change, 1850–1940.

figure are several operational assumptions. First, the delimiting of each generation depends upon the location of clear initial and terminal points for every realignment phase. Such precision is difficult because of the very nature of realignments. At times they have emerged nationwide only gradually because of their uneven development in different parts of the nation (such as during the Civil War and the New Deal). The task of specifying the realignment phases is made even more difficult by the fact that each has been preceded by a period of partisan instability which appears, on the surface, to be "of a piece" with the subsequent realigning phase. (Nonetheless, a graphical depiction of my theory of realignment dynamics requires precise delimitation of these rather imprecise phenomena, and thus I have attempted to determine initial and terminal points as carefully as possible by weighing the relevant historical evidence. At the same time, I must reiterate that this is an artificial precision and that these points may be moved within reasonable bounds without disturbing the essential features of the theory.)

The Civil War realignment phase seems to have begun with southern secession from the Union in 1861, not with the long period of partisan instability which preceded it, as is often supposed. The basic structure of this Civil War party system seems to have been set by the peace at Appomattox four years later. A number of scholars [14] contend that the Civil War realignment was completed by the beginning of the 1860's. Sundquist for example, concludes: "By 1858 the new alignment was firmly in place throughout the North." [15] Yet, in retrospect, this assessment seems to overestimate the importance of this time period for the development of long-term partisan orientations. As Sundquist adds: "The heightened polarization of the war years etched the slavery-secession-war-reconstruction-Negro-rights line of cleavage more deeply into the political pattern until old lines dividing the electorate were obliterated. More and more voters made their party choices on the basis of the new line of cleavage rather than the old, especially the new generation of voters just coming to political maturity." [16]

The period prior to the 1860's seems more an era during which the old party system was eroding rather than the new one forming. Pomper argues that the 1864 election, not an earlier election, first registered "the definite break with traditional sources of party support" [17] even in the North; he supports his contention by reporting low correlations between that election and the average of the four preceding presidential elections and high correlations between it and the average of the four subsequent elections. Furthermore, Lipset shows that the realignment in the South postdated the 1860 election, coming with the referenda over secession several months later. [18]

---

[14] Burnham, *Critical Elections;* Charles Sellers, "The Equilibrium Cycle in Two Party Politics," *Public Opinion Quarterly,* 29(1965):16–37; James L. Sundquist, *Dynamics of the Party System,* (Washington, D.C.: Brookings Institution, 1973).

[15] Sundquist, *Dynamics of the Party System,* p. 71.

[16] *Ibid.,* p. 87.

[17] Gerald Pomper, *Elections in America* (New York: Dodd, Mead, 1970), p. 114.

[18] Seymour Martin Lipset, *Political Man* (Garden City, N.Y.: Doubleday, 1960), chap. 11.

Scholars agree that the Panic of 1893 initiated the next realignment phase. Sundquist and Burnham ascribe to the Panic of 1893 the responsibility for the initial urbanite movement away from the Democrats.[19] This movement was surely crystallized by the Democrats' choice of an agrarian populist as their presidential candidate three years later. Bryan's nomination countered these losses partially by attracting rural, particularly western, voters to the Democratic party. Pomper's correlational analysis shows that the 1896 election was most unlike those that preceded and consistent with those that followed.[20] This realigning phase had clearly run its course by the reelection of McKinley over Bryan in 1900.

While Key identifies the beginnings of a realignment in New England during the 1928 election, it seems doubtful that the New Deal realignment was fully initiated throughout the nation, and even in that region, prior to the Depression of 1929.[21] The changes in voting patterns in the 1928 election were probably tied to the candidacy of Al Smith and would not have been permanent had the Depression of 1929 not reinforced the short-run lines of cleavage. As Sundquist puts it: "The heavy movement across party lines in presidential voting in the cities in 1928 was obviously caused by the issues that dominated public discussion in that election—religion and Prohibition. These were not the dominant issues of 1932 and 1936. The minor realignment of 1928 in the cities can therefore be considered an episode in American politics distinct from the realignment of the 1930's."[22] The realignment started by the Depression of 1929 and continued in the election of 1932 was probably not consummated until the 1936 election.

The second important assumption underlying figure 23.2 is that the period during which adults are most likely to change their partisan attitudes comes between the age at which they are first eligible to vote (twenty-one before 1970 and eighteen since) and age thirty. Both are arbitrary bounds for the "adult formative years" and serve only as a first approximation until more is known about the formation of political attitudes in adults.

A third assumption is that the average age differential between parents and children is the conventional twenty-five years. This assumption plays an important role in the spacing of the mobilization phases in figure 23.2. The generations available for mobilization are, by definition, those whose parents were not adults during the previous realigning phase. Thus, the children of normal politics begin to enter the electorate twenty-five years after the end of that phase. The mobilization phase begins twenty-five years after the termination of the preceding period of realignment and ends with the denouement of the new realignment phase. The children of normal politics may be in the electorate for some years (but no more than nine) before they are realigned.

---

[19] Sundquist, *Dynamics of the Party System;* Burnham, *Critical Elections.*
[20] Pomper, *Elections in America,* p. 107.
[21] Key, "A Theory."
[22] Sundquist, *Dynamics of the Party System,* pp. 181–82.

This theory of realignment suggests that the prior disengagement of young voters from the established party system is a necessary precondition for realignment. The purportedly weak childhood partisan socialization of the children of normal politics only nurtures the "ripeness for realignment," however; a societal trauma, often a depression, seems from past experience necessary to deteriorate the actual realignment. It is clear in retrospect that traumatic events will not have this effect if they are not set in the context of an electorate "ripe for realignment." Other traumas of at least equal magnitude—the economic depressions of 1873 and 1907, two world wars, and the anticommunist hysteria of the early cold war period, for example—had no more than short-lived impacts on partisan behavior.

Manifestations of a decline in the importance of parties are apparent *prior* to each of the realignments in the past. Third party movements were unusually successful in electoral politics in the 1850's, the early 1890's, and the 1920's. Split-ticket voting also seems to have peaked during the 1920's[23] and may well have risen in the earlier periods if the pre-1900 electoral system had not made ticket splitting virtually impossible.[24] The decline of parties during each of these periods was arrested abruptly by the advent of a traumatic realignment-producing event and the consequent resocialization of young voters to provide a realignment generation.

This theory cannot stand without substantial qualification. First, a certain tentativeness is inevitably involved in any theory which purports to explain a macropolitical phenomenon using micropolitical behavior, without much more than circumstantial evidence linking the two. Second, the operational assumptions incorporated in figure 23.2 are crude. The time interval between generations, the adult formative years, and the length of each realignment phase all resist precise quantification. Third, individuals in age-defined political generations do not necessarily share experiences during both childhood and the early years of adulthood. Political learning and experience are far too complex to be common for age-related individuals who differ substantially on other fundamental variables. The theory can withstand this qualification, however, because partisan realignments require only partial reshufflings of the electorate.

The most critical qualification to this theory is that it is grounded on assumptions about past individual-level political behavior which cannot be tested empirically. We simply cannot determine whether the partisan orientations of previous realignment generations were more deeply rooted than those of other generations of voters. Futhermore, we know virtually nothing about the relative intensities of partisan socialization when performed by realignment versus normal politics generations. Precise answers to these questions must await another realignment phase in American electoral poli-

---

[23] Milton C. Cummings, Jr., *Congressmen and the Electorate* (New York: Free Press, 1966), p. 37.

[24] Jerrold G. Rusk, "The Effect of the Australian Ballot Reform on Split Ticket Voting: 1876–1908," *American Political Science Review,* 64(1970):1220–38.

tics. Partial answers, on the other hand, may be suggested by contemporary political behavior, if they are researched. Even these answers, though, will not be forthcoming unless political socialization researchers recognize the importance of the early adult years for the formation of enduring political orientations and realize that substantial variations may exist in the success with which each successive generation socializes its young.

Contemporary American Electoral Politics

Recent American electoral politics has been marked by unusual instability. After a landslide victory of historic proportions in the 1964 presidential election, the Democratic party descended into bitter internecine strife and electoral defeat, followed by electoral disaster in 1972. During the same time period, pollsters plotted an increase in self-identified independents in the electorate, at the expense of both parties (see figure 23.3). This change in the distribution of partisan orientations has been paralleled by a remarkable increase in split-ticket voting, particularly in the two most recent presidential elections—1968 and 1972.

Some observers conclude that recent events in American electoral politics signal a new realignment phase. Phillips trumpets the emergence of a new Republican majority coalition.[25] Burnham, on the other hand, is more cautious: "It is particularly doubtful . . . that a new majority would be 'Republican' in any well-defined, party-identified sense of the terms; but such a

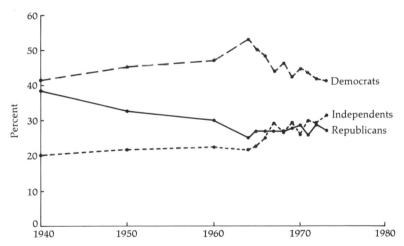

Figure 23.3 Distribution of party identification, 1940–1973. Source: The Gallup Opinion Index, Report No. 95, May 1973 (recent figures represent yearly averages).

[25] Kevin Phillips, *The Emerging Republican Majority* (Garden City, N.Y.: Doubleday, 1970).

majority, if derived from the 'great middle,' would surely be profoundly conservative."[26] If there has been any realignment, he concludes, its direction has been conservative, even though the dynamics of that realignment may well have set in motion a liberal-to-radical realignment to come in the future. A few political commentators have even perceived the birth of a new liberal majority in the politics of the sixties,[27] although they have been virtually silenced by the Nixon landslide in 1972.

Burnham also expresses considerable doubt that a realignment is possible any longer in American politics.[28] This important mechanism of electoral change has been rendered inoperable, he maintains, by the "depoliticizing and antipartisan" electoral reforms enacted by the Progressives at the turn of the century. To Burnham, the decline in the importance of party loyalties (and, hence, parties) to the electorate is a long-term trend which was briefly slowed, but not reversed, by the New Deal realignment.

It seems to me that neither the theory of realignment nor that of the decline of parties provide adequate explanations for contemporary electoral politics. Nor does Burnham's combination of the two theories in a single explanation seem satisfactory.[29] The best clues to the state of present politics are found in the political orientations of the youngest generation of voters. Change should be clearest, as well as most prophetic of the future, in this generation. Two logically intertwined characteristics of these maturing voters are conspicuous in recent years. First, this generation is much more heavily independent than older generations were at similar stages in the life cycle,[30] and there is every indication of increased independence among the young. (Data from the University of Michigan congressional election study in 1970 and from the Gallup Poll show that the generations which entered the electorate after 1968 were, if anything, more independent than their immediate predecessors.) Second, the heightened independence of this generation represents an erosion of support for both the Democrats and the Republicans.

Thus not only has there been no aggregate shift in a partisan direction, but there has been no tendency for young voters to flock to the banners of either party. Republican presidential victories in 1968 and 1972 were registered in spite of, not because of, the voting tendencies of this generation.

---

[26] Burnham, *Critical Elections*, p. 141.

[27] Frederick G. Dutton, *Changing Sources of Power*, (New York: McGraw-Hill, 1971).

[28] Walter Dean Burnham, "The End of American Party Politics," *Transaction*, 6(169):12–22; Burnham, *Critical Elections*.

[29] *Ibid.*

[30] In the past twenty years, young voters have continually identified themselves as independents more than have their elders. The common interpretation of this relationship is that it reflects life-cycle differences and that generations would become more partisan as they aged (Campbell et al., *The American Voter*, p. 162). While it is too early to determine whether the phenomenon will persist through the life cycle, the life-cycle differences in partisanship which have been common in past years appear to have been joined recently by pervasive generational differences.

II. PARTISAN REALIGNMENT

McGovern's showing among these voters in 1972 does not augur well for an emerging Democratic majority. In the absence of changes in the distribution of partisan loyalties in the electorate and of a noticeable disproportionate mobilization of young voters into one party, realignment explanations for present policies seem inadequate.

Recent changes in partisan orientations, principally the increase in independents, appear, on their face, to be explained better by the theory of the decline of parties. Upon closer examination, though, this theory too is found wanting. It fails to explain a signal characteristic of the increase in independents: its suddenness. (Sundquist has made this same point but with a different explanation for it than mine. [31])

As conceptualized by Burnham, the decline of parties has been inexorable since the beginning of the twentieth century. [32] Only the onset of the New Deal realignment slowed the spread of this fatal cancer in the party system, but it hardly effected a cure of it. Given this view, it is puzzling why the pace of the decline of parties accelerated so quickly in the sixties.

Beyond the theories of realignment and decline of parties lies an explanation of contemporary electoral politics. The socialization theory of realignment offers an explanation which fits both the present and the past. The 1960's and early 1970's bear striking resemblance to eras in American political history which preceded realignments. The electorate in each case—in the 1850's, the 1890's, the 1920's, and the present—contains a generation of young voters who, as children of normal politics, were (and are) ripe for realignment. The current ripe-for-realignment generation began to enter the electorate in full force in the 1960's (see figure 23.4), and the decline of parties has been manifest ever since.

What differentiates the present from the earlier mobilization periods is that almost a decade has passed without an event with sufficient force and direction to destroy the old party alignment and mobilize young voters in new partisan directions. A second differentiating feature, making the current decline of parties all the more pronounced, is that a higher proportion of the electorate is in the under-thirty age group than has been the case in the recent past. One of the more subtle effects of the post-World War Two "baby boom" and the recent reduction of the voting age to eighteen has been to quicken the pace of partisan decay.

The Future of American Electoral Politics

While my socialization theory of realignments can explain both the periodicity of past realignments and the current drift away from parties, it yields no clear predictions about the future. Several alternative future scenarios may be suggested, each of which seems plausible.

---

[31] Sundquist, *Dynamics of the Party System*, p. 353.
[32] Burnham, "The End of American Party Politics;" *Critical Elections*.

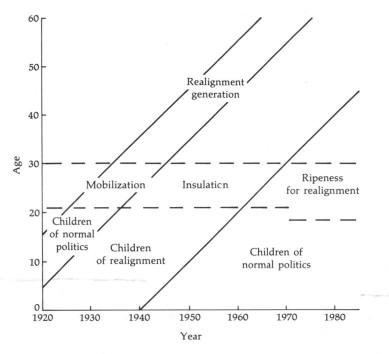

Figure 23.4 Population replacement and partisan change, 1920–1980.

The first scenario assumes that some critical, realigning event is "just around the corner." As in the past, this event may be economic in nature, though the major role government now plays in managing the economy would seem to preclude economic dislocations of the magnitude of past depressions. Current economic problems are sure to make their mark on political dispositions. But it is doubtful that they will catalyze a realignment, particularly since they reflect current partisan cleavages. Another potential realigning event may be the Watergate affair. Past revelations of political wrongdoing have never triggered a realignment, but one cannot be certain whether this is explained by their timing (none occurred when the electorate was ripe for realignment) or by the general nonpartisan "fallout" of such issues over the long run.

The conflict over civil rights for blacks may constitute a realigning issue. But unless there is considerable lag in the impact of events on partisanship, this issue does not seem to have generated the kind of traumatic force necessary to mobilize voters towards a new partisan alignment. Even though it seems premature to write an ending to the importance of this conflict and its realigning potential, there is little evidence that it will produce a realignment, especially since the major questions underlying this conflict are now juridical in nature and outside of the electoral arena.

An alternative scenario portrays a future almost wholly incongruous with the past. In the absence of a catalyzing traumatic event, the current ripeness for realignment may continue, contributing to an increasingly severe decline of party. Some voters in the generation ripe for realignment have already passed their thirtieth birthday and may no longer be available for partisan mobilization. This may lead to the increasing influence of "Madison Avenue politics" and to a perceptible decline in popular influence over public policy because, for all their faults, political parties are valuable instruments for democracy, and no institutions have yet emerged which can supplant them as vehicles for popular control.

A variation of this theme assumes that independence rarely constitutes a meaningful long-run partisan orientation and that independents over thirty will remain available for mobilization. If this assumption is valid, then we may expect a far more sweeping realignment in the future than has ever appeared in the past. Such a realignment could well endanger partisan competition in America by virtually vanquishing the party not favored in the realignment.

Whatever happens in the future, the socialization theory of realignment should considerably enhance our understanding of past and present electoral politics. Ripe for realignment in a system which has failed to generate any mobilizing forces in partisan directions, younger voters are drifting away from both parties to a haven of political neutrality. This drift could fundamentally alter the dynamics of American electoral politics by terminating the century-old cycle of realignments and normal politics. It could culminate in a paralysis in the making of public policy if confidence declines in political parties—the major forces for the policy coordination that occurs in American politics—and if no other institutions arise to take their place.

III. PARTY

DEALIGNMENT

24. Are Parties Becoming Irrelevant?

Turnout in American elections is declining. More and more people call themselves independents rather than Republicans or Democrats. More people are casting split-ticket ballots (voting Republican for some offices and Democrat for others). Cynicism about politics, especially party politics, has been on the rise. These trends are very clear when one looks at data through the 1974 election.

Many read in these trends "the end of parties," at least as we know them. Instead of realigning, the present party system is said to be "dealigning." The traditional coalition parties will die out, possibly to be replaced by a multiparty system of factions with narrowly defined viewpoints. Independent candidacies will become more frequent. Nominally partisan candidates will increasingly run without full support from their own parties. Thus, the current situation is seen as representing a significant juncture in the history of our party system.

But why are these things happening and will they continue? And if they continue, do they indeed signify the end of parties? These are the questions discussed in this section.

Of all the developments in contemporary electoral politics, the most remarkable is the increase in the number of independents after the mid-60's. As both the SRC/CPS and Gallup data show (see pp. 407 and 423), the proportion of independents was relatively constant throughout the 1940's, 1950's, and into the 1960's. Then the proportion suddenly jumped from a little over a fifth to about a third of the population. Significantly, the increase was greatest among the young, suggesting that the electorate may become still more independent as older voters who are more partisan die off.

This was not the only change, however. Split-ticket voting is on the increase, a fact widely publicized by journalists and popular writers. [1] People are relying less on their party identification as issue voting becomes the norm. Voters—especially independents—are more intelligent, more discriminating, and certainly more cynical than before. [2] George Wallace captured a large third-party vote in 1968. Prominent individuals like Senator Thurmond, John Lindsay, and John Connally changed parties. An independent was elected governor of Maine in 1974. A Conservative was elected senator from New York in 1970 and Conservatives talk hopefully about the possibility of becoming a new major party.

That these developments signify the end of parties appears even more reasonable when one realizes the large number of changes in American society that have affected the party system. When our current parties were formed, American society was still being shaped by the frontier. Instant communication was unknown, and parties served the necessary function of integrating the nation. Large numbers of immigrants had to be absorbed into the system, and the urban party served as a welfare system for them. Today, the mass media have permitted a revolution in campaign technology, but the basic structure of the parties remains unchanged. The urban machine has lost much of its original purpose. Even the nominative function has been taken away from the party machine and given to voters in political primaries. In short, the world in which our parties were formed no longer exists.

In today's circumstances, organized political parties may be an anachronism. Existing parties could be replaced by new party forms more attuned to an era of instant communication, but so far there seems little likelihood of media-based parties. Rather, candidates are increasingly turning to media, information, and management specialists in an effort to sell themselves rather than the party. "Candidate-centered technology" has become the new style of election campaigns. [3]

---

[1] Walter DeVries and V. Lance Tarrance, *The Ticket-Splitter* (Grand Rapids, Mich.: Eerdmans, 1972).

[2] On cynicism, see Arthur H. Miller, "Political Issues and Trust in Government: 1964-1970," *American Political Science Review*, 68(1974):951–72.

[3] Robert Agranoff, *The New Style in Election Campaigns* (Boston: Holbrook, 1972), chap. 1.

In the academic world, the "end of parties" argument is most strongly associated with Walter Dean Burnham, and it is a portion of his work which we reprint in chapter 25. Burnham cites some of the familiar data supporting the trends we have described. He then sets these data in a broader historical context which will be the heart of Section IV. Burnham sees these tendencies as part of a change in American electoral politics that has been underway since the end of the last century. Here the historical aspects of the argument need not concern us greatly. What is of chief concern is Burnham's interpretation of the trends as signaling the decline of parties in the electorate. It is conceivable, he writes later, that political leaders can forge a realignment which will rescue the party system, but more likely " . . . the party system may have already moved beyond the possibility of critical realignment because of the dissolution of party-related identification and voting choice at the mass base."[4]

Burnham does not necessarily like these developments. While the popular press often seems to glorify the decline of "party voting" in favor of "independent thinking," "independent candidates" as opposed to "party politicians," and even a cynical electorate as opposed to one "slavishly wedded to party," Burnham raises the question of what politics would be like without parties. He suggests " . . . that political decision-makers would have wider discretion, particularly in foreign and military issue areas, than they have even now, and that specific interest groups would enjoy even more influence on policy-making than they do now."[5] More generally, in the selection reprinted here, he argues that the decline of parties would favor the few who are powerful at the expense of large numbers who are individually powerless—presumably minorities (defined in terms of age and other characteristics as well as race), the poor, and generally those who do not belong to strong, organized pressure groups.

We have finally found an area where there is little disagreement as to the facts. The declines in turnout, partisanship, and party voting are obvious. On the surface, there is little doubt about what is happening; what is controversial is the explanation and interpretation of these facts. Is the cause of these trends really alienation, or is that merely an assumption by students and professors? Do the trends threaten the party system, or are they just part of cyclical change within the party system? These questions form the basis of a lively dispute.

The Persistence of Parties

Disagreement with the end-of-parties thesis centers on three questions: How serious are current trends? Is alienation the cause? Is the decline of parties likely to be the effect? Each of these should be considered briefly.

---

[4] Walter Dean Burnham, *Critical Elections and the Mainsprings of American Politics* (New York: Norton, 1970), p. 173.

[5] *Ibid.*, p. 174.

How low are turnout, party identification, and party voting today? Turnout in the 1972 presidential election was around 55 percent, a decline from the 60–65 percent turnout of the 1950's and 1960's. The 1972 turnout was admittedly low, especially in the nonsouthern states. Yet it was not unprecedentedly low. In 1948, turnout was only 54 percent. In the wartime election of 1944, it was 56 percent, and in the elections immediately following women's suffrage, turnout dropped below 50 percent. Part of the decline in 1972 was the inevitable result of the greater youth vote (due to enfranchising 18- to 20-year-olds as well as the increase in the number of voters in their twenties due to the postwar baby boom) since young voters generally vote less. Though this effect probably cannot account for more than a 3 percent drop, controlling for this factor means that the 1972 turnout was only slightly below that of recent elections. Moreover, figures from the 1920's through the 1940's show that turnout has been still lower in the past. Though turnout has declined for three presidential elections in a row (through 1972)—and though we should not be complacent about it—it is far from obvious that presidential voting is marked by growing indifference.

Many more people think of themselves as independents today than previously. Self-proclaimed independents increased from about 22 percent in 1952 to a third of the public in the early 1970's. Again, the independent figure is inflated by the effect of young voters, but there has been some genuine increase in independents.[6] Yet, as Converse points out in the reading reprinted here, there are several things to consider. For one thing, most voters still consider themselves closer to one party than the other. The "pure independent" category—those who do not consider themselves closer to either party—was still just 13 percent in 1972 (based on the CPS 1972 election study). Similarly, the suddenness of the rise in independents, the smaller increases in the mid-70's, and the timing of other "indicators" raise the question of whether the change is part of a continuing trend or is an isolated feature of the late 1960's and the 1970's. Independents have increased in number, but most people still identify with a party, and a new plateau may well have been reached.

Party voting has declined, as Nie charts in figure 11 of his paper in chapter 7. Yet party identification remains the best single predictor of the vote. Even in 1972, party identification was an excellent predictor. Any statement to the effect that party is no longer important is considerably exaggerated, especially since party identification still conditions our attitudes toward candidates and issues. Furthermore, the decline of party voting in 1964 and 1972 may signify little more than the idiosyncrasies of particular elections in which parties chose nominees who were unpopular with large segments of their own supporters. The relationship between party and vote has loosened up

---

[6] Percentages of independents come from surveys—chiefly SRC/CPS surveys and Gallup polls—and are bound to fluctuate a few percentage points due to sampling error. Too much reliance should not be placed on an exact number. However, the increase observed in the late 60's was too large to be dismissed as a random fluctuation.

enough to permit widespread defection in such a case, but that does not imply a permanent decrease in party voting.

The rise in split-ticket voting is a more complicated matter. There surely has been an increase, but its magnitude and meaning are difficult to estimate. Most popular accounts refer to outstanding examples of "split results" (e.g., a district that votes heavily Republican for presidential candidates and heavily Democratic for congressional ones) or are at least based on a collection of aggregate results. But inferring individual behavior from aggregate results is dangerous, and reliance on precise estimates would be doubly hazardous. Moreover, as Converse again indicates, the interpretation of survey results must proceed cautiously. Figures such as those cited by Burnham (table 25.1) seem to speak for themselves, but in fact they may be misleading.

Thus we have here a debate as to the seriousness of current trends. Some see the decline in turnout, partisanship, and party voting as critical. Others see it as a slight anomaly and partly due to the habits of the young voter and the idiosyncracies of particular election campaigns. There is no agreement about whether these changes are sufficiently large to have a major impact on the future of electoral politics.

The next question moves us to consider the cause of these trends. Alienation or distrust of the government is most often cited as the explanation. Alienation has indeed increased steadily and dramatically in the United States since 1964.[7] We need only refer to race problems, the Vietnam War, and Watergate to understand some of the reasons for this disaffection. But is alienation the cause of the recent trends? Possibly so, but empirical studies have notably failed to show it.

The impact of alienation has perhaps been studied most often with regard to turnout. Attitudinal and legal factors have been very important in explaining differences in turnout. But either these factors do not include cynicism[8] or it has been found that cynicism accounts for considerably less variation than other attitudinal factors, such as efficacy and indifference.[9]

Moreover, studies of nonvoting challenge the assumption that nonvoting among the young is due to alienation. First, lower turnout of young people was found even for the 1950's, well before young people began to adopt cynical attitudes. Second, lower turnout is also found among the very old, a group not noted for their alienation. The lower turnout for the older voters is due to the fact that it is often difficult for them to get to the polls. The same proves true of the young voter. Young people are unusually mobile, which made it difficult for them to meet the stringent residence require-

---

[7] Miller, "Political Issues and Trust."

[8] Angus Campbell, Philip E. Converse, Warren E. Miller, and Donald E. Stokes, *The American Voter* (New York: Wiley, 1960), chap. 5.

[9] Arthur H. Miller and Warren E. Miller, "Issues, Candidates and Partisan Divisions in the 1972 American Presidential Election," *British Journal of Political Science*, 5(1975):393-434; Richard A. Brody and Benjamin I. Page, "Indifference, Alienation, and Rational Decisions," *Public Choice*, 15(1973):1-17.

ments of the 1950's. Additionally, young people without families of their own and without their own homes have less of a stake in the community and are therefore less involved in politics. Thus, young people always tend to vote less because of the living conditions associated with being young, just as older people always tend to vote less because of conditions imposed by age. Neither phenomenon is true only of recent elections, and neither need be explained by alienation.

If these studies adequately operationalize alienation, then alienation would not seem to be a cause of the increase in nonvoting. It may be worth considering, however, whether more appropriate operationalizations of alienation are possible and whether those would better explain the decline in turnout. Many suspect that alienation is the true cause of nonvoting, but empirical studies so far have supported the contrary view.

Alienation is also cited as being responsible for the dissatisfaction with current party politics shown by such trends as the increase in the number of independents and the decline in partisan voting. But it is highly questionable at this point whether alienation is a cause of dissatisfaction or a result of it. The importance of this is that, if the parties succeed in satisfying the electorate, alienation should decline. This would be less likely to happen if alienation were independently fueling dissatisfaction with the parties. Though it hardly proves the point, the recent evidence that the electorate responds rationally to issues is consistent with the view that dissatisfaction with party policies causes alienation rather than the other way around.

Apart from the subject of cause and effect, there is a serious question as to just how strongly alienation and partisan behavior are related. Citrin, for example, argues that alienation seems to produce neither excessive apathy nor activism.[10] Arthur Miller, in contrast, suggests that a relationship exists, but that it depends on complex interaction with other factors.[11] In any case, nominal "pure" independents have been only as cynical as partisans of the party out of the White House, with the exception of 1968. Independent learners have been virtually indistinguishable from partisans.[12]

In short, alienation does not seem to be related in a simple, direct fashion to the decline in partisan identification and behavior, though more complex relationships may exist. Once again, the view that alienation is the explanation for the observed trends may be correct, but it does not receive much support from the empirical work to date.

The final part of the argument involves the likely effects of current trends. Burnham sees the changes as leading to the end of parties and the dissolution of the party system. An interesting contrasting view is the one given by Beck in chapter 23. Beck suggests that the United States was ripe for realign-

---

[10] Jack Citrin, "The Political Relevance of Trust in Government," *American Political Science Review,* 68(1974):973-88.

[11] Miller, "Political Issues and Trust."

[12] Citrin, "Political Relevance of Trust," p. 977.

ment in the 1960's. When realignment did not occur, that left a group of young voters who had been pulled away from traditional party alignments without being pulled into new ones. The result was the rapid change in indicators which Burnham cites. The large increase in the size of the under-thirty age group, coupled with their lack of partisanship, quickened the apparent pace of partisan decay. Thus the changes may reflect a potential realignment that failed rather than the decline of parties per se.

The conclusion of the Rusk and Weisberg article in chapter 21 interprets the trends as indicating increased volatility within the system. There would be low volatility if everyone identified with a party and always voted for that party, with higher volatility as independence and defection increased. Heightened volatility no doubt has a number of important effects. It means that the majority party will win elections less often, as when the majority Democrats won the presidency in all five elections from 1932 to 1948 but in only two of the six elections from 1952 to 1972. It may also increase the rate of split-ticket voting as voters are less inclined to vote solely for their own party. Increased volatility may also heighten the potential for realignment because of the presence of a large group of relatively uncommitted voters. But all of this does not necessarily presage the end of parties.

Thus, this last part of the debate indicates that there are many possible interpretations of the changes in the turnout, partisanship, and party voting indicators and that dealignment is not a necessary outcome. Realignment may occur instead, or the current alignment may continue with some in-crease in volatility. Moreover, the changes may be the natural result of the failure of a realignment to capture the imagination of a new generation, in which case it does not indicate a mortal flaw in our parties. Even if the traditional party system is someday replaced by new organizations which take better advantage of the revolution in campaign technology, this will not imply that the reason for the change was alienation from the old party system. An eventual demise of the current party system should not be taken as validation of one of the many conflicting theories of those who for dec-ades predicted its end.

Conclusions

The debate about the end of parties is unusual because it is both historical and contemporaneous. One need not accept the historical argument (which we consider in the next section of this book) to feel that current changes will lead to party dealignment. Yet one also need not feel that present-day trends are necessarily heading in that direction. Different interpretations compete with each other. People disagree as to the extent of the trends, how much they are caused by alienation, and whether they will end in dealignment.

This tale has four morals. First, beware of overinterpreting current changes. Newspapers have to interpret daily events, and a majority of their predictions are consequently flawed. The trends which seem so important today may prove trivial when viewed in historical perspective. Second, do not assume that change is impossible even if it is slow. The current party system is old—both in organizational form and in the basis of current party alignments—and it is weakening. Organizationally, it may eventually mutate to a form more compatible with current campaign technology. Ideologically, it is likely to undergo realignment—at least in the sense that the issue positions associated with each party may change, even if coalitional structures do not.

A third point is that one should not necessarily welcome the passing of parties if it does occur. Parties play a useful role in mediating the conflicts that are inevitable in a plural society and in representing interests that might otherwise go unrecognized.

Finally, don't expect political parties to be eliminated. To do so would be to ignore the fundamental law of political parties—they form because of a need for continuous organization regardless of whether provisions are made for them. The founders of the American Republic opposed parties and made no provisions for them, but they formed of their own right. They have always arisen naturally because of real needs rather than by careful plan and design. Thus, if the current parties die out in the United States, they will eventually be replaced. The party's never been over.

Further Readings

Change in American Politics

Walter Dean Burnham, *Critical Elections and the Mainsprings of American Politics* (New York: Norton, 1970). Argues that American party system is dealigning.

Richard M. Merelman, "Electoral Instability and the American Party System," *Journal of Politics,* 32(1970):115-39. Emphasis on the increasing instability of election results.

Norval D. Glenn, "Sources of the Shift to Political Independence: Some Evidence from a Cohort Analysis," *Social Science Quarterly,* 53(1972):494-519. Explanation of the increase in independents, finding a gradual increase nationwide and a sharp increase in the South.

Comparative Study of Alignment

Ronald Inglehart and Avram Hochstein, "Alignment and Dealignment of the Electorate in France and the United States," *Comparative Political Studies,* 5(1972):343-72. Contrasts forms of political change in the two countries.

Jack Dennis, "Support for the Institutions of Elections by the Mass Public," *American Political Science Review,* 64(1970):819–35. Study of dimensions of popular support for elections and party system.

Arthur H. Miller, "Political Issues and Trust in Government: 1964–1970," *American Political Science Review,* 68(1974):951–72. Finds decreased trust in government, caused by cynicism in the Left and in the Right.

Jack Citrin, "The Political Relevance of Trust in Government," *American Political Science Review,* 68(1974):973–88. Challenges the interpretations of Miller's findings, arguing that cynicism represents unhappiness with administration policies rather than permanent alienation from the political system.

25. The Onward March of Party Decomposition

WALTER DEAN BURNHAM

. . . . A longitudinal analysis of survey results over the past two decades, even at the grossest level, . . . shows an accelerating trend toward erosion of party linkages in the American electorate, and at two levels: that of voting behavior and that of a normally much more glacial measure, party identification. Since 1948 the Survey Research Center of the University of Michigan has asked its respondents whether they voted straight or split tickets for state and local officials, and since 1952 they have been asked whether they voted for the same party's candidates for president in all elections for which they were eligible, or for candidates of different parties. In table 25.1 these two series show a sharp break downward during the 1960's. [1]

Of even greater interest is the data on party identification. It has been widely assumed in the literature that although voting behavior in contemporary America is heavily influenced by short-term factors of varying kinds,

SOURCE: *Critical Elections and the Mainsprings of American Politics,* by Walter Dean Burnham, pp. 119-34. Copyright © 1970 by W. W. Norton & Company, Inc. Reprinted with permission of W. W. Norton & Company, Inc.

[1] The percentages are those of the total sample, excluding the categories coded as "don't knows" and "inappropriates." While the 1968 data have not become available in time for inclusion here, the Gallup organization found that only 43 percent of the 1968 voters chose a straight party ticket, a figure which closely fits the end of this series. See *Gallup Opinion Index,* December 1968, p. 9.

Table 25.1   The Decline of Party: Evidences from Survey Data, 1948-1966

Category	1948	1952	1956	1958	1960	1962	1964	1966
Straight ticket, state and local	72	74	71	70	73	58	60	50
Same party's presidential candidate	—	68	58	59	54	56	58	46

SOURCE: Courtesy of the Inter-University Consortium for Political Research.

Table 25.2   The Decline of Party: Movements in Party Identification, 1940-1969

Year	Independent	Strong Democratic	Strong Republican	Total Strong Identifiers
1940*	20			
1944*	20			
1948*	19			
1952	23	23	14	37
1956	20	23	16	39
1960	23	21	16	37
1962	22	24	13	37
1964	23	27	11	38
1965*	23			
1966	29	18	10	28
1967*	31			
1968	28	23	9	32
1969*	30			

*AIPO (Gallup) data were used for these years. Figures for the other years are based on Survey Research Center studies. For the latter, the three categories of independent leaning to Democratic, independent, and independent leaning to Republican are lumped together.

the structure of partisan identification in the electorate has tended to reflect far less change across time. Moreover, the standard work on American voting behavior in the 1950's, *The American Voter*, emphasizes that the voter who is weakly or not at all identified with either major party is less likely to be politically involved or aware than his strongly party-identified compatriot. [2] But during the 1960's, the hitherto glacial measures of party identification have also undergone comparatively abrupt change. As table 25.2 reveals, there has been a recent and rather sharp increase in independents which has paralleled a sharp decline in the proportion of strong party identifiers—and particularly Democratic Party identifiers—in the electorate.

It is tempting to speculate that the great Democratic collapse of 1966 was a direct outgrowth of the disarray and disillusion arising from the Vietnam

---

[2] Angus Campbell et al., *The American Voter* (New York: Wiley, 1960), pp. 143-45.

War, urban disorders and the nationalization of the race issue. In any case, the data reveal a sharp upward shift in independents which can be pinpointed with some assurance as falling between 1965 and 1966. This shift has apparently resulted in a durable change in state, with independents moving from one-fifth to nearly one-third of the total. For what is probably the first time since reliable survey data became available nearly a generation ago, the proportion of strong party identifiers in the total electorate is now no greater than the proportion of independent identifiers.

Moreover, there is some reason for supposing that the nature of political independence may have undergone a profound change since the 1950's. To be sure, the authors of *The American Voter* focus their attention upon individuals in discussing party identifications. Indeed, one lacuna occurring often in the survey literature is the failure to demonstrate a clearly developed relationship between the level of individual attachments to party and what might be described as the "demography" of party identification.[3] But even as dedicated a democrat as the late V. O. Key, Jr. was primarily concerned to show not that independent voters were other than as described in the survey literature, but that independent identifiers and those who switched from party to party in presidential elections were by no means the same voters.[4] There is probably wide consensus that the Survey Research Center view of the independent is the correct one:

> Far from being more attentive, interested and informed, independents tend as a group to be somewhat less involved in politics. They have somewhat poorer knowledge of the issues, their image of the candidates is fainter, their interest in the campaign is less, their concern over the outcome is relatively slight, and their choice between competing candidates, although it is indeed made later in the campaign, seems much less to spring from discoverable evaluations of the elements of national politics.[5]

There remain a number of imponderables in this question which are beyond the scope of this study to explore in their full detail. One notes from the above evaluation, however, that these are characteristics of relative political unawareness or ignorance. It is well known that, in terms of population groupings, the proportion of "know-nothingness" about our politics tends to be associated with the educationally and economically deprived, with women more than men, with people under thirty, and with those who live in parts of the country where local tradition and custom have not been favorable to mass participation in partisan electoral politics.

An examination in some detail of party identification as it relates to political response in the 1964 Survey Research Center study presents one side of the problem of the independent in the current decade. The 1964 study, which was made before the recent rapid increase in the independent share

---

[3] Compare, for example, *ibid.*, Chapter 6.

[4] V. O. Key, Jr., *The Responsible Electorate*, (Cambridge, Mass.: Harvard University Press, 1966), pp. 1-28.

[5] Campbell et al., *The American Voter*, p. 143.

of the total electorate, reveals that the demographic and certain other characteristics of independent identifiers do not correspond to what might have been expected. They are clearly not concentrated toward the bottom of the scales of income, occupation, and education; rather to the contrary, in fact. As table 25.3 reveals, the share of 1964 independents descends with occupational category, and monotonically with income; but along the educational dimension, the peak share of independents falls among high school graduates who have had some college education.

The significant point is that none of the groups among which independents have the largest share (leaving aside categories not discussed as yet, such as southerners or adults under thirty) is the kind of group associated with low political participation or efficacy. If it is indeed true that the profile of the 1964 independent can be read in terms analogous to those used by the authors of *The American Voter,* it would have to follow that there is a rather steep upward gradient in the proportion of individual voters who are political "know-nothings" as one ascends in each social category toward the top of the social scale. But this, if true, would be a significant political anomaly.

The problem is further complicated when one examines certain ranges of

Table 25.3   The Structure of Party Identification, 1964

Category	Number	Strong Dem.	Weak Dem.	Ind.	Weak Rep.	Strong Rep.
Occupation						
Professional-managerial	245	20	21	30	13	16
Clerical-sales	172	24	25	23	16	12
Skilled, semi-skilled	271	31	24	27	10	8
Unskilled, service	147	41	28	22	8	2
Farmers	44	32	32	9	16	11
Retired, not head of household	631	26	26	20	16	12
Income						
$10,000 and over	309	20	20	26	19	15
$7,500–$9,999	235	23	22	26	18	11
$6,000–$7,499	216	27	30	24	12	7
$4,000–$5,999	305	29	28	21	11	11
Under $4,000	471	33	26	20	11	10
Education						
Grades 0–8	373	39	27	17	11	7
Grades 9–11 +	302	30	28	23	10	8
High school graduate	329	23	28	23	16	10
High school graduate plus training	156	21	19	29	16	15
Some college	195	19	21	30	14	16
College graduate	172	19	21	23	17	20

political opinion among our party-identified groups. If the Survey Research Center's involvement index is studied, the result is quite clear: independents are indeed disproportionately concentrated at the lowest end of the scale, particularly by contrast with strong identifiers of either party.[6] On the other hand, a study of the efficacy index—a measure of the individual's sense of political competence—reveals an entirely different picture. Among 1964 independents, 36 percent scored high-to-very-high on this efficacy index, a proportion exceeded only by the 50 percent of strong Republican identifiers who also had a high-to-very-high score. Of the independents, 37 percent also scored low-to-very-low on this index, indicating a strongly bimodal distribution for this group; but 36 percent of strong Democratic identifiers also registered low-to-very-low, while only the strong Republican identifiers had a share of low-efficacy individuals (28 percent) which was significantly below that of the independents.

Viewing the two groups of strong party identifiers and independents as a whole, the strong Democratic Party identifiers tend to be high in terms of involvement and low on the efficacy scale; the strong Republican identifiers are very high on both; and the independents tend to be markedly low on the involvement continuum, but to have *bimodal* political-efficacy characteristics, with large proportions of both high and low scorers.

Again, on matters related to perceptions of parties and behavior in the electoral context of 1964, independents clearly showed evidence of lesser involvement—indeed, of much lesser involvement—than the strong identifiers with the two major parties. Thus, while 76 percent of the strong Democrats and 84 percent of the strong Republicans in the sample claimed to have cast ballots for one or the other of the major candidates, only 62 percent of the independents claimed to have done so. Similarly, favorable references to either party were, of course, much scarcer among independents than among either weak or strong party identifiers: 63 percent had no positive response to make concerning the Democrats (compared with 19 percent among strong identifiers), while 75 percent had no favorable references to make about the Republicans (compared with 20 percent among strong identifiers). On the other hand, the structure of opinions on two key issues and on the generalized question of the threat of growing governmental power reveals very little difference between the independents and any of the other four categories of identifiers, with the conspicuous exception of strong Republicans. Responses on the three questions are provided in table 25.4. As is evident, independents show up rather well on the "don't know" category in all three questions when compared with all other groups except the highly politically conscious and involved, though relatively small, group of strong Republi-

6 Of those with very high and high involvement scores, 54 percent are strong Democratic or strong Republican Party identifiers, while only 14 percent are independents. Of those with the lowest involvement scores (those in the three bottom units of the scale), 13 percent are strong party identifiers, while 38 percent are independents.

Table 25.4 Party Identification and Issue Questions, 1964

Response	Number	Strong Dem.	Weak Dem.	Ind.	Weak Rep.	Strong Rep.
A. Is the (federal) government getting too powerful?						
Yes						
Depends	468	16	24	30	43	66
No	49	3	3	5	2	2
Don't know, no	554	49	39	35	25	15
interest	465	32	34	30	30	17
B. Do you favor Medicare?						
Yes						
Depends	763	66	54	47	35	22
No	94	6	4	6	7	8
Don't know, no	435	12	24	30	39	62
interest	244	15	17	17	19	8
C. Do you favor government help to Negroes who can't find jobs?						
Yes, favor						
Depends	596	50	35	43	31	19
Leave to states	114	6	6	7	11	9
Don't know, no	618	33	41	36	44	63
interest	205	11	18	13	15	9

cans. Except on the question of help to Negroes, their general policy attitudes tend to fall in the middle, as one might expect.

The conclusion of this part of the study must remain ambiguous. It is
evident enough that the 1964 independents show less awareness of and
involvement in the existing instrumentalities of electoral politics than do
party identifiers. But it is equally clear that there is some kind of bimodality
in operation in their demographic profile: one finds small but suggestive
tendencies to peak among both professional-managerial *and* skilled-semi-
skilled occupations, for instance; among self-identified (or "class-conscious")
members of the middle class, but *also* among nonself-identified (or relatively
not "class-conscious") working-class people; and toward the top, but not at
the very top, of the educational scale. It is also clear that independents tend
to split between those with high-to-very-high scores of political efficacy and
those with low-to-very-low scores.

To note all this is not necessarily an attempt to demonstrate that independents are more politically conscious, at least during this decade, than those
examined in *The American Voter* but only to make clear that there seem to be
significant discrepancies in the data. It may be entirely likely that there are
at least *two* sets of independents: "old independents" who correspond to the
rather bleak classical survey-research picture, and "new independents" who
may have declined to identify with either major party not because they are
relatively politically unconscious, but because the structure of electoral poli-

tics at the present time turns upon parties, issues, and symbolisms which do not have much meaning in terms of their political values or cognitions.

These considerations bring us to the second aspect of the problem of independent identification: the steep post-1965 increase to a new level and, associated with this, the structure of these increases. If one compares the June 1965 Gallup survey with that of September 1967, when the proportion of independents reached what seems to be about its present level, it seems clear that the increase has been most heavily concentrated among those population groups where—barring a highly improbable distribution of individual voters—one would least expect to find disproportionate shares of the politically incompetent or the politically unaware. The array of increases is presented both for its minimum and maximum in table 25.5. The evidence seems strong, though not necessarily overwhelming, that the recent decline in Democratic identification and increase in independent adults is concentrated toward the top of the social structure, precisely where one might expect to find the most stable linkages between voters and existing party and other political structures. Not only the increase but the absolute proportion of independents has become increasingly identified with the comfortable urban-suburban middle class.

One further aspect of the political independent requires discussion: the fact that this characteristic is so high among young adults. If systematic change is occurring in the direction of erosion in party linkages among the youngest age cohorts, the long-range implications are likely to be profound. To be sure, this is a group which is the least politically socialized of any age-stratified group in the electorate; mobility is apt to be considerably greater than it will be later, social roles are not as fixed as they subsequently be-

Table 25.5   Growth of the "New Independent": Shifts in Proportion of Independents by Social Category, June 1965–September 1967

Category	Increase
Age 30–49	11
Highest income ($7,000 and over)	10
College educated	10
Nonwhite	10
Age 21–29	10
White-collar occupations	10
U.S.	8
Age 50 and over	6
Women	6
Grade-school education	5
Middle income ($5,000–$6,999)	5
Low income (under $3,000)	3
Farmers	2

Source: Based on published AIPO (Gallup) data.

come, and so on. This is reflected in the data, and along two dimensions. Taking the Gallup surveys of party affiliation from 1951 through 1968, voters in the twenty-one to twenty-nine age group had a larger share of independents than either the thirty to forty-nine age group or voters over fifty in each survey; and in each survey the proportion of independents fell monotonically from the youngest to the oldest group. Secondly, the variations over time are also monotonically arrayed: greatest among the twenty-one to twenty-nine-year-olds (standard deviation: 5.0), next among voters aged thirty to forty-nine (standard deviation: 3.4), and least among those fifty or over (standard deviation: 2.8).[7]

At the same time, the stratification pattern among young voters bears some similarity to that found in the larger population. The most significant of these differences is the far greater proportion of independents among whites (42 percent) than among nonwhites (24 percent); among men (44 percent) as compared with women (37 percent); and as between those with a college education (44 percent) and those with high school (39 percent) or grade school (38 percent) educations. Moreover, the "generation gap" has clearly widened: while in 1965 the difference between the proportion of independents among the youngest and oldest age classes was 12 percent, this widened in 1967-68 to 16 percent, the largest spread in this seventeen-year series. As one reaches college students in this analysis, the proportion of independents rises to a global total of 44 percent in early 1969, and to 53 percent by the end of the year.[8] Here there is a typical downward movement with age and school class.

Of much higher salience, however, is the very strong positive relationship between political and social radicalism and lack of party affiliation: while only 23 percent of students classifying themselves as "extremely conservative" are independents, the proportion rises steadily to a whopping 57 percent among those describing themselves as "extremely liberal." While those students who have stuck to the conventional collegiate dissipation—getting drunk on occasion—have an independent proportion nearly identical with that of college students as a whole (45 percent), those who have explored the drug scene score much higher: 60 percent among those who have tried marijuana, 65 percent among those who have tried barbiturates, and 82 percent among those who have experimented with LSD.

While a summary of all of these findings must remain ambiguous until further intensive work is done, the pattern of change in recent years seems fairly clear. The political parties are progressively losing their hold upon the electorate. A new breed of independent seems to be emerging as well—a person with a better-than-average education, making a better-than-average income in a better-than-average occupation, and, very possibly, a person whose political cognitions and awareness keep him from making identifica-

---

[7] *Gallup Opinion Index,* June 1968, p. 2.
[8] *Ibid.,* June 1969, p. 39; Jan. 1970, p. 14.

tions with either old party. The losses the two parties, particularly the Democrats, have suffered in this decade have largely been concentrated among precisely those strata in the population most likely to act through and in the political system out of proportion to their numbers. This may point toward the progressive dissolution of the parties as action intermediaries in electoral choice and other politically relevant acts. It may also be indicative of the production of a mass base for independent political movements of ideological tone and considerable long-term staying power.[9]

What are the policy implications of these movements toward electoral disaggregation? There is every reason to suppose that twentieth-century American politics has been pre-eminently marked by the decomposition and contraction of those partisan structures and functions which reached their widest, most cohesive form in the decades after the Civil War. This decomposition alone is enough to set the evolution of American electoral politics apart as something approaching the unique in the Western world, not least because its origins can be traced back so far in time. That is, it can be traced back to the time when the centralist imperatives of order and control implicit in mature industrial capitalism came more and more into collision with a pre-existing, fully mobilized party system of preindustrial origin. The "classical" American response to this confrontation was, after all, the partial destruction of these nineteenth-century partisan linkages.

Of course, the New Deal era was a time in which political power was reallocated, shifting somewhat from the hands of the business elite and its political ancillaries to a more pluralistic, welfare-oriented coalition of elites and veto groups. This was the minimum price, in all probability, of system survival. To that extent, parties resumed a good deal of their former importance as *instruments of collective social action.* This meant that not only the identity of individual office holders and the distribution of symbolic benefits but their role as a significant influence over the contours of public policy were at stake.

But while it was possible for traditional American governmental structures and the dominant American political formula to survive and adapt to the transition from business rule to disaggregated welfarism, it was—and has remained—considerably less clear that further major democratic adaptations to the collective pressures of mature industrialism could be achieved without the gravest cultural and institutional transformations. It seems evi-

---

[9] Here the Gallup survey is once again of interest. As of October 1968 (*Gallup Opinion Index*, October 1968, p. 27), 27 percent of American voters wished to see the establishment of a new political party whose principles are more in line with their views than either of the two major parties, while 67 percent expressed satisfaction with the status quo. The familiar loading occurs: the more deprived strata are less interested than the upper-middle strata, the South is somewhat disproportionately favorable to a new party (31 percent), and fully 41 percent of independent identifiers favor the idea, compared with 52 percent of independents who favor the existing partisan order.

dent in retrospect that the policy choices which even the New Dealers made in their heyday tended to fall short of radical innovation. [10]

Moreover, while quantitative indices support the qualitative judgment that party as an instrument of broadly national, collective initiatives was restored during the 1932–48 period, at no time during that period did new organizational forms of party emerge. Such forms might have served as a crystallized, action-oriented definition of party as an open system of action in which the many who were individually powerless could pursue collective political objectives under elites identified with them. But they did not, and it seems very likely that under American conditions, even at the height of the Great Depression, they could not. Mass voting behavior was transformed enormously during the 1930's; partisan organization and processes seem scarcely to have changed at all.

Moreover, the post-1952 resumption of the march toward electoral disaggregation leads one to suspect the possibility that, in terms of the history of American voting behavior at least, the New Deal might come to be regarded one day as a temporary if massive deviation from a secular trend toward the gradual disappearance of the political party in the United States. It is clear that the significance of the party as an intermediary link between voters and rulers has again come into serious question. Bathed in the warm glow of diffused affluence, vexed in spirit but enriched economically by our imperial military and space commitments, confronted by the gradually unfolding consequences of social change as vast as it is unplanned, what need have Americans of political parties? More precisely, what need have they of parties whose structures, processes, and leadership cadres find their origins in a past as remote as it is irrelevant?

It seems fairly evident that if this secular trend toward politics without parties continues to unfold, the policy consequences will be profound. To state the matter with utmost simplicity: political parties, with all their well-known human and structural shortcomings, are the only devices thus far invented by the wit of Western man which with some effectiveness can generate countervailing collective power on behalf of the many individually powerless against the relatively few who are individually—or organizationally—powerful. Their disappearance could only entail the unchallenged ascendancy of the latter unless new structures of collective power were developed to replace them and unless conditions in the social structure and the political culture were such that they could be effectively used. This contingency, despite recent publicity for the term "participatory democracy," seems precisely what is not likely to occur under at least immediately conceivable circumstances in the United States. Assuming that it does not, the

---

[10] For a useful comparative discussion of this and many other matters of interest to American political scientists, including a review of the genesis of the Social Security Act, see Andrew Shonfield, *Modern Capitalism* (New York: Oxford University Press, 1965), pp. 298–329.

policies of a politics without parties would certainly not be overtly similar in any detail to those of the 1920's. As American political and economic elites have learned to accept and use Keynesian economics to their and the country's profit, so they have learned to accept, and profit from, the disaggregated welfarism which was the political legacy of the New Deal era. Within those limits, however, there would be little reason to doubt that public policy would generally tend to be as system-maintaining or "conservative" for its time as was that of the 1920's for that time, even though punctuated from time to time by fire-brigade rescue operations.

26. The Erosion of Party Fidelity

PHILIP E. CONVERSE

With some regularity, journalists after each election seize upon some local instance of massive ticket-splitting to develop the thesis that partisanship has suddenly lost its meaning for the American voter. And the theme becomes particularly prevalent after such major "turning-point" elections as 1952, which broke 20 years of Democratic occupancy of the White House.

Most such accounts turn out to be exaggerated, to say the very least. With the benefit of hindsight, for example, the record shows nothing like a steady decline in the capacity of partisanship to predict voting choice at various levels of office in the period since the Second World War. The proportion of people calling themselves independents, rather than adherents of either party, was almost exactly the same in 1964 as it had been in 1944, with nothing more exciting than faint sampling variability in between. The other levels of partisan intensity registered in our measure have remained constant over the same period as well.

In 1966 and 1968, however, the proportion of self-styled "independents" increased rather markedly, from about 22 to 28 percent. If apoliticals are

SOURCE: "Change in the American Electorate," by Philip E. Converse in Angus Campbell and Philip E. Converse, eds., *The Human Meaning of Social Change*, pp. 317–32. Copyright © 1972 by Russell Sage Foundation.

added in among independents to accumulate all persons who refuse any party allegiance, the change is much less impressive (from an earlier norm of 26 percent to about 29 percent). Yet . . . the sharp decline of apoliticals in the 1960's can be traced exclusively to Southern blacks, and figure 26.1 makes clear that these apoliticals have not merely begun to call themselves independents but rather have tended to become clear partisans. It follows that any decline in partisanship in the national aggregate in the late 1960's would simply be more dramatic among whites taken alone. This development will be assessed briefly here.

There are a variety of "indicators" in our surveys that might be taken as reflective of the levels of party fidelity in the land available for examination over nearly a 20-year period. These include such items as reports of ticket-splitting incidence and proportions of the electorate indicating they have voted for different parties for President within their citizen lives. Several of these indirect measures have moved in a direction suggestive of lowered partisan fidelity since 1952, and none that we have explored show any noteworthy counter trend. Nevertheless, the changes registered in these measures do not coincide particularly with the swelling of independents in the late 1960's, and it is relatively easy to see that, while each of these indirect indicators can be affected by changes in levels of partisanship, they can be powerfully influenced by other factors as well.

For example, reports of voting for different parties for President can be strongly affected by particular sequences of candidate pairings and events

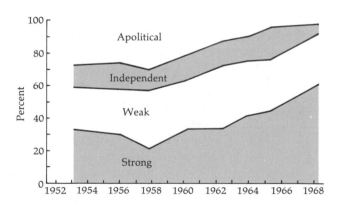

Figure 26.1 Growth in partisanship among Negroes in the South, 1952–68. (Responses to the intensity portion of the standard party identification question permit a division into strong and weak identifiers with a major party, independents, and persons who are "apolitical" by virtue of inability to relate themselves to the question at all. Partisanship so measured has intensified markedly among Southern blacks during the 1960's. Because of small case numbers for Southern blacks, adjacent samples have been combined to yield this trend graph, with observations located at the mean point in time for each cluster of samples.)

that throw up third-party intrusions. This index has in fact increased: setting aside blacks, who have been less likely to vary their presidential votes in recent years, we find that 30 percent of whites prior to the 1952 election reported having voted for different parties, a figure that had advanced to 45 percent in 1968. The lion's share of this change occurred between 1952 and 1954, however, and was centered in the South. After the long period of Democratic presidential dominance, many white Democrats voted Republican for the first time in 1952, and this large wave of defection to Eisenhower showed up first in the 1954 reports of past behavior. There was another smaller increase in the "different-party" proportion in 1966, after some relatively consistent Republicans had voted against Goldwater in 1964. It should increase again among whites in 1970, since all Wallace voters who have voted in at least one other election will now qualify. It might be argued that such increases are themselves evidence of declining party fidelity that is a mere extension of trends set in motion at the turn of the century. Yet, there is as much reason to believe that we happened upon a dramatic local minimum of this measure in 1952, and that event sequences have probably produced local maxima as great as 1966 or 1970 in the past. Consider, for example, the likely situation in 1934, after Roosevelt overturned an era of massive Republican dominance in 1932, in an electorate partially populated by voters who had also participated in the Wilson intrusion of 1916 or the La Follette intrusion of 1924 or (for the Solid Democratic South) the repudiation of Catholic Al Smith in 1928. It is hard to imagine that the proportion of "different-party" voters would have been much lower at such a conjuncture than in 1966–70. Obviously, these event sequences are of supreme political importance, and high proportions of different-party voters may well characterize realigning epochs. But the available data of this type do not provide very compelling evidence of a long-term, irreversible decline in the impact of partisanship.

Another measure that seems to hint at a secular erosion of party fidelity is an item that asks people whether they voted a straight party ticket for state and local offices. In 1952, 73 percent of the voting citizens claimed to have voted a straight ticket. Through 1960, the same figure hovered near 70 percent. In 1964, it fell suddenly to a point near 60 percent, and proceeded downward to 51 percent in both 1966 and 1968. Again, the case for diminishing partisanship seems straightforward. However, it is clear that other factors than individual feelings of party allegiance can affect such a measure. In particular, for an extended period prior to the 1950's, large areas of the country showed little partisan competition in general elections. Large numbers of Democrats could run unopposed at lower offices in the South, and Republicans could do so in the North. As partisan balance between regions began to increase after the Second World War, fueled largely by population redistribution, many districts both North and South began to be worth contesting by the minority party. Thus, the sheer possibility of ticket-splitting at lower levels of office must have increased in this period rather dramatically, quite independent of levels of partisan intensity. Moreover, the decline of straight-ticket reports for lower offices has been accompanied by a decline in proportions of persons claiming to have split their ticket fairly evenly, as opposed to a stray defecting vote or two. There have been coding and probing problems with this questionnaire item which militate against putting too much weight on such anomalies; nonetheless, they suggest ways in which straight-ticket voting might decrease while the incidence of crossing party lines might decrease as well.

It is in one sense pointless to deal with such indirect measures when much more direct measures are available, and we have done so only because of the hasty conclusions that have been drawn from some of these other indicators. Certainly the most direct measure is that which indexes the degree of felt partisan loyalty and, as we have seen, the relevant measure has shown no change in the period 1944-64, but indicates some loosening of partisanship in the late 1960's. However, some scholars are distinctly uncomfortable with such "soft" psychological measures and are apprehensive that people might routinely report normal identifications while progressively losing their inhibitions about crossing party lines. Perhaps the most direct behaviorally oriented measure, however, is also available in our data: the frequency with which partisans defect to cast ballots for the opposing party. For most of the biennial elections since 1952 we have been able to make such calculations covering most major offices, including votes cast for presidential, senatorial, gubernatorial and congressional candidates. We have set aside ballots cast in races not contested by major parties: thus, we focus here on individual propensities to cross party lines when proffered a genuine choice between party loyalty or defection. Between 1952 and 1964, this culling amounts to a sample of some 15,600 decisions over six elections, and it is of interest that in this period partisans defected on less than one vote in seven (13.5 percent of all ballots cast).[1] Our prime interest here is in how these defection rates have behaved over time, however, and the data are divided by election in table 26.1. Unfortunately, such a refined estimate was not as yet available for 1968, although it will become so in the future, and we have filled in this critical observation on the basis of raw rates of defection, adjusted very slightly in the direction that more refined estimates typically deviate from raw estimates.

The data attest to a significant decline of party fidelity in the late 1960's, a judgment that would be further enhanced if figures were presented for whites alone and if increases in pure independents were taken into account as well. On the other hand, they provide no proof whatever that party

---

[1] Note that another source of lability in party voting resides among pure independents, who refuse to indicate even a faint party "leaning," and whose ballots cannot therefore be judged as "loyal" or "defecting." While data cited earlier refer to a swelling of "independents" in the 1966-68 period which includes "leaners" who can be classed as loyal or defecting in above terms, much of the 1966-68 change in the party identification distribution has occurred in an expansion of the "pure" independents. This additional source of vote variability cannot be represented in table 26.1, although it is a highly meaningful contribution to evidence for a recent decline in partisanship.

Table 26.1 Rates of Voluntary Defection among Partisans Voting at Higher Levels of Office, 1952-68[a]

Year	Percent Defecting
1952	18.0
1956	13.2
1958	11.1
1960	10.3
1962	11.1
1964	15.9
1966	19.3
1968[b]	19.8

[a] Ballots accumulated here cover congressional and senatorial votes in all years, presidential votes quadrennially, and gubernatorial votes in years when these were requested. Generally speaking, there is remarkable similarity in levels of defection for the three types of national office in any given year, and strong temporal covariation as well. Gubernatorial votes tend to show somewhat higher rates of defection, by 3 to 6 percent. Since the votes for governor were not canvassed in 1956, 1960 or 1962, it may be wise to think of these estimates as properly a percent or two greater.

[b] Estimated. The estimate presented here excludes the presidential vote, clouded by the Wallace candidacy. The Wallace candidacy poses problems in part because of the likelihood that many Southern Democrats would not have thought of themselves as defecting to vote for fellow Southern Democrat Wallace, If all Wallace votes are considered automatically as voluntary defections, the appropriate value would be about 21.7 percent defecting. If Wallace voters were simply dropped from consideration, but loyal and defecting votes for Humphrey and Nixon were considered in 1968, the estimate would be 19.0 percent defecting.

allegiance has been steadily declining in salience since the turn of the century. Indeed, if anything, table 26.1 appears to have tapped into some more cyclical phenomenon, in the vague sense that moments of electoral realignment seem to have shown a rough periodicity in the past.[2] It is extremely plausible to imagine that the loosening of partisanship in the current period renders the electorate fallow for such a major transition. Generational fault lines in the 1968 presidential vote were apparent, with older voters outside the South attending to standard "New Deal" issues of social welfare and choosing between Humphrey and Nixon on these issues in ways conventional in the 1950's, while younger voters were more attentive to issues of the 1960's, including Vietnam, the racial crisis, and campus disorder. This meant that one stream of younger voters, including many Democrats, supported Wallace, and another stream was disillusioned by nothing better than the Humphrey choice on the left. Whether a full realignment does occur depends to some degree on the policy directions pursued by the Republican Party in the next few years. Nevertheless, the "Southern strategy" and the prominence of the Agnew backlash philosophy seem calculated to appeal

[2] Burnham among others has argued that full realignments occur once every "long generation," and that some less permanent dislocation seems to appear at the midpoint of such epochs—putatively, in the data of table 26.1, at the time of the 1952 election. See W. D. Burnham, *Critical Elections and the Mainsprings of American Politics* (New York: Norton, 1970), chap. 1.

both to the South generally and to many working-class elements elsewhere, previously Democratic, while alienating liberal Republicans of the more cosmopolitan urban sectors of the country.

At the same time, one can predict with some confidence that partisanship will not re-solidify immediately, and is likely in the aggregate to show signs of further loosening well toward 1980. This expectation hinges on the simple fact, thoroughly documented, that as a pure life-cycle phenomenon, young voters come into the electorate with much weaker levels of partisanship than more habituated voters. Under normal circumstances, there are about twice as many "independents" among people aged 21 to 24 than among those over 70.[3] The 1968 election was the first to be affected at all by the massive postwar boom in the birth rate, and some small portion of the increase in independents can be traced to this fact. Still, the impact of the young moving into the electorate was slight in 1968 compared to what may be expected over the next decade. Extension of the vote to 18-year-olds nationwide would simply speed and strengthen these effects. Thus, quite independent of political discontent or the attractiveness of party fidelity, the evolution of the age table for the country will produce an electorate that shows higher partisan volatility in the next decade.

Nonetheless, it would seem quite inappropriate to imagine that we have witnessed in 1966 and 1968 an "end of party" in American electoral politics. For one thing, even with the loosened levels of partisanship of 1968, party allegiance remained far and away the strongest determinant of most political cognitions and behavioral choices in the electorate. It could wane many times as much again without losing its dominant role. The fact that the influx of young voters is about to lower levels of conventional partisanship further means that we will hear a good deal about the "end of party" in the 1970's. And indeed, it is possible that, overlaid on the realigning discontents of the late 1960's, there are some seeds of a more truly secular decline of party fidelity. There is, however, no very conclusive evidence of such a development at this time. If we wish to consider irreversible trends in the nature of the country's electorate, we must turn in other directions.

---

[3] See Philip E. Converse, "Of Time and Partisan Stability," *Comparative Political Studies*, 2(1969):139–71.

IV. HISTORICAL AND INSTITUTIONAL PERSPECTIVES

27. Has Voting Changed Historically?

Numbers have invaded the study of history, and it will never be the same. "Cliometricians" like Fogel and Engerman have called into question time-honored beliefs about the economics of slave history and plantation life.[1] In political history, researchers have questioned such "truths" as the outpouring of democratic participation in the Jacksonian era. This represents a loss of sorts. Beard's colorful statement that "the roaring flood of the new democracy was . . . [by 1824] foaming perilously near the crest . . .," represents more mellifluous prose than McCormack's careful analysis of electoral statistics from that era.[2] Yet the gains in precision, in verifiability, and, presumably, in correctness of interpretation more than make up for what is lost.

But numbers must be interpreted. This is amply illustrated in the controversy surrounding the reinterpretation of slave history by a quantitative analysis. It is also well-documented in the controversy over changes in the American electorate during the past century, represented here in chapters 28 and 29. With the charting of the contemporary American electorate well

---

[1] Robert W. Fogel and Stanley L. Engerman, *Time on the Cross: The Economics of American Negro Slavery* (Boston: Little, Brown, 1974).

[2] Charles A. and Mary R. Beard, as quoted in Richard P. McCormack, "New Perspectives on Jacksonian Politics," *American Historical Review,* 65(1960):288–301.

under way, interest has turned to other countries and to our own history to see whether our understanding of and interpretation of elections in the current United States can be applied in other circumstances. The historical applications have generated considerable controversy about the nature of the nineteenth- and twentieth-century electorates and about the causes of the changes that have been observed. Unlike some of the other controversies represented in this book, the factions in this one are relatively well defined and few in number. Resolution of the debate seems relatively far off or impossible, but, nonetheless, it has extreme intrinsic interest and bears importantly on our understanding of electoral behavior and its causes. Hence, it is well worth considering.

The Twentieth Century:
Large Decline of Party by a Business Take-over

It is fun, if nothing else, to think of the nineteenth-century electorate as being extremely informed and politically active. Part of the charm of Lincoln's Gettysburg Address is that it was so short and roughhewn in contrast to the lengthy, polished oratory of the main speaker of the day, Edward Everett. "Politics as recreation played a much larger role in most people's lives in the earlier periods," to use Sellers's words. One has the distinct impression that "the press was almost exclusively devoted to political debate, that the populace submitted with apparent willingness to far more and infinitely longer political speeches than even the most politically avid moderns would endure, and that local party activity was more intense than at present."[3]

On a more serious and more quantitative level, one can cite numerous statistics which tend to support the view of the nineteenth-century electorate as being unusually involved in political affairs. Jensen has written delightfully about some of this activity. Newspaper statistics are so numerous that it is difficult to know which figures to select, but the statistic that "329 cities in 1880 (roughly speaking all those above 7,000 population) possessed *five or more* newspapers, including both dailies and weeklies," conveys the right impression.[4] In regard to political discussions, Jensen cites the 1892 election in Indiana, in which "the two parties held 5,000 schoolhouse meetings in the last week of the campaign alone."[5] As something of a surprise, he notes that "by 1880 statewide polls [though not of the modern kind] were common, and critical battlefields were surveyed two and three times during

---

[3] Charles Sellers, "The Equilibrium Cycle in Two-Party Politics," *Public Opinion Quarterly*, 29(1965):16–37, fn. 26. It should be pointed out that Sellers is one of the most prominent quantitative political historians and that the quotation is from a footnote.

[4] Richard Jensen, "American Election Campaigns: A Theoretical and Historical Typology," paper presented at the annual meeting of the Midwest Political Science Association, Chicago, 1968, p. 6.

[5] *Ibid.*, p. 17.

a campaign. In 1908, the Republican national chairman organized 50,000 poll takers to interview 5 million voters in 20 states. . . . The chairman recorded the information sent in by his workers on an elaborate card index that was the wonder of journalists and politicians both."[6]

Statistics such as these, though they seem to summarize the subjective impressions of many historians, might be criticized as relatively unsystematic. For this reason, Burnham's careful analysis of "The Changing Shape of the American Political Universe" represented a major contribution and in many respects initiated serious discussions of the apparent decline of the party in the electorate. It is this article which is reprinted in chapter 28. Burnham reported that since 1896 there has been a decline in voting turnout, an increase in split-ticket voting, much less voting in off years than during presidential elections ("drop-off"), a tendency to vote only for the highest offices on the ballot ("roll-off"), and greater partisan vote swing between elections.

At first glance, it would seem most difficult to dispute these statistics. Some of Burnham's conclusions are admittedly based on information from a small number of states, but his turnout figures, for example, are based on data from the entire country. Moreover, he shows that the decline after 1896 was evident in nonsouthern as well as southern states, so that it could not be attributed simply to disenfranchisement of blacks. Drop-off figures are similarly given for the entire country. One could quarrel with Burnham's measure of split-ticket voting,[7] which was necessitated by the absence of survey data from that era. But taken together, it initially seems clear that there has been a considerable change in political participation in the present century.

If participation was indeed considerably higher in the nineteenth century, Burnham correctly observes that this has important implications for understanding electoral behavior. One of the most interesting implications is the relationship between education and political participation. Since the advent of systematic polling in the 1930's, studies have almost invariably shown a strong relationship between number of years of schooling and degree of political participation. But if participation was uniformly high during the nineteenth century, at a time when fewer people were educated than at present, the relationship between education and participation itself must have been different or absent. Theoretically, this is possible, but why a relationship which is so widespread now—and one which is so eminently understandable—should have been absent a century ago is an interesting puzzle. Similarly, if participation was very high, the relationship between rising and falling turnout and the amplitude of partisan swings would necessarily differ in the two centuries.

---

[6] *Ibid.*, p. 4. This spills over into the twentieth century, but then historical events never fall into time periods quite the way quantitative analysts would like.

[7] See Andrew T. Cowart, "A Cautionary Note on Aggregate Indicators of Split Ticket Voting," *Political Methodology*, 1(1974):109–30.

Aside from the question of what behavioral changes have occurred is the interpretation of change. Following the depression of 1893, the Democratic party turned in 1896 from Cleveland to the populist William Jennings Bryan. A political realignment followed, one which lined up Democratic strength in the South, West, and poorer rural areas against Republican strength in the East, cities, and business elites. Importantly, this shift made the Republicans the dominant party throughout the first decades of this century, in contrast to the even party balance in the last decades of the previous century. Burnham sees the decline of competition between the parties, as well as other changes such as judicial decisions, as a lessening of the alternatives open to voters. The leaders of the industrial revolution, in effect, stole the electoral system away from the people without doing away with the procedures and traditions of a democratic system. This capture of the electoral system by the elite led to the beginning of the decline of the party system. With the importance of their decisions greatly reduced, voters gradually became alienated and regarded their participation as being relatively meaningless. Party loyalty similarly became weaker. This argument leads directly into Burnham's prediction of "the end of parties" in the current era, discussed in the previous section of this book.

Other interpretations are fully possible. Jensen and Kleppner emphasized the role of religious-ethnic variables in the latter part of the nineteenth century.[8] Kleppner sees these variables as continuing in importance throughout the 1890's. Jensen agrees with Burnham that a transition in politics was occurring in the 1890's, but differs substantially on the nature of that change. Jensen attributes the change largely to William McKinley, suggesting that McKinley brought an end to the religious battles of the previous years and introduced a politics of pluralism in which a broad coalition of interests could all benefit by working together to achieve electoral success. Importantly, as Rusk points out, Jensen "sees the consequences of the 1896 election as good, not bad," with McKinley "dampening and eventually stopping the religious wars by ousting the pietists from the party and starting a new pluralist politics in which groups learn to bargain, compromise and get along with one another."[9]

Thus we have a view of a nineteenth-century electorate that was active and informed compared with a twentieth-century electorate in which participation, and particularly partisanship, has declined. Why that change came about is a matter of some contention, with Burnham emphasizing economic variables and Jensen emphasizing the movement to a pluralist style of politics. Considerable dispute, however, has arisen over the extent of the partisan decay and the reasons for it, a conflict which has important

[8] Richard Jensen, *The Winning of the Midwest* (Chicago: University of Chicago Press, 1971); Paul Kleppner, *The Cross of Culture* (New York: Free Press, 1970).

[9] Jerrold G. Rusk, "The American Electoral Universe: Speculation and Evidence," *American Political Science Review*, 68(1974):1028–49, at p. 1038.

implications for our understanding of the way in which political behavior is altered. We now turn to the other side of this debate.

Little Decline of Party by Institutional Change

Disagreement exists, first of all, over precisely how large a change there was in voting behavior between the nineteenth and twentieth centuries. Taken at face value, the figures cited by Burnham make it incontrovertible that a major decline in turnout occurred at the end of the last century. However, the reliability of nineteenth-century turnout figures is open to question. The absence of personal registration systems and the party-printed unofficial ballots opened the way to a variety of forms of fraud, including "repeating votes," and "voting the graveyard." [10]

That such fraud existed, at least occasionally to a large degree, is not questioned. The question is whether such fraud sufficiently inflated turnout records so that if true figures were known, twentieth-century turnout would be little, if at all, lower than nineteenth-century turnout. [11] Unfortunately, though some of the fraud was committed openly and perhaps even served as "amusement," [12] accurate records of the amount of fraud, not surprisingly, are nonexistent. Thus the debate continues. The best conclusion at the moment is that the possibility of major fraud at least "casts some doubts on Burnham's claim of an enlightened era." [13]

Additonally, doubts have been raised about how informed and issue-conscious the voters were. Rusk points out that the strongly partisan behavior of the nineteenth-century electorate, so emphasized by Burnham, raises doubts as to just how "rationally" voters could have approached issues. [14] He reminds us that the local newspapers cited by Jensen were often little more than "propaganda rags stirring up party loyalty [rather] than conveyors of the in-depth information on the issues." [15] Similarly, Converse argues that there was a rather limited flow of information in the nineteenth century. His argument rests on more than the comparatively low levels of education at that time and allows for the possibility that informal social communications might have taken the place of today's mass media. [16] In addition, one might question the "entertainment value" of politics in the nineteenth century.

---

[10] Philip E. Converse, "Change in the American Electorate," in Angus Campbell and Philip E. Converse, eds., *The Human Meaning of Social Change* (New York: Russell Sage, 1972).

[11] Walter Dean Burnham, "Theory and Voting Research: Some Reflections on Converse's 'Change in the American Electorate,'" *American Political Science Review*, 68(1974):1002–23.

[12] Converse, "Change," p. 282.

[13] Rusk, "American Electoral Universe," p. 1033.

[14] *Ibid.*, p. 1033–34.

[15] *Ibid.*, p. 1034.

[16] Philip E. Converse, "Information Flow and the Stability of Partisan Attitudes," *Public Opinion Quarterly*, 26(1962):578–99.

Stories of heavily attended, hours-long lectures make interesting telling, but give no information about the frequency of such meetings and the attentiveness of the audience.

Serious questions can therefore be raised about the true nature and magnitude of the differences between politics in the nineteenth and twentieth centuries. Perhaps even more controversial, however, is the matter of interpreting differences that are agreed on.

The reason for a dispute is that, about 1896, changes were also occurring in the mechanics of conducting elections. In particular, the official and secret ("Australian") ballot was widely introduced about that time, as were personal registration systems. Philip Converse and Jerrold Rusk have argued that the trends which Burnham reports are due to such election reforms instead of being due to actions by the economic elite, or to a "decline of party." They attempt to prove this by careful analysis of the effects of election reforms which different states adopted at different times. The full set of analyses is found in a number of sources, but we have reprinted Rusk's paper on the Australian ballot reform here as the single most systematic, complete analysis relating to this problem. Rusk attempts to show that the changes in ballot form made split-ticket voting feasible for the first time. During the prior period, political parties distributed their own ballots, so that it was all but impossible to split a ticket. Thus, the new ballot form led directly to an increase in the incidence of split-ticket voting, more or less depending on the exact type of ballot used. Rusk also indicates that one of Burnham's other indicators—roll-off—would very likely be greater under the official ballot because this new form required greater effort on the part of the voter to vote for all offices. A separate analysis by Walker added that the type of official ballot used also affected this parameter. [17]

An analysis by Converse focuses on Burnham's other three indicators, particularly turnout. He argues that registration systems, which were most frequently introduced between 1890 and 1910, might explain the drop in turnout by a significant reduction in the amount of fraud, and by the lack of voting of those who failed to register but who would have voted otherwise (and did vote before personal registration was required). Although it is more difficult to show, the increase in drop-off and even in partisan swings might well be accounted for by a reduction of fraud and the imposition of registration. [18] In addition, Converse investigates the initiators of the reforms and suggests that there was certainly no conscious manipulation of electoral reforms by a corporate elite trying to insulate itself from the mass population. [19]

A related element of the debate over decreased turnout involves the "expanding electorate" theory—the view that enfranchising a new group de-

---

[17] Jack L. Walker, "Ballot Forms and Voter Fatigue: An Analysis of the Office Bloc and Party Column Ballots," *Midwest Journal of Political Science*, 10(1966):448–63.

[18] Converse, "Change," pp. 281–95.

[19] *Ibid.*, pp. 295–300.

presses overall turnout since many members of that new group (particularly older members who grew up in an era in which voting was not their business) will not vote immediately. This theory would explain the decline in turnout around 1920 by the implementation of women's suffrage. An analysis by Rusk and Stucker suggests that there was an immediate 10 percent decline in turnout associated with that reform. [20]

The debate between Burnham on the one side and Converse and Rusk on the other has continued in the Letter to the Editor columns of the *American Political Science Review*, Burnham's book on *Critical Elections and the Mainspring of American Politics*, and, more recently, an exchange in the September, 1974, *American Political Science Review*, which includes fresh analysis by Burnham, a comment by Converse, an integrative essay by Rusk, and rejoinder by Burnham. Burnham accepts the suggestion that institutional factors did apparently play some role in the changes he observed, but he argues that "the systemic factors at work during these periods were far broader in their scope and far heavier in their impact than any single change in the rules of the game or, in all probability, of all such things put together." [21]

This debate involves historical and institutional analysis, two areas which are too rarely explored in political science. To Converse and Rusk, changes in voting statistics need further interpretation only if they cannot be explained in terms of changes in the legal and institutional circumstances. Yet, for Burnham, the legal and institutional changes themselves have causes, and he argues that the changes were brought about by a capitalist elite which adopted reforms such as registration systems to weaken the opposition and capture control of the government. It is an argument over historical causes of reforms, the extent of vote fraud in earlier periods of history, the value of legal and institutional explanations of political change, and the extent to which such change helps explain the current trends. It is a dispute over the condition of the American electorate—whether it is deteriorating or improving and how it arrived at its present state.

Increasing Nationalization of Politics

Burnham's main thesis is that parties began to decline at the end of the previous century and continue to do so today. Converse and Rusk challenge this interpretation of twentieth-century trends and provide an alternate explanation. If parties did not decline, then how have they changed in the course of the last seventy to eighty years? Is there any way in which they could be said to have increased in vitality?

---

[20] Jerrold G. Rusk and John J. Stucker, "The Effect of Legal-Institutional Factors on Voting Participation: An Historical Analysis," paper presented at the annual meeting of the Midwest Political Science Association, 1973.

[21] Walter Dean Burnham, *Critical Elections and the Mainsprings of American Politics* (New York: Norton, 1970), p. 90.

Discussions of party decline have become so common that it is easy to overlook the ways in which political parties have gained strength. In particular, consider the entity known as the "national party." The national party was all but fiction a hundred years ago. There was no national party organization, beyond the presidential nominating convention at which delegates from the various state parties met to determine which would control the party during the presidential battle. After the election, the victorious party could use the congenial state parties to distribute patronage, but the defeated party had no organizational existence on a national scale until it met four years later to nominate a new presidential candidate. Today, the national parties maintain full-time organizations in Washington between, as well as during, election campaigns. They transact business and represent the parties on a continuous basis. If today's national parties look weak, they may still be infinitely stronger than the all-but-nonexistent national parties of the last century.

Concomitantly with these changes, the development of a modern communications system has helped nationalize politics. Presidential candidates cannot advocate different policies in different parts of the country since the media instantaneously transmit their proposals across the entire nation. The media have become so centralized that the local congressman is likely to receive less coverage than the theoretically more distant presidential contenders. As a result, national affairs become prominent and local issues recede.

Discussions of the nationalization of American politics often center on the so-called convergence of the South. The Civil War put the South into the Democratic camp where it remained solidly until 1948. Gradually, southern states began voting Republican, at least at the presidential level. Finally, by the 1964, 1968, and 1972 elections, the South was voting less Democratic for president than the rest of the nation. Yet in terms of party identification (and usually of voting below the presidential level), the South remains more Democratic than the non-South. Pomper, for example, reports 1972 figures of 50 percent Democratic identification in the South versus 37 percent Democratic in the non-South.[22] If the South has remained distinctive, it also shows signs of merging with the rest of the nation, for the 50 percent Democrat figure for 1972 is below a comparable 61 percent figure for 1960[23] and about a 68 percent figure for 1952.[24]

How nationalized is American politics? This question is addressed by Stokes in chapter 30. He considers the relative influence of district, state, and national factors on the congressional vote and on turnout in different regions and different years. His chief conclusions are that there has been a decline over the years in constituency influence on turnout and partisan

---

[22] Gerald M. Pomper, *Voters' Choice* (New York: Dodd, Mead, 1975), p. 29.
[23] *Ibid.*, p. 28.
[24] Adapted from Angus Campbell, Gerald Gurin, and Warren E. Miller, *The Voter Decides* (Evanston, Ill.: Row, Peterson, 1954), p. 93.

division in the United States, but that the constituency component is still greater in the United States than in Great Britain.[25] This, along with the decline in competitiveness in the United States, has kept our party system from becoming totally centralized.

Unfortunately, Stokes's conclusions have not been adequately incorporated into historical accounts of the American electorate, though Rusk notes that Jensen's and Kleppner's works, referred to above, largely emphasize local influences on elections while Burnham's theory emphasizes national economic influences.[26] Stokes's analysis is pregnant with implications for both historical and comparative studies of elections. We hope that in the future the historical changes and inter-nation differences it documents can be more fully incorporated into election research.

Stokes suggests that at the voter level, as well as the organizational level referred to above, the national parties have been strengthened over recent decades and local parties have been weakened. The nationalization of American politics is an important countertheme to Burnham's discussion of the decline of parties. To argue that American parties are dying is to miss an essential element in their evolution.

Conclusions

As promised, the disagreement which forms the heart of this section is not easily resolved, and we shall not try to do so here. If studies of contemporary events yield the controversies discussed in the other sections of this book, it is perhaps not surprising that historical interpretations are also controversial. Nonetheless, an explanation of our political present requires an understanding of the political past, and predictions of the future must be based on an analysis of the events that led to the present. Such analysis must not only be historical, but also both institutional (as when Rusk investigates the effects of various reforms) and comparative (as when Stokes compares American and British statistics).

What makes this sort of study so intriguing is that one cannot automatically assume that patterns of thought and events found in contemporary America necessarily occur either in other periods in our own history or in other countries. We hope to find consistent patterns, but the fact that a relationship exists at one time for one country does not mean it is universal.

Modern voting studies for the United States have developed a complex theory, one that has implications for earlier periods in history as well as for other countries. But the analysis of voting behavior cannot be limited either

---

[25] For a critique of the Stokes method, see Richard S. Katz, "The Attribution of Variance in Electoral Returns: An Alternative Measurement," *American Political Science Review,* 67(1973):817–28. However, Katz's point, if accepted, would probably not alter the direction of the trend observed by Stokes.

[26] Rusk, "American Electoral Universe," esp. p. 1032.

in time or in space if we are to achieve a broad-level theory. The historical analyses in this section begin to open up the time parameter. Simultaneously, scholars have been studying voting behavior in more than a dozen other countries in order to determine the spatial limitations of our understanding of voting. Our own space restrictions preclude us from reprinting any of the cross-national voting behavior research here (except for the comparisons made by Stokes), but that is not meant to disparage its importance in the slightest. Historians and comparative scholars are now using quantitative voting analysis to understand voting behavior at other points in time and space. This interest and their insights should pay off eventually in terms of a greater understanding of our own present. We cannot yet foresee the likely conclusions, though we are willing to place one bet with assurance— that controversies will remain, at least so long as elections are conducted.

Further Readings

Historical Trends and Their Interpretations

Philip E. Converse, "Information Flow and the Stability of Partisan Attitudes," *Public Opinion Quarterly,* 26(1962):578-99. Discusses the implications of absence of national media in nineteenth-century America.

Walter Dean Burnham, *Critical Elections and the Mainsprings of American Politics* (New York: Norton, 1970). Burnham's full analysis of historical trends in voting.

Walter Dean Burnham, "Theory and Voting Research: Some Reflections on Converse's 'Change in the American Electorate,'" *American Political Science Review,* 68(1974):1000-23. Argues that institutional ballot changes are not enough to explain the voting shifts he discovered.

Jerrold G. Rusk, "The American Electoral Universe: Speculation and Evidence," *American Political Science Review,* 68(1974):1028-49. Reply to Burnham, summarizing the controversy with new data on historical trends in the South and on women's suffrage.

Institutional Effects Relating to Voting

Jack L. Walker, "Ballot Forms and Voter Fatigue: An Analysis of the Office Block and Party Column Ballots," *Midwest Journal of Political Science,* 10(1966):448-63. How the form of the ballot affects actual voting.

J. Morgan Kousser, *Shaping of Southern Politics* (New Haven: Yale University Press, 1974). Effects of suffrage restriction on one-party dominance in the South.

Comparative Studies of Institutional Effects

Douglas W. Rae, *The Political Consequences of Electoral Laws,* rev. ed., (New Haven: Yale University Press, 1971). Cross-national study of effects of election laws on party systems.

Edward R. Tufte, "The Relationship Between Seats and Votes in Two-Party Systems," *American Political Science Review*, 67(1973):540–54. Analysis of how the number of legislative seats won by a party depends on their national vote totals.

Discussions of Possible Effects of Electoral College Reform

Neal R. Peirce, *The People's President* (New York: Simon and Schuster, 1968). Discusses problems of electoral college. Supports direct election of the president.

Wallace S. Sayre and Judith H. Parris, *Voting for President* (Washington, D.C.: Brookings Institution, 1970). Considers alternative reform proposals. Argues in favor of the electoral vote system.

Lawrence D. Longley and Alan G. Braun, *The Politics of Electoral College Reform* (New Haven: Yale University Press, 1972). Compares effects of electoral college with direct election of president.

28. The Changing Shape of the American Political Universe

WALTER DEAN BURNHAM

In the infancy of a science the use even of fairly crude methods of analysis and description can produce surprisingly large increments of knowledge if new perspectives are brought to bear upon available data. Such perspectives not infrequently require both a combination of methodologies and a critical appraisal of the limitations of each. The emergence of American voting-behavior studies over the last two decades constitutes a good case in point. Studies based on aggregate election statistics have given us invaluable insights into the nature of secular trends in the distribution of the party vote, and have also provided us with useful theory concerning such major phenomena as critical elections. [1] Survey research has made significant contributions to the understanding of motivational forces at work upon the individual voter. As it matures, it is now reaching out to grapple with problems which involve the political system as a whole. [2]

Source: *American Political Science Review,* 59(1965):7-28. Reprinted with permission of the publisher.

[1] The leading work of this sort thus far has been done by the late V. O. Key, Jr. See e.g., his "A Theory of Critical Elections," *Journal of Politics,* 17(1955):3-18, and his *American State Politics* (New York: Knopf, 1956). See also such quantitatively oriented monographs as Perry Howard, *Political Tendencies in Louisiana, 1812-1952* (Baton Rouge: Louisiana State University Press, 1957).

[2] The most notable survey-research effort to date to develop politically relevant theory regarding American voting behavior is Angus Campbell, Philip E. Converse, Warren E. Miller and Donald E. Stokes, *The American Voter* (New York: Wiley, 1960), especially chap. 20.

Not at all surprisingly, a good deal of well publicized conflict has arisen between aggregationists and survey researchers. The former attack the latter for their failure to recognize the limitations of an ahistorical and episodic method, and for their failure to focus their attention upon matters of genuine concern to students of politics.[3] The latter insist, on the other hand, that survey research alone can study the primary psychological and motivational building blocks out of which the political system itself is ultimately constructed. Not only are both parties to the controversy partly right, but each now seems to be becoming quite sensitive to the contributions which the other can make. As survey scholars increasingly discover that even such supposedly well established characteristics of the American voter as his notoriously low awareness of issues can be replaced almost instantaneously under the right circumstances by an extremely pronounced sensitivity to an issue, the importance of the time dimension and factors of social context so viewed become manifest.[4] Students of aggregate voting behavior, on the other hand, are turning to the data and methods of survey research to explore the structure and characteristics of contemporary public opinion.[5] A convergence is clearly under way. One further sign of it is the construction of the first national election-data archive, now under way at the Survey Research Center of the University of Michigan.[6] The completion of this archive and the conversion of its basic data into a form suitable for machine processing should provide the material basis for a massive breakthrough in the behavioral analysis of American political history over the last century and a half.

If controversies over method accompany the development of disciplines, so too does the strong tendency of the research mainstream to bypass signif-

---

[3] V. O. Key, Jr., "The Politically Relevant in Surveys," *Public Opinion Quarterly,* 24(1960):54–61; V. O. Key, Jr., and Frank Munger, "Social Determinism and Electoral Decision: The Case of Indiana," in Eugene Burdick and Arthur J. Brodbeck, eds., *American Voting Behavior* (Glencoe, Ill.: The Free Press, 1959), pp. 281–99.

[4] Warren E. Miller and Donald E. Stokes, "Constituency Influence in Congress," *American Political Science Review,* 57(1963):15–56. The authors observe that in the 1958 Hays-Alford congressional race in Arkansas, the normally potential nature of constituency sanctions against representatives was transferred under the overriding pressure of the race issue into an actuality which resulted in Hays' defeat by a write-in vote for his opponent. The normally low issue- and candidate-consciousness among the electorate was abruptly replaced by a most untypically intense awareness of the candidates and their relative positions on this issue.

For an excellent cross-polity study of voting behavior based on comparative survey analysis, see Robert R. Alford, *Party and Society* (Chicago: Rand McNally, 1963).

[5] V. O. Key, Jr., *Public Opinion and American Democracy* (New York: Knopf, 1961), based largely on survey-research data at the University of Michigan.

[6] This effort, to which the author was enabled to contribute, thanks to a Social Science Research Council grant for 1963-64, has been supported by the Council and by the National Science Foundation. This article is in no sense an integral part of that larger project. But it is proper to acknowledge gratefully here that the S.S.R.C., by making it possible for me to spend a year at the Survey Research Center, has helped to provide conditions favorable to writing it. Thanks are also due to Angus Campbell, Philip E. Converse, Donald E. Stokes and Warren E. Miller for their comments and criticisms. They bear no responsibility for the defects of the final product.

icant areas of potential inquiry, thus leaving many "lost worlds" in its wake. One such realm so far left very largely unexplored in the literature of American politics centers around changes and continuities in the gross size and shape of this country's active voting universe over the past century. Key, to be sure, made contributions of the greatest significance to our understanding of the changing patterns of party linkage between voters and government. Moreover, he called attention to the need for quantitative analysis of political data other than the partisan division of the vote for leading offices.[7] E. E. Schattschneider's discussion of the struggle over the scope of political conflict and his functional analysis of the American party system remain a stimulus to further research—not least in the direction of examining the aggregate characteristics of the American electorate over time.[8] Other recent studies, for example of the turnout of voters in Canada and Indiana, have added to our knowledge of contemporary patterns of mass political involvement.[9] The fact remains, however, that no systematic analysis over lengthy time periods has yet been made of the massive changes of relative size and characteristics in the American voting universe, despite their obvious relevance to an understanding of the evolving political system as a whole.

This article does not purport to be that systematic study. It is, rather, a tentative reconnaissance into the untapped wealth of a whole range of political data, undertaken in the hope of showing concretely some of the potentialities of their study. The primary objective here is the preliminary exploration of the scope of changes since the mid-nineteenth century in turnout and other criteria of voting participation, and the possible substantive implications of such changes.

There is also a second objective. The day is not far distant when a major effort will be undertaken to relate the findings of survey research to contemporary aggregate data and then to examine the aggregate data of past generations in the light of these derived relationships. Before such inquiry is undertaken, it will be a matter of some importance to ascertain whether and to what extent the basic findings of survey research about the present

[7] V. O. Key, Jr., *American State Politics*, pp. 71-73, 197-216.

[8] E. E. Schattschneider, *Party Government* (New York: Holt, Rinehart, & Winston, 1942) and *The Semi-Sovereign People* (New York: Holt, Rinehart, & Winston, 1960), pp. 78-96.

[9] Howard A. Scarrow, "Patterns of Voter Turnout in Canada," *Midwest Journal of Political Science*, 5(1961):351-64; James A. Robinson and William Standing, "Some Correlates of Voter Participation: The Case of Indiana," *Journal of Politics*, 22(1960):96-111. Both articles—one involving a political system outside of but adjacent to the United States—indicate patterns of contemporary participation which seem at variance with the conclusions of survey studies regarding the behavior of the American electorate. In Canada rural turnout is higher than urban, and no clear-cut pattern of drop-off between federal and provincial elections exists. Voter participation in Indiana apparently does not increase with the competitiveness of the electoral situation, and does increase with the rurality of the election jurisdiction. With the possible exception of the relationship between competitiveness and turnout, all of these are characteristics associated with nineteenth-century voting behavior in the United States; see below.

American electorate are actually relevant to earlier periods of our political history. Firm conclusions here as elsewhere must await much more comprehensive and detailed study. Even so, enough can be learned from the contours of the grosser data to warrant posting a few warning signs.

I

Several criteria of voting participation have been employed in this analysis: (1) estimated turnout; (2) drop-off; (3) roll-off; (4) split-ticket voting; (5) mean partisan swing. Turnout, the most indispensable of these criteria, is also unfortunately the "softest." A number of errors of estimate can arise from the necessary use of census data. For example, interpolations of estimates for intercensal years can produce significant error when abnormally large increases or decreases in population are bunched together within a few years. Estimates of the alien component in the total adult male population must also necessarily remain quite speculative for the censuses from 1880 through 1900, and are impossible to secure from published census data prior to 1870. No doubt this helps explain why students of voting-behavior research have avoided this area. But we need not reject these admittedly imprecise data altogether, because of their imperfections, when secular changes in turnout levels and variabilities from election to election are of far too great a magnitude to be reasonably discounted on the basis of estimate error.[10]

Moreover, the other criteria employed in this study not only share a very similar directional flow over time, but are directly derived from the voting statistics themselves. Free from the estimate-error problem, they are ordinarily quite consistent with the turnout data.[11] What is called "drop-off" here is the familiar pattern of decline in the total vote between presidential and succeeding off-year elections. The drop-off figures usually presented below are reciprocals of the percentage of the presidential-year total vote

---

[10] In computing turnout data, note that until approximately 1920 the criteria for eligibility to vote differed far more widely from state to state than they do now. In a number of states west of the original thirteen—for example, in Michigan until 1894 and in Wisconsin until 1908—aliens who had merely declared their intention to become citizens were permitted to vote. Woman suffrage was also extended piecemeal for several decades prior to the general enfranchisement of 1920. The turnout estimates derived here have been adjusted, so far as the census data permit, to take account of such variations.

[11] If one computes the off-year total vote of the years 1950–62 as a percentage of the total vote cast in the preceding presidential election, a virtually identical correspondence is reached with estimated off-year turnout as a percentage of turnout in the immediately preceding presidential year.

Year	Total Off-Year Vote as % of Vote in Last Presidential Year	Estimated Off-Year Turnout as % of Turnout in Last Presidential Year
1950	82.9	80.4
1954	69.2	67.5
1958	73.9	72.1
1962	74.4	73.6

which is cast in the immediately following off-year election. If the total vote for the two successive elections is the same, drop-off is zero; if the total vote in the off-year election exceeds that cast in the immediately preceding presidential election, drop-off is negative. Secular increases in the amplitude of drop-off could be associated with such factors as a declining relative visibility or salience of off-year elections, or with an increasing component of active voters who are only marginally involved with the voting process as such.

"Roll-off" measures the tendency of the electorate to vote for "prestige" offices but not for lower offices on the same ballot and at the same election. If only 90 percent of those voting for the top office on the ticket also vote for the lesser statewide office receiving fewest votes at the same election, for example, the roll-off figure stands at 10 percent. Secular increases in this criterion of voting participation could be associated with such variables as a growing public indifference to elections for administrative offices which might well be made appointive, or with a growing proportion of peripheral voters in the active electorate; or with changes in the form of ballots. Split-ticket voting has been measured rather crudely here as the difference between the highest and lowest percentages of the two-party vote cast for either party among the array of statewide offices in any given election. Zero on this scale would correspond to absolute uniformity in the partisan division of the vote for all offices at the same election. The amplitude of partisan swing is computed in this study without reference to the specific partisan direction of the swing, and is derived from the mean percentage of the two-party vote cast for either party among all statewide races in the same election. Both of these latter criteria are more directly related to changes in the strength of partisan linkage between voters and government than are the others employed in this study.

Two major assumptions underlie the use of these criteria. (1) If a secular decline in turnout occurs, and especially if it is associated with increases in drop-off and roll-off, we may infer that the active voting universe: (a) is shrinking in size relative to the potential voting universe; and (b) is also decomposing as a relative increase in its component of peripherally involved voters occurs. Opposite implications, of course, would be drawn from increases in turnout accompanied by decreases in these rough indices of voter peripherality. (2) If split-ticket voting and the amplitude of partisan swings are also increasing over time, we may infer that a decline in party-oriented voting is taking place among a growing minority of voters. Reductions in these criteria would suggest a resurgence of party-oriented voting.

NO

A recent study by Angus Campbell tends to support the view that the above criteria are actually related to the component of marginal voters and voters with relatively weak partisan attachments in today's active electorate. [12] Campbell argues that surge and decline in voting participation and in

---

[12] Angus Campbell, "Surge and Decline: A Study of Electoral Change," *Public Opinion Quarterly*, 24(1960):397–418.

partisan distribution of the vote result from two major factors: the entrance into the active electorate of peripherally involved voters who tend to vote disproportionately for such beneficiaries of partisan surges as President Eisenhower, and then abstain from the polls in subsequent low-stimulus elections; and the temporary movement of core voters with relatively low levels of party identification away from their nominal party allegiance, followed by their return to that allegiance in subsequent low-stimulus elections. Campbell's study reveals that split-ticket voting in the 1956 election tended to be heavily concentrated among two groups of voters: those who voted Republican for President in 1956 and did not vote in 1958, and those who voted Republican in 1956 but Democratic in 1958—in other words, among those with peripheral involvement in the political process itself and those with borderline partisan commitments. Moreover, roll-off—the failure to vote a complete ticket in 1956—was heavily concentrated among the non-voters of 1958. It is also suggestive that the level of drop-off in Campbell's panel from 1956 to 1958, 23 percent, very closely approximates the level of drop-off as measured by the aggregate voting data. [13]

II

Even the crudest form of statistical analysis makes it abundantly clear that the changes which have occurred in the relative size and shape of the active electorate in this country have not only been quantitatively enormous but have followed a directional course which seems to be unique in the contemporary universe of democratic polities. In the United States these transformations over the past century have involved devolution, a dissociation from politics as such among a growing segment of the eligible electorate and an apparent deterioration of the bonds of party linkage between electorate and government. More precisely, these trends were overwhelmingly prominent between about 1900 and 1930, were only very moderately reversed following the political realignment of 1928–1936, and now seem to be increasing once again along several dimensions of analysis. Such a pattern of development is pronouncedly retrograde compared with those which have obtained almost everywhere else in the Western world during the past century.

Probably the best-known aspect of the changing American political universe has been the long-term trend in national voter turnout: a steep decline from 1900 to about 1930, followed by a moderate resurgence since that time. [14] As the figures in table 28.1 indicate, nationwide turnout down through 1900 was quite high by contemporary standards—comparing favorably in presidential years with recent levels of participation in Western Europe—and was also marked by very low levels of drop-off. A good deal ·of the precipitate decline in turnout after 1896 can, of course, be attributed to the disfranchisement of Negroes in the South and the consolidation of its

---

[13] *Ibid.,* p. 413. The percentage of drop-off from 1956 to 1958, as computed from aggregate voting data, was 25.6 percent.

[14] See, e.g., Robert E. Lane, *Political Life* (Glencoe, Ill., Free Press, 1959), pp. 18–26.

Table 28.1 Decline and Partial Resurgence: Mean Levels of National Turnout and Drop-Off by Periods, 1848–1962*

Period (Presidential Years)	Mean Estimated Turnout (%)	Period (Off-Years)	Mean Estimated Turnout (%)	Mean Drop-Off (%)
1848–1872	75.1	1850–1874	65.2	7.0
1876–1896	78.5	1878–1898	62.8	15.2
1900–1916	64.8	1902–1918	47.9	22.4
1920–1928	51.7	1922–1930	35.2	28.7
1932–1944	59.1	1934–1946	41.0	27.8
1948–1960	60.3	1950–1962	44.1	24.9

*Off-year turnout data based on total vote for congressional candidates in off years.

Table 28.2 Sectionalism and Participation: Mean Turnout in Southern and Non-Southern States in Presidential Elections, 1868–1960

Period	Mean Turnout: Eleven Southern States (%)	Period	Mean Turnout: Non-Southern States (%)
1868–1880	69.4	1868–1880	82.6
1884–1896	61.1	1884–1896	85.4
1900 (transition)	43.4	1900	84.1
1904–1916	29.8	1904–1916	73.6
1920–1948	24.7	1920–1932	60.6
1952–1960	38.8	1936–1960	68.0

one-party regime. But as table 28.2 and figure 28.1 both reveal, non-Southern states not only shared this decline but also have current turnout rates which remain substantially below nineteenth-century levels. [15]

The persistence of mediocre rates of American voting turnout into the present political era is scarcely news. It forms so obvious and continuing a problem of our democracy that a special presidential commission has recently given it intensive study. [16] Two additional aspects of the problem, however, emerge from a perusal of the foregoing data. In the first place, it is quite apparent that the political realignment of the 1930's, while it restored

---

[15] There are, of course, very wide divergences in turnout rates even among non-Southern states. Some of them, like Idaho, New Hampshire and Utah, have presidential-year turnouts which compare very favorably with European levels of participation. A detailed analysis of these differences remains to be made. It should prove of the utmost importance in casting light upon the relevance of current forms of political organization and partisan alignments to differing kinds of electorates and political subsystems in the United States.

[16] *Report of the President's Commission on Registration and Voting Participation* (Washington, D.C., 1963), esp. pp. 5–9. Hereafter cited as *Report.*

Figure 28.1 Patterns of turnout: United States, 1860–1964, by region, and selected Western European nations, 1948–1961.

two-party competition to many states outside the South, did not stimulate turnout to return in most areas to nineteenth-century levels. Even if the mere existence of competitiveness precludes such low levels of turnout as are found in the South today, or as once prevailed in the Northern industrial states, it falls far short of compelling a substantially full turnout under present-day conditions. Second, drop-off on the national level has shown markedly little tendency to recede in the face of increases in presidential-year turnout over the last thirty years. The component of peripheral voters in the active electorate has apparently undergone a permanent expansion from about one-sixth in the late nineteenth century to more than one-quarter in recent decades. If, as seems more than likely, the political regime established after 1896 was largely responsible for the marked relative decline in the active voting universe and the marked increase in peripherality among those who still occasionally voted, it is all the more remarkable that the dramatic political realignment of the 1930's has had such little effect in reversing these trends.

At least two major features of our contemporary polity, to be sure, are obviously related to the presently apparent ceiling on turnout. First, the American electoral system creates a major "double hurdle" for prospective voters which does not exist in Western Europe: the requirements associated with residence and registration, usually entailing periodic re-registration at frequent intervals, and the fact that elections are held on a normal working day in this employee society rather than on Sundays or holidays. [17] Second, it is very probably true that nineteenth-century elections were major sources of entertainment in an age unblessed by modern mass communications, so that it is more difficult for politicians to gain and keep public attention today than it was then. [18] Yet if American voters labor under the most cumbersome sets of procedural requirements in the Western world, this in itself is a datum which tends to support Schattschneider's thesis that the struggle for democracy is still being waged in the United States and that there are profound resistances within the political system itself to the adoption of needed procedural reforms. [19] Moreover, there are certain areas—such as all of Ohio outside the metropolitan counties and cities of at least 15,000 population—where no registration procedures have ever been established, but where no significant deviation from the patterns outlined here appears to exist. Finally, while it may well be true that the partial displacement by TV and other means of entertainment has inhibited expansion of the active voting universe during the past generation, it is equally true that the structure of the American voting universe—i.e., the adult population—as it exists today was substantially formed in the period 1900-1920, *prior* to the development of such major media as the movies, radio and television.

III

As we move below the gross national level, the voting patterns discussed above stand out with far greater clarity and detail. Their divergences suggest something of the individual differences which distinguish each state subsystem from its fellows, as their uniformities indicate the universality of the broader secular trends. Five states have been selected for analysis here. During the latter part of the nineteenth century two of these, Michigan and Pennsylvania, were originally competitive states which tended to favor the Republican Party. They developed solidly one-party regimes after the realignment of 1896. These regimes were overthrown in their turn and vigorous party competition was restored in the wake of the New Deal realignment. In two other states, Ohio and New York, the 1896 alignment had no such dire consequences for two-party competition on the state level. These states have also shown a somewhat different pattern of development since the 1930's than Michigan and Pennsylvania. Our fifth state is Oklahoma, where a modified one-party system is structured heavily along sectional lines and operates in a socioeconomic context unfavorable to the classic New Deal articulation of politics along ethnic-class lines of cleavage.

Michigan politics was marked from 1894 through 1930 by the virtual

---

[17] *Ibid.,* pp. 11-14, 31-42.

[18] See, e.g., Stanley Kelly, "Elections and the Mass Media," *Law and Contemporary Problems,* 27(1962):307-26.

[19] E. E. Schattschneider, *The Semi-Sovereign People,* pp. 102-3.

eclipse of a state Democratic Party which had formerly contested elections on nearly equal terms with the Republicans. The inverse relationships developing between this emergent one-partyism on the one hand, and both the relative size of the active voting universe and the strength of party linkage on the other, stand out in especially bold relief.

A decisive shift away from the stable and substantially fully mobilized voting patterns of the nineteenth century occurred in Michigan after the realignment of 1896, with a lag of about a decade between that election and the onset of disruption in those patterns. The first major breakthrough of characteristics associated with twentieth-century American electorates occurred in the presidential year 1904, when the mean percentage Democratic for all statewide offices reached an unprecedented low of 35.6 and the rate of split-ticket voting jumped from almost zero to 17.1 percent. A steady progression of decline in turnout and party competition, accompanied by heavy increases in the other criteria of peripherality, continued down through 1930.

The scope of this transformation was virtually revolutionary. During the civil-war era scarcely 15 percent of Michigan's potential electorate appears to have been altogether outside the voting universe. About 7 percent could be classified as peripheral voters by Campbell's definition, and the remainder— more than three-quarters of the total—were core voters. Moreover, as the extremely low nineteenth-century level of split-ticket voting indicates, these active voters overwhelmingly cast party-line ballots. By the 1920's, less than one-third of the potential electorate were still core voters, while nearly one-quarter were peripheral and nearly one-half remained outside the political system altogether. Drop-off and roll-off increased sixfold during this period, while the amplitude of partisan swing approximately doubled and the split-ticket-voting rate increased by a factor of approximately eight to twelve.

For the most part these trends underwent a sharp reversal as party competition in Michigan was abruptly restored during the 1930's and organized in its contemporary mode in 1948. As the mean Democratic percentage of the

Table 28.3 Michigan, 1854–1962: Decay and Resurgence? (Percentages)

Period	Mean Turnout		Mean Drop-Off	Mean Roll-Off	Mean Split-Ticket Voting	Mean Partisan Swing	Mean % D of 2-Party Vote
	Pres. Years	Off-Years					
1854–1872	84.8	78.1	7.8	0.9	0.8	3.2	43.9
1878–1892	84.9	74.9	10.7	0.8	1.6	2.2	48.0
1894–1908	84.8	68.2	22.3	1.5	5.9	4.7	39.6
1910–1918	71.4	53.0	27.2	3.0	9.8	4.1	40.4*
1920–1930	55.0	31.5	42.9	6.0	10.0	7.3	29.8
1932–1946	63.6	47.3	25.9	6.7	6.0	7.4	47.9
1948–1962	66.9	53.6	19.1	4.1	5.8	4.9	51.0

*Democratic percentage of three-party vote in 1912 and 1914.

two-party vote increased and turnout—especially in off-year elections—showed a marked relative upswing, such characteristics of marginality as drop-off, roll-off, split-ticket voting and partisan swing declined in magnitude. Yet, as the means for the 1948–1962 period demonstrate, a large gap remains to be closed before anything like the *status quo ante* can be restored. Our criteria—except, of course, for the mean percentage Democratic of the two-party vote—have returned only to the levels of the transitional period 1900–1918. As is well known, exceptionally disciplined and issue-oriented party organizations have emerged in Michigan since 1948, and elections have been intensely competitive throughout this period.[20] In view of this, the failure of turnout in recent years to return to something approaching nineteenth-century levels is all the more impressive, as is the continuing persistence of fairly high levels of drop-off, roll-off and split-ticket voting.[21]

The Michigan data have still more suggestive implications. Campbell's discussion of surge and decline in the modern context points to a cyclical process in which peripheral voters, drawn into the active voting universe only under unusual short-term stimuli, withdraw from it again when the stimuli are removed. It follows that declines in turnout are accompanied by a marked relative increase in the component of core voters in the electorate and by a closer approximation in off years to a "normal" partisan division of the vote.[22] This presumably includes a reduction in the level of split-ticket voting as well. But the precise opposite occurred as a secular process—not only in Michigan but, it would seem, universally—during the 1900–1930 era. Declines in turnout were accompanied by substantial, continuous increases in the indices of party and voter peripherality among those elements of the adult population which remained in the political universe at all. The lower the turnout during this period, the fewer of the voters still remaining who bothered to vote for the entire slate of officers in any given election. The lower the turnout in presidential years, the greater was the drop-off gap between the total vote cast in presidential and succeeding off-year elections. The lower the turnout, the greater were the incidence of split-ticket voting and the amplitude of partisan swing. Under the enormous impact of the forces which produced these declines in turnout and party competitiveness after 1896, the component of highly involved and party-oriented core voters in the active electorate fell off at a rate which more than kept pace with the progressive shrinking of that electorate's relative size. These developments necessarily imply a limitation upon the usefulness of the surge-decline mod-

---

[20] Joseph La Palombara, *Guide to Michigan Politics* (East Lansing, Mich.: Michigan State University Press, 1960), pp. 22–35.

[21] This recalls Robinson and Standing's conclusion that voter participation in Indiana does not necessarily increase with increasing party competition. Of the eight Michigan gubernatorial elections from 1948 to 1962 only one was decided by a margin of 55 percent or more, while three were decided by margins of less than 51.5 percent of the two-party vote. Despite this intensely competitive situation, turnout—while of course much higher than in the 1920's—remains significantly below normal pre-1920 levels.

[22] Angus Campbell, "Surge and Decline," pp. 401–4.

el as it relates to secular movements prior to about 1934. They suggest, moreover, that the effects of the forces at work after 1896 to depress voter participation and to dislocate party linkage between voters and government were even more crushingly severe than a superficial perusal of the data would indicate.

Pennsylvania provides us with variations on the same theme. As in Michigan, the political realignment centering on 1896 eventually converted an industrializing state with a relatively slight but usually decisive Republican bias into a solidly one-party G.O.P. bastion. To a much greater extent than in Michigan, this disintegration of the state Democratic Party was accompanied by periodic outbursts of third-party ventures and plural party nominations of major candidates, down to the First World War. Thereafter, as in Michigan, the real contest between competing candidates and political tendencies passed into the Republican primary, where it usually remained until the advent of the New Deal. In both states relatively extreme declines in the rate of turnout were associated with the disappearance of effective two-party competition, and in both states these declines were closely paralleled by sharp increases in the indices of peripherality.

As table 28.4 demonstrates, the parallel behavior of the Michigan and Pennsylvania electorates has also extended into the present; the now-familiar pattern of increasing turnout and party competition accompanied by marked declines in our other indices has been quite visible in the Keystone State since the advent of the New Deal. On the whole, indeed, a better approximation to the *status quo ante* has been reached in Pennsylvania than in Michigan or perhaps in most other states. But despite the intense competitiveness of its present party system, this restoration remains far from complete.

A more detailed examination of turnout and variability in turnout below the statewide level raises some questions about the direct role of immigration and woman suffrage in depressing voter participation. It also uncovers a

Table 28.4 Voting Patterns in Pennsylvania, 1876–1962: Decline and Resurgence? (Percentages)

Period	Mean Turnout		Mean Drop-Off	Mean Roll-Off	Mean Split-Ticket Voting	Mean Partisan Swing	Mean % D of 2-Party Vote
	Pres. Years	Off-Years					
1876–1892	78.5	69.3	9.4	0.6	0.6	1.4	47.7
1894–1908	75.7	64.7	12.2	5.2	1.3	6.3	38.5
1910–1918	64.0	51.4	20.0	4.3	4.7	5.8	43.6*
1920–1930	50.4	39.5	28.0	5.2	8.9	7.1	32.8
1932–1948	61.5	51.9	14.9	2.2	1.4	6.1	49.0
1950–1962	67.5	56.3	12.2	1.8	3.1	3.3	49.3

*Combined major anti-Republican vote (Democrat, Keystone, Lincoln, Washington).

Table 28.5 Differentials in Aggregate Turnout and Variations of Turnout in Selected Pennsylvania Counties: Presidential Elections, 1876–1960*

County and Type	N	% Foreign Stock, 1920	1876-1896		1900-1916		1920-1932		1936-1960	
			Mean Turnout (%)	Coef. Var.	Mean Turnout (%)	Coef. Var.	Mean Turnout (%)	Coef. Var.	Mean Turnout (%)	Coef. Var.
Urban										
Allegheny	1	56.6	71.8	6.75	56.7	2.45	43.8	10.11	68.9	5.82
Philadelphia	1	54.3	85.2	4.61	72.9	6.42	50.5	12.57	68.8	4.40
Industrial-										
Mining	4	49.0	88.1	4.48	72.8	4.41	54.2	11.63	64.7	10.88
Rural	8	13.5	88.5	3.12	76.4	3.63	56.0	8.09	65.2	13.20

*The coefficient of variability is a standard statistical measure; see V. O. Key, Jr., *A Primer of Statistics for Political Scientists* (New York: Crowell, 1954), pp. 44-52. Since secular trends, where present, had to be taken into account, this coefficient appears abnormally low in the period 1900-1916. During this period many counties registered a straight-line decline in turnout from one election to the next.

significant transposition of relative voter involvement in rural areas and urban centers since about 1930.

It is frequently argued that declines in participation after the turn of the century were largely the product of massive immigration from Europe and of the advent of woman suffrage, both of which added very large and initially poorly socialized elements to the potential electorate.[23] There is no question that these were influential factors. The data in table 28.5 indicate, for example, that down until the Great Depression turnout was consistently higher and much less subject to variation in rural counties with relatively insignificant foreign-stock populations than in either the industrial-mining or metropolitan counties.

Yet two other aspects of these data should also be noted. First, the pattern of turnout decline from the 1876–1896 period to the 1900–1916 period was quite uniform among all categories of counties, though the rank order of their turnouts remained largely unchanged. It can be inferred from this that, while immigration probably played a major role in the evolution of Pennsylvania'a political system as a whole, it had no visible direct effect upon the secular decline in rural voting participation. Broader systemic factors, including but transcending the factor of immigration, seem clearly to have been at work. Second, a very substantial fraction of the total decline in turnout from

[23] Herbert Tingsten, *Political Behavior* (Stockholm, Stockholm Economic Studies, No. 7, 1937), pp. 10-36. See also Charles E. Merriam and Harold F. Gosnell, *Non-Voting* (Chicago: University of Chicago Press, 1924), pp. 26, 109-22, for a useful discussion of the effect of woman suffrage on turnout in a metropolitan area immediately following the general enfranchisement of 1920.

Table 28.6 Urban-Rural Differences in Stability of Political Involvement: 1936-60 Mean Turnout and Variability of Turnout as Percentages of 1876-96 Mean Turnout and Variability of Turnout, Pennsylvania

County and Type	N	1936-60 Turnout ——————— 1876-96 Turnout	1936-60 Variability ——————— 1876-96 Variability
Urban			
Allegheny	1	95.9	86.2
Philadelphia	1	80.8	95.4
Industrial-Mining	4	73.4	249.6
Rural	8	73.7	447.4

the 1870's to the 1920's—in some rural native-stock counties more than half—occurred *before* women were given the vote. Moreover, post-1950 turnout levels in Pennsylvania, and apparently in most other non-Southern states, have been at least as high as in the decade immediately preceding the general enfranchisement of women. If even today a higher percentage of American than European women fail to come to the polls, the same can also be said of such population groups as the poorly educated, farmers, the lower-income classes, Negroes and other deprived elements in the potential electorate. [24] In such a context woman suffrage, as important a variable as it certainly has been in our recent political history, seems to raise more analytical problems than it solves.

Particularly suggestive for our hypothesis of basic changes in the nature of American voting behavior over time is the quite recent transposition of aggregate turnout and variations in turnout as between our rural sample and the two metropolitan centers. In sharp contrast to the situation prevailing before 1900, turnout in these rural counties has tended during the past generation not only to be slightly lower than in the large cities but also subject to far wider oscillations from election to election. In Bedford County, for example, turnout stood at 82.5 percent in 1936, but sagged to an all-time low of 41.2 percent in 1948. The comparable figures in Philadelphia were 74.3 and 64.8 per cent, and in Allegheny County 72.5 percent (in 1940) and 60.6 percent.

———————————

[24] Survey-research estimates place current turnout among American women at 10% below male turnout. Angus Campbell et al., *The American Voter,* pp. 484-85. This sex-related difference in participation is apparently universal, but is significantly smaller in European countries which provide election data by sex, despite the far higher European level of participation by both sexes. The postwar differential has been 5.8 percent in Norway (1945-57 mean), 3.3 percent in Sweden (1948-60 mean), and 1.9 percent in Finland (1962 general election). While in 1956 only about 55 percent of American women went to the polls, the mean turnout among women in postwar elections was 76.1 percent in Norway and 79.4 percent in Sweden.

A major finding revealed by survey research is that the "farm vote" is currently one of the most unstable and poorly articulated elements in the American electorate. [25] It is said that since rural voters lack the solid network of group identifications and easy access to mass-communication media enjoyed by their city cousins, they tend to be both unusually apathetic and exceptionally volatile in their partisan commitments. As rural voting turnout was abnormally low in 1948, its rate of increase from 1948 to 1952 was exceptionally large and—fully consistent with Campbell's surge-decline model—was associated with a one-sided surge toward Eisenhower. A restatement of the data in table 28.5 lends strong support to this evaluation of the relative position of the rural vote as a description of the *current* American voting universe.

But the data strongly imply that virtually the opposite of present conditions prevailed during the nineteenth century. Such variables as education level, communications and nonfamily-group interaction were probably much more poorly developed in rural areas before 1900 than they are today. Not only did this leave no visible mark on agrarian turnout; it seems extremely likely that the nineteenth-century farmer was at least as well integrated into the political system of that day as any other element in the American electorate. The awesome rates of turnout which can be found in states like Indiana, Iowa and Kentucky prior to 1900 indicate that this extremely high level of rural political involvement was not limited to Pennsylvania. [26] As a recent study of Indiana politics demonstrates, the primarily rural "traditional vote" in that state was marked prior to 1900 by an overwhelming partisan stability as well. [27]

Perhaps, following the arguments of C. Wright Mills and others, we can regard this extraordinary change in rural voting behavior as a function of the conversion of a cracker-barrel society into a subordinate element in a larger mass society. [28] In any event, this rural movement toward relatively low and widely fluctuating levels of turnout may well be indicative of an emergent political alienation in such areas. It is suggestive that these movements have been accompanied generally in Pennsylvania as in states like West Virginia

---

[25] *Ibid.*, pp. 402–40.

[26] The estimated rates of turnout in presidential elections from 1876 through 1896, mean turnout in the period 1936–60, and estimated turnout in 1964 were as follows in these states.

State	1876	1880	1884	1888	1892	1896	1936–60 (Mean)	1964 (Prelim.)
Indiana	94.6	94.4	92.2	93.3	89.0	95.1	75.0	73.3
Iowa	89.6	91.5	90.0	87.9	88.5	96.2	71.7	72.0
Kentucky	76.1	71.0	68.0	79.1	72.6	88.0	57.6	52.6

[27] V. O. Key, Jr., and Frank Munger, "Social Determinism and Electoral Decision," pp. 282–88.

[28] C. Wright Mills, *The Power Elite* (New York: Oxford University Press, 1956), pp. 298–324. See also Arthur J. Vidich and Joseph Bensman, *Small Town in Mass Society* (New York: Doubleday, 1960), pp. 5–15, 202–27, 297–320.

Table 28.7 Patterns of Voter Participation in Ohio, 1857–1962: Decline Without Resurgence? (Percentages)

Period	Mean Turnout		Mean Drop-Off	Mean Roll-Off	Mean Split-Ticket Voting
	Pres. Years	Off-Years			
1857–1879	89.0	78.4	9.7	0.6	0.5
1880–1903	92.2	80.5	11.2	0.8	0.6
1904–1918	80.4	71.2	9.2	2.5	3.3
1920–1930	62.4	45.8	24.1	7.9	9.9
1932–1946	69.9	49.1	27.2	7.6	6.5
1948–1962	66.5	53.3	19.0	8.2	11.1

by a strongly positive Republican trend in these agrarian bailiwicks during the last thirty years.[29] The impression arises that the political realignment of the 1930's, which only imperfectly mobilized and integrated urban populations into the political system, had not even these limited positive effects in more isolated communities.

The behavior of the Ohio electorate down to about 1930 closely paralleled the patterns displayed in its neighbor states, Michigan and Pennsylvania. Since then a marked divergence has been manifest.

Two-party competition here was far less seriously affected by the sectional political alignment of 1896–1932 than in most other northern industrial states. Of the eighteen gubernatorial elections held in Ohio from 1895 to 1930, for example, Democrats won ten. But here as elsewhere are to be found the same patterns of decline in turnout and sharp increases in indices of voter peripherality after 1900. Indeed, while turnout bottomed out during the 1920's at a point considerably higher than in Michigan or Pennsylvania, it had also been considerably higher than in either of them during the nineteenth century. Here too such variables as woman suffrage seem to have played a smaller role as causal agents—at least so far as they affected the growing tendencies toward peripherality among active voters—than is commonly supposed. Drop-off from presidential to off-year elections began to assume its modern shape in Ohio between 1898 and 1910. As figure 28.2 shows, roll-off—an especially prominent feature in contemporary Ohio voting behavior—emerged in modern form in the election of 1914.

Ohio, unlike either Michigan or Pennsylvania, has demonstrated only an extremely limited resurgence since the realignment of the 1930's. Presidential-year voting turnout in the period 1948–60 actually declined from the mean level of 1932–44, and was not appreciably higher than it had been in the trough of the 1920's. If mean drop-off has declined somewhat in recent years, it still stands at a level twice as high as in any period before 1920.

---

[29] John H. Fenton, *Politics in the Border States* (New Orleans: Hauser Press, 1957), pp. 117–20.

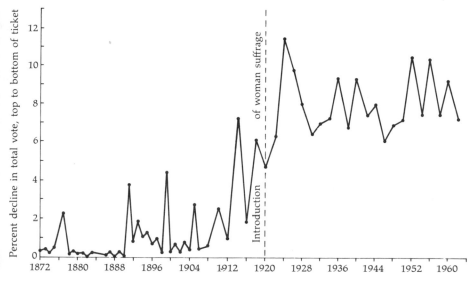

Figure 28.2 Increases in roll-off: the case of Ohio, 1872–1962.

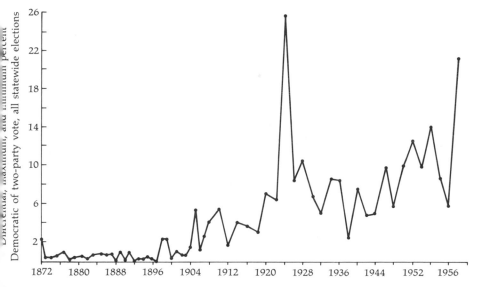

Figure 28.3 Increases in split-ticket voting: the case of Ohio, 1872–1962.

Moreover, roll-off and the rate of split-ticket voting have actually increased to unprecedented highs since 1948. By 1962 the latter ratio touched an all-time high of 21.3 percent (except for the three-party election of 1924), suggesting that Ohio politics may be becoming an "every-man-for-himself" affair. This pattern of behavior stands in the sharpest possible contrast to nineteenth-century norms. In that period turnout had reached substantially full proportions, drop-off was minimal and well over 99 percent of the voters cast both complete ballots and straight party tickets—an achievement that may have been partly an artifact of the party ballots then in use.[30] The political reintegration which the New Deal realignment brought in its wake elsewhere has scarcely become visible in Ohio.

Two recent discussions of Ohio politics may shed some light upon these characteristics. Thomas A. Flinn, examining changes over the past century in the partisan alignments of Ohio counties, concludes that until the first decade of the twentieth century the state had a set of political alignments based largely on sectionalism within Ohio—a product of the diverse regional backgrounds of its settlers and their descendants. This older political system broke down under the impact of industrialization and a national class-ethnic partisan realignment, but no new political order of similar coherence or partisan stability has yet emerged to take its place.[31] Flinn's findings and the conclusions which Lee Benson has drawn from his study of New York voting behavior in the 1840's are remarkably similar.[32] In this earlier voting universe the durability of partisan commitment and the extremely high levels of turnout appear to have had their roots in a cohesive and persistent set of positive and negative group referents. These, as Flinn notes, provided "no clear-cut class basis for statewide party following from the time of Jackson to that of Wilson."[33]

John H. Fenton, discussing the 1962 gubernatorial campaign, carries the argument one step further.[34] Basic to Ohio's social structure, he argues, is an unusually wide diffusion of its working-class population among a large number of middle-sized cities and even smaller towns. The weakness of the labor unions and the chaotic disorganization of the state Democratic Party seem to rest upon this diffusion. Ohio also lack agencies which report on the activities of politicians from a working-class point of view, such as have been set up by the United Automobile Workers in Detroit or the United Mine Workers in Pennsylvania or West Virginia. The result of this is that to a much greater extent than in other industrial states, potential recruits for a

---

[30] However, Ohio's modern pattern of split-ticket voting, formed several decades ago, seems to have been little (if at all) affected by the 1950 change from party-column to office-block ballot forms. See figure 28.3.

[31] Thomas A. Flinn, "Continuity and Change in Ohio Politics," *Journal of Politics,* 24(1962):521–44.

[32] Lee Benson, *The Concept of Jacksonian Democracy* (Princeton: Princeton University Press, 1961), pp. 123–207, 288–328.

[33] Flinn, "Continuity and Change," p. 542.

[34] John H. Fenton, "Ohio's Unpredictable Voters," *Harper's Magazine,* 225(1962):61–65.

cohesive and reasonably well-organized Democratic Party in Ohio live in an isolated, atomized social milieu. Consequently they tend to vote in a heavily personalist, issueless way, as the middle and upper classes do not. Such a state of affairs may provide clues not only for the relative failure of voter turnout to increase during the past generation, but for the persistent and growing indications of voter peripherality in Ohio's active electorate as well.

The development of the voting universe in New York is more analogous to the situation in Ohio than in either Michigan or Pennsylvania. In New York, as in Ohio, two-party competition was not as dislocated by the 1896-1930 alignment as a hasty survey of the presidential-election percentages during that period might suggest. Democrats remained firmly in control of New York City, and this control helped them to capture the governorship eight out of eighteen times from 1896 through 1930. There were other parallels with Ohio as well, for here too this persistence of party competition did not prevent the normal post-1896 voting syndrome from appearing in New York. Nor has there been any pronounced resurgence in turnout levels or convincing declines in the other variables since the 1930's. Drop-off, roll-off, split-ticket voting and partisan swing are not only quite high in New York by nineteenth-century standards, but have been twice as great as in neighboring Pennsylvania during the past decade. This relative failure of political reintegration is revealed not only by the data presented in table 28.8 but—in much more dramatic fashion—by the rise and persistence of labor-oriented third parties which are centered in New York City and have enjoyed a balance-of-power position between the two major party establishments. The existence of the American Labor and Liberal Parties, as well as the continuing vitality of anti-Tammany "reform" factions, are vocal testimony to the failure of the old-line New York Democratic Party to adapt itself successfully to the political style and goals of a substantial portion of the urban electorate.

Table 28.8 New York Voting Patterns, 1834-1962: Decline Without Resurgence? (Percentages)

Period	Mean Turnout (Pres. Years)	Mean Drop-Off	Mean Roll-Off	Mean Split-Ticket Voting	Mean Partisan Swing	Mean % D of 2-Party Vote
1834-1858	84.8	3.3	1.6	1.2	1.7	50.9*
1860-1879	89.3	7.9	0.4	0.6	2.6	50.1
1880-1898	87.9	10.4	1.2	1.6	5.0	50.5
1900-1908	82.5	8.3	1.1	2.2	3.7	47.2
1910-1918	71.9	10.9	5.1	3.3	3.8	46.2
1920-1930	60.4	17.3	5.5	9.5	8.3	49.6
1932-1946	71.3	22.5	4.9	3.4	3.2	53.2†
1948-1962	67.8	20.6	3.6	6.5	5.8	47.3†

* Elections from 1854 to 1858 excluded because of major third-party vote.

† The American Labor Party, 1936-46, and the Liberal Party, 1944-62, are included in Democratic vote when their candidates and Democratic candidates were the same.

Curiously enough, examination of the data thus far presented raises some doubt that the direct primary has contributed quite as much to the erosion of party linkages as has been often supposed.[35] There seems to be little doubt that it has indeed been a major eroding element in some of the states where it has taken root—especially in states with partially or fully one-party systems where the primary has sapped the minority party's monopoly of opposition. But comparison of New York with our other states suggests the need of further concentrated work on this problem. After a brief flirtation with the direct primary between 1912 and 1921, New York resumed its place as one of the very few states relying on party conventions to select nominees for statewide offices, as it does to this day. Despite this fact, the post-1896 pattern of shrinkage in turnout and increases in our other indices of political dissociation was virtually the same in New York as elsewhere. To take a more recent example, New York's split-ticket-voting ratio was 16.1 percent in 1962, compared with 21.3 in Ohio, 7.1 in Michigan and 6.8 percent in Pennsylvania. The overall pattern of the data suggests that since 1932 the latter two states may have developed a more cohesive party politics and a more integrated voting universe with the direct primary than New York has without it.

If the data thus far indicate some link between the relative magnitude of voter non-participation and marginality with the cohesiveness of the local party system, even greater secular trends of the same sort should occur where one of the parties has continued to enjoy a perennially dominant position in state politics. Oklahoma, a border state with a modified one-party regime, tends to support such an assumption.[36] The relatively recent admission of this state to the union naturally precludes analysis of its pre-1896 voting behavior. Even so, it is quite clear that the further back one goes toward the date of admission, the closer one comes to an approximation to a nineteenth-century voting universe. In Oklahoma, curiously enough, the secular decline in turnout and increases in the other indices continued into the New Deal era itself, measured by the off-year elections when—as in a growing number of states[37]—a full slate of statewide officers is elected. Since 1946 very little solid evidence of a substantial resurgence in turnout or of major declines in drop-off, roll-off or split-ticket voting has appeared, but there is some evidence that the minority Republican Party is atrophying.

---

[35] This would seem to suggest a limitation on Key's findings, *American State Politics*, pp. 169–96.

[36] This designation is given the state's political system in Oliver Benson, Harry Holloway, George Mauer, Joseph Pray and Wayne Young, *Oklahoma Votes: 1907–1962* (Norman, Okla.: Bureau of Government Research, University of Oklahoma, 1964), pp. 44–52. For an extensive discussion of the sectional basis of Oklahoma politics, see *Oklahoma Votes*, pp. 32–43, and V. O. Key, Jr., *American State Politics*, pp. 220–22.

[37] In 1936, 34 states (71 percent) elected governors for either two- or four-year terms in presidential years, and the three-year term in New Jersey caused major state elections to coincide with every fourth presidential election. By 1964, only 25 of 50 states (50 percent) still held some of their gubernatorial elections in presidential years. Two of these, Florida and Michigan, are scheduled to begin off-year gubernatorial elections for four-year terms in 1966.

Table 28.9   Voter Peripherality and Party Decay? Oklahoma, 1907–1962.
(Percentages)

Period	Mean Turnout (Off-Years)	Mean Drop-Off	Mean Roll-Off*	Mean Split-Ticket Voting*	State and Congressional Elections Uncontested by Republicans	
					Percent	Mean N†
1907–1918	52.9	12.1	6.1	3.6	2.1	32
1922–1930	40.1	13.0	13.9	9.7	2.1	31
1934–1946	37.1	32.2	16.4	8.1	14.8	32
1950–1962	44.5	26.3	14.0	10.5	41.3	29

*Roll-off and split-ticket voting are computed for contested elections only.
† Mean number of state and congressional races in each off-year election.

The magnitude of drop-off and roll-off has become relatively enormous in Oklahoma since the 1920's, with a very slight reduction in both during the 1950–1962 period. While turnout has correspondingly increased somewhat since its trough in the 1934–1946 period, at no time since 1914 have as many as one-half of the state's potential voters come to the polls in these locally decisive off-year elections. Still more impressive is the almost vertical increase in the proportion of uncontested elections since the end of World War II. The 1958 and 1962 elections, moreover, indicate that the trend toward decomposition in the Republican party organization and its linkage with its mass base is continuing. In 1958 the party virtually collapsed, its gubernatorial candidate winning only 21.3 percent of the two-party vote. Four years later the Republican candidate won 55.5 percent of the two-party vote. The resultant partisan swings of 34.2 percent for this office and 22.0 for all contested statewide offices was the largest in the state's history and one of the largest on record anywhere. But while 1962 marked the first Republican gubernatorial victory in the state's history, it was also the first election in which the Republican Party yielded more than half of the statewide and congressional offices to its opposition without any contest at all. Even among contested offices, the Oklahoma electorate followed a national trend in 1962 by splitting its tickets at the unprecedented rate of 17.3 percent.

As Key has suggested, the direct primary has almost certainly had cumulatively destructive effects on the cohesion of both parties in such modified one-party states as Oklahoma.[38] The rapidly spreading device of "insulating" state politics from national trends by holding the major state elections in off years has also probably played a significant role. Yet it seems more than likely that these are variables which ultimately depend for their effectiveness upon the nature of the local political culture and the socio-economic forces which underlie it. Pennsylvania, for example, also has a direct primary. Since 1875, it has also insulated state from national politics by holding its major state elections in off years. Yet since the realignment of the 1930's, both parties have contested every statewide office in Pennsylvania as a mat-

[38] Key, American State Politics, pp. 169–96.

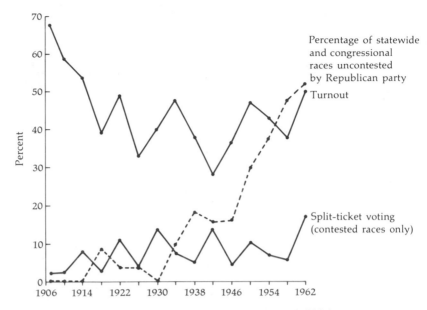

Figure 28.4 Patterns of political evolution: the case of Oklahoma, 1907–1962.

ter of course. Indeed, only very infrequently have elections for seats in the state legislature gone by default to one of the parties, even in bailiwicks which it utterly dominates.[39]

These five statewide variations on our general theme suggest, as do the tentative explorations below the statewide level in Pennsylvania, that an extremely important factor in the recent evolution of the voting universe has been the extent to which the imperatives of the class-ethnic New Deal re-alignment have been relevant to the local social structure and political culture. In the absence of an effectively integrating set of state political organizations, issues and candidates around which a relatively intense polarization of voters can develop, politics is likely to have so little salience that very substantial portions of the potential electorate either exclude themselves altogether from the political system or enter it in an erratic and occasional way. As organized and articulated in political terms, the contest between "business" and "government" which has tended to be the linchpin of our national politics since the 1930's has obviously made no impression upon many in the lowest income strata of the urban population. It has also failed

---

[39] In the period 1956–62 there have been 840 general-election contests for the Pennsylvania House of Representatives. Of these all but six, or 0.7 percent, have been contested by both major political parties. No Pennsylvania state Senate seat has been uncontested during this period. Despite the 1962 Republican upsurge in Oklahoma, however, there were no contests between the parties in 11 of 22 Senate seats (50.0 percent) and in 73 of 120 House seats (60.9 percent). All the uncontested Senate seats and all but two of the uncontested House seats were won by Democrats.

to demonstrate sustained organizing power in areas of rural poverty or among local political cultures which remain largely pre-industrial in outlook and social structure.

IV *Burnham's History of the US*

The conclusions which arise directly out of this survey of aggregate data and indices of participation seem clear enough. On both the national and state levels they point to the existence and eventual collapse of an earlier political universe in the United States—a universe in many ways so sharply different from the one we all take for granted today that many of our contemporary frames of analytical reference seem irrelevant or misleading in studying it. The late nineteenth-century voting universe was marked by a more complete and intensely party-oriented voting participation among the American electorate than ever before or since. Approximately two-thirds of the potential national electorate were then "core" voters, one-tenth fell into the peripheral category, and about one-quarter remained outside. In the four northern states examined in this survey the component of core elements in the potential electorate was even larger: about three-quarters core voters, one-tenth peripherals and about 15 percent non-voters.

In other ways too this nineteenth-century system differed markedly from its successors. Class antagonisms as such appear to have had extremely low salience by comparison with today's voting behavior. Perhaps differentials in the level of formal education among various groups in the population contributed to differentials in nineteenth-century turnout as they clearly do now. But the unquestionably far lower *general* level of formal education in America during the last century did not preclude a much more intense and uniform mass political participation than any which has prevailed in recent decades. Though the evidence is still scanty, it strongly implies that the influence of rurality upon the intensity and uniformity of voting participation appears to have been precisely the opposite of what survey-research findings hold it to be today. This was essentially a pre-industrial democratic system, resting heavily upon a rural and small-town base. Apparently, it was quite adequate, both in partisan organization and dissemination of political information, to the task of mobilizing voters on a scale which compares favorably with recent European levels of participation.

There is little doubt that the model of surge and decline discussed above casts significant light upon the behavior of today's American electorate as it responds to the stimuli of successive elections. But the model depends for its validity upon the demonstrated existence of very large numbers both of peripheral voters and of core voters whose attachment to party is relatively feeble. Since these were not pronounced characteristics of the nineteenth-century voting universe, it might be expected that abnormal increases in the percentage of the vote won by either party would be associated with very different kinds of movements in the electorate, and that such increases would be relatively unusual by present-day standards.

Even a cursory inspection of the partisan dimensions of voting behavior in the nineteenth century tends to confirm this expectation. Not only did the amplitude of partisan swing generally tend to be much smaller then than now,[40] but nationwide landslides of the twentieth-century type were almost non-existent.[41] Moreover, when one party did win an unusually heavy majority, this increase was usually associated with a pronounced and one-sided *decline* in turnout. Comparison of the 1848 and 1852 elections in Georgia and of the October gubernatorial and November presidential elections of 1872 in Pennsylvania, for example, makes it clear that the "landslides" won by one of the presidential contenders in 1852 and 1872 were the direct consequence of mass abstentions by voters who normally supported the other party.[42] Under nineteenth-century conditions, marked as they were by substantially full mobilization of the eligible electorate, the only play in the system which could provide extraordinary majorities had to come from a reversal of the modern pattern of surge and decline—a depression in turnout which was overwhelmingly confined to adherents of one of the parties.[43]

---

[40] Mean national partisan swings in presidential elections since 1872 have been as follows: 1872–92, 2.3 percent; 1896–1916, 5.0 percent; 1920–32, 10.3 percent; 1936–64, 5.4 percent.

[41] If a presidential landslide is arbitrarily defined as a contest in which the winning candidate received 55 percent or more of the two-party vote, only the election of 1872 would qualify among the 16 presidential elections held from 1836 to 1896. Of seventeen presidential elections held from 1900 through 1964, at least eight were landslide elections by this definition, and a ninth—the 1924 election, in which the Republican candidate received 54.3 percent and the Democratic candidate 29.0 percent of a three-party total— could plausibly be included.

[42] The total vote in Georgia declined from 92,203 in 1848 to 62,333 in 1852. Estimated turnout declined from about 88 percent to about 55 percent of the eligible electorate, while the Democratic share of the two-party vote increased from 48.5 percent in 1848 to 64.8 percent in 1852. The pattern of participation in the Pennsylvania gubernatorial and presidential elections of 1872 is also revealing.

Raw Vote	Governor, Oct. 1872	President, Nov. 1872	Absolute Decline
Total	671,147	562,276	− 108,871
Democratic	317,760	213,027	− 104,733
Republican	353,387	349,249	− 4,138

Estimated turnout in October was 82.0 percent, in November 68.6 percent. The Democratic percentage of the two-party vote was 47.3 percent in October and 37.9 percent in November.

[43] The only apparent exception to this generalization in the nineteenth century was the election of 1840. But this was the first election in which substantially full mobilization of the eligible electorate occurred. The rate of increase in the total vote from 1836 to 1860 was 60.0 percent, the largest in American history. Estimated turnout increased from about 58 percent in 1836 to about 80 percent in 1840. This election, with its relatively one-sided mobilization of hitherto apolitical elements in the potential electorate, not unnaturally bears some resemblance to the elections of the 1950's. But the increase in the Whig share of the two-party vote from 49.2 percent in 1836 to only 53.0 percent in 1840 suggests that that surge was considerably smaller than those of the 1950's.

This earlier political order, as we have seen, was eroded away very rapidly after 1900. Turnout fell precipitately from nineteenth-century levels even before the advent of woman suffrage, and even in areas where immigrant elements in the electorates were almost nonexistent. As turnout declined, a larger and larger component of the still-active electorate moved from a core to a peripheral position, and the hold of the parties over their mass base appreciably deteriorated. This revolutionary contraction in the size and diffusion in the shape of the voting universe was almost certainly the fruit of the heavily sectional party realignment which was inaugurated in 1896. This "system of 1896," as Schattschneider calls it, [44] led to the destruction of party competition throughout much of the United States, and thus paved the way for the rise of the direct primary. It also gave immense impetus to the strains of anti-partisan and anti-majoritarian theory and practice which have always been significant elements in the American political tradition. By the decade of the 1920's this new regime and business control over public policy in this country were consolidated. During that decade hardly more than one-third of the eligible adults were still core voters. Another one-sixth were peripheral voters and fully one-half remained outside the active voting universe altogether. It is difficult to avoid the impression that while all the forms of political democracy were more or less scrupulously preserved, the functional result of the "system of 1896" was the conversion of a fairly democratic regime into a rather broadly based oligarchy.

The present shape and size of the American voting universe are, of course, largely the product of the 1928–1936 political realignment. Survey-research findings most closely approximate political reality as they relate to this next broad phase of American political evolution. But the characteristics of the present voting universe suggest rather forcefully that the New Deal realignment has been both incomplete and transitional. At present, about 44 percent of the national electorate are core voters, another 16 or so are peripheral, and about 40 percent are still outside the political system altogether. By nineteenth-century standards, indices of voter peripherality stand at very high levels. Party organizations remain at best only indifferently successful at mobilizing a stable, predictable mass base of support.

The data which have been presented here, though they constitute only a small fraction of the materials which must eventually be examined, tend by and large to support Schattschneider's functional thesis of American party politics. [45] We still need to know a great deal more than we do about the specific linkages between party and voter in the nineteenth century. Systematic research remains also to be done on the causes and effects of the great post-1896 transition in American political behavior. Even so, it seems useful

----

[44] *The Semi-Sovereign People*, p. 81.

[45] *Ibid.*, esp. pp. 78–113. See also his "United States: The Functional Approach to Party Government," in Sigmund Neumann, ed., *Modern Political Parties* (Chicago: University of Chicago Press, 1956), pp. 194–215.

to propose an hypothesis of transition in extension of Schattschneider's argument.

The nineteenth-century American political system, for its day, was incomparably the most thoroughly democratized of any in the world. The development of vigorous party competition extended from individual localities to the nation itself. It involved the invention of the first organizational machinery—the caucus, the convention and the widely disseminated party press—which was designed to deal with large numbers of citizens rather than with semiaristocratic parliamentary cliques. Sooner than the British, and at a time when Prussia protected its elites through its three-class electoral system, when each new change of regime in France brought with it a change in the size of the electorate and the nature of *le pays légal,* and when the basis of representation in Sweden was still the estate, Americans had elaborated not only the machinery and media of mass politics but a franchise which remarkably closely approached universal suffrage. Like the larger political culture of which it was an integral part, this system rested upon both broad consensual acceptance of middle-class social norms as ground rules and majoritarian settlement (in "critical" elections from time to time), once and for all, of deeply divisive substantive issues on which neither consensus nor further postponement of a showdown was possible. Within the limits so imposed it was apparently capable of coherent and decisive action. It especially permitted the explicit formulation of sectional issues and—though admittedly at the price of civil war—arrived at a clear-cut decision as to which of two incompatible sectional modes of social and economic organization was henceforth to prevail.

But after several decades of intensive industrialization a new dilemma of power, in many respects as grave as that which had eventuated in civil war, moved toward the stage of overt crisis. Prior to the closing years of the century the middle-class character of the political culture and the party system, coupled with the afterglow of the civil-war trauma, had permitted the penetration and control of the cadres of both major parties by the heavily concentrated power of our industrializing elites. But this control was inherently unstable, for if and when the social dislocations produced by the industrial revolution should in turn produce a grass-roots counterrevolution, the party whose clienteles were more vulnerable to the appeals of the counterrevolutionaries might be captured by them.

The take-off phase of industrialization has been a brutal and exploitative process everywhere, whether managed by capitalists or commissars.[46] A vital functional political need during this phase is to provide adequate insulation of the industrializing elites from mass pressures, and to prevent their displacement by a coalition of those who are damaged by the processes of capital accumulation. This problem was effectively resolved in the Soviet

---

[46] Clark Kerr, John T. Dunlop, Frederick S. Harbison and Charles A. Myers, *Industrialism and Industrial Man* (Cambridge, Mass.: Harvard University Press, 1960), pp. 47–76, 98–126, 193, 233. Walt W. Rostow, *The Stages of Economic Growth* (Cambridge, England: Cambridge University Press, 1960), pp. 17–58.

Union under Lenin and Stalin by vesting a totalitarian monopoly of political power in the hands of Communist industrializing elites. In recent years developing nations have tended to rely upon less coercive devices such as non-totalitarian single-party systems or personalist dictatorship to meet that need, among others. The nineteenth-century European elites were provided a good deal of insulation by the persistence of feudal patterns of social deference and especially by the restriction of the right to vote to the middle and upper classes.

But in the United States the institutions of mass democratic politics and universal suffrage uniquely came into being *before* the onset of full-scale industrialization. The struggle for democracy in Europe was explicitly linked from the outset with the struggle for universal suffrage. The eventual success of this movement permitted the development in relatively sequential fashion of the forms of party organization which Duverger has described in detail.[47] In the United States—ostensibly at least—the struggle for democracy had already been won, and remarkably painlessly, by the mid-nineteenth century. In consequence, (the American industrializing elites were, and felt themselves to be, uniquely vulnerable to an anti-industrialist assault which could be carried out peacefully and in the absence of effective legal or customary sanctions by a citizenry possessing at least two generations' experience with political democracy.)

This crisis of vulnerability reached its peak in the 1890's. Two major elements in the population bore the brunt of the exceptionally severe deprivations felt during this depression decade: the smaller cash-crop farmers of the Southern and Western "colonial" regions and the ethnically fragmented urban working class. The cash-crop farmers, typically overextended and undercapitalized, had undergone a thirty-years' decline in the prices for their commodities in the face of intense international competition. With the onset of depression in 1893, what had been acute discomfort for them became disaster. The workers, already cruelly exploited in many instances during this "take-off" phase of large-scale industrialization, were also devastated by the worst depression the country had thus far known. Characteristically, the farmers resorted to political organization while the workers sporadically resorted to often bloody strikes. The industrializers and their intellectual and legal spokesmen were acutely conscious that these two profoundly alienated groups might coalesce. Their alarm was apparently given quite tangible form when the agrarian insurgents captured control of the Democratic Party in 1896.

But the results of that great referendum revealed that the conservatives' fears and the anti-industrialists' hopes of putting together a winning coalition on a Jacksonian base were alike groundless. Not only did urban labor *not* flock to William Jennings Bryan, it repudiated the Democratic Party on an unprecedented scale throughout the industrialized Northeast. The inten-

---

[47] Maurice Duverger, *Political Parties,* 2d ed. (New York: Wiley, 1959), pp. 1-60.

sity and permanence of this urban realignment was paralleled by the Democrats' failure to make significant inroads into Republican strength in the more diversified and depression-resistant farm areas east of the Missouri River, and by their nearly total collapse in rural New England. The Democratic-Populist effort to create a coalition of the dispossessed created instead the most enduringly sectional political alignment in American history—an alignment which eventually separated the Southern and Western agrarians and transformed the most industrially advanced region of the country into a bulwark of industrialist Republicanism.

This realignment brought victory beyond expectation to those who had sought to find some way of insulating American elites from mass pressures without formally disrupting the pre-existing democratic-pluralist political structure, without violence and without conspiracy. Of the factors involved in this victory three stand out as of particular importance. (1) The depression of 1893 began and deepened during a Democratic administration. Of course there is no way of ascertaining directly what part of the decisive minority which shifted its allegiance to the Republican Party reacted viscerally to the then incumbent party and failed to perceive that Cleveland and Bryan were diametrically opposed on the central policy issues of the day. But contemporary survey findings would tend to suggest that such a component in a realigning electorate might not be small. In this context it is especially worth noting that the process of profound break with traditional voting patterns began in the fall of 1893, not in 1896. In a number of major states like Ohio and Pennsylvania the voting pattern of 1896 bears far more resemblance to those of 1893–1895 than the latter did to pre-1893 voting patterns. Assuming that such visceral responses to the Democrats as the "party of depression" did play a major role in the realignment, it would follow that the strong economic upswing after 1897 would tend to strengthen this identification and its cognate, the identification of the Republicans as the "party of prosperity."

(2) The Democratic platform and campaign were heavily weighted toward the interests and needs of an essentially rural and semi-colonial clientele. Considerably narrowed in its programmatic base from the farmer-labor Populist platform of 1892, the Democratic Party focused most of its campaign upon monetary inflation as a means of redressing the economic balance. Bryan's viewpoint was essentially that of the smallholder who wished to give the term "businessman" a broader definition than the Easterners meant by it, and of an agrarian whose remarks about the relative importance of farms and cities bespoke his profound misunderstanding of the revolution of his time. Silver mine owners and depressed cash-crop farmers could greet the prospect of inflation with enthusiasm, but it meant much less to adequately capitalized and diversified farmers in the Northeast, and less than nothing to the depression-ridden wage-earners in that region's shops, mines and factories. Bryan's appeal at base was essentially Jacksonian—a call for a return to the simpler and more virtuous economic and political arrangements which he identified with that by-gone era. Such nostalgia

could evoke a positive response among the native-stock rural elements whose political style and economic expectations had been shaped in the far-away past. But it could hardly seem a realistic political choice for the ethnically pluralist urban populations, large numbers of whom found such nostalgia meaningless since it related to nothing in their past or current experience. Programmatically, at least, these urbanites were presented with a two-way choice only one part of which seemed at all functionally related to the realities of an emergent industrial society. With the Democrats actually cast in the role of reactionaries despite the apparent radicalism of their platform and leader, and with no socialist alternative even thinkable in the context of the American political culture of the 1890's, the Republican Party alone retained some relevance to the urban setting. In this context, its massive triumph there was a foregone conclusion.

(3) An extremely important aspect of any political realignment is the unusually intense mobilization of negative-reference-group sentiments during the course of the campaign. 1896 was typical in this respect. Profound antagonisms in culture and political style between the cosmopolitan, immigrant, wet, largely non-Protestant components of American urban populations and the parochial, dry, Anglo-Saxon Protestant inhabitants of rural areas can be traced back at least to the 1840's. Bryan was virtually the archetype of the latter culture, and it would have been surprising had he not been the target of intense ethnocultural hostility from those who identified with the former. He could hardly have appeared as other than an alien to those who heard him in New York in 1896, or to those who booed him off the stage at the Democratic Convention—also in New York—in 1924. Moreover, his remarks about the Northeast as "the enemy's country"—anticipating Senator Goldwater's views about that region in 1964—could only intensify a broadly sectional hostility to his candidacy and deepen the impression that he was attacking not only the Northeast's industrializing elites but the Northeast itself. Both in 1896 and 1964 this region gave every visible evidence of replying in kind.

As Schattschneider has perceptively observed, the "system of 1896" was admirably suited to its primary function. One of its major working parts was a judiciary which proceeded first to manufacture the needed constitutional restraints on democratic political action—a development presaged by such decisions as the Minnesota railroad rate case of 1890[48] and the income tax cases of 1894-1895[49]—and then to apply these restraints against certain sensitive categories of national and state economic legislation.[50] Another of the new system's basic components was the control which the sectional align-

[48] Chicago, Milwaukee & St. Paul Railway Co. v. Minnesota, 134 U.S. 418 (1890).

[49] Pollock v. Farmers' Loan & Trust Co., 157 U.S. 429 (1895); (rehearing) 158 U.S. 601 (1895).

[50] The literature on this process of judicial concept-formulation from its roots in the 1870's through its formal penetration into the structure of constitutional law in the 1890's is extremely voluminous. Two especially enlightening accounts are: Benjamin Twiss, *Lawyers and the Constitution* (Princeton: Princeton University Press, 1942), and Arnold M. Paul, *Conservative Crises and the Rule of Law* (Ithaca: Cornell University Press, 1960).

ment itself gave to the Republican Party, and through it the corporate business community, over the scope and direction of national public policy. Democracy was not only placed in judicial leading-strings, it was effectively placed out of commission—at least so far as two-party competition was concerned—in more than half of the states. Yet it was one of the greatest, if unacknowledged, contributions of the "system of 1896" that democratic forms, procedures and traditions continued to survive.[51] Confronted with a narrowed scope of effective democratic options, an increasingly large proportion of the eligible adult population either left, failed to enter or—as was the case with Southern Negroes after the completion of the 1890-1904 disfranchisement movement in the Old Confederacy—was systematically excluded from the American voting universe. The results of this on the exercise of the franchise have already been examined here in some detail. It was during this 1896-1932 era that the basic characteristics associated with today's mass electorate were formed.

These characteristics, as we have seen, have already far outlived the 1896 alignment itself. There seems to be no convincing evidence that they are being progressively liquidated at the present time. If the re-emergence of a competitive party politics and its at least partial orientation toward the broader needs of an urban, industrialized society were welcome fruits of the New Deal revolution, that revolution has apparently exhausted most of its potential for stimulating turnout or party-oriented voting in America. The present state of affairs, to be sure, is not without its defenders. The civics-minded have tended to argue that the visible drift away from party-oriented voting among a growing minority of voters is a sign of increasing maturity in the electorate.[52] Others have argued that mediocre rates of turnout in the United States, paralleled by the normally low salience of issues in our political campaigns, are indicative of a "politics of happiness."[53] It is further contended that any sudden injection of large numbers of poorly socialized adults into the active voting universe could constitute a danger to the Republic.[54]

But there is another side to this coin. The ultimate democratic purpose of issue-formulation in a campaign is to give the people at large the power to choose their and their agents' options. Moreover, so far as is known, the blunt alternative to party government is the concentration of political power, locally or nationally, in the hands of those who already possess concentrated economic power.[55] If no adequate substitute for party as a means for mobi-

---

[51] Paul, *Conservative Crises*, pp. 131-58.

[52] See, among many other examples, *Congressional Quarterly Weekly Report*, 22 (1 May 1964):801.

[53] Heinz Eulau, "The Politics of Happiness," *Antioch Review*, 16(1956):259-64; Seymour M. Lipset, *Political Man* (New York: Doubleday, 1960), pp. 179-219.

[54] *Ibid.*, pp. 216-19; Herbert Tingsten, *Political Behavior*, pp. 225-26.

[55] V. O. Key, Jr., *Southern Politics* (New York: Random House, 1949), pp. 526-28; E. E. Schattschneider, *The Semi-Sovereign People*, pp. 114-28.

lizing non-elite influence on the governing process has yet been discovered, the obvious growth of "image" and "personality" voting in recent decades should be a matter of some concern to those who would like to see a more complete restoration of the democratic process in the United States.

Moreover, recent studies—such as Murray Levin's examinations of the attitudes of the Boston and Massachusetts electorate—reveal that such phenomena as widespread ticket splitting may be associated quite readily with pervasive and remarkably intense feelings of political alienation.[56] Convinced that both party organizations are hopelessly corrupt and out of reach of popular control, a minority which is large enough to hold the balance of power between Republicans and Democrats tends rather consistently to vote for the lesser, or lesser-known, of two evils. It takes a mordant variety of humor to find a kind of emergent voter maturity in this alienation. For Levin's data are difficult to square with the facile optimism underlying the civics approach to independent voting. So, for that matter, are the conclusions of survey research about the behavior of many so-called "independent" voters.[57]

Findings such as these seem little more comforting to the proponents of the "politics of happiness" thesis. Granted the proposition that most people who have been immersed from birth in a given political system are apt to be unaware of alternatives whose explicit formulation that system inhibits, it is of course difficult to ascertain whether their issueless and apathetic political style is an outward sign of "real" happiness. We can surmise, however, that the kind of political alienation which Levin describes is incompatible with political happiness, whether real or fancied. (A great many American voters, it would seem, are quite intelligent enough to perceive the deep contradiction which exists between the ideals of rhetorical democracy as preached in school and on the stump, and the actual day-to-day reality as that reality intrudes on his own *milieu*. Alienation arises from perception of that contradiction, and from the consequent feelings of individual political futility arising when the voter confronts an organization of politics which seems unable to produce minimally gratifying results.) The concentration of socially deprived characteristics among the more than forty million adult Americans who today are altogether outside the voting universe suggests active alienation—or its passive equivalent, political apathy—on a scale quite unknown anywhere else in the Western world. Unless it is assumed as a kind of universal law that problems of existence which can be organized in political

---

[56] Murray B. Levin, *The Alienated Voter* (New York: Holt, Rinehart & Winston, 1960), pp. 58–75, and his *The Compleat Politician* (Indianapolis: Bobbs-Merrill, 1962), esp. pp. 133–78. While one may hope that Boston and Massachusetts are extreme case studies in the pathology of democratic politics in the United States, it appears improbable that the pattern of conflict between the individual's expectations and reality is entirely unique to the Bay State.

[57] Angus Campbell et al., *The American Voter*, pp. 143–45.

terms must fade out below a certain socio-economic level, this state of affairs is not inevitable. And if it is not inevitable, one may infer that the political system itself is responsible for its continued existence.

Yet such an assumption of fade-out is clearly untenable in view of what is known about patterns of voting participation in other democratic systems. Nor need it be assumed that substantial and rapid increases in American voting participation would necessarily, or even probably, involve the emergence of totalitarian mass movements. The possibility of such movements is a constant danger, to be sure, in any polity containing so high a proportion of apolitical elements in its potential electorate. But it would be unwise to respond to this possibility by merely expressing the comfortable hope that the apoliticals will remain apolitical, and by doing nothing to engage them in the system in a timely and orderly way. It is much more to the point to seek a way, if one can be found, to integrate the apolitical half of the American electorate into the political system before crisis arises.[58] Such integration need not be out of the question. The United States, after all, enjoyed intense mass political involvement without totalitarian movements during the last part of the 19th century, as do other Western democracies today.

No integration of the apoliticals can be carried out without a price to be paid. Underlying the failure of political organizations more advanced than the nineteenth-century middle-class cadre party to develop in this country has been the deeper failure of any except middle-class social and political values to achieve full legitimacy in the American political culture. It may not now be possible for our polity to make so great a leap as to admit non-middle-class values to political legitimacy and thus provide the preconditions for a more coherent and responsible mode of party organization. But such a leap may have to be made if full mobilization of the apolitical elements is to be achieved without the simultaneous emergence of manipulative radicalism of the left or the right. The heart of our contemporary political dilemma appears to lie in the conflict between this emergent need and the ideological individualism which continues so deeply to pervade our political culture. Yet the present situation perpetuates a standing danger that the half of the American electorate which is now more or less entirely out-

---

[58] The line of reasoning developed in this article—especially that part of it which deals with the possible development of political alienation in the United States—seems not entirely consistent with the findings of Gabriel A. Almond and Sidney Verba, *The Civic Culture* (Princeton: Princeton University Press, 1963), pp. 402-69, 472-505. Of course there is no question that relatively high levels of individual satisfaction with political institutions and acceptance of democratic norms may exist in a political system with abnormally low rates of actual voting participation, just as extremely high turnout may—as in Italy—be associated with intense and activist modes of political alienation. At the same time, the gap between American norms and the actual political activity of American individuals does exist, as Almond and Verba point out on pp. 479-87. This may represent the afterglow of a Lockean value consensus in an inappropriate socio-economic setting, but in a polity quite lacking in the disruptive discontinuities of historical development which have occurred during this century in Germany, Italy and Mexico. Or it may represent something much more positive.

side the universe of active politics may someday be mobilized in substantial degree by totalitarian or quasi-totalitarian appeals. As the late President Kennedy seemed to intimate in his executive order establishing the Commission on Registration and Voting Participation, it also raises some questions about the legitimacy of the regime itself. [59]

---

[59] "Whereas less than sixty-five percent of the United States population of voting age cast ballots for Presidential electors in 1960; and

"*Whereas popular participation in Government through elections is essential to a democratic form of Government;* and

Whereas the causes of nonvoting are not fully understood and more effective corrective action will be possible on the basis of a better understanding of the causes of the failure of many citizens to register and vote . . ." (emphasis supplied) The full text of the executive order is in *Report,* pp. 63-64. Compare with Schattschneider's comment in *The Semi-Sovereign People,* p. 112: "A greatly expanded popular base of political participation is the essential condition for public support of the government. This is the modern problem of democratic government. The price of support is participation. The choice is between participation and propaganda, between democratic and dictatorial ways of *changing consent into support, because consent is no longer enough.*" (Author's emphasis)

29. The Effect of the Australian Ballot Reform on Split Ticket Voting: 1876–1908

JERROLD G. RUSK

In the last two decades of political science, there has been considerable interest in the determinants of electoral behavior. Theories have been developed and tested on the sociological, psychological, and political antecedents of the vote. Virtually neglected in this search for determinants have been the institutional or structural properties of the electoral system itself. With a few notable exceptions,[1] such factors as electoral qualification requirements, registration laws, and ballot and voting systems have not generated much research enthusiasm. These institutional properties, however,

SOURCE: *American Political Science Review,* 64(1970):1220–38. Reprinted with permission of the publisher.

AUTHOR'S NOTE: This article is adapted from the author's doctoral dissertation of the same title (University of Michigan, 1968). Acknowledgments are due Angus Campbell, Warren E. Miller, Jack L. Walker, and Herbert F. Weisberg for their comments on the dissertation. A special debt of thanks is owed Philip E. Converse for reading and evaluating both the dissertation and this article.

[1] The few exceptions include Angus Campbell, Philip E. Converse, Warren E. Miller, and Donald E. Stokes, *The American Voter* (New York: Wiley, 1960), pp. 266–89; Stanley Kelley, Jr., Richard E. Ayres, and William G. Bowen, "Registration and Voting: Putting First Things First," *American Political Science Review,* 61(June 1967):359–79; V. O. Key, Jr., *American State Politics* (New York: Knopf, 1956); Donald R. Matthews and James W. Prothro, "Political Factors and Negro Voter Registration in the South," *American Political Science Review,* 57(June 1963):355–67; and Warren E. Miller, "Memorandum to the President's Commission on Registration and Voting Participation" (unpublished Michigan Survey Research Center paper, 1963).

provide the framework within which the effects of other independent variables must be judged. This applies to all basic electoral research—whether time specific or longitudinal—but especially to the latter. Too often longitudinal research tries to trace the causes of changing voting patterns without taking into account the institutional framework. A pointed example of this is Walter Dean Burnham's recent description of this country's "changing political universe" around the turn of the century[2]—a change which he ascribed to a breakdown in party competition and consequent voter alienation, but which undoubtedly could be partially, if not largely, explained by reference to the many institutional changes in voting rules which occurred during this period. The effects of institutional properties must be sorted out if the researcher is to establish reliable baselines against which to measure the effects of other variables.

The purpose of this study is to analyze the effects of one such institutional property of the electoral system—the Australian Ballot reform—on the changing split ticket voting patterns of the American electorate in the 1876-1908 time period. A theory is advanced to predict the ways in which ballot might be expected to affect split ticket voting. The theory encompasses not only the comparative effects of the Australian Ballot and the earlier unofficial "party strip" ballot, but also the differential effects of the varying internal formats the Australian Ballot assumed in the several states. A test of this theory is then made—involving a comparison of mean split ticket scores for the various ballot conditions across states within election years and within states across election years. Results show that the basic theory is confirmed. A test of Walter Dean Burnham's alternate theory of voting behavior for this time period is also made, and it is shown to be largely unsubstantiated insofar as it is dependent on the ticket-splitting phenomenon. Final interpretations are generalized to the role and influence of other institutional properties of the system on the voting decision.

The American Ballot System [3]

The Australian or "official" ballot was instituted in most states in the early 1890's. Massachusetts was the first to adopt it statewide in 1888[4] and, in less

---

[2] See Walter Dean Burnham, "The Changing Shape of the American Political Universe," *American Political Science Review,* 59(March 1965):7-28.

[3] The history of the American ballot system can be found in various sources such as Spencer D. Albright, *The American Ballot* (Washington, D.C.: American Council on Public Affairs, 1942); Eldon C. Evans, *A History of the Australian Ballot System in the United States* (Chicago: University of Chicago Press, 1917); Joseph P. Harris, *Election Administration in the United States* (Washington, D.C.: Brookings Institution, 1934); Arthur C. Ludington, *American Ballot Laws: 1888-1910* (Albany: New York State Library, 1911); and J. H. Wigmore, *The Australian Ballot System as Embodied in the Legislation of Various Countries,* 2d ed. (Boston: Boston Book Co., 1889). In general, these references give much better accounts of the Australian Ballot era than the voting systems in use prior to that time. An exception to this is the book by Evans.

[4] Although the first Australian Ballots were adopted in 1888 and 1889, they did not become effective in federal elections until 1890.

than eight years, approximately 90 percent of the states had followed suit. Rarely in the history of the United States has a reform movement spread so quickly and successfully. The example of Australia, which originated the Australian Ballot Law in 1856, and several other nations who adopted this law was sufficient to recommend the new system as a probable cure for the ills of the electoral administration of the time.

Before the introduction of the Australian Ballot, there was a separate ballot for each party called a "party strip" or "unofficial" ballot since it was prepared and distributed by the party instead of the government. Each party, in essence, made up its own ballot, listing only its candidates, and had "party hawkers" peddle it to the voters in what resembled an auctioneering atmosphere in and around the polling station. Each party also made its ballot distinctive by printing it in a different color and on a different sized sheet from those of the other parties. This assured instant recognition of the ballot by the voters, and, in turn, recognition by the party workers of which party's ballot a person picked up and voted. In addition, the fact that the actual act of voting was usually performed in the open further assured that the people had no right to a secret ballot. [5]

The Australian Ballot system changed all this. It was completely different from the earlier system in concept and orientation. The new ballot was state-prepared and state-administered—hence making it an "official" and uniform ballot which precluded the existence of party-prepared ballots. Secondly, the new ballot was a consolidated or "blanket" ballot, listing the candidates of all parties on it instead of only the candidates of one party. Last, the ballot was secret, an important complement to its being a consolidated ballot. The new system thus offered the voter an impartial, multiple-choice instrument, upon which he was allowed to deliberate and make a decision in the privacy of the polling booth. The intimidating party aura which so permeated the voting situation under the old system had been effectively dispelled.

Most states enacted ballot lows with the basic principles of the Australian Law—officiality, consolidation, and secrecy—intact. This still left them free to determine the internal format of the ballot, a matter on which there was not so much agreement among the states as there had been on the more basic provisions and general orientation of the Australian Law. Some states, following the lead of Massachusetts, looked once again to the original ballot law for cues and basically adopted its nonpartisan practice of aligning candidate names under office blocs. Some modification was made in this format,

---

[5] The party strip or unofficial ballot came into use in most states during the first half of the nineteenth century. Before that time, the states (or colonies) had other forms of paper balloting, voice voting, or such unorthodox procedures as letting corn or beans designate one's vote. At one time, in the early 1800's, several states allowed the voter to make up his own ballot. The parties, noting this, were motivated to print their own ballots in order to thwart the use of handwritten ballots. This practice of party-prepared ballots was upheld in a Massachusetts Supreme Court decision in 1829, setting a precedent which was not challenged until the beginning days of the Australian Ballot reform.

such as adding party names beside candidate names, but in general the ballot retained its objective, nonpartisan character. Other states followed the lead of Indiana in enacting a party column arrangement of candidate names on the official ballot. This format resembled a consolidation of the old party strips, placed side by side on the same sheet of paper. In essence, these states had overlaid their old party strip system onto the new Australian framework. Today, these two types of official ballot are known as the "Massachusetts office bloc" and "Indiana party column" arrangements.

The popularity of the two types of official ballot varied in this early time period. As figure 29.1 shows, the office bloc format was the favorite of states in the beginning, but the party column design predominated after 1890, generally increasing in popularity over the years. The inference can be drawn that the early popularity of the office bloc form was due to its association with the original Australian Ballot Law. But this type of ballot, even when modified by the addition of party names, was too objective and nonpartisan to be in keeping with the style and heritage of American politics. Americans soon changed the format of the ballot to party column to correspond more with the partisan nature of their political life. They perceived the important contribution of the Australian Law as lying in its basic provisions and not in its specific stipulation of internal format.

States also experimented in this period with adding certain features to the physical format of the ballot, such as straight ticket and party emblem devices. States would try a feature, evaluate its results, and then decide whether or not to keep it on the ballot. Figure 29.1 reveals certain trends in this experimentation and the resulting decisions made. For instance, the

Figure 29.1 Trends in state adoption of partisan ballot types and features.

488 straight ticket addition seems to have been well received, since its popularity gained over the years. In part, such a movement is to be understood in the light of the increasing popularity of the party column form, the straight ticket option adding to the partisan flavor of this kind of ballot. This is not to say that such an option could not be or was not offered on office bloc ballots but rather than the general trend was for its incorporation onto the party column format. Party emblem was less used, but it also increased in popularity during this period, primarily, again, as a complement to the party column ballot.

Basic Theory

The theory proposed here centers on the effects on voting of two key dimensions of the ballot as an institution—its structural properties and the electoral environment in which it is used. Such information about the ballot is obtainable from state statute books and historical accounts of the time. Certain logical developments of this information and the use of past research findings about voting behavior help us to understand how ballot law and usage define the parameters and alternatives of the decision-making process at the polls and how the individual reacts under different ballot conditions. Two central hypotheses on ballot effects can be formulated. The first is that the Australian Ballot system had a stimulating effect on split ticket voting relative to its predecessor, the unofficial party strip ballot. The second is that the different internal formats of the official ballot themselves had differential effects on split ticket voting; in particular, we may hypothesize that the incidence of such voting was related to the degree of partisan orientation the particular ballot format displayed. [6]

Under the old party strip system, the voter's decision was, for all practical purposes, limited to a single choice—that of which party's ballot to cast. If the voter was interested in several candidates of different parties, he would have to weigh their relative importance and make a decision either to go with the one he liked best, or to go with what he considered to be the best overall party slate of candidates. The same type of decision model could apply to parties as well, if the voter preferred this alternative to that of ranking individual candidates. The important point is that the ballot system encouraged the voter to reduce his several choices to one and then take the party ballot corresponding to that decision.

The party strip system did not deny the possibility of a split ticket vote being cast. There were ways to vote a split ticket if the individual had the

---

[6] These central hypotheses are based on a model of individual decision-making to be presented below. Testing such a model with aggregate election data is subject to the normal analytic cautions expressed by W. S. Robinson in his article, "Ecological Correlations and the Behavior of Individuals," *American Sociological Review*, 15(June 1950):351-57. For a discussion of the Robinson argument of "ecological fallacy" as it applies to this analysis, see Rusk, *Effect of the Australian Ballot Reform*, especially pp. 67-70.

motivation to find out how and to execute such a decision in an environment emphasizing partisan norms and allowing only an open vote. One method was to "scratch" a name off the ballot and write the name of another party's candidate above it. Another was to take two different party ballots, marking each for certain offices, and then have them attached together before depositing them in the ballot box. Certain variants of these voting schemes existed in other states. But it was rare to find instructions on how to vote "a split ticket" printed on the ballot or for a party hawker to mention such a possibility. The electoral environment discouraged deviant voting in most instances—the complete party control of the ballot encouraging and reinforcing a tendency toward straight ticket voting.

The voting situation was different under the Australian Ballot system. The voter no longer had to reduce his several choices to a single dominant choice: he could instead express his multiple preferences as they stood across the new consolidated ballot. If he needed guidance on how to do so, the ballot had voting instructions printed on it, and voting assistance was also obtainable from nonpartisan state officials. The presence of a secret vote gave further notice that the prevailing norms of the partisan world were capable of being broken at the polling station. In fact, the new system encouraged different norms more compatible with the changing milieu. Split ticket voting was on the rise because the opportunity clearly existed to be used. This did not mean that electorates immediately registered large split ticket tendencies overnight; voters had to adjust to the new ballot instrument and the new norms that the changing milieu created. Old habits had to be modified or broken to adjust to the new situation—habits that had been in existence for a long time.

Changes in voting habits (and the rate at which they took place) depended considerably on the internal format of the Australian Ballot. The two different formats of the official ballot could have effects of their own. For instance, the party column format, since it had consolidated the party strips of the earlier period, continued to suggest a more partisan vote than its counterpart, the office bloc ballot. The similarity in style of the Indiana format to its predecessor was compatible with previous voting habits, thereby making it more difficult to recognize and use the ticket-splitting potential of the new ballot. On the other hand, the Massachusetts ballot was conducive to an independent decision being made for each office. The alternatives it defined favored a multi-choice orientation rather than a single-choice one. The difference in orientation between it and the unofficial ballot probably prompted a faster adjustment to its split ticket capabilities than to those of the Indiana format.

The addition of straight ticket and party emblem features to the ballot could also have effects on voting behavior. Such partisan devices suggested some decrease in split ticket voting from the levels normally associated with ballot format alone, but the extent of this decrease depended on the ballot format on which they were displayed. The devices probably had only a small effect on the party column ballot since this format already provided a strong partisan orientation. But because these devices stood in greater contrast to the office bloc format, they were more salient to the voter and thereby considerably decreased the likelihood of split ticket voting on this ballot. In statistical terms, they must have had something akin to independent effects on the Massachusetts form, but only interactive effects on the Indiana ballot. [7]

Operational Definitions

The first step in testing any theory is to operationalize its basic concepts; the second, to evaluate the merit of such operations from a methodological point of view. In this study, only the dependent variable—split ticket voting—needs to be operationalized. The independent variables of ballot types and forms are usable for analysis purposes directly as they are taken from state laws.

The research literature provides few guidelines for operationalizing the dependent variable. A measure authored by Walter Dean Burnham has gained some currency in the field and is related to one theoretical interpretation of the voting patterns of this period. [8] The decision was made to use the Burnham measure, primarily for two reasons—tests show it to be capable of meeting our major analysis requirements, and use of it will facilitate contrasting our findings with those of Burnham in a later section of this paper. Results of experimentation performed with the Burnham measure in order to understand its behavior and its methodological strengths and weaknesses will be given below.

The Burnham measure is defined as the difference between the highest and lowest percentages of the two party vote cast for the Democratic party among the array of statewide races in any given state and election year. [9] For example, state A in a certain election year has the following statewide races, with the results expressed as Democratic percentages of the total vote cast for the two major parties: President, 51 percent; Governor, 49 percent; Secretary of State, 48 percent; State Treasurer, 48 percent; and Attorney General, 48 percent. The split ticket value for state A in this election year is 3 percent.

The central focus of the Burnham measure is on the competitive interac-

---

[7] In contemporary research on survey data, Angus Campbell and Warren E. Miller show the voting effects of one of these partisan devices, the straight ticket provision. They find that there is a greater tendency toward party slate voting when a ballot format has a straight ticket device than when it does not. However, it is difficult to tell to what extent such effects are separate from ballot format considered as a variable since the correspondence between straight ticket provisions and party column formats (or multi-choice provisions and office bloc formats) is very close today. See Campbell and Miller, "The Motivational Basis of Straight and Split Ticket Voting," *American Political Science Review*, 51(June 1957):293–312.

[8] Burnham, "Changing Shape," p. 9.

[9] The definition of a "statewide race" was expanded in this paper to include an aggregation of the district congressional vote. As a check on this operation, another measure was constructed excluding the congressional vote, and, when compared, both revealed similar behaviors and interpretations in the subsequent ballot analysis.

tion of the two major parties in an electoral situation. This requires the exclusion of uncontested races and the virtual exclusion of races with third party activity from consideration in the split ticket computations. [10] Third party intrusions of a sizable nature would especially create additional variation in the two party vote which could not be considered a true split ticket effect for Burnham's or our purposes. [11]

As an aggregate-based measure, the Burnham index suffers from the same liabilities as other such measures. For example, it assumes that the "gross difference value" it obtains is due solely to ticket-splitting, yet one realizes that some portion of this value is attributable to other causes. Election fraud, accidental miscounting of election returns, etc., can register artificial effects in the index. Also, since the measure is an aggregate difference figure, it would not detect mutual crossovers between the two parties which have the effect of canceling each other out. [12] After recognizing the weaknesses of an aggregate-based measure, the researcher must usually take the position that such problems are either minor or else distributed fairly randomly among the various cases in the data collection.

A fault more specific to the Burnham measure is that it does not provide for analysis of "comparable race sets" across states within a given election. The number and kinds of races from which it is computed can vary from state to state. The Burnham measure is rather best suited for analyzing ticket-splitting within states across election years as a means of controlling its "race composition factor." [13] A major part of the analysis in this paper uses the Burnham measure in this context. But an analysis across states is also an important interest. In this situation, use of the Burnham measure

---

[10] Burnham did not indicate what screening criteria he used to eliminate third party intrusions in his data. The rule established in this study was that no race would enter the computations if the third party vote contributed six or more percent to the total vote for that race. Admittedly, this figure was somewhat arbitrary and some might consider it too high; however, given the many and large third party movements in this period, the figure seems reasonable. To check this procedure, we also looked at those cases of states having third party vote figures greater than six percent for most of their races and yet where the percentage did not vary greatly across the set of contested races. These data, impure as they were, conformed to the same trendlines in the ballot analysis as the figures generated by the screening criterion selected for use with the Burnham measure. This gave increased confidence in the findings, and on two occasions in the ballot analysis below (tables 29.5 and 29.8), we display the "impure" values of states with the "pure" values of other states, carefully distinguishing the two in such instances.

[11] For certain research purposes, the third party vote would be a useful statistic to keep in the split ticket picture. Third parties broaden the alternatives open to the voter and in this way contribute to split ticket voting in certain areas. However, when the concern is with fluctuations in the two party vote space, third party figures can only be viewed as creating needless disturbances in the data.

[12] Aggregate election analyses usually assume that voters crossover or split their tickets mainly in one direction—the direction of national trends. But even if this were not the case, the phenomenon of mutual crossovers would not contaminate our ballot analysis unless it occurred, for some reason, far more often in unofficial than in official ballot states, a proposition that seems unlikely.

[13] By "race composition factor" is meant the types of races entering the Burnham index computations in any given state. Inspection of the data shows that this factor is fairly stable across elections though the index can in no way guarantee a complete control over this.

needs some intellectual justification since its values could fluctuate from state to state simply because of differences in the races composing it. Whether or not this is a disadvantage depends on how the index behaves as a function of the composition factor and what the relation of this behavior is to the predictions of ballot theory.

Several tests of the Burnham index were conducted, primarily to determine the effect of the race composition factor, but also for the more general purpose of checking to see if the measure was indeed tapping ticket-splitting. With regard to the latter purpose, the measure was found to behave as one might expect, both statistically and theoretically. That is, as one increased the number of races in the index, its value would generally rise as a function of the probability of rare outcomes entering the calculations. As one included the presidential race with two or more state-specific races, its value also tended to increase in keeping with the theory that the presidential race is a more powerful generator of short-term influences in elections. While these two tests suggested the validity of the measure, they also highlighted the possibility that states contesting larger numbers or given kinds of races could have higher split ticket values simply because of their particular race composition situations. Hence, another test was called for—and this revealed that the race composition factor was not spuriously affecting our own predictions as to ballot effects. That is, it indicated that there were not larger numbers of races or given types of races associated with those ballot conditions predicted by ballot theory to have greater incidences of split ticket voting. [14] A last test also confirmed this lack of spurious correlation and gave further evidence of validity. Three measures devised to have "comparable race sets," and hence to control for the variable factor of race composition, behaved similarly and gave similar results in the ballot analysis as the Burnham measure. [15] The results from all the tests indicated that, assum-

---

[14] While the primary purpose of this test was to examine the effects of the race composition factor on across-state, within-year analyses, it was also used in the within-state, across-year analysis context, once again revealing an absence of correlation between the race composition factor and the predictions of ballot theory.

[15] The three measures computed were based on the presidential-gubernatorial, presidential-congressional, and gubernatorial-congressional pairings of races. Ideally, they would have been the best measures to use in an analysis of ballot conditions across states within election years since they standardize race sets; however, there are several reasons why, in practice, they were not so useful. For one thing, they severely limit the number of cases entering the analysis. Even with the pairings mentioned above, one is assured of most states entering only the presidential-congressional computations since some of them do not contest the gubernatorial race in a presidential election year. With the addition of any third race to the index, more states would drop out of the computations for similar reasons. Second, the inclusion of but two races in an index for any given state does not allow much room for variation in the vote to occur. It certainly does not provide one with good esti-. mates of a state's split ticket voting behavior. Third, such an index does not provide an adequate comparison with the results generated by the Burnham measure within states across election years. Comparability of the two modes of analysis is best achieved by using the same measure rather than two differently constructed ones. Also, it is more appropriate to use the Burnham measure consistently in order to compare our results with those produced by Burnham for his interpretation of the voting behavior of this period.

ing some care with the number of races per state, the Burnham index reflected split ticket voting adequately and avoided any noticeable confounding or contaminating effects in its operations.

Introduction of The Australian Ballot

The Burnham split ticket values, when computed for the 1876–1908 time span, are quite revealing. Figure 29.2 displays a trendline of rising values in the years in which the Australian reform took place. [16] However, until ballot has been examined as an analysis variable, such a trend can only be regarded as indirect evidence of ballot's effect on voting. Perhaps there were other ticket-splitting stimuli that were particularly active in the Australian Ballot years. More direct tests of the central hypothesis need to be undertaken in order to determine the role ballot played in this split ticket voting picture.

One test is a within-year analysis of ballot conditions. Such a test also provides us with an election normalization device. Some control on different kinds and intensities of political stimuli can be put into effect by examining

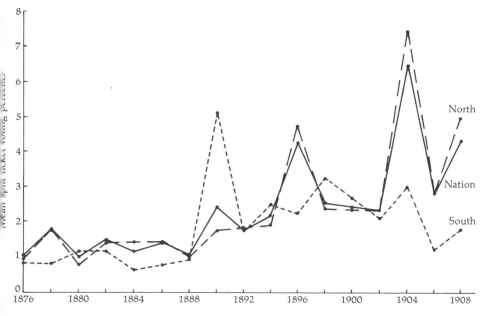

Figure 29.2 Means of split ticket voting index by election year for nation and region.

---

[16] Burnham, of course, also observed a rising split ticket trend in these years. His evidence for this was the split ticket scores of five states. See Burnham, "Changing Shape," pp. 13–14, 17–20.

the unofficial and official ballot systems with regard to ticket-splitting in the same year. The results of this analysis are presented in table 29.1.

A few points need to be made about table 29.1 before it can be analyzed effectively. First, the number of cases in the table is necessarily limited due to (1) the ballot reform being accomplished in a short period of time, leaving few data points in the unofficial ballot categories, and (2) part of this general period, 1890–1908, being marked by fervid third party activity, making it necessary to drop some of the states (mainly in the Australian Ballot category) from the analysis. Second, the table contains not one but two unofficial

Table 29.1 Split Ticket Voting Means of Unofficial and Australian Ballot States by Election Year for Nation and Region

Ballot Condition	Election Year										Overall Means 1890–1908
	1890	1892	1894	1896	1898	1900	1902	1904	1906	1908	
Nation											
Pure party strip	1.5	0.8	—	1.0	0.7	0.4	0.3	2.8	—	3.3	1.5
(1)	(16)	(3)	(0)	(1)	(1)	(2)	(2)	(2)	(0)	(2)	(29)
All party strip	2.5	1.0	0.6	4.0	0.7	1.4	0.5	2.6	0.1	4.3	2.2
(2)	(18)	(5)	(2)	(3)	(2)	(4)	(3)	(4)	(1)	(4)	(46)
Australian ballot	2.6	2.2	2.4	4.3	2.7	2.6	2.7	7.4	3.1	4.6	3.6
(3)	(7)	(13)	(11)	(34)	(26)	(36)	(20)	(21)	(13)	(21)	(202)
North											
Pure party strip	1.7	0.8	—	1.0	0.7	0.4	0.3	2.8	—	3.3	1.5
(1)	(13)	(3)	(0)	(1)	(1)	(2)	(2)	(2)	(0)	(2)	(26)
All party strip	1.6	0.8	0.9	1.7	0.7	1.6	0.5	2.7	0.1	4.8	1.7
(2)	(14)	(4)	(1)	(2)	(2)	(3)	(3)	(3)	(1)	(3)	(36)
Australian ballot	2.2	2.3	2.1	4.9	2.6	2.6	2.7	9.1	3.2	5.5	3.8
(3)	(6)	(11)	(9)	(28)	(24)	(27)	(19)	(15)	(12)	(16)	(167)
South											
Pure party strip	0.4	—	—	—	—	—	—	—	—	—	0.4
(1)	(3)	(0)	(0)	(0)	(0)	(0)	(0)	(0)	(0)	(0)	(3)
All party strip	5.4	1.9	0.3	8.5	—	0.9	—	2.2	—	2.6	3.8
(2)	(4)	(1)	(1)	(1)	(0)	(1)	(0)	(1)	(0)	(1)	(10)
Australian ballot	4.6	1.7	3.8	1.4	3.4	2.8	2.2	3.2	1.2	1.7	2.5
(3)	(1)	(2)	(2)	(6)	(2)	(9)	(1)	(6)	(1)	(5)	(35)

NOTE: Category (2) refers to all unofficial ballot states; category (1) refers to those unofficial ballot states which have all major statewide races on a single party strip ballot. Figures in parentheses denote the number of states on which the mean split ticket value was based for any given entry.

ballot categories. Row (1) refers to the general type of unofficial ballot in use during this period—the "pure party strip" which has been described in previous sections. Row (2) includes all unofficial ballot states, combining the ballot cases of row (1) with the very few states (never more than five in the United States at any particular time) that used a deviant form of the unofficial ballot. This deviant form was called the "separate party strip system"— its distinguishing characteristic being that a separate party strip ballot was used for each office contested by the party instead of following the modal pattern of placing all offices contested by the party on a single party strip ballot. Row (3) of the table is, of course, the official ballot category.

The main finding in table 29.1 follows the predictions of ballot theory. Regardless of whether one compares row (1) or (2) with row (3), the direction of mean values shows that the Australian Ballot states have more ticket-splitting than their unofficial counterparts in every election year in both the North and the nation.[17] The strength and consistency of this pattern of voting values attest to its own importance. The new official ballot allowed and encouraged split ticket voting. As a contrast, the South manifests a ragged, nonconsistent pattern. Partly this can be ascribed to inadequate cases for analysis purposes because of our data screening process. But also it is thought that the deviant form of unofficial ballot, which was used by a few southern states, motivated additional split ticket voting beyond that associated with the modal party strip ballot system. Such a tendency, given the few data cases in the table for the South, would accentuate the importance of this ballot in explaining the idiosyncrasies in this region's ticket-splitting picture.

A comparison of rows (1) and (2) by nation and region comments on the unique split ticket properties of the "separate party strip ballot system," the deviant form of unofficial ballot. For instance, in the nation, in all but one year the values of row (2) are greater than those of row (1). Since row (2) is an average of row (1) values and those of the deviant unofficial ballot states, one can easily infer that the deviant ballot is associated with the larger split ticket tendencies. The reason for this association lies in the fact that the voter had to choose a separate party ballot for each office for which he wished to vote; in so doing, he was faced with several possible decision-making situations, and unlike the voter in the modal party strip system, he did not have to reduce his several choices to a single dominant choice. The separate party strip system thus encouraged some modicum of ticket-splitting, at least generally greater than that evidenced in pure party strip ballot

---

[17] In some election years, the split ticket distributions (as pictured on a standard low-to-high percentage value scale) were skewed to the right. Because of this, medians were computed to compare with the pattern of means. As one might guess, the results were similar in direction although some of the differences were smaller. Variance figures in this and other tables also behaved predictably in accordance with the pattern of mean values. Another way to look at this basic relationship is conveyed in table 29.3 below, which presents the split ticket means for the ballot conditions for each state separately over all years, thereby holding constant the variation in the other states while viewing state X.

states. Its effects were more pronounced in the South than in the North, but the general tendency existed in both regions.

While the Australian Ballot and, to a lesser extent, the separate party strip system encouraged split ticket voting, a perusal of row (1) in the table reveals that the pure party strip states had very little split ticket voting in almost every election from 1890 through 1908. In fact, the values are similar in size to those registered in the same situation in earlier years before the Australian Ballot appeared in America. One might expect the values to rise in election years showing high split ticket values in the Australian Ballot states, but a comparison of rows (1) and (3) shows this rarely to be the case. For the separate party strip system, there seems to be some tendency in this direction as a result of its unique split ticket properties, but the modal party strip system presents a considerable obstacle to ticket-splitting in most elections, including some high ticket-splitting elections.

Another important aspect of table 29.1 is the consistency of the unofficial-official ballot comparisons, given the varied stimuli probably associated with the different election years. The arrangement of the data is the same across all years—high and low stimulus, or turnout, elections, "Republican" and "Democratic" years. A more rigorous analysis of this across-year consistency in the data would be through regression techniques. Such techniques can pinpoint the amount of temporal covariation in voting properties between the Australian and unofficial ballot conditions. The resulting slope lines and coefficients would comment on the relative sensitivity within each ballot condition to whatever short-term forces lead to more or less ticket-splitting over the years. Such regressions were performed on the values in table 29.1, considering the Australian Ballot values as the independent variable and the two unofficial ballot categories successively as dependent variables. The findings from both analyses revealed little variation in the effects of the unofficial ballot relative to the official one, indicating once again that people using the official ballot were more likely to translate whatever short-term forces there were in these years into greater split ticket voting. The official ballot provided the best opportunity for people to express their reactions to the short-term forces in the political environment.

A summary of the effects of the unofficial-official ballot conditions across all years can here serve to highlight the effects we have observed within given election years. As shown in table 29.2, the progression of split ticket values is as predicted and reflects the need to consider the two pre-Australian forms as separate categories with separate effects. This logic fits well with the idea that the two are conceptually different and that this difference is shown to have predictable influences on ticket-splitting behavior. The dominant theme of the two is, of course, registered by the pure party strip system with its low frequency of split ticket voting, since it was the type of unofficial ballot used by about 90 percent of the states. The contrast be-

Table 29.2 Split Ticket Voting Means of Unofficial and Australian Ballot States Over All Election Years, 1876–1908

Ballot Condition	Split Ticket Means
Pure party strip	1.2 (197)
Separate party strips	3.1 (20)
Australian ballot	3.6 (202)

SOURCE: The first two row categories refer to different types of the unofficial ballot.

tween the two pre-Australian categories and the Australian Ballot reflects the split ticket potential existing with a secret, consolidated ballot. The opportunity is presented by the ballot and stands in contrast to the party emphasis in the earlier voting system.

Another way to look at the effect of ballot is to take each state separately and compare its split ticket voting before it adopted the official ballot with such voting after adoption. The analysis mode then shifts from comparing mean split ticket scores of the unofficial and official ballot conditions across states within election years to within states across election years. Within this mode, comparisons will usually be made for similar types of elections—keeping presidential and off-year elections distinct because of the differing stimuli associated with each.

Practically speaking, the actual computations involve summing a state's split ticket values for elections of the same type, within each of the two ballot time periods, and then deriving a mean value for each period. Such an aggregation across elections within ballot periods has the advantage of sharpening the accounting of effects attributable to the ballot while dampening out (through mutual canceling) the effects of any unique election year stimuli. The end product of such aggregating and averaging operations should be good estimates of each state's ticket-splitting behavior in the two ballot environments. [18]

The data for presidential elections are presented in table 29.3 and resemble the other data sets with respect to the effects of the official ballot. All but one state—97 percent of the states in all—have a higher split ticket figure for their official ballot period than for their unofficial ballot period. In almost all of the states, the split ticket values of the two periods differ quite remarkably. Some states, such as Iowa, Massachusetts, Michigan, Oregon, and Rhode Island, reveal very little ticket-splitting in the party strip phase, but

---

[18] The voting estimates are "good" except for the fact that there is a rising split ticket curve in this period that makes sense substantively. Better estimates could be obtained by excluding the transition trends in the data.

mushroom in value when the reform movement took hold. What is important in this regard is the increment in split ticket voting from the unofficial ballot condition (as expressed in ratios of ballot categories) and not a given percentage increase taken to be a standard for all states to pass or fail. The relative increase is the item of interest, and, in most cases, such an increase is quite large. A doubling, tripling, or quadrupling of such voting is commonplace among the various states.

Some excellent summary information can also be gleaned from table 29.3. The import of its message is similar to earlier statements, but it can give us some indication of the average effect of the two ballot time periods. In the

Table 29.3 Split Ticket Voting Means of Unofficial and Official Ballot Periods of States in Presidential Election Years, 1876–1908

State	Unofficial Ballot Period	Official Ballot Period	Difference of Means	Category Cases	
				Unofficial Ballot	Official Ballot
Alabama	1.10	—	—	1	0
Arkansas	0.65	2.05	1.40	2	2
California	1.12	2.15	1.03	4	2
Colorado	2.62	3.88	1.26	4	5
Connecticut	0.60	—	—	4	0
Delaware	0.28	1.14	0.86	4	5
Florida	0.70	2.70	2.00	3	2
Georgia	—	—	—	0	0
Idaho	—	2.03	—	0	3
Illinois	1.18	1.20	0.02	4	2
Indiana	0.38	1.10	0.72	4	3
Iowa	0.93	3.40	2.47	3	3
Kansas	2.77	0.72	−2.05	4	4
Kentucky	0.45	1.58	1.13	4	4
Louisiana	1.10	—	—	2	0
Maine	—	—	—	0	0
Maryland	0.48	1.54	1.06	4	5
Massachusetts	1.15	6.58	5.43	2	6
Michigan	1.00	6.62	5.62	3	4
Minnesota	2.63	16.58	13.95	3	4
Mississippi	2.00	—	—	2	0
Missouri	1.57	2.00	0.43	6	1
Montana	—	12.90	—	0	3
Nebraska	2.05	3.65	1.60	4	4
Nevada	1.80	4.35	2.55	4	2

(continued)

NOTE: The unofficial ballot category covers the period from 1876 through the last presidential election before change from the unofficial ballot for each state. The official ballot category covers the period from the first presidential election in which the Australian Ballot was used through the 1908 election. The designation "category cases" refers to the number of elections entering the split ticket mean computations for the unofficial and official ballot periods of any given state.

Table 29.3 *(continued)* 499

State	Unofficial Ballot Period	Official Ballot Period	Difference of Means	Category Cases	
				Unofficial Ballot	Official Ballot
New Hampshire	0.72	4.08	3.36	4	5
New Jersey	1.28	—	—	9	0
New York	0.88	2.33	1.45	5	3
North Carolina	0.48	—	—	4	0
North Dakota	—	8.44	—	0	5
Ohio	0.65	1.98	1.33	4	4
Oregon	0.48	3.15	2.67	4	2
Pennsylvania	0.42	0.70	0.28	4	4
Rhode Island	0.55	5.46	4.91	4	5
South Carolina	—	—	—	0	0
South Dakota	—	1.40	—	0	2
Tennessee	1.70	2.30	0.60	4	4
Texas	0.55	3.40	2.85	2	2
Utah	—	18.65	—	0	2
Vermont	1.92	4.06	2.14	4	5
Virginia	0.30	5.73	5.43	3	3
Washington	—	3.23	—	0	3
West Virginia	0.73	2.40	1.67	3	5
Wisconsin	0.57	1.30	0.73	3	2
Wyoming	—	4.06	—	0	5
Means of state means	1.1	4.1	2.3	128	125

table, twenty-nine states qualify as having both unofficial and official ballot conditions. For these states, ticket-splitting goes from a mean value of 1.1 to 3.4 for the two ballot conditions, an increase of approximately three times. This is the average effect of the official ballot for states having both forms in presidential years. For all states, the figures deviate even more—1.1 to 4.1.

Several states, of course, were deleted from the first set of figures because of one or the other of two reasons—they used the unofficial ballot exclusively in this period, or, the converse, they adopted the official ballot, never having any previous ballot system. The incidence of ticket-splitting for the first category of states is very low—0.8 percent. The second category of states, those western states entering the Union in the early 1890's or later, go in the opposite direction—they display the highest split ticket average in the study, 7.2 percent. Obviously, variables other than ballot were contributing to this outcome. The entrance of a territorial entity into national politics in itself must promote some reactions similar in kind to those shown for the ballot. The presence of the ballot makes it easier to implement such reactions. However, even when the large split-ticket effects of these official ballot states are controlled for, the basic relationship between ballot and voting behavior still holds, as our example of the twenty-nine states above indicated.

The same story of ballot effects repeats itself in the off-year election figures so that little new information is to be gained from this data source. Approximately 85 percent of the states, in the off-year election context, show a rise in ticket-splitting in their Australian Ballot period. When off-year and presidential types of elections are merged, 91 percent of the states reveal the predicted direction.

Demonstration that ballot has an effect on split ticket voting is only one part of an analysis: for ballot theory to be substantiated, split ticket voting patterns must be shown to have changed in the states shortly after the new ballot was introduced. A reasonable prediction would be that, in accord with adjustment patterns, split ticket voting would show a rise in either the first or second election year in which a state used the new ballot. This proposition is first tested across states within these crucial years of ballot change. Table 29.4 presents mean split ticket values for three categories of states— unofficial ballot states (row 1 or 2), official ballot states in their first year of new ballot use, and official ballot states in their second year of use. According to the data, both the first and second years of ballot use seem to be good indicators of the effects of the official ballot. Sizable differences exist between the unofficial and official ballot states, as a comparison of either row (1) or row (2) with rows (3) and (4) indicates. States adopting the new ballot soon changed their voting patterns from those remaining steadfast to the existing system. Voters were seen to be adjusting to the new ballot and its ticket-splitting potential without much difficulty.

A second way to test this proposition of early ballot effects is within states across election years. In table 29.5, split ticket values are listed for each state

Table 29.4 Split Ticket Voting Means of Unofficial and Official Ballot States in Selected Years of Ballot Change

Ballot Condition		1890	1892	1894	1896	1898
Pure party strip	(1)	1.5	0.8	—	1.0	0.7
		(16)	(3)	(0)	(1)	(1)
All party strip	(2)	2.5	1.0	0.6	4.0	0.7
		(18)	(5)	(2)	(3)	(2)
First election year of official ballot use	(3)	2.6 (7)	1.9 (9)	2.6 (1)	19.0 (2)	— (0)
Second election year of official ballot use	(4)	— (0)	3.0 (4)	2.4 (8)	2.0 (2)	2.8 (3)

NOTE: It should be noted that in order to trace the same set of states from the first to the second year of official ballot use, one must compare a given election in category (3) with the succeeding election year in category (4) of the data set. Some states, however, will be missing in one or both years of the data set because of failure to meet its screening requirements.

in its last election year using the unofficial ballot and the first two elections using the official ballot. Also listed are "difference values" between the last unofficial ballot election and the second election year in which the official ballot was used. (Use of the second, instead of the first, election year in

Table 29.5 Split Ticket Values of States in Last Election Before and First and Second Election Years of Official Ballot Use, for Comparable Election Types

State	Last Election Year Using Unofficial Ballot (1)	First Election Year Using Official Ballot (2)	Second Election Year Using Official Ballot (3)	Difference Values (Column 3 Minus Column 1) (4)
California	0.7	(2.7)	4.0	3.3
Colorado	1.6	1.0	5.6	4.0
Delaware*	0.1	0.1	2.1	2.0
Illinois*	0.9	(0.5)	1.4	0.5
Indiana*	0.4	0.7	(0.5)	(0.1)
Iowa*	0.6	(0.8)	6.0	5.4
Kentucky*	0.2	—	0.6	0.4
Louisiana*	1.9	—	0.6	−1.3
Massachusetts	1.2	3.6	2.2	1.0
Michigan*	0.6	(2.2)	0.6	0.0
Minnesota	3.8	(6.3)	(6.4)	(2.6)
Nebraska	2.6	(8.1)	3.2	0.6
Nevada	2.7	(7.2)	4.9	2.2
New Hampshire	1.0	1.4	6.8	5.8
New York*	0.5	2.3	1.6	1.1
Ohio*	0.0	0.7	0.2	0.2
Oregon	0.7	—	3.9	3.2
Pennsylvania*	0.5	0.1	0.3	−0.2
Rhode Island	(0.4)	2.8	3.2	(2.8)
Tennessee	1.1	4.6	1.9	0.8
Vermont*	1.6	2.1	4.3	2.7
West Virginia*	0.5	0.4	0.2	−0.3
Wisconsin*	(1.4)	1.4	(1.1)	(−0.3)
Means	1.1	2.4	2.7	1.6

NOTE: Most values in the table met the screening requirements of the Burnham index. Those enclosed in parentheses did not but were included as "impure" cases as defined in footnote 10 above. In order for a state to be included in the table, it had to have split ticket values in both the last election before and the second election of official ballot use—thus excluding those states that has no pre-Australian period, those never adopting the official ballot in the 1876–1908 time period, and those screened out of even the "impure data set" in these heavily "third party" election years. For a given state, the "difference value" compares the split ticket scores of similar types of elections (either presidential or off-year), depending on when the ballot change took place. The designation "—" entered for some states in column (2) indicates that these states' split ticket values were not included because of failure to meet the requirements of either the Burnham index or its "impure version."
*Denotes states having the party column format in their second election year of official ballot use.

computing these "differences" rests on the assumption that it is less disturbed by adjusting tendency "noises" of the electorate toward the new ballot.) The type of election, presidential or off-year, used in these unofficial-official ballot comparisons is decided separately for each state, according to which year its change of ballot occurred.

Of first interest in the data is the fact that approximately 80 percent of the states had greater split ticket scores after they adopted the new ballot. The difference values in column (4) show this, and the trend is repeated when one compares columns (1) and (2). Certainly, this finding would be more impressive if higher, yet its consistency with our earlier tables is further evidence of this type of patterning in the data.

The ballot picture is improved if one considers a few additional features of the data. For one thing, the deviations in the difference values are very small for the remaining 20 percent of the states. This is because these states adopted the party column type of official ballot, which in many respects resembled the earlier unofficial ballot situation. Of note here too is the observation that most of the party column states showing the predicted direction also registered but small difference values. (Asterisks denote the party column states in table 29.5.) The next section will show that the party column form in the first few years revealed similar split ticket figures to the pre-Australian Ballot states. The habits formed by the party strip situation carried over to the party column form, with its arrangement of party strips and straight ticket provision facilitating the continuation of these habits.

Lending further weight to our ballot interpretation is the fact that with continued use of the party column format over time, the split ticket figures do increase. Admittedly, this tendency is not major, yet it does exist, as we shall see in figure 29.3 below. The reasons for the increased split ticket use of the party column form over time are probably twofold—a continuing adjustment to the new ballot and a given election producing a desire to use the split ticket property of the ballot.

Thus, an analysis within states across election years substantiates the earlier results found by examining data across states within election years. The new ballot has effects on voting behavior not only, generally speaking, across time, but also fairly immediately after it is introduced in the several states.

Types of Australian Ballots

The general conclusion of the last section was that the introduction and establishment of the official ballot facilitated a rise in split ticket voting. A more detailed question has to do with the relative contributions of the party column and office bloc types of this ballot to such ticket-splitting and also the contrast of their effects with those of the earlier unofficial ballot system.

Figure 29.3 presents the split ticket pictures for party column, office bloc, and unofficial ballot states in the North. The values in the figure are mean

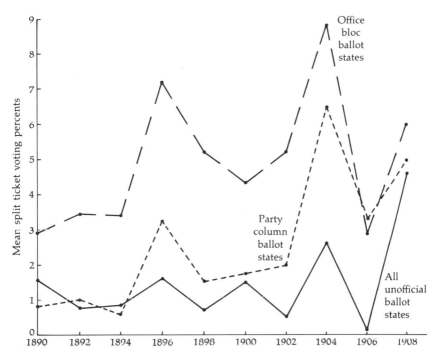

Figure 29.3 Split ticket means for three ballot conditions of states, North only.

scores for each ballot condition within the election years of the 1890–1908 time period. Looking first at just the two types of official ballot states, one notes the wide divergence in their respective split ticket values, suggesting the influence of differing internal ballot formats on voting behavior. Ticket-splitting is significantly higher under the less partisan arrangement of the office bloc form than under the party column type.

It is also interesting to contrast each form of the official ballot with the unofficial ballot. The spread between the office bloc and unofficial ballots is sizable, reflecting a marked difference in the ticket-splitting potentialities of the two. Smaller differences are shown between the party column and unofficial ballots, especially before the turn of the century. The correspondence in orientation and design of the two ballots undoubtedly has much to do with their closer split ticket values. Both ballots have "party" as their main focus and both provide an easy means of voting a straight ticket, if in somewhat different senses.[19] Identification of party, its column or strip arrange-

---

[19] There were two ways to vote a straight ticket in an unofficial ballot state—either deposit a given party strip in the ballot box unmarked or else mark it for all the candidates on it. Some states by law specified one way or the other, but some allowed both ways. In a party column state, one could vote a straight ticket by marking the entire ballot or by making a single mark if such an option was provided.

ment, and the attached emblem or color of ballot are conceptual parallels that could facilitate the task of straight ticket voting for the elector. [20]

In spite of this stress on the relatively close voting patterns of the party column and unofficial ballots, it is important to note, on the other hand, the very existence of divergence. As predicted, the party column form of the official ballot had somewhat greater ticket-splitting than the unofficial ballot, since its consolidation and secrecy features provided a better opportunity for this type of voting. [21] Across time this difference in voting between the two ballots became more marked as electorates adjusted to the split ticket potential of the new ballot. It took time for voting habits to change, and the similarity of the party column and unofficial conditions was an important reason why such habits changed more slowly under the party column than under the office bloc format.

These comparisons of the three trendlines in figures 29.3 can also give us a better understanding of the voting patterns earlier observed in table 29.1. The large differences between the official and unofficial ballot conditions were, to a large extent, a product of the effects of the office bloc states—at least in the first part of the Australian period. It was not only the fact that a state switched to the official ballot that prompted a rise in ticket-splitting— it was also the condition of imposing a specific internal format on this ballot, namely the office bloc arrangement, that facilitated the larger increments in voting fluidity. After the turn of the century, the split ticket trendline of the party column states deviated more seriously from the unofficial ballot trend-line—resulting in a greater contribution of the Indiana ballot to the sizable Australian Ballot ticket-splitting figures and, hence, to their differentiation from the unofficial ballot figures.

A different analysis of the party column, office bloc, and unofficial ballots, involving within-state, across-year comparisons, produced the same results as shown in figure 29.3. Office bloc states had higher mean split ticket scores than party column states, and both types of ballot states had greater mean split ticket scores in their official ballot period than in their unofficial ballot period. A study of those states that shifted ballot formats in their Australian years also revealed higher mean split ticket values for the period in which they used the office bloc format.

Within and across state comparisons have shown the impact of ballot format on voting habits. Obviously, this is a crucial variable in the overall ballot picture. But still there are other factors to consider—states could and

---

[20] The split ticket differences between the party column and party strip systems become even smaller if one contrasts the latter with only those party column states having emblem' and "single mark" features. The effects of these two devices will be explored in later tables.

[21] Two deviations occur in the data—for the years of 1890 and 1894. The deviation in 1890 is possibly due to the extremely small number of party column cases involved, 1890 being the first election in which this form of the Australian Ballot was used by any of the states. The deviation in 1894 is due to a separate party strip situation in one state. The differences between the two systems would have been larger and cleaner if one had con-trasted pure party strip values with party column values; this tact was not taken in figure 29.3 simply because two years had no values for the former condition.

Table 29.6 Relation of Ballot Form and Straight Ticket Provision to Split Ticket Voting, 1890-1908

Ballot Form	Presence of Straight Ticket	Absence of Straight Ticket	Marginals
Party column	2.7 (106)	3.0 (17)	2.7 (123)
Office bloc	3.7 (16)	5.3 (63)	5.0 (79)
Marginals	2.8 (122)	4.8 (80)	3.6 (202)

NOTE: Entries are split ticket means computed over all election years, 1890-1908, for states having the ballot combinations listed in the table.

did embellish these formats with straight ticket provisions and party emblems. Ballot formats did not have to exist in isolation, and the addition of these features could have added effects on electoral behavior.

The same sort of analysis was performed with these ballot features as with the party column-office bloc dichotomy in figure 29.3. That is, states were divided into those having and those not having straight ticket or party emblem features on their ballots. The results were similar in trend to the party column-office bloc contrast, and, indeed, the differences in split ticket scores between the straight ticket and non-straight ticket situations were comparable in magnitude to those found between the party column and office bloc formats.

The finding of associations between voting patterns and the two ballot features is a step in the right direction—but only the first step. These is a further question as to how these features relate to one another and to the format of the ballot.

All possible combinations of the two partisan features and ballot format were surveyed to answer the question about their interrelationships.[22] They showed ballot format to be the dominant explanatory factor. The most revealing pairing of variables was that of ballot format and the presence or absence of a straight ticket provision. As shown in table 29.6, both variables had considerable gross effects on voting, but larger differences occurred between types of ballot format when presence or absence of a straight ticket provision was controlled for than vice-versa.

The importance of the straight ticket provision depended on the ballot

---

[22] Originally, such combinations were viewed within election years and the direction of mean split ticket values was basically as predicted. However, one quickly confronted cells with few cases since several ballot configurations appeared with rare frequency in reality. Given these conditions, a better strategy was to aggregate ballot cases across time to better observe their effects and the following analysis is based on this procedure.

format on which it was placed. In the case of the party column ballot, the split ticket value seemed little affected by whether or not a straight ticket option was present. The party column format in itself was facilitative of straight ticket voting, and the straight ticket provision added only the ease of marking just one "X" instead of marking an "X" for each candidate. It took little extra effort to mark "X's" down a column, especially given the earlier experience with the party strip system.

The straight ticket variable, however, took on more importance when on the office bloc ballot. Here it cut down the ticket-splitting potential of a ballot offering many independent decision-making possibilities. The voter could escape the problem of deciding on each successive office how he would vote by relying on the straight ticket option. Apparently, many voters preferred this alternative.

The results of the table suggest the presence of some interaction. It is possible that people were viewing the party column ballot with its straight ticket device as a whole, as an entity, with the underlying format defining this basic orientation, whereas this would seem less to be the case with the office bloc-straight ticket ballot. Interaction of device with format could be occurring in the former case, while in the latter, the device would be having more of a separate effect from that of format. Interaction of effects would most likely occur if format and device were conceptually compatible and less likely if they were antithetical in purpose and orientation. [23]

The other two pairings of variables provided us with additional information. Their results will be discussed here, but the actual data patterns are presented in a summary table below, table 29.7. [24] The second pairing of variables, ballot format and party emblem, gave further evidence of the dominating explanatory power of ballot format. However, party emblem did have some influence in the party column case, making "party" even more salient to the voter and thereby decreasing split ticket voting tendencies slightly more than if it had not been present. Comparisons of the office bloc format with and without a party emblem could not be made since so few cases of the former pairing existed then and none do today. The problem of few cases made it difficult to hazard any test of interactive effects, although it seems plausible that people viewed the party column-emblem configuration as a single entity because of the compatible orientation.

The last pairing of variables, the two ballot provisions themselves, showed some modest decrease in split ticket voting when both partisan devices were

---

[23] This interpretation of interactive effects in the party column—straight ticket case is suggested but not necessarily confirmed by the data at hand. As one can observe, the important off-diagonal cell entries in table 29.6 have few cases and may not significantly depart from a value of 4.0, a condition indicating additive (separate) effects instead of interactive effects.

[24] A collapsing of some categories in table 29.7 is needed to recover the points discussed for these two pairings of variables. However, this is a simple mental exercise and saves us from presenting two further bivariate tables at this time which would only convey the same information as table 29.7.

Table 29.7 Relation of Particular Ballot Configurations to Split Ticket
Voting 1890–1908

Ballot Configuration	Party Column	Office Bloc	Marginals
Straight Ticket and Emblem	2.3 (57)	3.5 (2)	2.3 (59)
Straight Ticket Without Emblem	3.1 (49)	3.7 (14)	3.2 (63)
Neither Straight Ticket Nor Emblem	3.0 (17)	5.3 (63)	4.8 (80)
Marginals	2.7 (123)	5.0 (79)	3.6 (202)

NOTE: Entries are split ticket means computed over all election years, 1890–1908, for states having the ballot combinations listed in the table. The ballot combination of emblem but no straight ticket did not exist for any office bloc or party column cases; for this reason, it was not included as a category in the table.

present instead of just one. That is, the combination of a straight ticket and emblem provision reduced ticket-splitting in comparison to the "straight ticket only" type of ballot. The reason for this seems logical. The two devices share a common orientation and possibly interact in their effects, highlighting still further the partisan guideline. It is also of interest to note that the straight ticket-emblem combination, except for two cases, appeared only on the partisan-oriented Indiana format. The question of interactive effects between the two variables could not really be resolved since no state adopted a ballot form with an emblem but without a straight ticket.

The ballot combinations just presented can be summarized in one table. The cell cases decrease with an enlarged table, but the contrasts apparent in it are well worth the sacrifice. Table 29.7 presents these results.

Most of the discoveries of the pairwise comparisons mentioned above are repeated and highlighted here. The general influence of ballot format pervades the table. Some of the largest differences in the figures are attributable to it, and when the other variables are controlled, ballot format confronts one vividly as the dominant variable. The row marginals tell the story of decreasing split ticket voting with an increase in the number of partisan features in use. To understand this better, between-cell comparisons must be made. Reading the columns from bottom to top, one can see, in general, that adding a partisan provision to a given ballot type has the effect of decreasing the ticket-splitting. For instance, with the office bloc figures, ticket-splitting decreases by 1.6 percent when a straight ticket device is added. The counterpart party column cells show no decrease, this being the one deviant category in the data pattern. However, when going from straight ticket only to both straight ticket and emblem on the party column ballot, a decrease of 0.8 percent in split ticket voting is manifest.[25] When viewing the whole table from bottom right to top left, the decrease in split ticket voting progresses in a rather orderly and consistent fashion.

Thus ballot format, in its basic definition of the alternatives open to the voter, is a major key to understanding the incidence of ticket-splitting. The two partisan devices, straight ticket and emblem features, complement the party column format and, as a result, have some further role in heightening the salience of the "party vote" alternative. But clearly they are of secondary concern, interacting with the dominant theme portrayed by the ballot format. Such devices on an alien format, the Massachusetts type, stand in . contrast to the voting alternative suggested by its structure. Something more akin to separate effects is registered in this case by the partisan devices.

Summary

The findings of this study of the Australian Ballot can be summarized as follows:

1. The introduction and establishment of the Australian Ballot in the states led to an increase in ticket-splitting in comparison to the previous ballot system. Placing both major parties on the same ballot and guaranteeing a secret vote were the major new provisions of the Australian Ballot that allowed and encouraged the expression of cross-party preferences in the polling booth. Government preparation and regulation of the ballot assured the enforcement of the consolidation and secrecy provisions and made the ballot uniform and impartial throughout a state.

2. The unofficial ballot system in use previous to that time was distinguished by very little split ticket voting. This lack of ticket-splitting was explained by the existence of non-secret, easily identifiable, separate party ballots and the way in which the party workers peddled them to the voters. The situation forced a single choice on the voter—which party's ballot to take. A deviant form of this ballot system, using a separate party ballot for each office, revealed somewhat higher split ticket patterns. The possibility of voting a split ticket was more apparent in this situation.

3. The extent to which ticket-splitting rose from the unofficial to the Australian Ballot depended on the type of internal format used on the Australian Ballot. The party column format displayed a slightly higher split ticket pattern than the unofficial ballot. The remarkable conceptual and physical similarity of the two explains the closeness of the difference—voters were familiar with a certain kind of ballot and the party column format was compatible with their earlier voting habits. Voters only gradually adjusted to. the split ticket potential existing with this form of the Australian Ballot. The

---

[25] Comparison of the counterpart office bloc figures, 3.7 and 3.5, is unwarranted since the latter figure is based on so few cases. Also, the cells with 17 and 14 cases must be interpreted with caution, as footnote 23 earlier suggested.

office bloc format, on the other hand, was a complete contrast to the unofficial ballot and therefore revealed much higher split ticket patterns than its predecessor. A more immediate adjustment to it was forced on the voter.

4. By implication from the discussion in (3), the party column and office bloc forms themselves had very different split ticket voting patterns. The party column ballot was associated with a low level of ticket-splitting, since it was the more partisan-oriented of the two. The office bloc ballot displayed a much stronger split ticket pattern as a result of its multiple-choice orientation.

5. The inclusion of a partisan feature on a ballot format also had consequences on voting patterns. A straight ticket addition on an office bloc ballot decreased split ticket voting because it worked against the multi-choice orientation of this format. On the party column ballot, use of a straight ticket alone had no effect, but when an emblem was also added, some decrease in split ticket voting occurred. Throughout, however, the dominant variable was the ballot format itself. When the partisan devices were included, they decreased ticket-splitting within a narrow range of the levels imposed by ballot format.

6. The general picture is one of ballot being an important explanatory variable in the 1876-1908 time period. While other theories can be offered to explain split ticket voting trends, the contributing factor of the ballot cannot be denied its role in any such discussion. It allowed an element of flexibility to enter the system and, perhaps, helped to shape new trends in party organization, new boundaries of political competition. The system was more in flux, and ballot had helped to set it in motion.

Burnham's Theory

To date only one other theory has been advanced to explain the split ticket voting patterns of this period. The theory proposed by Walter Dean Burnham purports to explain the rise in ticket-splitting of this period by a breakdown in party organization and competition and a corresponding alienation of the voter from the political system. Before this breakdown, the electorate was, according to Burnham, quite firmly rooted in the party milieu and "party" served as the main reference group in the system.

Burnham's evidence for his theoretical conclusions is the split ticket records of five states, only four of which will concern us here. [26] But one could contend, given the above ballot analysis, that the increase in ticket-splitting observed by Burnham is, in fact, mainly due to the introduction and establishment of the official ballot in this period. The crucial question is how much variation in voting, if any, is there left to "explain" after ballot has explained all that it can. Any additional variation could be considered "fair game" for other variables, such as Burnham's, to interpret.

---

[26] Burnham's fifth state, Oklahoma, is not relevant to this analysis since it entered the Union at the end of the time period covered in this study.

In order to answer this question, a series of "expected" split ticket values for the four states were computed—"expected" in the sense that they encompassed the mean effects on split ticket voting of all other states using the same Australian Ballot configuration; then, these figures were compared with the "actual" values of the four states.[27] The results are presented in table 29.8 for each state's first election year of official ballot use, its second year of such use, and the remaining time spans for presidential and congressional election years, respectively.

The "difference values" in the table are the items to note. They sum up for the various years of interest the additional split ticket voting a state had left over after the effects of ballot were removed from the picture. Positive values indicate that some split ticket voting was left over; negative values indicated the reverse—that the states in question did not even achieve a split ticket value as high as the mean figure of other states using the same ballot configuration. A state-by-state analysis reveals that three of the four states had little or no additional split ticket voting for factors other than ballot to explain. The mean difference values for Ohio, New York, and Pennsylvania across these years are −.1, −.2, and .2, respectively. Only Michigan with a mean of 1.9 provides an exception to the general theme. The mean difference for all states over all years is 0.5, with Michigan providing most of the positive component in the computation. A value of zero would indicate that other explanatory factors were not needed for these states.

The reasons for such small difference values seem clear in the framework of previous ballot analyses. All four states had party column-straight ticket ballots and all save Pennsylvania had an emblem as well. Such states displayed only moderate split ticket increases in their Australian years relative to earlier ballot days. What increases in ticket-splitting there were to explain could easily be done by resort to the ballot variable alone. Only in Michigan did there seem to be other factors entering the picture.

The types of variables Burnham mentioned in his theory were supposed to be making widespread, not miniscule, changes in voting. While this could be the case in Michigan, it definitely is not so in the other three states. It is possible that a study of other states in this context might show additional

---

[27] The model used to compute these "expected" values is a simple additive one based on the formula, $Y = X + Z$. In the formula, X equals the state's pre-Australian split ticket effect, and Z refers to the net effect of other states with the same official ballot configuration as the state in question. The latter effect is computed by taking all such states for the election year (or year span) in question and subtracting their unofficial ballot mean from their official ballot mean. The type of election is held constant throughout the computations. An example for a state's first election year of official ballot use (year "A" in the table) will illustrate the procedure. The state of Ohio changed to a party column-straight ticket-emblem ballot in a presidential year. Therefore, its "X" value would be the mean split ticket value for presidential years in the unofficial ballot period. The "Z" value would find the same type of mean for all other states with that particular ballot configuration and subtract it from their mean value for the election year in which Ohio's ballot change occurred. Then, one merely adds the "X" and "Z" values together to get the "expected" split ticket value Y for Ohio in this particular election year.

Table 29.8 Expected and Actual Split Ticket Values in Selected Time Periods for Four States

Split Ticket Values	Michigan				Ohio				New York				Pennsylvania			
	A	B	C	D	A	B	C	D	A	B	C	D	A	B	C	D
Actual split ticket values (1)	(2.2)	1.5	6.6	3.5	0.7	(0.2)	2.4	0.9	2.3	0.8	2.4	0.1	0.1	0.2	0.8	6.1
Expected split ticket values (2)	1.2	1.0	2.1	2.1	1.0	0.1	2.3	1.1	1.2	0.7	3.3	1.1	0.1	1.1	3.0	2.2
Differences of (1) and (2) (3)	1.0	0.5	4.5	1.4	−0.3	0.1	0.1	−0.2	1.1	0.1	−0.9	−1.0	0.0	−0.9	−2.2	3.9

NOTE: Each state has actual and expected split ticket values for the following years: first election year of official ballot use, second election year of official ballot use, mean of the remaining presidential election years in the 1890–1908 time span, and mean of the remaining congressional election years in the 1890–1908 time span. These four time periods are designated in the table as "A," "B," "C," and "D," respectively. Those split ticket values enclosed in parentheses in row (1) are "impure" values as defined in footnote 10 above. The state of Pennsylvania was included as a data point in the official ballot period only until 1903 for three reasons. First, this state changed its ballot in 1903, providing a stimulus other states did not share—a stimulus that could contaminate the ensuing voter reactions in light of the previous experience with another official ballot format. Second, the time span for the second form (1904–1908) was too short to provide a reliable estimate of its split ticket effects. Third, the ballot change was to an office bloc–straight ticket combination, a virtual rarity among the states, thereby providing too few cases to ascertain its net effects in these other states.

ticket-splitting beyond what could be explained by ballot—but the crucial point is that the key examples of states used by Burnham do not confirm his theory. Even if other states showed such a tendency, Burnham would still have to account for other plausible features of this period which could cause ticket-splitting.

The ballot variable also seems to contribute to another of Burnham's findings. In his analysis, Burnham was concerned with not only the increased tendency toward ticket-splitting, but also toward "roll-off"—the tendency of the electorate to vote in greater numbers for high than for low prestige offices on the ballot. In the four states examined, Burnham found an increase in roll-off in the exact time period when the official ballot was adopted in these states. The official ballot contributed to roll-off since it was long and consolidated, requiring substantial effort on the part of the voter to mark all offices. But the unofficial ballot required less effort in voting than the official ballot—in many states, merely depositing the ticket in the ballot box, and, in some others, the marking of offices down a single column with no attendant decision-making involved as to partisan choices.[28]

The Institutional Environment

The position of this paper has been that the Australian Ballot had an important effect on split ticket voting behavior. But its broader position has been that the institutional properties of the electoral system, considered either as an entity or as a network of component parts, have played and continue to play a crucial role in influencing and shaping voting behavior—in essentially defining the conditions and boundaries of decision-making at the polls. Stanley Kelley and cohorts, in their excellent article on registration variables, probably stated it best—it is a matter of "putting first things first."

By "institutional properties" are meant those laws, customs, and norms that define and regulate the broader entity known as the electoral system. Such things as registration requirements, electoral qualification laws, voting systems (e.g., plurality, proportional representation systems), ballot and voting machine arrangements, and the like are the framework of the system. Introduction of new properties or changes in existing ones affect the voting setting and, in turn, the behavior and attitudes of people. Yet, all too often

---

[28] In an interesting piece of research, Jack Walker has shown that roll-off also varies according to the type of official ballot in use—the office bloc ballot contributing more to a roll-off effect than the party column ballot. Walker also views his findings as a possible modifying factor on Burnham's theory as the following quotation suggests: "The argument made by both Burnham and Stiefbold that increasing roll-off is an indication of increasing political alienation at least is weakened by our finding that changes in ballot forms directly affect the amount of roll-off" (p. 462). See Jack L. Walker, "Ballot Forms and Voter Fatigue: An Analysis of the Office Bloc and Party Column Ballots," *Midwest Journal of Political Science,* 10(November 1966):448-63.

the institutional environment has been taken for granted or as a "given" instead of being probed for its effects on political behavior.

The attempt of this study and a few others has been to demonstrate the importance of these variables. In this study, important and often large effects on voting have been shown to be associated with one such institutional variable when it was first introduced into the environment. Comparing these effects to contemporary election data tells us that ballot had its greatest effects in the period of this study because of its novelty and fairly immediate impact and then tapered off to a more normal, stable trendline as it became a commonplace in the political culture. Although the necessary research has yet to be done, the author would venture that the most crucial effects of any institutional property are visible in the early period of its use and then settle back to more normal differentiations in later years.

The explanatory power of institutional variables offers insight for future analyses. The introduction, establishment, or change in such factors can lend useful interpretations to shifts in electoral behavior. Take, for example, the changing vote turnout curve around the turn of the century, which cries for explanation. This sudden shift to lower turnout was another variable used by Burnham to justify his theory of party breakdown and voter alienation. But a more plausible explanation would be the effects of a newly enacted registration systems of the time, placing an additional barrier to the vote. Without much effort the reader can probably think of several other analytic uses to which this highly important set of variables could be put.

30. Parties and the Nationalization of Electoral Forces

DONALD E. STOKES

The fact that party systems have flourished in the modern world is at least partly due to the ease with which parties are seen as significant political actors by the mass public. Their presence can simplify wonderfully the *dramatis personae* of politics for a remote and very imperfectly informed audience, a fact that helps account for the durability of partisan attitudes once formed. [1] Among the gentle reifications by which the public makes sense of politics, imputing reality to the parties may be the most important of all. [2]

SOURCE: *The American Party Systems: Stages of Political Development,* by William Nisbet Chambers and Walter Dean Burnham. Copyright © 1967 by Oxford University Press, Inc. Reprinted with permission of the publisher.

AUTHOR'S NOTE: I am greatly indebted to Michael J. Kahan, Ronald May, and Arthur C. Wolfe for their aid in preparing this report. The immense task of assembling historical election returns was undertaken by Peter Axelrod, John Francis, Barbara Lazarus, Cathy Miller, Philip Quarterman, Margaret Squires, and Jill Wescott. Finally, I owe large debts to David Butler and Warren Miller, with whom I have explored various aspects of the British and American data discussed here.

[1] Graham Wallas wrote years ago that the citizen requires "something simpler and more permanent, something which can be loved and trusted, and which can be recognized at successive elections as being the same thing that was loved and trusted before; and party is such a thing." *Human Nature in Politics* (London, 1910), p. 83.

[2] One suspects that a majority of political scientists specializing in parties could be carried for the proposition that American parties as unitary entities don't exist; but the reasons that would lead them to think so trouble the American voter almost not at all. Perhaps the achievement represented by the reification of parties can be seen more clearly if we consider a rival schema for classifying leaders, such as that of Left and Right. As a means of typing political actors, liberal and conservative identifications probably are more real than party labels to many elite observers, but they have repeatedly been found to be of little meaning to the mass public.

Over the past quarter-century, survey studies of the American voter have detailed the importance of parties as cognitive objects.[3] Parties are among the first political objects visible to the very young, and the partisan identifications into which the child is "socialized" within the political culture of the family have a remarkable capacity to survive into adulthood. As an adult, the voter relies on his party allegiance to value new leaders and issues and to impose some order on the choices that are presented by a ballot of spectacular length and complexity.

Moreover, the conserving role of party identification by no means exhausts the significance of parties as objects of political attitude. The issues and events which deflect the partisan voter from his established allegiance, temporarily at least, and which can provide the whole grounds of choice for the independent voter of no fixed allegiance, may also be seen in our terms of party. To cite an example which has echoed through much of our political history, the cry to throw the rascals out has generally identified the rascals in party terms.

The reality which parties have as objects of mass perception is the more remarkable in view of the actual fragmentation of party structure and the diffusion of authority produced on all levels of government by the doctrine of separated powers. Indeed, the ambiguity of parties as stimulus objects suggests that the focus of partisan attitudes may vary a good deal and that the modern American experience may differ from that of other liberal democracies or earlier periods of our own politics. The very richness of contemporary American survey data poses the danger that conclusions of unwarranted generality will be drawn from the evidence at hand.[4]

This possibility is the backdrop to the empirical argument which I shall give. An analysis of election returns for the United States House of Representatives has made me feel that the past century has witnessed a profound change in the degree to which a local politics has produced the forces moving the electorate in our congressional elections. I shall describe this evolution here, drawing for purposes of contrast on comparable returns from parliamentary elections in Britain. Both the American development and the contrast with Britain seem to me to have important implications for political representation.

II

This analysis had its origin in a study of legislative representation in Britain and America, a study which has paid a good deal of attention to popular

---

[3] The empirical literature treating partisan attitudes in the adult and pre-adult years is by now vast. For a discussion of party identifications in the adult electorate, see Angus Campbell, Philip E. Converse, Warren E. Miller, and Donald E. Stokes, *The American Voter* (New York: Wiley, 1960), chaps. 6 and 7. For a seminal discussion of the development of partisan orientations in the young, see Fred I. Greenstein, *Children and Politics* (New Haven: Yale University Press, 1965), esp. 55–84.

[4] The need for restraint in extrapolating from contemporary survey evidence has been sensed by many writers, including a number of survey analysts. See the cautionary argument advanced by Walter Dean Burnham, "The Changing Shape of the American Political Universe," *American Political Science Review*, 59(1965):7–28.

influence on the cohesion of the parliamentary and congressional parties. Many influences affect the solidarity of a legislative party, but the members' perception of forces on their constituents' voting behavior is surely among them. Part of what is involved here is exactly the sort of cognitive question I have touched: what political actors are salient to the mass electorate? If the member of the legislature believes, on the one hand, that it is the national party and its leaders which are salient and that his own electoral prospects depend on the legislative record of the party as a whole, his bonds to the legislative party will be relatively strong. This is the situation posited by the model of responsible party government. But if the legislator believes, on the other hand, that the public is dominated by constituency influences and that his prospects depend on his own or his opponent's appeal or on other factors distinctive to the constituency, his bonds to the legislative party will be relatively weak. To these two levels of forces the intermingling of American elections adds a third: public response to statewide political leaders, whose coattails may extend into congressional contests via the long ballot.

To assess the relative importance of forces at these various levels I have utilized a statistical model which partitions the total variation of turnout and the party vote over a series of legislative elections into distinct components corresponding to the several levels at which influences on the electorate may arise. I shall say very little here about the model's formal properties since they are treated at length elsewhere.[5] The model detects the relative influence of forces at several levels by exploiting the nesting of a number of constituencies within a state or region and of a number of states or regions within the country as a whole. It can be seen intuitively that if the forces moving the electorate were perfectly idiosyncratic to individual constituencies, variations of turnout or party strength would show no more than a chance similarity across the constituencies of a state or region or across the whole nation. Detecting no more than chance similarity, the model would

---

[5] The model represents the proportion Y_{ijk} turning out or voting Republican in the jth congressional district of the ith state in the kth election year as a sum of three fixed and three random terms:

$$Y_{ijk} = \alpha + \beta_i + \gamma_{ij} + a_k + b_{ik} + c_{ijk} \tag{1}$$

where α is the fixed effect of national politics; β_i the fixed effect of politics in the ith state; γ_{ij} the fixed effect of politics in the jth district of the ith state; a_k the effect of national politics in the kth year; b_{ik} the effect of politics in the ith state in the kth year, and c_{ijk} the effect of politics in the jth district of the ith state in the kth year. It follows from this that the variance of Y_{ij} over the five congressional elections of a decade ($k = 1, \ldots, 5$) depends only on the variances and covariances of the three terms which vary over time; that is,

$$\text{Var } (Y_{ij}) = \text{Var } (a) + \text{Var } (b_i) + \text{Var } (c_{ij})$$
$$+ 2[\text{Cov } (a, b_i) + \text{Cov } (a, c_{ij}) + \text{Cov } (b_i, c_{ij})]. \tag{2}$$

A detailed discussion of the model appears in Donald E. Stokes, "A Variance Components Model of Political Effects," in John M. Claunch, ed., *Mathematical Applications in Political Science I* (Dallas: Arnold Foundation, 1965), 61-85. The paper gives the detailed formulas by which each of the terms of equation (2) may be calculated for individual congressional districts and averaged across the nation to reach explicit estimates of the magnitude of national, state, and constituency components of the total variance of turnout and party strength in the five elections of a given decade.

attribute all forces on electoral change to the constituency level. But if politics at the state or national level did have common effects across a number of constituencies, turnout or party strength would show parallel movements, and the model would attribute an influence to these higher levels of politics according to the degree of observed similarity. In this manner the total average variance of turnout or party strength can be partitioned into components due to forces acting on the electorate at each of several levels.

In the case of recent congressional voting, for example, there can be little doubt of the presence of national forces, especially when a congressional election is joined to a contest for the presidency. Likewise there can be little doubt that congressional voting reflects forces that arise in the individual constituency—the personal stature of the candidates, the hold of local party organizations, the intrusion of purely local issues. And it is part of the lore of American politics that statewide contests for governor or senator may also affect congressional races. The question therefore is not which of these forces are felt at all but rather what is their relative magnitude. It is this question which the model seeks explicitly to answer.

III

When applied to the congressional returns from the 1950's, the most recent full decade yielding the required data, the model gives strikingly dissimilar results for turnout and party choice. In the five elections from 1952 to 1960 by far the largest component of the variance of turnout was that measuring national influences. As shown in table 30.1a, forces beyond the constituency, especially those attendant on contests for the presidency, played the foremost role in the rise and fall of participation in congressional contests. Indeed, inspection of the components in the table's third column shows that

Table 30.1 Components of Variance of Vote for U.S. House of Representatives Over Five Elections, 1952-60

Political Level	Variance Component	Square Root of Variance Component	Normalized Variance component
a. Turnout			
National	72.87	8.54	.86
State	7.20	2.68	.08
Constituency	5.22	2.28	.06
			1.00
b. Party Vote			
National	9.32	3.05	.32
State	5.32	2.31	.19
Constituency	13.98	3.74	.49
			1.00

national forces accounted for nearly seven-eighths of the total variance of congressional turnout in this decade. It is interesting to note that statewide forces were at least as influential on congressional turnout as were forces arising within the constituency.

A very different pattern of variation of the party vote in the 1950's appears in table 30.1b. Much the largest component of the variance of party support is that measuring constituency influences; indeed, the third column of table 30.1b shows that almost half of the total variance could be attributed to this level. National forces were again substantial, although nothing like as influential as they were in the voter's decision whether or not to go to the polls. Apparently the coattails of presidential candidates are much more likely to pull voters to the polls than to govern what choices for Congress they make. The partisan influence of statewide contests on congressional races was by no means negligible, but was plainly the least important of the three.

Comparisons across the several political levels of table 30.1 suggest a good deal about the dynamics of voting for Congress in the recent past. These figures take on new sharpness, however, when they are compared to values obtained for other periods or other electoral systems. Indeed, no comparison is more instructive than that with Britain, the other great representational system to which I have given attention.

IV

Empirical comparisons across national frontiers are notoriously vulnerable to institutional and cultural dissimilarities extraneous to the problem at hand. Two structural differences between Britain and America have had to be dealt with in the comparison I shall give. The first of these has to do with the party system. The presence of the Liberals deprives British politics of a "pure" two-party character and confronts the investigator with a choice of ways to calculate variations of the electoral strength of the two main parties. Fortunately, for my purposes here it makes almost no difference which of several reasonable alternatives is chosen.[6]

------

[6] The differences between the several proposed measures of change turn on whether shifts of party strength are to be percentaged in terms of the total vote for one, two, or three parties, or the total registered electorate. I have chosen to use as a percentage base the combined total of the Conservative and Labour vote. For the kth election we may calculate for any parliamentary constituency the quantity

$$M_k = \frac{Con_k - Lab_k}{2}$$

where Con_k is the Conservative percent of the two-party vote, Lab_k the Labour percent. M_k can be thought of as the margin by which the Conservative share departed (positively or negatively) from 50 percent, that is, from being even with Labour's. Then the "swing" (positive or negative) to the Conservatives between a first and second election may be defined as $M_2 - M_1$, and the total variance of M_{ij}, that is, of the Conservative margin of the jth constituency of the ith region over a set of K elections ($k = 1, \ldots, K$), may be partitioned into national, regional, and constituency components by the model described above.

Table 30.2 Components of Variance of Party Vote Over
Five National Elections

Political Level	Variance Component	Square Root of Variance Component	Normalized Variance Component
a. For the U.S. House of Representatives, 1952-1960			
National	9.32	3.05	.32
State	5.32	2.31	.19
Constituency	13.98	3.74	.49
			1.00
b. For the British Parliament, 1950-1966			
National	5.13	2.26	.47
Regional	1.42	1.19	.13
Constituency	4.45	2.11	.40
			1.00

A more serious structural difference arises from the absence in Britain of the intermediate state level of the American federal system. The fact that single-member constituencies are the basis of representation in both the House of Representatives and the House of Commons provides the ground for comparing the national and constituency components in the two nations, but there is of course no direct British analogue to the effect of statewide contests on American congressional voting. I have nevertheless retained in the British analysis an intermediate "regional" component to detect common movements of party support in regional groupings of parliamentary constituencies.[7] This component keeps such regional movements from being falsely incorporated into the constituency component, but its interpretation must necessarily differ from that given the American state component.[8]

With these qualifications, the partisan components obtained from parliamentary election returns over the six British general elections of 1950, 1951, 1955, 1959, 1964, and 1966 show a profound divergence from the American congressional components of the past decade. These contrasts are set forth in table 30.2, which reproduces in 30.2a the American partisan components of table 30.1 for comparison with the partisan components for Britain, which are given in 30.2b. A first observation to be made from a comparison of tables 30.2a and 30.2b is that the electoral strength of the parties has been a good deal less variable in Britain than in America. Inspection of correspond-

[7] The definition of regions is very close to that given in the appendix to David Butler and Anthony King, *The British General Election of 1966* (London: Macmillan, 1966), 300-10.
[8] In particular, it is possible that regional effects are actually differential responses of regional clusters of constituencies to *national* forces. To some extent such "downward" deflections of forces are monitored by the model's covariance terms, as explained by Stokes, "A Variance Components Model of Political Effects," 74-5.

ing entries in the first two columns of table 30.2a and 30.2b shows the British figures to be uniformly smaller, in most cases markedly so. The more revealing comparison, however, is the relative size of the several partisan components within these two systems. In Britain the national component was the most important element of party change: very nearly half the total variance could be attributed to national forces. The constituency component contributed a somewhat smaller proportion of the total variance than in the United States. And when the contrast of constituency forces is made in terms of absolute magnitudes, rather than of proportions, the difference is remarkable. Indeed, the ratio of constituency components in the first column of tables 30.2a and 30.2b is three to one.

The marked difference of constituency forces in the two countries may be clearer if we take the simpler problem of change between two elections only and compare the dispersion of change across constituencies. For this comparison I have chosen pairs of elections in Britain and America which exhibit fairly equal average change: the mean swing between parties across the parliamentary constituencies of Britain from 1951 to 1955 was 1.8 percent; the mean swing across congressional districts contested both in 1952 and 1956 also was 1.8 percent. Variation about these means, however, was very unequal in the two countries, as the distributions superimposed in figure

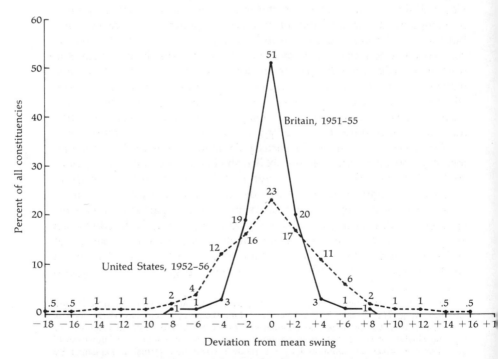

Figure 30.1 United States and Britain differentials in deviations from mean partisan swing, 1952-1956 and 1951-1955.

30.1 make clear. To focus attention on constituency influences in the two countries, both these distributions have been adjusted to remove the effect of state or regional, as well as national, forces. [9] The much sharper peak of the British curve makes clear how seldom forces centered on the individual parliamentary constituency yield a result which diverges strongly from a wider pattern of change.

There can be no doubt that table 30.2 and figure 30.1 describe a difference in electoral behavior which is of immense importance to representative government in Britain and America. The source of changes of voting for Congress lies a good deal within the individual constituency; of voting for Parliament, less so. Of course, these facts will give the legislator a national or constituency orientation only as he perceives the true source of electoral change. Interviews of congressmen and M.P.'s taken as part of the larger research project make clear, however, that the difference of electoral behavior reflected here is vividly apparent to the legislative elites of these two countries. [10]

Britain may well provide an extreme case of the nationalization of political attitude in the Western World; probably it is unique among nations which elect the national legislature from single-member constituencies. What is more, there is reason to believe that this aspect of the party system was strongly evident by the close of the last century, although the fissiparous behavior of nineteenth-century parliamentary elites and the displacement of the Liberals by Labour in this century make it difficult to submit this evolution to orderly analysis. For example, the homogeneity of change across the parliamentary constituencies of Britain between the general elections of 1892 and 1895 was already greater than the homogeneity of change in American congressional districts between successive elections of the 1950's. As shown by table 30.3 the standard deviation of swing over the life of the 1892 Parliament was 3.0 percent on an average swing of 4.0 percent; between the congressional elections of 1954 and 1958, for example, it was 6.3 percent on an average swing of 4.6 percent. The selected additional figures for Britain given in table 30.3 suggest that the nationalization of politics

[9] The correction for state or regional forces is a straightforward one. Adopting the notation of footnote 7, we may define M_{i1} as the average Conservative margin within the constituencies of the ith region in a first election; M_{i2} as the average Conservative margin in the ith region in a second election; M_{ij1} as the Conservative margin in the jth constituency of the ith region in the first election and M_{ij2} as the Conservative margin in the jth constituency of the ith region in the second election. The adjusted swing between elections in the jth constituency of the ith region is then calculated as

$$S_{ij} = M_{ij2} - M_{ij1} - (M_{i2} - M_{i1}).$$

[10] Data of this kind from American congressmen are reported in Donald E. Stokes and Warren E. Miller, "Party Government and the Saliency of Congress," *Public Opinion Quarterly*, 26(1962):532–46. The data from comparable interviews of Members of Parliament will be reported in a forthcoming analysis of representation in Britain and America. One of my parliamentary respondents, who stood in the Home Counties in 1964, wistfully reported that he had been delighted by the increase of his majority until he realized that his swing was dead on the national average.

Table 30.3 Some Swing Figures from Britain and the United States

Election Years	No. of Constituencies	Mean	Standard Deviation
a. Britain: General Elections			
1892–1895	307	4.0%	3.0%
1906–(Jan) 1910	419	4.9	4.4
1945–1950	135	4.5	3.7
1950–1951	224	.7	1.4
1951–1955	349	1.8	1.4
1955–1959	455	1.1	2.2
1959–1964	370	3.5	2.4
1964–1966	429	3.2	1.7

NOTE: The constituencies included in these analyses are those whose boundaries were not subject to marked change between the given pair of elections and whose patterns of candidature (i.e. Conservative vs. Labour, or Conservative vs. Labour vs. Liberal, etc.) were the same at both elections.

b. United States: Congressional Elections			
1952–1954	318	4.3	5.2
1954–1956	333	2.2	5.1
1956–1958	324	6.9	5.5
1958–1960	327	2.7	5.6
1952–1956	322	1.8	6.4
1954–1958	318	4.6	6.3
1956–1960	333	4.1	6.7

NOTE: Includes only constituencies contested both years of each pair of elections.

increased somewhat from the turn of the century to the present era, although the data would be much less clear for the intervening years of Liberal decline.

Casting the problem in these developmental terms inevitably carries our interest back to the historical antecedents of our American findings. If congressional voting in the middle of this century reveals substantial constituency influences on electoral change, what does the more distant past show? What patterns can be drawn from remote congressional returns by the model utilized for the present era?

V

The five congressional elections of a decade provide a natural group for such an analysis of historical returns. The Constitution's requirement that congressional seats be reapportioned among states after each decennial census has supplied an impetus every ten years for redrawing district boundaries. Once in a hundred years—after the 1920 census—Congress failed to discharge its constitutional mandate, and the courts in the 1960's have created special havoc with district lines. But the nine full decades of modern party development, from the 1870's through the 1950's, are accessible to an analysis of the development of congressional voting, and I have applied to the five congressional elections of each decade the statistical model utilized originally for the analysis of the 1950's.

Figure 30.2 gives the results of this historical analysis first of all for the constituency component of turnout. The results are impressive. Between the mid-nineteenth and mid-twentieth centuries variations of turnout became progressively less distinctive to congressional districts. Almost without a pause, the magnitude of constituency forces on turnout diminished over these nine decades to a level in the recent past which was very low indeed. While in large measure the electorate once went to the polls or stayed away according to the circumstances surrounding individual contests, this sort of influence has become exceedingly weak in recent times.

During this century there has been a complementary rise of national forces on turnout. The historical series of the national component, superimposed on the constituency series in figure 30.3, shows a marked rise over the five decades of this century. This rise followed a decline in the latter decades of the last century; the series indicates substantial national fluctuations of turnout, along with marked constituency variations, in the earliest decades after Reconstruction. In the twentieth century, however, the national and constituency series have diverged strongly, achieving a remarkable difference by the middle of the century. The series for the state component, also

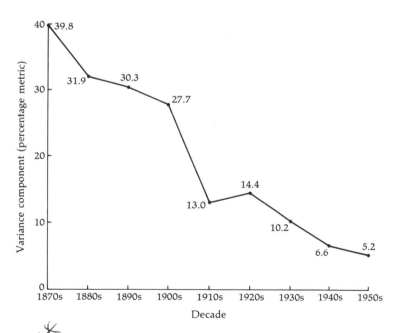

Figure 30.2 United States: changes in constituency influence on congressional-election turnout by decade. (Note: Only congressional districts with Democratic-Republican contests in all five elections of the decade are included.)

shown in figure 30.3, suggests that there has been a long-term secular decline of statewide forces on congressional turnout.

The decay of constituency influences on turnout has been paralleled by a
decline of constituency forces on the party vote in House races. The historical series for the constituency component of party strength is given by figure
30.4, where it is superimposed on the series for turnout. The two patterns
are broadly similar. The magnitude of constituency influences on the party
division did rise in the middle decades of this period but then fell away to a
level in the 1950's which was again, by comparison with the past, very low

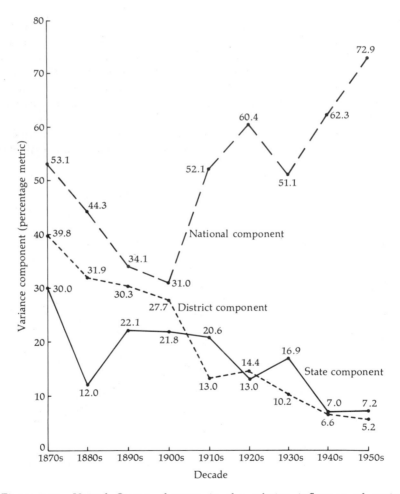

Figure 30.3 United States: changes in the relative influence of variance
components on congressional-election turnout, by decade. (Note: Only
congressional districts with Democratic-Republican contests in all five elections
of the decade are included.)

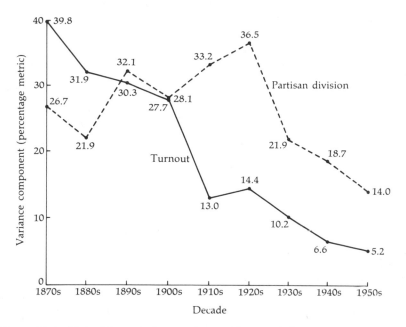

Figure 30.4 United States: changes in constituency influence on turnout and partisan division, by decade. (Note: Only congressional districts with Democratic-Republican contests in all five elections of the decade are included.)

indeed. The relative position of the two curves in the most recent decades suggests that constituency influences remain stronger in variations of party strength than of turnout, a finding detailed for the 1950's by table 30.1. And it is worth recalling that constituency influences on partisan voting for congressional candidates are stronger by a wide margin than constituency influences on partisan voting for British parliamentary candidates. But the primary conclusion to be drawn from the turnout and partisan components in the United States over most of a century is the substantial decline of the constituency as a distinct arena of conflict in congressional elections.[11]

The reasons for this decline must be several, and I shall offer little by way of grand explanation for the nationalization of politics on both sides of the Atlantic. Paradoxically, a fairly simple explanation may account for the major exception to the trend of these series, the temporary peaking of the partisan curve after the turn of the century. I suspect that the change of ballot form, which came in a rush in the closing years of the old century, may have been a main reason for this divergence. In 1888 "tickets" printed by the parties for their supporters were still almost universally in use, but by 1896 all but a few states had adopted some form of the Australian ballot,

---

[11] I shall defer to a later report an examination of the historical series of the national and state components of the partisan vote for Congress.

printed at public expense, carrying the names of all candidates for Congress and other offices contested in a general election, and allowing the citizen to vote in secrecy. [12] Coming at a time when the individual congressional district was a more vigorous arena of conflict than it is today, the encouragement which the consolidated secret ballot gave to variable party voting may well have produced the highs of the partisan component in the first decades of the new century. [13]

In many ways the decline of these historical series can be linked to more general processes of nationalization in American society. Probably one of the most important has to do with the changing structure of mass communications. In all eras of our politics, those contesting the congressional seat have had to compete for the attention of their electors. The quest for the voter's interest in the congressional district has never been easy, but in a day when the dissemination of news was controlled by local editors, abetted by the face-to-face communication networks of the American small town, it may have been a good deal easier. Certainly the rise of printed and broadcast media disseminating news to huge urban and hinterland audiences, of which any one congressional district is a small part, has worsened the lot of the congressional candidate, although it may in some cases have increased the visibility of state or urban candidates. Our interview studies of constituents in the present era show how much more salient to his voters is the congressman whose district comprises a "natural" community—Dayton, Ohio, let us say—than the congressman whose district is a fraction of a great metropolitan complex. The increasing mismatch of constituency and media audience can therefore have lessened steadily the visibility of congressional contests and, with it, the magnitude of forces distinctive to the constituency.

We can only believe that the centralization of mass communications has deeply influenced the nationalization of British politics. Today eight national morning newspapers achieve a coverage of four-fifths of British households, and very rarely does a single constituency provide the bulk of readers for a provincial daily. The centralization of news is even greater on radio and television which have never ventured into local broadcasting. The voter learns even less about his constituency from the mass media in Britain than he does in America.

And yet the evolution of mass communications in Britain should caution us against too facile an explanation of the nationalization of politics. It is true that the individual constituency counts for less today than it did prior to the rise of the national morning press in the first years of this century. But the strong parallelism of change across parliamentary constituencies appeared

---

[12] Frederick W. Dallinger, *Nominations for Elective Office in the United States* (New York, 1897), 173ff.

[13] This hypothesis ought to be checked in terms of the finer detail of electoral change, particularly by comparing, state by state, variations of the House vote before and after the exact year the ballot was changed. The source and magnitude of this influence would be clearer if a contrast were also drawn between the states adopting "straight-ticket" and "office-group" forms of the consolidated ballot.

earlier than that; indeed, we have already noted that this tendency was stronger in Britain during the 1890's than it was in America as late as the 1950's. The change that took place in British electoral politics somewhere in the latter half of the nineteenth century probably had more explicitly political origins, especially the great confrontation of Gladstone and Disraeli across the House, the extension of the franchise, and the rise of the national campaign. There may also have been critical political elements in the nationalization of congressional politics in the United States, especially the enormously increased salience of the federal government and the presidency in the period of Franklin D. Roosevelt and the New Deal.

Questions less of cause than of consequence, however, lay behind the analysis reported here. Whatever the factors in the decay of constituency influences over half a century or more, we may enquire into the effects of this development on political representation. A sure account of its effects would require evidence that is beyond reach, but I shall close with several observations on the nationalization of political attitude and representation in Parliament and Congress.

VI

The link between electoral forces and legislative behavior owes much of its elusiveness to the fact that it will depend on perceptions and motives held by the legislator himself. No electoral forces are likely to reach the man who knows his career is about to end by terminal illness, and the true forces acting on a constituency will not matter to the legislator who misperceives them totally. To enlarge what little we know of these perceptions in the current era, my colleagues and I have systematically interviewed Members of Congress and Members of Parliament, as well as samples of their constituents. But the fragmentary nature of such information from an earlier day precludes our measuring in any careful way the changes of perception which have accompanied the broadest changes of electoral forces.

The relationship between electoral patterns and legislative behavior would, however, be complex enough in terms of whatever it is in electoral "reality" that sensitizes the legislator to the forces on his electors. We may begin with the truism that the legislator who cares about his survival at the polls will defer more to electoral pressure, whatever its source, if his survival may depend on it. Hence, a nationalization of electoral forces will have greatest influence among those whose majorities can be swept away. There are of course many reasons—chairmanships, ministerial assignments, party loyalty, and the like—why a legislator can be concerned about the electoral fortunes of his party without his own seat being in danger. But we would expect electoral change to have a special poignancy for those whom it can put out of office.

The threat of defeat may be said to depend on two things, of which the first is the less tangible; for any existing majority, the possibility of defeat grows with the amplitude of change. If no more than 2 or 3 percent of voters can be expected to shift between elections, a majority of 10 percent will look impregnable; but if 20 or 30 percent can be expected to shift, such a lead will look very modest. Politicians rarely raise estimates of this kind to the level of an explicit calculus, but intuitive judgments as to the volatility of the vote constantly enter their assessments of the safeness of legislative seats.

The second, more tangible factor is of course the size of the legislator's majority. For any given amplitude of change, the threat of defeat will be greater where the margin has been narrow. As a means of classifying constituencies this factor is very often explicitly taken into account, and candidates, party managers, and the press all will make judgments as to the safeness of seats on the basis of the narrowness of prior victories.

It follows from this that we should heed the amplitude of change and the competitiveness of seats as we assess the legislative consequences of a change of the focus of electoral forces. These are matters on which Britain and America once again have differed profoundly. We have noted in table 30.2 that contemporary change is a good deal less extensive in Britain than in America. From 1950 to 1966—an interval which twice saw a turnover of party control—the average total variance of Labour or Conservative strength in British constituencies was less than half the average total variance of Republican or Democratic strength in America, and the contrast would be even greater if the congressional elections of the early 1960's were included in the comparison. If the two systems differed in this alone, the American congressman would live under the greater threat of defeat.

In fact, however, this difference is largely nullified by a contrast in the competitiveness of seats. The differences of partisan composition between the safest Conservative and safest Labour constituency is vast, but the massing of constituencies within a competitive range is somewhat more pronounced in Britain than America, even when a reasonable adjustment is made for what would have happened had the Republicans contested a greater number of Southern districts. For example, if we compare the congressional election of 1954 and the parliamentary election of 1955, elections in which the Democrats and Conservatives, respectively, won with comparable fractions of the two-party vote, the party winning the seat polled less than three-fifths of the two-party vote in 53 percent of Britain's constituencies but failed to exceed this margin in only 42 percent of congressional districts.

What is more, the competitiveness of American congressional districts is less today than it has been in some prior eras, particularly the era of the greatest change across the nation's constituencies, the decade of the 1890's and the first decades of this century. The distribution of Republican strength over the interval from 0 to 100 percent is shown in figure 30.5 for the elections of 1874, 1914, and 1958, elections which were once again won by comparable proportions of the whole two-party vote. By the standard of the classical era of Conservative-Liberal competition, the competitiveness of modern British constituencies also is less. The class basis of Conservative and Labour support and the class differences of constituencies have been

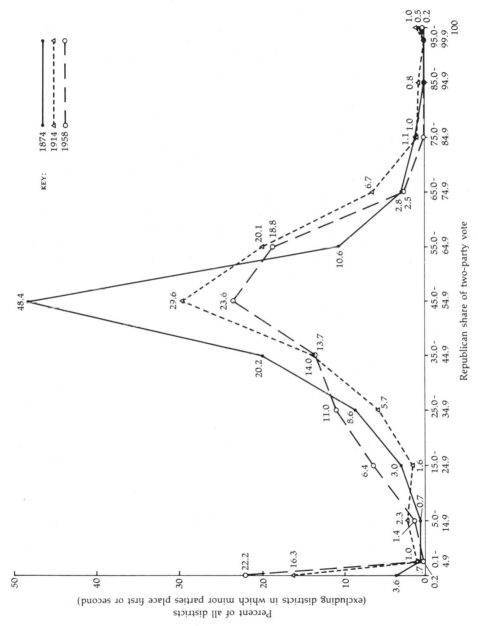

Figure 30.5 United States: decline in party competitiveness in congressional elections, 1874–1958.

enough to ensure this. But the concentration of constituencies over a middle range of party strength is still considerably stronger in Britain than it is in modern America. Even with the much greater amplitude of change in American congressional voting, congressmen are no more often than British M.P.'s under a threat of losing their seats in a general election.

This conclusion is borne out by the frequency with which seats change party hands in the two countries. In the parliamentary elections from 1950 to 1966 the average number of seats changing party control was less than 7 percent. In the congressional elections from 1952 to 1960 the average number of seats changing control was not greatly different. Despite the much greater amplitude of the fluctuations of party strength in the typical congressional district, comparable proportions of seats changed hands in the two countries, as shown by the first column of table 30.4. Since the typical parliamentary constituency lay closer to an even division of party strength, it could have the nearly same probability of changing hands on a much smaller average swing.

The pattern of turnover of party control also shows the greater nationalization of political attitude in Britain. Seats changed hands in Britain during this period almost completely in accord with the national trends of party strength. As shown in the second column of table 30.4, less than 8 percent of the changes of control within parliamentary constituencies were contrary to national movements of party strength. But in America during this period a very sizable minority of seats changed hands against the national tide. Indeed, if we note that a tide would run at all only as this figure is well below 50 percent, the actual 22 percent of changes against the national trend shows how strong were the influences on congressional voting distinctive to the individual district.

It would therefore be wrong to assume that the long-term decay of constituency forces in the United States has led the members of the congressional parties to identify their own fortunes strongly with the public's response to more national leaders and programs. If the competitiveness typical of congressional districts in the years after Reconstruction had survived the party realignment of the 1890's, the decline of the constituency as an arena of conflict might have done more to yield such a result. As it is, the congressman's usual majority and the remaining constituency influences are large

Table 30.4 Electoral Turnover in the United States House of Representatives and The British House of Commons (Percentages)

Country	Mean Proportion of Seats Changing Party Hands	Mean Proportion of Seats Changing Party Hands Which Moved Against Tide
United States, 1952–60	7.7	22.1
Britain, 1950–66	6.4	7.4

enough in American congressional parties to weaken the electoral logic of cohesion so clearly understood in Parliament.

And yet these qualifications in no way diminish the interest of the secular decline of constituency forces apparent in these data. Changes of party strength, and, even more, of turnout, over many decades show that by the middle of this century the public decided whether and how to vote for Congress less than ever before on the basis of influences distinctive to the constituency. If the nationalization of political forces has carried less far in America than in Britain it seems nevertheless an outstanding aspect of our elections for Congress over the life of the modern party system.

Name Index

Subject Index

Abstention. *See* Voting turnout
Age. *See* Issues, and the life cycle;
    Participation, and the life cycle; Party
    identification, and the life cycle;
    Voting choice, and the life cycle
Alienation. *See* Cynicism, political
American Independent Party. *See* Multiple
    parties; Political parties; Names of
    individual leaders in Name Index
Apathy, political, 27-29. *See also* Interest in
    politics
Australian Ballot, 445, 485-489

Ballot form, 468
    Australian Ballot, 445, 485-489
    effects of changes, 445, 449, 468n,
        488-490, 494-495, 497-502, 508-512,
        525-526
    and fraud, 444
    history of changes, 485-488
Belief systems. *See* Ideology
Blacks, 10, 78, 121n, 378-379, 389, 440
    participation, 27, 28n, 62-63, 327n, 366
    party identification, 307n, 327-330, 338,
        339-340, 353-354, 428, 434
    restrictions on voting, 456, 480
    voting behavior, 13, 309, 366
    See also Civil rights

Canada, 453
Candidates
    attitudes toward, 69, 164, 167, 174, 191n,
        202-203, 214-216, 234, 279-282,
        383-385
    distinguished from issues, 165, 168, 192n,
        201-202
    perceived differences, 51
    spatial representation, 174, 372-382
    thermometers, 28, 155-156, 214-216,
        371-372, 383-385
    and voting, 12, 47, 161-162, 164, 167,
        171, 174, 191-192, 202-204, 213
    See also Voting choice, determinants of;
        Voting choice, transmission between
        generations
Causal modeling, 168, 169, 174, 191-192,
    198-209, 235, 286
Chicago, 213

Citizen duty, 2, 26, 38-44, 54
Civil liberties, 5-7, 74, 75, 111-112, 129
Civil rights, 53, 87, 105, 162, 166, 182, 210,
    213-216, 220, 327, 363-364, 377-379,
    386, 389-394, 410
Civil War, 13, 362, 404, 430, 447, 460, 476
Closeness of elections. *See* Elections,
    closeness of
Cohort analysis, 205-206, 305-306, 317-330
Columbia voting studies, 9, 11-12, 162, 169
Competitiveness, 26, 40, 42, 448, 453n, 459,
    461, 470, 527-530
Comparative State Election Project, 10,
    168-169, 175, 244, 277
Congressional elections
    candidate, dimensions, 372-385
    and the economy, 238, 241-242, 251-252,
        255-257, 259-260, 263-265, 269,
        272-273
    importance of candidates, 238, 243, 244,
        246, 277-291, 452n, 516-517, 526
    incumbency, 238, 243-244, 245, 276-277,
        279-287, 289-291
    information level, 47, 238-239, 241, 245,
        272, 275-277, 279-283, 287, 291-292,
        452n
    party voting in, 238, 240-241, 243, 244,
        245, 276-277, 282-287, 289-291, 382,
        516-531
    and presidential popularity, 238, 241,
        242, 243, 245-246, 249n, 250-252,
        255-256, 259-260, 263-265, 271,
        272-273
    studies of, 9-10
    turnout in, 240-241, 454-456, 517,
        523-526
    voting choice, 282-285, 452n, 517-522
    See also Drop-off; Voting choice,
        determinants of for subpresidential
        races
Conservatism. *See* Ideology
Constituency effects, 247, 516-531
Controversies, role of, 15-16
Costs of voting, 13, 23, 25-27, 29-30,
    32-33, 36-43, 54
Critical elections. *See* Realignment
Cynicism, political, 3-4, 124-127, 413-414,
    421, 481-482